Beginning CSS: Cascading Style Sheets for Web Design

W9-AFW-432

Beginning CSS: Cascading Style Sheets for Web Design

Richard York

WILEY

Wiley Publishing, Inc.

Beginning CSS: Cascading Style Sheets for Web Design

Published by
Wiley Publishing, Inc.
10475 Crosspoint Boulevard
Indianapolis, IN 46256
www.wiley.com

Copyright © 2005 by Wiley Publishing, Inc., Indianapolis, Indiana

Published simultaneously in Canada

ISBN: 0-7645-7642-9

Manufactured in the United States of America

10 9 8 7 6 5 4 3 2 1

1B/QZ/RS/QU/IN

No part of this publication may be reproduced, stored in a retrieval system or transmitted in any form or by any means, electronic, mechanical, photocopying, recording, scanning or otherwise, except as permitted under Sections 107 or 108 of the 1976 United States Copyright Act, without either the prior written permission of the Publisher, or authorization through payment of the appropriate per-copy fee to the Copyright Clearance Center, 222 Rosewood Drive, Danvers, MA 01923, (978) 750-8400, fax (978) 646-8600. Requests to the Publisher for permission should be addressed to the Legal Department, Wiley Publishing, Inc., 10475 Crosspoint Blvd., Indianapolis, IN 46256, (317) 572-3447, fax (317) 572-4355, e-mail: brandreview@wiley.com.

LIMIT OF LIABILITY/DISCLAIMER OF WARRANTY: THE PUBLISHER AND THE AUTHOR MAKE NO REPRESENTATIONS OR WARRANTIES WITH RESPECT TO THE ACCURACY OR COMPLETENESS OF THE CONTENTS OF THIS WORK AND SPECIFICALLY DISCLAIM ALL WARRANTIES, INCLUDING WITHOUT LIMITATION WARRANTIES OF FITNESS FOR A PARTIC-ULAR PURPOSE. NO WARRANTY MAY BE CREATED OR EXTENDED BY SALES OR PROMO-TIONAL MATERIALS. THE ADVICE AND STRATEGIES CONTAINED HEREIN MAY NOT BE SUITABLE FOR EVERY SITUATION. THIS WORK IS SOLD WITH THE UNDERSTANDING THAT THE PUBLISHER IS NOT ENGAGED IN RENDERING LEGAL, ACCOUNTING, OR OTHER PRO-FESSIONAL SERVICES. IF PROFESSIONAL ASSISTANCE IS REQUIRED, THE SERVICES OF A COMPETENT PROFESSIONAL PERSON SHOULD BE SOUGHT. NEITHER THE PUBLISHER NOR THE AUTHOR SHALL BE LIABLE FOR DAMAGES ARISING HEREFROM. THE FACT THAT AN ORGANIZATION OR WEBSITE IS REFERRED TO IN THIS WORK AS A CITATION AND/OR A POTENTIAL SOURCE OF FURTHER INFORMATION DOES NOT MEAN THAT THE AUTHOR OR THE PUBLISHER ENDORSES THE INFORMATION THE ORGANIZATION OR WEBSITE MAY PROVIDE OR RECOMMENDATIONS IT MAY MAKE. FURTHER, READERS SHOULD BE AWARE THAT INTERNET WEBSITES LISTED IN THIS WORK MAY HAVE CHANGED OR DISAPPEARED BETWEEN WHEN THIS WORK WAS WRITTEN AND WHEN IT IS READ.

For general information on our other products and services or to obtain technical support, please contact our Customer Care Department within the U.S. at (800) 762-2974, outside the U.S. at (317) 572-3993 or fax (317) 572-4002.

Wiley also publishes its books in a variety of electronic formats. Some content that appears in print may not be available in electronic books.

Library of Congress Cataloging-in-Publication Data: 2004-024-101

Trademarks: Wiley, the Wiley Publishing logo, Wrox, the Wrox logo, Programmer to Programmer and related trade dress are trademarks or registered trademarks of John Wiley & Sons, Inc. and/or its affil-iates, in the United States and other countries, and may not be used without written permission. All other trademarks are the property of their respective owners. Wiley Publishing, Inc., is not associated with any product or vendor mentioned in this book.

About the Author

Richard York is a freelance web designer and a participant in the open source community. After attending website and graphic design courses at Indiana University-Purdue University, Indianapolis in Indianapolis, Indiana, Richard continued a course of self-study which involved mastering design of web sites using web technologies like CSS, XHTML, and PHP.

When not writing for Wrox or building a website, Richard works on open source webmail applications written for PHP PEAR, an open source repository of PHP applications. Richard also enjoys writing poetry, playing music, and painting. He maintains a website at www.smilingsouls.net that exhibits his personal and professional interests.

Credits

Senior Acquisitions Editor
Jim Minatel

Development Editors
Tom Dinse
Brian Herrmann
Jodi Jensen

Production Editor
Angela Smith

Technical Editor
Wiley-Dreamtech India Pvt Ltd

Copy Editor
Mary Lagu

Editorial Manager
Mary Beth Wakefield

Vice President & Executive Group Publisher
Richard Swadley

Vice President and Publisher
Joseph B. Wikert

Project Coordinator
Erin Smith

Graphics and Production Specialists
Lisa England
Carrie Foster
Denny Hager
Joyce Haughey
Jennifer Heleine

Quality Control Technician
John Greenough
Joe Niesen

Media Development Specialist
Angela Denny

Proofreading and Indexing
TECHBOOKS Production Services

Contents

Acknowledgments   xix

Introduction   1

Chapter 1: Introducing Cascading Style Sheets   9

Who Creates and Maintains CSS?   10
How the Internet Works   11
Abridged History of the Web   12
How CSS Came to Be   13
Advantages of Using CSS   14
Summary   14

Chapter 2: Document Standards   17

Choosing Which Markup Language to Use   17
How to Write Markup   18
Which Browser to Use   19
Microsoft Internet Explorer   20
Gecko: Mozilla, Mozilla Firefox, and Netscape   21
Opera   22
KHTML: Safari and Konqueror   22
Introduction to HTML   23
Single Tags and HTML Line Breaks   23
HTML Attributes   25
XML   28
XHTML   31
XHTML Is Case-Sensitive   31
All Attribute Values Must Be Enclosed in Quotes   31
No Attribute Minimization Allowed   32
All Elements Require Both an Opening and Closing Tag   32
Why XHTML Is the Future   33
The Document Type Declaration   36
DOCTYPE Sniffing   37
Common Document Type Declarations   40
HTML 4.01 Transitional   40
HTML 4.01 Frameset   40

Contents

HTML 4.01 Strict 41
XHTML 1.0 Transitional 41
XHTML 1.0 Frameset 41
XHTML 1.0 Strict 41
Summary 42
Exercises 42

Chapter 3: The Basics of CSS Anatomy and Syntax 43

CSS Rules 43
Introducing Selectors 44
Grouping Selectors and Declarations 44
Including CSS in a Document 49
Including an Embedded Style Sheet 49
Linking to External Style Sheets 50
Importing Style Sheets 50
How to Structure an External CSS Document 51
Inline Styles 52
CSS Comments 54
Summary 54
Exercises 55

Chapter 4: Data Types, Keywords, Color, Length, and the URI 57

Keywords 57
Strings 59
Length and Measurement Options 63
Inconsistencies with Absolute Measurements 64
Metric Measurements 64
Typographical Measurements 65
Relative Length Measurements 65
Measurements Based on the Height of the Lowercase Letter x 67
Pixel Measurements 67
Percentage Measurements 68
Integers and Real Numbers 68
Colors 69
Color Keywords 70
RGB Colors 70
Hexadecimal Colors 71
Short Hexadecimal and Web-Safe Colors 72
The URI 73
Summary 74
Exercises 75

Chapter 5: CSS Selectors   77

The Universal Selector   **77**
Contextual/Descendant Selectors   **78**
Direct Child Selectors   **85**
Direct Adjacent Sibling Combinator   **89**
Indirect Adjacent Sibling Combinators   **92**
Attribute Selectors   **93**
     Selection Based on the Presence of an Attribute   93
     Selection Based on the Value of an Attribute   94
     Attribute Substring Selectors   95
         Selection Based on Attribute Values That Begin with a String   95
         Selection Based on Attribute Values That End with a String   95
         Selection Based on Attribute Values That Contain a String   96
Class and ID Selectors   **100**
Summary   **105**
Exercises   **106**

Chapter 6: Pseudo-Element and Pseudo-Class Selectors   107

Pseudo-Elements   **107**
     ::first-letter and ::first-line   108
     ::selection   110
     ::before and ::after   111
Pseudo-Classes   **113**
     Dynamic Pseudo-Classes   113
         :link and :visited   113
         :hover   114
         :active   115
         :focus   116
     Structural Pseudo-Classes   120
         :root   120
         :first-child   121
         :last-child   121
         :empty   122
     The Negation Pseudo-Class :not   126
     The :target Pseudo-Class   128
Summary   **132**
Exercises   **133**

Contents

Chapter 7: Inheritance and the Cascade   135

Inheritance   **135**
The inherit Keyword   137
The Cascade   **137**
Calculating the Specificity of a Selector   139
!important Rules   155
Custom Style Sheets   **156**
Specifying a Custom Style Sheet Using MSIE   156
Specifying a Custom Style Sheet Using Mozilla   156
Customizing Mozilla Using CSS   158
Summary   **161**
Exercises   **162**

Chapter 8: Text Manipulation   163

The JT's Website   **164**
Developing a Design Strategy   164
Creating the Directory Structure   165
Settling on a Table of Contents   167
The letter-spacing Property   **175**
The word-spacing Property   **179**
Indenting Paragraph Text Using text-indent   **181**
Aligning Text with the text-align Property   **185**
Justifying Text   186
The text-decoration Property   **191**
The text-transform Property   **196**
The white-space Property   **199**
A Look Ahead to CSS 3   **200**
Summary   **201**
Exercises   **202**

Chapter 9: Font Manipulation   203

Specifying Fonts with the font-family Property   **203**
Generic Font Families   206
The font-style Property   **211**
The font-variant Property   **215**
The font-weight Property   **216**
Relative Values   218

The font-size Property **221**
Absolute Font Sizes 222
Relative Font Sizes 223
Percentage Font Sizes 225
The font Shorthand Property **230**
System Fonts 232
Summary **234**
Exercises **235**

Chapter 10: Liquid Design and the CSS Box Model **237**

Laying the Foundation for Liquid Design **238**
<table> versus <div> 239
Avoiding Tag Soup 241
Examining the Advantages of External Style Sheets 242
The media attribute and @media rule 242
The CSS Box Model **245**
Borders 248
border-width 248
border-style 250
border-color 255
Border Shorthand Properties 256
border 259
CSS 3 Border Properties 260
Calculating Dimensions 268
width 269
height 270
Auto Values for width and height 272
Percentage Measurements 274
Minimum and Maximum Dimensions 277
The line-height property 282
Padding 288
Margins 290
Aligning Block-Level Elements with margin: auto 291
Overflowing Content **302**
overflow: auto 302
overflow: scroll 304
overflow: hidden 305
overflow-x and overflow-y 305
Summary **306**
Exercises **307**

Contents

Chapter 11: CSS Buoyancy: Collapsing Margins, Floating, and Vertical Alignment **309**

Collapsing Margins **309**

The float Property **313**

Floating Box Model 315

Floating Inline Elements and the Inline Box Model 318

Applying Multiple Floats 322

Left and Right Floating 323

The clear Property **329**

The vertical-align Property **334**

Subscript and Superscript Text 334

The top, middle, and bottom Keywords 335

The text-top and text-bottom Keywords 338

Percentage and Length Value 338

Vertically Aligning the Contents of Table Cells 339

Summary **341**

Exercise **342**

Chapter 12: Styling Lists and the User Interface **343**

The list-style-type Property **343**

The list-style-image Property **348**

The list-style-position Property **349**

The list-style shorthand Property **350**

The cursor Property **351**

Summary **354**

Exercises **354**

Chapter 13: Backgrounds: Setting the Scene **357**

The background-color Property **357**

The background-image Property **362**

The background-repeat Property **365**

The background-position Property **369**

The background-attachment Property **375**

The background shorthand Property **377**

Summary **379**

Exercise **380**

Chapter 14: Positioning — 383

The position Property — **383**
Static Positioning — 384
Absolute Positioning — 384
Offset Properties — 387
Relative Positioning — 393
Fixed Positioning — 403
Controlling Layering with the z-index Property — **405**
Summary — **411**
Exercises — **412**

Chapter 15: Styling for Handheld Devices and Print — 413

Styling Web Documents for Handheld Devices — **413**
Styling Web Documents for Print — **421**
Controlling page breaks — 421
Summary — **427**
Exercises — **427**

Chapter 16: Styling Tables — 429

Optional Table Elements — **430**
Table Captions — **432**
caption-side — 432
Table Columns — **433**
Grouping Table Data — **435**
Other Table Styles — **444**
table-layout — 444
border-collapse — 451
border-spacing — 453
empty-cells — 455
Summary — **459**
Exercise — **459**

Contents

Chapter 17: Styling XML   461

XML Documents   **461**
Creating an XML Schema   **464**
  The XML Declaration   468
    XML Declaration Attributes   469
    The XML stylesheet Declaration   470
The display Property   **471**
  Styling Inline Elements with display: inline   472
  Styling Block Elements with display: block   473
  Styling List Items with display: list-item   473
    Generating Numbered Lists   474
  Table Display Values   478
    Applying display: table   479
    Adding a Caption with display: table-caption   479
    Applying display: table-column-group and display: table-column   480
    Styling Groupings, Table Rows, and Table Cells   480
Other Display Values   **488**
Summary   **489**
Exercise   **489**

Chapter 18: Cross-Browser Compatibility   491

Bugs in Microsoft Internet Explorer   **491**
  IE7   492
    What IE7 Is   492
    Getting the IE7 Source Code   492
    CSS Features Provided by IE7   492
    How IE7 Works   493
    Installing an HTTP Server   493
  Specific IE CSS Rendering Bugs and Work-Arounds   502
    The Peek-A-Boo Bug   502
    The Guillotine Bug   504
    The Three-Pixel Jog   507
    The Double-Margin Bug   508
    Floating Elements and Percentage Widths   510
Installing Multiple Versions of Internet Explorer   **512**
  The Caveats   512
Additional CSS Resources   **517**
Summary   **518**
Exercises   **518**

Contents

Appendix A: Exercise Answers   **521**

Appendix B: CSS Reference   **565**

Appendix C: CSS Colors   **591**

Appendix D: Browser Rendering Modes   **603**

Index   **607**

Acknowledgments

I would like to thank my very good friends Norman Trabulsy and Avery Sumner for allowing me to use their business—JT's Island Grill and Gallery—for the examples in this book. The food at JT's is unique, refreshing, and delicious. If you're ever in Chokoloskee, Florida (a tiny island in the heart of the Ten Thousand Islands on the western coast of Florida), I recommend that you stop in.

I'd like to thank the editors at Wiley: Jim Minatel, specifically, for giving me a break when no one else would, and my Development Editor, Jodi Jensen, who put up with my erratic submission schedule and has been immensely helpful to me. I'd also like to thank the rest of the staff at Wiley for their support, ideas, and encouragement throughout the writing process.

I'd like to thank Imar Spaanjaars for his suggestions and participation in the book, especially for being so vigilant in helping me to see content through the eyes of a beginner.

I would also like to thank my parents (Tammy and John) for their support.

Finally I'd like to thank my friends for their help and support: Keith, Mollie, Lisa, Richelle, etc.—thanks for being there! Especially, Eleanor, who's been my best friend through everything.

Introduction

Cascading Style Sheets (CSS) are the modern standard for website presentation. When combined with a structural markup language like HTML, XHTML, or XML (though not limited to these), Cascading Style Sheets provide Internet browsers with the information that enables them to present all the visual aspects of a web document. Cascading Style Sheets apply things like borders, spacing between paragraphs, headings or images, control of font faces or font colors, background colors and images, textual effects like underlined or strike-through text, layering, positioning, and a number of other presentational effects. CSS controls the presentational aspects of a web page's design, whereas HTML, XHTML, or XML control the structure of a web page, which means little more than determining that certain text is a heading, other text is a paragraph, still other text is a list of hyperlinks, and so on.

Beginning CSS: Cascading Style Sheets for Web Design covers all the details required to combine CSS with HTML, XHTML, or XML to create rich, aesthetically powerful designs. Throughout the book, I focus on combining CSS with XHTML specifically because XHTML is the standard hailed by Internet standards bodies as the successor to HTML and the present and future of website design. CSS and XHTML allow a web document to be presented with less code, resulting in a significantly smaller file size and greatly increased maintainability. CSS also enables the presentation of a web document to be centralized, which allows for the look and feel of an entire website to be written and centralized in one or a few simple documents, which makes updating a website a breeze. With only a few simple edits, the look and feel of an entire website can be completely changed.

By using modern standards like CSS and XHTML, you can drastically reduce the cost of building and maintaining a website when compared to legacy HTML-only pages. You can also greatly reduce the amount of physical bandwidth and hard disk space required, resulting in immediate long-term benefits for any website.

In this book, I also discuss how to style XML documents with CSS — XML being a more advanced markup language with multipurpose applications. XML will play an increasingly larger role in the production of XHTML documents in the future. The following sections tell you what *Beginning CSS: Cascading Style Sheets for Web Design* covers, who this book is intended for, how it is structured, what equipment you need to use it, where you can go if you have a problem or question, and the conventions used in writing it.

Who Is This Book For?

This book's primary audience is anyone seeking to learn how to use Cascading Style Sheets to present web documents. Because Cascading Style Sheets are used to control the presentational layout of a web document, people from backgrounds in art, graphic design, or those who prepare print layouts for publishing will feel at home using CSS. Regardless of your background, CSS is a simple and powerful language designed so that anyone can understand and use it.

To get the most out of this book, basic familiarity with HTML is helpful but not required. You need no prior experience creating web pages to use this book or work through the examples; all the necessary tools and steps to create a complete web document are provided.

What Does This Book Cover?

This book covers portions of the CSS level 1, 2, 2.1, and 3 specifications. These specifications are created by an independent, not-for-profit Internet standards organization called the World Wide Web Consortium (W3C) that plans and defines how Internet documents work. I show you which W3C standards have been implemented so far and which are available today in the most popular browsers. The most popular browsers include Microsoft Internet Explorer for Windows, Mozilla, Firefox, Netscape, Opera, and Safari. The major part of the book is written using what is defined in the CSS level 2.1 specification.

For your convenience, this book also includes an integrated CSS feature reference throughout the book, as well as notes on browser compatibility. A CSS reference is also included in Appendix B.

How This Book Is Structured

The first half of the book is focused on the background of CSS, the tools required to create and test web pages, the basic syntax used in CSS, and how CSS comes together with markup to create a web page. Beginning in Chapter 8, the focus shifts toward the properties CSS provides to control the different aspects of the presentation of markup in a web document. The following is a summary of the topics covered in each chapter:

❑ **Chapter 1, "Introducing Cascading Style Sheets":** In this first chapter, I talk about what CSS is, why it exists, who created it, where it is maintained, and how it has evolved. I also discuss some of the basic differences between the various CSS specifications — CSS Level 1, CSS Level 2, CSS Level 2.1, and CSS Level 3 — and how these specifications define what CSS is.

❑ **Chapter 2, "Document Standards":** I present an overview of the major web browsers. I also explore the various flavors of documents in which CSS is most commonly used in terms of day-to-day web design. I present examples of an HTML, XHTML, and XML document, as well as something called the Document Type Declaration (DTD), what it is, and why it's important to the CSS designer.

❑ **Chapter 3, "The Basics of CSS Anatomy and Syntax":** This chapter introduces the basics of CSS. Now that you have some knowledge of what types of documents use CSS, this chapter introduces CSS rules and how selectors and declarations are combined to create rules. I also demonstrate the various methods used to include CSS in a document.

❑ **Chapter 4, "Data Types, Keywords, Color, Length, and the URI":** Continuing the discussion on CSS basics, this chapter elaborates on some of the various widgets that can be included in CSS for property values. I discuss CSS keywords, length units, strings, integers, the URI, and the various mechanisms that CSS supports for referencing color.

❑ **Chapter 5, "CSS Selectors":** Building on the concept of the selector presented in Chapter 3, Chapter 5 discusses a multitude of selectors supported by the CSS Level 1, 2, and 3 specifications, which browsers support which selectors, and the usefulness of each selector in real-world context. This chapter utilizes an example for building a user feedback form throughout the chapter to demonstrate how you might apply selectors in a real project.

❑ **Chapter 6, "Pseudo-Element and Pseudo-Class Selectors":** Furthering the concept of the selector from Chapters 3 and 5, this chapter introduces some special selectors that apply only when certain events or conditions are present. For example, you can use pseudo-element and pseudo-class selectors to give the first letter of a paragraph a larger font than the rest of the paragraph, or allow a document to be styled based on whether the user is clicking something or where the mouse pointer is positioned.

❑ **Chapter 7, "Inheritance and the Cascade":** Inheritance plays a huge role in CSS. For instance, inheritance allows a style such as a font, font size, or font color to be set once for the body of a document and propagated throughout all the text in the body no matter where that text is positioned. Cascading allows more than one style sheet to be applied to a document gracefully; the cascade provides an organized way of dealing with the repetition of styles by giving styles precedence. In this chapter, I show you how to create your own custom style sheets for any website using features available in modern browsers. This chapter also provides demonstrations for how to invoke, override, and take advantage of inheritance in CSS. I present a preview of a real-world website and how the cascade is used in that website.

❑ **Chapter 8, "Text Manipulation":** Chapter 8 begins with a look at some of the strategies used in planning the production of a real-world website. In Chapter 7, you see the finished product of the JT's Island Grill and Gallery website, and you explore how inheritance and the cascade play a role in that design. In Chapter 8, you begin building that page from the ground up, and this project is revisted through most of the subsequent chapters. You learn what techniques and planning a professional website designer uses when beginning a project. Then throughout the rest of Chapter 8, I present the various properties that CSS provides for text manipulation. These properties provide effects such as controlling the amount of space between the letters of words, controlling the amount of space between the words of a paragraph, controlling text alignment, underlining, overlining, or strike-through text. I also show how to control the case of text by making text all lowercase, uppercase, or capitalized.

❑ **Chapter 9, "Font Manipulation":** After you have seen the properties that CSS provides for text manipulation in Chapter 8, Chapter 9 presents the CSS properties you can use to manipulate the presentation of fonts. These effects include applying bold text, setting a font face, setting the font size, setting an italic font, as well as learning to use a property that enables you to specify all CSS's font effects in one single property.

❑ **Chapter 10, "Liquid Design and the CSS Box Model":** Chapter 10 builds on the discussion of design techniques presented in Chapter 8 and elaborates on a design technique fundamental to CSS-based designs: liquid design. In this chapter, I discuss what rules to follow to create a lightweight design that is accessible on a variety of platforms and media, including presentation that adapts to multiple screen sizes and resolutions. I also cover the ideal markup to use for making a website accessibile to visually impaired users. Finally, I lay the foundation for adapting the website for display on a printed medium or handheld device. Building on the concept of liquid design, this chapter discusses a set of rules at the heart of CSS called the CSS box model. I tie these concepts together in a gardening website example utilized throughout the chapter.

❑ **Chapter 11, "CSS Buoyancy: Collapsing Margins, Floating, and Vertical Alignment":** In Chapter 11, I discuss a unique CSS phenomenon known as margin collapsing, which is what happens when top or bottom margins come into direct contact with other top or bottom margins in a web document. I also discuss the `float` and `clear` properties, two properties used to control the flow of layout in a web document and often used to create multicolumn layouts or flow text beside images. I also discuss the `vertical-alignment` property, which is used to create effects like subscript or superscript text, as well as to control vertical alignment in table cells.

❑ **Chapter 12, "Styling Lists and the User Interface":** In this chapter, I look at the properties CSS provides to control presentation of ordered and unordered lists. This discussion includes the options CSS provides for predefined list markers, custom list markers, and the position of list markers. I also discuss the `cursor` property and how you can use this property to control the style of the mouse cursor.

❑ **Chapter 13, "Backgrounds: Setting the Scene":** In Chapter 13, I present the properties CSS provides to control backgrounds in a web page. This includes properties that set a background color or background image, as well as those that control the position of a background, the tiling of a background, and whether a background remains fixed in place as a web page is scrolled or remains static. Finally, the chapter shows you how to use a property that combines all these individual effects into a single property.

❑ **Chapter 14, "Positioning":** I discuss four different types of positioning: static, relative, absolute, and fixed. You use positioning primarily to layer portions of a document, and in Chapter 14 I provide examples of how positioning works and how it can be applied to a real-world project.

❑ **Chapter 15, "Styling for Handheld Devices and Print":** In this chapter, I discuss what steps to take to use CSS to provide alternative style sheets for devices like cell phones, PDAs, and a printer-friendly version of a web document.

❑ **Chapter 16, "Styling Tables":** I present the different properties that CSS provides for styling HTML/XHTML tables. The properties presented in this chapter let you control the spacing between the cells of a table, the placement of the table caption, and whether empty cells are rendered. Additionally, I show you a property that provides a "stricter" mode for measurement of width in tables. I also look in detail at the available tags and options that HTML/XHTML provides for structuring tabular data.

❑ **Chapter 17, "Styling XML":** In this chapter, I show how you can use CSS to style XML content. This chapter focuses specifically on the CSS display property and how you use this property to change the behavior of tags in an XML or HTML/XHTML document.

❑ **Chapter 18, "Cross-Browser Compatibility":** In this final chapter of the book, I present the most common techniques used to make a CSS design compatible with Microsoft Internet Explorer for Windows. I also look at specific anomalies and bugs and present solutions for correcting these bugs in the Internet Explorer for Windows browser.

❑ **Appendixes:** Appendix A contains the answers to chapter exercises. Appendix B, "CSS Reference," provides a place for you to look up CSS features and browser compatibility on the fly. Appendix C, "CSS Colors," provides a reference of CSS named colors. Appendix D, "Browser Rendering Modes," provides a reference for the browser rendering modes invoked by the presence or absence of a Document Type Declaration (discussed in Chapter 2).

What Do You Need to Use This Book?

To make use of the examples in this book, you need the following.

❑ Several Internet browsers to test your web pages

❑ Text-editing software

Designing content for websites requires being able to reach more than one type of audience. Some of your audience may be using different operating systems or different browsers other than those you have installed on your computer. This book focuses on browsers available for the Windows operating system, although you can also apply CSS to browsers for Macintosh or Linux operating systems. In Chapter 2, I provide an overview of the most popular browsers for Windows, Macintosh, and Linux and where to go on the Internet to obtain the required software. The browsers used in the examples of this book are Microsoft Internet Explorer 6, Mozilla 1.7, and Opera 7.5.

The examples in this book also require that web page source code be composed using text-editing software. Chapter 2 discusses a few different options for the text-editing software available on Windows or Macintosh operating systems.

Conventions

To help you get the most from the text and keep track of what's happening, I've used a number of conventions throughout the book:

> **Boxes like this one hold important, not-to-be forgotten information that is directly relevant to the surrounding text.**

Tips, hints, tricks, and asides to the current discussion are offset and placed in italics like this.

As for styles in the text:

❑ I *highlight* important words when I introduce them.

❑ I show keyboard strokes like this: Ctrl+A.

❑ I show URLs and code within the text in a special monofont typeface, like this:
   `persistence.properties`.

❑ I present code in the following two ways:

```
In code examples I highlight new and important code with a gray background.
```

```
The gray highlighting is not used for code that's less important in the present
context, or has been shown before.
```

Source Code

As you work through the examples in this book, you may choose either to type all the code manually or use the source code files that accompany the book. All the source code used in this book is available for download at www.wrox.com. When you arrive at the site, simply locate the book's title (either by using the Search box or by using one of the title lists) and click the Download Code link on the book's detail page to obtain all the source code for the book.

Because many books have similar titles, you may find it easiest to search by ISBN; for this book the ISBN is 0-7645-7642-9.

After you download the code, just decompress it with your favorite compression tool. Alternatively, you can go to the main Wrox code download page at www.wrox.com/dynamic/books/download.aspx to see the code available for this book and all other Wrox books.

Errata

We make every effort to ensure that there are no errors in the text or in the code. However, no one is perfect, and mistakes do occur. If you find an error in one of our books, like a spelling mistake or faulty piece of code, we would be very grateful for your feedback. By sending in errata you may save another reader hours of frustration; at the same time, you will be helping us provide even higher quality information.

To find the errata page for this book, go to www.wrox.com and locate the title using the Search box or one of the title lists. Then, on the book details page, click the Book Errata link. On this page, you can view all errata that has been submitted for this book and posted by Wrox editors. A complete book list including links to each book's errata is also available at www.wrox.com/misc-pages/booklist.shtml.

If you don't spot "your" error on the Book Errata page, go to www.wrox.com/contact/techsupport.shtml and complete the form there to send us the error you have found. We'll check the information and, if appropriate, post a message to the book's errata page and fix the problem in subsequent editions of the book.

p2p.wrox.com

For author and peer discussion, join the P2P forums at p2p.wrox.com. The forums are a Web-based system for you to post messages relating to Wrox books and related technologies and interact with other readers and technology users. The forums offer a subscription feature to e-mail you topics of interest of your choosing when new posts are made to the forums. Wrox authors, editors, other industry experts, and your fellow readers are present on these forums.

At p2p.wrox.com you will find a number of different forums that will help you not only as you read this book, but also as you develop your own applications. To join the forums, just follow these steps:

1. Go to p2p.wrox.com and click the Register link.
2. Read the terms of use and click Agree.
3. Complete the required information to join as well as any optional information you wish to provide and click Submit.
4. You will receive an e-mail with information describing how to verify your account and complete the joining process.

You can read messages in the forums without joining P2P; but, in order to post your own messages, you must join.

After you join, you can post new messages and respond to messages other users post. You can read messages at any time on the Web. If you would like to have new messages from a particular forum e-mailed to you, click the Subscribe to this Forum icon by the forum name in the forum listing.

For more information about how to use the Wrox P2P, be sure to read the P2P FAQs for answers to questions about how the forum software works, as well as answers to many common questions specific to P2P and Wrox books. To read the FAQs, click the FAQ link on any P2P page.

1

Introducing Cascading Style Sheets

Cascading Style Sheets, fondly referred to as CSS, is a simple design language intended to simplify the process of making web pages presentable. Put simply, CSS handles the *look and feel* part of a web page. With CSS, you can control the color of the text, the style of fonts, the spacing between paragraphs, how columns are sized and laid out, what background images or colors are used, as well as a variety of other effects.

CSS was created in language that is easy to learn and understand, but it provides powerful control over the presentation of a document. Most commonly, CSS is combined with the markup languages HTML or XHTML. These markup languages contain the actual text you see in a web page — the paragraphs, headings, lists, and tables — and are the glue of a web document. They contain the web page's data, as well as the CSS document that contains information about what the web page should look like.

HTML and XHTML are very similar languages. In fact, for the majority of documents today, they are pretty much identical, although XHTML has some stricter requirements about the type of syntax used. I discuss the differences between these two languages in detail in Chapter 2, and I also provide a few simple examples of what each language looks like and how CSS comes together with the language to create a web page. In this chapter, however, I discuss the following:

- ❑ The W3C, an organization that plans and makes recommendations for how the web should function and evolve

- ❑ How Internet documents work, where they come from, and how the browser displays them

- ❑ An abridged history of the Internet

- ❑ Why CSS was a desperately needed solution

- ❑ The advantages of using CSS

The next section takes a look at the independent organization that makes recommendations about how CSS, as well as a variety of other web-specific languages, should be used and implemented.

Who Creates and Maintains CSS?

Creating the underlying theory and planning how Cascading Style Sheets should function and work in a browser are tasks of an independent organization called the World Wide Web Consortium, or W3C. The W3C is a group that makes recommendations about how the Internet works and how it should evolve. The W3C is comprised of member companies and organizations that come together to create agreed-upon standards for how the web should function. Many prominent companies and organizations are W3C members, including Microsoft, Adobe, The Mozilla Foundation, Apple, and IBM. The W3C oversees the planning of several web languages, including CSS, HTML, XHTML, and XML, all of which are mentioned in this book.

CSS is maintained through a group of people within the W3C called the CSS Working Group. The CSS Working Group creates documents called *specifications*. When a specification has been discussed and officially ratified by W3C members, it becomes a recommendation. These ratified specifications are called *recommendations* because the W3C has no control over the actual implementation of the language. Independent companies and organizations create that software.

The specifications created by the W3C are not limited only to web browsers; in fact, the specifications can be used in a myriad of software types, including word processor and spreadsheet applications, as well as by different types of devices, such as PDAs and cell phones. For that reason, the software implementing a specification is referred to by the W3C as the *user agent*, which is a generic term that encompasses all the different types of software that implement W3C specifications.

The W3C merely recommends that a language be implemented in a certain way to ensure that the language does what is intended no matter which operating system, browser, or other type of software is being used. The goal of this standardization is to enable someone using the Netscape browser, for example, to have the same Internet experience as someone using Internet Explorer. Common community standards provide web site developers with the tools they need to reach an audience, regardless of the platform the audience is using.

As I write this, CSS comes in four different versions, each newer version building on the work of the last. The first version is called CSS level 1 and became a W3C recommendation in 1996. The second version, CSS level 2, became a W3C recommendation in 1998. The third version, CSS level 2.1, is currently a candidate recommendation. A *candidate recommendation* is the status the W3C applies to a specification when it feels the specification is complete and ready to be implemented and tested. After the specification has been implemented and tested by at least a few of the member companies, the candidate recommendation can become a full recommendation. The fourth version is called CSS level 3 and portions of it are still in development.

This book discusses the portions of CSS available in browsers at the time of this writing — that includes most of CSS 2 and CSS 2.1, and a little of CSS 3. Some portions of CSS 2.1 contradict CSS 2 and are not yet implemented in any browser. Where appropriate throughout the book and before introducing a new CSS feature, I reference the W3C specification in which that CSS feature is documented by including the phrase *Documented in CSS* followed by the number. In Chapter 2, I discuss the browsers that you need to test and build CSS-enabled web documents.

You can find the W3C website at www.w3.org. Go there to find documents that browser makers refer to when they are looking to implement languages such as CSS into a browser or program. Be advised, these specifications lean heavily toward the technical side. They aren't intended as documentation for people who use CSS; rather, they are aimed at those who write programs that interpret CSS.

Now that you know a little about who is responsible for planning and outlining the development of CSS, the next section describes how a web document makes its way into your browser.

How the Internet Works

As you probably already know, the Internet is a complex network of computers. Most of what goes on behind the scenes is of little interest to the person developing content for a website, but it is important to understand some of the fundamentals of what happens when you type an Internet address into your browser. Figure 1-1 shows a simple diagram of this process.

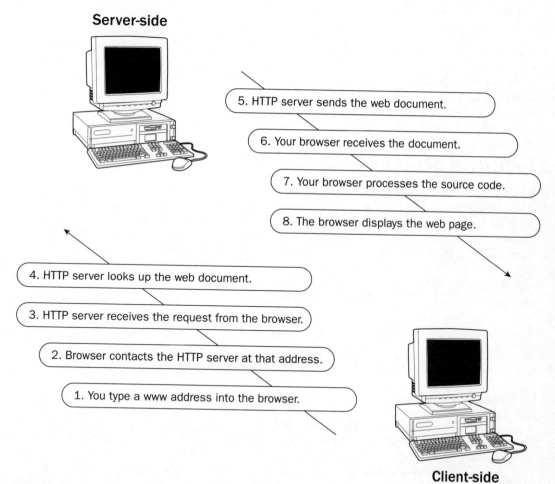

Server-side

5. HTTP server sends the web document.

6. Your browser receives the document.

7. Your browser processes the source code.

8. The browser displays the web page.

4. HTTP server looks up the web document.

3. HTTP server receives the request from the browser.

2. Browser contacts the HTTP server at that address.

1. You type a www address into the browser.

Client-side

Figure 1-1

At the top of the diagram in Figure 1-1, you see a computer labeled *server-side* and a computer labeled *client-side*. The server-side computer houses the documents and data of the website and is generally always running so that the website's visitors can access the website at any time of day. The client-side computer is, of course, your own computer.

The server-side computer contains HTTP server software that handles all the incoming requests for web pages. When you type an Internet address into a browser, the browser sends out a request that travels through a long network of computers that act as relays for that request until the address of the remote (server-side) computer is found. After the request reaches the HTTP server, the HTTP server sees what it is you are trying to find, searches for the page on the server's hard drive, and responds to the request you've made, sending the web page that you expect. That response travels back through another long chain of computers until your computer is found. Your browser then opens the response and reads what the HTTP server has sent back to it. If that server has sent an HTML document or another type of document that your browser can interpret, it reads the source code of that document and processes it into a displayable web page.

This is where CSS enters the picture. If CSS is present in the document, the CSS describes what the HTML page should look like to the browser. If the browser understands the CSS, it processes the web page into something you can see and interact with. If the browser only understands some of the CSS, it generally ignores what it doesn't understand. If the browser doesn't understand CSS at all, it usually displays a plain-looking version of the HTML document. I show you a few examples of this in some of the coming chapters, namely Chapters 5, 6, and 8.

Abridged History of the Web

Tim Berners-Lee (currently the director of the W3C) is credited with the invention of the *modern* Internet. That is the Internet as we know it and use it today to hop from one page to another by clicking colored hyperlinks. When Tim Berners-Lee came along with his invention, the Internet had already existed for several years in a different form. The earlier Internet was the result of the work and research of Vinton Cerf and Robert Kahn who devised a way for information to be transmitted over a network of computers. In a 1974 publication of a paper titled *A Protocol for Packet Network Intercommunication*, they outlined a protocol called Internet Protocol or IP. The IP is the underlying technology behind how information is accessed and transferred over the Internet today.

In 1989, Tim Berners-Lee came along with a proposal about how research could be shared more easily between physicists over the Internet. At the time, information sharing was difficult because there were so many different methods of doing it. He put together pieces of technology already used on the Internet for functions such as e-mail and named his invention the World Wide Web (WWW).

In the early 1990s, Berners-Lee created a standardized protocol by which computers in different places and running different software could communicate with one another. By typing in a simple address, any network-accessible documents could be accessed by any computer on the network that was capable of understanding this protocol. He called this protocol HyperText Transfer Protocol, or HTTP. This protocol would serve as the common ground where HyperText Markup Language (HTML) documents could be transmitted in a universally applicable way. You saw the details of what the HTTP protocol does in the diagram in Figure 1-1. Put simply, HTTP allows different computers, and even different devices, to communicate using a common language, giving us the World Wide Web of today.

How CSS Came to Be

During the mid-1990s, use of the Internet exploded. At that time, HTML was the only option for presenting a web page. As the Internet began to be used by more regular folks (as opposed to government, educational institutions, and researchers, as in the early days), users began demanding more control over the presentation of HTML documents. A great quandary arose; clearly HTML alone was not good enough to make a document presentable. In fact, not only was it not good enough, HTML alone simply wasn't suited for the job. HTML did not have the functionality that professional publishing required and had no way of making magazine- or newspaper-like presentations of an electronic document.

At the time, style sheets were not a new invention. In fact, style sheets were part of the plan from the beginning of HTML in 1990. Unfortunately, however, no standardized method of implementing style sheets was ever outlined, leaving this function up to the various browsers. In 1994, Tim Berners-Lee founded the World Wide Web Consortium, and a few days later, Håkon Wium Lie published his first draft of Cascading HTML Style Sheets. This draft was a proposal for how HTML documents could be styled using simple declarations.

Of those that responded to Håkon's draft of Cascading HTML Style Sheets was Bert Bos, who was working on a style sheet proposal of his own. The two joined forces and came up with Cascading Style Sheets. They dropped HTML from the title, realizing that CSS would be better as a general style sheet language, applicable to more than one type of document. CSS caused some controversy at its inception because part of the underlying fundamentals of the new style sheet language was that it created a balance between the browser's style sheet, the user's style sheet, and the author's style sheet. Some simply didn't like the idea that the user could have control over the presentation of a web document. Ultimately, however; the Internet community accepted CSS.

Among CSS supporters was Microsoft, who pledged support for the new style sheet language in its Internet Explorer web browser. Netscape, on the other hand, another popular web browser at the time, remained skeptical about CSS and went forward with a style sheet language of its own called JavaScript Style Sheets, or JSSS. Ultimately, Netscape's style sheets were not successful, and Microsoft's Internet Explorer browser grew more and more popular. At the time of this writing, IE is the dominant browser.

During the time that CSS was being planned, browsers began allowing HTML features that control presentation of a document into the browser. This change is the primary reason for much of the bloated and chaotic source code in the majority of websites operating today on the Internet. Even though HTML was never supposed to be a presentational language, it grew to become one. Unfortunately, by the time CSS level 1 was made a full W3C recommendation in 1996, the seed had already been planted. Presentational HTML had already taken root in mainstream website design and continues today.

However, all is not lost. Today, the most popular browsers have fantastic support for Cascading Style Sheets. Ironically, the browser exhibiting the least support is Microsoft's Internet Explorer for Windows, which still has enough CSS support to do away with most presentational HTML design. Among the browsers with the best CSS support is Netscape's browser (more on this in Chapter 2). This may beg the question: If Microsoft was such an avid supporter of Cascading Style Sheets in the beginning, why is Microsoft's browser the least standards-compliant today? The answer is that Microsoft did indeed follow through with its promise for CSS support, and it was the most comprehensive and impressive implementation of CSS even up to the release of Internet Explorer 6 in 2001. Even so, CSS implementation in Internet Explorer has been declining since the release of Internet Explorer 5. We can only speculate as to why Microsoft's browser no longer offers the best CSS support.

In Chapter 2, I discuss each of the browsers in use today. The next section presents some of the advantages of using CSS in a web document.

Advantages of Using CSS

By using Cascading Style Sheets for the presentation of a web document, you can substantially reduce the amount of time and work spent on composing not only a single document, but an entire website. Because more can be done with less, Cascading Style Sheets can reduce the amount of hard disk space that a website occupies, as well as the amount of bandwidth required to transmit that website from the server to the browser. Cascading Style Sheets have the following advantages:

❑ The presentation of an entire website can be centralized to one or a handful of documents, enabling the look and feel of a website to be updated at a moment's notice. In legacy HTML documents, the presentation was limited only to the document. CSS brings a much needed feature to HTML: the separation of a document's structure from its presentation.

❑ Users of a website can compose style sheets of their own, a feature which makes websites more accessible. For example, a user can compose a high-contrast style sheet that makes content easier to read.

❑ Browsers are beginning to support multiple style sheets, a feature which allows more than one design of a website to be presented at the same time. The user can simply select the look and feel that he or she likes most.

❑ Style sheets allow content to be optimized for more than one type of device. By using the same HTML document, different versions of a website can be presented for handheld devices such as PDAs and cell phones or for printing.

❑ Style sheets download much more quickly because web documents using CSS take up less hard disk space and consume less bandwidth.

Cascading Style Sheets allow the planning, production, and maintenance of a website to be incredibly simpler than HTML alone ever could be. By using CSS to present your web documents, you curtail literally days of development time and planning.

Summary

Cascading Style Sheets are the very necessary solution to a cry for more control over the presentation of a document. In this chapter, you learned that

❑ The World Wide Web Consortium plans and discusses how the Internet should work and evolve. CSS is managed by a group of people within the W3C called the CSS Working Group. This group of people makes recommendations about how browsers should implement CSS itself.

❑ The Internet is a complex network of computers all linked together. When you request a web document, that request travels through that network to a computer called an HTTP server that runs software. It sends a response containing the page you requested back through the network. Your browser receives the response and turns it into something you can see and interact with.

❑ Tim Berners-Lee invented the World Wide Web by creating the HyperText Transfer Protocol and the HyperText Markup Language.

❑ Vinton Cerf and Robert Kahn are credited with the invention of the Internet itself.

❑ CSS answers a need for a style sheet language capable of controlling the presentation of not only HTML documents, but several types of documents.

❑ CSS has many advantages. These include being accessible, applicable to more than one language; applicable to more than one type of device, and allowing a website to be planned, produced, and maintained in much less time. CSS also enables a website to take up significantly less hard disk space and bandwidth than formerly possible.

In Chapter 2, I describe the most popular browsers and the languages that support CSS in much more detail.

2

Document Standards

This chapter explores the various options for a document foundation. CSS is a dynamic tool, in that you can use it in more than one type of document, including HTML, XHTML, and XML documents. Each type of document may have several variations, flavors, or degrees of strictness. This chapter describes what's involved in creating each type.

Document standards are something very important to the aspiring CSS web designer. Inclusion of a Document Type Declaration (explained in a moment) and a well-formed document may mean the difference between a splitting, grueling headache and a mark-up document including CSS that works as expected in all the major browsers. Chapter 1 discussed the W3C body, the group assembled to decide on web standards. This chapter examines the various documents into which you can incorporate CSS, describing what each document looks like and giving you a few very basic examples of each document in action.

The explanation of each topic in the following list is quite lengthy and can easily fill an entire book. This chapter covers only the basics, including

- ❑ Writing mark-up
- ❑ Obtaining the required web browsers
- ❑ Introduction to HTML, XML, and XHTML
- ❑ Introduction to the Document Type Declaration
- ❑ DOCTYPE sniffing and how to invoke standards mode
- ❑ Creating web documents that survive and perpetuate into the foreseeable future

Choosing Which Markup Language to Use

HTML, XHTML, and XML are all based on SGML, which stands for Standard Generalized Markup Language. SGML is the parent of tag-based languages like HTML, XHTML, and XML, although it is not limited to these three examples. SGML defines what it means to be a tag-based language. Like SGML, HTML, XHTML, and XML are acronyms for more complex names:

❑ **HTML:** HyperText Markup Language

❑ **XHTML:** eXtensible HyperText Markup Language

❑ **XML:** eXtensible Markup Language

Some debate exists about which markup language is best and why. Most HTML coders don't bother to follow the W3C standards, which (you may recall from Chapter 1) provide a way to create web documents that behave predictably from browser to browser and from platform to platform. Standards provide a level-playing field for development. They allow the document to be designed in such a way that it can reach the largest audience with the least amount of effort. The <font> tag, for example, a simple HTML tag that can set a font face, size, and color, has been *deprecated* (a programming term meaning outdated, obsolete, or slated for deletion) since 1996 (the same year as the inception of CSS level 1). Yet the <font> tag has lingered, bloating documents, despite the fact that CSS font controls have existed for a good many years now and are well supported by today's browsers.

Any professional website designer would tell you to prepare your documents for the future while maintaining backward-compatibility. However, that's easier said than done unless you have years of website designing experience under your belt. This book takes the middle road by using XHTML, which is, generally speaking, backward-compatible, and is also (from the standpoint of the W3C) HTML's successor and the future of HTML.

The following sections examine one example of each of these markup languages.

How to Write Markup

HTML, XHTML, and XML are best written using a plain text editor. WYSIWYG (What You See Is What You Get) editors such as Microsoft Word aren't ideally suited for mark-up because the environment is not ideal for the composition of source code. WYSIWYG programs often have features like AutoCorrection and line wrapping; a plain text editor is more appealing precisely because it does not have these automatic features. Furthermore, the more automated WYSIWYG editors are designed to write the source code for you behind the scenes, so you don't have complete control over the structure and formatting of the source code. In contrast, a plain text editor doesn't insert anything into the source code beyond what you type into the text editor.

The Windows Notepad program is one example of a text editor that is ideal for composing source code. To launch Notepad, choose Start ➪ Run and then type Notepad in the Open text box. You can also use Microsoft FrontPage, but FrontPage is best used in *view source* mode where you can edit the source code directly instead of via the WYSIWYG interface. The same holds true for Macromedia Dreamweaver MX.

If Notepad is just too basic for your tastes, a text editor that highlights markup and CSS syntax might suit your needs better. The following are full-featured alternative text editors for Windows:

❑ Crimson Editor: www.crimsoneditor.com (free)

❑ HTML-kit: www.chami.com/html-kit (free)

Here are some alternative text editors that work with Mac OS X:

❏ CreaText: `http://creatext.sourceforge.net` (free)

❏ BBEdit: `www.barebones.com` (shareware)

Using Windows, you must create HTML files with the .html extension. If you use Notepad, beware of Windows saving your files with a .txt extension, which does not display files properly in a browser. To ensure that your files are saved properly, choose Start⇨Run and type `Explorer` (or right-click Start and choose Explore from the pop-up window) to open Windows Explorer. After Windows Explorer is open, choose Tools⇨Folder Options to open the Folder Options window; click the View tab, and uncheck the Hide Extensions for Known File Types box (see Figure 2-1). Then click OK.

HTML files are not the only file type in which the document extension is important; other file types require specific extensions as well. Those file types are covered later in this chapter.

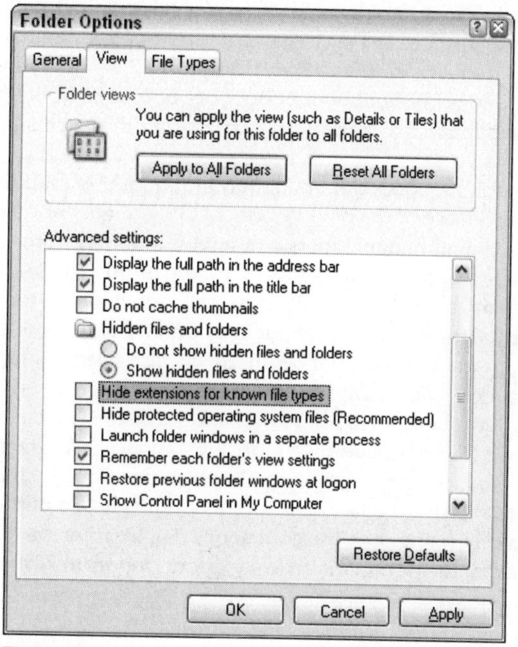

Figure 2-1

Now that you're armed with a text editor to compose your source code, the next section discusses the various browsers in use today.

Which Browser to Use

Throughout the course of the book, I jump between Mozilla 1.7, Microsoft Internet Explorer 6, and Opera 7.54. To help you fully understand each example, I recommend that you have access to all three browsers. Some examples work on one or two of these browsers, but not all three. I use Mozilla most frequently for this book's examples because it exhibits the most complete support for CSS specifications.

The following sections outline each of these browsers and what role they play in web development.

Microsoft Internet Explorer

Internet Explorer is Microsoft's browser that comes preloaded with the Windows operating system. The current version, as of this writing, is version 6.

Microsoft discontinued development of the Internet Explorer browser as a standalone application for Windows and announced that Internet Explorer will no longer be developed for other operating systems. That translates into no more Internet Explorer for the Macintosh. Instead, Microsoft plans for Internet Explorer to be completely integrated with its next operating system, codenamed Longhorn. Internet Explorer will no longer be its own application but a smaller part of the larger operating system. Consequently, updates to Internet Explorer will only be available with operating system updates and upgrades. In the meantime, updates to the current Internet Explorer 6 browser will come in the form of service packs and updates to the Windows XP and Windows 2000 operating systems via the Windows Update mechanism provided with Windows. According to Microsoft, this will not include updates to Internet Explorer's CSS capabilities or increased support for other web standards.

What does this mean for users and developers? Internet Explorer 6, released in 2001, is the last version of Internet Explorer until the release of the next Windows OS, Longhorn, currently projected for 2006. That leaves a gap of several years before developers will have access to improved support for CSS and other web standards in Microsoft's flagship browser. At the time of this writing, Internet Explorer is already aging rapidly. This means developers are likely to be stuck developing for Internet Explorer 6 for a good few years, coding around features that it does not support and dealing with bugs in the features that it does support. Internet Explorer's global market share has also been on the decline. At the time of this writing, this decline in market share is mostly among technically inclined people. People in the information technology industry have been switching more and more to Mozilla, an open-source browser with far more advanced support for web standards. Current statistics indicate that some websites receive as many as 20% of visitors using a Mozilla browser, although this figure can be much higher or lower depending on the website and its target audience. This figure should not to be taken lightly, however, as the number has been steadily rising over the course of 2004. Despite the decline in its use for some websites, Internet Explorer is still the dominant browser, garnering from 70% to 90% of the browser market share for most websites.

IE 6 provides the least support for the CSS standards discussed in this book; because of this fact, it receives the least attention. However, I couldn't very well write a successful book on website design without addressing how to design a website for the world's most popular browser. Internet Explorer's CSS bugs are well known; when and where appropriate, I discuss how to get around non-existent functionality and how to fix bugs in Internet Explorer without compromising standards. The bulk of this discussion is presented in Chapter 18 where I examine a few of Internet Explorer's most well-known CSS bugs and explore an emerging solution that actually implements CSS support in Internet Explorer 5, 5.5, and 6 for Windows.

You should use the Internet Explorer browser for some of this book's examples. If you don't currently have this browser, you can get it by going to the Internet Explorer homepage at www.microsoft.com/ie.

For Macintosh users, I recommend not using Internet Explorer for Mac because the capabilities and bugs of Internet Explorer for Windows and Internet Explorer for Mac are very different. Internet Explorer for the Macintosh has much better support for CSS, but it is an entirely different browser. The name may be the same, but the browsers themselves are very different. For Mac users, I recommend the Safari and Gecko browsers, which I discuss further in the coming sections. If you don't have Internet Explorer for Windows, you still can work through most exercises and examples presented in this book, with the exception of Chapter 18. That chapter is largely focused on identifying and correcting Internet Explorer for Windows bugs.

Gecko: Mozilla, Mozilla Firefox, and Netscape

Gecko was created in January 1998. At that time, Netscape announced that it was making its browser free to its users and that its browser would be *open source*, meaning that its source code would be freely available for modification and distribution. This led to the creation of Mozilla, the organization that develops and manages the Netscape code. America Online later purchased Netscape, and until July 2003, Mozilla remained a part of Netscape. In July 2003, the Mozilla Foundation was created, making Mozilla an independent, not-for-profit corporation. When the Netscape browser became open source, its rendering engine, the part of the browser software responsible for making the source code of a web page into something you can see and interact with, was given the name Gecko.

Gecko is the foundation that a whole suite of browsers relies on to do the behind-the-scenes work of rendering web pages. Gecko is included in AOL for OS X, Netscape 6, Netscape 7, Mozilla, and Mozilla Firefox browsers.

Netscape's browser market share has greatly diminished, whereas Mozilla continues to gain in popularity, occupying the number-two spot by most statistical estimates. The following table charts the relationship between Mozilla and Netscape browsers; the version relationships here show the corresponding version of Gecko shared between the two browsers.

Netscape Browser	Mozilla Browser
Netscape 7.2	Mozilla 1.7
Netscape 7.1	Mozilla 1.4
Netscape 7.0.2	Mozilla 1.0.2
Netscape 7.0.1	Mozilla 1.0.1

For instance, Netscape 7.2, which is the latest Netscape browser at the time of this writing, is based on the Gecko software inside Mozilla 1.7; and the two can be expected to behave the same as far as CSS is concerned.

The Mozilla browser is more than just a browser. It includes an e-mail client, an Internet Relay Chat (IRC) client, and a web page-authoring tool. However, this extra functionality doesn't appeal to everyone who uses a web browser. In fact, an average web user is unlikely to use anything but the browser itself. All this extra functionality also significantly increases the size of a Mozilla download. This, and other considerations, led the Mozilla foundation to create yet another browser. An application that includes only the browser was initially released under the name Phoenix, a name symbolic of a browser rising from the ashes of the overly complicated Mozilla browser and its Netscape predecessor. It was later renamed Firebird because of threats of trademark infringement from a company already using the Phoenix name; still later, the name was changed to Firefox to avoid conflicts with another open source project named Firebird. Now, settled on the name Firefox, Mozilla Firefox also uses the Gecko rendering engine to present web pages; it can be thought of as the browser part of the Mozilla browser.

The following table shows the relationship between the Mozilla and Mozilla Firefox browsers.

Mozilla Browser	Firefox Browser
Mozilla 1.7	Firefox 0.9
Mozilla 1.6	Firefox 0.8

Firefox 0.9 and Mozilla 1.7 can be expected to behave identically where CSS and design layout is concerned.

For the purpose of this book, I make heavy use of the Mozilla 1.7 browser, although Firefox 0.9 (or a later version) is also suitable. You can obtain either browser by visiting ww.mozilla.org. The Mozilla browser is available for Apple, Linux, and Windows operating systems.

> Each chapter of this book features browser-compatibility notes before a new CSS feature is introduced. These compatibility notes indicate the CSS specification that is referenced (see Appendix B for a detailed explanation) and which popular browsers you can expect to support the CSS feature (at the time of this writing). For those browsers that use the Gecko engine to present web documents — Mozilla, Netscape, Firefox, and AOL for the Mac — I list only Mozilla in the compatibility notes.

Opera

Opera is a lesser-known, Norwegian-based company. Opera users are fewer, accounting for only a few percent market share by most statistical estimates. Again, that figure can be much higher or lower depending on a website's audience. Also be aware that Opera and Mozilla Firefox browsers can be configured to identify themselves to a website as Microsoft Internet Explorer browsers. This, of course, can distort statistical analysis. This spoofing is done because websites often create content targeting Microsoft Internet Explorer and Netscape specifically, leaving everyone else out in the cold — even though third-party browsers like Mozilla Firefox and Opera probably support the required functionality.

At the time of this writing, the current version of the Opera browser is 7.54. You can download this browser for free from www.opera.com. The free version of Opera includes a window that displays advertisements. The Opera browser receives some attention in this book for a few CSS features that neither Mozilla nor Internet Explorer support, but which are worth mentioning. The Opera browser is available for Windows, Macintosh, Linux, and a variety of other platforms.

KHTML: Safari and Konqueror

The last browser that I discuss is Safari, which is based on Konqueror, itself an open-source browser available for Linux operating systems. The rendering engine used in the Safari and Konqueror web browsers is called KHTML. Safari is developed by Apple and is the browser included with Macintosh OS X operating systems. Previous to Safari, Internet Explorer and Gecko had been dominant on the Mac. Safari behaves in much the same way as Gecko.

For the purpose of this book, I note Safari compatibility when appropriate; however, none of the examples are dependent upon it. Safari is available only for Mac OS X and can be obtained from `www.apple.com/safari`. Konqueror is only available for Linux at this time; it can be found at `www.konqueror.org`.

Having discussed the browsers required for this book, I now introduce the various types of markup documents used with CSS.

Introduction to HTML

Plain old HTML is the oldest markup language. It is composed of a variety of tags. This section is intended as an HTML crash course. HTML is a book-length subject by itself. Unfortunately, I can cover only basic concepts here.

The following shows a set of HTML tags:

```
<HTML></HTML>
```

Tags begin with a left angle bracket (<), also known as the less-than symbol, followed by a tag name, and ending with a right angle bracket (>), or greater-than symbol. Most HTML tags have both an opening and closing tag; the closing tag contains a forward slash before the tag name (/>). Each HTML tag has a predefined purpose. The <HTML> tags in this example denote the beginning and end of an HTML document.

Single Tags and HTML Line Breaks

Some tags in HTML don't come in pairs, such as

```
<BR>
```

This is the HTML line break tag. You use it when you want to break text onto another line. Otherwise, HTML continues putting text on the same line — even if you've pressed the Return or Enter key.

In HTML, you combine tags to structure a document. Each tag tells the browser about the data contained in the document. The following example demonstrates a simple HTML table:

```
<TABLE BORDER=1 WIDTH=500>
    <TR>
        <TD>
            HEAT 1/2 OF BUTTER SLOWLY
            ADD BROWN SUGAR STIRRING UNTIL DISSOLVED
            ADD GINGER, RUM, VANILLA & REMAINING BUTTER
            TAKE OFF HEAT & STIR UNTIL ALL BUTTER IS MELTED
        </TD>
    </TR>
</TABLE>
```

In this example, each tag comes together to define a table. A table is used in HTML to show the relationship between data in much the same way a spreadsheet does. The `<TABLE>` tag begins the table, the `<TR>` tag defines a row of data and the `<TD>` tag defines a cell of data. Figure 2-2 shows the text contained in the `<TD>` element. An *element* is a term often used to refer to a *set* of HTML tags. In this usage, for example, it refers to the opening `<TD>` tag, the closing `</TD>` tag, and all the data between those two tags. If only one tag is required, as in the `<BR>` tag, that single tag constitutes the element.

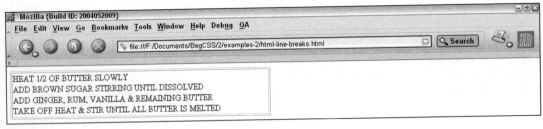

Figure 2-2

When viewed in a browser, the text between the `<TD>` and `</TD>` tags appears on one line, or the text wraps around to the next line when it reaches the end of the table cell, table, or window — whichever comes first. Here is the same code snippet with line breaks added:

```
<TABLE BORDER=1 WIDTH=500>
    <TR>
        <TD>
            HEAT 1/2 OF BUTTER SLOWLY<BR>
            ADD BROWN SUGAR STIRRING UNTIL DISSOLVED<BR>
            ADD GINGER, RUM, VANILLA & REMAINING BUTTER<BR>
            TAKE OFF HEAT & STIR UNTIL ALL BUTTER IS MELTED<BR>
        </TD>
    </TR>
</TABLE>
```

As you can see in Figure 2-3, when this code is viewed in a browser, the lines break wherever you inserted a `<BR>` tag.

Figure 2-3

HTML Attributes

You can use HTML attributes to alter some feature offered by a specific element. For instance, you can alter features pertaining to the presentation of a particular element, or you can alter features to uniquely identify that element. In the following example, the ID=mytable attribute uniquely distinguishes the table from other HTML tables. The COLSPAN=2 attribute in an HTML table tells the browser that a specific cell of table data spans two columns. The BORDER=1 attribute tells the browser that a border should go around the table, and the WIDTH=250 attribute tells the browser how wide the <TABLE> should be:

```
<TABLE ID=mytable BORDER=1 WIDTH=250>
    <TR>
        <TD COLSPAN=2>
            Some text.
        </TD>
    </TR>
    <TR>
        <TD>
            Some more text.
        </TD>
        <TD>
            Yet some more text.
        </TD>
    </TR>
</TABLE>
```

Figure 2-4 shows the result of this source code.

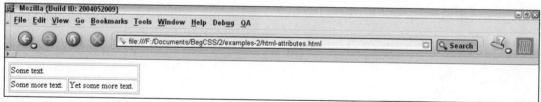

Figure 2-4

Now that I've shown you some HTML basics, work through the following Try It Out. The example uses a recipe to demonstrate HTML table-based design, which is a very common HTML design method.

Try It Out   Creating an HTML Document

Example 2-1. Follow these steps to create an HTML table:

1. In your favorite text editor, type the following HTML:

```
<!DOCTYPE HTML PUBLIC "-//W3C//DTD HTML 4.01 Transitional//EN">
    <HTML>
        <HEAD>
            <TITLE>Hummus</TITLE>
        </HEAD>
        <BODY>
            <TABLE BORDER=0 WIDTH=500>
```

```
<THEAD>
    <TR>
        <TH COLSPAN=4 BGCOLOR=#000000>
            <FONT COLOR=#FFFFFF>
                Hummus
            </FONT>
        </TH>
    </TR>
    <TR>
        <TH BGCOLOR=#000000>
            <FONT COLOR=#FFFFFF>
                #
            </FONT>
        </TH>
        <TH BGCOLOR=#000000>
            <FONT COLOR=#FFFFFF>
                Measurement
            </FONT>
        </TH>
        <TH BGCOLOR=#000000>
            <FONT COLOR=#FFFFFF>
                Product
            </FONT>
        </TH>
        <TH BGCOLOR=#000000>
            <FONT COLOR=#FFFFFF>
                Instructions
            </FONT>
        </TH>
    </TR>
</THEAD>
<TBODY>
    <TR>
        <TD>1</TD>
        <TD>#10 can</TD>
        <TD>CARBONZO BEANS</TD>
        <TD>DRAIN 1/2 CAN</TD>
    </TR>
    <TR>
        <TD>15</TD>
        <TD>CLOVES</TD>
        <TD COLSPAN=2>FRESH GARLIC</TD>
    </TR>
    <TR>
        <TD>2</TD>
        <TD>TEASPOONS</TD>
        <TD COLSPAN=2>SALT</TD>
    </TR>
    <TR>
        <TD>8</TD>
        <TD>TABLESPOONS</TD>
        <TD COLSPAN=2>REAL LEMON JUICE</TD>
    </TR>
    <TR>
        <TD>2</TD>
```

```
                    <TD>CUPS</TD>
                    <TD COLSPAN=2>TAHINI</TD>
                </TR>
                <TR>
                    <TD>2</TD>
                    <TD>TABLESPOONS</TD>
                    <TD>PARSLEY</TD>
                    <TD>CHOPPED</TD>
                </TR>
            </TBODY>
            <TFOOT>
                <TR>
                    <TD COLSPAN=4 BGCOLOR=#808080>
                        <FONT COLOR=#FFFFFF>
                            BLEND IN FOOD PROCESSOR
                        </FONT>
                    </TD>
                </TR>
            </TFOOT>
        </TABLE>
    </BODY>
</HTML>
```

2. Save the file as example2-1.html. In your browser of choice, you should see the output shown in Figure 2-5.

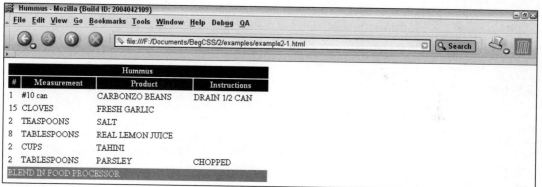

Figure 2-5

How It Works

Nothing fancy here. Notice that the text between the `<TITLE>` and `</TITLE>` tags now appears in the title bar of your web browser's window, and the browser window now contains the text between the `<BODY>` and `</BODY>` tags in the form of a simple recipe card, organized in a table format. So, HTML gives a document some basic structure and gives the browser a predefined way of organizing the data. Presentational markup includes the `<FONT>` tag and the `BGCOLOR` attribute. The `<FONT>` tag is used in markup to set the face, size, and color of a font, and the `BGCOLOR` attribute allows a solid color to be specified for the background of an element using a hexadecimal notation that I explain in more detail in Chapter 4. This book demonstrates why CSS is a much better solution for presentation. Can you imagine having to update 26 table cells just to change the font or background color of each individual cell? With

CSS, the presentational aspects of a document require only a few lines in a style sheet, which can eliminate redundancy. The old way of writing HTML is time-consuming and inefficient on multiple levels.

XML

I discuss XML next because it is, in many ways (especially with its rigid rules), the opposite of HTML. I could spend the entire book discussing XML, but I'm going to cover only the very basic stuff here. Unlike HTML, every XML tag absolutely must have both an opening and closing tag. XML is also case-sensitive, so title isn't the same thing as TITLE. In a nutshell, XML uses tags and attributes to describe what they enclose:

```
<movies>
    <movie>Big Fish</movie>
    <movie>Lord of the Rings</movie>
</movies>
```

Although having the tags describe what they enclose is one of the primary benefits of XML, it's not required. The following is equally valid XML:

```
<asdfgh>
    <lkj>Big Fish</lkj>
    <lkj>Lord of the Rings</lkj>
</asdfgh>
```

XML is useful not only for web presentation, but for an entire suite of applications, including complex programming languages, databases, and many other applications. But again, going into all the deep, dark details of XML is beyond the scope of this book.

To reiterate, the important differences between XML and HTML are primarily the following:

❑ XML is case-sensitive; HTML is not.

❑ XML absolutely requires both an opening and closing tag on all elements or the use of a special shortcut syntax in which only one tag is required. (This shortcut syntax allows both the opening and closing tag to be written as one tag.) Conversely, HTML does not always require both an opening and closing tag.

❑ Unlike HTML, XML tags do not have a predefined meaning. The author (not the browser) creates the meaning of each tag, which makes XML dynamic and adaptable to more than one application.

❑ XML documents are opened with an XML declaration instead of with an <HTML> tag.

You can find out more about applying CSS to an XML document in Chapter 17, or you might consider buying Wrox's Beginning XML, 3rd Edition

Now that you know what an XML document is, the following Try It Out demonstrates how the recipe card used in the preceding Try It Out example is formatted when written in XML.

Try It Out   An XML Document

Example 2-2. Follow these steps to create a simple XML document.

1.   Continuing the recipe example, fire up your favorite text editor and enter the follow XML:

```xml
<?xml version="1.0" encoding="ISO-8859-1" ?>
<recipe>
    <title>Hummus</title>
    <ingredients>
        <ingredient>
            <quantity>1</quantity>
            <measurement>#10 can</measurement>
            <product>CARBONZO BEANS</product>
            <instructions>DRAIN 1/2 CAN</instructions>
        </ingredient>
        <ingredient>
            <quantity>15</quantity>
            <measurement>CLOVES</measurement>
            <product>FRESH GARLIC</product>
        </ingredient>
        <ingredient>
            <quantity>2</quantity>
            <measurement>TEASPOONS</measurement>
            <product>SALT</product>
        </ingredient>
        <ingredient>
            <quantity>8</quantity>
            <measurement>TABLESPOONS</measurement>
            <product>REAL LEMON JUICE</product>
        </ingredient>
        <ingredient>
            <quantity>2</quantity>
            <measurement>CUPS</measurement>
            <product>TAHINI</product>
        </ingredient>
        <ingredient>
            <quantity>2</quantity>
            <measurement>TABLESPOONS</measurement>
            <product>PARSELY</product>
            <instructions>CHOPPED</instructions>
        </ingredient>
    </ingredients>
    <directions>
        BLEND IN FOOD PROCESSOR
    </directions>
</recipe>
```

2.   Save the file as example2-2.xml. Figure 2-6 shows what the XML document looks like when loaded into a browser.

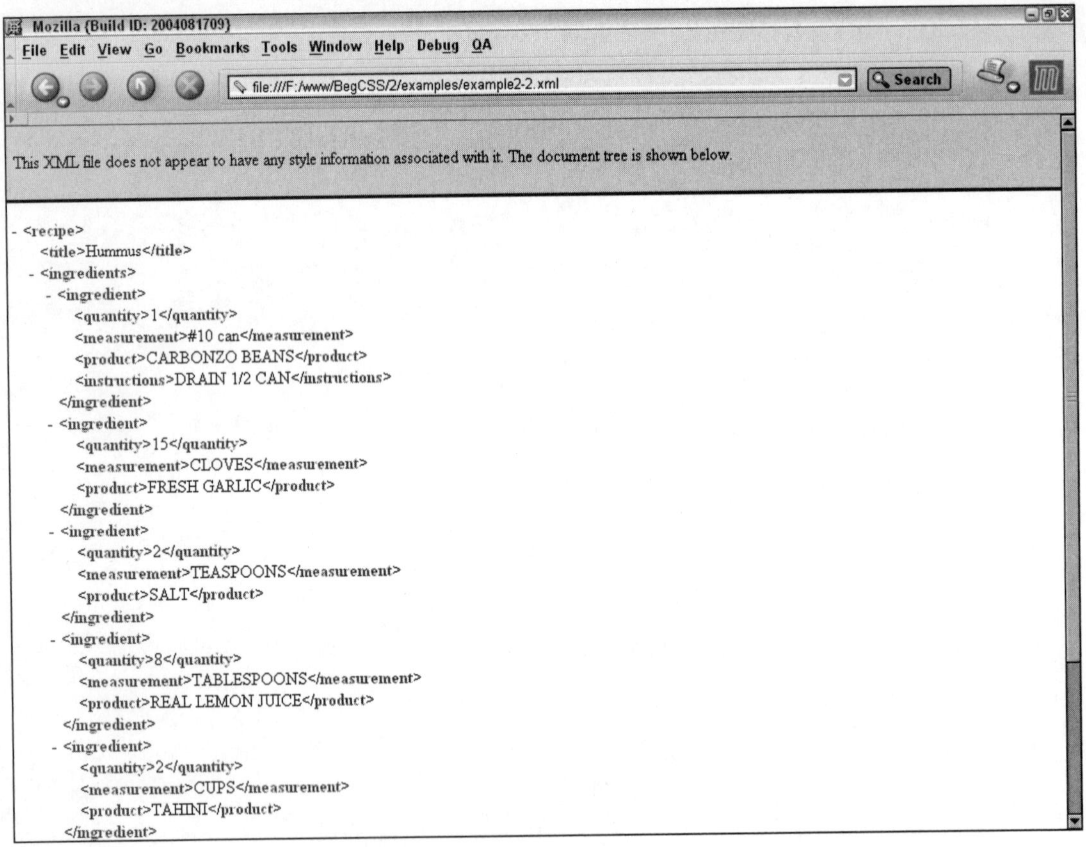

Figure 2-6

How It Works

The browser has no information about how to present the document, so the browser shows a tree of the XML source code. Often, the browser also provides a way to expand and collapse portions of the XML source code tree by displaying plus and minus signs that act as navigation buttons for the XML source code.

XML not only structures data; it also describes data. (Although this isn't required, it is one of XML's advantages.)

Chapter 17 explores in greater detail how to style XML documents, as well as offers more discussion on its background, structure, and uses. For now, simply note that XML is a more advanced method of structuring data that is applicable to more than one medium, not just end-user presentation.

XHTML

XHTML, the marriage of HTML and XML, is the document structure on which this book focuses. Put more simply, XHTML is a reformulation of HTML that conforms to the strict rules of XML syntax. For the purpose of this book, the XML part of XHTML is ignored, primarily because without XML, XHTML is the same as HTML except that it must conform to a stricter set of rules. Without XML, the examples are less confusing and more straightforward. Furthermore, and perhaps most important, Internet Explorer 6 — the world's most popular browser — does not currently properly support XHTML documents that contain both HTML and XML. Because I ignore the XML piece of XHTML, the examples presented in this book can work in the largest percentage of browsers.

Even though I have ignored the XML portion of XHTML, the use of XHTML-compliant HTML allows the documents presented in this book to be forward-compatible. That way, when XHTML support is improved and becomes more widespread, integration of XML becomes effortless.

XHTML provides the same predefined tags as HTML, while offering the user the extensibility of XML. XHTML differs from HTML in the following ways:

❑   XHTML, like XML, is case-sensitive, so you must write all HTML tags in all lowercase letters to achieve their associated HTML meaning.

❑   All attribute values must be enclosed in quotes.

❑   No attribute minimization (described shortly) is allowed.

❑   All tags must have both an opening and closing tag.

This set of rules allows XHTML to take on the extensibility of XML. The following sections discuss each rule in greater depth.

XHTML Is Case-Sensitive

The HTML part of XHTML basically includes the same tags with the same functionality used in HTML. More tags in HTML are used than in XHTML; for the most part, however, the two languages include the same tags with the same functionality.

One of the major differences between XHTML and HTML is that HTML is a very loose language; it doesn't care how a tag is written. For instance, <HTML> and <html> is the same tag in HTML. However, XML is case-sensitive, so when it came to marrying XML with HTML, certain aspects of HTML had to be made more rigid. In XHTML, <HTML> and <html> are not the same tag. In XHTML, all HTML tags must appear in all lowercase letters to achieve their associated HTML meaning.

All Attribute Values Must Be Enclosed in Quotes

Just as HTML is not case-sensitive, it is also very forgiving of attribute values not enclosed within quotation marks. The following is an example of an attribute value not enclosed within quotations:

```
<TD COLSPAN=2>
```

This attribute value causes an HTML table cell to span across two columns instead of just one. The following is an XHTML acceptable equivalent:

```
<td colspan="2">
```

The tag and attributes must be written in lowercase, and the value of the attribute must be enclosed within quotation marks. You may use either single or double quotation marks, as shown in the following example:

```
<td colspan='2'>
```

This all begs the question, "What happens if I don't follow the syntax rules?" The simple answer is that the document ceases to be valid XHTML. The complex answer is that when XML is added to an XHTML document and the XHTML document is not well formed, the browser refuses to display the document and displays an error indicating what went awry. I go into further detail about these errors in Chapter 17.

Well formed describes an XML document that strictly follows the syntax rules outlined here.

No Attribute Minimization Allowed

Scattered throughout HTML are a few oddball attributes that can be written with only one word. This syntax is referred to as *attribute minimization*. For example, suppose you're writing an HTML form with a select field or a field that shows a drop-down box. The following code specifies the option to allow the preselection of a value that appears in the drop-down list:

```
<SELECT NAME='some_field' SIZE='5'>
    <OPTION VALUE='1' SELECTED>Some selection</OPTION>
    <OPTION VALUE='2'>Another selection</OPTION>
</SELECT>
```

The SELECTED syntax used in the <OPTION> element is an example of attribute minimization. In XHTML this is not allowed. The following code is an XHTML-acceptable equivalent:

```
<select name='some_field' size='5'>
    <option value='1' selected='selected'>Some selection</option>
    <option value='2'>Another selection</option>
</select>
```

For backward compatibility, you generally write the SELECTED attribute as selected="selected". In more general terms, wherever there is attribute minimization, write attribute="attribute". This method works best in all browsers, including the older ones.

All Elements Require Both an Opening and Closing Tag

Like XML, XHTML requires both an opening and closing tag for every element, which means that the simple HTML line break, <BR>, is unacceptable in XHTML. Likewise, the <IMG> tag, which is used to insert an image into a document, is also not acceptable in XHTML. The same is true for a plethora of other tags.

XHTML allows you to write the HTML <BR> tag in two ways. The first is by using both opening and closing tags:

```
<br></br>
```

However, this presents a problem with backward compatibility. Modern browsers don't ignore the closing </br> tag, meaning that browsers treat </br> like another line break instead of as a closing tag. Therefore, instead of adding a closing tag, the W3C devised a shortcut syntax: a way to write the opening and closing tags as a single tag, as shown in the following:

```
<br/>
```

This time, the tag includes a forward slash before the closing angle bracket; the forward slash is used to close the tag. This is a shorthand way to write two tags when only one tag is technically required, as is the case for line breaks, images, and other special elements requiring no closing tag. This syntax allows the rule (that all elements requiring both an opening and closing tag) to be honored. This method presents a problem for older browsers, although modern browsers correctly interpret this tag. Older browsers ignore the tag altogether. For the tag to work on all browsers, include a single space between the end of the tag text and the forward slash, like this:

```
<br />
```

The single space allows the XHTML single slash syntax to work in older browsers. Either the <br/> syntax (no space) or the
 (including a space) are perfectly valid ways of writing the break tag.

Apply this shortcut syntax to any tag that doesn't require two tags, such as the image tag (<img />), the HTML form input (<input />), and so on.

The following section outlines why XHTML is important and why this book focuses on XHTML as the delivery method for web-based content.

Why XHTML Is the Future

XHTML is what HTML should have been from the very beginning. The following list details what makes XHTML so exciting to web developers.

❑ **XHTML is a cleaner representation of HTML.** The language is not bloated with presentational markup like the <font> tag and other HTML features that exist purely for presentation.

❑ **XHTML's rules are consistent.** You always know what to expect when viewing an XHTML page. Its rules define everything so that every XHTML page contains lowercase tags and attributes and attribute values are always quoted.

❑ **XHTML is far more dynamic than HTML.** XML capabilities make XHTML a better fit for complex projects.

❑ **XHTML documents download faster.** You can design XHTML files to be as much as two-thirds smaller in size when compared to presentation-oriented HTML documents. Smaller file sizes save hard disk space as well as expensive bandwidth.

❑ **XHTML files are easier to manage and update on multiple levels.** XHTML documents use less markup to structure the data of a document, so updating and managing XHTML becomes that much easier. When combined with CSS, you can centralize presentation into a single file. This functionality saves the maintainer the headache of editing each individual XHTML file. CSS also allows you to alter the entire look and feel of a website with a single file. Because you can link externally to CSS files (discussed in Chapter 3), a browser can cache them. This means you avoid re-download of every page requested by the visitor, which again saves expensive bandwidth.

Now that you are familiar with XHTML documents, it's time to revisit the recipe card example. The following Try It Out builds on Example 2-1, but it rewrites the original HTML document in XHTML, including all XHTML-acceptable syntax.

Try It Out　　**An XHTML Document**

Example 2-3. Follow these steps to rewrite the original HTML recipe document in XHTML.

1. Enter the following XHTML code in your text editor.

```
<!DOCTYPE html PUBLIC "-//W3C//DTD XHTML 1.0 Strict//EN"
"http://www.w3.org/TR/xhtml1/DTD/xhtml1-strict.dtd">
    <html>
        <head>
            <title>Hummus</title>
            <style type='text/css' media='all'>
                table {
                    border-width: 0px;
                    width: 500px;
                }
                th {
                    background: black;
                    color: white;
                }
                tfoot td {
                    background: #808080;
                    color: white;
                }
            </style>
        </head>
        <body>
            <table>
                <thead>
                    <tr>
                        <th colspan='4'>
                            Hummus
                        </th>
                    </tr>
                    <tr>
                        <th>
                            #
                        </th>
                        <th>
                            Measurement
```

```
                </th>
                <th>
                        Product
                </th>
                <th>
                        Instructions
                </th>
            </tr>
        </thead>
        <tbody>
            <tr>
                <td>1</td>
                <td>#10 can</td>
                <td>CARBONZO BEANS</td>
                <td>DRAIN 1/2 CAN</td>
            </tr>
            <tr>
                <td>15</td>
                <td>CLOVES</td>
                <td colspan='2'>FRESH GARLIC</td>
            </tr>
            <tr>
                <td>2</td>
                <td>TEASPOONS</td>
                <td colspan='2'>SALT</td>
            </tr>
            <tr>
                <td>8</td>
                <td>TABLESPOONS</td>
                <td colspan='2'>REAL LEMON JUICE</td>
            </tr>
            <tr>
                <td>2</td>
                <td>CUPS</td>
                <td colspan='2'>TAHINI</td>
            </tr>
            <tr>
                <td>2</td>
                <td>TABLESPOONS</td>
                <td>PARSLEY</td>
                <td>CHOPPED</td>
            </tr>
        </tbody>
        <tfoot>
            <tr>
                <td colspan='4'>
                        BLEND IN FOOD PROCESSOR
                </td>
            </tr>
        </tfoot>
    </table>
  </body>
</html>
```

2.   Save the file as example2-3.html. Figure 2-7 shows the output of this source code in the browser.

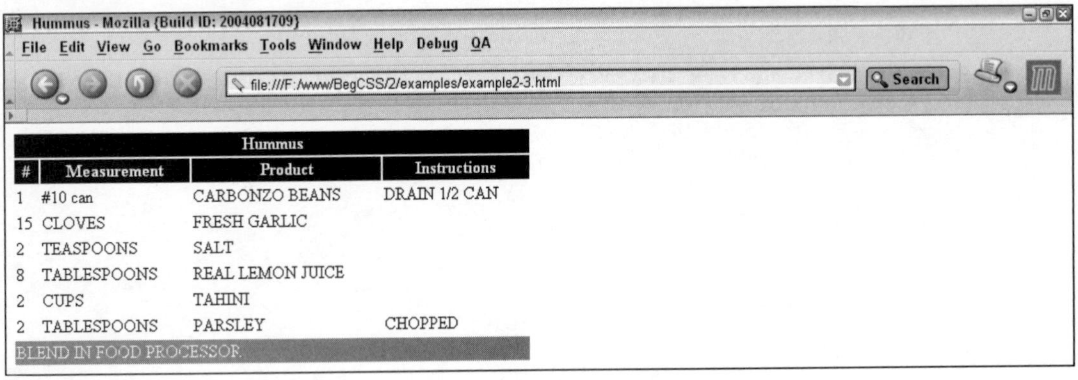

Figure 2-7

How It Works

Figure 2-7 shows that this output is identical to what's shown in Figure 2-5. This example demonstrates that XHTML is a little more rigid than HTML in terms of its syntax and structure. In this example, I remove the deprecated, presentational HTML that I used in Example 2-1 and replace it with the cleaner, more concise syntax of XHTML and CSS.

CSS brings a great deal of flexibility to the table by centralizing the document's presentation in a single place instead of scattering it all over the document, as was the case in Example 2-1. XHTML extends HTML by offering the flexibility of XML along with the predefined tags of HTML. Although this example does not demonstrate XML within an XHTML document, the subtle differences between XHTML and HTML are clear. The presentational aspects of Example 2-1 — the BGCOLOR, BORDER, and WIDTH attributes, and the <FONT> tag — are now all declared using a cascading style sheet that's embedded directly in the document. The tags and attributes are all written in lowercase letters, and the attribute values are enclosed in quotations. The HTML line break tag is written with the shortcut syntax for closing a tag: <br /> instead of <BR>.

> *Thanks to my good friends at JT's Island Grill and Gallery in Chokoloskee, Florida, for the delicious recipe.*

The Document Type Declaration

The Document Type Declaration (commonly abbreviated DTD) is a single line of code that appears before the opening <html> tag in HTML and XHTML documents. It's a rather complicated topic; however, it is a crucial component of writing standards-compliant XHTML documents with CSS. The Document Type Declaration looks like this:

```
<!DOCTYPE html PUBLIC "-//W3C//DTD XHTML 1.0 Strict//EN"
"http://www.w3.org/TR/xhtml1/DTD/xhtml1-strict.dtd">
<html>
    <head>
        <title> My webpage </title>
```

The inclusion of this code, more or less announces to the browser what type of document it can expect. It tells the browser about the markup syntax used in the document and provides some rules for its behavior. The example shown here is used to indicate to the browser that the document is an XHTML document that strictly follows the W3C recommendation of what XHTML 1.0 is. For introductory purposes, this is a bit of an over-simplification of the DTD. Understanding the inner components of what it is and does, however, is not essential knowledge for designing web pages with XHTML and CSS.

The inclusion of the DTD is an important component of designing standards-oriented XHTML documents. But in relation to CSS, the DTD has a more important effect on designing web pages: DOCTYPE sniffing.

DOCTYPE Sniffing

DOCTYPE sniffing, also known as the DOCTYPE switch, is a process used by modern browsers to select a rendering mode based on the inclusion or absence of a DTD. In Internet Explorer 6, the DTD is used to invoke one of two rendering modes. The first rendering mode is known as quirks mode, and the second rendering mode is known as standards-compliant mode. Essentially this behavior makes Internet Explorer 6 two browsers in one. Standards-compliant mode is used to make web pages that follow the W3C standards to the letter. Quirks mode relies on nonstandard methods to render web pages that were created before the W3C standards were implemented and came into widespread use. Quirks mode exists as a way to provide backward-compatibility for the millions of websites in existence today that were either created before W3C standards were implemented, or for websites whose authors are not yet standards savvy.

The two rendering modes have very significant differences in Internet Explorer 6. The choice of rendering mode may have an adverse effect on authoring CSS-enabled documents because Microsoft has made some CSS features available only when Internet Explorer 6 is in standards-compliant mode.

Other browsers like Mozilla, Opera, and Safari also have standards-compliant and quirks modes. In fact, these browser introduce an additional rendering mode known as *almost standards mode*. Appendix D provides a detailed table of which DTDs invoke which mode in which browser. However, even though the less popular browsers also provide these rendering modes, the differences between these modes is not nearly as significant as Internet Explorer 6's, which is why I have focused on Internet Explorer 6 here.

Throughout this book, all the examples invoke standards-compliant mode in all browsers. The following Try It Out demonstrates how Internet Explorer renders a web page in quirks mode. After this example, I provide an example of how Internet Explorer renders content in standards-compliant mode, and I highlight the differences between the two.

Try It Out   Experimenting with Quirks Mode and Standards Mode

Example 2-4. To demonstrate the nuances in rendering your web page according to these two rendering modes in Internet Explorer 6, follow these steps.

1. Using your favorite text editor, type the following HTML document:

```
<html>
    <head>
        <title> Doctype Sniffing </title>
        <style type='text/css' media='all'>
```

```
                    table {
                        margin: auto;
                    }
                    td {
                        background: green;
                        margin: 10%;
                        border: 5px solid black;
                        padding: 10%;
                        width: 100%;
                        color: black;
                        font-size: 200%;
                        text-align: center;
                    }
                    div {
                        background: green;
                        border: 5px solid black;
                        font-size: 200%;
                        padding: 1%;
                    }
                    #div1 {
                        float: left;
                        width: 30%;
                    }
                    #div2 {
                        margin-left: 34%;
                        width: auto;
                    }
                </style>
            </head>
            <body>
                <table>
                    <tr>
                        <td>
                            Some content.
                        </td>
                    </tr>
                </table>
                <div id='div1'>
                    This div smells funny.
                </div>
                <div id='div2'>
                    This div has a <em>strange</em> and rather pleasing odor about it.
                </div>
            </body>
        </html>
```

2. Save the file as example2-4.html.

3. Using the example2-4.html file, add the following DTD before the opening `<html>` tag to see how this example renders according to W3C standards:

```
<!DOCTYPE html PUBLIC "-//W3C//DTD XHTML 1.0 Strict//EN"
"http://www.w3.org/TR/xhtml1/DTD/xhtml1-strict.dtd">
<html>
    <head>
        <title> Doctype Sniffing </title>
```

4. Save the modified file as example2-5.html.

5. Open Internet Explorer and load example2-4.html in one browser window and example2-5.html in another.

Figure 2-8 shows example2-4.html in quirks mode in Internet Explorer.

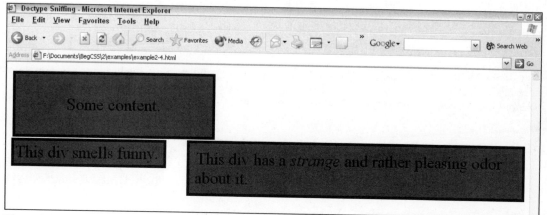

Figure 2-8

Figure 2-9 shows example2-5.html in standards-compliant mode in Internet Explorer.

Figure 2-9

How It Works

When compared side-by-side, the effects of the DTD become obvious. In example2-4.html, the table is not centered, but it is centered in the rendering of example2-5.html. Furthermore, the <div> elements do not have the same dimensions. These two examples demonstrate a few of the very important differences between quirks mode and standards-compliant mode. You do not encounter any of these differences between these two modes when you view the same two pages using the Mozilla browser. This indicates to you that the quirks mode of one browser isn't the same as the quirks mode of another browser. Furthermore, through this example it becomes obvious that using Internet Explorer in quirks mode limits the scope of available CSS functionality.

Microsoft itself provides a detailed accounting for these inconsistencies in available CSS functionality. These are documented for each CSS feature at the following URL:

```
http://msdn.microsoft.com/library/default.asp?url=/workshop/author/css
/reference/attributes.asp
```

In summary, for CSS design, cross-browser consistency is dependent upon the browser's interpretation of the W3C standards. Using the standards-compliant mode provided by the browser is one way to avoid inconsistency. The following section outlines some of the possible DTDs that are available.

Common Document Type Declarations

The following sections summarize the most common DTDs in use and include a brief description of what the DOCTYPE is used for. The examples in this book primarily use the XHTML 1.0 Strict DOCTYPE.

HTML 4.01 Transitional

HTML transitional is the loosest document type. It allows the use of deprecated HTML, such as the <font> tag, which was one feature of HTML that necessitated the creation of CSS in the first place. The HTML 4.01 Transitional DOCTYPE is not case-sensitive. For example, <HTML> is the same as <html>. This principle applies to all HTML 4.01 DOCTYPEs. When this DOCTYPE appears with a URL to the DTD, it invokes the standards mode:

```
<!DOCTYPE HTML PUBLIC "-//W3C//DTD HTML 4.01 Transitional//EN"
"http://www.w3.org/TR/html4/loose.dtd">
```

If the URL does not appear in the DTD, as in the following example, the DOCTYPE invokes quirks mode:

```
<!DOCTYPE HTML PUBLIC "-//W3C//DTD HTML 4.01 Transitional//EN" >
```

In fact, if the DTD URL is incorrect in any way, the DOCTYPE invokes quirks mode instead of standards mode.

HTML 4.01 Frameset

HTML frameset is the same declaration as HTML transitional, but with the inclusion of *framesets*. Framesets enable the browser window to be partitioned (or separated) into more than one window, allowing the author to display and reference more than one HTML page at once. HTML frameset also allows the use of inline frames, which enables you to include external HTML documents inside another HTML document. You specify HTML frameset like this:

```
<!DOCTYPE HTML PUBLIC "-//W3C//DTD HTML 4.01 Frameset//EN"
"http://www.w3.org/TR/html4/frameset.dtd">
```

Like HTML 4.01 transitional, this DOCTYPE also invokes standards mode. If it appears without the DTD URL or with an invalid URL, it invokes quirks mode.

HTML 4.01 Strict

HTML strict (theoretically, at least) does not allow the use of deprecated HTML. Like the example of the XHTML strict Document Type Declaration that I discussed earlier in this chapter, the HTML 4.01 Strict DTD implies that the document strictly follows the W3C's definition of what HTML 4.01 is. You specify HTML strict like this:

```
<!DOCTYPE HTML PUBLIC "-//W3C//DTD HTML 4.01//EN"
"http://www.w3.org/TR/html4/strict.dtd">
```

This DOCTYPE invokes standards mode regardless of whether it appears with the DTD URL. But an incorrect URL may invoke quirks mode in some browsers.

XHTML 1.0 Transitional

Similar to HTML 4.01 Transitional, XHTML transitional implies that the markup is not perfect. You specify XHTML transitional like this:

```
<!DOCTYPE html PUBLIC "-//W3C//DTD XHTML 1.0 Transitional//EN"
"http://www.w3.org/TR/xhtml1/DTD/xhtml1-transitional.dtd">
```

All XHTML DOCTYPEs invoke standards mode regardless of whether a DTD URL appears in the declaration.

XHTML 1.0 Frameset

Similar to HTML 4.01 frameset, XHTML frameset is essentially XHTML transitional but allows the use of frames. Note, however, not including a frameset DOCTYPE generally has no effect on frame usage. You specify the XHTML frameset DOCTYPE like this:

```
<!DOCTYPE html PUBLIC "-//W3C//DTD XHTML 1.0 Frameset//EN"
"http://www.w3.org/TR/xhtml1/DTD/xhtml1-frameset.dtd">
```

As stated previously, this XHTML DOCTYPE invokes standards mode.

XHTML 1.0 Strict

XHTML 1.0 Strict is the DOCTYPE appearing in all of this book's examples. It implies that the document conforms to the more rigid XHTML syntax rules and does not allow deprecated HTML tags and attributes. The browser ignores deprecated HTML tags or attributes if they appear in an XHTML document with a strict DOCTYPE. You specify XHTML strict like this:

```
<!DOCTYPE html PUBLIC "-//W3C//DTD XHTML 1.0 Strict//EN"
"http://www.w3.org/TR/xhtml1/DTD/xhtml1-strict.dtd">
```

Again, XHTML strict invokes standards mode.

Summary

CSS is designed to work with a variety of documents. Although not limited to HTML, XHTML, and XML, you find CSS most commonly used in those types of documents. In this chapter you learned that the following:

❑ Internet Explorer 6, Gecko, Opera, and KHTML browsers make up the majority of browsers in use today, with Internet Explorer 6 being the world's most popular browser.

❑ Markup languages are used to structure data.

❑ HTML is the oldest markup language and allows the loosest syntax.

❑ XML is the extreme opposite of HTML in terms of syntactical strictness in that it is very rigid and very defined.

❑ XHTML is the middle road and the chosen delivery medium for most of this book's examples.

❑ XHTML is stricter than HTML in terms of its basic syntactical rules.

❑ XHTML is case-sensitive, and you must write all its HTML tags in lowercase letters and all attribute values must be enclosed within quotation marks.

❑ XHTML does not allow attribute minimization.

❑ All XHTML tags must contain both an opening and a closing tag, although XHTML provides a shortcut syntax that allows the opening and closing tags to be written together as a single tag.

❑ The Document Type Declaration is a line of code that appears before the opening <html> tag; it provides the browser with some basic information about the document's syntax.

❑ DOCTYPE sniffing (the DOCTYPE switch) is used to select one of two rendering modes in Internet Explorer 6, and one of three rendering modes in all other browsers.

❑ Internet Explorer 6 quirks mode limits the scope of available CSS functionality, which results in huge inconsistencies between Internet Explorer 6 quirks mode and Internet Explorer 6 standards-compliant mode.

Chapter 3 begins a discussion of basic CSS syntax.

Exercises

1. Using a structure similar to that of the recipe paradigm, create HTML, XML, and XHTML documents listing your favorite movies. Include information for the lead actor or actress, the title, and the genre.

2. Explain the differences between quirks mode and standards mode.

The Basics of CSS Anatomy and Syntax

CSS documents aren't terribly complicated. However, if you've ever treaded through the CSS specifications made available at the W3C website at www.w3.org, CSS may seem like a daunting undertaking. In all truth, it isn't. A CSS document may consist of nothing but CSS rules or it may be included directly in HTML, XHTML, or XML. In this chapter, you learn how to recognize CSS rules and the basic syntax used to form them. Because CSS is a language used to describe aesthetic layout, its very design makes it easy to use in more than one type of document (the folks at the W3C even did that intentionally!). Most commonly, you find CSS in HTML, XHTML, and XML documents.

In this chapter, I discuss the following:

- ❑ Basic CSS syntax
- ❑ CSS rules, selectors, and declarations
- ❑ How to include CSS in a document

CSS Rules

The following is an example of a CSS *rule*. You can set the layout of the rule according to your preferences:

```
body {
    color: black;
}
```

The next line is identical to the preceding example.

```
body {color: black;}
```

Like HTML, XHTML, and XML, CSS can use white space and line breaks for purposes of readability. The interpreter reading the CSS doesn't care how much white space appears in the style sheet or how many line breaks are used. Humans, however, must often add some sort of structure to prevent eye strain.

`body` in this example refers to the `<body>` tag in an HTML or XHTML document and is what is known as the *selector*, or more specifically a *type selector*. The selector is followed by a curly-brace–delimited list of one or more semicolon-separated *declarations*. A declaration is a property followed by a colon, followed by a value. Each declaration formats the element or elements specified in the selector list for presentation to web visitors.

In the preceding rule example, all text and all CSS properties for color receive a value of black unless specified otherwise elsewhere. (This is where the Cascade comes in. I discuss specifying elements in Chapter 7.)

Introducing Selectors

In CSS, a selector is the target element or elements to which each CSS rule is applied. Put simply, the selector tells the browser where and what to format. A selector may be user-specified via the `class=""` or `id=""` attributes, or it may simply be the HTML or XML tag name itself. But CSS doesn't stop there. CSS also supports more complex selectors that function based on the context in which the target element appears in the document. I discuss each type of selector in depth in Chapter 5; for now, look at the following rule:

```
td
{
    font-family: Arial;
}
```

This rule applies an Arial font to every `<td>` element. If there are 160 `<td>` elements in the web page, the CSS rule is applied 160 times. Using deprecated HTML to create the same formatting requires a `<font>` tag to be included in each and every `<td>` element. With CSS, the font is specified just once. That's right, once.

Grouping Selectors and Declarations

A style sheet wouldn't be very useful if it didn't contain a mechanism for grouping selectors and declarations. Complex style sheets can save resources by combining repetitive rules to create a single rule. The following example groups selectors and declarations:

```
p, h1, h2, h3, h4, h5
{
    font-family: Arial;
    color: black;
}
```

Each selector is separated by a comma, whereas a semicolon separates each declaration. In this example an Arial font and black text is applied to `<p>`, `<h1>`, `<h2>`, `<h3>`, `<h4>` and `<h5>` elements.

Declarations may also be grouped. The following code:

```
body {font-family: Arial;}
body {font-size: 10pt;}
body {color: black;}
```

is identical to this format:

```
body
{
    font-family: Arial;
    font-size: 10pt;
    color: black;
}
```

Both are valid in CSS.

The following Try It Out demonstrates how to apply styles to a selected HTML element in the body, as well as how to group selectors and declarations.

Try It Out   Selectors and Grouping

Example 3-1. To see how a selector is used to select HTML elements in the body, follow these steps.

1.   Fire up your favorite text editor and type the following XHTML:

```
<!DOCTYPE html PUBLIC "-//W3C//DTD XHTML 1.0 Strict//EN"
"http://www.w3.org/TR/xhtml1/DTD/xhtml1-strict.dtd">
<html>
    <head>
      <meta http-equiv="content-type" content="text/xhtml; charset=windows-1252" />
      <meta http-equiv="content-language" content="en-us" />
        <title>Selectors and Grouping</title>
        <style type="text/css" media="all">
            p {
                font-family: Arial;
                font-size: 14pt;
            }
            h1 {
                color: black;
                border: 5px solid black;
            }
            h2 {
                color: orange;
                border: 4px solid orange;
            }
            h3 {
                color: blue;
                border: 3px solid blue;
            }
            h1, h2, h3 {
                letter-spacing: 5px;
                padding: 10px;
```

```
        }
      </style>
  </head>
  <body>
      <h1>
          Heading 1
      </h1>
      <h2>
          Heading 2
      </h2>
      <h3>
          Heading 3
      </h3>
      <p>
          Selectors choose the element to apply formatting to.  These may also be
          grouped together.
      </p>
  </body>
</html>
```

2. Save this as example3-1.html.

3. Fire up your favorite browser and load the file.

Figure 3-1 shows how CSS selects the different headings in the body of the HTML document to which it applies different text colors and borders and few other effects.

How It Works

This example demonstrates how CSS uses selectors to determine where and to what you apply presentation. It also demonstrates how selectors may be grouped together so that formatting changes can be applied to multiple elements without specifying a separate rule for each individual element. I have used a number of properties to apply font, font size, text color, borders, spacing between letters, and padding to the specified elements. The following reviews each individual component of the style sheet.

The first rule selects all the <p> elements in the document:

```
p {
    font-family: Arial;
    font-size: 14pt;
}
```

The preceding rules apply an Arial font face and a font size of 14 points. font-family is a CSS property, and Arial is the value of that property; together they make a declaration. p is the selector; the selector combined with the declarations make a rule. This rule applies an Arial font face and 14-point font size to the following snippet of markup:

```
<p>
    Selectors choose the element to apply formatting to.  These may also be
    grouped together.
</p>
```

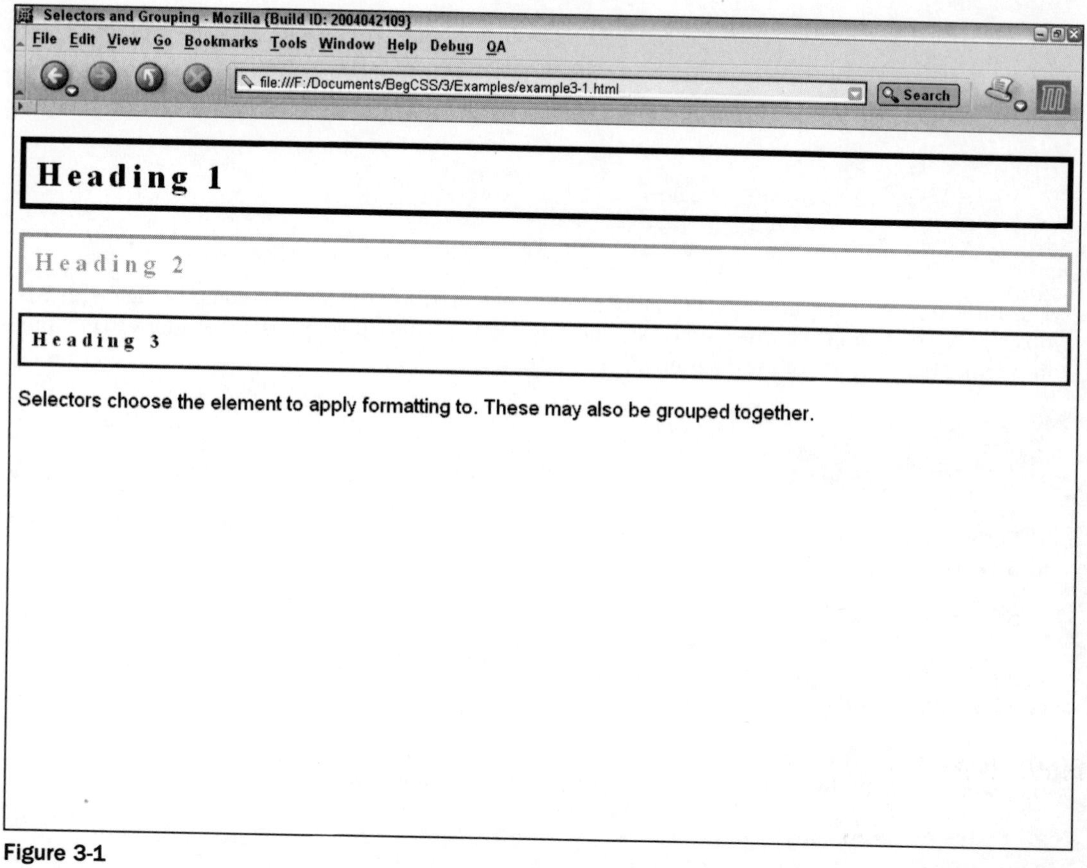

Figure 3-1

Wherever a <p> element occurs in the HTML document, the type has an Arial font face, 14 points in size. In Chapter 4, I take a more in-depth look at the different units of measurement CSS allows. In Chapter 9, I cover the syntax of font properties.

The next rule selects all <h1> elements that occur in the HTML document:

```
h1 {
    color: black;
    border: 5px solid black;
}
```

Every <h1> element will have black text and a 5-pixel thick, solid, black border around it. This selects the following snippet of markup:

```
<h1>
    Heading 1
</h1>
```

Because you include h1 as the selector, the browser knows to associate it with <h1> elements that appear later in the body of the document.

Similar declarations appear in the next rule:

```
h2 {
    color: orange;
    border: 4px solid orange;
}
```

This time, the element is an <h2> instead of an <h1> element, and the text is colored orange with a 4-pixel thick, solid, orange border placed around the element. This rule applies declarations to the following element in the body of the document:

```
<h2>
    Heading 2
</h2>
```

The browser knows that the h2 as the selector refers to the <h2> element. The same concept is applied by the next rule:

```
h3 {
    color: blue;
    border: 3px solid blue;
}
```

This time it's an <h3> element, the text is blue, and a 3-pixel thick, solid, blue border is placed around the element. Finally, the last rule selects all three heading elements at the same time:

```
h1, h2, h3 {
    letter-spacing: 5px;
    padding: 10px;
}
```

This rule selects all the <h1>, <h2>, and <h3> elements appearing in the body of the document. It includes a declaration that increases the amount of space between the letters inside each heading. *Padding*, a term that refers to the amount of space between the inside border edge and the edge of the content inside of an element, is also applied. In this example, it's the space between the sentences inside each heading and the inside border edge. This rule groups three selectors together; it selects all three heading elements in the document and applies the declarations to the following snippet of markup:

```
<h1>
    Heading 1
</h1>
<h2>
    Heading 2
</h2>
<h3>
    Heading 3
</h3>
```

Now that you've had an overview of how selectors work in a CSS document, the next section discusses the various ways in which you can include CSS in a document.

Including CSS in a Document

CSS is very flexible regarding how you call it in a document. You can include CSS in a document in four ways:

❑ CSS can be included in a document by using embedded style sheets, which are included between `<style>` and `</style>` tags directly in an HTML or XHTML document.

❑ CSS can be included in its own document and linked to an HTML or XHTML document by using the `<link>` element.

❑ CSS can be imported from within another style sheet by using an `@import` rule.

❑ CSS can be included directly in an element in an HTML or XHTML document by using inline styles with the `style=""` attribute.

Each method has its own particular usefulness. The upcoming sections describe how each of these methods can be used to include CSS in an HTML or XHTML document.

Including an Embedded Style Sheet

You use the `<style></style>` tag set to include embedded style sheets directly in the document. This is one of the style sheet methods I demonstrated in Example 3-1. You can include HTML comment tags if you want to hide style sheet rules from non-equipped browsers. Since HTML's early days, HTML has supported the capability to add comment text to a document. Comment text gives the web author the ability to add notes to a project so he can recall why he did something in a certain way or to mark the sections of a document. In HTML, you add a comment by typing a left angle bracket, an exclamation mark, two dashes, at least one space, and then the comment text itself. You close the comment by typing at least one space, two more dashes, and the right angle bracket. Here's what a comment looks like:

```
<!-- Hi I'm comment text -->
```

Comments are useful for a number of reasons. After figuring out how to do something complex, you may want to make a note of what steps you followed to solve the problem. Otherwise, when you return to the project a day, a week, a month, or a year later, you may look at the code and have no idea why you did what you did.

In the context of an embedded style sheet, comments have a special meaning. Because they appear inside the `<style>...</style>` tags, they tell browsers that don't support CSS to ignore the text that appears between them. Modern CSS-equipped browsers, on the other hand, read the sequence of `<style>`, followed by `<!--`, and know that style sheet rules appear there. This allows CSS to be hidden from browsers that are incapable of interpreting it. The following snippet shows how you can use comment tags to hide CSS from older browsers:

```
<style type='text/css'>
    <!--
        body, td {
            color: blue;
        }


    -->
</style>
```

Older browsers simply ignore any CSS rules defined inside the HTML comments.

For the `<style>` tag to be strictly formed XHTML syntax, a `type` attribute is required for the `<style>` tag. This is intended to tell the browser what type of syntax follows.

The next section describes how CSS can be written in its own document and included in an HTML or XHTML document.

Linking to External Style Sheets

`<link/>` and `@import` are supported in IE 5.5, IE 6, Mozilla 1.7, Opera 7.5, and Safari 1.2.

The authors of CSS recognized that HTML-template creation is a common need. As such, the W3C body made recommendations that allow external style sheets to be included in a document from within HTML or XHTML by use of the `<link>` element or from within a style sheet itself using the `@import` rule. External style sheets are the preferred method of CSS inclusion in a web document. External style sheets can be cached by the user's browser. This frees the user, who no longer needs to download the web page or website's style sheet on every page request. This also ensures that documents load very quickly, another feature of CSS that conserves expensive bandwidth.

Here's a demonstration of the `<link>` element method:

```
<link rel="stylesheet" href="path/to/cssdoc.css" type="text/css" />
```

The following attributes are required to use the `<link>` element for linking to a CSS document:

❑ `rel=""`: Defines the relation between the external document and the calling document. In this case, the relation is that the external document is the style sheet for the calling document.

❑ `href=""`: Like the anchor tag, `<a>`, `href` stands for hyperlink reference. It accepts an absolute or relative path to the style sheet document.

❑ `type=""`: Refers to the MIME type of the external file.

An *absolute* path means the complete path to the file. For instance, `http://www.somesite.com` is an absolute path. A *relative* path triggers the application to find the document relative to the requesting document. So if the example file's URL is `http://www.somesite.com/example.xhtml`, and the CSS document is stored in the style_sheets directory as cssdoc.css, the relative path included in `<link>` is `style_sheets/cssdoc.css` and the absolute path to the document is `http://www.somesite.com/style_sheets/cssdoc.css`.

Importing Style Sheets

You can also link to an external style sheet by using the `@import` rule. Here's a demonstration:

```
<style type="text/css">
    @import url(path/to/cssdoc.css);
</style>
```

This example uses the `<style></style>` method but includes the `@import` notation. It's very straight-forward: Plug in the `@import` rule followed by the `url()`, which may contain an absolute or relative path.

The `@import` method is not supported by older browsers, and it is sometimes used as a hack to hide styles from browsers that would crash horribly if these styles were present. One such browser is Netscape Navigator 4, which has horrible CSS support and has been known to lock up when certain styles are present.

How to Structure an External CSS Document

External style sheets are essentially the same thing as embedded style sheets; the key difference is that no markup exists in a CSS file. When you create an external, independent CSS document, it must be created using the .css file extension.

An external CSS document may contain nothing but CSS rules or comments; you see how to include comments within CSS later in this chapter. A CSS document cannot contain any markup.

The following Try It Out shows you how to link to an external style sheet from an XHTML document.

Try It Out   **Linking to an External CSS Document**

Example 3-2. To see how external style sheets are linked from an XHTML document, follow these steps.

1. Fire up that trusty text editor once more and type the following CSS, which is a modification of Example 3-1.

```css
p {
    font-family: Arial;
    font-size: 14pt;
}

h1 {
    color: black;
    border: 5px solid black;
}
h2 {
    color: orange;
    border: 4px solid orange;
}
h3 {
    color: blue;
    border: 3px solid blue;
}

h1, h2, h3 {
    letter-spacing: 5px;
    padding: 10px;
}
```

2. Save this file as example3-2.css.

3. Go back to the XHTML document you created for the last Try It Out (example3-1) and modify it to reflect the following changes:

```
<!DOCTYPE html PUBLIC "-//W3C//DTD XHTML 1.0 Strict//EN"
"http://www.w3.org/TR/xhtml1/DTD/xhtml1-strict.dtd">
<html>
    <head>
     <meta http-equiv="content-type" content="text/xhtml; charset=windows-1252" />
     <meta http-equiv="content-language" content="en-us" />
        <link rel="stylesheet" href="example3-2.css" type="text/css" />
        <title>Linking to External Style Sheets</title>
    </head>
    <body>
        <h1>
            Heading 1
        </h1>
        <h2>
            Heading 2
        </h2>
        <h3>
            Heading 3
        </h3>
        <p>
            Selectors choose the element to apply formatting to.  These may also be
            grouped together.
        </p>
    </body>
</html>
```

4. Save this file as example3-2.html in the same directory as example3-2.css.

5. View example3-2.html in your browser. You should see output identical to that in Figure 3-1.

How It Works

The embedded style sheet between the `<style>... </style>` tags has been replaced with an external style sheet by placing the rules inside the embedded style sheet into their own document, saving that document with a `.css` file extension, and then linking to the new file by including the `<link/>` element in the XHTML document. One of the benefits of an external style sheet is that it allows the same style rules to be applied to as many documents as the author wishes. This is one of the key benefits of CSS-based design. An external style sheet offers flexibility to the author that saves both time and resources.

The next section describes how styles can be included inline, directly on elements, by using the `style` attribute.

Inline Styles

The last method for including CSS in a document is from within the XHTML elements themselves. Sometimes it doesn't make sense to clutter your external or embedded style sheets with a rule that will be used on only one element in one document. This is where the `style=""` attribute comes into play; it's demonstrated by the following markup:

```
<table style="border: 1px solid black; margin: auto;">
    <tr>
        <td style="text-align: right; font-size: 18pt;">
            Some text aligned left.
        </td>
    </tr>
</table>
```

This method allows for the text to be formatted from within the document and may be applied to any rendered element.

The following Try It Out demonstrates how the `style` attribute is used to add styles directly to the elements of a web document.

Try It Out   The style Attribute

Example 3-3. To use the `style` attribute to apply styles directly to the elements of a document, follow these steps:

1. Using the documents you created for Example 3-2, return to your text editor and enter the following XHTML:

```
<!DOCTYPE html PUBLIC "-//W3C//DTD XHTML 1.0 Strict//EN"
"http://www.w3.org/TR/xhtml1/DTD/xhtml1-strict.dtd">
<html>
    <head>
     <meta http-equiv="content-type" content="text/xhtml; charset=windows-1252" />
     <meta http-equiv="content-language" content="en-us" />
        <title>The Style Attribute</title>
    </head>
    <body>
        <h1 style="color: black;
                border: 5px solid black;
                letter-spacing: 5px;
                padding: 10px;">
            Heading 1
        </h1>
        <h2 style="color: orange;
                border: 4px solid orange;
                letter-spacing: 5px;
                padding: 10px;">
            Heading 2
        </h2>
        <h3 style="color: blue;
                border: 3px solid blue;
                letter-spacing: 5px;
                padding: 10px;">
            Heading 3
        </h3>

        <p style="font-family: Arial;
                font-size: 14pt;">
            Selectors choose the element to apply formatting to.
```

```
                These may also be grouped together.
          </p>
       </body>
    </html>
```

2.   Save as example3-3.html.

How It Works

Note that the output is identical to output of the earlier examples depicted in Figure 3-1. The style attribute allows CSS declarations to be included directly in the XHTML element. The style attribute, however, is not as dynamic as a style sheet. It gives you no way to group repetitive rules or declarations. The style attribute should only be used when a more efficient method is not available (if, for example, the element to be styled does not appear on multiple pages).

Continuing the discussion of basic syntax, the next section discusses how to include comments in a CSS document.

CSS Comments

Like the HTML comments I described earlier in this chapter, comment text can be added inside style sheets. In a multipage template, this helps you remember which CSS rule applies to what or why it was added in the first place. CSS supports multiline comments that begin with a forward slash and an asterisk (/*) and terminate with an asterisk and a forward slash (*/):

```
/*  This rule applies to the design.html file */

table {
      padding: 50px;
      background-color: red;
      color: white;
      }
/*
 * CSS comments may span multiple lines.  (extra asterisks not required)
 */
```

CSS comments provide a mechanism that allow you to insert notes about what the styles in the style sheet do and why they were added in the first place. As I mentioned for HTML comments, the design of a website can get complicated, and often it's helpful to make notes that help you remember why you added one thing or another.

Summary

CSS consists of selectors and declarations that, when put together, form CSS rules. Selectors may be grouped using commas, and declarations may be grouped using semicolons. CSS styles may be embedded using style sheets that appear inside a web document. Alternatively, CSS styles may be linked externally via two methods, one which uses the <link> tag and another from within embedded style sheets using the @import notation. CSS styles may also be included inline, via the style="" attribute.

In this chapter, you learned what CSS looks like and a little of what it can do. You established the following facts:

❏ CSS selectors determine where and to what you can apply presentational declarations.

❏ CSS may be included directly in the document using embedded styles that appear directly in an HTML or XHTML document between the `<style></style>` tags.

❏ Style sheets may be included externally via the `@import` notation or the `<link/>` tag.

❏ Styles may be applied directly to an HTML or XHTML element by using the `style` attribute.

❏ CSS supports comments. Comments can help you remember the purpose of the styles in a style sheet — why they were added in the first place and what they do.

Having discussed some of the basic syntax of CSS, I continue this discussion in the next chapter by talking about data types, the units of measurement CSS allows for length, the different methods of specifying colors, and the syntax used to include things like background images.

Exercises

1. Using an inline style sheet, design a CSS document with two headers contained in `<h1>` and `<h2>` tags in which `<h1>` and `<h2>` elements both are in green, 22pt, Times New Roman font. Add a paragraph of text also in black, Times New Roman font, but 12pt in size. No declaration may be repeated. Include comments to signify what each rule does.

2. Using the scenario in Exercise 1, redesign the document so that the CSS document is included externally.

3. Again using the scenario in Exercise 1, rewrite the document so that each rule appears in each HTML element using the style attribute. (Declarations may be repeated.)

Data Types, Keywords, Color, Length, and the URI

CSS is comprised of a variety of smaller widgets and syntactical rules that come together to enhance the functionality and the wealth of features in style sheets. These features enable you to use different units of measurement and different methods for referencing colors; they also let you insert content into a document directly from CSS and call on external files through universally recognized file paths. This chapter explores how these widgets are used as property values in CSS. In this chapter I discuss

- ❑ Keywords and how keywords are used to define the functionality of a property in CSS
- ❑ Strings—a data type used in CSS that enables content to be inserted from a style sheet
- ❑ Absolute and relative lengths
- ❑ Integers and floating-point decimals—data types used in CSS to measure lengths
- ❑ Color keywords, RGB, and hexadecimal colors
- ❑ The URI

These pieces of CSS help make it a powerful presentational tool. Although CSS isn't really a programming language, its syntax and components are designed to mirror programming language components. In Chapter 3, you saw that declarations are composed of properties and values. This chapter explains the values a CSS property can have: colors, lengths, keywords, strings, and URLs. The first value you'll learn about is the keyword value.

Keywords

A *keyword* value is used to invoke some special functionality. For example, red, green, and blue are CSS keywords, although, keywords can have uses in CSS other than just specifying colors. Keywords are used in CSS as property values, as in this example:

```
table {
    background-color: red;
}
```

The keyword in this example is red. The background-color property applies a solid background color, red in this case, to the HTML / XHTML <table> element.

Many types of keywords are used in CSS, and sometimes a single keyword can have different meanings depending on the element to which it is applied. The auto keyword, for example, is used by CSS to apply some default style or behavior, and its meaning depends on the way it's used. For example

```
<table style='width: auto;'>
```

Figure 4-1 shows width: auto; applied to the <table> element.

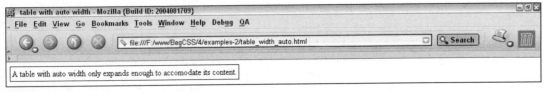

Figure 4-1

When width: auto; is applied to a <table> element, it invokes a different mechanism for width measurement than when it is applied to a <div> element:

```
<div style="width: auto;'>
```

Figure 4-2 shows width: auto; applied to the <div> element.

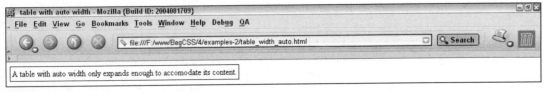

Figure 4-2

All elements with a width property have an auto value by default, but not all elements behave the same way when width is applied. The <table> element, for instance, only expands horizontally to accommodate its data, a method called *shrink-to-fit*. A <div> element, on the other hand, expands horizontally as far as there is space, which is called *expand-to-fit*.

I've added a border around each element in Figures 4-1 and 4-2 so that you can see its width. The border outlines the edges of each element, showing exactly how much space each element occupies. I discuss the finer details of the width property in Chapter 10.

Keywords always invoke some special, predefined behavior. In the case of the borders I added for Figures 4-1 and 4-2, each border contains three separate keywords that define how it appears when the browser renders it:

```
<div style='border: thin solid black;'>
```

This example defines a property with three keyword values: thin, solid, and black. Each value refers to a different characteristic of the border's appearance: thin refers to its measurement, solid to its style, and black to its color.

Keywords are cousin to another type of value, one that accepts any kind of input. This value is known as a string.

Strings

Keywords and strings are very different in both their syntax and their effect on your pages. Unlike keywords, which you use to control the appearance of your pages, strings can be used to add content to a web page. A *string is* any sequence of characters; for example, "Hello, World" is a string. In most languages and in CSS, strings are enclosed within either single or double quotation marks. A string is what is known as a data type. *Data types* are used to classify information. Integers, real numbers, and strings are examples of data types. Strings may contain text, numbers, symbols—any type of character.

One use of strings in CSS is to include content in a document from the style sheet instead of adding the content within HTML / XHTML tags. You can add content directly from the style sheet. For example, instead of typing the following:

```
<div>
    Hello, World!
</div>
```

you can apply a rule using the content property with a string value, like this:

```
div {
    content: "Hello, World!";
}
```

The string in this example is "Hello, World!". In this context, I use the content property to insert content into a <div> element directly from the style sheet. This type of functionality is referred to in CSS as *generated content*. The content property is not yet widely supported; however, it does work with Opera 7, and it works in Mozilla as well—but only when used with a special type of selector (more on this in Chapter 6). While using Opera 7, if I make an XHTML document with an empty <div> element and add a style sheet rule that includes the content property with a string value, the string in the content property is inserted into the <div> element, as depicted in this next example:

```
<!DOCTYPE html PUBLIC "-//W3C//DTD XHTML 1.0 Strict//EN"
"http://www.w3.org/TR/xhtml1/DTD/xhtml1-strict.dtd">
<html>
    <head>
        <title> The content property </title>
```

```
            <style type='text/css' media='all'>

                div {
                    content: "Hello, world!";
                }


            </style>
        </head>
        <body>
            <div></div>
        </body>
    </html>
```

Figure 4-3 shows that the string "Hello, world!" is inserted into the `<div>` element using the content property.

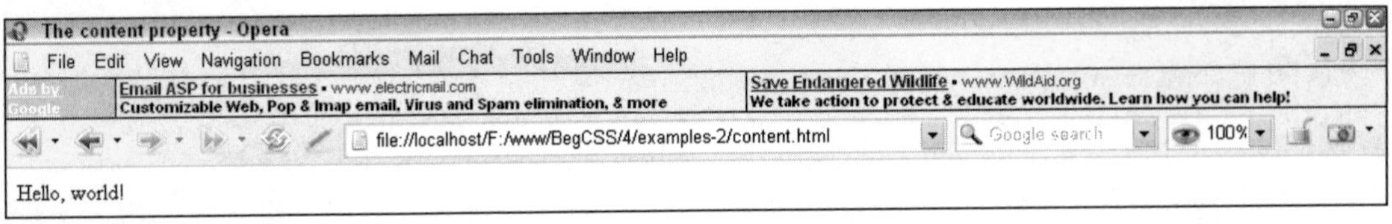

Figure 4-3

Strings and keywords differ in use and in syntax. Strings are used to insert content into a web page, and keywords invoke special predefined functionality. Keywords are always referenced without quotation marks, and strings are always referenced with quotation marks. If you were to apply quotation marks to keywords, you would not achieve the desired effect. The following does not give you the results you want:

```
div {
    border: "thin" "solid" "black";
}
```

Enclosing keywords within quotation marks means that a border is not applied to the `<div>` element. If you apply this rule to an element, nothing happens. When quotation marks are added, keywords become strings. CSS is generally forgiving of such errors, but as of this writing, no browser reports errors in CSS syntax.

Strings may contain any sequence of characters of any length — even quotation marks are allowed. However, strings may contain quotation marks only if they're *escaped* using another special character, the backslash character. When you *escape* quotation marks, you tell the browser: "Ignore the quotation mark; it is part of the string." The backslash is used to quote Foghorn Leghorn in the following code:

```
div {
    content: "Foghorn said: \"Get away from me son, you bother me.\"";
}
```

Figure 4-4 shows that the quotation marks have made it into the rendered page, but the backslashes don't show.

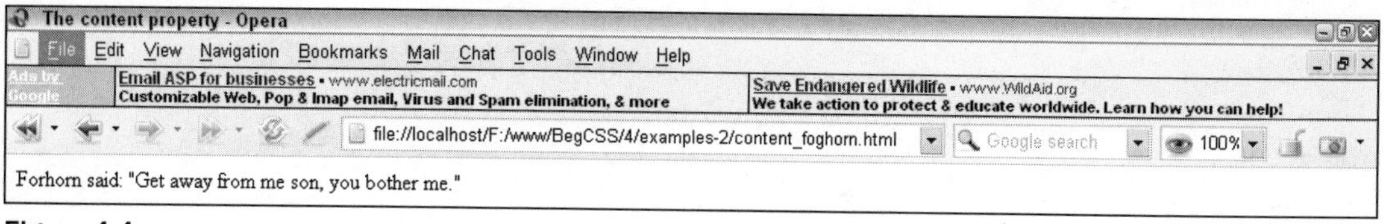

Figure 4-4

As an escape character, a backslash is only included to tell the browser to ignore the quotation mark that appears directly after it. The same backslash character is used to escape single quotes as well, if the string is enclosed by single quotes:

```
div {
    content: 'Foghorn said: \'Get away from me son, you bother me.\'';
}
```

The browser also ignores the single quotes in the middle with the use of the backslash character before the quote mark. Quotation marks do not have to be escaped if single quotes are used within a string enclosed by double quotes or vise versa. In this example

```
div {
    content: "Foghorn said: 'Get away from me son, you bother me.'";
}
```

the single quotes do not have to be escaped because double quotes enclose the string.

In CSS, strings exist primarily to allow content to be inserted from the style sheet, although they do have some other uses in attribute selectors that I discuss in Chapter 5.

Now that you've seen what keywords and strings are, you can create a very simple document that uses both with the following Try It Out.

Try It Out   Keywords and Strings

Example 4-1. Follow these steps to create a simple document with keyword and string property values:

1.   Fire up your text editor and enter the following markup and CSS.

```
<!DOCTYPE html PUBLIC "-//W3C//DTD XHTML 1.0 Strict//EN"
"http://www.w3.org/TR/xhtml1/DTD/xhtml1-strict.dtd">
<html>
    <head>
        <title> The content property </title>
        <style type='text/css' media='all'>

            div {
                content: "This string is placed inside of all div elements.";
                border: thick solid black;
                background: skyblue;
                color: black;
                font-size: xx-large;
```

```
                padding: 20px;
            }

        </style>
    </head>
    <body>
            <div></div>
            <div></div>
    </body>
</html>
```

2. Save as example4-1.html.

3. Open the page in the Opera 7.5 browser. It should look like the page shown in Figure 4-5.

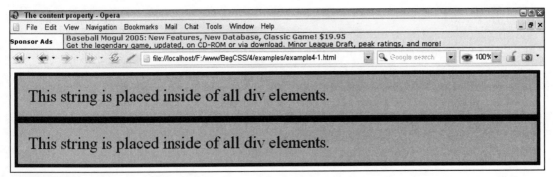

Figure 4-5

How It Works

The preceding Try It Out demonstrates the effect of several CSS keywords and one CSS string. To see how this is put together, examine each declaration in the rule. The first declaration uses the content property to insert a string into all <div> elements in the document:

```
content: "This string is placed inside of all div elements.";
```

To see the effects of the content property, you must use Opera 7 because Mozilla only partially supports this property. Internet Explorer does not support it at all. Its effects are simple: The content property allows content to be placed inside CSS instead of in the body of the document. Each of the following declarations has keyword values:

```
border: thick solid black;
background: skyblue;
color: black;
font-size: xx-large;
```

The border property, demonstrated in Figures 4-1 and 4-2, may have up to three keyword values, each defining how the border is styled. Here the border is thick, solid, and black. (I discuss the border property in further detail in Chapter 10.) The next declaration applies a skyblue background color to each <div> element. Next comes a declaration making the text black, even though all browsers make text black by default. The last declaration makes the font size extra, extra large.

Finally, I add padding to the example with the `padding: 20px;` declaration. Padding is space between the content of an element and the inner border edges. I added padding to make the text readable; without the padding the text of each `<div>` is flush with the border.

Now that you've seen some examples of CSS property values, the following section shows how length values such as `width` and `length`, can be specified in CSS to define a document's layout.

Length and Measurement Options

Two kinds of lengths are used in CSS: relative and absolute. *Absolute* lengths are not dependent on any other measurement. An absolute measurement retains its length regardless of the environment (operating system, browser, or screen resolution of a computer monitor) in which it is applied. *Relative* lengths, on the other hand, depend on the environment in which they're used, such as the computer monitor's screen resolution or the size of a font.

Absolute length units supported by CSS are shown in the following table.

Unit Abbreviation	Description
in	Inches
cm	Centimeters
mm	Millimeters
pt	Points, 1 point is equal to 1/72th of an inch
pc	Picas, 1 pica is equal to 12 points

Absolute lengths are supposed to maintain their size across multiple screen resolutions and platforms. For example:

```
p {
    font-size: 1in;
    margin: 0;
}
```

renders a font that is 1 inch tall, as shown in Figure 4-6.

Figure 4-6

Inconsistencies with Absolute Measurements

I said earlier that absolute measurements are *supposed* to maintain their size, but that doesn't mean that they actually *do*. The business of coding real-world physical lengths in a computer isn't nearly as easy as it may seem. Figure 4-6 becomes much larger when viewed at an 800 x 600 screen resolution than when viewed at 1024 x 768. These physical measurements are based on pixels, albeit very poorly. Pixels are tiny dots that a computer monitor uses to create the image you see, and the number of pixels displayed depends on the monitor's screen resolution. A computer monitor set to an 800 x 600 screen resolution displays 800 pixels horizontally and 600 pixels vertically for a possibility of 480,000 total pixels. Windows XP typically defines 1 inch as 96 pixels, but that depends on the operating system's display settings. It can be far from accurate because the length of a pixel changes depending on the screen resolution setting. Using Mac OS X, 1 inch is equal to 72 pixels (again, this might be far from accurate).

Figure 4-7 shows two <div> elements: The top <div> element has a height and width of 1 inch, and the bottom <div> has a height and width of 96 pixels. Both have a black background with white text for clarity. Switching the screen resolution from 800 x 600 pixels to 1280 x 1024 shows that the measurement of 1 inch remains the same as the 96-pixel measurement. Furthermore, because there is a difference between how Windows and Mac platforms interpret an inch, absolute measurements are unreliable for designing content to display on a computer monitor. To make things even more confusing and inconsistent, Mozilla enables you to switch from 96 pixels per inch to 72 pixels per inch using the preferences panel. In fact all the popular browsers render content based on 96 pixels per inch because of Windows legacy, including Apple's own Safari 1.2 browser.

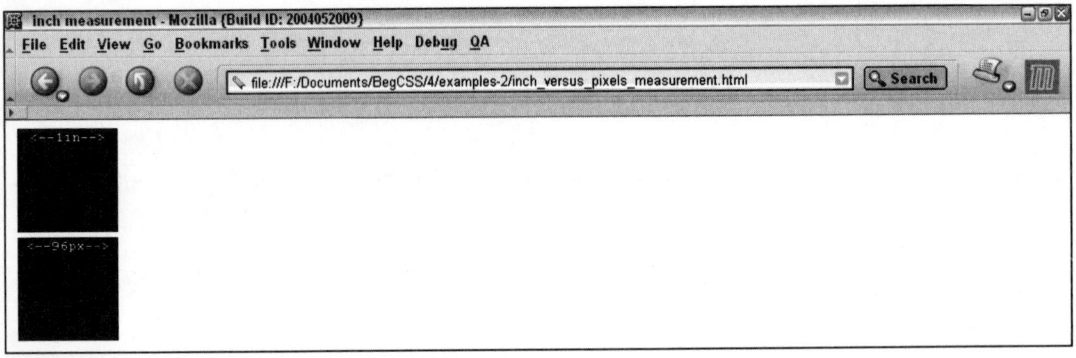

Figure 4-7

So, if physical lengths are so inconsistent and so difficult to get right, why does the CSS specification include them? It does so because, even though they're unreliable for designing content that displays on a computer monitor, these units of measurement are perfectly fine and universally applicable when you are designing content for print. In Chapter 15 you explore how to use CSS to alter the presentation of a web document for print. In that case, these units are most useful.

Metric Measurements

Understandably, CSS supports metric units because 99% of the world uses them. Centimeters and millimeters are allowed, and they produce the lengths you would find on a ruler. However, these measurements are subject to the same inconsistencies as inches and should not be used to design content for display on a computer screen.

Typographical Measurements

The *pt* unit stands for *points*, a unit of measurement heavily used in typographical design. One point is equal to one seventy-second of an inch. Because points are based on the measurement of an inch, points are also inaccurate. The *pc* measurement stands for *picas*, another typographical unit of measurement. One pica is equal to 12 points.

Relative Length Measurements

As I mentioned earlier, relative lengths depend on the environment in which they're used. The following table shows the relative units allowed by CSS.

Unit Abbreviation	Description
em	Length relevant to the nearest font-size.
ex	The x-height of the relevant font (height of the letter x).
px	Pixels, relative to the viewing device, for example, a computer monitor.

The *em* measurement unit depends on the nearest font size. For example:

```
div {
    font-size: 12px;
    height: 2em;
}
```

This rule defines a font size of 12 pixels and a height of 2em. Because em depends on the font size, this results in a height of 24 pixels for the `<div>` element. If I had not defined a font size, the em unit would depend on the font size of the `<div>` element's parent element.

To get a better idea of how em works, the following Try It Out shows how em units relate to the font-size of the element.

Try It Out   Measuring Using em Units

Example 4-2. The following steps show you how to measure using em measurement.

1. Enter the following markup into your text editor.

```
<!DOCTYPE html PUBLIC "-//W3C//DTD XHTML 1.0 Strict//EN"
"http://www.w3.org/TR/xhtml1/DTD/xhtml1-strict.dtd">
<html>
    <head>
        <title> em measurement </title>
        <style type='text/css' media='all'>
            body {
                border: 1em solid black;
                margin: 0;
                padding: 10px;
```

```
            }
        div {
            font-size: 24px;
            height: 3em;
            border: 1em solid black;
        }
    </style>
  </head>
  <body>
    The body's border is 1em thick. The body doesn't have a font
    size defined, so the em measurement here goes by the browser's
    default font size, which may vary from browser to browser.
    <div>
        This font is 24 pixels tall and this div is 3 ems tall,
        which results in a div 72 pixels tall (3 * 24 = 72). Its
        border is 1em thick, or 24 pixels thick.
    </div>
  </body>
</html>
```

2. Save the file as example4-2.html

3. Load the document in a browser; you should see output like that shown in Figure 4-8.

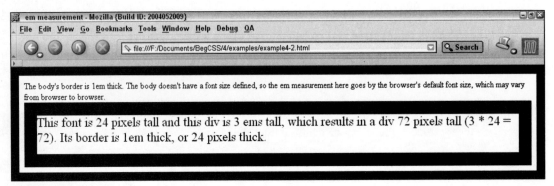

Figure 4-8

How It Works

The output in Figure 4-8 shows how em units are calculated. The first selector in the style sheet applies style to the <body> element:

```
body {
    border: 1em solid black;
    margin: 0;
    padding: 10px;
}
```

Em units are calculated using the font size of the element, but in this case the <body> element has no font size defined, nor does its parent element, the <html> element. When no font size is specified and no ancestor elements have a font size defined, the em unit is based on the browser's default font size. The default font size in Mozilla is 16 pixels. So in this example, if Mozilla is the browser and it's running with default settings, the 1em measurement for the border around the <body> element is 16 pixels. The <div> element, on the other hand, does have a font size defined — it's set to 24 pixels:

```
div {
    font-size: 24px;
    height: 3em;
    border: 1em solid black;
}
```

The height of the <div> element is set to 3em, or three times the font size. The font size is 24 pixels, so the height of the <div> element is 72 pixels. Likewise, the border for the <div> element specifies a 1em thickness, meaning the border is 24 pixels thick.

Measurements Based on the Height of the Lowercase Letter x

The *ex* measurement, also known as *x-height*, is (like the em) based on the font size. However, the ex measurement is relative to the height of the lowercase letter *x*. The ex measurement is another unit of measurement derived from typography.

Like measurement in inches, ex measurement is unreliable, but for different reasons. Because it is difficult to determine the actual height of the lowercase letter *x* for a given font, most browser creators take a shortcut in implementing the ex measurement. Instead of relying on the height of the lowercase letter *x*, ex measurement is defined by taking the measurement of half of 1 em, or 0.5 em. Because of its inconsistencies, ex measurement is yet another unit of measure to be avoided when designing for display on a computer monitor.

Pixel Measurements

Pixels, the *px* measurement, are measured relative to the computer monitor's settings. This measurement depends on the resolution of the user's monitor. For instance, a 1px measurement viewed at a resolution of 800 x 600 is larger than a 1px measurement viewed at a resolution of 1024 x 768.

Pixels are easiest to understand when they specify the width and height of an image because images are created based on the number of pixels they contain. Pixel measurements have some advantages and disadvantages. Pixel measurements use the actual pixels on your computer monitor. Although that is often fine for screen display, it is not as precise when it comes to printing documents. The size of a pixel can change depending on many factors, among which are monitor size and resolution and the fine-tuning settings that stretch and shrink the display output. Therefore, defining a pixel measurement for print leaves lots of room for browser inconsistencies. This is an area best-suited for the absolute units that I discussed earlier in the chapter. I discuss this issue further in Chapter 15.

Percentage Measurements

Percentage measurements are always dependent on something else; therefore, percentage measurements are also a form of relative measurement. The behavior of a percentage measurement changes depending on the element to which the measurement is being applied. For instance:

```
body {
        margin: 0;
}
div {
        width: 100%;
        color: white;
        background: black;
}
```

As you can see in Figure 4-9, the `<div>` element takes up 100% of the available area. In this example, I removed the margin from the `<body>` element with the `margin: 0;` declaration. I did this because the body's default margin affects the `<div>` element's rendering. The `width: 100%;` measurement is based on the size of the `<body>` element; therefore, the `<div>` element's width is relative to the width of the `<body>` element. Because percentage measurements change depending on what they're applied to, I continue to revisit this topic throughout the book, as I introduce and explain each property.

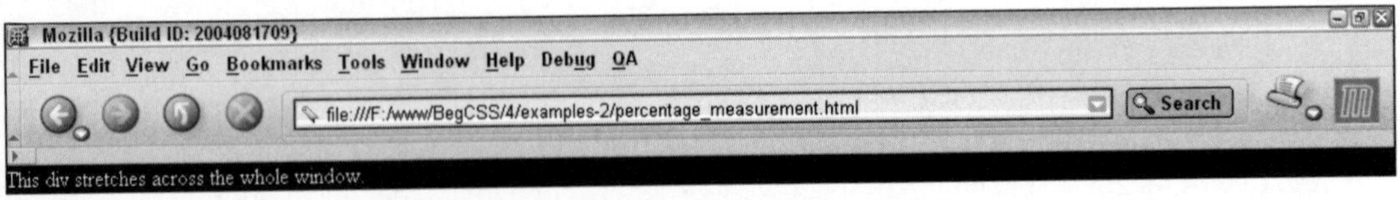

Figure 4-9

Because it's a presentational language, most of CSS is affected in some way by length and units of measurement. The fundamental unit for all measurements when you design for display on a computer monitor is the pixel, because computers display images in pixels. You can define lengths relative to font sizes, using em units as the most practical and consistent solution. Absolute lengths, on the other hand, are better suited for print because of the multitude of inconsistencies that occur when absolutes are used for presentations on a computer monitor. In the next section, I continue the discussion of CSS property values with a look at how CSS interprets numbers.

Integers and Real Numbers

CSS allows numbers as values for several properties. Two types of numbers are accepted by CSS: *integers* and *real numbers*. Like strings, integers and real numbers are data types and are often used in CSS for the measurement of length. The first type, integers, are exclusively whole numbers, meaning no decimals are allowed. In CSS, an integer may be preceded by a plus (+) or minus (-) to indicate the sign. Although some properties do not accept negative values, many do. As you can see in the following code, one property that allows negative values is the margin property:

```
body {
        margin: 0;
}
```

```
div {
    font-size: 24pt;
    width: 100%;
    color: white;
    background: black;
    margin: -10px;
}
```

The rendering depicted in Figure 4-10 shows what happens when these rules are applied to an XHTML document. As I did with the percentage width example, I removed the default margin from the `<body>` element to observe the effect of the margin property on the `<div>` element. I also made the font size large, the text white, and the background color black to clarify the dimensions of the `<div>` element. With a negative margin applied, the `<div>` is shifted partially off-screen.

Figure 4-10

Real numbers are the second type of number allowed by CSS. Real numbers can have a decimal value, and decimal values increase the precision of measurements in CSS.

Real numbers in CSS can be preceded by plus (+) or minus (-) to indicate the number's sign. The value 1.2em, for example, means 1.2 times the font size. As in mathematics, a positive sign is assumed if no sign is present. If I have a declaration that says `margin-left: -1.2em;`, this causes an element to shift to the left 1.2 times the font size.

CSS as of this writing does not allow expressions. For instance, I could not write the following:

```
div {
    width: 5px + 8px;
}
```

`5px + 8px` is an expression, and CSS is not capable of evaluating it (although a future CSS specification might include this functionality).

CSS provides some basic and reasonable rules for the specification of integers and real numbers in property values. CSS is also very flexible with how colors are specified, a topic I discuss in the following section.

Colors

CSS has a number of options for specifying colors, ranging from a 216-color, web-safe pallet to the full range of colors available in the RGB format, a total of 16,777,216 colors! More specifically, those options are as follows:

❏ **Color keywords:** These enable you to specify a color by its name.

❏ **RGB values:** These enable you to specify a color via a Red, Green, Blue representation, which provides access to millions of colors.

❏ **RGB Percentage:** This option is the same as RGB but uses percentages.

❏ **RGBA (RGB with Alpha channel [available in CSS 3]):** The RGB palette is used with the addition of an alpha channel to specify transparency.

❏ **Hexadecimal:** This enables you to specify a color by a special hexadecimal number.

❏ **Shorthand Hexadecimal:** This is a shortened representation of hexadecimal numbers; it is limited to a special 216-color, web-safe pallet.

Each method is a means to accomplish the same thing: specifying a color. These methods may be used to specify text color, border color, or background color. Next, you see what each of these methods looks like when used in the context of a style sheet rule.

Color Keywords

The first method for specifying color, mentioned previously, is to use a color keyword. This is the most intuitive method because all you need to do is reference the name of the color itself. Here are some examples:

```
div {
    color: black;
    background-color: red;
    border: thin solid orange;
}
```

As I mentioned in Chapter 3, this is a simple element name selector. This rule applies style to any <div> element contained in the document. I have specified that each <div> element should have black text, a red background, and a thin, solid orange border around the element. In this example, black, red, and orange are color keywords, so a color keyword is simply the name of the color.

In CSS 3, 147 colors are named. Browser support for these colors has been very good in the tests I have run. I found only a single color not supported by Internet Explorer 6. That color is lightgray, spelled with an *a*; however, the browser does support lightgrey, spelled with an *e*. This is an obscure bug that arises because Internet Explorer only allows the British spelling of *grey* and not the American English *gray*. The CSS specification supports both spellings of gray. Netscape 7 and Mozilla support the full list of colors defined in CSS 3, as do Opera 7 and Safari 1.

> **A complete table of CSS-supported color keywords is available in Appendix C.**

RGB Colors

RGB stands for Red, Green, and Blue. These are the primary colors used to display the color of pixels on a computer monitor. Using these three colors in various combinations, it is possible to create every color of the rainbow. This is done through different colored lights either overlapping each other or appearing side by side in different intensities to display color. RGB is also known as *luminous* or *additive* color. Luminous means that RGB uses light in varying intensities to create color, and additive means colors are added to one another to produce the colors of the spectrum. Many computers monitors are capable of displaying millions of colors: 16,777,216 colors, in fact. CSS RGB color is specified using a special three-number syntax, with each one representing a color channel. This first number is red, the second green, and the third blue:

```
body {
    background-color: rgb(128, 128, 128);
}
```

This produces the same color as the CSS color keyword `gray`. Equal amounts of all three channels form a variation of gray, where 0,0,0 is black and 255,255,255 is white.

Here's another example:

```
body {
    background-color: rgb(135, 206, 235);
}
```

This produces the same color as the CSS color keyword `skyblue`. The number 135 refers to the red channel, 206 to the green channel, and 235 to the blue channel. RGB color is also often specified in hexadecimal format.

RGB values may also be represented using percentages:

```
body {
    background-color: rgb(50%, 50%, 50%);
}
```

This also produces the same color as the CSS color keyword `gray`.

CSS 3 is to introduce one more variation on the rgb scheme, with rgba. This specification includes the specification of an alpha channel, which is used to make an element transparent. The alpha channel of rgba is specified in the same manner as regular RGB with the A to indicate how transparent the color is, with 0 being fully opaque and 255 being fully transparent. No browser yet supports the rgba specification.

Hexadecimal Colors

Hexadecimal colors were used in old, presentation-based HTML documents. *Hexadecimal* refers to a numbering scheme that uses 16 characters as its base, expressed in a combination of letters and numbers. The decimal numbering system, on the other hand, uses 10 numbers as its base. A hexadecimal system uses 0-9 for the first 10 digits and A-F to represent the remaining 6 digits. Letter *A* corresponds to the number 10, *B* to 11, *C* to 12, and so on up to 15, which is represented by *F*. Hexadecimal values are another way of expressing an RGB value. For instance, #FFFFFF refers to white, which is expressed in RGB as 255, 255, 255. To switch from RGB values to hexadecimal, each channel is converted to its hexadecimal equivalent, so each 255 becomes FF in hexadecimal. To calculate the hexadecimal value, divide the RGB number by 16. The result is the first hexadecimal digit. The remainder from the division becomes the second hexadecimal digit. The RGB value 255 divided by 16 equals 15 with a remainder of 15. In hexadecimal, 15 are represented by F, so applying this formula results in FF. The process is repeated for each RGB color channel, so the hexadecimal notation of 255, 255, 255 is FF, FF, FF or #FFFFFF. In CSS, hexadecimal colors are included just as RGB or color keywords are, as shown in the following example.

```
div {
    color: #000000;
    background-color: #FF0000;
    border: thin solid #FFA500;
}
```

#000000 is the hexadecimal representation of black; the same as RGB 0, 0, 0 or simply the black color keyword. #FF0000 is a hexadecimal representation of red, or RGB 255, 0, 0, or the red color keyword. Finally, #FFA500 is a hexadecimal representation of orange, or RGB 255, 165, 0, or the orange color keyword.

Short Hexadecimal and Web-Safe Colors

There are 216 web-safe colors. A *web-safe color* is a hexadecimal color comprised of any combination of the following: FF, CC, 99, 66, 33, 00, for a potential of 216 colors. These colors were originally identified and given their web-safe name by Lynda Weinman, a graphic and web design guru and author of numerous graphic and web design books. These 216 colors were identified as colors safe for cross-platform, cross-browser use on computer systems capable of displaying only 256 colors; in other words, 8-bit systems. There are 216 colors, minus 40 colors reserved for use by operating systems Different operating systems, such as Macintosh OS and Windows OS, do not reserve the same 40 colors. So these 40 colors cannot be relied upon. If one attempts to use a color outside of the 216-color pallet on a system only capable of displaying 256 colors, the operating system may attempt to display the color through a process called dithering. *Dithering* is a process in which the operating system attempts to mix two colors that it is capable of displaying to get the requested color.

Figure 4-11 shows a dithered image.

Figure 4-11

Figure 4-12 shows the image undithered.

Figure 4-12

These images have been converted to grayscale for publication, but if you look close, you should be able to see the effects of dithering. The image in Figure 4-11 is pixilated and grainy; the image in Figure 4-12 is smooth and fluid.

Dithering causes all sorts of nasty things to happen to an image or solid color. In some cases a grid appears on a solid background where the operating system attempts to display the color using two colors.

Hexadecimal notation is capable of expressing all 16,777,216 colors allowed by RGB. If a color outside the web-safe pallet is used, this leads to dithering. Short hexadecimal notation, on the other hand, allows only the 216-color, web-safe pallet:

```
div {
    color: #000;
    background-color: #F00;
    border: thin solid #FFA500;
}
```

Only FF, CC, 99, 66, 33, and 00 are allowable in the web-safe pallet, so the notation for these can be simplified. FF becomes simply F, CC becomes C, 99 becomes 9, and so on. A single digit rather than two represents the pair. So in this example, #000 refers to black and #F00 refers to red. #FFA500 is not representable in short hexadecimal notation because A5 cannot be simplified to a single digit. Only pairs in which both numbers have the same value can be converted to short hexadecimal notation.

Although in the past the web-safe pallet was frequently necessary for designers, today advanced graphic cards capable of displaying millions of colors have become so common that the number of 8-bit systems capable of displaying only 256 colors has fallen dramatically. Today, it is safer to design creatively with color. The browser-safe pallet is not yet completely dead — it still has a place in designing web content for display on PDAs and cell phones, most of which are limited to 256 colors.

The URI

CSS uses a special term — URI (Universal Resource Indicator) — when the location of a resource or data file must be specified. The acronym *URI* is related to two other acronyms, URL (Universal Resource Locator), and URN (Universal Resource Name). The ideas behind both of these specifications are combined to get the URI, the term used in the W3C CSS specifications. URIs are most used in CSS for two purposes:

❑   The inclusion of style sheets.

❑   The inclusion of background images.

The URI is referenced using a special method, as show in the following example.

```
background: url(mypicture.jpg);
```

The url() syntax is used to enclose the URI of the file being referenced. Like the @import and <link/> tag discussed in Chapter 3, this URI can be either a relative or an absolute path to the resource. So in this example, mypicture.jpg must exist in the same directory as the style sheet. If the style sheet is named *mystyle.css* and it's located at http://www.mysite.com/styles/mystyle.css, the *mypicture.jpg* file must also exist in the *styles* directory, where its path is http://www.mysite.com/styles/mypicture. jpg. The complete, absolute path or the shortened relative paths are both acceptable references to the file. I address this topic again in Chapter 8, where I outline some of the techniques that professional website designers use to manage the files of a website and in Chapter 13 where I discuss the background property and the syntax it allows.

Summary

CSS properties may have a wide range of values that can include keywords, strings, lengths, colors, and URIs. In this chapter you learned that the following:

❑   Keywords are used in CSS to invoke special behavior or styles for an element, such as how a border appears or how width is handled.

❑   Strings are used in CSS primarily to insert content dynamically.

❑   Absolute lengths are more suited for print than for screen.

❑   Pixel length measurements are more suited for screen than for print.

❑   RGB colors are luminous or additive colors that are combined to create a possibility of over 16 million colors. In CSS, these can be expressed in three channels by including a number between 0 and 255 for each channel or by a percentage real number.

❑   Hexadecimal colors are RGB colors values written in a system using a 16 alphanumeric character base (instead of a 10 number base as with the common decimal system).

❑   Short hexadecimal notation is a representation of the 216-color, web-safe pallet

❑   URIs are used to reference external files in CSS. External files are imported from other sources and can be, for example, background images and other style sheets.

The discussion of CSS basics is continued in Chapter 5, which takes an in-depth look at the various types of selectors that CSS supports.

Exercises

1. Compose a web page with a heading of `<h1>` and a paragraph of text `<p>`. Specify the font size in the selector for the `<body>` element as 12 pixels. Specify the heading font size as 1.2em. Give the paragraph a font size of 0.9em. Give the heading a thin, black, solid border and a pink background. Give the paragraph a thin, solid, black border, white text, and a gray background. Give both the heading and the paragraph a padding of 1em.

2. Repeating the scenario from Exercise 1, specify all sizes using pixels instead of em units, and use RGB instead of color keywords to specify the colors for the document. Calculate the pixel measurements so that they are exactly the same lengths as the em measurements you used in Exercise 1.

5

CSS Selectors

In Chapter 3, I touched on the topic of type selectors. You learned that CSS Selectors choose where and what to format in a document. CSS, however, supports a wide range of options for the selector. This chapter covers

- ❑   The universal (wild card) selector
- ❑   Contextual/descendant selectors
- ❑   Child selectors
- ❑   Direct/indirect adjacent sibling combinators
- ❑   Attribute selectors
- ❑   User-defined class and id selectors

At the time of this writing, no universal support exists for all selector types. For that reason, most of this chapter's examples are designed to work in Netscape 7, Mozilla, or Mozilla Firefox. Mozilla has an excellent implementation of the CSS recommendations as outlined by the W3C, whereas other browsers still lack this support in some areas.

The Universal Selector

Documented in CSS 3 and supported in IE 5.5, IE 6, Mozilla 1.7, Opera 7.5, and Safari.1.2.

The universal selector is an asterisk. When used alone, the universal selector tells the CSS interpreter to apply the CSS rule to the entire document and all conceivable elements:

```
* {
    font-family: Arial;
    color: black;
}
```

This rule is applied to all elements contained in the document unless specified elsewhere by the cascade—covered in Chapter 7. The universal selector applies to everything, including form input fields and tables of data. It applies style to any and every element present in a document. The universal selector can also be used with other types of selectors, such as descendant selectors, which is the focus of the next section.

Contextual/Descendant Selectors

Documented in CSS 3 and supported in IE 5.5, IE 6, Mozilla 1.7, Opera 7.5, and Safari 1.2.

Descendant selectors apply style based on whether one element is a descendant of another. In CSS, *descendant* means an element that is a child, grandchild, great grandchild, and so on of another element. This type of relationship is referred to as an *ancestral* relationship.

> *In the CSS level 1 specification, descendant selectors are referred to as contextual. The name change was made in the CSS level 2 specification. The name change likely resulted from new selectors in CSS 2, several of which can also be considered contextual because their selection is based on the context in which the target element appears in the document.*

The following rule demonstrates a descendant selector:

```
div h1 {
    color: darkolivegreen;
}
```

This example applies a color of `darkolivegreen` to `<h1>` elements, but only if somewhere in the document hierarchy the `<h1>` element appears nested inside a `<div>` element. That is to say the `<h1>` could appear inside a `<table>` or a paragraph of text, as long as each of these is nested inside at least one `<div>` element.

For example, you could have the document hierarchy represented in Figure 5-1.

In Figure 5-1, `<html>` is the root element; each element following `<html>` is a child of `<html>`; `<div>` is a child of `<body>`; `<table>` is a child of `<div>`; and so on. The descendant selector, `div h1`, says that if an `<h1>` element has an ancestor `<div>` element, you should apply the style declarations contained in the rule. This selector applies style whether `<h1>` is a direct child of `<div>` or a distant grandchild.

If `div h1` is the descendant selector, that selector applies to the following markup:

```
<div>
    <h1>Some header text</h1>
</div>
```

as well as to this markup:

```
<div>
    <table>
        <tr>
            <td>
                <h1> Some header text </h1>
            </td>
        </tr>
    </table>
</div>
```

Both hierarchies are valid for the div h1 descendant selector.

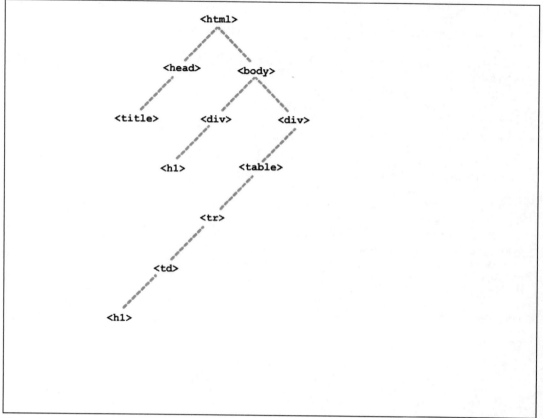

Figure 5-1

Descendant selectors are not limited as to how many elements are referenced in the element hierarchy; therefore, using the preceding example, all the following rules also reference the <h1> element appearing inside the table.

```
div table td h1 {
    color: darkolivegreen;
}

div table h1 {
    color: darkolivegreen;
}

div td h1 {
    color: darkolivegreen;
}
```

The <h1> element inside the table applies darkolivegreen-colored text.

In the last section, I mentioned the universal selector could be combined with other selectors, like the descendant selector. Take for instance, the following rule:

```
div * {
    color: lavender;
}
```

The selector in this rule applies to all descendants of the <div> element; every descendant of the <div> element receives lavender text.

Now that you have an overview of how the universal and descendant selectors work, the following Try It Out puts that knowledge into a tangible real-world example. Each example in this chapter builds a user input form for feedback for the Widgets and What's-its company to demonstrate the various CSS selectors in action. This example lays the input form's foundation and shows you how to apply styles to elements with the universal selector, descendant selectors, and plain old type selectors introduced in Chapter 3.

Try It Out   Descendant Selectors

Example 5-1. This example begins with the basic form look and feel and the input-form questions.

1. Return to your favorite text editor and type the following markup:

```
<!DOCTYPE html PUBLIC "-//W3C//DTD XHTML 1.0 Strict//EN"
"http://www.w3.org/TR/xhtml1/DTD/xhtml1-strict.dtd">
<html>
    <head>
        <title>Feedback Form - Widgets and What's-its</title>
        <style type="text/css">

            * {
                font-family: sans-serif;
                color: white;
            }
```

```
/**
 * Apply this style to all h1 elements regardless of where they
 * appear in the page.
 **
 */

h1, form h2 {
    background: gray;
}

h1, h2, form {
    margin: 0;
}

h1 {
    font-size: 24px;
    padding: 5px;
    border-bottom: 5px solid black;
    letter-spacing: -2px;
    width: 510px;
    -moz-border-radius-topleft: 10px;
    -moz-border-radius-topright: 10px;
}

form {
    background: lightgrey;
    padding: 10px;
    width: 500px;
    -moz-border-radius-bottomleft: 10px;
    -moz-border-radius-bottomright: 10px;
}

/**
 * Apply these styles label elements, but only if they
 * appear inside of an input form
 **
 */

form label {
    display: block;
    font-weight: bold;
    margin: 5px;
    width: 225px;
    text-align: right;
    background: black;
}

/**
 * These styles are shared between h2 and label elements
 * that appear inside of a form
 **
 */

form h2, form label {
    font-size: 15px;
```

```
                     -moz-border-radius: 10px;
                     padding: 3px;
                }
          </style>
     </head>
     <body>
          <h1>Widgets and What's-its</h1>
          <form>
               <h2>Tell us what's on your mind..</h2>
                    <label>Name:</label>
                    <label>Email:</label>
                    <label>Address:</label>
                    <label>Comments:</label>
                    <label>How'd you hear about us?</label>
          </form>
     </body>
</html>
```

2.   Save the file as example5-1.html. You should see output similar to what is shown in Figure 5-2.

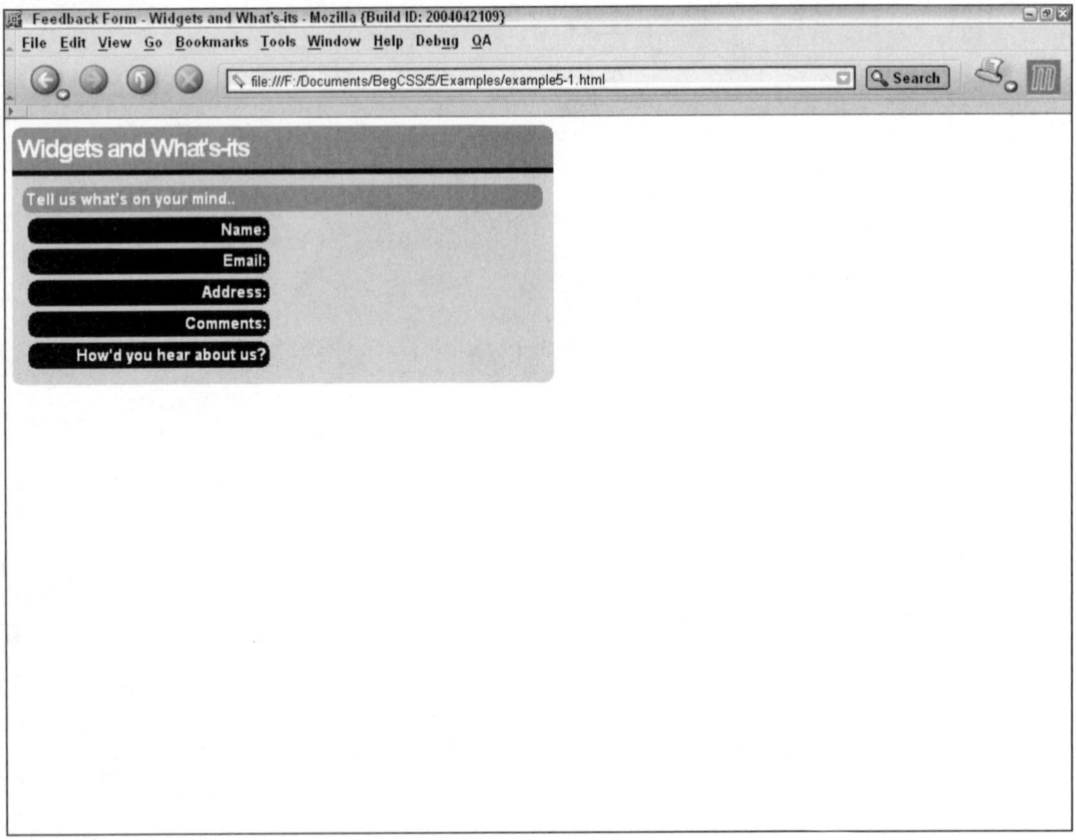

Figure 5-2

How It Works

This example lays the foundation for the user-input form example used throughout this chapter. Because this example is much more complex than previous examples, take a look at each rule individually. The style sheet begins with the universal selector:

```
* {
    font-family: sans-serif;
    color: white;
}
```

This rule applies the properties contained in it to all rendered elements. This example applies a generic font, sans-serif, with the `font-family` property. Web page authors use generic fonts to avoid specifying an operating-system–specific font. For instance, Tahoma is a Windows-only font, whereas Helvetica is a Macintosh/Linux-specific font. (Chapter 9 discusses generic fonts in greater detail.) The color property follows `font-family` property, which applies white text to the entire document.

Next comes the first example of a descendant selector. This rule groups two selectors. First it selects all <h1> elements, and then all <h2> elements, but only if they appear inside of a <form> tag. If the <form> element is a parent, grandparent, or ancestor of the <h2> element it receives a gray background:

```
h1, form h2 {
    background: gray;
}
```

The next rule removes preset margins from the <h1>, <h2>, and <form> elements, which squishes every-thing together and gives the form a nice, seamless look. This rule specifies that the black border on the bottom of the top <h1> header is flush with the input form:

```
h1, h2, form {
    margin: 0;
}
```

This style sheet contains comment text to help you understand what each rule does:

```
/**
 * Apply this style to all h1 elements regardless of where they
 * appear in the page.
 **
 */
```

Next comes another familiar selector from Chapter 3. This rule selects all <h1> elements:

```
h1 {
    font-size: 24px;
    padding: 5px;
    border-bottom: 5px solid black;
    letter-spacing: -2px;
    width: 510px;
    -moz-border-radius-topleft: 10px;
    -moz-border-radius-topright: 10px;
}
```

This rule applies an absolute width to the <h1> element with the width: 510px; declaration. It also applies some padding with the padding: 5px; declaration, which adds some space between the text inside the <h1> element and the inside border edge, a 24-pixel font size, and a thick, black border under the heading. The letter-spacing property squishes the header's letters together. The letter-spacing property's negative value causes the letters to appear closer together. This rule contains two new properties: -moz-border-radius-topleft and -moz-border-radius-topright. These are proprietary CSS properties that work only in Gecko browsers and round the top-left and top-right edges of the header. Although many developers discourage its use, it is harmless to include proprietary CSS because browsers that don't recognize the styles simply ignore them. For example, the proprietary -moz-border-radius property is included in CSS 3 as the border-radius property, but no browser support has yet emerged for this property.

After the header, you style the element that contains the input form itself, the <form> element.

```
form {
    background: lightgrey;
    padding: 10px;
    width: 500px;
    -moz-border-radius-bottomleft: 10px;
    -moz-border-radius-bottomright: 10px;
}
```

This rule includes a light grey background. Grey is spelled with an *e* here (its British spelling) because Internet Explorer doesn't recognize it with an *a* (its American spelling). All CSS color constants with grey in the name are laid out by the W3C to be spelled with either an *e* or an *a* to accommodate either spelling.

The form here also includes a width of 500 pixels, as opposed to the header's width of 510 pixels. Why the difference? This concept is known in CSS as the box model, and I discuss it in detail in Chapter 10. *The box model* is a set of rules that governs the fundamentals of web page layout. To give you a brief overview of how the box model works, there are four areas where the space of each element is measured: margins, border, padding, and width, in that order. These four come together to form a box. The width of an element is measured from inside padding edge to inside padding edge—known as the *content area*—where the text and images inside an element appear. Around the content is the padding, around the padding are the borders, and around the borders is the margin. You can refer to the diagram presented in the first figure in Chapter 10 (Figure 10-1) for a visual representation.

In CSS, the background of each element is the area from outside border edge to outside border edge, which includes the borders, padding, and content area. The form has a padding of 10 pixels, and the header has a padding of 5 pixels. In order to line up the <h1> heading with the <form> element, the amount of padding you add to each element's width must be equal because the padding plus the width equals the background area. Each padding size is doubled to get the amount of padding used on both the left and right sides of the element, and that amount is then added to the element's width. The form's width, including padding, is 520 pixels; the header's width including padding is also 520 pixels. Because the box model is a fundamental concept of CSS design, I continue to revisit this topic throughout the book.

Next you style the form questions:

```
form label {
    display: block;
    font-weight: bold;
```

```
        margin: 5px;
        width: 225px;
        text-align: right;
        background: black;
    }
```

In this example, `<label>` elements contain the form questions. The `<label>` element is intended exclusively for form input controls. Each `<label>` element can be tied to a specific form input control, which you see demonstrated in Example 5-2. This rule also employs a descendant selector; the styles are applied only if the `<label>` element appears inside a `<form>` element. The first declaration applied to each `<label>` element makes all of them block-level elements; this is a complicated adjustment that changes the way the `<label>` element handles the box model. The addition of `display: block;` causes the `<label>` element to take on an entirely different behavior where margin, borders, padding, and width are concerned. The effects of this change are too complicated to explain here, so I revisit this in Chapters 10 and 17.

The text of each question in the feedback form is made bold with the `font-weight: bold;` declaration; then some margin is applied to each `<label>`, which provides some space between the bottom of one `<label>` and the top of the next. Each is given a width of 225 pixels; this width leaves room for the form input controls, which you add in Example 5-2. The text of each `<label>` is then right-aligned with the `text-align: right;` declaration, and each is given a black background.

Finally, you apply styles common to `<h2>` and `<label>` elements that appear inside forms:

```
form h2, form label {
    font-size: 15px;
    -moz-border-radius: 10px;
    padding: 3px;
}
```

The `<h2>` element is used as the form's header, and the `<h1>` heading contains the company name. This rule applies some padding, a font size, and once more, the proprietary `-moz-border-radius` property, which rounds the edges of `<h2>` and `<label>` elements appearing inside a form.

The next section continues the discussion of selectors with the direct child selector, a selector that works in a similar fashion to the descendant selector.

Direct Child Selectors

Documented in CSS 3 and supported in Mozilla 1.7, Opera 7.5, and Safari 1.2.

Direct Child selectors operate much like descendant selectors in that they also rely on an ancestral relationship to decide where to apply style. Descendant selectors, however, are more ambiguous because they apply to any descendant of an element. Child selectors apply only to immediate children of the element. This is achieved by introducing a new syntax for the selector. This example shows a direct child selector:

```
h2 > em {
    color: blue;
}
```

It uses the greater than sign (>) to show the relationship between the two elements. In this example, <em> must be a direct child of an <h2> element before it becomes blue. For example

```
<h2>Welcome to <em>What's-its</em> and Widgets</h2>
```

results in the application of this rule. Whereas

```
<h2>Welcome to <strong><em>Widgets</em></strong> and What's-its</h2>
```

does not apply this rule, because <em> isn't a direct child of <h2>. The <strong> element is the direct child of <h2>, and <em> is the direct child of <strong>.

In this Try It Out, you build on the document presented in Example 5-1. You add form input fields to the Widgets and What's-its feedback form and implement direct child selectors in the embedded style sheet.

Try It Out   Direct Child Selectors

Example 5-2. The following steps show you how to use direct child selectors:

1. Open example5-1.html and modify the embedded style sheet, adding the following highlighted rules:

```
/**
 * These styles are shared between h2 and label elements
 * that appear inside of a form
 **
 */

form h2, form label {
    font-size: 15px;
    -moz-border-radius: 10px;
    padding: 3px;
}

/**
 * Direct Child Selectors
 **
 */

form > div > label {
    float: left;
}
form > div {
    clear: left;
}
div > input, div > select {
    margin: 3px;
    padding: 4px;
}
```

```
            select > option {
                padding: 4px;
            }
        </style>
        <title>Feedback Form - Widgets and What's-its</title>
    </head>
```

2. Next, add form input controls to the document body, a `for` attribute to each `<label>` element, and enclose each form question and input control with `<div>` elements:

```
<h1>Widgets and What's-its</h1>
<form>
    <h2>Tell us what's on your mind..</h2>
    <div>
        <label for='feedback[name]'>Name:</label>
        <input type='text' size='25' name='feedback[name]' />
    </div>
    <div>
        <label for='feedback[email]'>Email:</label>
        <input type='text' size='25' name='feedback[email]' />
    </div>
    <div>
        <label for='feedback[address]'>Address:</label>
        <textarea name='feedback[address]'
                  cols='40' rows='3' wrap='virtual'>
        </textarea>
    </div>
    <div>
        <label for='feedback[message]'>Comments:</label>
        <textarea name='feedback[message]'
                  cols='40' rows='6' wrap='virtual'>
        </textarea>
    </div>
    <div>
        <label for='feedback[heard]'>How'd you hear about us?</label>
        <select name='feedback[heard]'>
            <option value=''>Choose...</option>
            <option value='newspaper'>Newspaper</option>
            <option value='magazine'>Magazine</option>
            <option value='television'>Television</option>
            <option value='radio'>Radio</option>
            <option value='other'>Other</option>
        </select>
    </div>
</form>
```

3. Save this file as example5-2.html. Loading the file into Mozilla/Firefox/Netscape, you should see output like that which is shown in Figure 5-3.

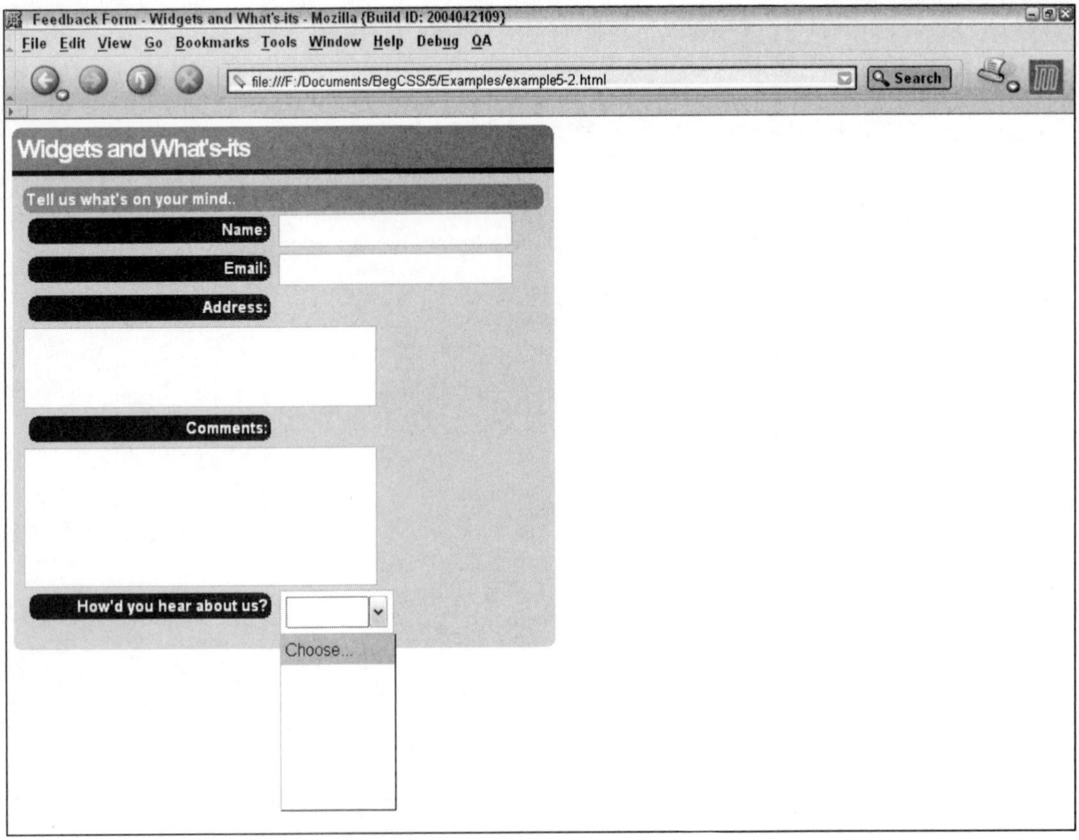

Figure 5-3

How It Works

With this round of modifications, your feedback form looks more like a feedback form, although it's still not quite complete. The first rule you applied selects the `<label>` element if it is a direct child of a `<div>`, which, in turn, is a direct child of a `<form>` element:

```
form > div > label {
    float: left;
}
```

It wasn't really necessary to add another rule that selects the `<label>` element because you created a rule using the `form label` selector in Example 5-1 to select `<label>` elements. You added this rule simply to see how the direct child selector works. Here you applied a `float: left;` declaration; this is another complicated property that I discuss at great length in Chapter 11. The addition of this declaration, `float: left;` causes the `<input>` and `<select>` elements to appear to the right of the `<label>` element. In fact, when the `float` property is applied to an element, it causes all the elements that follow the floated element to float to the left or right of the element (if there is room for those subsequent elements to fit in terms of their dimensions). So to limit the effects of the `float` property you applied another rule:

```
form > div {
    clear: left;
}
```

The `clear` property is a companion property to the `float` property. The `clear` property tells the `<div>` element to ignore the `float` property on the `<label>` element and allows the `<div>` element to stay on its own line, preventing the `<div>` element from floating, too. With the `float` property on the `<label>` element, the inputs you add and every subsequent `<label>` element and `<div>` element try to put themselves beside the first `<label>` element. This works for everything but the `<textarea>` elements, which stay on their own line because they're bigger than the space between the `<label>` element and the edge of the form. This looks a little strange, but you fine-tune this in Example 5-3. Again, these are complicated properties that are discussed again in Chapter 11. Now that the `<input>` elements and the `<select>` element are on the same line as the question, you need to tweak the spacing and enter the next rule:

```
div > input, div > select {
    margin: 3px;
    padding: 4px;
}
```

This rule says if `<input>` and `<select>` elements are direct children of `<div>` elements, apply a 3-pixel margin and a 4-pixel padding to those elements. This adjusts the spacing so that the inputs match up with the questions vertically. And finally the last rule is the following:

```
select > option {
    padding: 4px;
}
```

With CSS, you can style the options of drop-down menus individually. Browsers like Mozilla have impressive CSS support for styling drop-down menus, whereas Internet Explorer 6 doesn't support quite as many properties as Mozilla does. The rule says that if `<option>` elements are direct children of the `<select>` element (which they always are) give them 4 pixels-worth of padding.

Continuing the discussion of selectors, the next section discusses a selector much like the direct child selector, but instead of child elements, it selects siblings.

Direct Adjacent Sibling Combinator

Documented in CSS 3 and supported in Mozilla 1.7, Opera 7.5, and Safari 1.2.

Adjacent sibling selectors, just as the name sounds, select based on whether two elements appear side by side in a document as siblings. Referring back to the diagram in Figure 5-1, `<head>` and `<body>` are siblings because they appear side by side and share the same parent, the `<html>` element. Likewise, the two `<div>` elements in the diagram are siblings because they also appear side by side and share the same parent, the `<body>` element. Whereas the direct child selector in the previous section relied on a parent-child relationship, direct adjacent sibling combinators rely on a sibling relationship.

CSS 2 simply refers to these selectors as adjacent sibling selectors. CSS 3 changes the name slightly to direct adjacent sibling combinator. The name change is due to an expansion of CSS 3 to also include indirect adjacent sibling combinators (discussed in the next section). The word combinator is based on the word selector and what the syntax does.

For example, a rule using a direct adjacent sibling combinator selector looks like this:

```
<!DOCTYPE html PUBLIC "-//W3C//DTD XHTML 1.0 Strict//EN"
"http://www.w3.org/TR/xhtml1/DTD/xhtml1-strict.dtd">
<html>
    <head>
        <style type="text/css">
            h2 + p {
                text-indent: 20px;
                color: red;
            }
        </style>
    </head>
    <body>
        <div>
            <h2>
                Welcome to CSS widgets.
            </h2>
            <p>
                This paragraph of text is red and is indented 20 pixels.
            </p>
        </div>
        <p>
            This paragraph of text is not indented, it does not have the same
            parent as an h2 element.
        </p>
    </body>
</html>
```

The `<p>` element directly follows the `<h2>` element, making the `<p>` element a direct sibling of the `<h2>` element. The `h2 + p` selector makes the text of the paragraph that follows the `<h2>` element, red and indented 20 pixels.

Building on the document that you completed for Example 5-2, this Try It Out continues building on the feedback form for Widgets and What's-its with the application of a rule that uses the direct adjacent sibling combinator.

Try It Out   Direct Adjacent Sibling Combinator

Example 5-3. In the following steps, the input form is expanded with the inclusion of a style rule that uses the direct adjacent sibling combinator.

1   Once more in your text editor, open the document example5-2.html and make the following changes to the Widgets and What's-its embedded style sheet:

```
select > option {
    padding: 4px;
}

/**
 * Direct Adjacent Sibling Combinators
 **
 */

label + input, label + select, label + textarea {
    background: darkgray;
}
```
```
    </style>
    <title>Feedback Form - Widgets and What's-its</title>
</head>
<body>
```

2.   Save the file as example5-3.html. Loading the file in Mozilla/Firefox/Netscape, you see output like that shown in Figure 5-4. I've typed some text into each input field so you can see how the text of each field is styled.

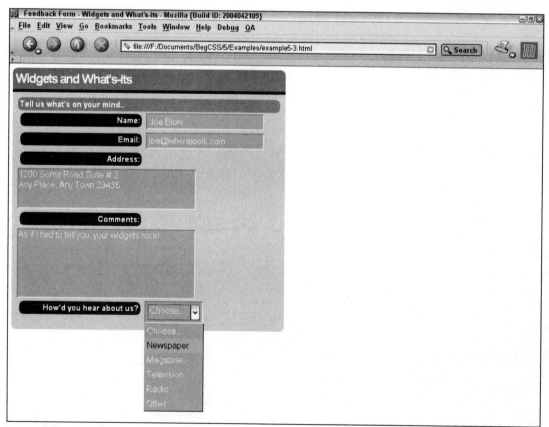

Figure 5-4

How It Works

This example is very straightforward. The new rule selects three different elements. It says if an `<input>` element follows a `<label>`, give the element a dark gray background. If a `<select>` element follows a `<label>`, do the same. If a `<textarea>` element follows a `<label>`, do the same.

The next section introduces the indirect adjacent sibling combinator — another contextual selector similar to the direct adjacent sibling combinatory.

Indirect Adjacent Sibling Combinators

Documented in CSS 3 and supported in Safari 1.2.

Like the direct adjacent sibling combinator selector discussed in the preceding section, the indirect adjacent sibling combinator selector also selects elements based on sibling relationships. This new selector loosens up the rules a bit, however. Indirect adjacent sibling combinators do not require the elements to appear side by side in the document, but the elements still must share the same parent element. You use a tilde (~) instead of a plus sign (+) in the syntax for an indirect adjacent sibling combinator selector.

The embedded style sheet of the following XHTML document shows the syntax for this rule:

```
<!DOCTYPE html PUBLIC "-//W3C//DTD XHTML 1.0 Strict//EN"
"http://www.w3.org/TR/xhtml1/DTD/xhtml1-strict.dtd">
<html>
    <head>
        <style type="text/css">
            h2 ~ h3 {
                text-decoration: underline;
                font-size: 22px;
                color: lightgreen;
            }
        </style>
    </head>
    <body>
        <div>
            <h2>
                Welcome to CSS widgets.
            </h2>
            <p>
                This paragraph of text is indented 20 pixels.
            </p>
            <h3>
                Some underlined text.
            </h3>
        </div>
    </body>
</html>
```

The `<h2>` and `<h3>` element must have the same parent for the selector to work, and element `<h2>` still precedes element `<h3>`. But the two elements do not have to be side by side. This selector results in the `<h3>` element receiving underlined, light green text with a font size of 22 pixels.

Browser support for the indirect adjacent sibling is yet to emerge at the time of this writing. Currently, it is supported only by Safari.

The next section continues discussion of CSS selectors by introducing a new kind of selector, one that selects elements based on that element's attributes.

Attribute Selectors

Documented in CSS 3 and supported in Mozilla 1.7, Opera 7.5, and Safari 1.2.

Attribute selectors may decide where to apply style declarations based on the presence of attributes or attribute values that appear in the HTML, XHTML, or XML tag.

The syntax looks like this:

```
input[type='text'] {
    background: green;
}
```

This rule selects `<input/>` elements that contain the `type='text'` attribute, as in the following:

```
<input type="text" name="some_input" />
```

There are, however, several types of attribute selectors. CSS provides attribute selectors that select elements based on the following:

- ❑ The presence of an attribute
- ❑ The value of an attribute
- ❑ Whether one of several possible values is present in an attribute
- ❑ Whether the attribute value begins with a specific string
- ❑ Whether the attribute value ends with a specific string
- ❑ Whether the attribute value contains a specific string anywhere in the value, be it at the beginning, end, or middle

The following sections examine each type of attribute selector in greater depth and provide examples of the syntax for each.

Selection Based on the Presence of an Attribute

Documented in CSS 3 and supported in Mozilla 1.7, Opera 7.5, and Safari 1.2.

A simple attribute selector selects elements based on the presence of a particular attribute. The syntax looks like this:

```
input[type] {
    background: lightcoral;
    border: 2px dotted darkorange;
}
```

In this example, the selector begins with a simple type selector preceded by the attribute name enclosed in square brackets. This rule applies to <input> elements, but only <input> elements that contain a type attribute. This selector is related to the type selector introduced in Chapter 3; but instead of only selecting an element, the selection is made based on whether that element contains a particular attribute.

The next section discusses attribute selectors that select based on whether the attribute contains a particular value.

Selection Based on the Value of an Attribute

Documented in CSS 3 and supported in Mozilla 1.7, Opera 7.5, and Safari 1.2.

Attribute value selectors delegate style declarations based on an attribute's presence and value. Here is the selector I showed at the opening of this "Attribute Selectors" section:

```
input[type='text'] {
    background: green;
}
```

CSS, however, also supports the specification of multiple values via the following syntax:

```
input[type~='text' 'file' 'password'] {
    border: 2px dotted darkorange;
}
```

The tilde indicates multiple values. In this example, the style sheet rule is applied to <input> elements that have a type attribute value of text, file, and password, as in

```
<input type='text' name='some_field' /><br />
<input type='password' name='some_password' /><br />
<input type="file" name='some_user_file' /><br />
```

A 2 pixel-wide dotted border appears around each field. However, the style sheet rule is not applied to <input> elements with a type attribute value of radio or checkbox, or to an <input> element with a type attribute containing any other value.

No major browser yet supports the tilde multiple value syntax.

However, you are not limited to the presence of only one attribute. An element may also be selected based on the presence and value of multiple attributes:

```
input[type='text'][name='some_field']
```

This would match any input element that has a type attribute of "text" and a name attribute of "some_field".

The values don't necessarily have to be enclosed in quotes. The following selector is also valid.

```
input[type=text][name=some_field]
```

The following section discusses attribute substring selectors that select elements based on where in an attribute's value a string appears.

Attribute Substring Selectors

Documented in CSS 3 and supported in Mozilla 1.7 and Safari 1.2.

Taking the flexibility of attribute selectors even further, the selectors in the following sections choose elements based on whether a particular string appears at the beginning of an attribute's value, at the end of an attribute's value, or anywhere inside an attribute's value. A string that appears inside another string is often referred to as a *substring*.

Selection Based on Attribute Values That Begin with a String

The first type of substring attribute selector chooses elements with an attribute value that begins with a particular string. This is demonstrated in the following rule:

```
a[href^='ftp://'] {
    background: orange;
}
```

This rule selects links (`<a/>` elements) that have an `href` attribute when the value of the `href` attribute begins with the string "`ftp://`". The rule selects all FTP links in a web page and gives them orange backgrounds.

This attribute substring selector introduces the caret (^) character in the selector syntax, which indicates that the attribute value begins with "`ftp://`". Each `href` attribute prefixed with "`ftp://`" is then styled according to the declarations defined in the rule.

Another example of this syntax in action is to match all e-mail links in a page:

```
a[href^='mailto'] {
    color: burlywood;
}
```

This code changes the color of all e-mail links to `burlywood`!

The next section examines the attribute substring selector that chooses elements with attribute values ending with a string.

Selection Based on Attribute Values That End with a String

The next substring attribute selector chooses elements with attributes whose value ends with a string. The syntax of this selector is demonstrated in the following rule:

```
a[href$='.html'] {
    color: indianred;
}
```

The selector of the preceding rule uses the dollar sign to signify that the selector matches the end of the attribute value. This changes all links that end in an .html suffix to `indianred`. Here's an example of this in the document itself:

```
<a href='http://www.somesite.com/index.html'>Hello, World!</a>
```

The `href` attribute in the link ends in an .html extension, so it receives a text color of `indianred`. Conversely, this principle does not apply to the `href` attribute of the following `<a>` element:

```
<a href='http://www.somesite.com/index.php'>A .php page</a>
```

The attribute's value in this example ends with a .php suffix, so it does not receive a text color of `indianred`.

The next section discusses an attribute substring selector that chooses elements based on whether a string appears anywhere in an attribute's value.

Selection Based on Attribute Values That Contain a String

The final type of attribute substring selector is more of a wild card. It selects an element that contains an attribute whose value contains a string anywhere in the value: at the beginning, end, or anywhere in between. This attribute substring selector uses an asterisk in the syntax to indicate that the selector is looking anywhere inside the value:

```
a[href*='.php'] {
    background-color: thistle;
}
```

This matches any URL that contains a .php extension regardless of whether the URL contains anchors or query strings, as shown in this example:

```
<a href='/index.php?content=341&amp;sid=a0da625a83123f133e72436f20254baf'>Some link
text</a>
```

All that garbage after the question mark is called the *query string*, which holds special meaning for programming languages such as PHP, ASP, Perl, and others. What that stuff does isn't important. What is important is that using this style sheet rule, the selector finds the .php extension even though it is in the middle of the value. The selector also finds the .php value if it appears at the beginning or the end of the URL:

```
<a href='http://www.somesite.com/index.php'>A .php page</a>
```

Both links receive the `thistle` color.

The following Try It Out continues to build on the Widgets and What's-its input form. This time you apply attribute selectors.

Try It Out   Attribute Selectors

Example 5-4. The following steps demonstrate the usefulness of attribute selectors in an input form.

1.   In your text editor, open example5-3.html and modify the embedded style sheet to include the following highlighted block:

```
        label + input, label + select, label + textarea {
            background: darkgray;
        }

        /**
         * Attribute Selectors
         **
         */

        option[value] {
            letter-spacing: 2px;
        }
        option[value='newspaper'] {
            background: orange;
        }
        option[value='magazine'] {
            background: red;
        }
        option[value='television'] {
            background: black;
        }
        option[value='radio'] {
            background: green;
        }
        option[value='other'] {
            background: blue;
        }
        input[name$='[name]'] {
            color: darkred;
        }
        input[name$='[email]'] {
            color: darkblue;
        }
        textarea[name$='[address]'] {
            color: purple;
        }
        textarea[name$='[message]'] {
            color: black;
        }
        select[name$='[heard]'] {
            color: darkgreen;
        }
        input[name^='feedback'],
        select[name^='feedback'],
        textarea[name^='feedback'] {
            font-weight: bold;
        }
    </style>
    <title>Feedback Form - Widgets and What's-its</title>
</head>
<body>
```

2. Save as example5-4.html. Viewing the example in Mozilla, Netscape 7, or Firefox, you see output that looks like Figure 5-5.

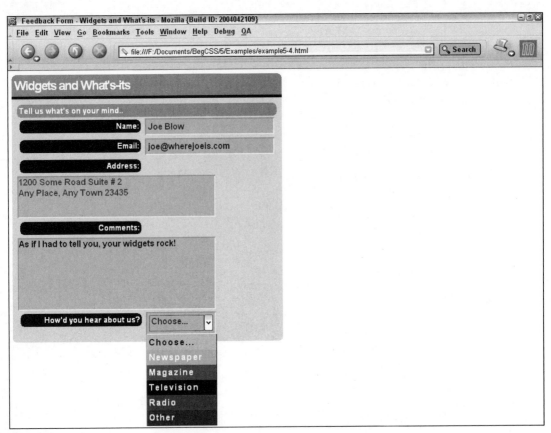

Figure 5-5

How It Works

Following is a review of each rule applied:

```
option[value] {
    letter-spacing: 2px;
}
```

This rule applies some letter spacing to each individual <option> element. Mozilla has impressive styling capability for form inputs. The <select> element is styled separately from the individual options contained inside of it. In the Widgets and What's-its feedback form, for example, the selected value has a gray background, bold, dark green text (thanks to a rule discussed later), and a different style for each option in the drop-down list. The next set of rules applies more styles to each individual <option> element to further differentiate them:

```
option[value='newspaper'] {
    background: orange;
}
option[value='magazine'] {
```

```
        background: red;
}
option[value='television'] {
    background: black;
}
option[value='radio'] {
    background: green;
}
option[value='other'] {
    background: blue;
}
```

These rules give each <option> element a different background color based on the value of the value attribute.

The next set of rules applies a different text color to each input field:

```
input[name$='[name]'] {
    color: darkred;
}
input[name$='[email]'] {
    color: darkblue;
}
textarea[name$='[address]'] {
    color: purple;
}
textarea[name$='[message]'] {
    color: black;
}
select[name$='[heard]'] {
    color: darkgreen;
}
```

The first rule specifies that darkred text be applied if the name attribute of <input> elements ends with the string '[name]'. The other input elements receive a different text color based on what the name attribute's value ends with. This leads me to the final rule:

```
input[name^='feedback'],
select[name^='feedback'],
textarea[name^='feedback'] {
    font-weight: bold;
}
```

The last rule specifies that <input> elements, <select> elements, and <textarea> elements receive bold text if the name attribute's value begins with the string "feedback".

The next section continues the discussion of selectors with class and id selectors.

Class and ID Selectors

Documented in CSS 3 and supported in IE 5.5, IE 6, Mozilla 1.7, Opera 7.5, and Safari 1.2.

The last of the selectors to be discussed in this chapter are those defined by the author using the `class=""` or `id=""` attributes. Class and id selectors are the most widely supported selectors. In fact, they are as widely supported as the type selector introduced in Chapter 3. There are two types of selectors. The `class` attribute is more generic, meaning it may encompass many elements in a given document, even elements of different types or purposes. On the other hand, you can only use the `id` attribute once per page. The name `id` tells you that the id must be unique. Besides using it in CSS, you can also use the `id` to access the element that contains it via a scripting language like JavaScript. You can also link to the location of the element with an `id` name using anchors. Anchors are appended to URLs to force a browser to go to a specific place in a document. I discuss anchors in more detail in Chapter 6. So the `id` attribute serves more than one purpose. Think of it as an element's address inside a document—no two addresses can be the same.

The following is an example of a class selector:

```
.someclass {
    color: mediumseagreen;
}
```

The user-defined class contains a dot before the class name. In the document body, you reference the class like this:

```
<div class="someclass">
    Some div text.
</div>
```

The dot appearing before the class name in the CSS rule tells CSS that you are referencing a class selector. The dot does not need to appear in the `class` attribute value itself; in fact it cannot.

When used in this context, the type of element doesn't matter. In other words, you can also apply the class to other elements, as in the following:

```
<span class="someclass">
    Some span text.
</span>
```

The same rule applies to the `<span>` element as applies to the `<div>` element. Both now have medium seagreen text. Elements can also be assigned more than one class. The following markup is an example of this:

```
<div class="foo bar">
    Some div text.
</div>
```

The value of this `class` attribute actually contains two class names, `foo` and `bar`. Each class name in the attribute is separated by a space. In the corresponding style sheet, the two classes may be referenced by two separate rules:

```
.foo {
    font-family: monospace;
}
.bar {
    color: goldenrod;
}
```

This results in the <div> element receiving a monospace font and goldenrod colored text. The class names may also be chained together, which is demonstrated by the following rule:

```
.foo.bar {
    font-weight: bold;
}
```

The preceding rule applies only to elements that reference both class names in their class attribute.

Internet Explorer incorrectly interprets chained class names; only the last class name in the chain is recognized. In the preceding example, Internet Explorer would interpret the .foo.bar *selector as* .bar *only.*

To reference an id, you precede the selector syntax with a hash mark (or pound sign, #):

```
#someid {
    color: mediumseagreen;
}
```

Following the same concept, any element in the document body may contain the id.

```
<div id="someid">
    Some div text.
</div>
```

You can make both class and id selectors more specific by appending the name of the element to the beginning of the selector. For instance, if in the last examples you only want <div> elements for each rule, the selectors look like the following:

```
div.someclass {
    color: mediumseagreen;
}
div#someid {
    color: mediumseagreen;
}
```

Now each rule is applied only to <div> elements that contain the corresponding class and id names.

Although the id must be unique, in these examples you can name only one element someid. The CSS style sheet, however, may contain as many references to that id as are necessary. The uniqueness rule only applies to naming the elements, not the references to them. You can apply classes, on the other hand, to as many elements in the body as necessary.

The following Try It Out finishes the Widgets and What's-its feedback form, this time incorporating user-defined selectors.

Try It Out   User-Defined Selectors

Example 5-5. By following these steps, you can see how to work with user-defined selectors.

1. Using example5-4.html, enter the modifications in the highlighted block to the embedded style sheet:

```
input[name^='feedback'],
select[name^='feedback'],
textarea[name^='feedback'] {
    font-weight: bold;
}

/**
 * Class Selectors
 **
 */

label.spanform {
    float: none;
    width: auto;
    text-align: left;
}
div.spanform {
    text-align: center;
}

/**
 * ID Selectors
 **
 */

div#buttons {
    text-align: right;
}

input#button {
    background: black;
    font-weight: bold;
    border: 1px solid white;
}
div#copyright {
    margin-top: 10px;
    border-top: 1px dashed black;
    padding-top: 10px;
    font-size: 8pt;
    text-align: center;
    color: black;
}
    </style>
    <title>Feedback Form - Widgets and What's-its</title>
</head>
<body>
```

2. Make the highlighted modifications to the body of the document:

```html
<h1>Widgets and What's-its</h1>
<form>
    <h2>Tell us what's on your mind..</h2>
    <div>
        <label for='feedback[name]'>Name:</label>
        <input type='text' size='25' name='feedback[name]' />
    </div>
    <div>
        <label for='feedback[email]'>Email:</label>
        <input type='text' size='25' name='feedback[email]' />
    </div>
    <div class='spanform'>
        <label for='feedback[address]' class='spanform'>Address:</label>
        <textarea name='feedback[address]'
                  cols='40' rows='3' wrap='virtual'>
        </textarea>
    </div>
    <div class='spanform'>
        <label for='feedback[message]' class='spanform'>Comments:</label>
        <textarea name='feedback[message]'
                  cols='40' rows='6' wrap='virtual'>
        </textarea>
    </div>
    <div>
        <label for='feedback[heard]'>How'd you hear about us?</label>
        <select name='feedback[heard]'>
            <option value=''>Choose...</option>
            <option value='newspaper'>Newspaper</option>
            <option value='magazine'>Magazine</option>
            <option value='television'>Television</option>
            <option value='radio'>Radio</option>
            <option value='other'>Other</option>
        </select>
    </div>
    <div id='buttons'>
        <input type='submit'
               name='feedback[action]' value='Submit' id='button' />
    </div>
    <div id='copyright'>
        &copy; Copyright 2004 What's-its and Widgets, All Rights Reserved.
    </div>
</form>
</body>
</html>
```

3. Save the file as example5-5.html. You should see output similar to what appears in Figure 5-6.

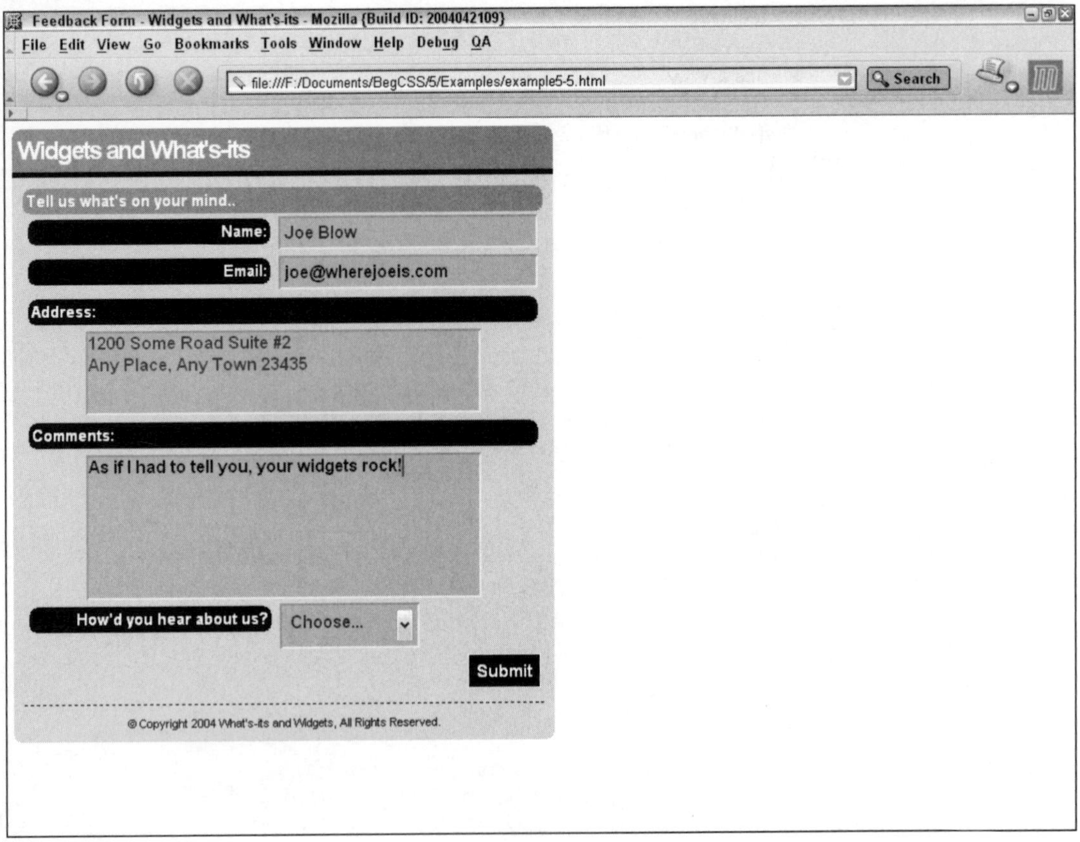

Figure 5-6

How It Works

Here is a review of each new style sheet rule:

```
label.spanform {
    float: none;
    width: auto;
    text-align: left;
}
div.spanform {
    text-align: center;
}
```

The first rule is a class selector referring specifically to `<label>` elements. The class is glued specifically to `<label>` elements containing the class declaration because you use the same class name for two different sets of elements. The second rule contains the same class name, but applies only to `<div>` elements.

Reviewing each declaration in the first rule, you apply a `float: none` declaration to prevent the float property from being applied to `<label>` elements containing the spanform class. Recall from Example 5-2 that you applied a `float: left` declaration to all `<label>` elements to achieve a two-column effect.

This property repeals that declaration, but only where the class spanform is defined inside <label> elements. The remaining <label> elements still have a float: left applied. The next property is width: auto. The width property has a value of auto by default. Although in Example 5-1 you applied a width of 225 pixels to all <label> elements, this rule repeals that declaration so that <label> elements with a spanform class definition span the entire form horizontally. The last declaration aligns text left, once again repeating a declaration from Example 5-1 that right aligns all text in <label> elements. The next rule for spanform class declarations that apply only to <div> elements centers the <textarea> fields.

The next set of rules applies a Submit button to the form:

```
div#buttons {
    text-align: right;
}
input#button {
    background: black;
    font-weight: bold;
    border: 1px solid white;
}
```

The first rule uses an id selector named buttons to align the button to the right of the div. Another id selector named button refers to the input button itself and follows the first id selector. It applies a black background, bold face font, and a thin white border around the button. Recall from Example 5-1 that all elements receive white text via the universal selector, which is why you do not need to specify a text color.

The last rule applies some styling to the copyright text added to the bottom of the input form:

```
div#copyright {
    margin-top: 10px;
    border-top: 1px dashed black;
    padding-top: 10px;
    font-size: 10px;
    text-align: center;
    color: black;
}
```

To provide some spacing between the thin, black, dashed border and the bottom of the input form, 10 pixels of margin are added. Next, you apply some space between the thin, black, dashed border and the content of the copyright <div> by adding 10 pixels of padding. A small, 10-pixel font size and black coloring for the text are applied as well, and the text is aligned to the center of the <div>.

Summary

CSS selectors provide a flexible and diverse array of options for applying style to a document. CSS 2 greatly expanded the options made available in CSS 1, and CSS 3 has again expanded selector options.

In this chapter you learned the following:

❑   The universal selector applies style to all conceivable page elements.

❑   Descendant selectors apply style based on document hierarchy and ancestral relationships.

❑   Using child selectors makes the methodology created for descendant selectors more specific.

❑   Direct adjacent sibling combinators (that's a mouthful) apply style if two elements, appearing back to back in a document as siblings, have the same parent.

❑   Indirect adjacent sibling combinators take the methodology created for direct adjacent sibling combinators and loosen up the rules so that the elements don't have to appear back to back, just in the same block.

❑   Attribute selectors delegate style depending on the presence of attributes or attribute values.

❑   Selectors may also be user-defined using the `class` and/or `id` attributes.

Chapter 6 continues the discussion of selectors, covering pseudo-class and pseudo-element selectors, which are special CSS selectors that apply style when certain conditions are present in the document.

Exercises

1.   Using what you already know about selectors, rewrite the Widgets and What's-its input form to simplify the embedded style sheet. Make the selectors cross-browser compatible (Internet Explorer, Mozilla, and Opera), and remove redundant references to elements. For example, if the various selectors in the Widgets and What's-its input form refer to the same element but appear more than once in the style sheet (even when written differently, such as a direct child selector and an adjacent sibling selector that refer to the same element), combine the rules so that only one rule exists for that selector. If the selectors aren't compatible with Internet Explorer 6, rewrite the style sheet so that it uses compatible selectors. Avoid repeating declarations.

2.   Using what you've learned about input forms, create your own company feedback form. Apply common fields and your own color scheme to your input form (consulting Appendix C if necessary). Your input form must contain at least three fields: a name field, an e-mail field, and a comments field.

6

Pseudo-Element and Pseudo-Class Selectors

This chapter expands on the selectors presented in Chapter 5 and introduces special types of CSS selectors. These selectors apply only when certain user-initiated events occur or when certain conditions are present in the document. A user-initiated event can be a mouse click or the mouse pointer hovering over an element. One example of a special condition is a case where you are styling only the first letter or the first line of a paragraph of text. Another example is a situation in which you want to access an element in the document but you don't know its name. You do, however, know where it resides in the document tree. In CSS these special circumstances are answered with pseudo-element and pseudo-class selectors. In this chapter, I discuss

- ❑ Pseudo-elements
- ❑ Pseudo-classes
- ❑ Dynamic pseudo-classes
- ❑ Structural pseudo-classes

These selectors are called *pseudo* because they are represented by conditions but are not necessarily representable with normal markup. They provide a simplified approach to what might otherwise be a complicated undertaking.

As was the case in Chapter 5, this chapter's examples rely exclusively on the Mozilla browser because it supports nearly all the features discussed. You should run these examples in Mozilla 1.7 or greater.

Pseudo-Elements

Pseudo-elements represent certain aspects of a document not easily modifiable with plain markup. Pseudo-elements may be used to modify the formatting of the first letter of a paragraph, the first line of a paragraph, to dynamically insert content within an element, or to change the style of the text currently selected by the user's mouse.

Following are the pseudo-elements currently supported by browsers that are discussed in this chapter:

- ❏   **::first-letter:** styles only the first letter of an element
- ❏   **::first-line:** styles only the first line of an element
- ❏   **::selection:** styles mouse highlighted text
- ❏   **::before:** inserts content into a document from CSS before an element
- ❏   **::after:** inserts content into a document from CSS after an element

Although CSS 3 contains far more pseudo-elements than those mentioned, this chapter focuses primarily on those implemented in the major browsers at the time of this writing. Let's explore each pseudo-element.

The double colon (::) syntax preceding each pseudo-element is new in CSS 3 and is used on pseudo-elements only. For example, p::first-letter refers to the first letter of a paragraph instead of p:first-letter. This syntax distinguishes pseudo-elements from pseudo-classes, which use single colon syntax, as in a:hover, which is a reference to a pseudo-class. Many modern browsers support the new syntax, but it is not widely supported in older browsers. You must use the old single colon (:) syntax specified in CSS 1 and 2 in order for pseudo-elements to work in older browsers.

::first-letter and ::first-line

Documented in 3 and supported in IE5.5, IE 6 , Mozilla 1.7, Opera 7.5, and Safari 1.2.

The pseudo-elements ::first-letter and ::first-line refer to the first letter and first line of an element containing text. When designing a website, it is helpful to have control over how you present content. With the ::first-letter and ::first-line pseudo-elements, you can control the formatting of the first letter and first line of a paragraph completely from CSS. You may add an increased font size or other font effects, apply a background color or image, or use just about any text effect supported by CSS and the browser.

You can apply pseudo-elements to a specific element, via a selector, or to all elements. The following rule applies an 18-pixel font and a yellow background to the first letter of every paragraph element <p> contained in a document.

```
p::first-letter {
    font-size: 18px;
    background-color: yellow;
}
```

The following rule applies an 18-pixel font and yellow background to the first letter of all elements contained in a document.

```
::first-letter {
    font-size: 18px;
    background-color: yellow;
}
```

If only the pseudo-element is used as the selector, the style declarations are applied to all elements in the document.

The following Try It Out shows you what the `::first-letter` and `::first-line` pseudo-elements look like in a style sheet and demonstrates some of the textual effects you can apply. As you did in Chapter 5, you build a web page to follow along with an example of each pseudo-element and pseudo-class in action. This example lays the groundwork for a Quotations web page

Try It Out   Styling a Paragraph

Example 6-1. In the following steps, I start off with a famous quote by Albert Einstein and apply a little formatting to the quote.

1.   Type the following into your text editor:

```
<!DOCTYPE html PUBLIC "-//W3C//DTD XHTML 1.0 Strict//EN"
"http://www.w3.org/TR/xhtml1/DTD/xhtml1-strict.dtd">
<html>
    <head>
        <title> Albert Einstein </title>
        <style type='text/css' media='all'>

            * {
                font-family: sans-serif;
            }
            p::first-letter {
                font-size: 200%;
                background-color: lightgray;
                border: 1px solid black;
            }
            p::first-line {
                letter-spacing: 5px;
            }

        </style>
    </head>
    <body>
            <p>
            You see, wire telegraph is a kind of a very, very long cat.
            You pull his tail in New York and his head is meowing in Los
            Angeles. Do you understand this? And radio operates exactly
            the same way: you send signals here, they receive them there.
            The only difference is that there is no cat.
            </p>
    </body>
</html>
```

2.   Save the file as example6-1.html. This markup results in the rendered output depicted in Figure 6-1.

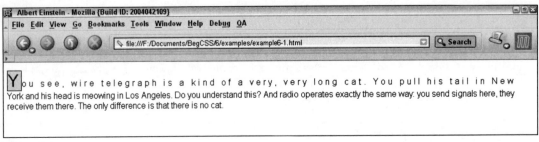

Figure 6-1

How It Works

This is a very simple example that begins with the universal selector, which applies the font sans-serif to all rendered elements via the `font-family` property. The first letter of text is styled to be 200% in size, to receive a light gray background, and a thin, solid black border. The paragraph's first line is styled with the `letter-spacing` effect, which spaces each letter 5 pixels apart.

::selection

Documented in CSS 3 and supported in Mozilla 1.7 (Alternative) and Safari 1.2.

New in CSS 3, the `::selection` pseudo-element refers to text the user selects with the mouse (mouse highlighted text). According to the CSS 3 specification, the `::selection` pseudo-element accepts only the following properties: `color`, `cursor`, `background`, and `outline`. At the time of this writing, support for this pseudo-element is yet to emerge and is supported only by Apple's Safari browser; it is supported by Mozilla 1.7, as `::-moz-selection`. For example, the following document demonstrates the `::-moz-selection` pseudo-element supported by Mozilla 1.7 and the `::selection` pseudo-element supported by Safari 1.2.

```
<!DOCTYPE html PUBLIC "-//W3C//DTD XHTML 1.0 Strict//EN"
"http://www.w3.org/TR/xhtml1/DTD/xhtml1-strict.dtd">
<html>
    <head>
        <style type="text/css">
            ::selection {
                backgroud: crimson;
                color: pink;
            }
            ::-moz-selection {
                background: crimson;
                color: pink;
            }
        </style>
    </head>
<body>
    <div>
        <p>
            Some paragraph text.
        </p>
```

```
    <p>
        Some more paragraph text.
    </p>
    <p>
        Even more paragraph text.
    </p>
        </div>
    </body>
</html>
```

When combined with markup in the body of the document and when text is highlighted with the mouse cursor, the highlighted text is displayed with a crimson background and pink text instead of the default gray background with black text.

To highlight text in a web document, click and hold down your mouse button; then move the cursor to select a sentence, paragraph, or all the text in the document.

As you saw in the preceding example, Mozilla provides the `::-moz-selection` pseudo-element with a browser-specific `-moz-` prefix. You saw this prefix in the examples in Chapter 5 with the `-moz-border-radius` property. This prefix is applied in Mozilla to proprietary CSS features that have been created by Mozilla developers and that don't appear in any W3C CSS specification. This prefix is also applied to standard W3C CSS features that the Mozilla developers don't feel are quite ready for prime time. It is also used for CSS features that appear in a draft of a W3C CSS specification but have not yet been ratified by the world community in an official recommendation. Therefore, you should use these features with the caution that many are intended by developers primarily for testing purposes. They may not live up to what the W3C defines in the official CSS specification. The functionality and the syntax used for these features may also change without notice in future releases of Mozilla. Eventually, in some future release of Mozilla, the `::-moz-selection` pseudo-element will become the `::selection` pseudo-element.

At the time of this writing, the `::-moz-selection` pseudo-element may not be grouped with the `::selection` pseudo-element because of a bug in Mozilla. To apply styles with the `::-moz-selection` pseudo-element, place the pseudo-element in its own rule.

::before and ::after

Documented in CSS 3 and supported in Mozilla 1.7, Opera 7.5, and Safari 1.2.

The `::before` and `::after` pseudo-elements allow you, using the `content` property, to insert content before and after the content inside an element. The `content` property enables you to insert text, image files, or sound files from CSS. This property is useful in situations where repetition occurs in a document or where updating a few CSS rules is much easier than editing each document individually across many pages.

Support for the `content` property or the `::before` and `::after` pseudo-elements has not yet reached Internet Explorer, and Mozilla's implementation is minimal because the `content` property works only when used in conjunction with the `::before` and `::after` pseudo-elements. This is consistent with the CSS 2 and 2.1 specifications. However, a CSS 3 draft specifies the `content` property is applicable without the use of the `::before` and `::after` pseudo-elements.

Continuing with the Quotations website, the following Try It Out demonstrates the simplest use of `::before` and `::after` pseudo-elements.

Try It Out Dynamically Inserting Content

Example 6-2. The following steps demonstrate how CSS uses the `::before` and `::after` pseudo-elements to dynamically insert content.

1. Using the example6-1.html document you created earlier, type the following (highlighted) changes to the embedded style sheet for your Quotations website:

```
          p::first-line {
              letter-spacing: 5px;
          }

          /* :: before and ::after */

          h1#top::before, h1#top::after {
              content: "::";
          }
      </style>
  </head>
```

2. Enter the following changes to the body of the document:

```
  <body>
          <h1 id='top'>Albert Einstein</h1>
          <p>
            You see, wire telegraph is a kind of a very, very long cat.
```

3. Save as example6-2.html. The output should look like what appears in Figure 6-2.

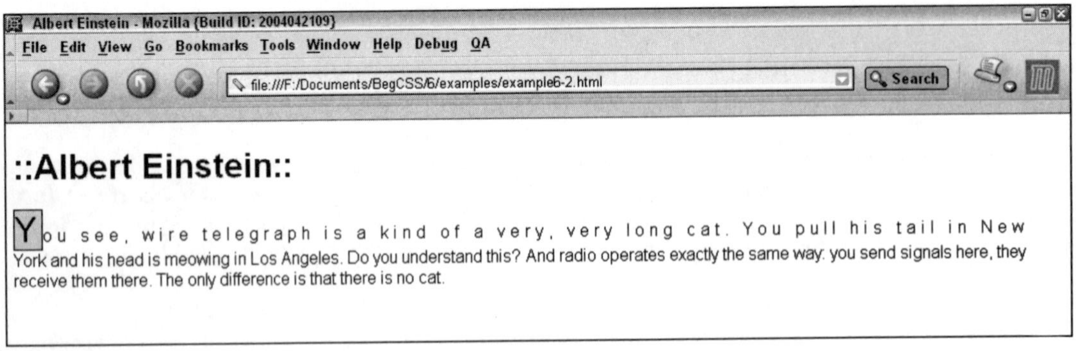
Albert Einstein - Mozilla (Build ID: 2004042109)
File Edit View Go Bookmarks Tools Window Help Debug QA
file:///F:/Documents/BegCSS/6/examples/example6-2.html
Search
::Albert Einstein::
You see, wire telegraph is a kind of a very, very long cat. You pull his tail in New York and his head is meowing in Los Angeles. Do you understand this? And radio operates exactly the same way: you send signals here, they receive them there. The only difference is that there is no cat.

Figure 6-2

How It Works

This simple demonstration inserts a header for your Quotations website. Using the `::before` and `::after` pseudo-elements, you insert two colons before and after the heading text.

The `::before` and `::after` pseudo-elements are from a portion of CSS referred to as the *generated content module*. These pseudo-elements provide a mechanism for including redundant content in web pages. In this example, the demonstration was very simple. As in the Example 4-1 from Chapter 4 where you created a page that includes content using the `content` property, the `::before` and `::after` pseudo-elements are designed to be used with the `content` property and allow insertion of content either before or after the content of an element.

Pseudo-Classes

Pseudo-classes are used to represent dynamic events, a change in state, or a more general condition present in the document that is not easily accomplished through other means. This may be the user's mouse rolling over or clicking on an element. In more general terms, pseudo-classes style a specific state present in the target element. This state may be an input element marked as disabled or enabled. Pseudo-classes allow the author the freedom to dictate how the element should appear under either condition.

Unlike pseudo-elements, pseudo-classes contain a single colon before the pseudo-class property.

Dynamic Pseudo-Classes

The following are considered dynamic pseudo-classes. They are a classification of elements that are only present after certain user actions have or have not occurred:

- ❑ **:link:** signifies unvisited hyperlinks
- ❑ **:visited:** indicates visited hyperlinks
- ❑ **:hover:** signifies an element that currently has the user's mouse pointer hovering over it
- ❑ **:active:** signifies an element on which the user is currently clicking
- ❑ **:focus:** indicates elements that currently have focus (input form elements, for example)

CSS 3 includes several more dynamic pseudo-classes; however, at the time of this writing, only those presented here are widely available in browsers.

:link and :visited

Documented in CSS 3 and supported in: IE 5.5, IE 6, Mozilla 1.7, Opera 7.5, and Safari 1.2.

The `:link` pseudo-class refers to an unvisited hyperlink, whereas `:visited`, of course, refers to visited hyperlinks. These two pseudo-classes are used to separate styles based on user actions. An unvisited hyperlink may be red and contain no underlined text, whereas a visited hyperlink may be green and have the underline applied. Dynamic pseudo-classes change document styles based on specific user actions.

The following document demonstrates how these pseudo-classes are applied:

```
<!DOCTYPE html PUBLIC "-//W3C//DTD XHTML 1.0 Strict//EN"
"http://www.w3.org/TR/xhtml1/DTD/xhtml1-strict.dtd">
<html>
    <head>
        <style type='text/css'>
            a:link {
                background: blue;
                color: white;
            }
            a:visited {
                background: white;
                color: black;
            }
        </style>
    </head>
    <body>
        <a href='http://www.google.com'>Google</a> |
        <a href='http://www.wrox.com'>Wrox</a> |
        <a href='http://www.php.net'>PHP</a> |
        <a href='http://www.quirksmode.org'>Quirks Mode</a>
    </body>
</html>
```

In this example, unvisited links are styled with the :link dynamic pseudo-class. They receive a blue background and white text. Visited links, on the other hand, are given a crimson background and pink text. The order in which the :link and :visited dynamic pseudo-classes appear in the style sheet is important and has to do with the cascade, which I discuss in Chapter 7. If the :link pseudo-class is defined after the :visited pseudo-class in the style sheet, the :link pseudo-class takes precedence. The declarations with the :link pseudo-class override those defined for the :visited pseudo-class. As you see in Chapter 7, this has to do with how specific the selector is; in this example, the specificity is the same.

> **A mnemonic device used to remember the order in which dynamic pseudo-classes (as applied to links) must appear in style sheets is LoVe HAte, or** :link, :visited, :hover **and** :active.

The next section continues the discussion of dynamic pseudo-classes with the :hover pseudo-class.

:hover

Documented in CSS 3 and supported in: IE 5.5 (partial), IE 6 (partial), Mozilla 1.7, Opera 7.5, and Safari 1.2.

The :hover pseudo-class refers to an element over which the user's mouse pointer is currently hovering. While the user's mouse pointer is over the element, the specified style is applied; when the user's mouse pointer leaves the element, it returns to the previously specified style. The :hover pseudo-class is applied in the same way that the :link and :visited pseudo-classes are applied. Using the example I presented for the `:link` and `:visited` pseudo-classes, the following appends a rule that includes the `:hover` pseudo-class.

```css
a:link {
    background: blue;
    color: white;
}
a:visited {
    background: white;
    color: black;
}
a:hover {
    background: black;
    color: white;
}
```

If you apply this rule, the background color changes to black and the text color changes to white when the mouse cursor is on top of a link.

In IE, the `:hover` pseudo-class applies only to hyperlinks (which is incorrect under the CSS 2 specification), whereas other browsers recognize the `:hover` pseudo-class on any rendered element, per the CSS 2 specification.

:active

Documented in CSS 3 and supported in: IE 5.5 (partial), IE 6 (partial), Mozilla 1.7, Opera 7.5. and Safari 1.2.

The `:active` pseudo-class refers to an element that the user is currently clicking on. The specified style remains in place while the user holds down the mouse button, and the element does not return to its original state until the user releases the mouse button. In the following, I modify the example I presented for the `:hover` pseudo-class:

```css
a:link {
    background: blue;
    color: white;
}
a:visited {
    background: white;
    color: black;
}
a:hover {
    background: black;
    color: white;
}
a:active {
    background: red;
    color: white;
}
```

If you add this rule, the background color of the link turns red and the color of the link turns white when the user clicks and holds down the mouse button over a link.

Like the :hover *pseudo-class,* :active *only applies to hyperlinks in IE; whereas, in other browsers it applies to any rendered element, per the CSS specification.*

:focus

Documented in CSS 3 and supported in Mozilla 1.7, Opera 7.5, and Safari 1.2.

The :focus pseudo-class refers to the element that has focus, such as an input field or form button. Focus refers to the active element in a document. Only one element can be active at a time. A focused element is the element that currently has control; one example is when you click an input field and see the blinking vertical bar or when you press the Tab key to navigate through the links and input fields present in a web document. The Tab key shifts focus from one link or input field to the next. A dashed box around a link typically indicates that a link has focus (although not all browsers treat hyperlinks as focusable). A blinking vertical bar indicates that a text input element has focus. The following example applies the :focus pseudo-class to the example you saw for the :active pseudo-class in the preceding section:

```
a:link {
    background: blue;
    color: white;
}
a:visited {
    background: white;
    color: black;
}
a:hover {
    background: black;
    color: white;
}
a:active {
    background: red;
    color: white;
}
a:focus {
    background: gray;
    color: white;
}
```

When you load the preceding example into Mozilla and tap the Tab key to navigate through the links, you see the background of each link become gray and the color of each link become white. This shows the focus shifting from one link to the next; if you press the Return key, you navigate to the URL in the hyperlink. While a link has focus, its style becomes controllable with the :focus pseudo-class. Similarly, you can style form input controls when they have focus.

Opera 7.5 does not support *focus* when applied to hyperlinks. Opera 7.5 applies the :focus pseudo-class only to form input controls like text fields and drop-down menus.

> **In terms of the LoVe HAte mnemonic device introduced earlier in this chapter,** :focus **may be applied last.**

Now that you have seen what each dynamic pseudo-class looks like and a little of what each does, the next Try It Out demonstrates each of these in a realistic, real-world application. It expands on your Quotations website and provides a demonstration of dynamic pseudo-classes through the implementation of a navigational bar.

Try It Out   **Dynamic Pseudo-Classes**

Example 6-3. In the following steps, you can see how dynamic pseudo-classes work.

1. Using the example6-2.html document you completed in the preceding Try It Out, type the following (highlighted) changes to the embedded style sheet:

```
h1#top::before, h1#top::after {
    content: "::";
}
```

```
/* Dynamic pseudo-classes */
ul {
    list-style: none;
}
li {
    border: 1px solid black;
    padding: 5px;
    margin: 2px;
    float: left;
}
li a {
    padding: 2px;
    color: black;
    font-size: 15pt;
    text-decoration: none;
}
li a:link {
    background-color: white;
    color: black;
}
li a:visited {
    background-color: black;
    color: white;
}
li a:active {
    background-color: lightgray;
    color: black;
}
li a:hover, li a:focus {
    background-color: gray;
    color: white;
}
```

```
    </style>
  </head>
```

2. Enter the following changes to the body of the document:

```
<body>
    <h1 id='top'>Albert Einstein</h1>
    <ul>
        <li><a href='http://www.google.com'>Google</a></li>
        <li><a href='http://p2p.wrox.com'>Wrox P2P</a></li>
        <li><a href='http://www.mozilla.org'>Mozilla</a></li>
        <li><a href='http://pear.php.net'>PEAR</a></li>
    </ul>
    <p>
        You see, wire telegraph is a kind of a very, very long cat.
```

3. Save the file as example6-3.html. You should see output like that shown in Figure 6-3:

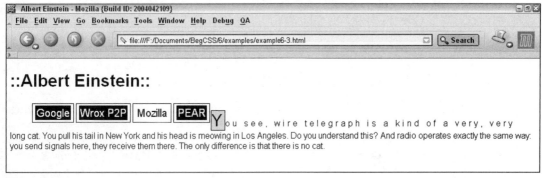

Figure 6-3

How It Works

This example utilizes all five dynamic pseudo-classes to build a navigational menu, admittedly one that doesn't really have anything to do with the Quotations website.

Take a look at each new style sheet rule and what each does to the document. The navigational menu is contained in an unordered list, which is used to give the document structure and to make it accessible to visually impaired users. Using an unordered list makes the web site's structure more predictable, just as using heading elements and paragraph elements make the structure describe itself. The concept of accessibility is explored further in Chapter 10. The first CSS rule strips away the preformatted list style, which usually causes each list item to appear with a bullet.

```
ul {
    list-style: none;
}
```

With this CSS property, the list now appears without any bullets next to each list item. Next, some formatting is applied to each <li> item.

```
li {
    border: 1px solid black;
    padding: 5px;
    margin: 2px;
    float: left;
}
```

First, each <li> element receives a thin, black border, some padding, and 2 pixels of margin to put space between one element and another. Next a `float: left` is applied. If you recall the example of the `float` property from Chapter 5, it reorients each <li> element so that each appears on the same line instead of on separate lines. So instead of being laid out like a list, elements appear side-by-side. The `float` property also causes the paragraph text to appear after the navigation bar, which isn't very aesthetically pleasing (but that's fine). An upcoming example takes advantage of that to make the navigation bar appear to be layered. Next, the dynamic pseudo-classes add some foundation to each link:

```
li a {
    padding: 2px;
    color: black;
    font-size: 15pt;
    text-decoration: none;
}
```

Until the dynamic pseudo-classes kick in, this rule provides a foundation for how all links contained within a <li> element should look. Some padding, black text, and a 15-point font are applied to each link. The `text-decoration: none` property strips away the default underline that appears under every link. When you have the foundational styles in place for each link, next comes styling the unvisited links on the page:

```
li a:link {
    background-color: white;
    color: black;
}
```

This rule is not much different from the last style. It simply says to give unvisited links a white background and black text. For visited links, the opposite is true:

```
li a:visited {
    background-color: black;
    color: white;
}
```

Visited links receive a black background and white text instead. What about links currently being clicked on? The next style applies the declarations while the user's mouse button is clicked. When the user releases the mouse button, the styles return to those applied before the mouse button was clicked.

```
li a:active {
    background-color: lightgray;
    color: black;
}
```

This style once more changes the background color. Based on whether or not the link is being clicked, the rule applies a `lightgray` background and `black` text. The last rule is two-fold:

```
li a:hover, li a:focus {
    background-color: gray;
    color: white;
}
```

This rule applies style when one or both of two conditions are present: when the user's mouse cursor is hovering over the link and/or when the link has focus. In order to give the link focus in Mozilla, use the Tab key to navigate to the link. The background then turns gray and the text turns white. You can apply focus to hyperlinks and input form elements. The `:hover` pseudo-class is intended to be applied to all elements. Mozilla implements the `:hover` pseudo-class correctly; Internet Explorer only recognizes the `:hover` pseudo-class on links.

Structural Pseudo-Classes

The following selection of CSS 3 pseudo-classes are not yet widely supported; only Mozilla and Safari browsers support all three of them, and Opera 7.5 supports two of them. Structural pseudo-classes apply style based on where in the document tree the element resides:

- ❑ **:root:** refers to the root element of a document; in HTML, this is the `<html>` element.

- ❑ **:first-child:** refers to the first child element of an element.

- ❑ **:last-child:** refers to the last child element of an element.

- ❑ **:empty:** refers to an element that has no content, no children, and no white space.

These pseudo-classes also apply style based on the structure of the document. Whereas dynamic pseudo-classes change styles based on user actions, structural pseudo-classes have no actions associated with them and apply style based on the document's structure. For instance, the names of tags in an XML document may change. You may not know the name of the tag, but you know where in the document tree the element resides. CSS answers this kind of situation with structural pseudo-classes.

The following sections examine each structural pseudo-class in detail and in what type of situation each is useful.

:root

Documented in CSS 3 and supported in Mozilla 1.7 and Safari 1.2.

The `:root` pseudo-class refers to the root element of a document. In HTML or XHTML documents, the root element is the `<html>` element; in XML documents, it is the top-level element. The `:root` element exists primarily for use in XML documents, and because XML documents have the capability to contain invented tags and attributes, you may not always know what the `:root` element is called. In HTML, however, the root element is guaranteed to be the `<html>` element.

:first-child

Documented in CSS 3 and supported in Mozilla 1.7, Opera 7.5, and Safari 1.2.

The :first-child pseudo-class refers to the first-child of an element. For instance:

```
div > p:first-child
```

This selector matches any <p> element that is the first-child of a <div> element. The following markup fits the scenario:

```
<div>
    <p> Some text </p>
</div>
```

Because <p> is the first-child, it matches the selector's criterion. Yet the following markup does not match the criterion:

```
<div>
    <h1> Some header </h1>
    <p> Some Text </p>
</div>
```

In this example, <h1> is the first-child of the <div> element. The div > p:first-child selector could have just as easily been represented with just div > p, if you recall the purpose of the direct child selector from Chapter 5. However, the :first-child pseudo-element matches only the first child, whereas the direct child selector matches any child.

Like the :root pseudo-class, the :first-child pseudo-class is more useful in XML documents where the various elements in the document aren't guaranteed to be the same from document to document, but where the underlying structure may remain identical. Using the preceding example, the following selector applies style to whichever element is the first-child of a <div> element:

```
div > :first-child
```

This selector matches both the first example <p> Some text </p> and the second example <h1> Some header </h1>.

:last-child

Documented in CSS 3 and supported in Mozilla 1.7, Opera 7.5, and Safari 1.2.

The opposite of the :first-child pseudo-class, this pseudo-class matches the last-child of an element. For instance

```
div > p:last-child
```

The preceding selector matches the <p> element in the following markup:

```
<div>
    <h1> Some header </h1>
    <p> Some Text </p>
</div>
```

However, if the <p> were first and the <h1> last, it would not match:

```
<div>
     <p> Some Text </p>
     <h1> Some header </h1>
</div>
```

:empty

Documented in CSS 3 and supported in Mozilla 1.7 and Safari 1.2.

The :empty pseudo-class refers to elements that have no child elements, text, or content of any kind, including white space. Therefore

```
div:empty
```

matches this

```
<div></div>
```

but not this:

```
<div> Hello, world! </div>
```

Mozilla incorrectly applies the :empty *pseudo-class to elements that contain white space.*

After reviewing a few structural pseudo-classes, the next Try It Out demonstrates them in action and continues the Quotations web page from the earlier examples:

Try It Out   Structural Pseudo-Classes

Example 6-4. The following steps continue the Quotations website via the implementation and demonstration of structural pseudo-classes.

1. Using the example6-3.html document you created in the last Try It Out, type the following changes to the embedded style sheet:

```
li {
    border: 1px solid black;
    padding: 5px;
    margin: 2px;
    float: left;
}
```

```
/* Structural pseudo-classes */

:root {
    border: 35px solid black;
    -moz-border-radius: 10%;
    margin: 35px auto;
    padding: 35px;
    background-color: lightgray;
    width: 550px;
```

```
        }
        div:empty {
            height: 30px;
            background: black;
            -moz-border-radius: 10%;
        }
        div p:first-child {
            border: 10px solid black;
            padding: 40px;
            -moz-border-radius: 10%;
            background-color: gray;
            font-weight: bold;
        }
        div h1:first-child {
            padding: 0;
            border-bottom: 1px dashed black;
            letter-spacing: 2px;
        }
        div h1:last-child {
            padding: 10px;
            letter-spacing: -3px;
        }
    </style>
</head>
```

2. Enter the following changes to the document's body:

```
<body>
    <div></div>
    <div>
        <h1>Famous Quotes</h1>
        <h1 id='top'>Albert Einstein</h1>
    </div>
    <div></div>
    <ul>
        <li><a href='http://www.google.com'>Google</a></li>
        <li><a href='http://p2p.wrox.com'>Wrox P2P</a></li>
        <li><a href='http://www.mozilla.org'>Mozilla</a></li>
        <li><a href='http://pear.php.net'>PEAR</a></li>
    </ul>
    <div>
        <p>
            You see, wire telegraph is a kind of a very, very long cat.
            You pull his tail in New York and his head is meowing in Los
            Angeles. Do you understand this? And radio operates exactly
            the same way: you send signals here, they receive them there.
            The only difference is that there is no cat.
        </p>
    </div>
    <div></div>
</body>
</html>
```

3. Save the file as example6-4.html. You should see output like that shown in Figure 6-4, if you're using a Gecko browser.

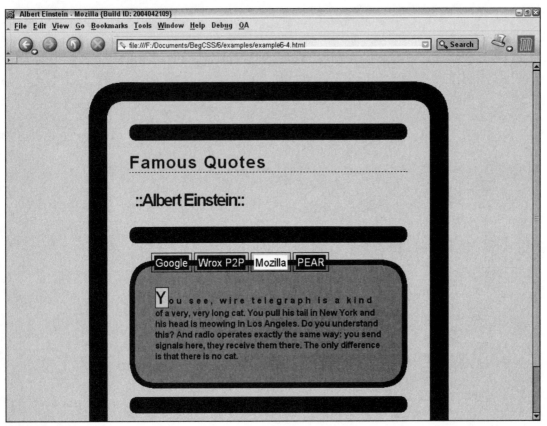

Figure 6-4

How It Works

As you can see from the output, structural pseudo-classes greatly improve the look and feel of the Quotations website. The exploration of the new style rules begins with the :root pseudo-class.

```css
:root {
    border: 35px solid black;
    -moz-border-radius: 10%;
    margin: 35px auto;
    padding: 35px;
    background-color: lightgray;
    width: 550px;
}
```

The :root pseudo-class applies style to the base element of a document. In HTML documents, the <html> element is the base element. In XML documents, the base element might change from document to document because the entire tag schema can be completely different, which is why the `:root` pseudo-class element exists. In HTML, you could simply refer to the base element using the `html` type selector. This rule applies a very thick, black border around the document, and it rounds corners with the proprietary `-moz-border-radius` property. Then it adds more box properties, some padding, and an absolute width. The `margin` property used here is shorthand. The first value applies to the top and bottom sides, and the second value applies to the left and right sides. In this case, a value of `auto` centers block-level elements. The specifics of how margin, padding, borders, and width work together are explored in greater depth in Chapter 10.

The next rule applies to all `<div>` elements that don't contain anything.

```
div:empty {
    height: 30px;
    background: black;
    -moz-border-radius: 10%;
}
```

Using the `:empty` pseudo-class you can pick out all the elements that don't contain anything; no text, no children elements, nothing. The empty `<div>` elements in the body are used purely for presentation. They receive a height of 30 pixels, black backgrounds, and rounded edges with the proprietary `-moz-border-radius` property. The next rule selects the paragraph element containing the quote itself.

```
div p:first-child {
    border: 10px solid black;
    padding: 40px;
    -moz-border-radius: 10%;
    background-color: gray;
    font-weight: bold;
}
```

This is somewhat fancier than it needs to be. In a simple document like this, it makes more sense to select the paragraph using the p type selector because more browsers support it. For the sake of demonstration, however, the `div p:first-child` selector selects the `<p>` element because it is the first child of a `<div>` element. This is where you take advantage of the float applied to the `<li>` elements in the navigation menu in Example 6-3. This rule applies just enough padding to make the navigational menu appear layered on top of the paragraph. If I had done this

```
<div style='clear: left;'>
    <p>
        You see, wire telegraph is a kind of a very, very long cat.
```

the effect wouldn't have worked because the `<div>` would have been forced onto its own line, killing the layered effect. The next style rule formats the heading that you add to the body:

```
div h1:first-child {
    padding: 0;
    border-bottom: 1px dashed black;
    letter-spacing: 2px;
}
```

This says if `<h1>` is the first child of a `<div>` element: Give it no padding, a dashed black border along the bottom, and 2 pixels of letter spacing. The final rule is another fancy way to reference the other `<h1>` element remaining from previous examples:

```
div h1:last-child {
    padding: 10px;
    letter-spacing: -3px;
}
```

This rule condenses the letters of the text and gives the header 10 pixels of padding on all sides.

The Negation Pseudo-Class :not

Documented in CSS 3 and supported in Mozilla 1.7 and Safari 1.2.

This pseudo-class, again not yet widely supported, applies style based on what the element is not. The `:not` pseudo-class takes an argument for what it is *not* to match. In programming, the term *argument* means information passed to a method or function. *Methods* and *functions* are subprograms that perform a predefined task or set of tasks; in this application, the function is the delegation of a style sheet rule. The argument refers to the data needed to perform the task. In most languages, functions take their arguments between parentheses, which are used to delimit the argument list:

```
:not(div)
```

This selector matches every element present except `<div>` elements. The `:not` pseudo-class also accepts attributes and attribute values in the argument. This selector matches all `<a>` elements that do not contain an `href` attribute.

```
a:not([href])
```

The selector matches all `<a>` elements that don't link to the URL specified:

```
a[href]:not([href='http://www.somesite.com'])
```

This selector matches all elements that are not `<div>` elements with an id of `content`:

```
body:not(div#content)
```

As is the case with attribute selectors, you can use that syntax in the `:not` pseudo-class. Therefore, the following example matches all elements inside a `<form>` element where the name attribute doesn't begin with `"some_form"`:

```
form:not([name~='some_form'])
```

The `:not` pseudo-class applies styles based on what an element is not. The next Try It Out is a brief demonstration of this concept.

Try It Out   The Negation Pseudo-Class

Example 6-5. Building again on the Quotations website, the following steps implement an example of the `:not` pseudo-class.

1. Using the document you created for Example 6-4, make the following changes to the embedded style sheet:

```
div h1:last-child {
    padding: 10px;
    letter-spacing: -3px;
}

/* :not pseudo-class */

h1:not(#top) {
    font-size: 12pt;
}

    </style>
</head>
```

2. Save the file as example6-5.html. You should see output like that shown in Figure 6-5.

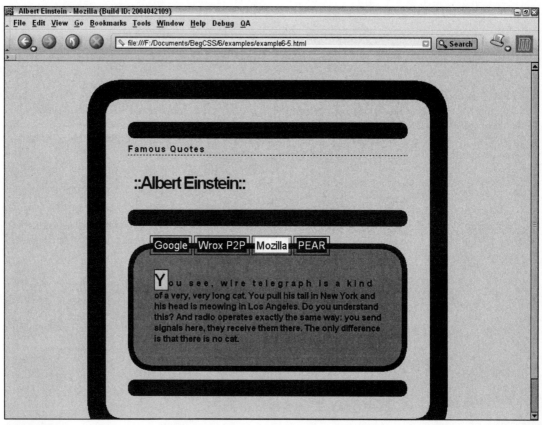

Figure 6-5

How It Works

This is a very simple demonstration of the `:not` pseudo-class, adding only one new rule to the Quotations website embedded style sheet. This rule says that all `<h1>` elements that don't have `id="top"` get a 12-point font size.

The :target Pseudo-Class

Documented in CSS 3 and supported in Mozilla 1.7 and Safari 1.2.

The last pseudo-class covered in this chapter is the `:target` pseudo-class. Like several of the CSS3 pseudo-classes, this was previously a proprietary, Mozilla-only pseudo-class, adopted by the W3C in the CSS 3 specification. This pseudo-class applies style based on HTML anchors.

Say, for instance, that you have an extensive FAQ page. After the user clicks on one of the questions on the page, the browser directs him somewhere further down the page to find the answer. The question looks something like this:

```
Q. <a href="#widgets">What are Widgets?</a>
```

The answer to the question is located somewhere after the previous line:

```
A. <span id="widgets">Widgets are things!</span>
```

When the question is clicked, the browser scrolls automatically to where the answer is. You may have to add lots of text or HTML line breaks between the question and the answer to see the browser scroll down to the answer. This feature is called an *anchor*. Anchors allow the author to makes links within the same document because some HTML pages can get quite lengthy. Anchors eliminate the need for lots of scrolling. An anchor is set up using a hash mark and the name of the anchor at the end of a hyperlink. Such as

```
Q. <a href="#widgets">What are Widgets?</a>
```

The anchor's name is `#widgets`. You should recall from Chapter 5 that referencing an `id` selector in CSS takes the same syntax, so naturally anchors point to an element containing that `id` name and use an identical syntax to link to them.

The `:target` pseudo-class was introduced to make it possible to change the style of the target so that it can stand out from any other targets on the page.

Using the `:target` pseudo-class, it is possible for you to change the style of the target element with the following CSS.

```
:target {
    background-color: yellow;
}
```

This CSS changes the background color of any target to yellow. When a new target is clicked, the background color moves to that element instead, and the first element returns to its normal background color. It is also possible to restrict the styles to one target or another:

```
span#widgets:target {
    background-color: yellow;
}
```

This CSS restricts the color change to only the <span> element.

Now that you have a feel for what the :target pseudo-class does and what HTML anchors are, you can take it all for a test drive. The next Try It Out adds the :target pseudo-class to the Quotations website example.

Try It Out   **:target Pseudo-Class**

Example 6-6. In the following steps, you put the finishing touches on the Quotations website by adding a picture of Albert Einstein and some :target effects:

1. Building on the example6-5.html document that you created in the last Try It Out, type the highlighted changes into the embedded style sheet:

```
h1:not(#top) {
     font-size: 12pt;
}

/* :target pseudo-class */

div#quoteimage:target {
    background-color: black;
    border: 1px solid white;
}
h1#top:target {
    background-color: black;
    border: 1px solid white;
    color: white;
}
h1 a {
    color: inherit;
    text-decoration: none;
}

div#quoteimage {
    margin: 10px;
    text-align: center;
}
img#albert {
    width: 305px;
    height: 240px;
    border: 5px solid black;
    margin: 10px;
}
```

```
        </style>
    </head>
    <body>
```

2. Make the following changes to the body of the document:

```
        <div></div>
        <div>
            <h1>Famous Quotes</h1>
            <h1 id='top'><a href='#quoteimage'>Albert Einstein</a></h1>
        </div>
        <div></div>
        <ul>
            <li><a href='http://www.google.com'>Google</a></li>
            <li><a href='http://p2p.wrox.com'>Wrox P2P</a></li>
            <li><a href='http://www.mozilla.org'>Mozilla</a></li>
            <li><a href='http://pear.php.net'>PEAR</a></li>
        </ul>
        <div>
            <p>
             You see, wire telegraph is a kind of a very, very long cat.
             You pull his tail in New York and his head is meowing in Los
             Angeles. Do you understand this? And radio operates exactly
             the same way: you send signals here, they receive them there.
             The only difference is that there is no cat.
            </p>
        </div>
        <div></div>
        <div id='quoteimage'>
            <a href='#top'>
                <img src='albert.jpg' id='albert' alt='Albert Einstein' />
            </a>
        </div>
    </body>
</html>
```

3. Save as example6-6.html. You should see output like that which appears in Figure 6-6.

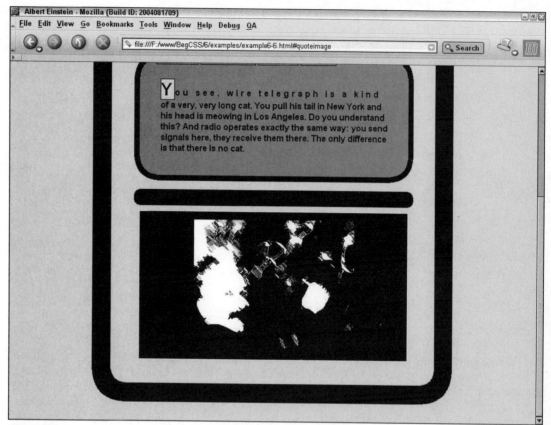

Figure 6-6

How It Works

This example puts the finishing touches on the Quotations page by adding a picture that appears when a user clicks the Albert Einstein heading. When a user clicks the image, the Albert Einstein heading is highlighted in black, with a thin, white border, and the text is inverted to white. Examining each rule individually, the first rule applies some styles for the image as a target:

```
div#quoteimage:target {
    background-color: black;
    border: 1px solid white;
}
```

It gives the `<div>` a black background and a thin, white border, but only when it's the active target. The next rule applies styles to the header labeled top or the Albert Einstein header:

```
h1#top:target {
    background-color: black;
    border: 1px solid white;
    color: white;
}
```

131

When the `<h1>` element with `id="top"` is the active target, it also receives a black background and thin, white border, as well as white text, so that the text is readable. The next rule styles the link that relocates the browser window to the picture of Albert Einstein:

```
h1 a {
    color: inherit;
    text-decoration: none;
}
```

It says if `<h1>` is an ancestor of `<a>`, make the color inherit, which means make the color of the link whatever is specified for `<h1>` at the moment. And then, the `text-decoration: none` declaration removes the underline from the link. The next rules apply style to the image and the `<div>` containing the image:

```
div#quoteimage {
    margin: 10px;
    text-align: center;
}
img#albert {
    width: 305px;
    height: 240px;
    border: 5px solid black;
    margin: 10px;
}
```

This rule applies a margin to the `<div>` to space it away from everything else, which results in the space between the `<div>` and the empty `<div>` element above it. Next, the `text-align: center` declaration centers the image. And finally the image itself receives some styles: A thick, black border is added; its width and height are specified in pixels; and yet another margin is applied to space the image edges from the inside of the `<div>` containing it.

Summary

CSS offers dynamic solutions to problems that might otherwise require a great deal more effort to solve. Pseudo-elements and pseudo-classes provide the solution to problems without requiring extra markup or complex scripting languages. Pseudo-elements and pseudo-classes are special types of CSS selectors that apply style only when certain conditions are present in the document or after certain user actions occur. In this chapter, you learned that

- ❏ `::first-letter` and `::first-line` alter the first letter and line of a paragraph.

- ❏ `::selection` alters the style of mouse-selected text, when browser support for it emerges.

- ❏ `::before` and `::after` insert content before and after content appearing inside of an element.

- ❏ Dynamic pseudo-classes alter styles based on user actions, which include visiting (or not visiting) a link, hovering the mouse pointer over an element, clicking on an element, or by giving an element focus.

- ❏ Structural pseudo-classes apply style based on where an element appears in the document tree. The element can be the root element, the first child of another element, the last child of another element, or it may contain no children or content.

❑ The negation pseudo-class :not applies style based on what an element is not.

❑ The :target pseudo-class applies style to an element that is the target of another element.

The next chapter discusses inheritance, the cascade, and how it affects document layout.

Exercises

1. Using a technique similar to those described in this chapter, create a navigational bar for the Widgets and What's-Its website. Use the document you created in Chapter 5, exercise 1. Include styles for :link, :visited, :hover, :active, :focus, and links for home, contact us, products, services, and faq. As was the case in that example, the navigational bar must also be cross-browser compatible, where possible. Use the unordered list technique discussed in this chapter. Add the navigation bar between the heading and <form> element. Also add a :focus pseudo-class to each of the input field elements: <input>, <select>, and <textarea>.

Hint: Add the clear: left property to the <form> element's selector to prevent it from floating up beside your links.

2. Write an FAQ page for Widgets and What's-its. Be creative in your questions and answers, and style the page so that it is identical to the feedback form example in Chapter 5. Include styling using the :target pseudo-class.

Hint: Use the <div> element instead of a <form> element for the body.

7

Inheritance and the Cascade

In Chapter 6, I discussed pseudo-element and pseudo-class selectors. In this chapter, now that you have some understanding of the basic nuts and bolts that make up CSS, you learn about inheritance and the cascade. In CSS, inheritance and the cascade are as fundamental as selectors and properties. In fact, the importance of precedence is implied by the name of the language itself: Cascading Style Sheets. *Cascading* is a term used to describe precedence. Because CSS declarations can appear more than once for a single element, the CSS specification includes a set of guidelines defining which declarations can take precedence over others and how this is decided. In this chapter, I discuss the following:

❑ Inheritance and why the values of some properties are inherited and some are not

❑ The inherit keyword and how to force inheritance

❑ The *cascade* and how style sheets and some selectors take precedence over others

❑ The !important rule and how to force precedence

❑ Custom style sheets and how to override website styles with custom style sheets

Inheritance

CSS is designed to simplify web document creation, enabling a property to be applied to all elements in a document. To put it another way, after a property has been applied to a particular element, its children retain those property values as well. This behavior is called *inheritance*.

Many properties in CSS are inheritable, and inheritance makes writing style sheets a snap. Two types of properties that can be inherited are most text properties and font properties. After they're applied to an element, they are inherited by that element's descendants. Take, for instance, this rule:

```
div#parentdiv {
    text-align: center;
}
```

The preceding rule creates center-aligned text, regardless of whether the same text appears in its child elements, as the following code illustrates:

```
<div id='parentdiv'>
    Some text aligned center.
  <div>
       Because the text-align property is inherited,
       this text is also aligned center.
  </div>
</div>
```

In the preceding code, the rule is applied to the <div> element with the 'parentdiv' id, and the property is inherited by the <div> element contained within the 'parentdiv' <div> element. The advantage of inherited properties is that you don't have to specify a property again for each nested element.

This results in the rendering shown in Figure 7-1. As you can see, the text in both elements is center aligned.

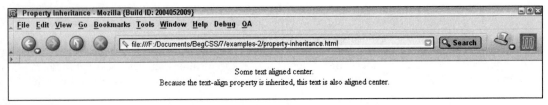

Figure 7-1

Some properties, such as border, margin, and padding, are not inherited because inheriting would not be appropriate. Most of the time, you want these to be set only on a selected element and not on that selected element's children. The following rule is an example of a property that is not inherited:

```
div#parentdiv {
    border: thin solid black;
}
```

This rule puts a thin, solid, black border around the element selected:

```
<div id='parentdiv'>
    This div has a border around it.
  <div>
       This div does not have a border around it.
  </div>
</div>
```

The border property (discussed in detail in Chapter 10) is a box model property. Box model properties handle things like borders, margins, and padding. These aren't inherited because their effects are, more often than not, to be used only on the element, not on its children.

> **Inheritance for each property is outlined in Appendix B.**

Now that you've had this brief overview of inheritance, in the next section I discuss the `inherit` keyword, which you can use to force inheritance — to determine that a given property inherits.

The inherit Keyword

The `inherit` keyword was introduced in CSS 2; all properties can have `inherit` as a value. This keyword allows you to state explicitly whether a property should inherit a value from its parent element, as shown in the following rules:

```
div#parentdiv {
    border: thin solid black;
}
div#childdiv {
    border: inherit;
}
```

When these rules are applied to the following markup, the thin, solid, black border is inherited by the child `<div>` because the child `<div>` has a border property with a value of `inherit`:

```
<div id='parentdiv'>
    This div has a border around it.
    <div id='childdiv'>
        This div also has a border around it.
    </div>
</div>
```

This results in the rendering shown in Figure 7-2.

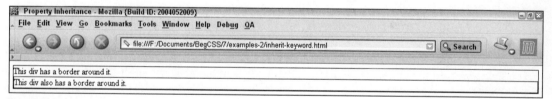

Figure 7-2

Both `<div>` elements have a thin, solid, black border.

In the next section, I discuss the cascade and how this concept determines precedence among style sheets and selectors.

The Cascade

With CSS, style sheets can come from more than one place. A style sheet can originate from any of the following sources:

❑   From the browser (default look and feel).

❑   From the user visiting the website (a custom, user-defined style sheet).

❑   From the web page itself (the website's author).

Because a style sheet can originate from more than one source, it is necessary to establish an order of precedence to determine which style sheet applies style for the page the user is seeing. The first style sheet comes from the browser itself, and this style sheet applies some default styles for a web page such as the default font and text color, how much space is applied between each line of text, and how much space is applied between each letter of text. In a nutshell, it controls the look and feel of the web page by controlling the behavior of each element when no styles are specified.

A style sheet can also be applied by a user visiting the website via a custom style sheet, which is discussed later in this chapter. This allows the user to specify his or her own look and feel. This aspect of CSS makes the web more accessible: A user with visual disabilities can write a style sheet to accommodate his or her needs, or the browser can provide options that generate the user's style sheet behind the scenes. No knowledge of CSS is required.

Finally, the author of the web page can specify a style sheet (of course). The precedence of each style sheet is as follows.

❑   The browser's style sheet is the weakest.

❑   The user's style sheet takes precedence over the browser's style sheet.

❑   The author's style sheet is the strongest and takes precedence over the user's style sheet.

A user's style sheet wins out over the browser's style sheet, but the author's style sheet wins over both. Lastly, the order in which style sheets appear in a document is also important, and generally speaking the last included has the highest precedence.

Take for instance this external style sheet:

```
@import(styles.css);
div {
    color: black;
}
```

The style sheet included for the @import notation is weaker than the style sheet including it because the rules in that style sheet appear before those in the style sheet importing it. Likewise, an embedded style sheet is more important than style sheets that are included externally. Finally, the HTML/XHTML style attribute is more important than any style sheet.

The order of rules inside a style sheet is also important:

```
div {
    text-align: left;
    color: white;
}
div {
    text-align: center;
    color: blue;
}
```

This results in the output depicted in Figure 7-3.

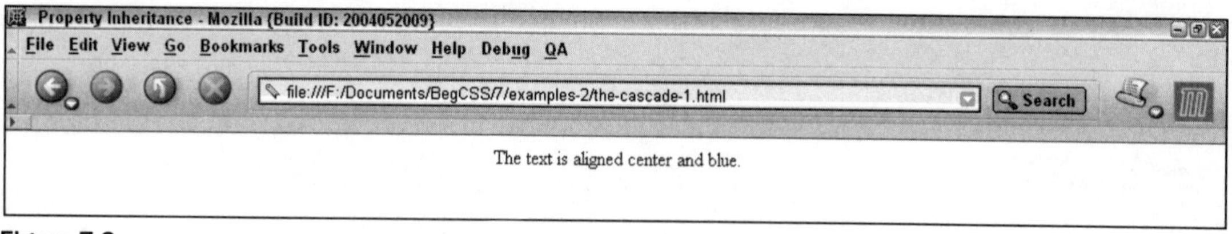

Figure 7-3

The second rule wins because it appears after the first one, so the `<div>` elements appearing in the document are center-aligned and in blue text.

Calculating the Specificity of a Selector

In addition to style sheet precedence, an order of precedence exists for the selectors contained in each style sheet. This precedence is determined by how specific the selector is. For instance, an id selector is the most specific, and the universal selector is the most general. Between these, the specificity of a selector is calculated using the following formula:

❑ Count the number of ID attributes in the selector; this is variable a

❑ Count the number of attributes, pseudo-classes, and class names in a selector; this is variable b.

❑ Count the number of element names in the selector; this is variable c.

❑ Ignore pseudo-elements.

Concatenate each number together to get the specificity of the selector. *Concatenate* is a programming term that means *glue together*. In this case if I concatenate a, b, and c I get abc, instead of the sum of a, b, and c, which I might refer to as x. Following are some examples.

Selector	Selector Type	Specificity
*	Universal Selector	000 ($a = 0$, $b = 0$, $c = 0$)
li	Element Name	001 ($a = 0$, $b = 0$, $c = 1$)
ul li	Element Name	002 ($a = 0$, $b = 0$, $c = 2$)
div h1 + p	Element Name	003 ($a = 0$, $b = 0$, $c = 3$)
input[type='text']	Element Name + Attribute	011 ($a = 0$, $b = 1$, $c = 1$)
.someclass	Class Name	010 ($a = 0$, $b = 1$, $c = 0$)
div.someclass	Element Name + Class Name	011 ($a = 0$, $b = 1$, $c = 1$)
div.someclass.someother	Element Name + Class Name + Class Name	021 ($a = 0$, $b = 2$, $c = 1$)
#someid	ID Name	100 ($a = 1$, $b = 0$, $c = 0$)

I have included the leading zeros in the specificity chart to clarify how concatenation works, but these are actually dropped. To determine the order of precedence, simply determine the highest number. The selector with the highest number wins. For instance, consider this example:

```
* {
    font-family: sans-serif;
}
div {
    font-family: "Times New Roman";
}
```

Apply this to the following markup:

```
<body>
    This font is sans-serif.
    <div>
        This font is Times New Roman.
    </div>
</body>
```

The result looks like the output shown in Figure 7-4.

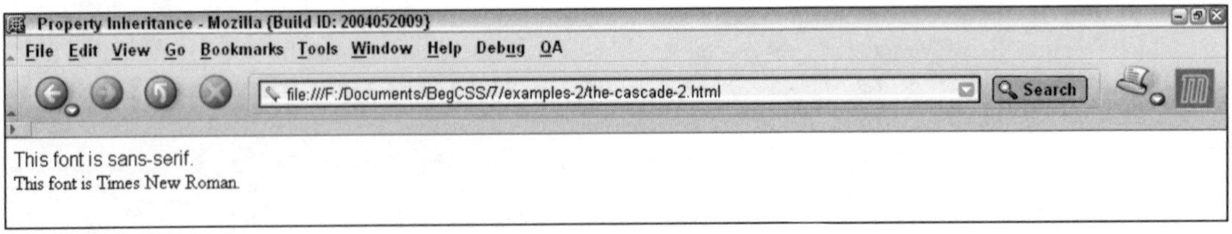

Figure 7-4

The `div` selector wins over the universal selector because the `div` selector is more specific. Using the chart, the universal selector has a specificity of zero, so it's the broadest and most general. The `div` selector has a specificity of one, so it wins — by just one. Here's another example:

```
ul li {
    border: thin solid black;
}
li#navigation {
    border: thick solid black;
}
```

Apply this to the following markup:

```
<ul>
    <li> This list item has a thin border around it. </li>
    <li id='navigation'> This list item has a thick border around it. </li>
</ul>
```

The result is shown in Figure 7-5.

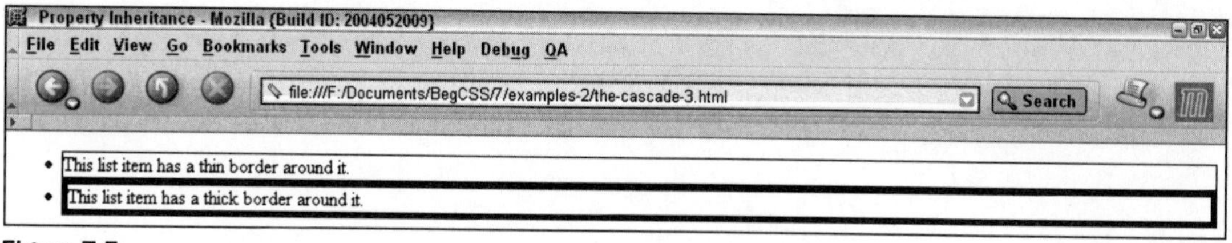

Figure 7-5

The first selector is the descendant selector that you saw in Chapter 5. It selects the `<li>` element because it is a descendant of the `<ul>` element. Both rules apply a border. The first rule has a specificity of 2 because it contains two element names: `<ul>` and `<li>`. But it doesn't have an id or any attributes in the selector. The second rule is an id selector, but it contains an element name, too. So its specificity is 101. It has one id name, no attribute selectors, no class names, no pseudo-classes, and one element name. So it wins by 99, and the border around the `<li>` is thick instead of thin. If I removed the `id='navigation'` from the second list item, it would also have a thin border because it, too, is a descendant of the `<ul>` element.

When an HTML `style` attribute is applied, it is considered the most specific of any selector on the page. That's because according to the CSS specification, it is defined as having the specificity of a selector with an id name. Because the `style` attribute appears after any styles appearing in style sheets, it also takes precedence over the id selector. Therefore, the `style` attribute takes precedence over all other rules.

In the following Try It Out, I show you a few examples of the cascade and inheritance from a complex real-world web page. The web page in this example is a dinner menu from JT's Island Grill and Gallery website, a real website for a restaurant in Chokoloskee, Florida. Don't be intimidated by the amount of source code you see here. You're going to focus only on some specific examples of cascading and inheritance that can be observed in this example. Then, beginning with Chapter 8 and on through Chapter 14, you see how to build this web page from the ground up. Having seen the design of the completed web page here, it will be easier for you to follow along in Chapter 8 and subsequent chapters as each piece of the puzzle fits into place. You can download the images and source code for this example from www.wrox.com.

Try It Out   Examining the Effects of the Cascade and Inheritance

Example 7-1. The following steps show examples of the cascade and inheritance in a real-world website.

1.   Enter the following markup into your text editor:

```
<!DOCTYPE html PUBLIC "-/pp/W3C//DTD XHTML 1.0 Strict//EN"
"http://www.w3.org/TR/xhtml1/DTD/xhtml1-strict.dtd">
<html>
    <head>
        <title>
            JT's Island Grill and Gallery - Chokoloskee, Florida
        </title>
        <link rel='stylesheet' type='text/css'
            href='base_styles.css' media='screen'/>
```

```
            <link rel='stylesheet' type='text/css'
                href='menu_system.css' media='screen'/>
            <link rel='stylesheet' type='text/css'
                href='dinner_menu.css' media='screen'/>
    </head>
    <body>
        <div id='nav'>
            <div>
                <ul id='gifts'>
                    <li id='leftedge'>
                        <span>Unique Gifts</span>
                        <ul class='menu'>
                            <li><a href=''>Gallery</a></li>
                        </ul>
                    </li>
                    <li>
                        <span>Chokoloskee</span>
                        <ul class='menu'>
                            <li><a href=''>Visiting Chokoloskee</a></li>
                            <li>
                                <a href=''>The Everglades and Ten
                                    Thousand Islands</a></li>
                            <li><a href=''>Recreation in South
                                    Western Florida</a></li>
                        </ul>
                    </li>
                </ul>
                <a href='index.html'>
                    <img src='jts_sign.jpg'
                        alt='JTs sign'
                        title='Go home.'/>
                </a>
                <ul id='food'>
                    <li id='rightedge'>
                        <span>Delicious Food</span>
                        <ul class='menu'>
                            <li><a href=''>Lunch at JT's</a></li>
                            <li><a href=''>JT's Lunch Menu</a></li>
                            <li><a href=''>Dinner at JT's</a></li>
                            <li>
                              <a href='dinner_menu.html'>
                                JT's Dinner Menu
                              </a>
                              </li>
                        </ul>
                    </li>
                    <li>
                        <span>Employment</span>
                        <ul class='menu'>
                            <li><a href=''>Contact JT's</a></li>
                            <li><a href=''>Seasonal Employment
                                    Opportunities</a></li>
```

```
                            </ul>
                    </li>
                </ul>
        </div>
</div>
<div id='body'>
    <h1>
        JT's at Night
    </h1>
    <div id='content'>
        <img src='dinner_plate.jpg'
            id='dinnerplate'
            alt='dinner plate'/>
        <h3>Appetizers</h3>
            <h4>Stone Crab Claws <em>Market Price</em></h4>
                <p>
                    1/2 lb of claws straight from local docks served
                    cracked with a house stone crab mustard sauce.
                </p>
            <h4>Sesame Seared Tuna <em>$8</em></h4>
                <p>
                    Sashimi grade yellowfin tuna encrusted in sesame
                    seeds lightly seared and served with soy dipping
                    sauce and wasabi.
                </p>
            <h4>Pita and Hummus <em>$4</em></h4>
                <p>
                    Our homemade hummus drizzled with olive oil,
                    accompanied with warm pita bread.
                </p>
            <h4>JT's Triple Crab Cakes <em>$7</em></h4>
                <p>
                    A rich blend of stone crab, blue crab and snow crab
                    sautéed to order, seasoned with Old Bay and fresh
                    parsley.
                </p>
            <h4>Spicy Coconut Shrimp <em>$8</em></h4>
                <p>
                    Gulf shrimp sautéed in coconut served with our
                    spicy peanut sauce.
                </p>
            <h4>Black Bean Quesadilla <em>$6</em></h4>
                <p>
                    Cheddar cheese, onions, green peppers, raisins,
                    almonds &amp; black beans grilled in a spinach
                    tortilla with fresh salsa.
                </p>
        <h3>Soups and Salads</h3>
            <h4>Key Lime-Cilantro Grilled Seafood Salad
                <em>$9</em>
            </h4>
                <p>
                    Grilled fish, shrimp &amp; scallops atop bed of
```

```
                            mixed organic greens with home-made key
                            lime-cilantro vinaigrette.
                    </p>
                <h4>Tomato Avocado Salad   <em>$9</em></h4>
                    <p>
                            Organically grown avocados and tomatoes atop a
                            fresh organic spring mix, with home-made roasted
                            tomato vinaigrette and freshly baked pita chips.
                            <em>(add shrimp for $1.25)</em>
                    </p>
                <h4>Florida Citrus Salad <em>$7</em></h4>
                    <p>
                            Almonds, coconut and mandarin oranges atop fresh
                            organic greens with a house honey-orange dressing.
                    </p>
                <h4>Spinach Salad with Warm Bacon Dressing <em>$7</em></h4>
                    <p>
                            Fresh spinach topped with a sizzling bacon
                            vinaigrette garnished with tomatoes and hard
                            boiled egg.
                    </p>

                <h4>Tonight's Salad   <em>ask</em></h4>
                    <p>
                            Chef's specialty salad changes nightly.
                    </p>
                <h4>Soup of da' day <em>ask</em></h4>
                    <p>Prepared fresh daily</p>
        <h3>Entrees</h3>
            <p class='menucaption'>
                    Entrees come with tonight's small salad and fresh baked
                    ciabatta bread.
            </p>
            <h4>Stone Crab Claws <em>Market Price</em></h4>
                <p>
                        One lb locally caught stone crab claws served
                        cracked with our key lime mustard sauce.
                </p>
            <h4>Apricot Pork Tenderloin <em>$16</em></h4>
                <p>
                        Tenderloin rolled and baked with apricot &amp;
                        spinach with a parmesan crust and apricot sauce,
                        fanned over rice and seasonal vegetables.
                </p>
            <h4>Crab Cakes and Mango Salsa <em>$18</em></h4>
                <p>
                        Blend of fresh stone crab, snow crab, and blue crab
                        topped with a black bean-ginger sauce and mango
                        salsa, with pineapple jasmine rice.
                </p>
            <h4>Red Wine Grilled Portobello <em>$17</em></h4>
                <p>
```

```
                    Portobello mushroom broiled with goat cheese and a
                    red wine-shallot sauce over linguine, with
                    pan-fried yams, apples, and scallions.
                </p>
        <h4>Jamaican Jerk Shrimp &amp; Scallops <em>$17</em></h4>
            <p>
                    Shrimp &amp; scallops cooked in our home-made
                    authentic Jamaican marinade served with pineapple
                    jasmine rice and veggies.
                </p>
        <h4>Yellowfin Tuna in Flambé Vanilla Rum <em>$21</em></h4>
            <p>
                    Sashimi Grade Yellowfin tuna seasoned with adobo
                    &amp; cinnamon, seared, and flambéed in
                    vanilla-rum, with garlic buttermilk mashed
                    potatoes and fresh sautéed veggies.
                </p>
        <h4>Coconut Sesame Chicken <em>$17</em></h4>
            <p>
                    Chicken Breast sautéed with glazed walnuts and a
                    sesame sauce, over black bean cakes and
                    stir-fried vegetables, sprinkled with nutmeg.
                </p>
        <h4>Picadillo <em>$14</em></h4>
            <p>
                    Olives &amp; raisins cooked with ground beef,
                    onions, peppers and Cuban spices, atop rice
                    with fresh baked bread.
                </p>
        <h4>Blackened New York Steak <em>$20</em></h4>
            <p>
                    Spiced and blackened New York Strip with garlic
                    buttermilk mashed potatoes, a papaya-basil
                    marmalade, and marinated mushrooms.
                </p>
<h3>Children</h3>
        <h5>Pasta &amp; Tomato Sauce <em>$4</em></h5>
        <h5>Pasta topped with Cheese <em>$4</em></h5>
        <h5>Mini Crab Cakes <em>$7</em></h5>
        <h5>Grilled Cheese Sandwich <em>$3</em></h5>
        <h5>Peanut Butter &amp; Jelly Sandwich <em>$3</em></h5>
<h3>Beverages</h3>
        <h5>Soft drink cans <em>$1.50</em></h5>
        <h5>Iced tea (sweet or not) <em>$1.50</em></h5>
        <h5>Home-made Key Limeade <em>$1.50</em></h5>
        <h5>Coffee, hot tea, hot chocolate <em>$1.50</em></h5>
        <h5>Juice, milk <em>$1.50</em></h5>
<h3>Local Flavor</h3>
        <h5>Hot Pressed Cuban Sandwich <em>$8</em></h5>
        <h5>JT's Classic Cheeseburger <em>$7</em></h5>
        <h5>BBQ Pork Sandwich <em>$7</em></h5>
<h3>Dessert</h3>
        <h5>Home-made Key Lime Pie <em>$4</em></h5>
```

```
                <p>
                    The best in the Everglades
                </p>
              <h3>Local Music &amp; Arts</h3>
                <img src='dinner.jpg'
                    id='dinner'
                    alt='Dinner Table'/>
                <p class='copy'>
                    We hope you enjoy tonight's live music. To help keep
                    the local arts alive we book musicians from here in
                    south Florida. Many of them have music CD's or tapes
                    for sale in our shop. If you haven't already done so,
                    check out our walls and shelves. We like to consider
                    them a gallery of Florida.  We feature local artists,
                    crafters, musicians and authors. When you purchase
                    something you like, not only are you taking home a
                    true piece of this area, you are helping to preserve
                    its art and culture.
                </p>
            </div>
            <h6>
                &copy; Copyright 2003-2004 Panther's Crossing, Inc.
            </h6>
        </div>
    </body>
</html>
```

2. Save this file as dinner_menu.html.

3. Enter the following style sheet into your text editor:

```
body {
    background: url('palms.jpg') no-repeat fixed center bottom;
    padding: 5em 0 1.2em 0;
    margin: 0;
    font-family: "Courier New", Courier, monospace;
    text-transform: lowercase;
}
a {
    text-decoration: none;
}
a:hover {
    text-decoration: underline;
}
div#body {
    margin: 0 auto;
    width: 50em;
}
h1, h6 {
    background-color: lightsteelblue;
    border-left: 0.05em solid black;
    border-right: 0.05em solid black;
```

```
}
h1, h2, h3, h4, h5, h6 {
    margin: 0;
}
h1 {
    clear: both;
    padding: 0.5em 1.1em;
    border-top: 0.05em solid black;
    -moz-border-radius-topleft: 0.8em;
    -moz-border-radius-topright: 0.8em;
    font-family: "Monotype Corsiva", cursive;
    letter-spacing: 4px;
    font-size: 1.5em;
}
h2 {
    margin: 0 1.2em;
    padding: 0.9em 1.1em 0;
    border-bottom: 0.05em dotted black;
}
h3 {
    border-bottom: 1px dotted black;
    font-size: 0.9em;
}
h6 {
    padding: 1em 0;
    -moz-border-radius-bottomleft: 0.8em;
    -moz-border-radius-bottomright: 0.8em;
    border-bottom: 0.05em solid black;
    font-size: 0.8em;
    text-align: center;
}
div#content {
    padding: 1.2em;
    border: 0.05em solid black;
    font-size: 0.9em;
    word-spacing: 5px;
    letter-spacing: 1px;
}
p.copy {
    padding: 1.2em;
    margin: 0 1.2em;
    line-height: 2em;
    border-bottom: 0.05em dotted black;
    font-size: 1.2em;
    font-family: "Times New Roman", Times, serif;
    text-indent: 20px;
    text-align: justify;
}
img {
    margin: 1.7em;
    border: 0.05em solid black;
}
```

4. Save the preceding style sheet as base_styles.css.

5. Enter the following style sheet into your text editor.

```css
div#nav {
    position: fixed;
    right: 0;
    left: 0;
    top: 0.8em;
}
div#nav > div {
    position: relative;
    margin: auto;
    width: 50em;
    text-align: center;
}
div#nav > div > a > img {
    position: relative;
    clear: left;
    display: block;
    margin: 0 auto;
    width: 17em;
    height: auto;
    z-index: 1;
}
div#nav ul {
    position: absolute;
    list-style-type: none;
    margin: 0;
    padding: 0;
}
div#nav > div > ul {
    top: 2.92em;
    width: 50%;
}
ul#gifts {
    left: 0;
}
ul#food {
    right: 0;
}
div#nav span {
    display: block;
    overflow: hidden;
    height: 2.1em;
    line-height: 2.2em;
}
div#nav > div > ul > li {
    position: relative;
    background-color: lightblue;
    padding: 0.5em;
    border: 0.05em solid black;
    font-size: 0.9em;
    padding: 0 0.5em;
```

```
        width: 8.35em;
        height: 2.2em;
}
div#nav > div > ul > li:hover {
        background-color: lightsteelblue;
}
ul#gifts > li {
        float: left;
}
ul#food > li {
        float: right;
}
div#nav > div > ul > li#leftedge {
        border-right-width: 0;
        -moz-border-radius-topleft: 1em;
        -moz-border-radius-bottomleft: 1em;
        margin-left: 0.3em;
}
div#nav > div > ul > li#leftedge:hover {
        -moz-border-radius-bottomleft: 0;
}
div#nav > div > ul > li#rightedge {
        border-left-width: 0;
        -moz-border-radius-topright: 1em;
        -moz-border-radius-bottomright: 1em;
        margin-right: 0.3em;
}
div#nav > div > ul > li#rightedge:hover {
        -moz-border-radius-bottomright: 0;
}
ul.menu {
        top: 2.19em;
        background-color: lightblue;
        width: 15em;
        -moz-border-radius-bottomleft: 1em;
        -moz-border-radius-bottomright: 1em;
        border: 0.05em solid black;
        display: none;
}
ul#food ul.menu {
        -moz-border-radius-topleft: 1em;
         right: -0.07em;
}
ul#gifts ul.menu {
        -moz-border-radius-topright: 1em;
        left: -0.05em;
}
div#nav > div > ul > li:hover > ul.menu,
ul.menu:hover {
        display: block;
}
ul.menu li {
        text-align: left;
        color: black;
```

```
}
ul.menu a {
    margin: 0.4em;
    padding: 0.5em;
    color: black;
    display: block;
    border: 0.05em solid lightblue;
}
ul.menu a:hover {
    background-color: lightsteelblue;
    -moz-border-radius: 0.8em;
    border: 0.05em solid black;
    text-decoration: none;
}
div#nav ul a:active {
    background-color: steelblue;
}
```

6. Save the preceding style sheet as menu_system.css.

7. Enter the following style sheet into your text editor:

```
div#content * {
    font-family: "Times New Roman", Times, serif;
}
div#content h3 + p, div#content h4 + p  {
    margin: 0 0 1.8em 0;
}
div#content h3 {
    margin-top: 1.8em;
    border-bottom: none;
    font-family: "Monotype Corsiva", cursive;
    text-decoration: underline;
    font-size: 2em;
}
div#content img + h3 {
    margin-top: 0;
}
h3 + p.menucaption {
    font-style: italic;
    text-align: center;
}
h4, h5 {
    font-size: 1.3em;
}
h3, h4, h5, h4 + p, h5 + p {
    text-align: center;
}
h4 em, h5 em {
    margin-left: 0.9em;
    font-weight: lighter;
}
h5 + p {
    margin-top: 0;
}
h5 {
```

```
    font-weight: normal;
}
p.copy {
    padding-top: 0;
}
div#content {
    background: lightyellow url('dinner_glass.jpg') no-repeat fixed center center;
}
div#body img {
    float: right;
    height: auto;
}
img#dinnerplate {
    width: 9em;
}
img#dinner {
    width: 16em;
}
```

8. Save the preceding style sheet as dinner_menu.css.

9. Open dinner_menu.html in Mozilla, Mozilla Firefox, or Netscape. You should see output like that shown in Figure 7-6.

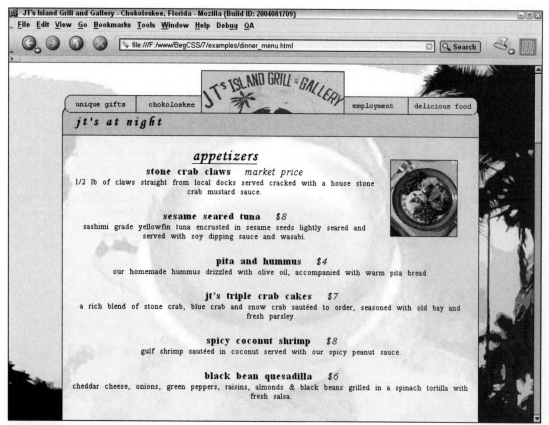

Figure 7-6

How It Works

In this example, you see three style sheets and a markup document that contains the data for the JT's dinner menu. The three style sheets each have a specific purpose and divide the styles of the JT's website into three different categories. The base_styles.css style sheet is broader. It is intended to be applied not only to the dinner menu, but to all the other pages of the JT's website as well. The second style sheet, menu_system.css, houses the styles specific to the navigation bar that floats with the document as you scroll down the page. The third style sheet, dinner_menu.css, houses styles specific to the dinner menu. Although the JT's dinner menu is quite a lengthy example, it contains several simple examples of cascading and inheritance that you can easily identify.

First, let's review some examples of inheritance taking place in the dinner menu. The first example of inheritance appears in the first rule of the base_styles.css style sheet:

```
body {
    background: url('palms.jpg') no-repeat fixed center bottom;
    padding: 5em 0 1.2em 0;
    margin: 0;
    font-family: "Courier New", Courier, monospace;
    text-transform: lowercase;
}
```

I'll explain the second line of the highlighted declaration in this rule first. The text-transform: lowercase; declaration can be readily observed in the whole web page. By applying the text-transform: lowercase; declaration to the <body> element, you've made all the text in the entire document appear in lowercase letters—a style that is not always desirable; but in this case, it seems to make the dinner menu more artistic. The style is applied beginning with the <body> element and propagates to all its descendants.

Now, look back at the first line of the highlighted declaration in the preceding rule. This declaration sets the font. I look at the font-family property in detail in Chapter 9. For this immediate discussion, the font-family property is also an example of a property that is inherited. If you set the font-family property on the <body> element, it propagates to all the children, grandchildren, and distant descendants of the <body> element. You can observe this in the font face of the menu headings and drop-down menus at the top of the document, which all have a Courier New font.

Inheritance can also be overridden. You can see this in the *jt's at night* heading under the page's navigation. This heading has a Monotype Corsiva font instead of the Courier New font set for the <body> element:

```
h1 {
    clear: both;
    padding: 0.5em 1.1em;
    border-top: 0.05em solid black;
    -moz-border-radius-topleft: 0.8em;
    -moz-border-radius-topright: 0.8em;
    font-family: "Monotype Corsiva", cursive;
    letter-spacing: 4px;
    font-size: 1.5em;
}
```

The `<h1>` element is a descendant of the `<body>` element, so I could have allowed the Courier New font to inherit from the `<body>` element to the `<h1>` element. But I decided a Monotype Corsiva font would look better for the heading. Additionally, different fonts were utilized in the body of the dinner menu. The following rule is set in the dinner_menu.css file:

```css
div#content * {
    font-family: "Times New Roman", Times, serif;
}
```

The preceding rule uses a combination of the id and universal selector that you saw in Chapter 5, and it gives all the descendant elements of the `<div>` with a `content` id name a Times New Roman font. In this rule, inheritance is *not* being utilized. Although all the descendant elements are given the Times New Roman font, they are given this font in a different way. By using the universal selector, each descendant element is given a Times New Roman font explicitly instead of through inheritance. This means that if you set the font family on a descendant element of the `content` `<div>`, the application of that font is subject to the cascade. The following rule, which also appears in the dinner_menu.css style sheet, is an example of this:

```css
div#content h3 {
    margin-top: 1.8em;
    border-bottom: none;
    font-family: "Monotype Corsiva", cursive;
    text-decoration: underline;
    font-size: 2em;
}
```

The `<h3>` heading contains the headings for the different parts of the menu: *appetizers, soups and salads, entrees,* and so on. The `<h3>` element is selected as a descendant of the `content` `<div>`. Because the specificity of the universal selector is zero, and the specificity of the h3 selector is 1, the font specified in the h3 selector wins. However, as you may remember from Chapter 5, the universal selector selects *everything*. If the `<h3>` element has any children elements, those elements still have a Times New Roman font. Because the universal selector applies to everything, its selection takes precedence over inheritance. I have included the example utilizing the universal selector merely to emphasize it as a possibility and to show that selecting an element takes precedence over inheritance.

The cascade of the JT's dinner menu is important, as I explained. Each style sheet has a specific purpose — going from broader to more specific. The base_styles.css style sheet is the weakest because it is included first. The menu_system.css style sheet takes precedence over the base_style.css style sheet because it appears after it. The dinner_menu.css style sheet takes precedence over both the base_styles.css and menu_system.css style sheets because it appears last. The following is a review of some examples of the cascade that appear in the JT's dinner menu. The first example comes from the menu_system.css style sheet:

```css
div#nav > div > ul > li {
    position: relative;
    background-color: lightblue;
    padding: 0.5em;
    border: 0.05em solid black;
    font-size: 0.9em;
    padding: 0 0.5em;
    width: 8.35em;
    height: 2.2em;
}
```

```
div#nav > div > ul > li:hover {
    background-color: lightsteelblue;
}
```

Both rules refer to the same <li> elements, which in this case are the navigational headings *unique gifts, chokoloskee, employment,* and *delicious food.* A light blue background color is specified for each of these list items in the first rule. In the proceeding rule, that background color is changed to light steel blue when the user's mouse cursor hovers over the top of one of the list items. This is done via the cascade. The selector of the first rule, div#nav > div > ul > li, has a specificity of 104 because it has one id selector and four element names in the selector. The selector of the following rule, div#nav > div > ul > li:hover, has a specificity of 114 because it has an id selector, four element names, and a pseudo-class in the selector. This allows it to take precedence over the preceding rule and to apply a different background color when the user's mouse cursor hovers over a navigational heading.

Another example of the cascade appears in one rule in the base_styles.css style sheet and in one rule in the dinner_menu.css style sheet. The following rule is from the base_styles.css style sheet:

```
p.copy {
    padding: 1.2em;
    margin: 0 1.2em;
    line-height: 2em;
    border-bottom: 0.05em dotted black;
    font-size: 1.2em;
    font-family: "Times New Roman", Times, serif;
    text-indent: 20px;
    text-align: justify;
}
```

The following rule is from the dinner_menu.css style sheet:

```
p.copy {
    padding-top: 0;
}
```

The rules have the same specificity: 11. The rule from base_styles.css comes first and sets the padding on all four sides of <p> elements with a copy class name. I decided that I didn't want any top padding on the copy <p> element in the dinner menu. This ensures that the content of the copy <p> is flush with the heading above it, *local music & arts.* This is an example of the cascade; I've partially overridden the padding set in the first rule appearing in the base_styles.css style sheet by applying a new rule in the dinner_menu.css style sheet.

The JT's dinner menu plays an important role in the coming chapters. From Chapter 8 to Chapter 14 you see how this design was built from the ground up and how CSS features work. Having seen the final product here, you'll be able to follow along more easily with each new feature introduced because you already know the goal of the project.

The next section continues discussion of the cascade with the !important rules.

!important Rules

Along with the need for the cascade in CSS came the need to override it. This is where !important rules come in. The !important syntax appears within a declaration after the property value and before the semicolon that terminates the declaration. Two components make up this syntax: an exclamation mark, used here as a delimiter, and the important keyword. A delimiter marks the ending of one thing and the beginning of another. Here the exclamation mark signals the end of the declaration. The important keyword must appear next, followed by a semicolon to terminate the declaration:

```
div {
    color: black !important;
}
```

A declaration containing the !important rule, like the preceding one, takes precedence over any other declaration.

```
div#someid {
    color: orange;
}
```

Under the cascade, the id selector takes precedence over the element name selector. However, if the !important rule appears in a declaration, that declaration takes precedence. In this case, as illustrated by the preceding code, the result is black text color rather than orange.

The !important rule also takes precedence over the style attribute.

```
<div style='color: purple;'>
    some text
</div>
```

The color for the div is still black because the !important rule takes precedence over all other declarations.

Although the cascade dictates that the website author's style sheet takes precedence over the user's, the !important rule allows the user to override author specified styles.

> Under CSS 1, an author's !important rule takes precedence over a user's !important rule; under CSS 2, a user's !important rule takes precedence over the author's. The change makes CSS more accessible, enabling people with visual disabilities to write their own custom style sheets.

If more than one !important rule appears in a style sheet, and the style sheet has the same origin — that is, both rules come from the author's style sheet or both come from the user's style sheet — the latter rule wins out over any specified previously.

Custom Style Sheets

CSS is not limited to use by website designers. In modern browsers, it is a feasible solution to make websites more accessible. It enables users to create custom style sheets and apply them to all websites they visit. This is done via a feature offered in some browsers that allows a custom style sheet to be referenced. After the sheet is referenced, its rules can be made to override those of the website's authors. In the following sections I describe how to do this with Microsoft Internet Explorer and Mozilla.

Specifying a Custom Style Sheet Using MSIE

Custom style sheets are specified in IE by choosing Tools ➪ Internet Options. Click the Accessibility button, check the box labeled Format Documents Using My Style Sheet, and click the Browse button to locate a CSS document (with the .css extension) on your hard disk. The Accessibility panel is depicted in Figure 7-7.

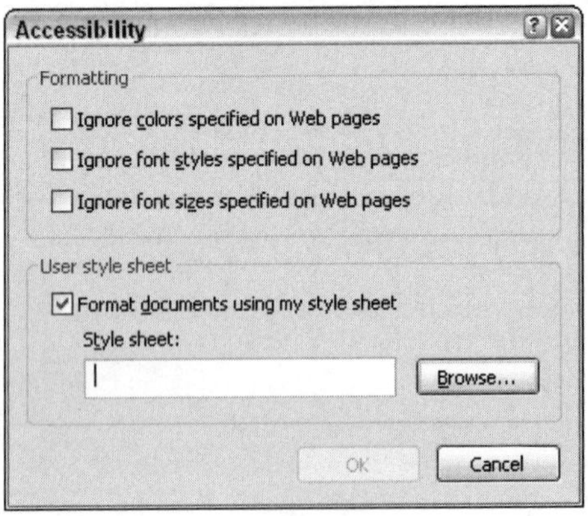

Figure 7-7

Remember to take into account that website author style sheets take precedence over user-specified style sheets. To override the author's style sheet, create declarations in the custom CSS file using the `!important` rule to override author-specified styles.

Specifying a Custom Style Sheet Using Mozilla

The process for specifying a custom style sheet isn't as intuitive when you are using Mozilla. I outline the process here for specifying a custom style sheet using Windows XP, although a custom style sheet can be specified for Mozilla using any operating system. Mozilla offers a simplified method of specifying colors, fonts, and other aspects of presentation that requires no knowledge of CSS. These options are used to create a user-defined style sheet behind the scenes. They are available from the Edit ➪ Preferences menu in Mozilla. Select the Appearance category from the left panel of the Preferences window. Expand the category, and options for the Font and Color are exposed. The preferences menu is depicted in Figure 7-8.

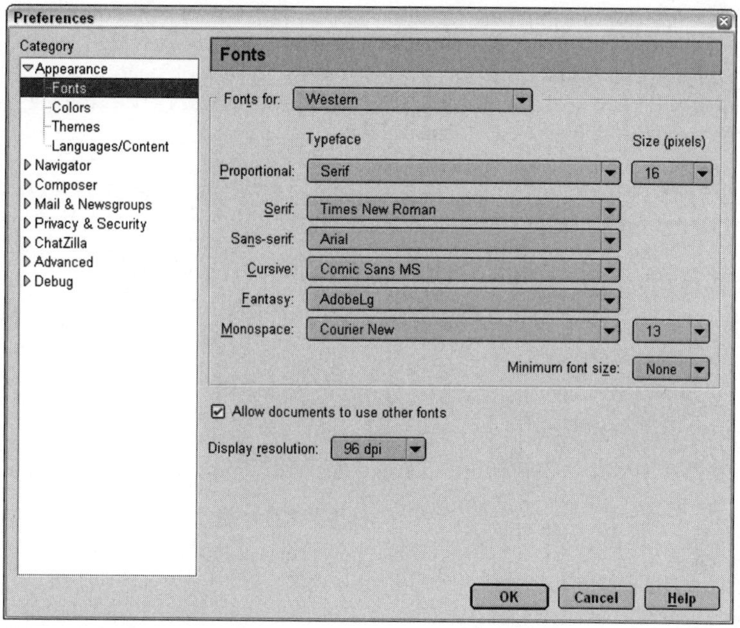

Figure 7-8

Although this built-in, idiot-proof method of controlling presentation is perfectly fine for those who know nothing about CSS, Mozilla has a slightly more complicated method of getting around this built-in specification of styles so that a completely customized style sheet can be used. This method requires you to find a special file titled *chrome* in a hidden directory (in Windows XP). Therefore, before I can show you how to specify a custom style sheet, a little background information is necessary so you will be able to locate this hidden folder.

First, Mozilla creates a profile for each user so multiple people can use Mozilla and all have different preferences and settings. To specify a custom style sheet for Mozilla, you must locate the folder that contains your Mozilla profile settings. The default profile is titled *default* by default, unless specified otherwise during the installation process. With this information, you may now begin the task of locating the folder titled *chrome*, which is located in a folder that goes by the same name as your Mozilla profile.

Before you can locate this folder, you must make some configuration changes because this folder resides in a hidden folder. In order to be used, hidden folders must be visible. To make hidden folders visible, open Windows Explorer by going to the Start menu and clicking the Run option. When the Run dialog opens, type `explorer` in the Open text box. After Windows Explorer opens, choose Tools ⇨ Folder Options. (Recall from Chapter 2 that the same menu was required to show extensions for all file types. The Folder Options menu is depicted in Figure 2-1.) Click the View tab and then click the option labeled Show Hidden Files and Folders. Finally, click OK to activate the changes. Now all files and folders are visible.

To navigate to the profile folder, click through the following sequence of folders using Windows Explorer. Start with My Computer ⇨ C:\ (or the drive letter where Windows is installed) ⇨ Documents and Settings. Then open the folder with the Windows XP user name that Mozilla is installed under.

Continue with the following sequence of folders: Application Data ➪ Mozilla ➪ Profiles. Open the folder with the Mozilla profile name for which you'd like to specify a custom style sheet. Within the folder for your profile name, you may find a folder with some gobbledegook for a title—a seemingly random sequence of letters. Within that folder, click the folder titled *chrome*. Figure 7-9 depicts the complete folder tree required to access the *chrome* folder.

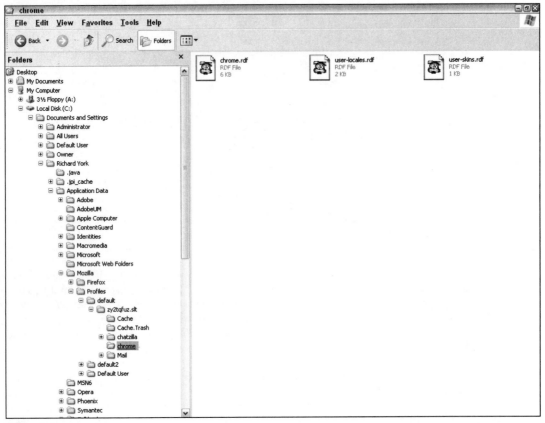

Figure 7-9

The CSS file used as a custom style sheet for Mozilla must also have a special name: userContent.css. Add a CSS file named userContent.css to the chrome directory, and Mozilla will attempt to apply the styles specified in it to the websites you visit while you're logged on to Mozilla using the profile name of the directory userContent.css was saved in. I say *attempt* because the cascade still applies; because this is a user style sheet, a website author's style sheet still takes precedence over the user's style sheet. As I discussed earlier in this chapter, in the section "!important Rules," declarations must be made with the !important rule to override declarations made by the website author.

Customizing Mozilla Using CSS

Mozilla doesn't stop with allowing a custom style sheet for content. You can also make a style sheet for certain aspects of the look and feel of the browser itself. In fact, Mozilla itself is written mostly in web programming languages like CSS, JavaScript, and XML, and because Mozilla is open source, this makes it very easy to enhance—and to participate as a Mozilla developer. The style sheet for the browser differs slightly from that of the content. First, this file must be named userChrome.css; however, it must be placed in the same directory as the userContent.css file. Second, the userChome.css file contains a reference to something called XUL, which stands for the Extensible User-interface Language. Aside from a single reference to XUL, the rest of this file is written in plain CSS. Mozilla provides some prewritten examples of the userContent.css and userChrome.css file. You can view these with Windows Explorer at the following location:

```
C:\Program Files\mozilla.org\Mozilla\defaults\profile\US\chrome
```

With a default installation, Mozilla is located in C:\Program Files\. However, it can be installed on any drive. Mozilla's example files are titled userChrome-example.css and userContent-example.css.

Now that I've explained where the file goes and what it does, follow the steps in this Try It Out to create a custom style sheet for Microsoft Internet Explorer and Mozilla.

Try It Out Creating a userContent.css Style Sheet for Mozilla and IE

Example 7-2. In this exercise, you learn how to use a custom style sheet to change styles in IE and Mozilla.

1. Open your text editor and add the following CSS:

```css
* {
    color: white !important;
    -moz-border-radius: 0 !important;
}
a:link, a {
    color: royalblue !important;
}
a:active {
    color: red !important;
}
a:visited {
    color: purple !important;
}
body {
    background: black !important;
}
div, table, td, h1, h2, h3, h4, h5, h6 {
    background: inherit !important;
}
input, select, textarea {
    padding: 5px !important;
    border: thin solid gray !important;
    background-color: blue !important;
    margin: 5px !important;
}
input:focus {
    background-color: red !important;
}
input[type='image'] {
    display: none !important;
}
img {
    display: none !important;
}
```

2. Save the file as userContent.css.

3. To use the style sheet with Mozilla, save the file to the Mozilla user profile *chrome* directory described in the section "Customizing Mozilla Using CSS" earlier in this chapter.

4. Apply the style sheet using Internet Explorer's accessibility panel, also described in this chapter in the section "Specifying a Custom Style Sheet Using MSIE."

How It Works

This style sheet overrides all styles specified on a website. It uses a high contrast color scheme, white text on a black background. It sets all unvisited links to royal blue, and changes visited links to purple at any website the user visits. Let's review each style rule. The first style rule makes all text white, and it removes any border radius effects:

```
* {
    color: white !important;
    -moz-border-radius: 0 !important;
}
```

Next, the linking color scheme is defined:

```
a:link, a {
    color: royalblue !important;
}
a:active {
    color: red !important;
}
a:visited {
    color: purple !important;
}
```

Unvisited links are made royal blue, active links are made red, and visited links are made purple. Next, the background is applied to all elements. I've done this by applying a black background to the <body> element; then other elements are told to inherit their background color.

```
body {
    background: black !important;
}
div, table, td, h1, h2, h3, h4, h5, h6 {
    background: inherit !important;
}
```

This forces all the other elements to go along with whatever is defined for the <body> element. Next I want to control the look and feel of input <form> elements. In this rule, I make <input>, <select>, and <textarea> elements have a blue background.

```
input, select, textarea {
    padding: 5px !important;
    border: thin solid gray !important;
    background-color: blue !important;
    margin: 5px !important;
}
```

Some padding and margins are added for clarity, and a thin, gray border is placed around each input element. As I did for :active links, I also want <input> fields to turn red when in focus, and I do that with this rule:

```
input:focus {
    background-color: red !important;
}
```

Finally, because images are annoying, I get rid of them. Luckily, CSS provides me with that capability. Making background colors black ought to get rid of most background images. For the <img> element and input buttons that use images, I add the following rules:

```
input[type='image'] {
    display: none !important;
}
img {
    display: none !important;
}
```

The display: none; declaration takes the images out of the rendered document as though they never existed. All these styles combined create a high contrast design that loads quickly because images are not displayed.

Custom style sheets offer a great deal of flexibility for people with visual disabilities, for people using low bandwidth Internet connections, and for people who simply like to customize their Internet experience. Mozilla and Internet Explorer provide easy-to-use tools to create them.

Summary

Inheritance and the cascade are fundamental to CSS. Inheritance makes controlling the effects of property values a breeze, because each property is defined either to inherit or not, as is appropriate to its purpose. The cascade provides some rules for precedence to determine which styles win when multiple style sheets and rules containing the same declarations come into play. Precedence is determined by a simple formula that calculates which selector wins.

In this chapter you learned that the following:

❑   Some properties are inherited, which reduces redundancy in the document by eliminating the need for declarations to be written multiple times.

❑   Some properties are not inherited, which also reduces redundancy by preventing the effects of declarations from being applied to the element's decendants.

❑   The cascade provides both some ground rules and a simple formula to determine the precedence of style sheets and selectors.

❑   Custom style sheets allow users to specify their own styles for the websites they visit.

Now that you know the background of CSS, Chapter 8 begins with a look at the strategies used in beginning a real-world website design project and introduces you to CSS's text manipulation properties.

Exercises

1. Open the file for example5-5.html and calculate the specificity for each selector used in this example. (If you go to www.wrox.com and download the entire folder structure of files for the book, you can find example5-5.html under Chapter 5\Try It Out.)

    Hint: Don't forget that selectors can be grouped.

2. Write your own userContent.css file. Make all backgrounds white and all text black. Make all unvisited links blue, visited links purple, and active links red. Have all input fields use a white background with a black border and black text. Don't display any images.

8

Text Manipulation

In Chapter 7 you learned how certain properties in CSS are inherited and how the cascade determines which style rules are the most important. In this and subsequent chapters, I begin an in-depth look at the individual properties of CSS and how these come together to style a document. In this chapter, I also present the beginning of a real-world website project that forms the basis for the examples in this chapter and every chapter that follows. Each example builds on the JT's Island Grill and Gallery website that I presented in Chapter 7 to demonstrate the effects of the cascade and inheritance. Although in Chapter 7 you have already seen what the completed JT's Island Grill and Gallery home page looks like, here I begin the process of building the JT's website from scratch, step by step, to demonstrate how I achieved the design presented in Chapter 7.

In this chapter, I also present some of the techniques and strategies required to make a success of a real-life website, such as basic planning and best markup practices. I also look specifically at properties that manipulate the presentation of text. You can manipulate text in a variety of ways, from the length of space between letters in words of text, to the length of space between the words of a sentence, to the spacing between sentences in a paragraph, to how much space is used to indent the text contained in a paragraph of text. I discuss design strategy — how to approach a real-world website design project — and I look ahead to what's in store in CSS 3.

I cover the various CSS text-manipulation properties:

- ❑ The letter-spacing property and how it is used to add or subtract space between the letters that make up a word

- ❑ The word-spacing property and how it is used to add or subtract space between the words of a sentence

- ❑ The text-indent property and how it is used to indent the text of a paragraph

- ❑ The text-align property and how it is used to align the text of a document

- ❑ The text-decoration property and how it is used to underline, overline, and strikethrough text

- ❑ The text-transform property and how it is used to capitalize text or convert text to uppercase or lowercase letters

- ❑ The white-space property and how it is used to control the flow and formatting of text

The text manipulation properties of CSS allow you to design the layout of a document in much the same way as you use a word processing application. Before I get into the discussion of the various CSS text-manipulation properties, however, I provide an overview of the JT's Island Grill and Gallery website to show you what's involved in designing a website for the real world using CSS and XHTML.

The JT's Website

In Chapter 7 you got a sneak peek at what the completed JT's Island Grill and Gallery restaurant home page looks like. What I did not mention in Chapter 7 is that this is a real-life website. The restaurant's owners (and friends of yours truly) graciously agreed to my including their website in my book for the purpose of demonstrating what CSS can do. Thrilled at the opportunity to present a real website, I completely rewrote the entire website so that it makes optimal use of most CSS properties. From this chapter onward, each "Try It Out" example focuses on how to build a real-life website from scratch using CSS as the primary designing tool. As the book progresses, new properties are introduced and added to the JT's style sheet. This easy-to-follow approach makes the benefits and effects of each property apparent.

To understand what is involved in creating a real website, you must first learn the strategies and techniques required to build it, and this is the focus of the coming sections.

Developing a Design Strategy

Before I continue with the discussion of CSS, you should understand each step required in planning the JT's website, particularly which methods to use so that the website can propagate seamlessly across a variety of screen resolutions, browsers, platforms, and devices. This includes deciding what techniques to employ to create a website that is accessible, easy to maintain, and fluid to the user's environment. This type of design is referred to as liquid design. Liquid design refers to the design of web pages that are adaptive to the user's environment—page that increases or decreases in size with the user's screen resolution and that are available on a variety of platforms, browsers, and devices. I discuss the techniques involved in creating a liquid design in more detail in Chapter 10, so the strategies I discuss here lead directly to those strategies.

Building a website requires you to have a strategy for the layout of the website, for the storage and management of the website's files, and for how people visiting the website will interact with the website to locate the information they are looking for. Although these strategies are important, you must also settle on a strategy for how the markup within each document will be structured because this is part of how the website will be managed and updated. The following list outlines the requirements for successfully building the JT's website. Your plan should include the following:

❑ A logical and organized directory structure, where the website's images and the different XHTML pages and style sheets will be stored.

❑ A table of contents that determines what the different pages of the website will contain and what they will be called, and all the required photos, artwork, or other images that will make up the content and creative presentation of the website.

❑ A color scheme.

❑ A list of browsers to support—the website must work on a variety of platforms and browsers to reach the most users possible. The most common browsers include Internet Explorer 5.5 and 6 for Windows, Safari for Mac OS X, Gecko (Netscape 7, Mozilla and Mozilla Firefox), and Opera 7.

❏ A provision for accessibility for visually impaired users and people who are accessing the content of the website with the aid of a browser that reads content with a voice synthesizer.

❏ Alternative versions of the website for print and for handheld devices like PDAs and cell phones.

Each step is important to create a website that adheres to standards that ensure the website can propagate seamlessly across a variety of platforms. Browsers and devices that implement agreed-upon standards make this possible. I postpone the discussion of the last three points in the preceding list until later chapters because each is a lengthy topic in itself.

In terms of browser compatibility, many of the examples that I present don't function properly using the Microsoft Internet Explorer 5.5 and 6 browsers for Windows. However, I have not ignored Internet Explorer; in fact, I mentioned it as an important browser to design for. In Chapter 19, I cover techniques that work around problems you face when displaying content in Internet Explorer. This discussion merits its own chapter because Internet Explorer has the most problems and the least amount of CSS functionality.

You should use Mozilla to test the examples unless I specify otherwise.

As for the last two bullet points in the preceding list, I discuss accessibility in more detail in Chapter 10 and how to write style sheets for print, handheld devices, and PDAs in Chapter 15. The techniques that I use between now and then play into those discussions and will become more obvious when those topics emerge.

As for color schemes, because I am using CSS, I don't need to absolutely settle on a certain scheme at the beginning of the project. The color scheme can be updated from one or a few CSS files later and take effect immediately for the entire website.

For the coming sections, I limit the discussion to the basic directory structure, the pages required in the JT's website, and a simple example of how the markup is structured.

Creating the Directory Structure

The directory structure houses all the files required for the website. The directory structure must be organized and easy to maintain so that the website's files are easy to find, edit, or remove. The JT's website is comprised primarily of the following types of documents:

❏ XHTML documents that contain the markup and copy for each page of content

❏ Images: photos, artwork, and other graphical content

❏ Style sheets

The directory structure is an important part of designing a website, even for a small website like JT's. Planning the directory structure makes the project easy to manage should the website expand and become more complicated. With an organized directory structure in place, a website can grow more easily — it becomes scalable.

The required files for the JT's website are available from www.wrox.com. However, if you do not have access to the Wrox website, the following Try It Out outlines how to create the required directory structure.

Try It Out   **Creating the Required Directory Structure**

Example 8-1. To set up the required directory structure for the JT's website, follow these steps:

1. Create a directory named *chokoloskee-island*.

2. Inside the chokoloskee-island directory, create a directory called *style_sheets* and a directory called *images*.

3. Inside the images directory, create a directory named *backgrounds* and a directory named *photos*. Your directory structure should look like the one in Figure 8-1.

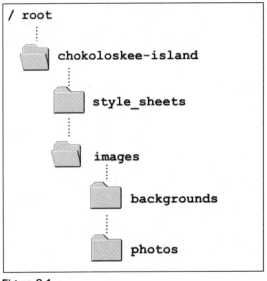

Figure 8-1

How It Works

Figure 8-1 shows a basic tree view representation of the JT's website directory structure. The *root* directory shown in Figure 8-1 is the directory in which you've created the chokoloskee-island directory, and this can be any directory that you like.

The directory structure is very important because a well-thought–out directory structure makes the files easy to manage. A clean, logical, and organized directory structure that categorizes the files required for the website is one step in the process of creating a website. Your clients and colleagues will appreciate the professionalism of this approach to organizing the website's files, particularly as the website grows larger and becomes more complicated. Locating important files will remain a relatively easy task for those charged with maintaining the site.

The approach here is simple: The chokoloskee-island directory is named after the domain that the clients have chosen, chokoloskee-island.com. Within that directory, another directory is dedicated to the website's images, naturally enough called Images. Within that directory are two other directories, one for background images and one for photos. Additionally, there is a directory for the style sheets. Should the website be expanded, subcategories of these directories (such as a subdirectory to the Images directory named *Artwork* or a subdirectory to the Photos directory named *Employees*) would be easy to add. The style sheets directory can also be expanded. For instance, if the clients decide they want a different color scheme or skins, additional style sheet directories can be added to accommodate that.

Now that a directory structure is in place, let's look at the different pages required for the website.

Settling on a Table of Contents

Norman and Avery, the clients, have indicated to me what pages they would like on their website. Luckily for me, they have been gracious enough to also supply the required copy for each page. I have taken several photos related to the restaurant and surrounding area with my digital camera, and my clients have also provided several photos of their own. They have outlined the information contained on each page as follows:

- ❑ Welcome page
- ❑ Contact JT's
- ❑ Seasonal jobs and employee housing
- ❑ JT's gift shop
- ❑ Calendar of upcoming events
- ❑ Chokoloskee
- ❑ The Everglades and Ten Thousand Islands
- ❑ Recreational information
- ❑ Lunch at JT's
- ❑ Lunch menu
- ❑ Dinner at JT's
- ❑ Dinner menu

With the copy and the images supplied, I begin the task of assembling the required markup for each page, as well as deciding which images I'm likely to include in the website. For the purposes of this chapter, I have chosen one of these pages to use as an example: the dinner menu. The concepts presented to style these pages are applicable to all the pages of the website.

At this point, the creation of a mockup would be appropriate. A *mockup* is typically a simple image file that shows your client what the finished product will look like. It can be created with image-editing programs such as Macromedia Flash, Macromedia Fireworks, or Adobe Photoshop. The mockup is often just a static image that requires no coding, so the creative vision can be portrayed by the designer with little effort. The mockup is often the primary vehicle for selling your creativity to the client. In this case, I've already prepared a mockup and gained the client's approval for the graphical design, navigation, and creative layout of the website. The mockup for this design was presented in Chapter 7. I've already written all the code, and the examples in the coming chapters illustrate how I put together the markup and CSS to achieve that design.

The following Try It Out demonstrates the basic strategies applied to create the markup itself. The markup presented in this example is not identical to that presented in Chapter 7 because it is impossible to foresee all the necessary elements in an initial design. As the design progresses, additional elements might become necessary; but using the techniques presented here in the initial planning reduces the need to include additional elements, class names, or id names. This example presents very basic strategies for including markup that explains the data contained in the document based on the copy provided by the client.

Try It Out   **Structuring the Markup**

Example 8-2. Follow these steps to create the markup for the JT's dinner menu:

1.   Type the following markup or open the dinner_menu.html file provided in the code download from www.wrox.com:

```
<!DOCTYPE html PUBLIC "-/pp/W3C//DTD XHTML 1.0 Strict//EN"
"http://www.w3.org/TR/xhtml1/DTD/xhtml1-strict.dtd">
<html>
    <head>
        <title>
            JT's Island Grill and Gallery - Chokoloskee, Florida
        </title>
    </head>
    <body>
        <div id='nav'>
            <ul>
                <li>
                    Unique Gifts
                    <ul>
                        <li><a href=''>Gallery</a></li>
                    </ul>
                </li>
                <li>
                    Chokoloskee
                    <ul>
                        <li><a href=''>Visiting Chokoloskee</a></li>
                        <li>
                            <a href=''>The Everglades and Ten
                                        Thousand Islands</a></li>
                        <li><a href=''>Recreation in South
                                        Western Florida</a></li>
                    </ul>
                </li>
            </ul>
            <a href='/chokoloskee-island/'>
                <img src='images/photos/jts_sign.jpg'
                    alt='JTs sign'
                    title='Go home.'/>
            </a>
            <ul>
                <li>
                    Employment
                    <ul>
                        <li><a href=''>Contact JT's</a></li>
```

```
                    <li><a href=''>Seasonal Employment
                            Opportunities</a></li>
            </ul>
        </li>
        <li>
            Delicious Food
            <ul>
                <li><a href=''>Lunch at JT's</a></li>
                <li><a href=''>JT's Lunch Menu</a></li>
                <li><a href=''>Dinner at JT's</a></li>
                <li>
                 <a href='dinner_menu.html'>
                    JT's Dinner Menu
                 </a>
                </li>
            </ul>
        </li>
    </ul>
</div>
<div id='body'>
    <h1>
        JT's at Night
    </h1>
    <div id='content'>
        <img src='images/photos/dinner_plate.jpg'
            alt='dinner plate'/>
        <h3>Appetizers</h3>
            <h4>Stone Crab Claws <em>Market Price</em></h4>
                <p>
                    1/2 lb of claws straight from local docks served
                    cracked with a house stone crab mustard sauce.
                </p>
            <h4>Sesame Seared Tuna <em>$8</em></h4>
                <p>
                    Sashimi grade yellowfin tuna encrusted in sesame
                    seeds lightly seared and served with soy dipping
                    sauce and wasabi.
                </p>
            <h4>Pita and Hummus <em>$4</em></h4>
                <p>
                    Our homemade hummus drizzled with olive oil,
                    accompanied with warm pita bread.
                </p>
            <h4>JT's Triple Crab Cakes <em>$7</em></h4>
                <p>
                    A rich blend of stone crab, blue crab and snow crab
                    sautéed to order, seasoned with Old Bay and fresh
                    parsley.
                </p>
            <h4>Spicy Coconut Shrimp <em>$8</em></h4>
                <p>
                    Gulf shrimp sautéed in coconut served with our
                    spicy peanut sauce.
```

```
            </p>
        <h4>Black Bean Quesadilla <em>$6</em></h4>
            <p>
                Cheddar cheese, onions, green peppers, raisins,
                almonds &amp; black beans grilled in a spinach
                tortilla with fresh salsa.
            </p>
<h3>Soups and Salads</h3>
        <h4>Key Lime-Cilantro Grilled Seafood Salad
            <em>$9</em>
        </h4>
            <p>
                Grilled fish, shrimp &amp; scallops atop bed of
                mixed organic greens with home-made key
                lime-cilantro vinaigrette.
            </p>
        <h4>Tomato Avocado Salad  <em>$9</em></h4>
            <p>
                Organically grown avocados and tomatoes atop a
                fresh organic spring mix, with home-made roasted
                tomato vinaigrette and freshly baked pita chips.
                <em>(add shrimp for $1.25)</em>
            </p>
        <h4>Florida Citrus Salad <em>$7</em></h4>
            <p>
                Almonds, coconut and mandarin oranges atop fresh
                organic greens with a house honey-orange dressing.
            </p>
        <h4>Spinach Salad with Warm Bacon Dressing <em>$7</em></h4>
            <p>
                Fresh spinach topped with a sizzling bacon
                vinaigrette garnished with tomatoes and hard
                boiled egg.
            </p>

        <h4>Tonight's Salad  <em>ask</em></h4>
            <p>
                Chef's specialty salad changes nightly.
            </p>
        <h4>Soup of da' day <em>ask</em></h4>
            <p>Prepared fresh daily</p>
<h3>Entrees</h3>
        <p class='menucaption'>
            Entrees come with tonight's small salad and fresh baked
            ciabatta bread.
        </p>
        <h4>Stone Crab Claws <em>Market Price</em></h4>
            <p>
                One lb locally caught stone crab claws served
                cracked with our key lime mustard sauce.
            </p>
        <h4>Apricot Pork Tenderloin <em>$16</em></h4>
            <p>
```

```
                        Tenderloin rolled and baked with apricot &amp;
                        spinach with a parmesan crust and apricot sauce,
                        fanned over rice and seasonal vegetables.
                   </p>
              <h4>Crab Cakes and Mango Salsa <em>$18</em></h4>
                   <p>
                        Blend of fresh stone crab, snow crab, and blue crab
                        topped with a black bean-ginger sauce and mango
                        salsa, with pineapple jasmine rice.
                   </p>
              <h4>Red Wine Grilled Portobello <em>$17</em></h4>
                   <p>
                        Portobello mushroom broiled with goat cheese and a
                        red wine-shallot sauce over linguine, with
                        pan-fried yams, apples, and scallions.
                   </p>
              <h4>Jamaican Jerk Shrimp &amp; Scallops <em>$17</em></h4>
                   <p>
                        Shrimp &amp; scallops cooked in our home-made
                        authentic Jamaican marinade served with pineapple
                        jasmine rice and veggies.
                   </p>
              <h4>Yellowfin Tuna in Flambé Vanilla Rum <em>$21</em></h4>
                   <p>
                        Sashimi Grade Yellowfin tuna seasoned with adobo
                        &amp; cinnamon, seared, and flambéed in
                        vanilla-rum, with garlic buttermilk mashed
                        potatoes and fresh sautéed veggies.
                   </p>
              <h4>Coconut Sesame Chicken <em>$17</em></h4>
                   <p>
                        Chicken Breast sautéed with glazed walnuts and a
                        sesame sauce, over black bean cakes and
                        stir-fried vegetables, sprinkled with nutmeg.
                   </p>
              <h4>Picadillo <em>$14</em></h4>
                   <p>
                        Olives &amp; raisins cooked with ground beef,
                        onions, peppers and Cuban spices, atop rice
                        with fresh baked bread.
                   </p>
              <h4>Blackened New York Steak <em>$20</em></h4>
                   <p>
                        Spiced and blackened New York Strip with garlic
                        buttermilk mashed potatoes, a papaya-basil
                        marmalade, and marinated mushrooms.
                   </p>
         <h3>Children</h3>
              <h5>Pasta &amp; Tomato Sauce <em>$4</em></h5>
              <h5>Pasta topped with Cheese <em>$4</em></h5>
              <h5>Mini Crab Cakes <em>$7</em></h5>
              <h5>Grilled Cheese Sandwich <em>$3</em></h5>
              <h5>Peanut Butter &amp; Jelly Sandwich <em>$3</em></h5>
```

```
            <h3>Beverages</h3>
                <h5>Soft drink cans <em>$1.50</em></h5>
                <h5>Iced tea (sweet or not) <em>$1.50</em></h5>
                <h5>Home-made Key Limeade <em>$1.50</em></h5>
                <h5>Coffee, hot tea, hot chocolate <em>$1.50</em></h5>
                <h5>Juice, milk <em>$1.50</em></h5>
            <h3>Local Flavor</h3>
                <h5>Hot Pressed Cuban Sandwich <em>$8</em></h5>
                <h5>JT's Classic Cheeseburger <em>$7</em></h5>
                <h5>BBQ Pork Sandwich <em>$7</em></h5>
            <h3>Dessert</h3>
                <h5>Home-made Key Lime Pie <em>$4</em></h5>
                <p>
                    The best in the Everglades
                </p>
            <h3>Local Music &amp; Arts</h3>
                <img src='images/photos/dinner.jpg'
                    alt='Dinner Table'/>
                <p>
                    We hope you enjoy tonight's live music. To help keep
                    the local arts alive we book musicians from here in
                    south Florida. Many of them have music CD's or tapes
                    for sale in our shop. If you haven't already done so,
                    check out our walls and shelves. We like to consider
                    them a gallery of Florida.  We feature local artists,
                    crafters, musicians and authors. When you purchase
                    something you like, not only are you taking home a
                    true piece of this area, you are helping to preserve
                    its art and culture.
                </p>
        </div>
        <h6>
            &copy; Copyright 2003-2004 Panther's Crossing, Inc.
        </h6>
    </div>
  </body>
</html>
```

2. Save this file in the chokoloskee-island directory as dinner_menu.html. When displayed, the page should look like Figure 8-2.

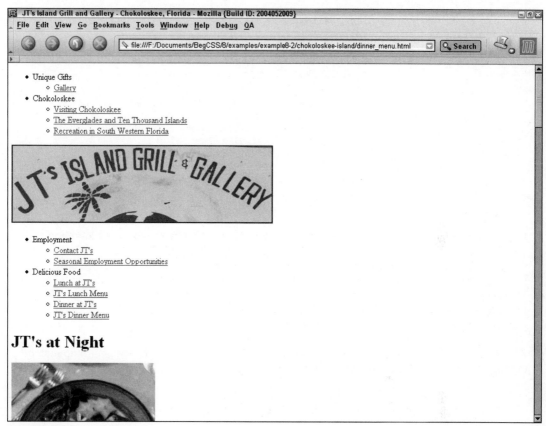

Figure 8-2

How It Works

As you can see from Figure 8-2, the markup alone is very mundane when viewed in a browser. However, there is a strategy in place for the markup. First, the markup used in the dinner menu must describe the data that makes up the dinner menu itself. HTML lists define the website's navigation because the navigation menus are really just a list of links. In Chapter 12, I demonstrate how to style these lists with CSS; and in Chapter 14, I demonstrate how these navigational lists are converted — using only CSS — into dynamic drop-down menus that appear only when the user's mouse cursor is over a navigation heading. This resembles the behavior of the different drop-down menus that are part of the browser itself. For example, when the user clicks the File menu in a browser, a menu appears containing various options. The drop-down menus that you create for the JT's website behave in a similar manner; the only difference is the mouse cursor only has to hover over the menu for it to appear. The user need not click it. The following is an excerpt from the dinner_menu.html document showing how the navigation is organized using list the elements, `<ul>` and `<li>`. The nested lists become the drop-down menus that you observed in Chapter 7:

```
                        <ul>
                            <li>
                                Unique Gifts
                                <ul>
                                    <li><a href=''>Gallery</a></li>
                                </ul>
                            </li>
                            <li>
                                Chokoloskee
                                <ul>
                                    <li><a href=''>Visiting Chokoloskee</a></li>
                                    <li>
                                        <a href=''>The Everglades and Ten
                                            Thousand Islands</a></li>
                                    <li><a href=''>Recreation in South
                                            Western Florida</a></li>
                                </ul>
                            </li>
                        </ul>
```

I've divided the navigation between two lists: The first appears before the company logo, and the second appears after the company logo. This allows the navigation to be divided into four headings: *Unique Gifts,* which contains a link to a page with information about the restaurant's gift shop; *Chokoloskee,* which contains links to information about the local area, Chokoloskee, the Everglades, and Recreation; *Employment*, with links to a page containing contact information and a page with employment information; and the last heading, *Delicious Food*, which contains links to pages containing information about the restaurant's menus, daily events, and dining atmosphere.

Each section of the page has also been given id names — at least those parts of the markup that are obvious and easy to name at this early stage of planning:

```
        <title>
            JT's Island Grill and Gallery - Chokoloskee, Florida
        </title>
    </head>
    <body>
        <div id='nav'>
            <ul>
```

The navigation is wrapped inside a <div> element and given the name nav. The body of the document is wrapped in a <div> element named body that includes both the heading and the footer, which are contained inside of <h1>, and <h6> tags respectively. The <h1> element contains the name of the page, and the <h6> element contains the footer text. The content of the menu is contained inside of a <div> element named content. Then the data of the menu itself is divided into different headings and paragraphs:

```
            <div id='content'>
                <img src='images/photos/dinner_plate.jpg'
                    alt='dinner plate'/>
                <h3>Appetizers</h3>
                    <h4>Stone Crab Claws <em>Market Price</em></h4>
                        <p>
```

```
                1/2 lb of claws straight from local docks served
                cracked with a house stone crab mustard sauce.
        </p>
        <h4>Sesame Seared Tuna <em>$8</em></h4>
```

Each section of the menu—Appetizers, Entrees, and so on—is contained within <h3> headings. Beneath those headings, each menu item is also contained inside a heading, and the price of the menu item is contained within <em> tags. (em is short for *emphasis*.) Using the <em> tag allows the price of each menu item to be styled independently from the heading element that contains the menu item. The description of the menu item is itself contained within <p> tags because these are really just paragraphs of text.

Using this strategy of writing markup—using as little markup as possible, only enough markup to describe the data itself—keeps the file size small and the markup manageable. Although the page appears quite mundane, every aspect of it is now controllable using CSS. The font sizes, the text layout, margins, and every other aspect of presentation are controlled directly from the style sheet.

Finally, a strategy employed in this markup—and the markup of previous chapters—is that the markup is indented to make it easy to read and troubleshoot:

```
<html>
    <head>
        <title>
            JT's Island Grill and Gallery - Chokoloskee, Florida
        </title>
    </head>
    <body>
```

Using this discipline of indenting tags makes it obvious where each tag begins and ends. If you use text editors like Crimson Editor (that I mentioned in Chapter 2), the process of indenting and un-indenting tags is very easy. Entire blocks of markup can be indented at once by highlighting the block with the mouse cursor and pressing the tab key while the block is highlighted. Conversely, entire blocks can be un-indented by pressing Shift+Tab while a block is highlighted. The benefit of indented markup is that errors are easier to spot and prevent; secondly, it's simply good practice.

Other text editors and development environments like Macromedia Dreamweaver MX also provide code beautification tools that make the life of a website designer much easier.

Now that you've read about the strategies for starting a website project, in the remainder of the chapter I discuss the various CSS properties used to manipulate text, beginning with the letter-spacing property.

The letter-spacing Property

Documented in CSS 2.1 and supported in IE 5.5, IE 6, Mozilla 1.7, Opera 7.5, and Safari 1.2.

The letter-spacing property, as I have demonstrated briefly in previous chapters, controls the amount of space between the letters. The following table shows its allowable values.

Property	Value
letter-spacing	normal | <length> | inherit Initial value: normal

The letter-spacing property is a simple property that accepts a length as its value. A length value is any length value supported by CSS, as I discussed in Chapter 4.

This style sheet

```
p {
    letter-spacing: 10px;
}
```

and this paragraph

```
<p>
    Each letter of each word is ten pixels apart.
</p>
```

result in the output shown in Figure 8-3. As you can see in the figure, each letter of each word is spaced 10 pixels apart.

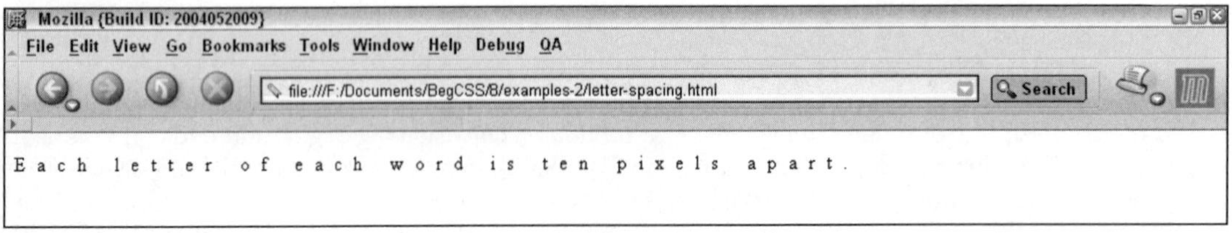

Figure 8-3

The letter-spacing property may have either a positive or negative value. When given a negative value, the letters of words are closer together. Given this style rule

```
p {
    letter-spacing: -2px;
}
```

and this paragraph

```
<p>
    Two pixels of space have been subtracted from between each letter.
</p>
```

you get the result shown in Figure 8-4.

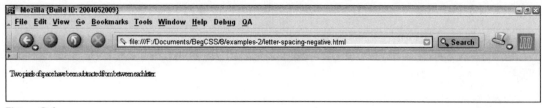

Figure 8-4

As you can see in this figure, the letters of the paragraph are condensed together because the value of the letter-spacing property is a negative value.

The letter-spacing property can be used to add or subtract space between letters. In the following Try It Out, you add the letter-spacing property to the style sheet for the JT's website.

Try It Out   The letter-spacing Property

Example 8-3. To apply the letter-spacing property to the JT's website, follow these steps:

1.   Create a new style sheet and add the following rules:

```
h1 {
    letter-spacing: 4px;
}
div#content {
    letter-spacing: 1px;
}
```

2.   Name the new style sheet base_styles.css and save it in the style_sheets directory you created in Example 8-1.

3.   Open dinner_menu.html and add the following markup to link to the new style sheet:

```
<link rel='stylesheet' type='text/css' href='style_sheets/base_styles.css'/>
```

4.   Save dinner_menu.html. When viewed in Mozilla, it should look like the page shown in Figure 8-5.

177

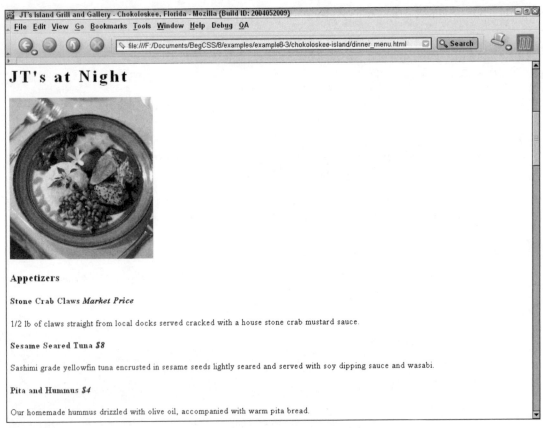

Figure 8-5

How It Works

Figure 8-5 shows the `<h1>` heading and beginning of the dinner menu, where the effects of the `letter-spacing` property are most noticeable.

The base_styles.css file contains styles that can be reused for the entire website, meaning that the base_styles.css style sheet is included for all the pages of the JT's website. This example shows the first addition to the JT's style sheet. The letters in the `<h1>` element, which contains the topic for the page, are spaced 4 pixels apart. Then, in the `<div>` element that contains the content of the site, 1 pixel of space is added between all the letters. The `letter-spacing` property is a simple effect that adds or subtracts space between the letters of words.

The `word-spacing` property, covered in the following section, is closely related to the `letter-spacing` property.

The word-spacing Property

Documented in CSS 2.1 and supported in IE 5.5, IE 6, , Mozilla 1.7, Opera 7.5, and Safari 1.2.

The word-spacing property, in essence, functions identically to the letter-spacing property. However, instead of controlling the space between letters, the word-spacing property controls the space between words. The following table shows its allowable values.

Property	Value
word-spacing	normal | <length> | inherit Initial value: normal

To demonstrate the effect of the word-spacing property, consider the following style sheet rule

```
p {
    word-spacing: 10px;
}
```

and this paragraph

```
<p>
    Each of the words of this paragraph are spaced ten pixels apart.
</p>
```

which together result in the output shown in Figure 8-6. Ten pixels of space now separate each word of the paragraph.

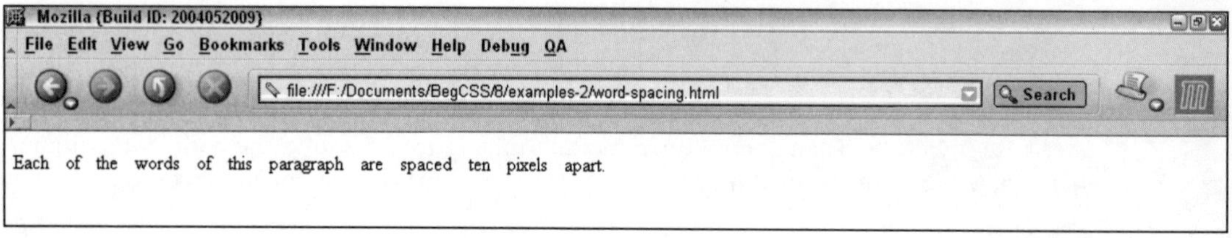

Figure 8-6

Additionally, like the letter-spacing property, the word-spacing property can contain a negative value. If given a negative value, the effects are less space between each word. So, the following rule

```
p {
    word-spacing: -5px;
}
```

and this paragraph

```
<p>
    Each word contained in this paragraph appear closer together since the word-
    spacing property has a negative value.
</p>
```

result in the output shown in Figure 8-7. As you can see, all the words in the paragraph appear close together.

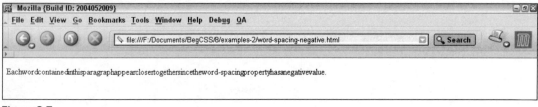

Figure 8-7

> *Naturally, the next property on the agenda should be a property that controls the spacing between the lines of a paragraph; this is done with the* line-height *property, which accepts a length value just as the* letter-spacing *and* word-spacing *properties do. Although this could easily be discussed here as well, I discuss the* line-height *property in detail in Chapter 10 as part of a discussion about controlling width and height in a document.*

As you did with the letter-spacing property in example8-3, in the following Try It Out you apply the word-spacing property to the JT's website.

Try It Out   The word-spacing Property

Example 8-4. In the following steps, you apply the word-spacing property to the JT's website.

1.   Open the base_styles.css file that you created in Example 8-3 and add the following declaration:

```
div#content {
    word-spacing: 5px;
    letter-spacing: 1px;
}
```

2.   Save base_styles.css. Then open dinner_menu.html. Figure 8-8 shows the body of the dinner menu, where the effects of adding the word-spacing property are most noticeable.

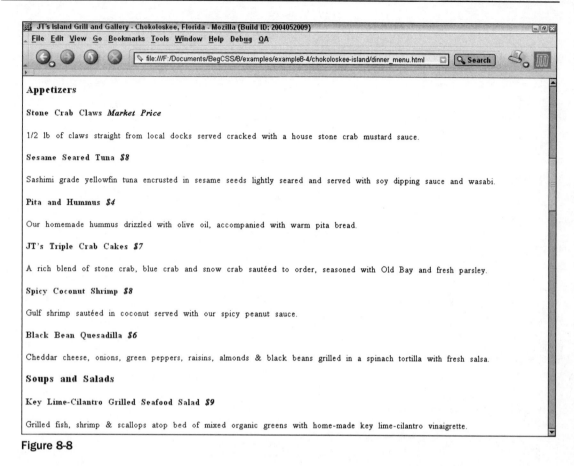

Figure 8-8

How It Works

Another relatively simple addition to the JT's style sheet, this property spaces the words of each sentence of text in the content `<div>` five pixels apart. This property is useful for spreading out the copy of the page Additionally, the spacing between each letter is increased. Both these effects enhance the background image applied to the dinner menu. (The background image is introduced in Chapter 13.)

The next section covers a property that controls the space inserted to indent a paragraph.

Indenting Paragraph Text Using text-indent

Documented in CSS 2.1 and supported in IE 5.5, IE 6, Mozilla 1.7, Opera 7.5, and Safari 1.2.

Indenting text in CSS is done using the `text-indent` property. The `text-indent` property identifies the first line of text of a paragraph and inserts the specified length before the first line of text; thus indenting the text. The following table shows this property's allowed values.

Property	Value
text-indent	<length> | <percentage> | inherit Initial value: normal

The text-indent property accepts either a normal length value or a percentage value. If a percentage value is specified, the percentage is based on the width of the containing element. To illustrate this, consider this example

```
p {
    text-indent: 25%;
    width: 200px;
}
```

and this markup:

```
<body>
    <p>
        "There are two ways of constructing a software design; one way is to make
        it so simple that there are obviously no deficiencies, and the other way is
        to make it so complicated that there are no obvious deficiencies. The first
        method is far more difficult." - C. A. R. Hoare
    </p>
</body>
```

Figure 8-9 shows the result of this rule and markup: the text-indent property with a percentage width.

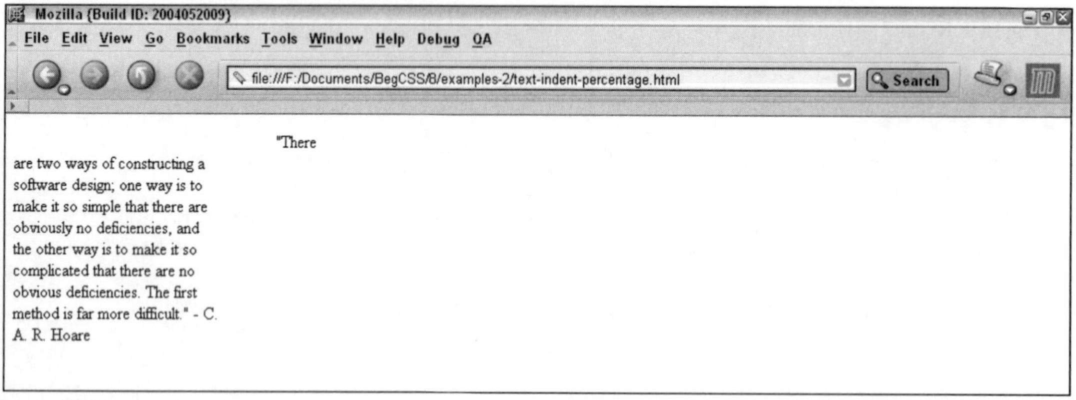

Figure 8-9

The percentage width assigned by the text-indent property depends on the width of the <p> element's parent element. In this example, the parent element is the <body> element. By default, the <body> element's width expands horizontally, filling the entire browser window.

The `<p>` element is assigned a fixed width of 200 pixels, but the indentation for the `<p>` element is based on the width of the `<body>` element (which is more than 200 pixels). That's why the first line of the `<p>` element text in Figure 8-9 is so far to the right: it's indented 25% of the width of the `<body>` element, not the width of the `<p>` element.

In contrast to percentage values, a simple length value is illustrated by the following rule:

```
p {
    text-indent: 25px;
    width: 200px;
}
```

and this paragraph of text:

```
<p>
    "There are two ways of constructing a software design; one way is to make it so
    simple that there are obviously no deficiencies, and the other way is to make
    it so complicated that there are no obvious deficiencies. The first method is
    far more difficult." - C. A. R. Hoare
</p>
```

Figure 8-10 shows that the first line of the paragraph of text is indented.

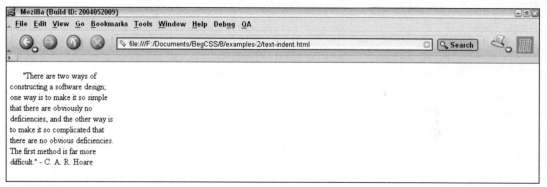

Figure 8-10

In the markup, I've added a fixed width of 200 pixels to clarify the effects of the `text-indent` property.

Like `letter-spacing` and `word-spacing`, the `text-indent` property can also accept a negative value. For instance, I can alter the style sheet rule presented for Figure 8-10 to a negative value, like this:

```
p {
    text-indent: -25px;
    width: 200px;
}
```

Figure 8-11 shows that the text is shifted the other way, and in this case a portion of the first word of the paragraph is clipped.

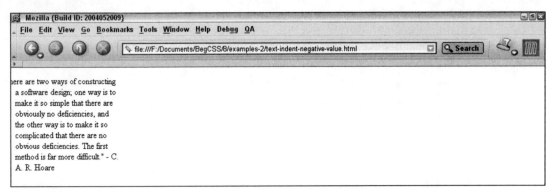

Figure 8-11

Now that you've seen some examples of the text-indent property, you apply the text-indent property to the JT's style sheet in the following Try It Out.

Try It Out   **Applying the text-indent Property**

Example 8-5. The following steps show you how to apply the text-indent property to the JT's style sheet.

1. Add the following rule to the base_styles.css style sheet:

```
div#content {
  word-spacing: 5px;
    letter-spacing: 1px;
}
p.copy {
    text-indent: 20px;
}
```

2. Save the base_sstyles.css file.

3. Modify dinner_menu.html by making the following changes:

```
<img src='images/photos/dinner.jpg'
        alt='Dinner Table'/>
    <p class='copy'>
        We hope you enjoy tonight's live music. To help keep
        the local arts alive we book musicians from here in
```

4. Save dinner_menu.html. When viewed in Mozilla, your page should look like the one in Figure 8-12.

We hope you enjoy tonight's live music. To help keep the local arts alive we book musicians from here in south Florida. Many of them have music CD's or tapes for sale in our shop. If you haven't already done so, check out our walls and shelves. We like to consider them a gallery of Florida. We feature local artists, crafters, musicians and authors. When you purchase something you like, not only are you taking home a true piece of this area, you are helping to preserve its art and culture.

© Copyright 2003-2004 Panther's Crossing, Inc.

Figure 8-12

How It Works

As you can see from the output in Figure 8-12, the last paragraph of text is now indented 20 pixels. Recall from earlier examples that I mentioned the base_styles.css file is a file intended to apply style to the entire website. I've created a class named `copy` and identified it from the base_styles.css style sheet using the class selector `p.copy`, which selects only paragraphs with a class named `copy`. This naming allows me to identify and give special styles to certain paragraphs, and it allows the other paragraphs contained in the dinner_menu.html file to be styled independently from those designated as *copy*.

Continuing the discussion of text manipulation properties, the next section covers the `text-align` property.

Aligning Text with the text-align Property

Documented in CSS 1, 2, and 3 and supported since IE 4, NS 4, Opera 4, and Safari 1.

The purpose of the `text-align` property is simple: It aligns text! The following table outlines each of the possible values for the `text-align` property.

Property	Value
text-align	left | right | center | justify | inherit Initial value: left

From earlier discussion in the book, it should be obvious what `text-align: left;`, `text-align: right;` and `text-align: center;` do. Here is a brief reiteration of what these values do

```
p#left {
    text-align: left;
}
p#right {
    text-align: right;
}
p#center {
    text-align: center;
}
```

when combined with this markup:

```
<p id='left'>
    This text is aligned left.
</p>
<p id='right'>
    This text is aligned right.
</p>
<p id='center'>
    This text is center aligned.
</p>
```

Figure 8-13 shows that the `text-align` property aligns the text contained in each paragraph based on the supplied value.

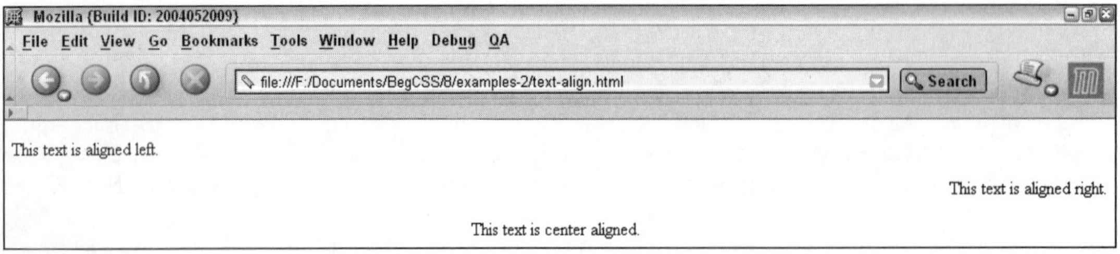

Figure 8-13

Justifying Text

You haven't yet seen what `text-align: justify;` does. At first glance, including `text-align: justify;` in a document has the same effect as `text-align: left;`. Consider this example:

```
p {
    text-align: justify;
    border: 1px solid lightgrey;
    text-indent: 25px;
    width: 200px;
}
```

Figure 8-14 depicts what the text looks like with `text-align: justify;` applied.

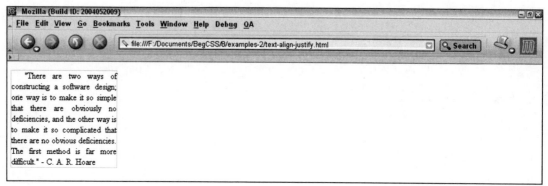

Figure 8-14

If you refer back to Figure 8-10, you can see what the text of the C.A.R. Hoare quote looks like aligned left; left alignment is the default behavior. To clarify the effects of `text-align: justify;` in Figure 8-14, I added a thin, light gray border. When you compare the output of `text-align: justify;` in Figure 8-14 to the effects of `text-align: left;` in Figure 8-10, the effects become obvious. When justified, each line of text is lined up with the paragraph's margin on both the left and right sides. Extra space is applied between the words of each sentence to achieve this.

In the following Try It Out, you continue building the JT's website with the inclusion of the `text-align` property.

Try It Out   **Applying the text-align Property**

Example 8-6. In the following steps, you add the `text-align` property to the JT's website.

1.   Make the following modifications to the base_styles.css style sheet:

```
h1 {
    letter-spacing: 4px;
}
h6 {
    text-align: center;
}
div#content {
    word-spacing: 5px;
    letter-spacing: 1px;
}
p.copy {
```

```
        text-indent: 20px;
        text-align: justify;
}
```

2. Save base_styles.css.

3. Create a new .css file and name it menu_system.css. Add the following rule:

```
div#nav {
    text-align: center;
}
```

4. Save menu_system.css in the style_sheets directory that you created for Example 8-1.

5. Create a new css file and name it dinner_menu.css. Add the following rules:

```
h3 + p.menucaption {
    text-align: center;
}
h3, h4, h5, h4 + p, h5 + p  {
    text-align: center;
}
```

6. Save dinner.menu.css in the style sheets directory you created for Example 8-1.

7. Make the following modifications to dinner_menu.html to link to the base_styles.css and menu_system.css style sheets you just created:

```
<head>
    <title>
        JT's Island Grill and Gallery - Chokoloskee, Florida
    </title>
    <link rel='stylesheet'
        type='text/css' href='style_sheets/base_styles.css'/>
    <link rel='stylesheet'
        type='text/css' href='style_sheets/menu_system.css'/>
    <link rel='stylesheet'
        type='text/css' href='style_sheets/dinner_menu.css'/>
</head>
```

8. Save dinner_menu.html. When viewed in Mozilla, it looks like Figure 8-15.

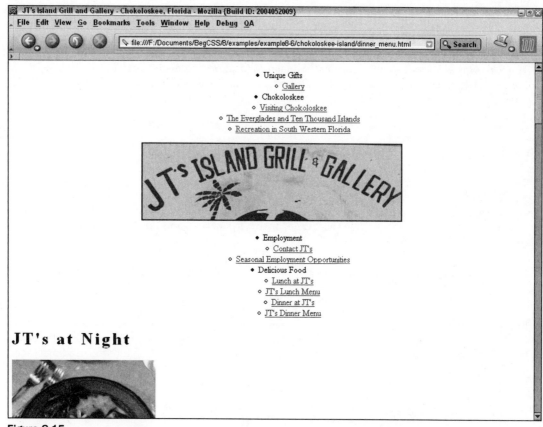

Figure 8-15

How It Works

Figure 8-15 shows that the navigational menu is center aligned. However, most of the body of the menu itself is also center-aligned, and the paragraph of text at the bottom of the menu is justified.

This example seems to complicate things a bit, but not really. Before I get into why I placed the properties where I have, I want to discuss another strategy. That strategy is dividing the CSS rules among different files. The base_styles.css file is used to apply styles to the entire website; the menu_system.css file deals specifically with the navigation menu that's contained in the unordered lists. Last, dinner_menu.css contains styles that are specific to the dinner menu page. Modularizing and organizing the style sheets is one more strategy to make the website easy to maintain.

Recall from Chapter 7 (where I discussed the cascade) that the order in which style sheets are included in a document is important: The last style sheet included in the document trumps the one before it and the one before that, and so on. In this example, the base_styles.css style sheet is included first because it's the weakest. It is followed by the menu_system.css style sheet, and if any rule in the menu_system.css style sheet is identical to a rule in the base_styles.css style sheet, the rule in the menu_system.css file takes precedence. Lastly, the dinner_menu.css file takes precedence over both previous files because this style sheet contains styles specific to the presentation of the dinner menu.

Why did I include these styles where I have? The styles are separated into different style sheets to make each style sheet easier to manage. Broader styles that apply to the whole website are placed in the base_styles.css style sheet. Styles specific to the navigation are placed in the menu_system.css style sheet, and finally the style sheet for the dinner menu itself is placed in the dinner_menu.css style sheet. The following is a review of why each individual modification was made. First, I made two modifications to the base_styles.css style sheet. The first modification is the addition of a rule, and it centers the footer text contained in the <h6> element at the bottom of the page.

```
h6 {
    text-align: center;
}
```

The second modification adds the text-align: justify; declaration to the p.copy rule. This justifies all paragraphs with a class named copy, which means that the words are spaced so the beginning and end of each line is flush with the left and right margins, respectively, of the paragraph. The next modification involved creating a new style sheet called menu_system.css, and this file houses all styles used for navigation. One rule is added to this style sheet:

```
div#nav {
    text-align: center;
}
```

Recall from Chapter 7 that all text properties are inherited by their descendants. So setting the text-align: center; declaration on the <div> with an id named nav causes the image and all the content inside the lists to be centered. The idea behind adding this declaration is to center the headings for each set of links and the JT's logo. The last modification is the creation of a style sheet that houses all the rules specific to the dinner menu. Here, again, rules are added to center the text:

```
h3 + p.menucaption {
    text-align: center;
}
h3, h4, h5, h4 + p, h5 + p  {
    text-align: center;
}
```

These two rules center all the headings and paragraphs contained in the menu body. The first rule uses the adjacent sibling selector. If you recall from Chapter 5, the adjacent sibling selector chooses the element based on what it's next to. That means if an <h3> element is followed by a <p> element with a class name of menucaption, it chooses the markup highlighted in the following code:

```
<h3>Entrees</h3>
    <p class='menucaption'>
        Entrees come with tonight's small salad and fresh baked
        ciabatta bread.
    </p>
```

It chooses the paragraph because it is next to an <h3> element.

Now that you've had an overview of text alignment with CSS, the next section covers the text-decoration property.

The text-decoration Property

Documented in CSS 2.1 and supported in IE 5, IE 6, Mozilla 1.7, Opera 7.5, and Safari 1.2.

The `text-decoration` property applies underlining, overlining, and strikethrough to text. The following table outlines the `text-decoration` property and the values it allows.

Property	Value
text-decoration	none | [underline || overline || line-through || blink] | inherit Initial value: none

No version of IE supports the blink value. `text-decoration` support began in IE 4, NS 4, and Opera 3, however these only partially implement the `text-decoration` property. Support listed is for browsers that support the underline, overline, and line-through values.

Because this property is a little more complicated than those covered previously, a simple explanation of its use is warranted.

To demonstrate the various styles available using this property, consider this example:

```
p#underline {
    text-decoration: underline;
}
p#overline {
    text-decoration: overline;
}
p#line-through {
    text-decoration: line-through;
}
p#blink {
    text-decoration: blink;
}
```

and this markup:

```
<p id='underline'>
    This text is underlined.
</p>
<p id='overline'>
    This text is overlined.
</p>
<p id='line-through'>
    This text has a line through it.
</p>
<p id='blink'>
    This text blinks in those browsers that support it.
</p>
```

Example 8-16 shows the various effects provided by the `text-decoration` property as specified by the preceding code.

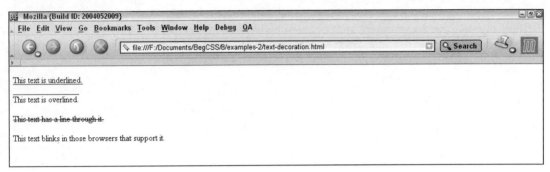

Figure 8-16

However, this is not all that is possible with the `text-decoration` property. This notation:

```
[ underline || overline || line-through || blink ]
```

means that the `text-decoration` property can accept one or more of these values. To specify more than one value, each value is separated by a single space. For instance:

```
p {
    text-decoration: underline overline;
}
```

This rule makes the text of the paragraph both underlined and overlined, as Figure 8-17 shows.

Figure 8-17

The notation for the `text-decoration` property indicates that it can accept up to four values. Those values can be any combination of `underline`, `overline`, `line-through`, and `blink`. The values `none` or `inherit` can be used instead of any of the four values; if either of these values are used, however, only that lone value may appear. Consider this rule:

```
p {
    text-decoration: underline overline line-through blink;
}
```

This rule makes the text underlined, overlined, strikethrough, and blinking, as shown in Figure 8-18.

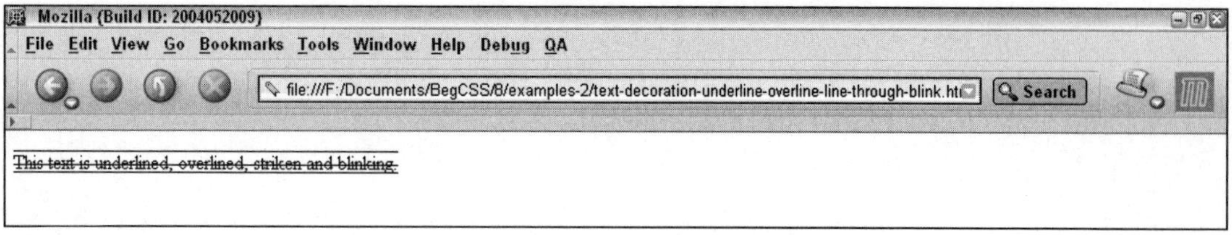

Figure 8-18

Now that you have some understanding of the `text-decoration` property, the following Try It Out applies the `text-decoration` property to the JT's style sheet.

Try It Out   Applying the text-decoration Property

Example 8-7. In the following steps you apply the `text-decoration` property to the JT's website.

1. Make the following modifications to the base_styles.css file:

```
a {
    text-decoration: none;
}
a:hover {
    text-decoration: underline;
}
h1 {
    letter-spacing: 4px;
}
h6 {
    text-align: center;
}
```

2. Save base_styles.css.

3. Make the following modifications to the menu_system.css file:

```
div#nav {
    text-align: center;
}
ul.menu a:hover {
    text-decoration: none;
}
```

4. Save menu_system.css.

5. Make the following modifications to the dinner_menu.css file:

```
h3 {
    text-decoration: underline;
}
```

```css
h3 + p.menucaption {
    text-align: center;
}
```

6. Modify the dinner_menu.html file, adding the following class names:

```html
<ul>
    <li>
        Unique Gifts
        <ul class='menu'>
            <li><a href=''>Gallery</a></li>
        </ul>
    </li>
    <li>
        Chokoloskee
        <ul class='menu'>
            <li><a href=''>Visiting Chokoloskee</a></li>
            <li>
                <a href=''>The Everglades and Ten
                        Thousand Islands</a></li>
            <li><a href=''>Recreation in South
                        Western Florida</a></li>
        </ul>
    </li>
</ul>
<a href='index.html'>
    <img src='images/photos/jts_sign.jpg'
        alt='JTs sign'
        title='Go home.'/>
</a>
<ul>
    <li>
        Employment
        <ul class='menu'>
            <li><a href=''>Contact JT's</a></li>
            <li><a href=''>Seasonal Employment
                        Opportunities</a></li>
        </ul>
    </li>
    <li>
        Delicious Food
        <ul class='menu'>
            <li><a href=''>Lunch at JT's</a></li>
            <li><a href=''>JT's Lunch Menu</a></li>
            <li><a href=''>Dinner at JT's</a></li>
            <li>
              <a href='dinner_menu.html'>
                JT's Dinner Menu
              </a>
            </li>
        </ul>
    </li>
```

7. Save dinner_menu.html. When viewed in Mozilla, your page should now look like the one shown in Figure 8-19.

Figure 8-19

How It Works

The effects of this style sheet are simple. First, styles are added for links. The underline is removed from links with the `text-decoration: none;` declaration:

```
a {
    text-decoration: none;
}
a:hover {
    text-decoration: underline;
}
```

Then an underline is added to links when the user's mouse cursor rolls over a link with the `:hover` pseudo-class. The underline appears *only* when the mouse cursor is on top of a link. The addition of an underline when the user's mouse cursor is over a link is a cool effect; however, it is used only for links that appear in the body of the document. For the navigational menus, I have other effects in mind that I add in later chapters. The underline effect can be removed for the navigational menus using the following code:

```
ul.menu a:hover {
    text-decoration: none;
}
```

The menu class name is added to each embedded list so that these can be distinguished from the other lists. Now the underline doesn't show up when the mouse rolls over links in the navigational menu. Last, each section heading of the JT's dinner menu is underlined:

```
h3 {
    text-decoration: underline;
}
```

The next section continues the discussion of text manipulation properties with the text-transform property.

The text-transform Property

Documented in CSS 2.1 and supported in IE 5.5, IE 6, Mozilla 1.7, Opera 7.5, and Safari 1.2.

The text-transform property exists purely to manipulate the case of text, for instance to capitalize or make all characters uppercase or all characters lowercase. The following table shows the text-transform property and its possible values.

Property	Value
text-transform	capitalize | uppercase | lowercase | none | inherit Initial value: none

The text-transform property is used to manipulate the case of text. Consider this example

```
p#capitalize {
    text-transform: capitalize;
}
p#uppercase {
    text-transform: uppercase;
}
p#lowercase {
    text-transform: lowercase;
}
```

and this markup:

```
<p id='capitalize'>
    every word of this sentence is capitalized.
```

```
</p>
<p id='uppercase'>
    every word of this sentence is in uppercase.
</p>
<p id='lowercase'>
    EVERY WORD OF THIS SENTENCE IS IN LOWERCASE.
</p>
```

Figure 8-20 shows that the `text-transform` property overrides the case of the text, no matter how it appears in the source code.

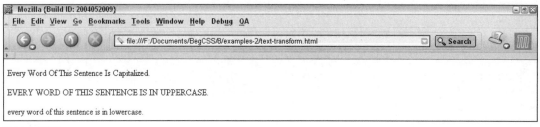

Figure 8-20

In the first paragraph, even though in the source the sentence appears in all lowercase, if you apply the `text-transform: capitalize;` declaration, each word of the sentence is capitalized. Likewise, in the next paragraph, even though the source code contains all lowercase letters, with the addition of the `text-transform: uppercase;` declaration, each word of the sentence appears in all uppercase letters in the rendered output. Finally, in the last paragraph, each word appears in uppercase in the markup source code, but with the addition of the `text-transform: lowercase;` declaration, each word of the sentence appears in all lowercase in the actual output rendered by the browser.

Now that you've seen an example of what the `text-transform` property does, the following Try It Out adds the `text-transform` property to the JT's Island Grill and Gallery style sheet.

Try It Out   Apply the text-transform Property

Example 8-8. In the following steps, you apply the `text-transform` property to the JT's website.

1. Add the following rule to the base_styles.css style sheet:

```
body {
    text-transform: lowercase;
}
a {
    text-decoration: none;
}
```

2. Save base_styles.css. The JT's website now looks like 8-21.

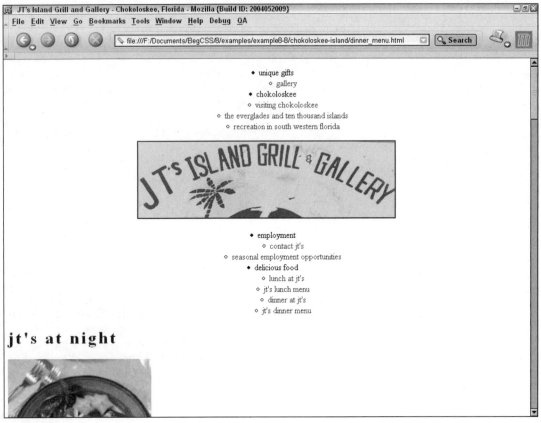

Figure 8-21

How It Works

Adding the text-transform property to the <body> element using the body selector in the base_styles.css style sheet makes all text on all pages of the JT's Island Grill and Gallery website appear in lowercase. Like other text properties, the text-transform property is inherited by all descendant elements, which makes all the text appearing in the dinner_menu.html page appear in lowercase, regardless of how it appears in the source code of the markup itself.

The idea of making all of the text lowercase may seem like a bad idea to some. My rationale for applying this effect is to give the text a more consistent look and feel. If my clients decide that all lowercase text is too pretentious or otherwise undesirable, the beautiful part about CSS is that I can easily remove the property, after which the capitalization applied in the source code returns instantly on all the pages of the website.

The following section continues the discussion of text manipulation properties with the white-space property.

The white-space Property

Documented in CSS 2 and supported in IE 5.5 (partial), IE 6 , Mozilla 1.7, Opera 7.5, and Safari 1.2.

The `white-space` property allows you to control text formatting in the source code of the web document. The following table outlines the possible keyword values of the `white-space` property as of CSS 2.

Property	Value
white-space	normal | pre | nowrap | inherit Initial value: normal

IE 5.5 only supports `white-space: nowrap;`*. IE 6 supports* `white-space: pre;` *but only when in standards mode.*

Here is an example of the `white-space: pre;` declaration:

```
p {
    font-family: monospace;
    white-space: pre;
}
```

I've specified a monospace font for clarity. When the preceding declaration is combined with this markup

```
<p>
From        the        moment
I           picked          up
your        book        until
I           laid           it
down,       I           was
convulsed with  laughter.
Some        day            I
intend      reading        it.
                Groucho Marx
</p>
```

the result looks like Figure 8-22.

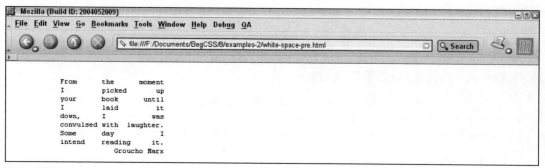

Figure 8-22

199

In the source code for the output shown in Figure 8-22, I've added lots of spaces between the words and extra line breaks. With the `white-space: pre;` declaration those spaces are preserved in the browser's rendered output.

By default the browser will collapse the extra spaces between words and ignore the line breaks, which is the behavior of the `white-space: normal;` declaration. The `white-space: pre;` declaration preserves that extra space and keeps the line breaks where they appear in the source code. Under normal circumstances, if there is too much text to appear on a single line, the extra text overflows onto the following line or lines. The `white-space: nowrap;` declaration prevents that overflow from happening and forces the text to stay on one line, unless an HTML line break `<br/>` element is encountered. That forces a line break.

```
p {
    white-space: nowrap;
}
```

Figure 8-23 shows that the text has flowed off the screen to the right because there is more text than can fit on the screen.

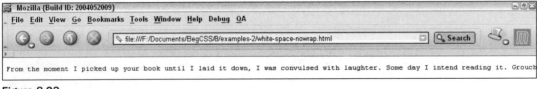

Figure 8-23

Compare the output in Figures 8-22 and 8-23 to that in Figure 8-24 where no `white-space` property is applied. That is, applying the `white-space: normal;` declaration is the same as applying no `white-space` property because `normal` is the initial value of the `white-space` property.

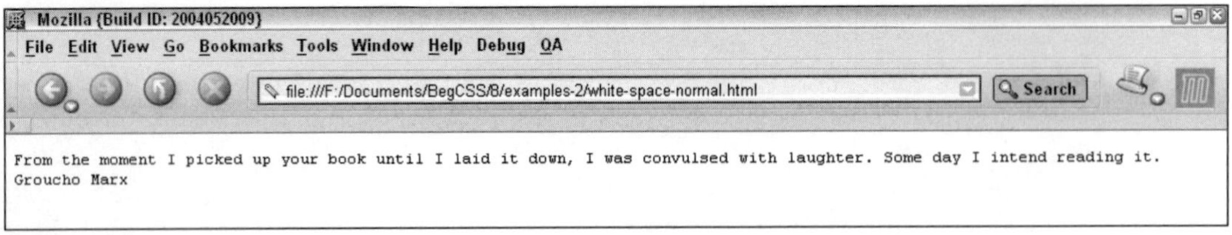

Figure 8-24

A Look Ahead to CSS 3

The CSS 3 Text module was recently made a candidate recommendation by the W3C. Candidate status means that the W3C feels the proposed changes to CSS are ready to be implemented and tested by the various browser makers. Therefore, the text properties appearing in CSS 3 should begin to be implemented in browsers and available for developers to use in websites in the months and years to come. The additions to CSS 3 are too numerous to list here, but here is a brief summary of some new properties in CSS 3:

❑ Several internationalization properties that aid in styling content are presented in different languages. These properties help to style languages that are read from right to left and also to display Oriental text. Such properties are used to style mixed language content in XML documents.

❑ More control over preformatted text will be available with the inclusion of several new white-space properties.

❑ The capability to change the style of underlined, overlined, and line-through text will be provided. For instance, you'll be able to change the style of the line used for underlines, overlines, and line-through. Line options will include dotted, dashed, double line, and so on. You will also have the capability to specify a different color and a different width for the underline, overline, and line-through.

❑ Other properties will help you control text overflow. For instance, you'll have the capability to hide extra text if it does not fit in a specified area and replace the hidden text with an ellipsis.

In general, CSS 3 introduces more control over the formatting and manipulation of text.

Summary

In this chapter, I presented a variety of techniques for planning the layout and design of a website, as well as how to employ CSS's text manipulation properties. The techniques and strategies for approaching a website design project include

❑ Planning how the files are to be stored so you can create an effective, scalable, and organized directory structure.

❑ Determining the different pages that will appear in the website and gathering the website's copy. These activities determine the website's navigation.

❑ Creating a mockup and then implementing an initial strategy for approaching the markup of the document. This helps you include only the necessary markup to describe the data contained in the document.

I also discussed a variety of CSS text-manipulation properties, which include

❑ The letter-spacing property, which is used to specify the length of space between letters.

❑ The word-spacing property, which is used to specify the length of space between words.

❑ The text-indent property, which is used to indent text.

❑ The text-align property, which is used to align the text of a document.

❑ The text-decoration property, which is used to apply decorative styling to text, such as underlining, overlining, strikethrough, or blinking text.

❏ The `text-transform` property, which is used to control the case of text regardless of what case is used in the document's source code.

❏ The `white-space` property, which is used to control text formatting as it relates to how the text appears in the document's source code.

In addition, I presented a brief look ahead to CSS 3, which expands your capability to manipulate and control the presentation of text. Chapter 9 continues the coverage of text manipulation, with a discussion of the font properties in CSS.

Exercises

1. You've been hired to design a website for an artist, who has indicated that the website will contain photography, oil paintings, poetry, and creative writing. Your client has also indicated a desire to present alternative skins of the website by including alternative styles sheets. How might you approach storing the website's files?

2. Continuing with the artist's website from Exercise 1, design a page with a poem (that you create or copy). Taking a minimalist approach to the markup, format the poem so that it appears in the rendered output as it does in the source code. Write the poem so that it appears in all lowercase.

3. Using your work from exercise 2, wrap each line of the poem in <p> tags, indent each line 25 pixels, and capitalize the first letter of every line and the title by using the `::first-letter` pseudo-element. Center-align the title text. Add 2 pixels of space between each letter and 5 pixels of space between each word of the poem itself. Give the <body> a fixed width of 200 pixels. Underline the poem's title.

9

Font Manipulation

Chapter 8 presented a variety of text manipulation properties and outlined some of the techniques and strategies involved in beginning a website design project. This chapter continues the discussion of text manipulation with CSS's font manipulation properties. CSS includes a variety of properties that change the face, size, and style of a font. This chapter covers:

❑ The font-family property and how it is used to change the face of a font

❑ The font-style property and how it is used to make a font italic or oblique

❑ The font-variant property, a property similar to the text-transform property presented in Chapter 8, and how this property is used to create a small-caps effect

❑ The font-weight property and how it is used to increase or decrease how bold or light a font appears

❑ The font-size property and how it is used to increase or decrease the size of a font

❑ The font property and how it is used as shorthand to specify a number of other font properties.

Specifying Fonts with the font-family Property

Documented in CSS 2.1 and supported in IE 5.5, IE 6, Mozilla 1.7, Opera 7.5, and Safari 1.2.

The font-family property is used to specify fonts. The following table outlines the font-family property and the values that it allows.

Property	Value
font-family	[[<family-name> | <generic-family>] [, <family-name> | <generic-family>]*] | inherit Initial value: Varies depending on the browser or user agent.

Here is an example of the basic use of the `font-family` property:

```
p#times-new-roman {
    font-family: "Times New Roman";
}
p#arial {
    font-family: Arial;
}
```

The preceding rule, combined with this markup:

```
<p id='times-new-roman'>
    This font is Times New Roman.
</p>
<p id='arial'>
    This font is Arial.
</p>
```

results in the display shown in Figure 9-1.

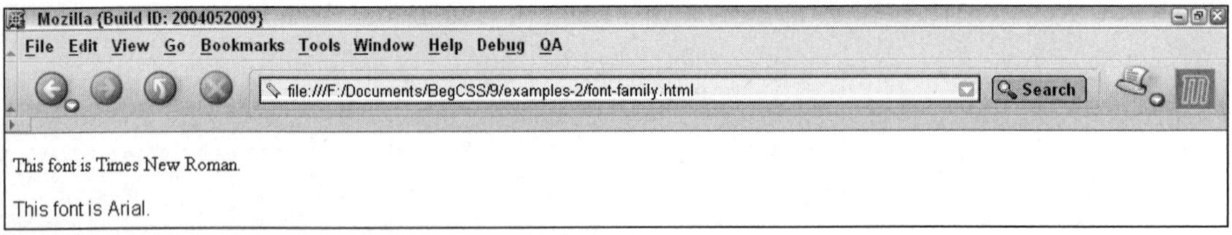

Figure 9-1

The example is pretty straightforward. The first rule applies a Times New Roman font to the paragraph with the id name `times-new-roman`, and the second rule applies an Arial font to the paragraph named `arial`. There is one fundamental difference between the two: Times New Roman appears enclosed in double quotes. The name of the font itself contains white space, and so enclosing the name of the font in quotes prevents the browser from getting confused. The second example, which specifies an Arial font, does not appear enclosed in quotes because no white space appears in the name of the font.

The documentation of the `font-family` property specifies the following notation:

```
[[ <family-name> | <generic-family> ] [, <family-name> | <generic-family>]* ] |
inherit
```

This notation indicates that the `font-family` property can accept one or more fonts for its value, which is what is meant by the repetition of the syntax in the notation and the presence of the asterisk. The asterisk indicates that the syntax may be repeated one or more times. The `inherit` value may also be supplied instead of any font. Two types of fonts can be specified. The first is documented as `<family-name>` in the preceding table. The `<family-name>` notation refers to fonts installed on the user's computer, which means that the available fonts depend on the user's operating system and the fonts available to that operating system. The `<generic-family>` notation refers to a small subset of predefined fonts that can be expected to always be available; this is discussed in more detail in the next section.

The available font families that can be specified vary depending on the operating system. Windows does not provide the same fonts as Macintosh. Furthermore, the available fonts also vary depending on the programs installed on the user's computer. For instance, Microsoft Office installs a number of extra fonts in addition to those that ship with Windows. For this reason, the `font-family` property is dynamic because it can accept more than one font as its value. This capability is provided because it is difficult to foresee which fonts will be available on the user's computer. It is usually best to test on several different platforms using various browsers on different operating systems. To ensure the consistency of fonts, the `font-family` property allows fallback fonts to be specified in the event that the first choice is not available. The following rule

```
p {
    font-family: "Times New Roman", Times;
}
```

combined with this markup:

```
<p>
    This text appears in Times New Roman font, if Times New Roman is installed. It
    appears in Times if Times New Roman is not installed, but Times is. If neither
    font is installed, the browser's default font is used.
</p>
```

produces the results shown in Figure 9-2.

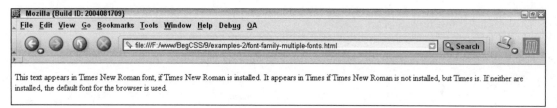

Figure 9-2

In this example, two fonts are specified as the value of the `font-family` property. This allows you to specify a fallback font. In this case, if Times New Roman (common to Windows computers) is not installed on the user's computer, the browser attempts to display the Times font (common to Macintosh computers). If neither font is available, the browser uses its default font, which is the same as the font used when no font is specified and varies depending on the browser. The `font-family` allows a potentially unlimited list of fonts to be specified, meaning that you can specify as many fonts as you'd like to fallback on.

The effect of the following code is that the browser goes through the list of comma-separated fonts until it finds one that it is capable of displaying:

```
p {
    font-family: Arial, Shruti, "Microsoft Sans Serif", Tahoma, Mangal, Helvetica;
}
```

Generic Font Families

Documented in CSS 2.1 and supported in IE 5.5, IE 6, Mozilla 1.7, Opera 7.5, and Safari 1.2.

As I mentioned in the first section, the available fonts vary from operating system to operating system. They can vary even more with individual user's computer systems because even more fonts can be installed along with certain programs. The only way to maintain consistency displaying from platform to platform is to provide either a list of font families (so a fallback font can be called upon if the desired font is not installed) or to specify a generic font. Generic fonts are a set of basic fonts that are available regardless of the user's operating system. The following table outlines the generic font family names defined in CSS.

Generic Font	Resembles
serif	Times, Times New Roman
sans-serif	Helvetica, Arial
cursive	Zapf-Chancery
fantasy	Western
monospace	Courier, Courier New

The generic font names display fonts similarly in different browsers and operating systems. Figure 9-3 shows generic font output in Mozilla.

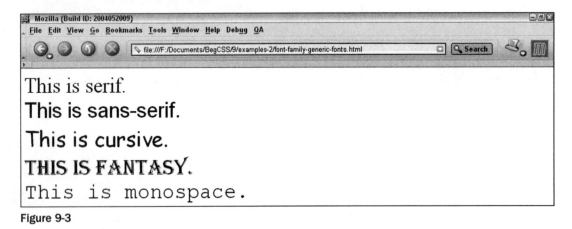

Figure 9-3

Figure 9-4 shows generic font output in IE 6.

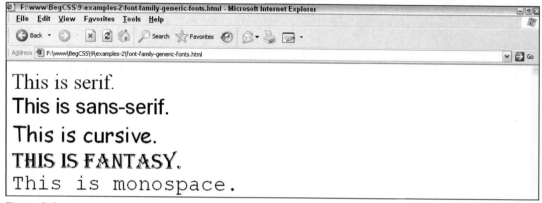

Figure 9-4

Figure 9-5 shows generic font output in Opera 7.5.

Figure 9-5

Figures 9-3, 9-4, and 9-5 show how Mozilla, IE, and Opera 7 render generic fonts on a Windows XP platform. From the output shown in those figures, you can see that generic font rendering is not exactly identical between browsers. Fonts that display consistently are serif, sans-serif, and monospace. In the notation for the `font-family` property documentation, `<generic-family>` refers to the possible specification of a generic font name. Often a generic font is included as a last fallback option, as shown in the following rule:

```
p {
    font-family: Arial, Shruti, "Microsoft Sans Serif", Tahoma, Mangal, Helvetica,
sans-serif;
}
```

The addition of sans-serif to the end of the font list for the `font-family` property means that as a last resort, if none of the other fonts specified are installed on the user's computer, the generic sans-serif font should be used.

The following Try It Out continues to build on the JT's Island Grill and Gallery website presented in Chapter 8, this time applying the font-family property to the style sheet.

Try It Out   **Applying the font-family Property**

Example 9-1. Follow these steps to add the font-family property to the style sheet.

1.   Make the following modifications to the base_styles.css style sheet:

```
body {
    font-family: "Courier New", Courier, monospace;
    text-transform: lowercase;
}
a {
    text-decoration: none;
}
a:hover {
    text-decoration: underline;
}
h1 {
    font-family: "Monotype Corsiva", cursive;
    letter-spacing: 4px;
}
h6 {
    text-align: center;
}
div#content {
    word-spacing: 5px;
    letter-spacing: 1px;
}
p.copy {
    font-family: "Times New Roman", Times, serif;
    text-indent: 20px;
    text-align: justify;
}
```

2.   Save base_styles.css.

3.   Make the following modifications to the dinner_menu.css style sheet:

```
div#content * {
    font-family: "Times New Roman", Times, serif;
}
h3 {
    font-family: "Monotype Corsiva", cursive;
    text-decoration: underline;
}
```

4. Save dinner_menu.css. The result of these modifications is shown in Figure 9-6.

Figure 9-6

How It Works

This example applies a specific font face to all aspects of the JT's website. Specifying a font face is beneficial because not all browsers use the same default font. By adding these rules, the font is explicitly set, making display on different browsers more consistent. The first font is applied to the <body> element:

```
body {
    font-family: "Courier New", Courier, monospace;
    text-transform: lowercase;
}
```

This declaration specifies a fixed width font for the <body> element. However, the font-family property is another example of a property that is inherited by its descendant elements. So, if you add only this declaration, all text on every page of the JT's website is rendered in a fixed-width, monospace font. I specified Courier New first because that font is specific to Windows platforms, then the Courier font because that is specific to Macintosh, and finally, as a last resort, the monospace generic font. This declaration makes the navigational menu appear in a fixed-width, monospace font. The next addition changes the font of the <h1> element:

```
h1 {
    font-family: "Monotype Corsiva", cursive;
    letter-spacing: 4px;
}
```

The Monotype Corsiva font adds a touch of elegance to the <h1> heading, which contains the topic of the page. Later, after loading up the website on Macintosh and Linux operating systems, I can add fonts that appear similar to Monotype Corsiva. However, because the style is centralized in one place with CSS, fine-tuning the style sheet for other operating systems becomes much easier. All that's required is a simple edit of the base_styles.css file, so adding additional fonts for those systems takes less than a minute. The changes are instantaneous to all pages of the JT's website. The last declaration added to the base_styles.css style sheet applies a sans-serif font to any paragraph with a class name of copy:

```
p.copy {
    font-family: "Times New Roman", Times, serif;
    text-indent: 20px;
    text-align: justify;
}
```

Thanks to the cascade, the font-family declaration applied to the <h1> element takes precedence over the one specified for the <body> element. The selectors have the same specificity, if you recall the discussion from Chapter 7, but because the selector for the <h1> element appears later in the style sheet, it trumps the selector for the <body> element. The same concept is used for the selection of the <p> element with a copy class name, which has a greater specificity than the <body> selector. So this selector has two things going for it as far as the cascade is concerned. It both appears later in the style sheet and has a greater specificity, which makes all text appearing in <p> elements with a copy class name appear in Times New Roman for Windows, Times for Macintosh, and the generic serif font otherwise.

The last two modifications made in this exercise are to the dinner_menu.css style sheet:

```
div#content * {
    font-family: "Times New Roman", Times serif;
}
h3 {
    font-family: "Monotype Corsiva", cursive;
    text-decoration: underline;
}
```

The first selector combines two different selectors. The id selector selects the <div> element with an id name of content, and it also uses the universal selector. In this context, this combination of selectors selects all descendants of the <div> element with an id name of content. This has exactly the same effect as this selector:

```
div#content {
    font-family: "Times New Roman", Times serif;
}
```

They have the same effect, first, because they have the same specificity in terms of the cascade, and second because the font-family property is inherited by all descendants of the element that it is applied to.

Adding these two fonts does two things. First, it gives the menu a serif font, which overrides the monospace font specified in the selector for the <body> element for the base_styles.css style sheet earlier in this example. Second, each <h3> element is given the same Monotype Cursiva font specified for the <h1> element in the base_styles.css file, which again is intended to add a touch of elegance to the menu.

The next section continues this discussion of font manipulation with the font-style property.

The font-style Property

Documented in CSS 2.1 and supported in IE 5.5, IE 6, Mozilla 1.7, Opera 7.5, and Safari 1.2.

The font-style property is used to switch between styles provided by a particular font. Those styles are italic or oblique, and they are a part of the font itself. The following table outlines the possible values for the font-style property.

Property	Value
font-style	normal | italic | oblique | inherit Initial value: normal

The italic and oblique values are, with most fonts, indistinguishable in how they render. Consider this example:

```
p {
    font-family: sans-serif;
    font-size: 25px;
}
p#normal {
    font-style: normal;
}
p#italic {
    font-style: italic;
}
p#oblique {
    font-style: oblique;
}
```

Combine the preceding rules with the following markup:

```
<p id='normal'>
    This font is normal.
</p>
<p id='italic'>
    This font is italic.
</p>
```

211

```
<p id='oblique'>
    This font is oblique.
</p>
```

Figure 9-7 shows that the oblique and italic values are identical.

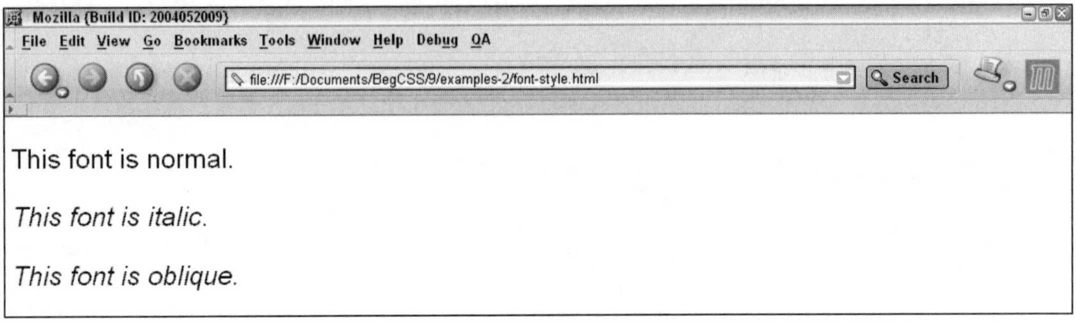

Figure 9-7

This test of the oblique and italic values shows that if the font has an italic style, that italic style is used when either the italic or oblique values are specified. This behavior is identical when viewed in IE 6, Opera 7, or Mozilla. However, not all fonts have an italic style or an oblique style. Consider the following example, which demonstrates what happens when a font has neither an italic nor an oblique style:

```
p {
    font-family: "Monotype Corsiva";
    font-size: 25px;
}
p#normal {
    font-style: normal;
}
p#italic {
    font-style: italic;
}
p#oblique {
    font-style: oblique;
}
```

Combine this style sheet with the following markup:

```
<p id='normal'>
    The font is normal.
</p>
<p id='italic'>
    This font is italic.
</p>
<p id='oblique'>
    This font is oblique.
</p>
```

Figure 9-8 shows Monotype Corsiva, a font that has neither an italic style nor an oblique style — it has only one style.

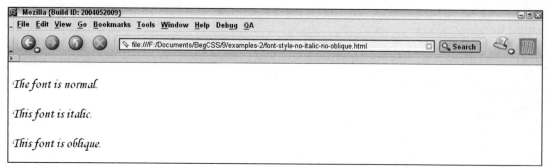

Figure 9-8

The following Try It Out continues the JT's Island Grill and Gallery website with the addition of the `font-style` property.

Try It Out   Applying the font-style Property

Example 9-2. Follow these steps to apply the font-style property to the JT's Island Grill and Gallery website.

1.   Open the dinner_menu.css style sheet and make the following modification:

```
h3 + p.menucaption {
    font-style: italic;
    text-align: center;
}
```

2. Save the dinner_menu.css file. The results are shown in Figure 9-9.

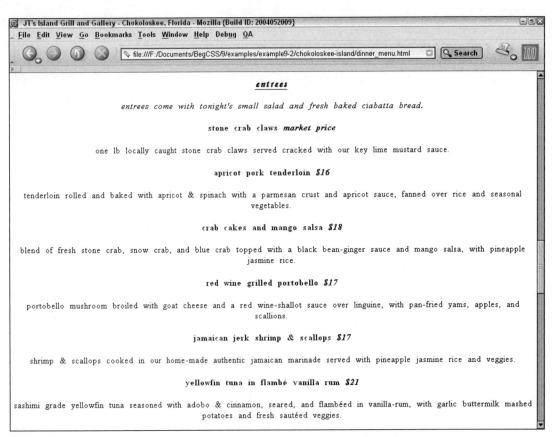

Figure 9-9

How It Works

This addition to the JT's style sheet makes the following highlighted paragraph appear in italics:

```
<h3>Entrees</h3>
    <p class='menucaption'>
        Entrees come with tonight's small salad and fresh baked
        ciabatta bread.
    </p>
```

The addition of the `font-style: italic;` declaration is a natural styling for the *Entrees* caption, which says what each entrée comes with.

The next section continues the discussion of font manipulation properties by introducing the `font-variant` property.

The font-variant Property

Documented in CSS 2.1 and supported in IE 5.5 (incorrectly), IE 6, Mozilla 1.7, Opera 7.5, and Safari 1.2.

The `font-variant` property provides an effect that is only slightly different from that of the `text-transform: uppercase;` declaration presented in Chapter 8. The following table outlines the `font-variant` property and its possible values.

Property	Value
font-variant	normal | small-caps Initial value: normal

Internet Explorer 4, 5, and 5.5 treat the `font-variant: small-caps;` *effect as identical to the* `text-transform: uppercase;` *effect. IE 6 displays the* `font-variant: small-caps;` *effect correctly.*

The `font-variant: small-caps;` declaration causes letters to appear in uppercase but scaled slightly smaller than capitalized letters. Consider the following example:

```
p#text-transform {
    text-transform: uppercase;
}
p#font-variant {
    font-variant: small-caps;
}
```

Combine the preceding style sheet with this markup:

```
<p id='text-transform'>
    This demonstrates the use of the text-transform: uppercase; effect.
</p>
<p id='font-variant'>
    This demonstrates the use of the font-variant: small-caps; effect.
</p>
```

The result is shown in Figure 9-10.

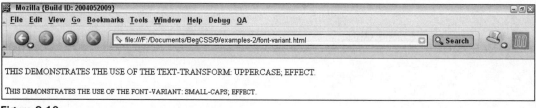

Figure 9-10

Figure 9-10 shows that when compared side by side with the text-transform: uppercase; declaration, the effect of the font-variant: small-caps; declaration is obvious. The capitalized letter maintains its case and size, but all lowercase letters are displayed as capital letters scaled slightly smaller than any *real* capital letters appearing in the markup's source code.

The next section continues the discussion of font manipulation properties with the font-weight property.

The font-weight Property

Documented in CSS 2.1 and supported in IE 5.5, IE 6, Mozilla 1.7, Opera 7.5, and Safari 1.2.

The font-weight property provides the functionality to specify how bold a font is. The following table outlines the font-weight property and the values that it allows.

Property	Value
font-weight	normal | bold | bolder | lighter | 100 | 200 | 300 | 400 | 500 | 600 | 700 | 800 | 900 | inherit Initial value: normal

The font-weight property is used to specify how bold or how light a font appears, as is demonstrated by the following example, illustrated in Figure 9-11:

```
<p style='font-weight: normal;'>
    This font is normal.
</p>
<p style='font-weight: bold;'>
    This font is bold.
</p>
<p style='font-weight: bolder;'>
    This font is bolder.
</p>
<p style='font-weight: lighter;'>
    This font is lighter.
</p>
<p style='font-weight: 100;'>
    This font is 100 weight.
</p>
<p style='font-weight: 200;'>
    This font is 200 weight.
</p>
<p style='font-weight: 300;'>
    This font is 300 weight.
</p>
<p style='font-weight: 400;'>
    This font is 400 weight.
</p>
<p style='font-weight: 500;'>
```

```
        This font is 500 weight.
    </p>
    <p style='font-weight: 600;'>
        This font is 600 weight.
    </p>
    <p style='font-weight: 700;'>
        This font is 700 weight.
    </p>
    <p style='font-weight: 800;'>
        This font is 800 weight.
    </p>
    <p style='font-weight: 900;'>
        This font is 900 weight.
    </p>
```

Mozilla {Build ID: 2004052009}

File Edit View Go Bookmarks Tools Window Help Debug QA

file:///F:/Documents/BegCSS/9/examples-2/font-weight.html   Search

This font is normal.

This font is bold.

This font is bolder.

This font is lighter.

This font is 100 weight.

This font is 200 weight.

This font is 300 weight.

This font is 400 weight.

This font is 500 weight.

This font is 600 weight.

This font is 700 weight.

This font is 800 weight.

This font is 900 weight.

Figure 9-11

Figure 9-11 illustrates the possible values for the font-weight property. This example demonstrates that for the majority of fonts, the font is either bold or it isn't. The rendering of all values appears identical in IE 6, Opera 7, and Mozilla 1.7. The 600 through 900 values appear the same as the bold value. The 100 through 500 values don't appear different from normal text. This is what happens when the font is a simple, standard font, like that used here.

> **The 100 through 900 values really exist for fonts that have eight different bold faces defined, as is the case with high-end professional quality fonts used for publishing. What this means is that to display a font as bold, italic, oblique, or any other style, a separate font file is used.**

Figure 9-12 is a snapshot of the directory containing the various font files. Take for example the Agaramond font shown in the figure. Four font files are associated with the Agaramond font: one for the normal font with no style applied (Regular), one for bold, one for italic, and one for bold and italic. To achieve the effect of a font that becomes increasingly bold—to make use of the 100 through 900 values—a separate font definition file is required for each variation in the font. Most major browsers, however, will show more limited font output—like that shown in Figure 9-11 where the font used had only one bold face and not several. The `bolder` and `lighter` keywords are relative values.

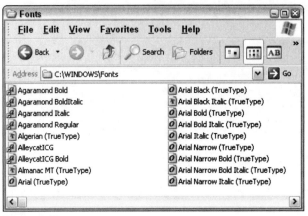

Figure 9-12

Relative Values

In the preceding section, the `bold`, and `100-900` values of the `font-weight` property are *absolute* values because their meaning does not change. The `bolder` and `lighter` values of the `font-weight` property are *relative* values, which means their meaning depends on how bold their parent or ancestor element's font appears. The following code is a demonstration of this:

```
body {
    font-family: monospace;
}
div {
    font-weight: bolder;
}
```

Accompany the preceding rule with this markup:

```
<body>
    This font is normal.
    <div>
        This font is bolder than the font for the &lt;body&gt; element.
    </div>
</body>
```

The result looks like the display shown in Figure 9-13.

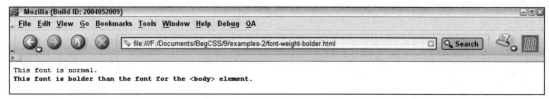

Figure 9-13

The `bolder` and `lighter` keywords make the text bolder or lighter based on the font-weight of the element's parent or ancestor. In this case, the `<body>` element is the `<div>` element's parent. The `<body>` element has no `font-weight` applied, so it appears normal; and the font for the `<div>` element appears bolder because of the `font-weight: bolder;` definition. As is the case with the 100-900 values, if a sophisticated font is available on the user's computer that has several variations from light to bold, the bolder value would trigger the browser to display the variation that is bolder than the one before it. Likewise, the lighter value would display a less bold variation. The following style sheet

```
body {
    font-family: monospace;
    font-weight: bold;
}
div {
    font-weight: lighter;
}
```

accompanied by this markup:

```
<body>
    This font is bold.
    <div>
        This font is lighter than the font for the &lt;body&gt; element.
    </div>
</body>
```

results in the display shown in Figure 9-14.

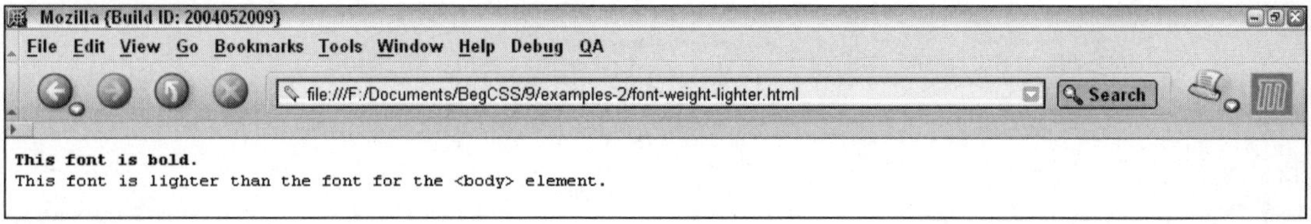

Figure 9-14

Now that you've seen an overview of the `font-weight` property's capabilities, the following Try It Out lets you apply the `font-weight` property to the JT's website.

Try It Out   Applying the font-weight Property

Example 9-3. Follow these steps to apply font weight variations to the JT's website.

1.   Make the following modifications to the dinner_menu.css style sheet:

```
h3, h4, h5, h4 + p, h5 + p  {
    text-align: center;
}
h4 em {
    font-weight: lighter;
}
h5 {
    font-weight: normal;
}
```

The result is shown in Figure 9-15.

Figure 9-15

How It Works

Figure 9-15 shows the effects of these two rules. The first rule added to the dinner_menu.css style sheet makes the text in the `<em>` element lighter than that of its parent element (the `<h4>` element).

```
h4 em {
    font-weight: lighter;
}
```

This rule selects only `<em>` elements that are descendants of `<h4>` elements, which for this project selects the menu item price. The result is that the font used for the `<em>` element is lighter than that used for the `<h4>` element, which is bold by default. The `font-weight: normal;` declaration would have had an identical effect; however, describing the price text as lighter than the menu item text is more intuitive. What I really want is the text for the price to be lighter than that used for the `<h4>` heading.

The next rule removes the default bold face font from the `<h5>` elements used in the menu. Its purpose is to make these elements appear more natural and consistent with the rest of the menu's layout.

```
h5 {
    font-weight: normal;
}
```

Because the font for all heading elements `<h1>` through `<h6>` is boldfaced by default, the `font-weight: normal;` declaration removes the boldfaced effect.

For the majority of web design projects, a font is either bold or it isn't. The average web surfer is unlikely to have installed sophisticated fonts capable of displaying eight variations of bold. In summary, the most used values of the `font-weight` property are likely to be normal, bold, bolder, or lighter (with more emphasis on the first two). I continue the discussion of font manipulation properties by introducing the `font-size` property.

The average price tag of professional publishing-industry quality fonts like these ranges from $50 to $300 for the package, depending on the company providing the fonts.

The font-size Property

Documented in CSS 2 and supported in IE 5.5, IE 6, Mozilla 1.7, Opera 7.5, and Safari 1.2.

The `font-size` property is, of course, used to control the size of fonts. The following table outlines the `font-size` property and its possible values.

Property	Value
font-size	\<absolute-size> | \<relative-size> | \<length> | \<percentage> | inherit Initial value: medium

The bad news, as I mentioned in Chapter 4 in the discussion of CSS length units, is the number of caveats and fallbacks attached to each measurement. Some are better suited for screen and some are better suited for print, and not all length units are interpreted consistently on different browsers. The same is true of the keyword values for the font-size property that I discuss in the following sections.

Absolute Font Sizes

The <absolute-size> value notation of the font-size property refers to one of seven keyword values. Absolute values for the font-size property are defined using keywords that range from xx-large to xx-small. The following table outlines the absolute values and their relation to HTML heading sizes as of CSS 2.

Absolute Keyword	xx-small	x-small	small	medium	large	x-large	xx-large
HTML Heading	n/a	<h6>	<h5>	<h4>	<h3>	<h2>	<h1>

These keywords specify the font size based on a scaling factor of 1.2. The *scaling factor* is the ratio between two shapes. The scaling factor is determined by multiplying the font size by 1.2 to determine the next font size relative to the previous one. For instance, if a font size of 16 pixels is assumed for the medium keyword value, the large keyword would be approximately 19 pixels, rounding down from 19.2 because 16 multiplied by 1.2 equals 19.2

These keywords exist for sizing fonts relative to the browser user's font-size preferences. The browser precalculates the value of each keyword depending on those preferences. The name *absolute* is somewhat misleading because each keyword is *relative* to the user's font-size preferences. The actual length unit size of each keyword varies depending on a number of factors, such as:

❑ The browser's default font size.

❑ The user's font size preferences.

❑ The font family being used.

Despite all of these variables, this is one place where the three browsers, IE 6, Mozilla 1.7, and Opera 7.5, seem to be consistent.

Figure 9-16 shows each absolute font size in relation to the default HTML heading size and a size specified in points.

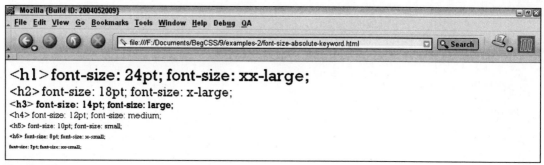

Figure 9-16

Although this association between font size keywords and length units works for the Rockwell font I used in Figure 9-16, the point sizes depicted are approximations and might not be the same point unit values when another font is used. If you increase or decrease the size of the text using the zoom feature of the browser, you'd notice that the point sizes change in response to the absolute keyword values if you are using Opera and Mozilla. However, Internet Explorer 6 ignores the user's adjustments to font size preferences on font sizes specified in points (or any other absolute length unit, like inches or centimeters). Therefore, the point sizes do not change with the size of the absolute keywords when adjustments to the user's font size preferences are made. Adjustments in the size of the font can be made in Internet Explorer from the View ➪ Text Size menu. In Mozilla, changes to font size can be made by pressing Ctrl + + or Ctrl + -, or from the View ➪ Text Zoom menu. In Opera, the font size can be adjusted using the same shortcuts as in Mozilla, or from the View ➪ Zoom menu.

Relative font-size keywords, covered in the following section, are closely associated with the absolute font size keywords.

Relative Font Sizes

The `<relative-size>` notation of the `font-size` property refers to two values: `larger` and `smaller`. When either of these two values is used, the font size is determined by the values appearing in the table for absolute size keywords discussed in the previous section. Take, for instance, the following example:

```
body {
    font-size: medium;
}
p {
    font-size: larger;
}
```

Combine this with the following markup:

```
<body>
    This font is medium in size.
    <p>
```

```
            This size of this font corresponds to font-size: large;, which is the next
            value in the absolute font-size keyword table.
            <span style='font-size: large;'>This is demonstrated by placing the text
            next to text with a font-size: large; explicitly specified.</span>
        </p>
    </body>
```

The results are shown in Figure 9-17.

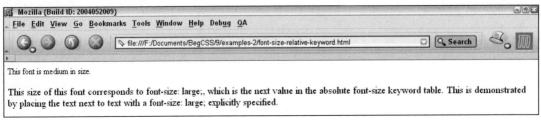

Figure 9-17

Figure 9-17 demonstrates how the next value in the absolute font-size keyword table is chosen. Because the font for the <body> element is made medium in size with the font-size: medium; declaration, when font-size: larger; is applied to the <p> element, the browser chooses the next larger value in the absolute keyword table and applies a font size that is the same as would be generated by the font-size: large; declaration. If the value is specified with a length unit—say, for instance, as pixels—the browser simply applies a 1.2 scaling factor to that size to get the larger size.

Figure 9-18 shows how a font size specified as 16 pixels gets increasingly larger when font-size: larger; is applied to descendant elements. This also shows how the font-size: larger; and font-size: smaller; declarations are very similar to the font-weight: bolder; and font-weight: lighter; declarations.

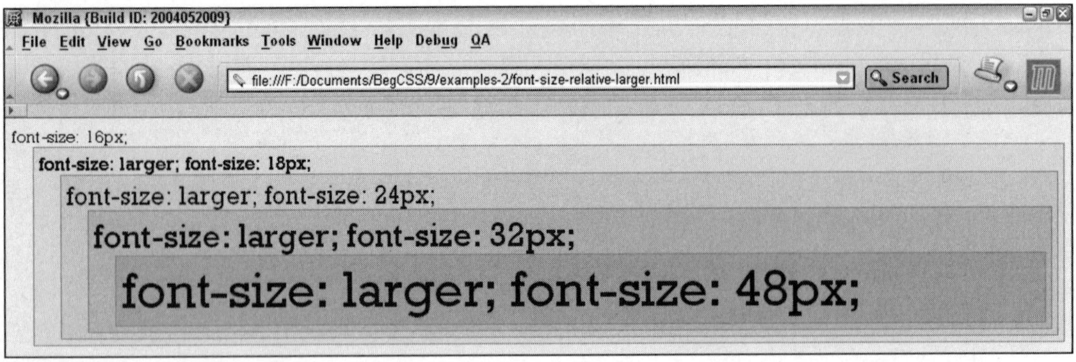

![Mozilla browser window showing nested font sizes: font-size: 16px; font-size: larger; font-size: 18px; font-size: larger; font-size: 24px; font-size: larger; font-size: 32px; font-size: larger; font-size: 48px;](file:///F:/Documents/BegCSS/9/examples-2/font-size-relative-larger.html)

Figure 9-18

In contrast to the font-size: larger; declaration, Figure 9-19 shows what happens when the font-size: smaller; declaration is used instead.

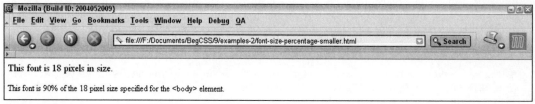

Figure 9-19

The `font-size: smaller;` declaration performs the same scaling factor changes that the `font-size: larger;` declaration does, but does them in reverse.

Percentage Font Sizes

Percentage font sizes work much like the em units discussed in Chapter 4. Consider the following example:

```css
body {
    font-size: 18px;
}
p {
    font-size: 90%;
}
```

Combine this with the following markup:

```html
<body>
    This font is 18 pixels in size.
    <p>
        This font is 90% of the 18 pixel size specified for the &lt;body&gt;
        element.
    </p>
</body>
```

The result is shown in Figure 9-20.

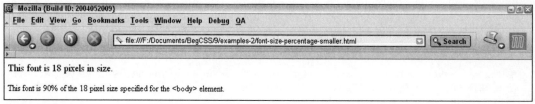

Figure 9-20

Figure 9-20 shows that percentage values are based on the element's ancestry. The font size for the <p> element is 90% of the size specified for the <body> element. This works much the same as the em unit does for font sizes. However, unlike the em unit, the meaning of a percentage measurement varies depending on the CSS property that it is used with. An em unit, you should recall, always refers to the font size. Most designers prefer em units to other types of measurements because the size of an em unit depends on the font size. The em units create the possibility for liquid, accessible designs that increase or decrease in size to accommodate the user's font size preferences. I discuss this in more detail in Chapter 10.

A percentage font size measurement might also be used to increase the size of a font. Take, for instance, the following example:

```
body {
    font-size: 150%;
}
```

When applied to the following markup

```
<body>
    This font is 150% of the size of the user's font size preferences.
    <p>
        This font is 100% of the size of the font used for the &lt;body&gt; element.
    </p>
</body>
```

it renders the results shown in Figure 9-21.

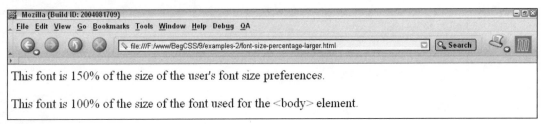

Figure 9-21

The font for the <body> element in Figure 9-21 is 50% larger than the user's default font size preferences. In Mozilla, the default font size is set to 16 pixels, so the font for the <body> element in Figure 9-21 is 50% larger than 16 pixels or 24 pixels in size. Specifying the font size as 150% is the same, in this case, as it would be had you specified a font size of 1.5em. The font for the <p> element is 100% of the font size used for the <body> element. The <p> element's font size is only 100% of the <body> element's font size because the font-size property is inherited. If the <p> element were to have any descendants, their font size would be that of the font size specified on the <p> element. This demonstrates that percentage font sizes are dependant on the element's ancestry.

After this overview of how the font-size property works, in the following Try It Out you add the font-size property to the JT's Island Grill and Gallery style sheets.

Applying a Font Size

Example 9-4. By following these steps, you add the `font-size` property to the JT's website style sheets.

1. Make the following highlighted modifications to the base_styles.css style sheet:

```css
h1 {
    font-family: "Monotype Corsiva", cursive;
    letter-spacing: 4px;
    font-size: 1.5em;
}
h3 {
    font-size: 0.9em;
}
h6 {
    font-size: 0.8em;
    text-align: center;
}
div#content {
    font-size: 0.9em;
    word-spacing: 5px;
    letter-spacing: 1px;
}
p.copy {
    font-size: 1.2em;
    font-family: "Times New Roman", Times, serif;
    text-indent: 20px;
    text-align: justify;
}
```

2. Save the base_styles.css style sheet.

3. Make the following modifications to the dinner_menu.css style sheet.

```css
div#content h3 {
    font-family: "Monotype Corsiva", cursive;
    text-decoration: underline;
    font-size: 2em;
}
h3 + p.menucaption {
    font-style: italic;
    text-align: center;
}
h4, h5 {
    font-size: 1.3em;
}
```

4. Save the dinner_menu.css style sheet. The results of these modifications can be seen in Figure 9-22.

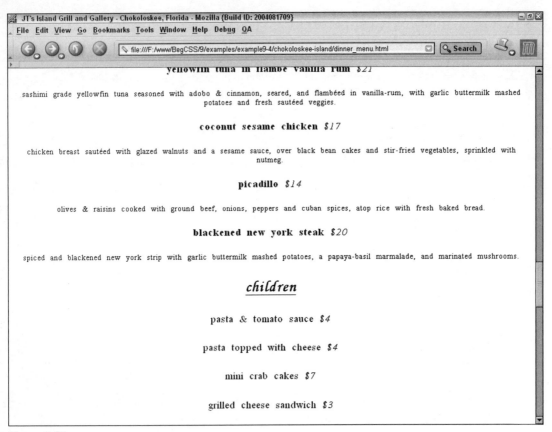

Figure 9-22

How It Works

Each of these rules specifies a font size for the JT's dinner menu. I have chosen to specify each font size using the em unit that I discussed in Chapter 4 so that font sizes will change with the user's font size preferences. If the font size of the browser is increased, the font size of the menu also increases accordingly. Although similar results can be achieved using absolute keywords or percentage font sizes, this approach facilitates the overall design of the website, because I plan to apply padding, borders, margins, and other elements of document layout using em units. This approach enables the site's design to adapt completely to the user's font size preferences—scaling larger or smaller depending on how large the user has the font size set. This makes the design accessible because people with poor vision tend to crank up the font sizes to make reading easier. Because I've used em measurements, making the font size larger is like applying a magnifying glass to the whole page. I go into more detail on this throughout Chapter 10.

The approach here is quite simple. I have adjusted the heading sizes in the dinner menu and the heading sizes of <h1> heading containing the document's title, as well as the <h6> heading containing the document's footer:

```
h1 {
    font-family: "Monotype Corsiva", cursive;
    letter-spacing: 4px;
    font-size: 1.5em;
}
h3 {
    font-size: 0.9em;
}
h6 {
    font-size: 0.8em;
    text-align: center;
}
```

The <h1> heading is increased to one and one-half sizes larger than the user's font setting, and the <h6> heading is adjusted to 0.8 of the user's font-size setting. The <h3> element is also made slightly smaller. (Although the <h3> element is not used in the dinner menu, it is used on the other pages of the JT's website.)

The next rule adjusts the size of the text appearing in the <div> with an id name of content:

```
div#content {
    font-size: 0.9em;
    word-spacing: 5px;
    letter-spacing: 1px;
}
```

This makes the text size just slightly smaller. Next, I increase the size of text appearing in a <p> element with an id name of copy:

```
p.copy {
    font-size: 1.2em;
    font-family: "Times New Roman", Times, serif;
    text-indent: 20px;
    text-align: justify;
}
```

Remember, however, that the copy <p> appears inside of the content <div>, so the 1.2em size is based on the 0.9em size of the content <div>. This means that the size of the copy <p> font becomes 0.2 larger than 0.9em, which is itself 0.1 less than the size of the default font. Then adjustments are made to the dinner_menu.css style sheet to fine-tune the different menu headings:

```
div#content h3 {
    font-family: "Monotype Corsiva", cursive;
    text-decoration: underline;
    font-size: 2em;
}
```

The <h3> elements used for each menu section heading — appetizers, entrees, and so on — are made double the size of the font used for the content <div>. Therefore, the size of the <h3> elements inside the content <div> are made two times 0.9em because the em unit depends on the element's ancestry and the font size of parent elements, just as the percentage font size does. Finally, <h4> and <h5> elements are increased in size:

```
h4, h5 {
    font-size: 1.3em;
}
```

These also appear inside of the content `<div>`, so their sizes are also based on the font size of the content div, which is 0.3em larger than the 0.9em size specified for the content `<div>`.

The next section examines a special short hand property used to specify several font properties in one.

The font Shorthand Property

Documented in CSS 1, 2, and 3, and supported since IE 4, NS 6, Opera 4, and Safari 1.

The `font` property is a shorthand property that allows several properties to be written in a single property. The following table outlines the `font` property and the values that it allows.

Property	Value
font	[<'font-style'> || <'font-variant'> || <'font-weight'>]? <'font-size'> [/ <'line-height'>]? <'font-family'>] caption | icon | menu | message-box | small-caption | status-bar | inherit

The notation for the `font` property is somewhat more complicated than those presented in previous examples. For now, just ignore the caption, icon, menu, message-box, small-caption, and status-bar values — these are called system fonts, and I discuss them in the next section. As for the first part of the notation, here's a break down of each portion:

```
[ <'font-style'> || <'font-variant'> || <'font-weight'> ]?
```

This indicates that either a `font-style`, `font-variant`, or `font-weight` value can be provided. The question mark indicates that this part is optional. The double vertical bars indicate that each value is optional, so one, two, or all three of these may appear, but none of them is required.

The next part indicates that a font size must be specified:

```
<'font-size'>
```

The font size is not optional, so a `font-size` value must always be provided.

The next part indicates that a line height may be specified, but because a question mark follows it, the line height is optional:

```
[ / <'line-height'> ]?
```

The forward slash in the notation indicates that if a line height is specified, a forward slash must separate the `font-size` and `line-height` properties. The question mark after the closing square bracket indicates that this portion of the syntax is optional.

The last portion indicates that a font family must be specified:

```
<'font-family'>
```

So at the very least, a `font-size` value and a `font-family` value must be specified. Now that you understand the notation, here's an example of this property including all its optional values:

```
p {
    font: italic small-caps bold 1em/1.5em sans-serif;
}
```

When applied to this markup:

```
<p>
    This font is italic, small-caps, bold, 1em in size, with a 1.5 em line height
    and a sans-serif font.
</p>
```

the result shown in Figure 9-23 is generated.

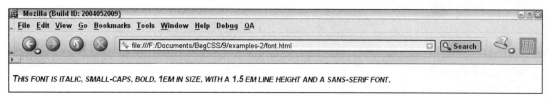

Figure 9-23

This rule includes all the values possible with the `font` property shorthand. Figure 9-23 shows that this rule makes the font italic, small-caps, bold, 1em in size with a 1.5 em line-height and a sans-serif font. I haven't discussed the `line-height` property yet because this property is discussed in Chapter 10, but essentially the `line-height` property accepts a normal length value, which sets the height for each line of text.

In contrast to the previous example, this example shows the `font` property with a minimal set of values:

```
p {
    font: 1em sans-serif;
}
```

When combined with this markup:

```
<p>
    This font is 1 em in size and sans-serif.
</p>
```

the result shown in Figure 9-24 is generated.

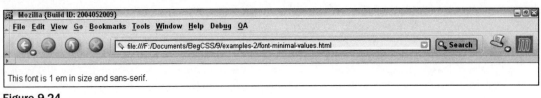

Figure 9-24

The notation indicates that at least a font size and a font family must be provided, as is reflected in the preceding example. Figure 9-24 shows output with a sans-serif font 1em in size.

Here are a few more possible variations of the font property:

```
font: bold 1.2em Arial, Helvetica, sans-serif;
```

This makes the font bold and 1.2em in size. Then, like the font-family property, the font property accepts a list of fonts. I've specified an Arial font, which is common to Windows systems. If that font isn't found on the user's computer, the Helvetica font is used, which is common to Macintosh systems. Then as a last resort, the generic sans-serif font is used:

```
font: italic 1.2/2em "Times New Roman", Times, serif;
```

The preceding rule makes the font italic and 1.2em in size with a 2em line height. Those specifications are followed by a list of font families.

Now that you've had an overview of the font shorthand property, the next section introduces you to the system font keywords.

System Fonts

Documented in CSS 2.1 and supported since IE 5.5, IE 6, Mozilla 1.7, Opera 7.5, and Safari 1.2.

System fonts are keywords that refer to a font predefined by the user's operating system. The following table outlines each available system font.

Font Name	Font Description
caption	Refers to the font used for captioned controls.
icon	Refers to the font used to label icons like those found on the desktop.
menu	Refers to the font used in menus, drop-down menus, and menu lists.
message-box	The font used in dialog boxes.
small-caption	The font used for labeling small controls.
status-bar	The font used in window status bars.

System fonts may only be set as a whole: When a system font is specified using the font shorthand property, the `font-family`, `font-size`, `font-weight` properties, and all other aspects of font display are set at once. The following example demonstrates each of the system fonts:

```
p#caption {
    font: caption;
}
p#icon {
    font: icon;
}
p#menu {
    font: menu;
}
p#message-box {
    font: message-box;
}
p#small-caption {
    font: small-caption;
}
p#status-bar {
    font: status-bar;
}
```

It is combined with the following markup:

```
<p id='caption'>
    This is the caption font.
</p>
<p id='icon'>
    This is the icon font.
</p>
<p id='menu'>
    This is the menu font.
</p>
<p id='message-box'>
    This is the message-box font.
</p>
<p id='small-caption'>
    This is the small-caption font.
</p>
<p id='status-bar'>
    This is the status-bar font.
</p>
```

The output is shown in Figure 9-25.

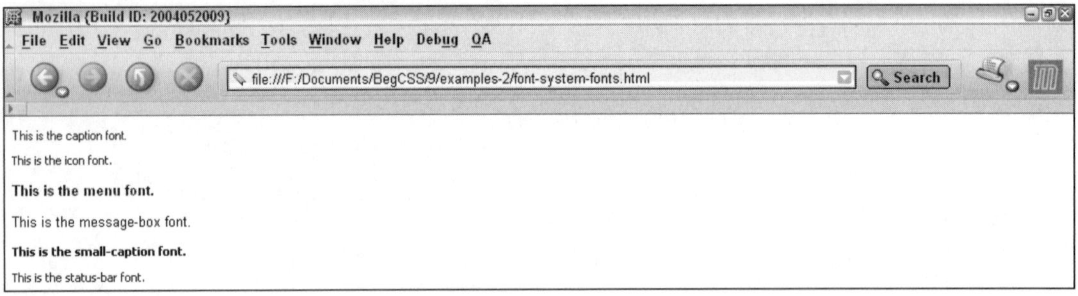

Figure 9-25

This figure shows what the system fonts look like rendered in a browser. The fonts, font sizes, and styles are specific to my configuration of Windows XP and may look different than when rendered in your browser. The display depends on the fonts, font sizes, and styles used by your operating system. System fonts provide a way of referencing the fonts found on the user's operating system, including the size, style, and weight of the system font. This allows a web page to adapt to the user's font preferences because operating systems often offer some method to customize the fonts they use.

Additionally, different aspects of system fonts can be overridden via the cascade by specifying the different font properties after a font declaration with a system font value. This is demonstrated by the following rule:

```
p {
    font: caption;
    font-size: 2em;
    font-style: italic;
}
```

In the preceding example, the font size and font style replace those specified for the system font.

Summary

This chapter demonstrated several properties CSS provides for manipulating font display. These properties allow both simple and complex control over how fonts are presented to the end user. In this chapter you learned

❑ How to specify the font face using the `font-family` property.

❑ How to make the font style oblique or italic with the `font-style` property.

❑ How to style the small-caps effect using the `font-variant` property.

❑ How to control the lightness and boldness of a font using the `font-weight` property.

❑ How to take advantage of specifying a font size that adjusts based on the user's font size preferences with the `font-size` property and absolute keywords.

❑   How to increase the size of a font based on the font size of an element's parent using relative keywords, percentage font sizes, or em units with the `font-size` property.

❑   How to combine the various font properties into one using the `font` shorthand property.

After learning some of CSS's simpler properties for text manipulation in Chapter 8 and going over font manipulation in this chapter, you now investigate the CSS box model and liquid design in Chapter 10.

Exercises

1.   Using Exercise 3 from Chapter 8, modify the style sheet, removing the `width: 200px;` and `text-align: justify;` declarations. Make the poem's title appear in normal font face, removing the bold styling. Make the first letter of each line of the poem 20% larger than the rest of the line and italic. Make the title of the poem appear in Monotype Corsiva or a font of your choice.

2.   Based on Exercise 1 that you just completed, use the `font` shorthand property to specify a Monotype Corsiva font family (or another font of your choice) for the first letter of each line appearing in the poem. Keep the remaining font size and style specified in Exercise 1.

Liquid Design and the CSS Box Model

Throughout this book, you have learned about standards, which ensure that the Internet is an enjoyable experience for everyone. Standards enable you to deliver a web document through more than one medium. On computer systems, standards allow web content to behave predictably when viewed on different browsers and different operating systems. Standards also allow web content to be delivered to more than one type of device: handheld computers, cell phones, aural browsers (where the content is read using a voice synthesizer), and a variety of other devices. This chapter discusses liquid design, a concept that allows content to adapt to the medium of presentation. Liquid design adjusts to the medium of content delivery regardless of screen size, resolution, or platform. As I discussed in Chapter 9, the layout stretches to accommodate any increase or decrease in screen resolution or the user's font-size preferences.

In this chapter, I discuss

❑ Laying the foundation for liquid design

❑ `<table>` versus `<div>`

❑ Tag soup

❑ The advantages of external style sheets: one page to rule them all

❑ The `media` attribute and `@media` rule

❑ The CSS box model

❑ CSS box model properties, padding, margins, borders, width, and height

❑ Controlling line height

❑ Establishing minimum and maximum dimensions

❑ Overflowing content

Each component is essential for fluid designs, which make a website accessible through more than one medium. Throughout this book you may have noticed that compatibility with older browsers (such as Netscape 4, Internet Explorer 4, and others whose support for things such as CSS and XHTML is virtually non-existent) is completely ignored. The concepts presented in this chapter would look quite mundane, if they render at all, in older browsers. The truth is simply this: Why sacrifice all the benefits of CSS-based design for a handful of designers still using a version 4 browser issued nearly seven years ago? In short, there comes a time in standards evolution when you must sacrifice backward compatibility in the name of better things.

This chapter begins by discussing the dos and don'ts of liquid design. Later, the chapter tackles the CSS Box model, a set of properties that is quite possibly the single most important component of CSS-based designs, affecting all rendered elements on a page. Its theory and implementation are the cornerstones of liquid design and require a vastly different way of thinking than do designs created with purely presentational markup like HTML tables.

Laying the Foundation for Liquid Design

In Chapter 8, I presented some of the strategies to begin designing a website from the ground up. The concept of liquid design plays an important role in this process. I postponed discussion of the strategies involved in creating liquid design until this chapter because they are closely related to the CSS box model properties that I also cover in this chapter. The following sections go into more detail about the theory behind the markup techniques I presented in Chapter 8.

Most websites adhere to some sort of template: a fixed definition of headings, content, and navigation that remain the same from page to page. In programming terms, this consistency of presentation is referred to as the *UI*, or user interface. The user interface is the general term for the buttons and switches and gizmos that formulate what a website is, and, you guessed it, how the user interfaces with the website. It involves a schema of navigation and a color scheme; put simply, the UI determines the look and feel of a website. A reusable foundation is important because it greatly increases maintainability. The following list outlines the ground rules for your liquid design project:

❑ No tables are allowed, except where data must be organized.

❑ Avoid using `<br />`, `<b>`, `<i>` and other unnecessary tags (*tag soup*).

❑ Styles sheets must be organized by media, and your web documents must use external style sheets to reduce file size and loading times.

This formulation of ground rules produces a design that is very lightweight, quick to download, and easy to port to other devices where size is a very big consideration, such as cell phones and PDAs. The structure becomes self-describing and easier to maintain. It no longer takes hours or days to make simple adjustments to the template. The design also becomes accessible, meaning that users accessing the website with a voice synthesizer can quickly navigate through each page without having to listen to every word on every page before finding a topic of interest.

If you think accommodating voice synthesizers isn't important, a multitude of accessibility organizations are ready to take offense. This is the software commonly used to access the Internet by people with visual or other types of disabilities or impairments. Software such as IBM's Home Page Reader (available from `http://www.ibm.com/able/hpr`) is bringing the web to people with disabilities. By following a few simple design guidelines, a disabled person's Internet experience can be greatly improved and enriched. In the United States, a set of Federal guidelines, known as Section 508, requires all government websites to be accessible to the disabled. In the coming sections, I present a few simple design techniques that take care of accessibility and maintainability in one fell swoop.

<table> versus <div>

Before CSS, you simply had no way to achieve an aesthetically pleasing design without using tables. However, these days, using tables is not desirable for a couple of reasons. The first and weakest argument is that table-based designs were not the original intention of the W3C. Early on, there wasn't a better alternative to table-based design, and even though CSS level 1 was written in 1996, support for it was not widespread. It did not become a feasible solution until 2001. Today, however, better methods exist, even on Internet Explorer 6, which at the time of this writing has the worst CSS support among the browsers.

Many of today's designs still make heavy use of HTML tables; in fact, it is quite common to find table piled on top of table on top of table in older HTML designs. At one time, this was considered quite elegant and creative. In the early days of table design the question was, "In what new way can I twist and mangle a table before it works on all browsers without breaking my design and still have it convey the look and feel that my client wants?" In the early days, the Internet was primarily a medium for educational institutions, corporations, and the military to pass around information. Like any early technology, the Internet was quite crude and lacked the capability to absolutely control the presentation of content.

As the Internet evolved, the first signs of presentational markup crept into the earlier versions of HTML. Then Netscape Communicator was the dominant browser, and customers began demanding more control over the presentation of content. Netscape responded with the <font> tag, and Microsoft followed suit with an implementation of its own. Around the same time, HTML tables also became quite popular for establishing the look and feel of a website. The truth is that it is just as difficult to maintain table-based design as it is to control all the fonts on a page with <font> tags. Tables, like <font> tags, cause the size of a file to increase significantly. All the extra markup in a document causes the price of file maintenance to increase almost proportionately to the file size. Tags and content become difficult to single out, and consistency of the template decreases because the presentation is contained in each individual document. On the other hand, designs that use generic <div> containers instead of tables are the opposite: They are easily maintained, result in smaller file sizes, and allow for *skinning* of the design. In other words, you can write new style sheets that give a completely different look and feel using the same content. This flexibility also opens up the door to delivery on more than one medium. In addition to designing for home computers, you can write style sheets for delivery on cell phones, PDAs, aural browsers, and a plethora of other devices.

Following is a snippet of markup bloated with presentational tags and attributes:

```
<table width="100%"  border="0" cellspacing="0" cellpadding="0">
    <tr>
        <td width="100" valign="top">
            <font face="Arial, Helvetica, sans-serif" color="#FF0000">
                The Menu
            </font>
        </td>
        <td>
            <font face="Arial, Helvetica, sans-serif" color="#000000">
                The Content
```

```
            </font>
        </td>
    </tr>
</table>
```

Using CSS, this entire block of markup can be reduced to only six lines.

```
<div id='menu'>
    The Menu
</div>
<div id='content'>
    The Content
</div>
```

You can also move the presentational markup to a style sheet that looks something like this:

```
* {
    font-family: Arial, Helvetica, sans-serif;
    color: black;
}
#menu {
    float: left;
    width: 100px;
    color: red;
}
```

Not only is the <div> and CSS approach simpler with smaller file sizes, many of extra attributes aren't required in the <div> design. These include valign='top', border='0', cellspacing='0', and so on. Because these attributes are all specific to HTML tables, <div> elements don't require their use. You could simply eliminate all the presentational markup from the <table> and style the <table> using CSS, but for the sake of complete flexibility and a smaller, simpler document structure, using <div> elements makes more sense.

The last huge argument against table-based designs is that they impede accessibility. All too often, table-based designs do not divide the site into headings (using HTML heading tags) and paragraph tags for text. They also use images heavily (some that serve no other purpose than spacing content), but don't provide *alternate text* with the image. As a result, blind visitors cannot have the full experience or they can become confused. Alternate text is presented in the alt attribute of the <img/> tag. This is the text displayed (or read if using a voice synthesizer), if the user cannot see the image or has disabled the viewing of images in the browser.

```
<img src="my.jpg" alt="This text is presented to the user if the image isn't
available" title="This is tooltip text and this text is displayed if the user's
mouser cursor is resting over the image" />
```

Table-based designs may also rely heavily on *image maps* — a design technique in which a link is mapped to certain coordinates on an image. Image maps are a useful tool as long as they don't make the website inaccessible. With CSS, you can completely eliminate or incorporate many of these techniques without compromising aesthetic design and quality.

To recap, table-based designs

❑ Are meant for data organization, not aesthetic layout.

❑ Are labor-intensive to maintain.

❑ Have a significantly larger file size, and thereby consume more bandwidth and more hard disk space. This results in longer download times for dial-up users and an all-around more expensive website.

❑ Are not ideal for PDAs and other mobile devices.

❑ Impede accessibility.

Using CSS, you can completely circumvent these complex table-based designs, as this chapter shows you. In the next section, I explore which tags you should avoid.

Avoiding Tag Soup

The next rule of fluid design is avoiding *tag soup*. What is tag soup you ask? Tag soup describes unnecessary or useless markup. Using CSS and properly formed markup, you can completely avoid the HTML line break tag, `<br>`, or `<br />` in XHTML. You can get around the line break tag by employing a number of very useful techniques that not only eliminate meaningless markup but also make a website more accessible and enable the source code to describe its content more intuitively.

Here are some techniques to help you avoid using the line break tag:

❑ Use unordered lists for navigational links (`<ul>`).

❑ Always enclose headings in HTML heading tags (`<h1>–<h6>`).

❑ Always enclose content text in paragraph tags (`<p>`).

These techniques remove the clutter of the break tag and allow the document structure to describe itself. You may recall the markup that I used to build JT's dinner menu in Chapter 8. There, I employed these techniques to make the structure of the document itself more intuitive and self-describing. These techniques also play a role in liquid design: By closely following the guidelines presented here, you can create a document that adapts to the user's environment. I show you how all this comes together throughout this chapter, especially with the addition of the CSS box model properties that I discuss a bit later.

A good way to avoid tag soup is to avoid the `<b>` (bold) tag and `<i>` (italic) tags. For the `<b>` tag, use the `<strong>` tag instead, as in:

```
<strong>Some bold text.</strong>
```

The W3C does not consider the `<strong>` tag to be presentational markup because the `<strong>` tag adds meaning to the markup's structure. You can use the `<strong>` tag in aural browsers to trigger a loader voice or a more emphasized voice. Most browsers associate the `<strong>` tag with bold-faced text, although this isn't part of the W3C's definition of the `<strong>` tag. On the other hand, `<b>` is used purely for presentation and has no extra meaning to the document structure. In addition to the `<strong>` tag, you can also use a generic `<span>` container combined with CSS, as in the following:

```
<span style='font-weight: bold;'>Some bold text.</span>
```

The <span> container is a generic inline-level tag that serves no purpose other than the delivery of style. The <span> container adds no real meaning to the document's structure, but is a standards-acceptable method of applying style to specific text. You can use the <span> element to partition part of a paragraph or line of text for styling. It can be used, for example, to highlight a portion of text with a different background color or to underline or strike through text that pertains solely to presentation. The <strong> tag is better suited for simply bolding text because it conveys both structural meaning and style.

Instead of using the <i> tag, consider using<em>, which stands for emphasis. Again, <em> is another tag that the W3C doesn't consider to be presentational markup because <em> adds meaning to the structure, as in the following:

```
<em>Some italic text.</em>
```

Nothing in the W3C recommendations states that the <em> element must be rendered in italics; however, most browsers interpret it that way. Again, the italic effect provided by using the <em> tag can also be accomplished by the generic <span> container with CSS:

```
<span style='font-style: italic;'>Some italic text.</span>
```

Additional obsolete HTML tags exist; but as a rule, you should avoid tags that exist purely for presentation and replace them with CSS tags that contribute additional meaning to the document structure. In fact, not only are <b> and <i> obsolete HTML tags, these tags do not function at all when included in an XHTML document. They are not part of the XHTML specification and, therefore, must be replaced with suitable replacements if XHTML is the medium of delivery.

Examining the Advantages of External Style Sheets

If you recall from Chapter 3, one advantage of external style sheets is that the browser caches them. This substantially reduces requests for style sheets as pages load. The browser looks in the cache, sees that the style sheet is already downloaded, and applies the styles to the page in question. Besides this advantage of external style sheets, their use enables you to specify different style sheets based on the *media* — the method of presentation. You can write one style sheet for a handheld computer or PDA; you can write another for presentation on a cell phone. You can hide images or resize divs and tables. In a word, you can optimize the presentation for a particular method of delivery. You optimize presentation with the media attribute and with @media rules. The media attribute and @media rules don't clutter the document with styles not relevant to the form of presentation you are using, further increasing efficiency.

The media attribute and @media rule

Media *attribute: Documented in CSS 2.1 and supported in IE 5.5, IE 6, Mozilla 1.8, Opera 7.5, and Safari 1.2.* @media: *Documented in CSS 2.1 and supported in IE 5.5, IE 6, Opera 7.5, and Safari 1.2.*

The media attribute is something you can add to the <link> element or <style> element that selects the method of presentation. As mentioned earlier, the media attribute allows the presentation of a completely different style sheet depending on what type of device being used to access the website.

The media attribute and @media rule support the values shown in the following table.

Value	Purpose
all	Suitable for all devices.
Braille	Intended for Braille tactical feedback devices.
embossed	Intended for paged Braille printers.
handheld	Intended for handheld devices.
print	Intended for presentation to a printer (in a browser use print preview to view the print style sheet).
projection	Intended for projected presentations.
screen	Intended for presentation on a color computer screen.
speech | aural	Intended for presentation to a speech synthesizer (called aural in CSS 2 and speech in CSS 2.1).
tty	Intended for media using a fixed-pitch character grid (such as teletypes, terminals, or portable devices with limited display capabilities).
tv	Intended for television (low resolution, low color, limited scrollability).

Note: PC browsers only recognize screen, print, *and* all *values.*

Recalling the `<link>` element from Chapter 3, the following is the `<link>` element with the addition of the media attribute:

```
<link rel='stylesheet'
      href='path/to/some_css_doc.css'
      type='text/css'
       media='screen'/>
```

The inclusion of the `media='screen'` attribute applies the styles in `some_css_doc.css` only for those users accessing the website using a normal PC. In the same way, you can apply the `media` attribute to an embedded style sheet using the following:

```
<style type='text/css' media='screen'>
```

Using the `media='screen'` attribute with the embedded style sheet has an effect that is identical to using the `media='screen'` attribute for the `<link>` element. The `@media` rule, on the other hand, is a method of selecting the media within the style sheet itself. In this example

```
@media print {
    body {
        font-size: 10pt;
    }
}
```

```
@media screen {
    body {
        font-size: 1em;
    }
}
```

the first rule results in a 10-point font size for print (if the user prints the web page from the browser, for example), and the second rule results in a 1em font size on the computer screen. The @media rule is the least-supported method, especially in older browsers. For that reason, the examples in this book stick with the media attribute, which is widely supported.

At this point, the examples focus only on styling for the screen. Chapter 15 explores what's involved in writing a style sheet for print and for a handheld device.

The following Try It Out adds the media attribute to JT's dinner menu to separate the style sheets referenced there by media.

Try It Out   **Separating Style Sheets by Media**

Example 10-1. In the following steps, you separate the JT's style sheets by media.

1.   Make the following adjustments to the dinner_menu.html file:

```
<!DOCTYPE html PUBLIC "-/pp/W3C//DTD XHTML 1.0 Strict//EN"
"http://www.w3.org/TR/xhtml1/DTD/xhtml1-strict.dtd">
<html>
    <head>
        <title>
            JT's Island Grill and Gallery - Chokoloskee, Florida
        </title>
        <link rel='stylesheet'
              type='text/css'
              href='style_sheets/base_styles.css'
              media='screen'/>
        <link rel='stylesheet'
              type='text/css'
              href='style_sheets/menu_system.css'
              media='screen'/>
        <link rel='stylesheet'
              type='text/css'
              href='style_sheets/dinner_menu.css'
              media='screen'/>
    </head>
```

2.   Save dinner_menu.html. Open the page in Mozilla, Firefox, or Netscape. You can see that there is no visible change from the output you saw in Figure 9-22.

How It Works

The inclusion of the `media='screen'` attribute limits the styles of the `base_styles.css`, `menu_system.css`, and `dinner_menu.css` style sheets so that they are only applied to normal home computers for content displayed on-screen. If you click the Print Preview feature of Mozilla, you can see that no styles are applied to the document, which demonstrates how the `screen` value limits the styling of elements for display on a computer screen only.

In Chapter 15, I present examples of how you can use the `media` attribute to provide alternative style sheets for handheld devices and print. This really demonstrates the power of separating content by media with CSS.

The next section begins a discussion of the CSS box model and how this formulation of properties governs the basic principles of CSS design.

The CSS Box Model

The next topic on the agenda is the CSS box model, discussed briefly in Chapter 2 and depicted in Figure 10-1. The CSS box model is how the browser measures things such as width, padding, borders, and margins within a box, and it is quite possibly the most important component of CSS-based designs. Figure 10-1 shows a detailed diagram of the CSS box model.

At the bottom of the diagram, the Internet Explorer width is noted. If you recall from Chapter 2, I made note of some differences in the Internet Explorer quirks mode rendering of the box model as opposed to the Internet Explorer standards mode interpretation of the box model. This diagram reflects how Internet Explorer quirks mode interprets the box model from outside border edge to outside border edge.

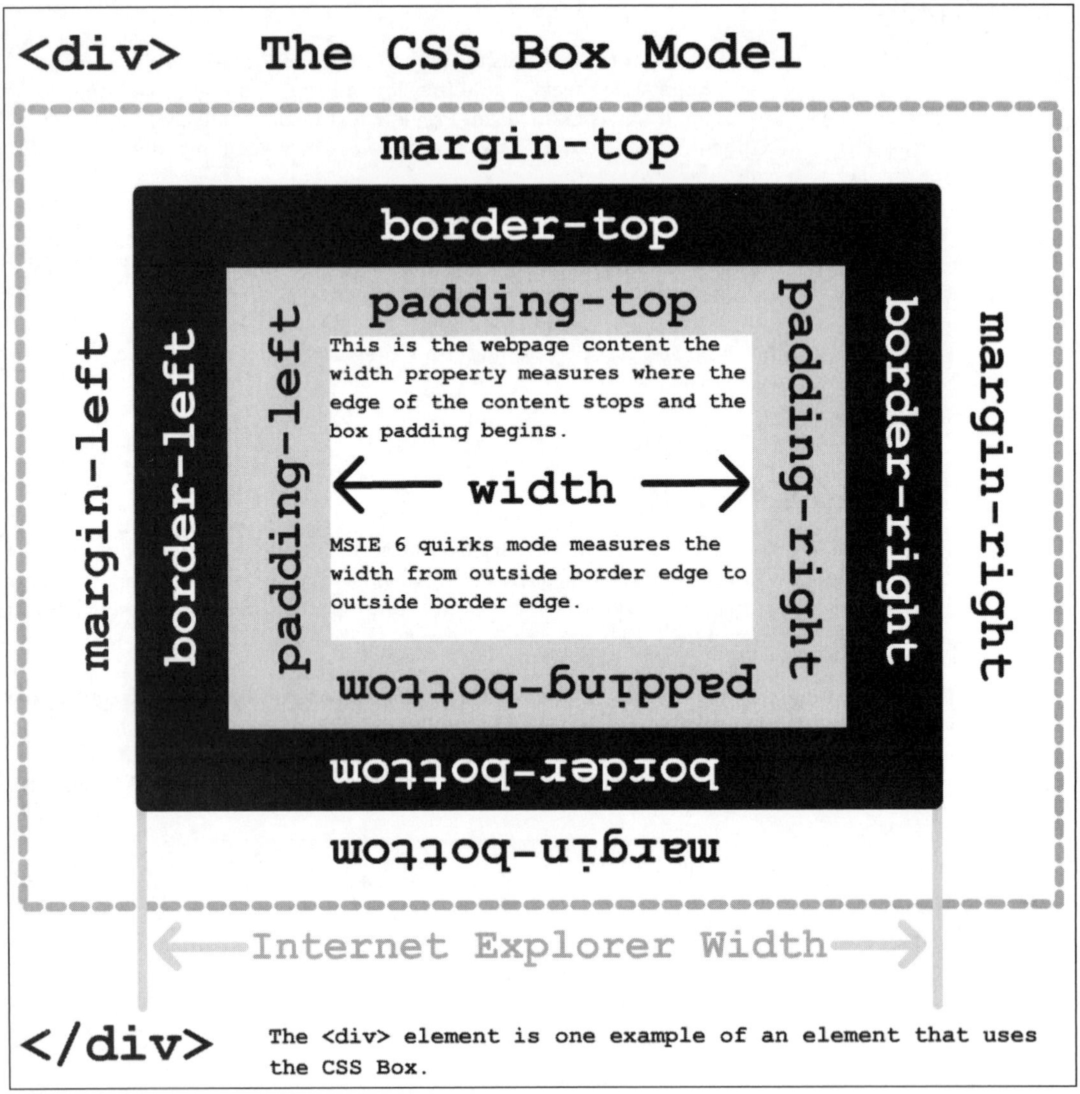
<div> The CSS Box Model
margin-top
border-top
padding-top
margin-left
border-left
padding-left
This is the webpage content the width property measures where the edge of the content stops and the box padding begins.
width
MSIE 6 quirks mode measures the width from outside border edge to outside border edge.
padding-right
border-right
margin-right
padding-bottom
border-bottom
margin-bottom
Internet Explorer Width
</div>
The <div> element is one example of an element that uses the CSS Box.

Figure 10-1

As a refresher from previous chapters, the following example provides a brief overview of box model properties and how they play into designing a website's layout:

```
p#paragraph-1 {
    padding: 10px;
    width: 200px;
    border: 1px solid black;
    margin: 10px;
    background: gray;
}
p#paragraph-2 {
    padding: 20px;
    width: 180px;
    border: 1px solid black;
    margin: 10px;
    background: lightgrey;
}
```

Combine this with the following markup:

```
<p id='paragraph-1'>
    This paragraph has a 200 pixel width and 10 pixels of padding.
</p>
<p id='paragraph-2'>
    This paragraph has a 180-pixel width and 20 pixels of padding, and yet the
    backgrounds of both paragraphs are lined up together.
</p>
```

Figure 10-2 demonstrates that these two <p> elements result in the perfect alignment of backgrounds when displayed in the browser window.

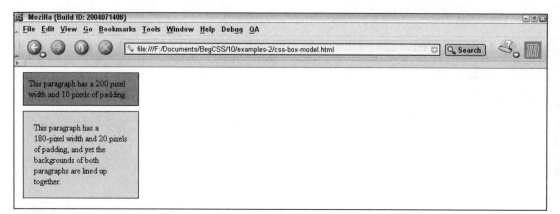

Figure 10-2

In CSS, the background appears from inside border edge to inside border edge. Width is measured from inside padding edge to inside padding edge. In order to achieve backgrounds that line up, you must add the width, the left padding, and the right padding together to get the background width. In the first <div>, this figure comes out to 220 pixels total; in the second <div>, this also comes out to 220 pixels total. Margins, on the other hand, do not include the background; rather, they are an invisible edge around the outside of the container. The border, margin, padding and width properties are examples of box model properties. The following sections discuss each of these properties, in addition to other properties closely related to the box model.

Borders

Borders appear between the margin and padding in the box model depicted in Figure 10-1. I begin discussion of the CSS box model with borders because the effects of the other box model properties become more obvious after applying borders. It's obvious that borders put lines around boxes. The following sections examine each individual border property.

border-width

Documented in CSS 2.1 and supported in IE 5.5 , IE 6, Mozilla 1.7, Opera 7.5, and Safari 1.2.

The `border-width` properties all control the width of a box border in some fashion. The following table outlines each `border-width` property.

Property	Value
border-top-width border-right-width border-bottom-width border-left-width	<border-width> | inherit Initial value: medium
border-width A <border-width> value refers to one of the following: thin | medium | thick | <length>	<border-width> {1,4} | inherit Initial value: medium

The individual `border-top-width`, `border-right-width`, `border-bottom-width`, and `border-left-width` properties exist for setting the width of the individual sides of a box.

Each of these properties can be combined into the single `border-width` shorthand property.

Borders aren't allowed to have percentage values; however, they are capable of accepting any length measurement supported by CSS (em, pixel, centimeter, and so on). In addition to length units, the border width may also be specified using one of three keywords: `thin`, `medium`, and `thick`. Figure 10-3 shows the rendered output of these three keywords.

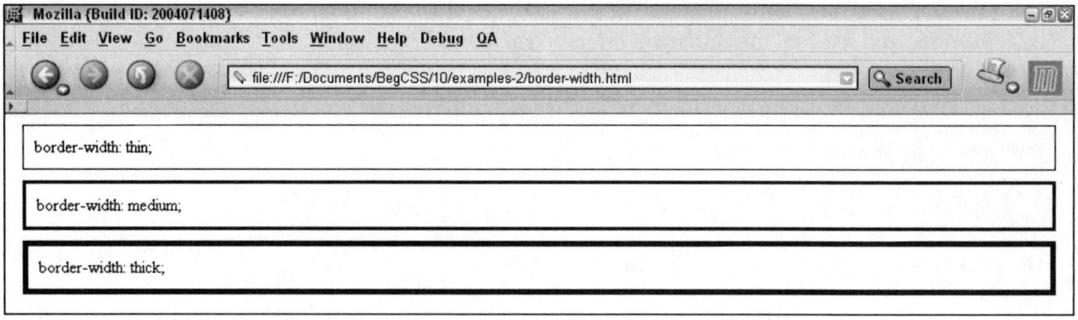

Figure 10-3

Like the `font` property discussed in Chapter 9, the `border-width` property is a combination of the individual `border-width` properties. The `border-width` shorthand property can be written in one of four ways. It can include from one to four values, which is what is meant by the {1,4} notation in the table describing its possible syntax. First, it can be written by including a value for all four sides of the box. The notation looks like this:

```
border-width: <border-top-width> <border-right-width> <border-bottom-width>
<border-left-width>;
```

In real usage, an example declaration looks like this:

```
border-width: 1px 4px 2px 3px;
```

Each value sets a border width for each side of the box; the 1px measurement refers to the top border, the 4px measurement refers to the right border, the 2px measurement refers to the bottom border, and the 3px measurement refers to the left border. This shorthand is the same thing as writing the following:

```
border-top-width: 1px;
border-right-width: 4px;
border-bottom-width: 2px;
border-left-width: 3px;
```

The next example of the `border-width` shorthand includes of three values:

```
border-width: <border-top-width> <border-right-width/border-left-width> <border-
bottom-width>;
```

In real usage, an example declaration looks like this:

```
border-width: 2em 5em 3em;
```

This time, the 2em measurement refers to the top border, the 5em measurement refers to the left and right borders, and the 3em measurement refers to the bottom border. This is the same thing as writing the following:

```
border-top-width: 2em;
border-right-width: 5em;
border-bottom-width: 3em;
border-left-width: 5em;
```

The next version of the `border-width` property includes only two values:

```
border-width: <border-top-width/border-bottom-width> <border-right-width/border-
left-width>;
```

An example declaration looks like the following:

```
border-width: 5px 2px;
```

In this example, the 5px measurement refers to the top and bottom borders of the box, and the 2px measurement refers to the left and right borders of the box. This is the same thing as writing the following:

```
border-top-width: 5px;
border-right-width: 2px;
border-bottom-width: 5px;
border-left-width: 2px;
```

Finally, the last possibility is to write the property with only one value specified:

```
border-width: <border-top-width/border-right-width/border-bottom-width/border-left-
width>;
```

An example looks like this:

```
border-width: 5px;
```

This example sets the border width for all four sides of the box at once. The next section continues the discussion of borders with the `border-style` property.

border-style

Documented in CSS 2.1 and supported in IE 5.5, IE 6, Mozilla 1.7, Opera 7.5, and Safari 1.2.

You use the `border-style` property to specify the style of border to be used. The `border-style` property is very similar to the `border-width` property presented in the previous section in that it uses an identical syntax to specify the style of border to be used for each side of the box. The following table outlines the `border-style` family of properties.

Property	Value
border-style A <border-style> value refers to one of the following: none | hidden | dotted | dashed | solid | double | groove | ridge | inset | outset	<border-style> {1,4} | inherit Initial value: none
border-top-style border-right-style border-bottom-style border-left-style	<border-style> Initial value: none

Like the `border-width` property, the `border-style` property is also a shorthand property, which combines the individual `border-top-style`, `border-right-style`, `border-bottom-style`, and `border-left style` properties into the single `border-style` property. Figure 10-4 shows the rendered representation of each of the `border-style` keywords.

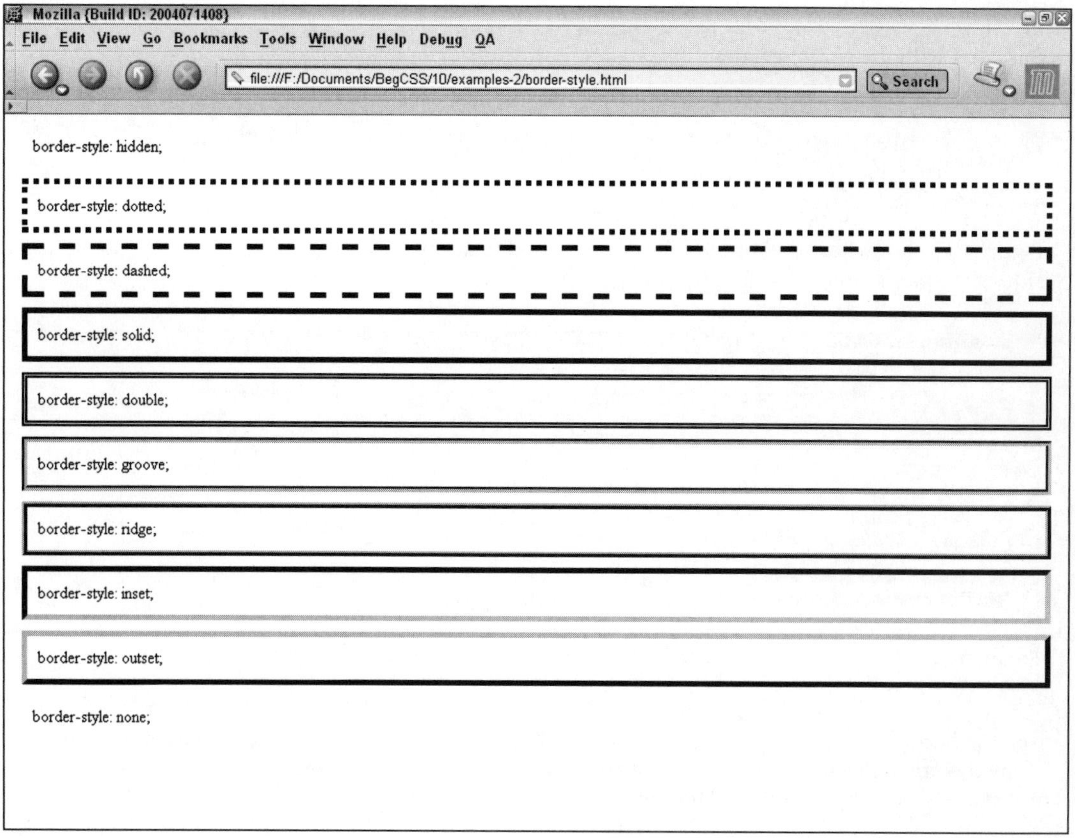

Figure 10-4

Like the `border-width` property, the `border-style` property can accept up to four values to specify the style for each side of the box. The concept presented for the `border-width` property is the same for most of the box model shorthand properties. Its syntax follows an easy-to-memorize schema for setting a value for each side of the box. To reiterate the concept, here is a more generalized run down of how box model shorthand properties work.

To specify all four values, use the following syntax:

```
theoretical-shorthand-property: <top-value> <right-value> <bottom-value> <left-value>;
```

An example of this syntax in action is demonstrated by the following rule:

```
p {
    margin: 20px;
    padding: 20px;
    width: 200px;
    border-width: thin medium 30px thick;
    border-style: solid dashed double dotted;
}
```

It is used with this markup:

```
<p>
    I hear and I forget. I see and I remember. I do and I understand.
        - Confucius
</p>
```

Figure 10-5 shows how the four-value syntax is used to apply a different border style and width to each side of the paragraph.

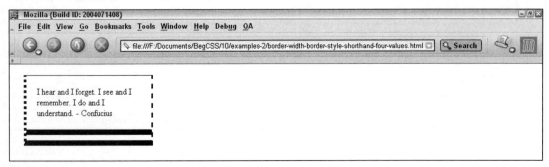

Figure 10-5

The top border is given a thin width and a solid style. The right border is given a medium width and a dashed border. The bottom border is given a 30-pixel width and a double border, and the left border is given a thick width and a dotted border.

To specify three values, the syntax is the following:

```
theoretical-shorthand-property: <top-value> <right-value/left-value> <bottom-value>;
```

An example of this syntax in action is demonstrated by the following rule:

```
p {
    margin: 20px;
    padding: 20px;
    width: 200px;
    border-width: thin medium thick;
    border-style: solid dashed dotted;
}
```

It is combined with this markup:

```
<p>
    A lie can travel halfway around the world while the truth is putting on
    its shoes.
        - Mark Twain
</p>
```

Figure 10-6 demonstrates how the three-value syntax is used to apply the border width and style.

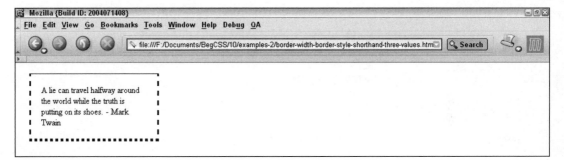

Figure 10-6

The top border is given a thin width and a solid border. The left and right borders are given a medium width and a dashed style, and the bottom border is given a thick width and a dotted style.

To specify two values, use the following syntax:

```
theoretical-shorthand-property: <top-value/bottom-value> <right-value/left-value>;
```

This syntax is demonstrated by the following rule:

```
p {
    margin: 20px;
    padding: 20px;
    width: 200px;
```

```
    border-width: thin thick;
    border-style: solid dotted;
}
```

It is applied to the following markup:

```
<p>
    I never forget a face, but in your case I'll be glad to make an exception.
        - Groucho Marx
</p>
```

Figure 10-7 shows how the two-value shorthand syntax behaves when applied to markup.

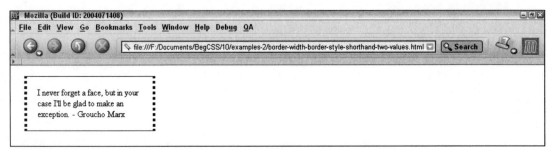

Figure 10-7

In this example, the top and bottom borders are given a thin width and a solid style, and the left and right borders are given a thick width and a dotted border style.

To specify only one value, use the following syntax:

```
theoretical-shorthand-property: <top-value/right-value/bottom-value/left-value>;
```

The syntax for the last example of box model shorthand properties is demonstrated by the following rule:

```
p {
    margin: 20px;
    padding: 20px;
    width: 200px;
    border-width: thick;
    border-style: dotted;
}
```

It is applied to this markup:

```
<p>
    Only two things are infinite, the universe and human stupidity, and I'm not
    sure about the former.
        - Albert Einstein
</p>
```

Figure 10-8 shows that the thick width and dotted border style are applied to all four sides of the box.

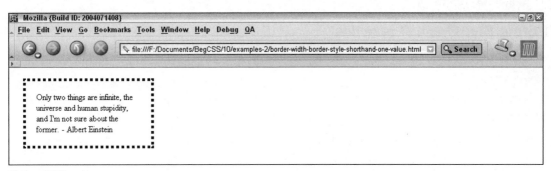

Only two things are infinite, the universe and human stupidity, and I'm not sure about the former. - Albert Einstein

Figure 10-8

The next section continues the discussion of borders with the `border-color` properties.

border-color

Documented in CSS 2.1 and supported in IE 5.5, IE 6, Mozilla 1.7, Opera 7.5, and Safari 1.2.

The `border-color` property is another shorthand property. Like the `border-style` and `border-width` properties, you can use `border-color` to control how a border is styled. The `border-color` property, as you may have guessed, specifies the border color for each side of the box. The following table outlines the `border-color` family of properties.

Property	Value
border-color	<color> {1,4} | transparent | inherit Initial value: the value of the 'color' property.
border-top-color border-right-color border-bottom-color border-left-color	<color> | transparent | inherit Initial value: the value of the 'color' property.

Internet Explorer does not support the `transparent` *keyword.*

Like `border-style` and `border-width`, this property can accept up to four values. This property accepts a <color> value, meaning that it can accept a color keyword, a hexadecimal value, short hexadecimal value, or an RGB value; any color value accepted by the `color` property is also acceptable to the `border-color` properties.

As you saw in Figures 10-5, 10-6, 10-7, and 10-8, specifying the `border-width` and `border-style` properties on their own—without specifying the `border-color` property—demonstrates that when a `border-color` is not specified, the border color is the same color as specified for the `color` property. In those figures, no `color` property was provided, so the border color was the same as the browser's default color for text.

With an overview of what is possible with borders, the upcoming sections discuss the border shorthand properties.

Border Shorthand Properties

Documented in CSS 2.1 and supported in IE 5.5, IE 6, Mozilla 1.7, Opera 7.5, and Safari 1.2.

The `border-top`, `border-right`, `border-bottom`, and `border-left` properties combine the `border-width`, `border-style`, and `border-color` properties into single properties for each side of the box. The following table outlines the possible values for these four properties.

Property	Value
border-top border-right border-bottom border-left	[<border-width> || <border-style> || <color>] | inherit

The notation for the `border-top`, `border-right`, `border-bottom`, and `border-left` properties indicates that one to three values are possible; each value refers to a `border-width` value, a `border-style` value and a `border-color` value. The syntax for all three values is as follows:

```
border-top: <border-width> <border-style> <color>;
```

The preceding snippet translates into this declaration:

```
p {
    border-top: 1px solid black;
}
```

It is applied to this markup:

```
<p>
    The top border of this paragraph has is 1 pixel width, solid and black.
</p>
```

Figure 10-9 shows that this code results in a 1-pixel-wide, solid, black border across the top of the <p> element.

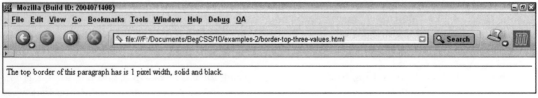

Figure 10-9

The preceding shorthand is equivalent to this:

```
p {
    border-top-width: 1px;
    border-top-style: solid;
    border-top-color: black;
}
```

The shorthand properties condense all that code into one property. Like the individual `border-color`, `border-style`, and `border-color` properties discussed in previous sections, more than one type of syntax is possible. This example provides only the `border-width` and `border-style`.

```
border-top: <border-width> <border-style>;
```

As you saw in Figures 10-5, 10-6, 10-7, and 10-8, in this syntax the border color becomes the same as that defined for the color property. In this case, no color is defined, so the border color becomes the same color as the default color for text in the browser. The following rule demonstrates the `border-top` property with two values:

```
p {
    border-top: thin solid;
}
```

It is applied to this markup:

```
<p>
    The top border of this paragraph is the same color as the text color.
</p>
```

Figure 10-10 shows that the border receives the same color as the color defined for the text; in this case, it's the browser's default color for text, which is black.

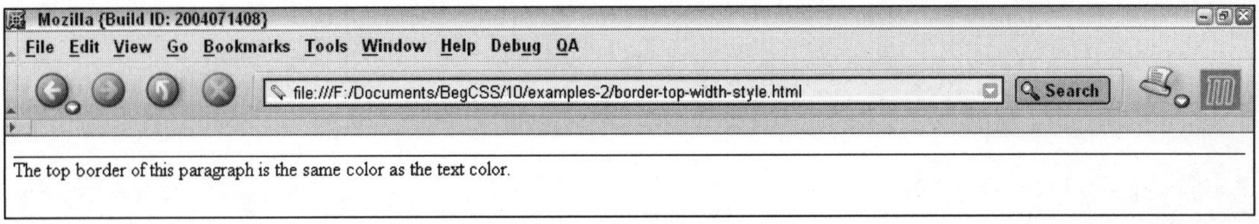

Figure 10-10

The `border-top: thin solid;` declaration is the same thing as saying the following:

```
p {
    border-top: thin solid black;
}
```

The `border-top` declaration inherits the value of the color property. Here's another variation of the syntax:

```
border-top: <border-style> <border-color>;
```

The initial value of the `border-width` properties is `medium`. In this usage, `medium` is assumed and the value of the `border-width` property, the style, and the color are applied accordingly.

```
p {
    border-top: solid black;
}
```

They are applied to this markup:

```
<p>
    The top border of this paragraph is of medium thickness.
</p>
```

Figure 10-11 demonstrates that this code results in a black border of medium thickness.

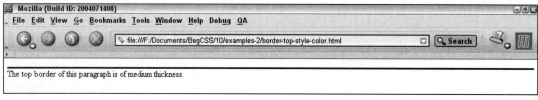

Figure 10-11

These omissions of style do not work for the `<border-style>` value. Its initial value is `none`, so when you omit the style value, no border appears, although it is technically possible to specify only a single value in this way. The final possibility is a single value because the initial value of the `border-style` property is none; single value syntax applies a visible border only when the `border-style` is specified. This can be demonstrated with the following rule:

```
p {
    border-top: solid;
}
```

It is applied to this markup:

```
<p>
    The top border of this paragraph has a medium width and the color specified for
    text.
</p>
```

Figure 10-12 demonstrates how the initial value of the `border-width` property is applied when no `border-width` is specified and how the color of the border is the color specified for the text of the paragraph when no other color is specified.

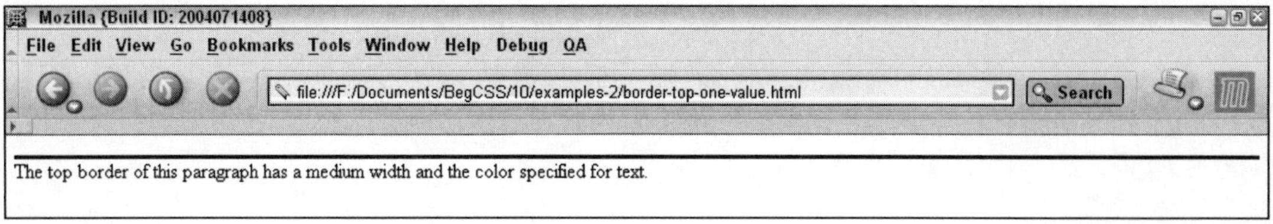

Figure 10-12

Because the initial value of the `border-style` property is none, specifying a single value by using the `border-top`, `border-right`, `border-bottom`, and `border-left` properties is best done by specifying a `border-style`.

The `border-top`, `border-right`, `border-bottom`, and `border-left` properties combine the values of the `border-width`, `border-style`, and `border-color` properties into a single property. The next section continues the discussion of borders with the `border` shorthand property.

border

Documented in CSS 2.1 and supported in IE 5.5, IE 6, Mozilla 1.7, Opera 7.5, and Safari 1.2.

The `border` property combines all four border properties (`border-top`, `border-right`, `border-bottom`, `border-left`) and all three style properties (`border-width`, `border-style`, `border-color`) into a single property. The following table outlines the border shorthand property.

Property	Value
border	[<border-width> || <border-style> || <color>] | inherit

The syntax used for the `border` property is identical to the syntax used for the `border-top`, `border-right`, `border-bottom` and `border-left` properties. The only difference is that the `border` property sets the `border-width`, `border-style`, and `border-color` values for all four sides of the box at once.

```
border: <border-width> <border-style> <color>;
```

The `border` property sets each side in one fell swoop. This is demonstrated by the following example:

```
p {
    border: 1px solid black;
}
```

It is used with this markup:

```
<p>
    This paragraph has a 1 pixel thick, solid black border around it.
</p>
```

Figure 10-13 shows the paragraph has a 1px, solid, black border around it on all four sides.

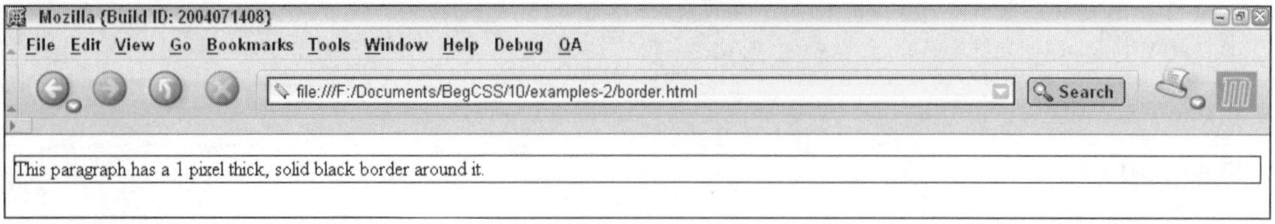

Figure 10-13

This one property replaces four separate properties, as shown in this example.

```
p {
    border-top: 1px solid black;
    border-right: 1px solid black;
    border-bottom: 1px solid black;
    border-left: 1px solid black;
}
```

This rule provides output identical to that depicted in Figure 10-13. The next section touches briefly on what's in store in CSS 3.

CSS 3 Border Properties

The CSS 3 set of border properties has been expanded to include even more flexibility in border styling. At the time of this writing, the CSS 3 border module has not yet reached candidate recommendation status, meaning that the W3C CSS working group can still make modifications to the properties proposed for inclusion in CSS 3. Rather than discuss each of these potential additions to CSS 3 in detail, this section simply summarizes what's proposed for inclusion.

First are the `border-radius` properties. Almost identical to the proprietary `-moz-border-radius` property used in previous examples in Chapter 5, this property rounds box edges. These properties include the following:

❑   `border-top-right-radius`

❑   `border-bottom-right-radius`

❑   `border-bottom-left-radius`

❑   `border-top-left-radius`

❑   `border-radius` (shorthand for the individual properties)

The `border-radius` properties answer a need for CSS designs to break out of the square box designs, which are often prevalent in CSS design. These differ from the `-moz-border-radius` properties you saw in Chapter 5, but only slightly. The Mozilla properties refer to each corner as `-moz-border-radius-topright`, `-moz-border-radius-bottomright`, and so on.

Next are the `border-image` properties, which are a collection of properties used to set an image for each side and corner of a box, which allows completely customizable borders. The `border-image` properties have no proprietary counterpart and have not yet been implemented in a browser, so no further elaboration is necessary.

The following Try It Out walks you through the steps for applying a border.

Try It Out   Applying Borders

Example 10-2. Follow these steps to see how borders play into the JT's website.

1.   Apply the following changes to the base_styles.css file:

```css
body {
    font-family: "Courier New", Courier, monospace;
    text-transform: lowercase;
}
a {
    text-decoration: none;
}
a:hover {
    text-decoration: underline;
}
h1, h6 {
    border-left: 0.05em solid black;
    border-right: 0.05em solid black;
}
h1 {
    border-top: 0.05em solid black;
    -moz-border-radius-topleft: 0.8em;
    -moz-border-radius-topright: 0.8em;
    font-family: "Monotype Corsiva", cursive;
    letter-spacing: 4px;
    font-size: 1.5em;
}
h2 {
    border-bottom: 0.05em dotted black;
}
h3 {
    border-bottom: 1px dotted black;
    font-size: 0.9em;
}
h6 {
    -moz-border-radius-bottomleft: 0.8em;
    -moz-border-radius-bottomright: 0.8em;
    border-bottom: 0.05em solid black;
    font-size: 0.8em;
    text-align: center;
}
div#content {
    border: 0.05em solid black;
    font-size: 0.9em;
    word-spacing: 5px;
```

```
        letter-spacing: 1px;
}
p.copy {
        border-bottom: 0.05em dotted black;
        font-size: 1.2em;
        font-family: "Times New Roman", Times, serif;
        text-indent: 20px;
        text-align: justify;
}
img {
        border: 0.05em solid black;
}
```

2. Save base_styles.css

3. Make the following modifications to the menu_system.css file:

```
div#nav {
        text-align: center;
}
div#nav > ul > li {
        border: 0.05em solid black;
        font-size: 0.9em;
}
div#nav > ul > li#leftedge {
        border-right-width: 0;
        -moz-border-radius-topleft: 1em;
        -moz-border-radius-bottomleft: 1em;
}
div#nav > ul > li#leftedge:hover {
        -moz-border-radius-bottomleft: 0;
}
div#nav > ul > li#rightedge {
        border-left-width: 0;
        -moz-border-radius-topright: 1em;
        -moz-border-radius-bottomright: 1em;
}
div#nav > ul > li#rightedge:hover {
        -moz-border-radius-bottomright: 0;
}
ul.menu {
        -moz-border-radius-bottomleft: 1em;
        -moz-border-radius-bottomright: 1em;
        border: 0.05em solid black;
}
ul#food ul.menu {
        -moz-border-radius-topleft: 1em;
}
ul#gifts ul.menu {
        -moz-border-radius-topright: 1em;
}
ul.menu a {
        color: black;
        display: block;
```

```
    border: 0.05em solid lightblue;
}
ul.menu a:hover {
    -moz-border-radius: 0.8em;
    border: 0.05em solid black;
    text-decoration: none;
}
```

4. Save the menu_system.css file.

5. Make the following modifications to the dinner_menu.css file:

```
div#content * {
    font-family: "Times New Roman", Times, serif;
}
div#content h3 {
    border-bottom: none;
    font-family: "Monotype Corsiva", cursive;
    text-decoration: underline;
    font-size: 2em;
}
h3 + p.menucaption {
    font-style: italic;
```

6. Save the dinner_menu.css file.

7. Make the following modification to the dinner_menu.html file:

```
<body>
    <div id='nav'>
        <ul id='gifts'>
            <li id='leftedge'>
                Unique Gifts
```

8. Make the following medication to the dinner_menu.html file:

```
        <a href='index.html'>
            <img src='images/photos/jts_sign.jpg'
                alt='JTs sign'
                title='Go home.'/>
        </a>
        <ul id='food'>
            <li>
                Employment
                <ul class='menu'>
                    <li><a href=''>Contact JT's</a></li>
                    <li><a href=''>Seasonal Employment
                                Opportunities</a></li>
                </ul>
            </li>
            <li id='rightedge'>
                Delicious Food
                <ul class='menu'>
```

9. Save dinner_menu.html and open dinner_menu.html in Mozilla, Firefox, or Netscape. You should see output like that shown in Figure 10-14.

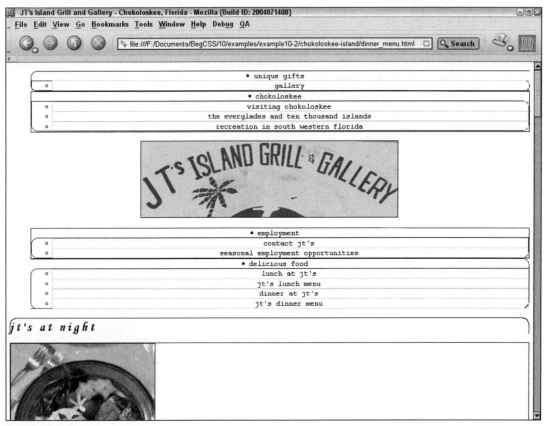

Figure 10-14

How It Works

This example defines borders for the JT's dinner menu. From a design standpoint, the addition of borders makes the effects of applying width, margins, and padding (which I introduce in upcoming sections) easier to see. The styles applied in base_styles.css, as I have said in previous examples, outline the basic look and feel that I want to be applied to the entire website. In this style sheet I apply borders to the `<h1>` and `<h6>` elements and the content `<div>` element that contains the copy for each page. I also choose to use the proprietary `-moz-border-radius` property to round the edges of the corners of the `<h1>` and `<h6>` elements. This property, although not standard, provides some insight into what the CSS 3 border-radius property will be used for, if it becomes a part of the final CSS 3 standard. Here is an explanation of the theory behind these additions to the base_styles.css style sheet. The first rule applies a left and right border to the `<h1>` and `<h6>` headings.

```
h1, h6 {
    border-left: 0.05em solid black;
```

```
        border-right: 0.05em solid black;
}
```

In the final design, I want the bottom of the <h1> element to be completely flush with the top of the content <div>, and the top of the <h6> element to be flush with the bottom of the content <div>. This effect becomes more obvious when I apply padding and margins to the design. Essentially, if I specify a border for all sides of the <h1> and <h6> element, I create a double border when I style the <h1> and <h6> elements to be flush with the content <div>. The next rule follows along with this logic.

```
h1 {
        border-top: 0.05em solid black;
        -moz-border-radius-topleft: 0.8em;
        -moz-border-radius-topright: 0.8em;
        font-family: "Monotype Corsiva", cursive;
        letter-spacing: 4px;
        font-size: 1.5em;
}
```

Because I want to give the illusion that the <h1>, content <div>, and <h6> elements are seamless, to appear to be a single element, this rule specifies a top border for the <h1> element and rounds the top-left and top-right corners with the -moz-border-radius property. The next rules apply to my plan for the other pages of JT's website; <h2> and <h3> are simply intended to contain headings for subtopics.

```
h2 {
        border-bottom: 0.05em dotted black;
}
h3 {
        border-bottom: 0.05em dotted black;
        font-size: 0.9em;
}
```

The <h3> element is also used in the dinner menu, but it has a different meaning for the dinner menu than it does for the rest of the site. The rule applied for the dinner menu cancels the effect of <h3> element.

```
div#content h3 {
        border-bottom: none;
        font-family: "Monotype Corsiva", cursive;
        text-decoration: underline;
        font-size: 2em;
}
```

Because the dinner menu has a style that is different from other pages of the site (where the <h3> element is used), the border applied in base_styles.css is canceled out via the cascade with border-bottom: none; in the dinner_menu.css file. The next modification to the base_menu.css file applies styles to the <h6> element.

```
h6 {
        -moz-border-radius-bottomleft: 0.8em;
        -moz-border-radius-bottomright: 0.8em;
        border-bottom: 0.05em solid black;
```

```
        font-size: 0.8em;
        text-align: center;
    }
```

This follows the same logic that I used for the `<h1>` element: A bottom border is specified and the bottom-left and bottom-right corners are rounded with the `-moz-border-radius` property. Continuing the logic of designing the `<h1>` content `<div>` and `<h6>` elements borders relate to each other, the next rule specifies a border for the content `<div>`.

```
    div#content {
        border: 0.05em solid black;
        font-size: 0.9em;
            word-spacing: 5px;
```

The next rule places a thin, dotted border on the bottom of all paragraphs with a copy class name:

```
    p.copy {
        border-bottom: 0.05em dotted black;
        font-size: 1.2em;
        font-family: "Times New Roman", Times, serif;
```

This style provides a simple effect that places a dotted border under paragraphs designated as copy. The last rule added to the base_styles.css style sheet is a border around all images.

```
    img {
        border: 0.05em solid black;
    }
```

The next group of changes appears in the menu_system.css file. The changes made here are intended to achieve the following goals: to make the *unique gifts* and *chokoloskee* headings eventually appear to the left of the JT's logo; to make the *employment* and *delicious food* headings appear to the right of the JT's logo; to turn the list of links under each heading into drop-down menus. The border styles applied to the menu_system.css file also foster these goals. The first addition applies a thin border around each `<li>` element that appears in the top-level menu. This is done with the following rule:

```
    div#nav > ul > li {
        border: 0.05em solid black;
        font-size: 0.9em;
    }
```

I select the `<li>` element using the direct child selector. As you saw in Chapter 5, this selector chooses an element based on its immediate descendant. The selector says: If the `<ul>` element is a child of a `<div>` with an id of nav and `<li>` is a child of the `<ul>` element, apply these declarations to the `<li>` element. I also decide that I want a slightly smaller font for the `<li>` elements containing the navigational headings, so I also apply a `font-size` declaration. The effects of adding this border are difficult to see, but become more obvious as other box model properties are applied. The next rule applies styles to the `<li>` element containing the *unique gifts* heading.

```
    div#nav > ul > li#leftedge {
        border-right-width: 0;
        -moz-border-radius-topleft: 1em;
        -moz-border-radius-bottomleft: 1em;
    }
```

The goal of this rule is similar to the technique I used for the <h1>, content <div>, and <h6> elements. For the menu system, the layout plan is for the *unique gifts* and *chokoloskee* headings to appear side by side to the left of the JT's logo and the *employment* and *delicious food* headings to appear side by side at the right of the JT's logo. Because I intend the two headings on the left and on the right side of the logo to appear side by side, I have the problem of double borders. To correct this, I specify a zero width border on the <li> element that will eventually be the left-most heading. This leaves a single border separating the *unique gifts* and *chokoloskee* headings. I also round the top-left and bottom-left corners of the *unique gifts* <li> element. The next rule provides an effect using the :hover pseudo-class:

```
div#nav > ul > li#leftedge:hover {
    -moz-border-radius-bottomleft: 0;
}
```

This effect plays directly into my plan to make the navigation into drop-down menus. This becomes more obvious in Chapter 14. The next rule applies similar effects to the heading that will eventually become the right-most heading that I applied to the *unique gifts* heading (that will eventually become the left-most heading):

```
div#nav > ul > li#rightedge {
    border-left-width: 0;
    -moz-border-radius-topright: 1em;
    -moz-border-radius-bottomright: 1em;
}
```

Again, the concept is that the *employment* and *delicious food* headings will be side by side on the right side of the logo. This rule prevents a double border from appearing between the *employment* and *delicious food* headings with the border-left-width: 0; declaration. The top-right and bottom-right corners of the *delicious food* <li> element are rounded with the -moz-border-radius property. Like the :hover effect applied to the left-most *unique gifts* heading, the effects of the next rule become more obvious in Chapter 14:

```
div#nav > ul > li#rightedge:hover {
    -moz-border-radius-bottomright: 0;
}
```

The next rule styles what will eventually become the drop-down menus. These are identified by a menu class name:

```
ul.menu {
    -moz-border-radius-bottomleft: 1em;
    -moz-border-radius-bottomright: 1em;
    border: 0.05em solid black;
}
```

The styles applied in this rule put a thin, solid, black border around each of the nested <ul> elements, designated as submenus. Here again, I round the border corners with the -moz-border-radius property. In this rule, I only apply the -moz-border-radius property to the bottom-left and bottom-right corners. I want the rounded corners to be different depending on which side of the logo they appear. The next two rules help reach this goal:

```
ul#food ul.menu {
    -moz-border-radius-topleft: 1em;
}
ul#gifts ul.menu {
    -moz-border-radius-topright: 1em;
}
```

With the first rule, the top-left corner of the nested `<ul>` menus that appear in the `<ul>` with an id name of `food` are given a rounded top-left corner. The following rule rounds the top right corner of `<ul>` menus that appear in the `<ul>` element with a `gifts` id name. This is another effect that becomes more obvious in Chapter 14. The final two rules apply styles to the links in the submenus:

```
ul.menu a {
    color: black;
    display: block;
    border: 0.05em solid lightblue;
}
ul.menu a:hover {
    -moz-border-radius: 0.8em;
    border: 0.05em solid black;
    text-decoration: none;
}
```

These two rules apply styles to the links of the menus. The first declaration ensures that links in the navigational menus stay black in color, even if I decide to change the color of links that appear elsewhere in the document. The next declaration `display: block` is a special declaration that makes the `<a>` element behave like a `<div>` element. I go into more detail about the display property in Chapter 17. The purpose of including it here is to make the entire `<li>` element clickable as a link, instead of only the link text. The next declaration specifies a light blue border around each link in the menu. The light blue was chosen because the background color for each menu will eventually be made light blue, whereas this border will be invisible, but it will still take up 0.05em of space. I could have also specified the declaration with the `transparent` keyword, but Internet Explorer does not support it. The reason why the 0.05em of space is preserved is observable in the next rule, which applies a `:hover` effect to each navigation link. This rule rounds the edges of each border and makes the border black. If I were to remove the `border: 0.05em solid lightblue;` declaration, you would observe that the whole menu flickers when the mouse cursor hovers over each link applying the `border: 0.05em solid black;` declaration.

If you recall the final design of the JT's website from Chapter 7, the goal of these styles should be obvious. After the borders are applied, the effects of the other box model properties also become more obvious. The next section continues the discussion of box model properties with the dimension properties.

Calculating Dimensions

CSS 1 introduces the width and height properties as part of the CSS box model. CSS 2 expands on those properties providing minimum and maximum dimensions when variable lengths are involved, as is the case with percentage width and height values. A liquid design provides lots of opportunities to take advantage of the full set of box model controls.

The following sections examine each of CSS's dimension properties individually.

width

Documented in CSS 2.1 and supported since IE 5.5, IE 6, Mozilla 1.7, Opera 7.5, and Safari 1.2.

The `width` property is a pretty simple property; it sets the width of an element. According the CSS box model diagram presented in Figure 10-1, width is the space measured from inside padding edge to inside padding edge. The following table outlines the `width` property and its possible values.

Property	Value
width	\<length\> | \<percentage\> | auto | inherit Initial value: auto

The width property accepts a length unit, which is indicated in the preceding table with the \<length\> notation. The following is a simple example of the `width` property using a length unit:

```
p {
    border: thin solid black;
    text-align: justify;
    width: 150px;
}
```

It is used in this markup:

```
<p>
    Peter Piper picked a peck of pickled peppers.
    Did Peter Piper pick a peck of pickled peppers?
    If Peter Piper picked a peck of pickled peppers,
    where's the peck of pickled peppers Peter Piper picked?
</p>
```

Figure 10-15 shows the \<p\> element is 100 pixels wide and the height of the box adjusts automatically to accommodate the text inside.

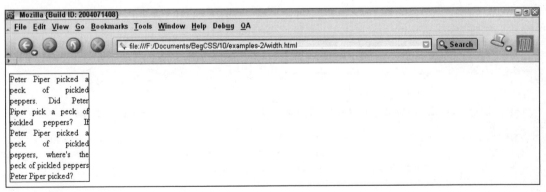

Figure 10-15

I applied a thin, solid, black border to highlight the width of the <p> element. In this example, the text is flush with the border. This is further highlighted by the use of the `text-align: justify` declaration. Therefore, the width can be thought of as the portion of the element that contains the actual copy, text, or images.

The next property is the `height` property, and it behaves identically to the width property. The difference is, of course, that it measures the vertical content space.

height

Documented in CSS 2.1 and supported in IE 5.5, IE 6, Mozilla 1.7, Opera 7.5, and Safari 1.2.

Like the `width` property, the `height` property sets the amount of space between the top-inside padding edge and the bottom-inside padding edge. The following table outlines the `height` property and its possible values.

Property	Value
height	<length> | <percentage> | auto | inherit Initial value: auto

The `height` property causes an element to behave somewhat differently than its HTML height attribute counterpart in standards-compliant browsers. When you explicitly specify a height, the height remains the same regardless of how much text you place inside the element. Consider the following example:

```
p {
    border: thin solid black;
    text-align: justify;
    width: 150px;
    height: 150px;
}
```

Combine it again with tongue-twisting markup:

```
<p>
    Peter Piper picked a peck of pickled peppers.
    Did Peter Piper pick a peck of pickled peppers?
    If Peter Piper picked a peck of pickled peppers,
    where's the peck of pickled peppers Peter Piper picked?
</p>
```

Figure 10-16 demonstrates that in Mozilla, the specified height causes the text to spill over the element's bottom border because there is more text than the height allows.

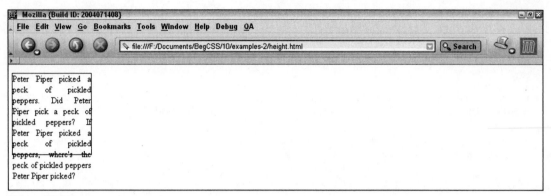

Figure 10-16

As of this writing, Internet Explorer does not correctly interpret CSS dimensions. Internet Explorer inter-prets the height property in a manner closer to the CSS definition for the `min-width` and `min-height` properties (although not exactly the same). Because of this, if you set height using the `height` property, Internet Explorer ignores the setting if the text or object contained inside that element is larger than the dimensions of that element. Figure 10-17 demonstrates Internet Explorer's incorrect interpretation of the CSS height property.

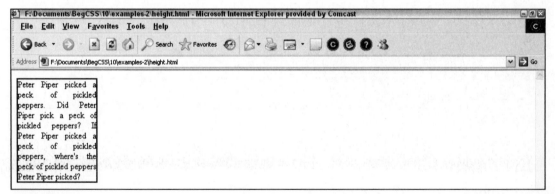

Figure 10-17

All is not lost. Solutions for getting around Internet Explorer's lack of support and incorrect interpreta-tion of certain properties are discussed in Chapter 18. For now, Internet Explorer 6 simply adjusts the height to accommodate the extra text, just as though a `height: auto;` were applied. If the text is smaller than the element, the `height` property applies as it should. The same behavior occurs if the con-tent is wider than the element's width allows:

```
p {
    border: thin solid black;
    width: 100px;
}
```

This is shown in the following example, where I use the longest word I could think of:

```
<p>
    Supercalifragilisticexpialidocious!
</p>
```

Figure 10-18 demonstrates that the same behavior occurs whether the content is wider than the element's width allows or whether the content is more than the height allows.

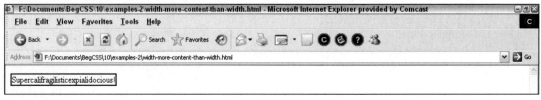

Figure 10-18

This is another place where Internet Explorer behaves incorrectly; it forces the element's width to expand to accommodate the extra content, which is also incorrect behavior according to the W3C CSS specifications. Figure 10-19 demonstrates IE 6's incorrect interpretation of the CSS width property with a fixed-width length.

Figure 10-19

The next section continues the discussion of dimensions with auto values for width and height.

Auto Values for width and height

By default, width and height properties have an auto value. The meaning of the auto keyword changes depending on the type of element that it is applied to. When used on a <div> element, the element spans all the horizontal space available to it and expands vertically to accommodate any content inside of it, including text, images, or other boxes. Elements with this behavior are called *block* elements. Some examples of block elements are <div>, <p>, <h1> through <h6>, <form> and <ul> elements. The following example demonstrates this:

```
p {
    border: thin solid black;
    width: auto;
    height: auto;
}
```

It is used with this markup:

```
<p>
    How much wood would a woodchuck chuck if a wooodchuck could chuck wood?
    A woodchuck would chuck all the wood a woodchuck could chuck if a woodchuck
    could chuck wood.
</p>
```

Figure 10-20 demonstrates how the <p> element takes up all the space available to it and expands vertically to accommodate the content inside.

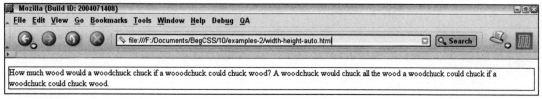

Figure 10-20

The width of the <p> element also adjusts to any changes in the window size. The same behavior occurs with other block elements like <div> or headings <h1> through <h6>. By definition, block elements are to occupy the entire line.

The auto value can also have different meanings depending on the type of element with which you use it. The CSS specifications say that the intrinsic dimensions of the element determine the auto value. In terms of block elements, that means that they span the whole line and expand vertically just enough to accommodate the elements contained inside of that element. The <table> element is an example of an element that is not a block element. <table> elements are in a class all of their own. By default, <table> elements expand and contract only enough to accommodate the text they contain. In CSS this type of behavior is called *shrink-to-fit*. This is demonstrated in the following example:

```
table {
    border: thin solid black;
    width: auto;
    height: auto;
}
```

It is combined with this markup:

```
<table>
    <tr>
        <td>
            The table only expands enough for the content inside of it.
        </td>
    </tr>
</table>
```

Figure 10-21 demonstrates that a `<table>` element's intrinsic dimensions are not the same as a `<p>` or `<div>` element's intrinsic dimensions.

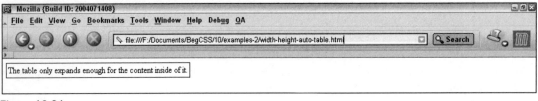

Figure 10-21

The `<img />` element is another example of an element that has different *intrinsic dimensions*. When the `auto` keyword is used on images, the `auto` value allows the image to be displayed as is. If the image is 500 pixels by 600 pixels, the auto `value` displays the image as 500 by 600 pixels. In that light, the graphics program that generated the image determines the image's intrinsic dimensions. When you use `height: auto;` on an image, and you explicitly specify the image's width, the image's height scales in aspect ratio to the image's width.

Percentage Measurements

Using percentage width and height measurements in CSS is somewhat different from using the `width` or `height` HTML attributes. Using percentage measurements with the `width` and `height` properties requires factoring in margin, padding, and borders. Consider the following example:

```
p {
    width: 100%;
    height: 100%;
    margin:  10px;
    padding: 10px;
    border:  1px solid black;
    background: lightgray;
}
```

The preceding is applied to this markup:

```
<p>
    It is not a bad idea to get in the habit of writing down one's thoughts. It
    saves one having to bother anyone else with them.
        - Isabel Colegate
</p>
```

Figure 10-22 shows that the `<p>` hasn't become any larger vertically.

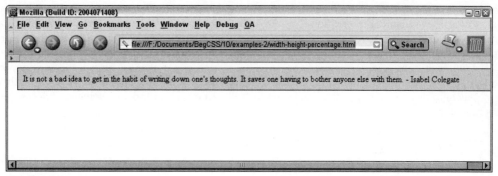

Figure 10-22

The height of the containing element determines the percentage height. By default, that means the containing element has a declaration of `height: auto;`. In this case, the containing elements are the `<html>` and `<body>` elements. If you include style sheet rules for the `<html>` and `<body>` elements and give them 100 percent heights by adding the following rule:

```
html, body {
    height: 100%;
}
```

You can see, in Figure 10-23, that the page stretches both horizontally and vertically larger than the window.

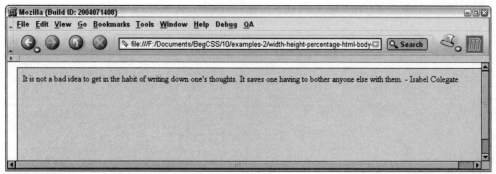

Figure 10-23

Margin is applied to the `<body>` element by default, in addition to the border. Margin and padding are applied to the `<p>` element. If you refer back to the CSS box model in Figure 10-1, you remember that width is measured from inside padding edge to inside padding edge. As I pointed out in the section on height, the same is also true of height. At this time, current implementations of CSS offer no feasible work-around to prevent the scroll bar from appearing while you are applying margins, padding, or borders to the <div> element in addition to a 100% width and height. Because of margins, padding, and borders, the element stretches larger than the window. You have a few possible solutions to the problem. You can specify a smaller percentage, but doing so does not guarantee the text will appear the same on all screen resolutions. CSS 3 may offer a solution to this problem, but at the time of this writing, the W3C working group has yet to settle on one. Instead, standards-compliant browsers allow you to utilize a different technique, one using positioning. Using the following rule for the <p> element achieves the desired effect.

```
p {
    padding: 10px;
    margin: 10px;
    border:  1px solid black;
    background: lightgray;
    position: absolute;
    top: 0;
    right: 0;
    bottom: 0;
    left: 0;
}
```

Figure 10-24 shows that the desired effect of horizontal and vertical fluidity has been achieved.

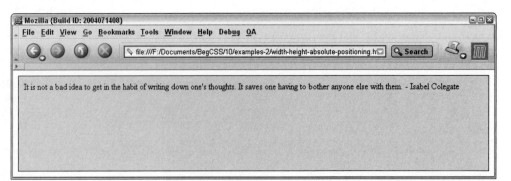

Figure 10-24

This technique uses absolute positioning to stretch the <p> element so that it fills the entire window to do what you couldn't do with height: 100%; and width: 100%;. Although this technique does not work in IE 6, it does work in Mozilla, Opera, and Safari. The concept of *positioning* is one I've yet to discuss. Essentially, the element is delivered to a specific place on the browser window. The top, right, bottom, and left properties tell the browser where to position the element. In the CSS specifications, these are known as *offset properties* because they position an element offset to something else. In this example, these are positioned relative to the browser window. Each accepts a value for length, and the length is the amount of the offset. Offset properties are generally used in pairs, such as top: 5px; left: 5px;, to position the content relative to the top and left sides of the window. Using all four properties causes the content to be stretched, creating vertical and horizontal fluidity. Chapter 14 covers positioning in greater detail. The next section discusses a set of properties related to the width and height properties, and these are properties that specify minimum and maximum dimensions.

Minimum and Maximum Dimensions

The `min-width`, `max-width`, `min-height`, and `max-height` properties define minimum and maximum boundaries when it is necessary to constrain a width or height from expanding or contracting past a certain point. In a liquid design, that scales to fit the user's screen size. It is sometimes helpful to define where you want the document to stop stretching. For instance, if you have designed primarily with an 800 x 600 or 1024 x 768 screen resolution in mind, a user viewing your website at 1600 x 1200 pixels may see the content stretched pretty thin if an `auto` keyword or percentage values are used to define the width. This is where the CSS properties `min-width`, `max-width`, `min-height`, and `max-height` come into play.

min-width

Documented in CSS 2.1 and supported in Mozilla 1.7, Opera 7.5, and Safari 1.2 (partial).

The `min-width` property defines a lower-size constraint on an element. The available values for the `min-width` property are outlined in the following table.

Property	Value
min-width	<length> | <percentage> | inherit Initial value: 0

Safari 1.2 does not support the `min-width` property when used on positioned elements. I discuss positioned elements in Chapter 14.

The `min-width` property defines when an element using an `auto` keyword or percentage width should stop shrinking to fit the user's window. Consider the following code:

```
p {
    padding: 10px;
    margin: 10px;
    border: thin solid black;
    width: auto;
    min-width: 200px;
}
```

It is used with the following markup:

```
<p>
    About the most originality that any writer can hope to achieve honestly is to
    steal with good judgment.
        - Josh Billings
</p>
```

Figure 10-25 demonstrates that, if you run this snippet in a browser, when the browser window or containing element becomes smaller than 200 pixels, the <p> stops shrinking and a scroll bar appears across the bottom of the browser window.

Figure 10-25

If the <p> is inside another element and that element becomes smaller than the <p> element's min-width, the <p> element overflows the edges of that element. The opposite scenario, defining a maximum width, is covered in the next section.

max-width

Documented in CSS 2.1 and supported in Mozilla 1.7, Opera 7.5, and Safari 1.2

In contrast to the min-width property, the max-width property is used to set an upper constraint for width with elements using either an auto keyword or percentage measurement for width. The max-width property is defined in the following table.

Property	Value
max-width	\<length> | \<percentage> | none | inherit Initial value: none

Safari 1.2 does not support the max-width property when used on positioned elements. I discuss positioned elements in Chapter 14.

The max-width property allows you to define a maximum length if the area available to the element becomes larger. Consider a <p> element with the following declarations:

```
p {
    padding: 10px;
    margin: 10px;
    border: thin solid black;
    width: auto;
    max-width: 500px;
}
```

This is put together with the following markup:

```
<p>
    You have to know how to accept rejection and reject acceptance.
        - Ray Bradbury
</p>
```

Figure 10-26 shows that the <p> element stops expanding horizontally when it reaches a 500-pixel width.

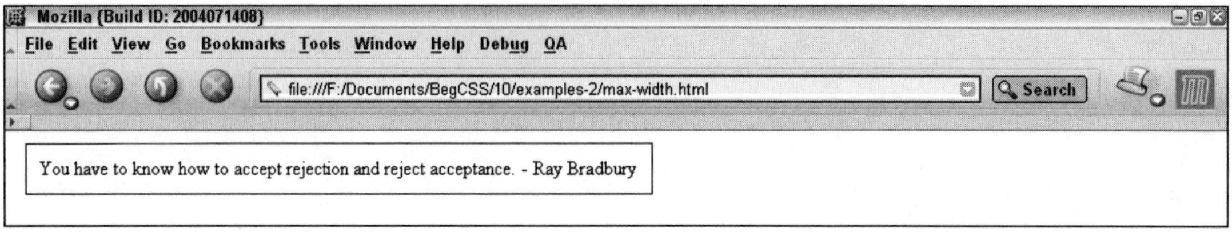

Figure 10-26

As a block-level element, the <p> element expands horizontally, filling all the available space. In this light, it is fluid. On a high-resolution monitor set to 1280 x 1024 pixels, for instance, the content inside of the <p> element could potentially get stretched very thin. The minimum and maximum width properties allow an upper and lower limit to be set for the size of an element and allow an author to take advantage of fluid design that adjusts to accommodate the user's environment. CSS also offers identical properties to set upper and lower limits for height.

min-height

Documented in CSS 2.1 and supported in IE 6 (partial), Mozilla 1.7, and Opera 7.5.

If you are using a variable or percentage height, the min-height property lets you specify when you want the element to stop shrinking vertically. The following table outlines the possible values for the min-height property.

Property	Value
min-height	<length> | <percentage> | inherit Initial value: 0

IE 6 supports the min-height property only when used on <td>, <th>, and <tr> elements.

Recalling the discussion on percentage heights, you have to use a certain combination of properties to achieve vertical fluidity without overstepping the boundaries of the window. This is done with absolute positioning and by including all four offset properties. The following demonstrates the required rule and markup:

```
p {
    padding: 10px;
    margin: 10px;
    border:  1px solid black;
    background: lightgray;
    position: absolute;
    top: 0;
    right: 0;
    bottom: 0;
    left: 0;
    min-height: 200px;
}
```

It is applied to the following paragraph of text:

```
<p>
    A positive attitude may not solve all your problems, but it will annoy enough
    people to make it worth the effort.
        - Herm Albright
</p>
```

Figure 10-27 demonstrates that if the vertical area available to the element is less than 200 pixels, as defined with the min-height: 200px; declaration, a vertical scroll bar appears and the <p> element stops shrinking when the 200-pixel threshold is met.

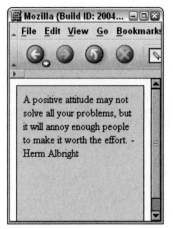

Figure 10-27

Continuing the discussion on minimum and maximum dimensions, I cover the max-height property next.

max-height

Documented in CSS 2.1 and supported in Mozilla 1.7 and Opera 7.5.

The opposite of the `min-height` property is the `max-height` property, which allows the author to tell the browser when an element should stop expanding. It allows an upper height constraint to be specified for the element. The `max-height` property is outlined in the following table.

Property	Value
max-height	<length> | <percentage> | none | inherit Initial value: none

The `max-height` property does for height what the `max-width` property does for width. This is demonstrated with the following rule and markup:

```
p {
    padding: 10px;
    margin: 10px;
    border:  1px solid black;
    background: lightgray;
    position: absolute;
    top: 0;
    right: 0;
    bottom: 0;
    left: 0;
    max-height: 200px;
}
```

It is applied to the following paragraph:

```
<p>
    A positive attitude may not solve all your problems, but it will annoy enough
    people to make it worth the effort.
        - Herm Albright
</p>
```

Figure 10-28 demonstrates that the <p> element stops expanding vertically at 400 pixels.

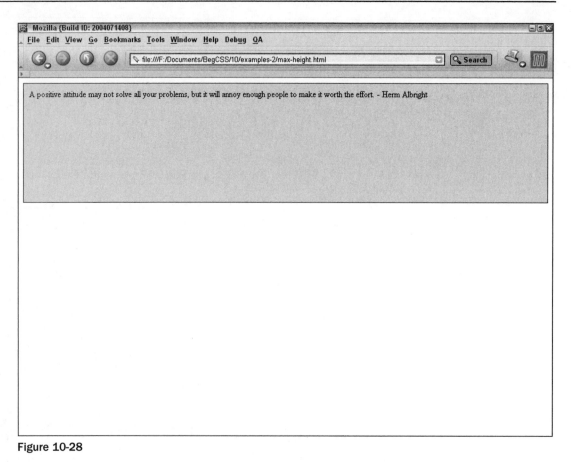

A positive attitude may not solve all your problems, but it will annoy enough people to make it worth the effort. - Herm Albright

Figure 10-28

The next section wraps up discussion of dimensions with the line-height property.

The line-height property

Documented in CSS 2.1 and supported in IE 5.5, IE 6, Mozilla 1.7, Opera 7.5, and Safari 1.2.

As I mentioned in Chapter 9, the line-height property refers to the height of the line on which each line of text appears. The line-height property and its possible values are outlined in the following table.

Property	Value
line-height	normal | <number> | <length> | <percentage> | inherit Initial value: normal

This property allows an explicit length to be defined for each line of text. Consider the following rule and markup:

```
p {
    margin: 10px;
    padding: 10px;
    color: black;
    border: thin solid;
    width: 250px;
    line-height: 3em;
    font-size: 1em;
}
```

It is applied to the following paragraph of text.

```
<p>
    Home computers are being called upon to perform many new functions, including
    the consumption of homework formerly eaten by the dog.
        - Doug Larson
</p>
```

Figure 10-29 shows that each line of text is contained in a `line-height` 3em high. This produces the effect of quadruple-spaced text because a 1em `font-size` is specified

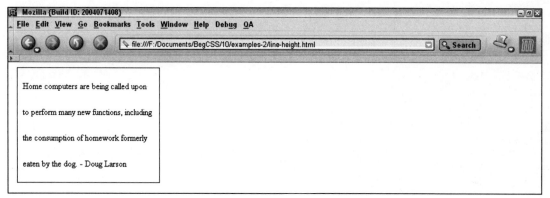

Figure 10-29

Now that you have some background knowledge about how dimensions work in CSS, the following Try It Out lets you apply some dimensions to the JT's Island Grill and Gallery style sheet.

Try It Out   **Applying Dimensions**

Example 10-3. Follow these steps to apply dimensions to the JT's style sheet.

1.   Add the following rule to the base_styles.css style sheet:

```
a:hover {
    text-decoration: underline;
}
div#body {
    width: 50em;
}
```

```
h1, h6 {
    border-left: 0.05em solid black;
    border-right: 0.05em solid black;
}
```

2. Add the following declaration to the base_styles.css style sheet:

```
p.copy {
    line-height: 2em;
    border-bottom: 0.05em dotted black;
    font-size: 1.2em;
    font-family: "Times New Roman", Times, serif;
    text-indent: 20px;
    text-align: justify;
}
```

3. Save base_style.css.

4. Make the following modifications to the menu_system.css style sheet:

```
div#nav {
    width: 50em;
    text-align: center;
}
div#nav > a > img {
    width: 16em;
    height: auto;
}
div#nav > ul > li {
    border: 0.05em solid black;
    font-size: 0.9em;
}
div#nav > ul > li#leftedge {
    border-right-width: 0;
    -moz-border-radius-topleft: 1em;
    -moz-border-radius-bottomleft: 1em;
}
div#nav > ul > li#leftedge:hover {
    -moz-border-radius-bottomleft: 0;
}
```

```
div#nav > ul > li#rightedge {
    border-left-width: 0;
    -moz-border-radius-topright: 1em;
    -moz-border-radius-bottomright: 1em;
}
div#nav > ul > li#rightedge:hover {
    -moz-border-radius-bottomright: 0;
}
ul.menu {
    width: 15em;
    -moz-border-radius-bottomleft: 1em;
    -moz-border-radius-bottomright: 1em;
    border: 0.05em solid black;
}
```

5. Save menu_system.css.

6. Add the following style attribute to the dinner_menu.html document:

```
<h1>
    JT's at Night
</h1>
<div id='content'>
    <img src='images/photos/dinner_plate.jpg'
        style='width: 9em; height: auto;'
        alt='dinner plate'/>
    <h3>Appetizers</h3>
        <h4>Stone Crab Claws <em>Market Price</em></h4>
```

7. Add the following style attribute to the dinner_menu.html document:

```
<h3>Local Music &amp; Arts</h3>
    <img src='images/photos/meta_playing.jpg'
        style='width: 16em; height: auto;'
        alt='meta playing'/>
    <p class='copy'>
        We hope you enjoy tonight's live music. To help keep
```

8. Save dinner_menu.html. Open dinner_menu.html in the Mozilla browser; you should see output like that shown in Figure 10-30.

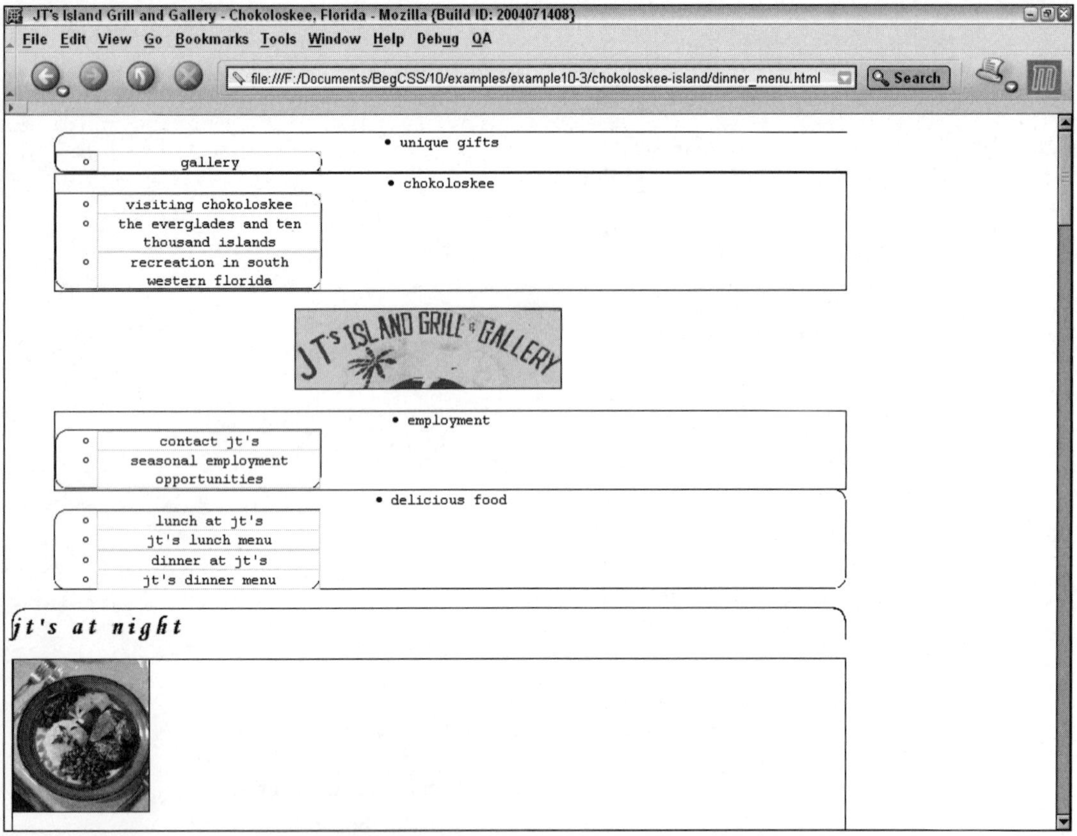

Figure 10-30

How It Works

Figure 10-30 shows the result of applying the dimension properties. Though still quite crude, with the addition of these properties, the design is beginning to take on a more definitive shape. The goal of these additions is to put as few constraints on the design as possible so that the design adapts fluidly to the user's environment. Although I could have utilized the minimum and maximum properties, I decided to go with a different approach to achieve a liquid design. As you may have noticed in this and previous examples, I have used the em unit to specify all lengths. The use of em units, if you recall from Chapter 4, makes each measurement dependent on the value of the font-size property.

For this design, I also specified font sizes using the em unit, which makes the entire design dependent on the user's font size preferences, while preserving the aesthetic intent of the page. If you increase or decrease Mozilla's font size setting, the design of the JT's dinner menu scales fluidly with that design, including the images! For each image, I also use images slightly larger than I need so that the design scales gracefully, leaving little possibility of artifacts appearing in the JPEG images. Here is a brief reiteration of each modification and why it was made. The rule that I included in the base_styles.css style sheet sets a size constraint on the <div> element with a body id name:

```
div#body {
    width: 50em;
}
```

The value specified for the width is 50em, or 50 times the value of the font size. Because the body `<div>` wraps all the headings and copy that appear in the dinner menu, this constraint is enough to achieve a fluid design. Those headings and paragraphs, because they are block elements, adjust their size according to the space available to them. The next modification to the base_styles.css style sheet applies a `line-height` of 2em:

```
p.copy {
    line-height: 2em;
    border-bottom: 0.05em dotted black;
    font-size: 1.2em;
    font-family: "Times New Roman", Times, serif;
    text-indent: 20px;
    text-align: justify;
}
```

This declaration makes the size of each line double the size of the font, which results in the copy being more spread out. The next three modifications set some constraints on the menu navigational system via the menu_system.css style sheet. The first modification sets a constraint on the `<div>` element containing the navigation:

```
div#nav {
    width: 50em;
    text-align: center;
}
```

Again, a 50em width is specified. This is to keep the navigation proportionate with the body `<div>`. The next modification scales down the JT's logo image:

```
div#nav > a > img {
    width: 16em;
    height: auto;
}
```

Another em unit is used to tie the size of the image to the size of the user's font. An auto height is used to keep the aspect ratio of the image, which allows the image to scale in perfect proportion with increases or decreases in the user's font size. The final modification sets a width for each list of links that will eventually become drop-down menus.

```
ul.menu {
    width: 15em;
    -moz-border-radius-bottomleft: 1em;
    -moz-border-radius-bottomright: 1em;
    border: 0.05em solid black;
}
```

The final modifications are made to the dinner_menu.html file itself:

```
<img src='images/photos/dinner_plate.jpg'
```

```
                        style='width: 9em; height: auto;'
                        alt='dinner plate'/>
```

Each of these styles is included directly in the dinner_menu.html file because they are only applied to one element. Both are included to scale down the images. The next section continues the discussion of the CSS box model with the `padding` property.

Padding

Documented in CSS 2.1 and supported in IE 5.5, IE 6 , Mozilla 1.7, Opera 1.7, and Safari 1.2.

Padding is the space between the content of an element and its borders, as has been mentioned briefly in previous examples. The following table shows the various padding properties.

Property	Value
padding	[<length> | <percentage> {1,4}] | inherit
padding-top padding-right padding-bottom padding-left	<length> | <percentage> | inherit

The `padding` property is a shorthand property, meaning that it is a simplified representation of other properties. In the preceding table, the square brackets are used to group the values. In this context, the `padding` property can accept either what is contained between the brackets as a value or the `inherit` keyword, but not both.

Here's a brief review on how CSS properties are documented. The <length> syntax (no, not an HTML tag) is a placeholder, which means that the property may accept any CSS length value, be it pixels, centimeters, inches, or any other measurement supported by CSS. The vertical bar means *or* in this context and can accept either a <length> value or a <percentage> value, or any combination of either. The {1,4} syntax means that the property can accept up to four values, but it must contain at least one value. To illustrate what all this means, examine each of the acceptable syntaxes for the `padding` short-hand property. The first syntax is the `padding` property accepting four separate values:

```
padding: <padding-top> <padding-right> <padding-bottom> <padding-left>;
```

This usage includes all four of the separate padding properties in one; each value represents a side of the box. Consider the following example:

```
p {
    padding: 10px 0 0 10px;
}
```

This results in 10 pixels of padding on the top and left sides of the box. It's the same thing as saying:

```
p {
    padding-top: 10px;
    padding-right: 0;
    padding-bottom: 0;
    padding-left: 10px;
}
```

The separate properties are combined into a single property. The next possible syntax contains three values:

```
padding: <padding-top> <padding-right/padding-left> <padding-bottom>;
```

This syntax combines the left and right padding values in the middle value, which is equivalent to this example:

```
p {
    padding: 10px 5px 10px;
}
```

This is the same thing as saying:

```
p {
    padding-top: 10px;
    padding-right: 5px;
    padding-bottom: 10px;
    padding-left: 5px;
}
```

All four values are represented with only three values. The next syntax combines the top and bottom in the first value and the left and right in the second value:

```
padding: <padding-top/padding-bottom> <padding-right/padding-left>;
```

This syntax is equivalent to this usage:

```
p {
    padding: 10px 5px;
}
```

This usage results in 10 pixels of padding on the top and bottom sides, and 5 pixels of padding on the left and right sides. It's the same thing as saying:

```
p {
    padding-top: 10px;
    padding-bottom: 10px;
    padding-left: 5px;
    padding-right: 5px;
}
```

When the `padding` property contains only a single value, it applies to all four sides at once:

```
padding: <padding-top/padding-right/padding-bottom/padding-left>;
```

In the context of actual usage this appears as the following:

```
p {
    padding: 10px;
}
```

The preceding is the same thing as saying:

```
p {
    padding-top: 10px;
    padding-right: 10px;
    padding-bottom: 10px;
    padding-left: 10px;
}
```

Each use of the shorthand property is a method of representing all four sides of the box in a simple and concise manner.

> **The padding property cannot have a negative value; if one is supplied, it is ignored.**

The next property, `margin`, follows an identical syntax to the padding properties.

Margins

Documented in CSS 2.1 and supported in IE 5.5, IE 6, Mozilla 1.7, Opera 7.5, and Safari 1.2.

Whereas padding puts space between the inside of the box border and the content itself, the `margin` property applies space outside the box, between the box and the browser window, or between the box and the other elements in the document. The following table shows the various margin properties.

Property	Value
margin	[\<length> | \<percentage> | auto {1,4}] | inherit
margin-top margin-right margin-bottom margin-left	\<length> | \<percentage> | auto | inherit

The only difference between the `padding` and `margin` properties is the name and where they apply space to the box; otherwise they are identical. The syntax is exactly the same.

The `margin` property, like the `padding` property, is also a shorthand property, which simplifies its usage:

```
margin: <margin-top> <margin-right> <margin-bottom> <margin-left>;
```

The following is an example of its actual usage:

```
p {
    margin: 10px 0 5px 20px;
}
```

This syntax is again the same thing as saying:

```
p {
    margin-top: 10px;
    margin-right: 0;
    margin-bottom: 5px;
    margin-left: 20px;
}
```

In this example, however, instead of adding space between the inside border and the content, you add the space between the outside border and the window. The margin is an invisible box around the border.

Also like the `padding` property, the `margin` property supports the combined usage syntax:

```
margin: <margin-top> <margin-right/margin-left> <margin-bottom>;
margin: <margin-top/margin-bottom> <margin-right/margin-left>;
```

The `margin` property also supports the single usage syntax:

```
margin <margin-top/margin-right/margin-bottom/margin-left>;
```

This syntax applies the value simultaneously to all four sides. That leads me to the next topic, aligning boxes using margins.

The following section outlines how to align block elements using the `margin` property with the `auto` keyword.

Aligning Block-Level Elements with margin: auto

In previous chapters, you may have noticed a curious use of the `margin` property to center or align block-level elements. This use is intended to make centering more intuitive and to separate box aligning from text aligning. Consider the following rule:

```
p {
    padding: 2em;
    margin: 2em;
    border: thin solid black;
    width: 10em;
    margin-right: auto;
}
```

It is combined with this markup:

```
<p>
    Peter Piper picked a peck of pickled peppers.
    Did Peter Piper pick a peck of pickled peppers?
```

```
        If Peter Piper picked a peck of pickled peppers,
      where's the peck of pickled peppers Peter Piper picked?
  </p>
```

Figure 10-31 shows that the <p> element is aligned to the left in the browser window with the inclusion of the margin-right: auto; declaration.

Figure 10-31

By the same token, using margin-left: auto; aligns the block to the right of the browser window, resulting in the output shown in Figure 10-32.

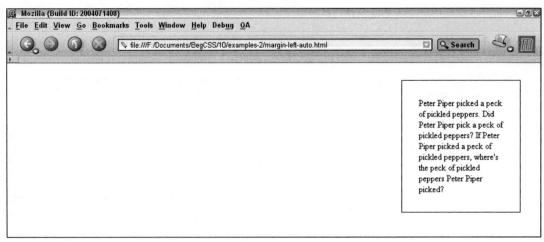

Figure 10-32

And finally, using simply `margin: auto;` results in the block being centered in the browser window, resulting in the output in Figure 10-33.

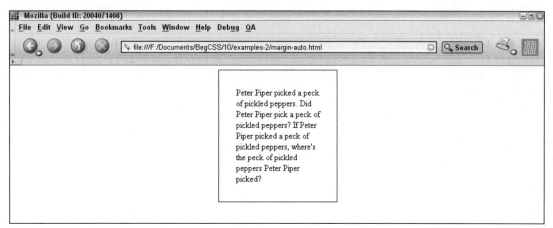

Figure 10-33

Using the `auto` keyword on `margin-top` and `margin-bottom`, however, does not affect vertical aligning. This requires positioning, which I discuss in Chapter 14. The `auto` value applies exclusively to the `margin-left` and `margin-right` properties for block alignment.

Now that I've discussed the padding and margin properties in more detail, the next Try It Out lets you apply these properties to the JT's Island Grill and Gallery style sheets.

 Try It Out   **Applying Margins and Padding**

Example 10-4. Follow these steps to add margins and padding to the JT's style sheets.

1.   Make the following changes to the base_styles.css style sheet:

```css
body {
    padding: 5em 0 1.2em 0;
    margin: 0;
    font-family: "Courier New", Courier, monospace;
    text-transform: lowercase;
}
a {
    text-decoration: none;
}
a:hover {
    text-decoration: underline;
}
```

```
div#body {
    margin: 0 auto;
    width: 50em;
}
h1, h6 {
    border-left: 0.05em solid black;
    border-right: 0.05em solid black;
}
h1, h2, h3, h4, h5, h6 {
    margin: 0;
}
h1 {
    padding: 0.5em 1.1em;
    border-top: 0.05em solid black;
    -moz-border-radius-topleft: 0.8em;
    -moz-border-radius-topright: 0.8em;
    font-family: "Monotype Corsiva", cursive;
    letter-spacing: 4px;
    font-size: 1.5em;
}
h2 {
    margin: 0 1.2em;
    padding: 0.9em 1.1em 0;
    border-bottom: 0.05em dotted black;
}
h3 {
    border-bottom: 1px dotted black;
    font-size: 0.9em;
}
h6 {
    padding: 1em 0;
    -moz-border-radius-bottomleft: 0.8em;
    -moz-border-radius-bottomright: 0.8em;
    border-bottom: 0.05em solid black;
    font-size: 0.8em;
    text-align: center;
}
div#content {
    padding: 1.2em;
    border: 0.05em solid black;
    font-size: 0.9em;
    word-spacing: 5px;
    letter-spacing: 1px;
}
p.copy {
    padding: 1.2em;
    margin: 0 1.2em;
    line-height: 2em;
    border-bottom: 0.05em dotted black;
    font-size: 1.2em;
    font-family: "Times New Roman", Times, serif;
```

```
        text-indent: 20px;
        text-align: justify;
}
img {
        margin: 1.7em;
        border: 0.05em solid black;
}
```

2. Save base_styles.css

3. Make the following changes to the menu_system.css style sheet:

```
div#nav {
        margin: auto;
        width: 50em;
        text-align: center;
}
div#nav > a > img {
        margin: 0;
        width: 16em;
        height: auto;
}
div#nav ul {
        margin: 0;
        padding: 0;
}
div#nav > ul > li {
        padding: 0.5em;
        border: 0.05em solid black;
        font-size: 0.9em;
}
```

4. Continue with modifying the menu_system.css style sheet, with the addition of declarations to the following rule:

```
ul.menu a {
        margin: 0.4em;
        padding: 0.5em;
        color: black;
        display: block;
        border: 0.05em solid lightblue;
}
```

5. Save menu_system.css.

6. Make the following changes to the dinner_menu.css style sheet:

```
div#content * {
        font-family: "Times New Roman", Times, serif;
}
```

```
div#content h3 + p, div#content h4 + p  {
    margin: 0 0 1.8em 0;
}
div#content h3 {
    margin-top: 1.8em;
    border-bottom: none;
    font-family: "Monotype Corsiva", cursive;
    text-decoration: underline;
    font-size: 2em;
}
div#content img + h3 {
    margin-top: 0;
}

h3 + p.menucaption {
    font-style: italic;
    text-align: center;
}
h4, h5 {
    font-size: 1.3em;
}
h3, h4, h5, h4 + p, h5 + p  {
    text-align: center;
}
h4 em, h5 em {
    margin-left: 0.9em;
    font-weight: lighter;
}
h5 + p {
    margin-top: 0;
}
h5 {
    font-weight: normal;
}
p.copy {
    padding-top: 0;
}
```

7.   Save dinner_menu.css. Open dinner_menu.html in Mozilla; you should see output like that in Figure 10-34.

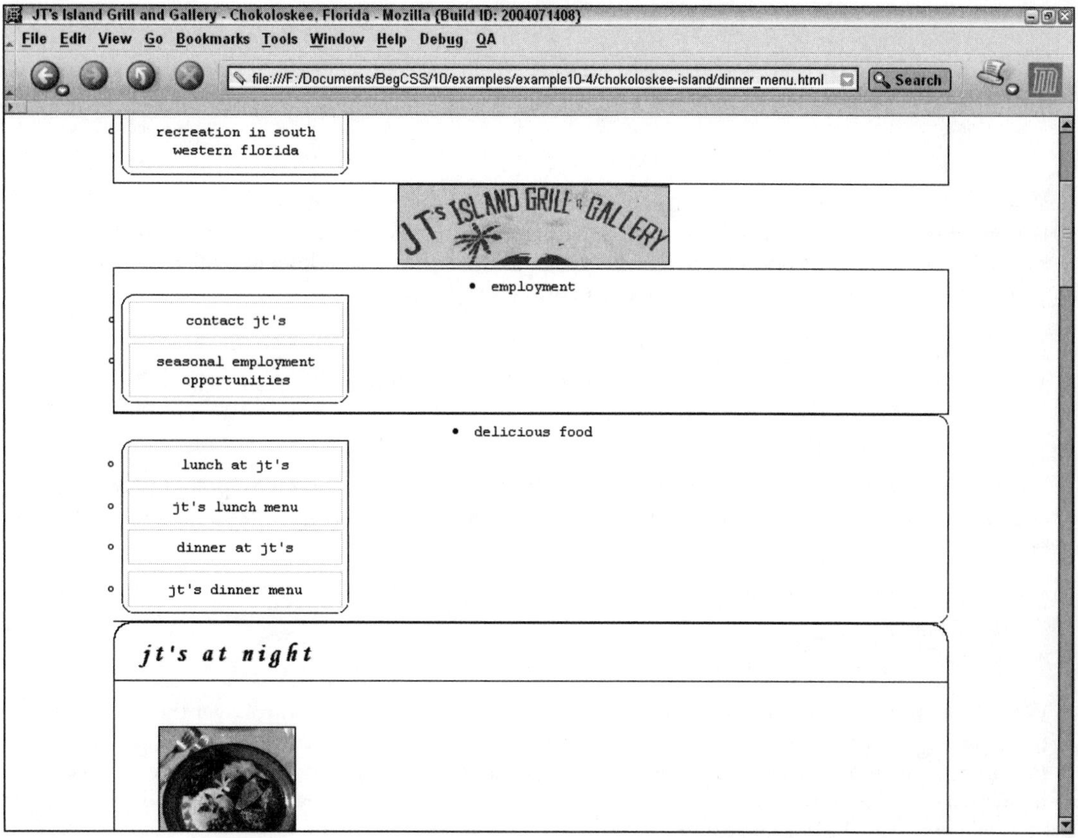

Figure 10-34

How It Works

Figure 10-34 shows that the design for the JT's Island Grill and Gallery dinner menu has again improved by leaps and bounds with the addition of margins and padding. The main objective for applying margins and padding is to eliminate default margins applied to headings and to give the text inside each element some breathing room. To illustrate the theory behind each modification, here's a brief look at each modification. The first additions are to the rule applying style to the <body> element in the base_styles.css style sheet.

```
body {
    padding: 5em 0 1.2em 0;
    margin: 0;
    font-family: "Courier New", Courier, monospace;
    text-transform: lowercase;
}
```

The first declaration adds 5em of padding to the top of the <body> element, and 1.2em of padding to the bottom of the <body> element. With the second declaration of margin: 0; all default margins applied by the browser are removed. The next modification centers the <div> element with a body id that wraps around the headings and copy of the dinner menu:

```
div#body {
    margin: 0 auto;
    width: 50em;
}
```

No margin is applied to the top and bottom margins and the auto keyword is applied to the left and right margins to center the block element. The next rule removes all default margins from heading elements:

```
h1, h2, h3, h4, h5, h6 {
    margin: 0;
}
```

With all default margins applied by the browser removed, I have more control over the presentation of the heading elements. The addition of this style also causes the <h1>, content <div>, and <h6> elements to appear flush and seamless, which was one of my objectives when I applied the borders to these elements. The next modification uses the padding property to put some space between the text inside the <h1> element and the border around it:

```
h1 {
    padding: 0.5em 1.1em;
    border-top: 0.05em solid black;
    -moz-border-radius-topleft: 0.8em;
}
```

The next rule doesn't apply to the dinner menu because it doesn't contain any <h2> elements, but it is applicable to other pages of the JT's website:

```
h2 {
    margin: 0 1.2em;
    padding: 0.9em 1.1em 0;
    border-bottom: 0.05em dotted black;
}
```

Just ignore the preceding rule for now. The next modification applies some space between the text inside the <h6> element and the top and bottom borders:

```
h6 {
    padding: 1em 0;
    -moz-border-radius-bottomleft: 0.8em;
    -moz-border-radius-bottomright: 0.8em;
}
```

The next addition puts some space around all the copy inside the content <div>:

```
div#content {
    padding: 1.2em;
    border: 0.05em solid black;
    font-size: 0.9em;
```

This declaration puts some space between the content in the dinner menu itself and the border around it. The next modification is also made to give the text room to breathe:

```
p.copy {
    padding: 1.2em;
    margin: 0 1.2em;
    line-height: 2em;
    border-bottom: 0.05em dotted black;
```

1.2em of padding is applied to all sides of copy <p> elements. No margin is added on the top and bottom sides, but 1.2em of margin is added to the left and right sides. The last rule applied puts margins around all images:

```
img {
    margin: 1.7em;
    border: 0.05em solid black;
}
```

Here 1.7em of margin is applied to all four sides of all images contained in the document. The objective of this spacing is to give the text breathing room. With margins applied to all the images in the document, the content of the document doesn't run up against each image. The effect of this application of margin to the images become more obvious in Chapter 11, where these images are adjusted so that the text and content run up beside each image. The next modifications are made to the navigational menu at the top of the page. The first modification centers the nav <div> that contains the lists of links, headings, and the JT's logo:

```
div#nav {
    margin: auto;
    width: 50em;
    text-align: center;
}
```

The margin: auto; declaration centers the <div>; however, I wrote this declaration simply as margin: auto; instead of margin: 0 auto; to demonstrate that the top and bottom margins are not affected by the use of the auto keyword. The following modification removes the margin from the logo image applied with the general img rule in the base_styles.css style sheet:

```
div#nav > a > img {
    margin: 0;
    width: 16em;
    height: auto;
}
```

The navigation list that is now above the logo will appear to the left of the logo, and the navigation list now situated below the logo will appear to the right of the logo. Removing the margin is one step in achieving that effect. The next rule removes margin and padding from the <ul> elements:

```
div#nav ul {
    margin: 0;
    padding: 0;
}
```

The <ul> element has padding applied by default in most browsers; however, Internet Explorer uses margins instead of padding. Therefore both are removed by applying margin: 0; and padding: 0; declarations. The next rule puts some space around each of the navigation headings:

```
div#nav > ul > li {
    padding: 0.5em;
    border: 0.05em solid black;
    font-size: 0.9em;
}
```

Again, this rule keeps the text from running up against the borders of the <li> elements. Finally, the last modification to the menu_system.css style sheet follows along the same lines:

```
ul.menu a {
    margin: 0.4em;
    padding: 0.5em;
    color: black;
    display: block;
```

In Example 10-2, with the application of borders, the <a> element was made into a block element instead of retaining its default behavior as an inline element. This modification made the whole list element clickable as a link (instead of only the text). The modifications made here spread out each link more with margin outside each <a> element and padding inside each element. The modifications made to the dinner_menu.css style sheet, like those made to the other style sheets, deal mostly with controlling the default padding and margins applied by the browser:

```
div#content h3 + p, div#content h4 + p  {
    margin: 0 0 1.8em 0;
}
```

The addition of this rule selects <p> elements that follow <h3> or <h4> elements appearing in the markup by using the adjacent sibling selector. The selector first uses the descendant selector to select <h3> and <h4> elements that are descendants of the content <div>; then, it selects only the <p> elements that appear after these headings. So by using this selector, both the descriptions for each menu item and the captions that appear after menu section headings are selected. This modification puts some space between the bottom of each paragraph and the next heading in the menu, while at the same time keeping the top of the paragraph flush with the bottom of the headings appearing before them. The next modification adds a top margin to each <h3> element that contains headings for the different parts of the menu:

```
div#content h3 {
    margin-top: 1.8em;
```

```
border-bottom: none;
font-family: "Monotype Corsiva", cursive;
```

The addition of this space further distinguishes each section of the menu from the others. The next modification removes the top margin from the first <h3> element appearing in the dinner menu, which is the *Appetizers* heading:

```
div#content img + h3 {
    margin-top: 0;
}
```

When the image is shifted to the right and the text is shifted up beside the image, the first <h3> element appears closer to the top border of the content <div>. The next modification puts some space between the text for each menu item and the <em> element containing the menu item's price:

```
h4 em, h5 em {
    margin-left: 0.9em;
    font-weight: lighter;
}
```

Another selector is also added to the rule so that both the prices of menu items in <h4> elements and the prices inside <h5> elements are chosen. The next rule removes the default top margin from <p> elements that appear directly after <h5> elements by using the adjacent sibling selector.

```
h5 + p {
    margin-top: 0;
}
```

This rule selects the following paragraph and causes its text to appear flush with the bottom border of the <h5> element:

```
<h3>Dessert</h3>
    <h5>Home-made Key Lime Pie <em>$4</em></h5>
    <p>
        The best in the Everglades
    </p>
<h3>Local Music &amp; Arts</h3>
```

Finally, the last modification to the dinner_menu.css style sheet removes the top padding from the copy <p> appearing at the bottom of the menu:

```
p.copy {
    padding-top: 0;
}
```

Like the modification made for the first <h3> element, which contains the *Appetizers* heading, this modification makes the text at the top of this paragraph flush with the bottom of the <h3> heading above it. The effect of this becomes more obvious in Chapter 11 when the image is moved to appear beside the text instead of above it.

Padding and margins are — along with the other box model properties — quite possibly the most important properties of CSS. Their theory and implementation are fundamental to the core of CSS design. The CSS box model properties allow the markup of the document to be minimal; lengthy table-based designs and tag soup become unnecessary as the presentation of the document can be completely controlled using only CSS. Although the JT's style sheet is still far from an elegant design, at this point, the complexity and power of CSS becomes increasingly more obvious with each new property introduced to its design.

The following sections discuss a property closely related to the box model family of properties: the `overflow` property.

Overflowing Content

Documented in CSS 2.1 and supported in IE 6, Mozilla 1.7, Opera 7.5, and Safari 1.2.

The CSS `overflow` property exists to manage content that is susceptible to dimensional constraints, where the content could possibly overflow the boundaries of those dimensional constraints. The following table outlines the `overflow` property and its possible values.

Property	Value
overflow	visible | hidden | scroll | auto | inherit Initial value: visible

The two most common uses of the `overflow` property are to hide content when more content than space is available or to apply scroll bars so that the extra content can be accessed. By default, the value of the `overflow` property is the `visible` keyword, the effects of which you saw in Figure 10-16. This figure showed that when the width and height specified are smaller than the content allows, the content overflows the edges of the box containing it. The following sections discuss each of the other possible values for the `overflow` property.

overflow: auto

The `overflow: auto` property tells the browser to decide whether the content is larger than its container, as demonstrated by this rule

```
p {
    padding: 10px;
    margin: 10px;
    border: thin solid black;
    width: 150px;
    height: 150px;
    overflow: auto;
}
```

It is then combined with some markup:

```
<p>
    Peter Piper picked a peck of pickled peppers.
    Did Peter Piper pick a peck of pickled peppers?
    If Peter Piper picked a peck of pickled peppers,
    where's the peck of pickled peppers Peter Piper picked?
</p>
```

When you use the overflow: auto; declaration, a vertical scroll bar appears if the width and height are set to 150px each and the content is larger than those constraints allow (see Figure 10-35). The scroll bar gives the user access to the overflowing content.

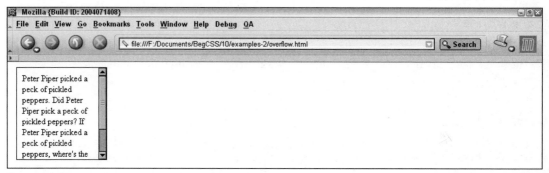

Figure 10-35

To put it more simply, a vertical scroll bar appears because the content is larger than the box containing it. By the same token, if you want the text contained in the element not to wrap as it fills up the container, you can apply another CSS declaration to prevent wrapping: white-space: no-wrap;. This declaration was discussed in Chapter 8 and prevents the content from automatically wrapping inside the container. With white-spance: nowrap; applied, line breaks now occur only where you apply them with XHTML explicitly. This is demonstrated by the following rule:

```
p {
    padding: 10px;
    margin: 10px;
    border: thin solid black;
    width: 150px;
    height: 150px;
    overflow: auto;
    white-space: nowrap;
}
```

Figure 10-36 shows that the white-space: nowrap; declaration, when rendered in a browser, causes a horizontal scroll bar to appear (instead of a vertical scroll bar, as was the case in Figure 10-35).

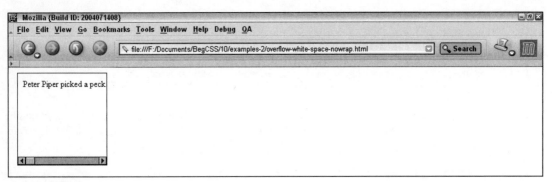

Figure 10-36

The next section discusses the effects of the `scroll` keyword when used in conjunction with the `overflow` property.

overflow: scroll

Using the `overflow: scroll;` declaration ensures that the horizontal and vertical scroll bar tracks always appear regardless of how much content is inside the box. This is demonstrated by the following rule:

```
p {
    padding: 10px;
    margin: 10px;
    border: thin solid black;
    width: 150px;
    overflow: scroll;
}
```

With the `overflow: scroll;` declaration applied to the rule, Figure 10-37 demonstrates that scroll bars appear regardless of whether the content overflows or not.

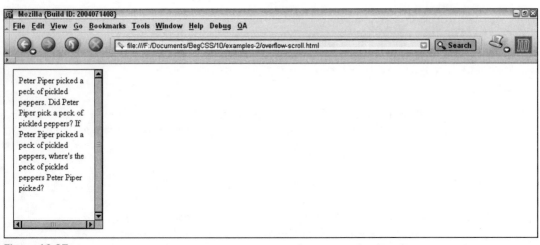

Figure 10-37

Removing the height constraint from the rule in the "Peter Piper" snippet of markup would normally result in no overflow because by default, as a block element, the `<p>` element expands vertically to accommodate the content inside it.

The final value discussed here for the `overflow` property is the `hidden` keyword.

overflow: hidden

The `overflow: hidden;` declaration clips any content that doesn't fit inside the box, essentially ignoring whatever doesn't fit. This is demonstrated by the following rule.

```
p {
    padding: 10px;
    margin: 10px;
    border: thin solid black;
    width: 150px;
    height: 150px;
    overflow: hidden;
}
```

Using this property results in the output depicted in Figure 10-38.

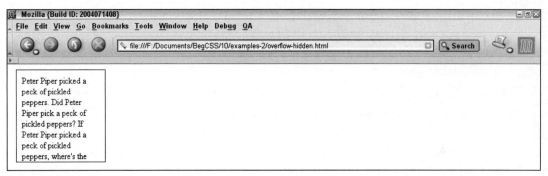

Figure 10-38

It's obvious from this figure that the content that doesn't fit inside the box is simply invisible and inaccessible to the user. The final section of this chapter discusses two properties proprietary to Internet Explorer and planned for possible inclusion in CSS 3 as part of the CSS standard: `overflow-x` and `overflow-y`.

overflow-x and overflow-y

The `overflow-x` and `overflow-y` properties are currently proprietary Internet Explorer properties that are proposed additions to the CSS 3 specification. These properties currently work only in Internet Explorer 6 when Internet Explorer 6 is provided with a standards mode Document Type Declaration.

Like the `overflow` property, `overflow-x` and `overflow-y` control overflow content, but they also allow users to control the overflowing content with a scroll bar: only a vertical scroll bar for the `overflow-y` property, and only a horizontal scroll bar for the `overflow-x` property. Each of these properties accepts the same values as the `overflow` property.

Summary

Liquid design is a combination of techniques that allow web content to be delivered to more than one medium. The most important principle of liquid design is content that adapts to the user's environment. Using some basic ground rules, you can minimize document markup not only for speedy delivery but also to make the document easy to maintain and manage. Markup, which has nothing to do with structure, is left out. Headings are enclosed in heading tags, text in paragraph tags, and lists of links are enclosed in unordered lists, following the principles behind the groundwork laid for the JT's dinner menu that I presented in Chapter 8. These techniques assist visually impaired users accessing the website with the aid of a voice synthesizer. Accessibility is increased because the document is more clearly structured in headings, paragraphs, and lists. With the media attribute and @media rule, you can design content for delivery to a specific medium, be it for the PC, for print, for handheld devices, or for a plethora of other devices. Finally, by using em units, you can design a web page that scales to the user's font-size preferences without compromising the aesthetic intention of your design.

The CSS box model is a set of rules that tells the browser how to handle the width of a box, padding, borders, and margins. The box model offers the designer consistency across multiple platforms and browsers. Margin and padding are essential to a document and prevent the document from rendering in complete chaos. Borders offer more aesthetic possibilities. CSS dimensions offer controls over how wide and high an element can be. Finally, overflow allows the simulation of inline frames and gives you control over content when it is larger than the element containing it.

To recap the material presented in this chapter, you learned the following:

❑ Why table-based designs increase the size and expense of maintaining a website

❑ Why tables should only be used to show relation between data

❑ Why using the <div> element is best for partitioning the different parts of a document

❑ How defining the content of a web page in headings, paragraphs, and lists increases the accessibility of a website and makes more sense than tag soup

❑ How to apply border widths, border styles, and border colors with the border family of properties

❑ How to apply dimensions to the elements of a document using the width and height family of properties

❑ How to control the line height of text using the line-height property

❑ How to apply padding to a document with the padding property

❑ How to apply margins to a document with the margin property

❑ How you can use the overflow property to manage content in cases where the content of an element is bigger than the element itself

Now that you've had a fairly in-depth exposure to the properties fundamental to CSS design, Chapter 11 discusses CSS buoyancy, a topic involving the float and vertical-align properties of CSS.

Exercises

1. Using the exercise completed for Chapter 6, Exercise 2, convert the Widgets and What's-its FAQ page to a liquid design that adapts to the user's font size using em units. Remove all width constraints and proprietary CSS from the document, and then convert the length units to em units, keeping as close to possible to the look and feel of the original units specified in pixels. Use Mozilla's default font size to achieve this. Remove any margin separating the elements from the edge of the browser window.

2. Using the design completed for Exercise 1, write another version of the Widgets and What's-its FAQ, one in which the design stops expanding at a 60em width and stops contracting at a 30em width. The document should be centered if the 60em maximum width is met. Meet these requirements by adding only a single rule with three declarations to the document.

3. Writing yet another variation of the Widgets and What's-its FAQ page, add a <div> wrapping all the content of the FAQ page. Rewrite the rule that you created in Exercise 2 to reference the wrapper <div>. With two <div> elements in the page at this point, give each a unique name and rewrite the selectors for both <div> elements accordingly. Include in the rule for the wrapping <div> an upper constraint on the height of 30em, where scroll bars appear to access the content overflowing that height. Ensure that there is still no margin between the elements themselves and the top edge of the browser window.

CSS Buoyancy: Collapsing Margins, Floating, and Vertical Alignment

In Chapter 10, I presented a subset of properties that combine to define a concept known as the CSS box model. In this chapter, I continue introducing new properties, this time focusing on two properties most often misunderstood by users new to CSS design: the `float` and `clear` properties. These properties are often misunderstood because of their unique effect on the elements in a document. The `float` property is also closely related to the discussion of the CSS box model that I presented in Chapter 10. In this chapter I discuss:

❑ Margin collapsing and how this phenomenon affects the layout of block elements

❑ The `float` property and how it is used to change the flow of elements in a document — for instance, to place text beside an image

❑ The `clear` property and how this property is used to cancel the effects of the `float` property

❑ The `vertical-align` property and how this property is used to control the vertical alignment of text to create subscript or superscript text or control vertical alignment in table cells

Before I begin the discussion of the float property, I have to rewind to margins, a concept discussed in Chapter 10 with the CSS box model. The following section explains *margin collapsing*, which, in turn, helps you understand why the `float` property behaves as it does.

Collapsing Margins

Learning CSS involves more than simply memorizing its properties, selectors, widgets, and syntax. CSS is full of anomalies and idiosyncrasies, so sometimes you don't reach your goal by following the most obvious path. In this section, I discuss margin collapsing, which users often fully understand only after a long and tedious process of trial and error. I discuss it here because it helps to explain some inconsistencies with the CSS `float` property, covered in the next section.

In CSS, *margin collapsing* occurs when top or bottom margins of one element come into contact with the top or bottom margins of another element. Margin collapsing is demonstrated in the following example:

```
p {
    margin: 20px;
    padding: 20px;
    border: thin solid black;
    background: rgb(218, 218, 218);
}
```

In the markup, set up two paragraphs, one after the other:

```
<body>
    <p>
        This is the first paragraph.
    </p>
    <p>
        This is the second paragraph.
    </p>
</body>
```

Figure 11-1 shows margin collapsing in two places. You can see the margin collapsing between the top border of the top paragraph and the bottom border of the browser window. If you recall from Chapter 10, the browser often applies margin and padding to elements, although not every browser applies the same type of spacing to the same elements. Mozilla applies a small margin to the <body> element, which roughly translates to about 8 pixels. In Figure 11-1, margin collapsing occurs between that default margin in the <body> element and the top margin of the <p> element. Margin collapsing causes one of the two margins to be absorbed into the other; the collapsed margin is always the lesser of the two. In this case, the <body> element has a margin of about 8 pixels, and the top paragraph has a top margin of 20 pixels. Because the 20-pixel length is larger than the margin specified for the <body> element, the body's margin is collapsed. Therefore, only 20 pixels separate the text of the first paragraph from the bottom border of the browser window, instead of the 28 pixels you might expect. Also note in the example that the left and right margins have not collapsed; this is proper behavior. Margin collapsing affects only top and bottom margins.

Figure 11-1

The second place in the example where margin collapsing can be observed is between the two paragraphs. Only 20 pixels of space separate the paragraphs, which can again be attributed to margin collapsing. Margin collapsing can also occur if the elements are nested (as you can see in the preceding figure) because the <p> elements are nested inside the <body> element, and margin collapsing occurs between the top paragraph and the <body> element. This is highlighted by the following example

```
div {
    margin: 20px;
    background: rgb(178, 178, 178);
}
p {
    margin: 20px;
    padding: 20px;
    background: rgb(218, 218, 218);
}
```

combined with the following markup:

```
<div>
    <p> No margins, ey?</p>
</div>
```

Figure 11-2 shows that the top margin of the <p> element has collapsed with the top margin of the <div> element, and both have collapsed the default margin of the <body> element. Not quite what you expected right?

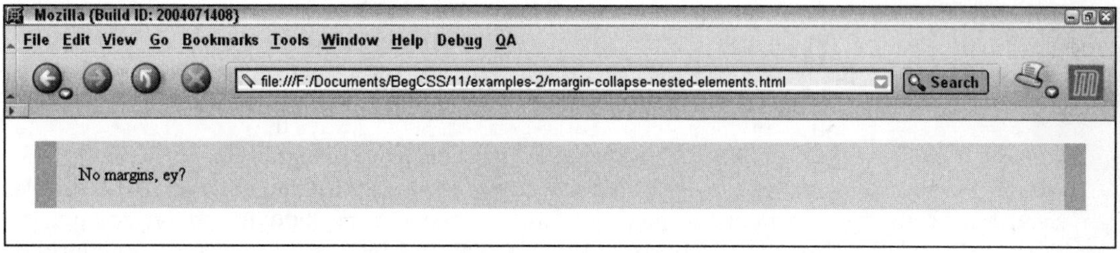

Figure 11-2

To prevent margins from collapsing, you must use either borders or padding to prevent the margins from contacting one another:

```
div {
    margin: 20px;
    padding: 20px;
    background: rgb(178, 178, 178);
}
p {
    margin: 0;
    padding: 20px;
    background: rgb(218, 218, 218);
}
```

Figure 11-3 shows what happens when padding is used.

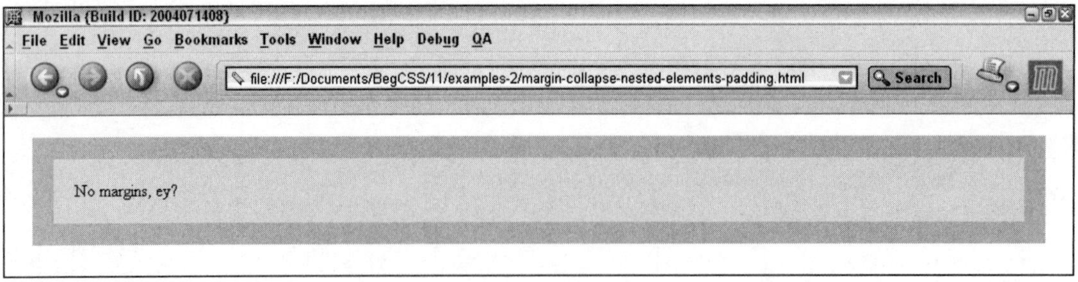

Figure 11-3

Figure 11-3 shows that the desired effect has been achieved. In this example, it was also necessary to remove the default margin from the <p> element so only 20 pixels separate the outside edge of the <p> element from the outside edge of its <div> parent—otherwise applying the default margin of the <p> element would result in more than 20 pixels between top of the div and the top of the paragraph and the bottom of the div and the bottom of the paragraph. This is demonstrated by leaving off the `margin: 0;` declaration:

```
div {
    margin: 20px;
    padding: 20px;
    background: rgb(178, 178, 178);
}
p {
    padding: 20px;
    background: rgb(218, 218, 218);
}
```

Figure 11-4 shows that with padding applied to the <div> element, the default margin of the <p> element appears between the bottom outside edge of the <div> element's padding and the top outside edge of the <p> element, as well as between the bottom outside edge of the <p> element and the bottom outside edge of the <div> element's padding.

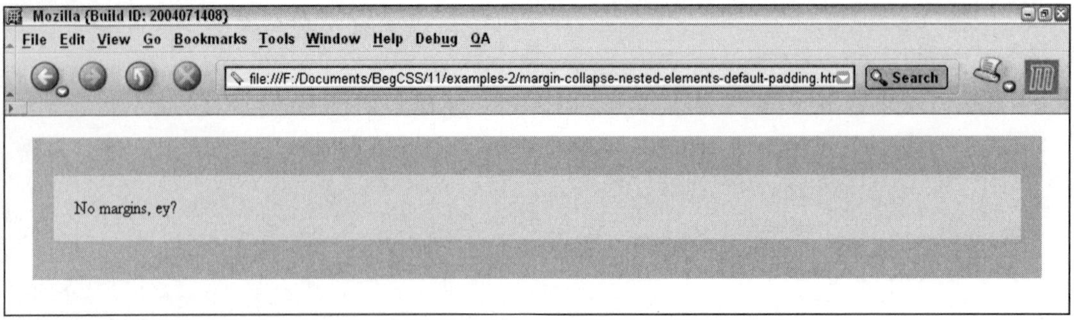

Figure 11-4

Margin collapsing is an important, often subtle effect of CSS design. If you understand it, you can often pinpoint why the space between vertical margins doesn't always appear as you might anticipate. Margin collapsing also plays an important role in setting up consistent test cases for the float property, discussed in the next section.

The float Property

Documented in CSS 2.1 and supported in IE 5.5, IE 6, Mozilla 1.7, Opera 7.5, and Safari 1.2.

As you have seen in the examples in previous chapters (such as the Einstein quote page in Chapter 6), the simple explanation of the float property is that it is used to put content side by side. In the coming sections, you look in depth at the float property, its idiosyncrasies, and how you can use it to lay out a web page. The following table outlines the float property and its possible values.

Property	Value
float	left | right | none | inherit Initial value: none

At this point, the float property appears fairly simple. It accepts keyword values of left, right, and none, and like all other properties, it also accepts a value of inherit. The effects of the float property are intrinsically tied to the CSS box model. After the float property is applied to an element, regardless of the type of element, that element takes on the behavior of a block element, where its dimensions are defined by width, height, padding, borders, and margins. Before you see some examples of this, the following snippet shows you how the float property affects a document's layout:

```
p#floated {
    float: left;
}
p {
    border: thin solid black;
}
```

Apply the preceding rule to the following markup:

```
<p id='floated'>
    This paragraph is floated left.
</p>
<p id='normal'>
    The text of this paragraph is beside the floated paragraph.
</p>
```

The output in Figure 11-5 shows the text of the normal paragraph is to the right and slightly above the floated paragraph.

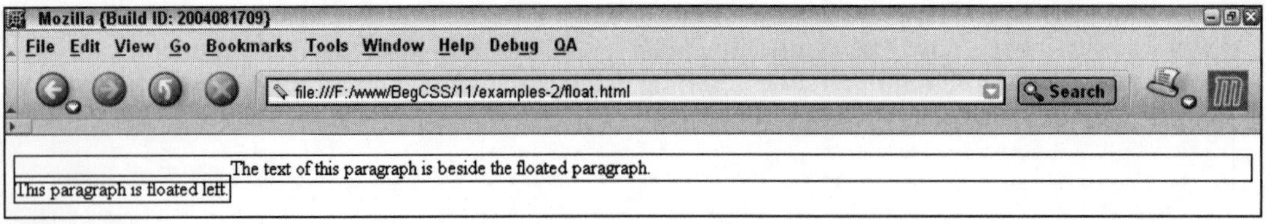

Figure 11-5

The output in Figure 11-6 is output from Opera, and it shows the two paragraphs perfectly level on the same line.

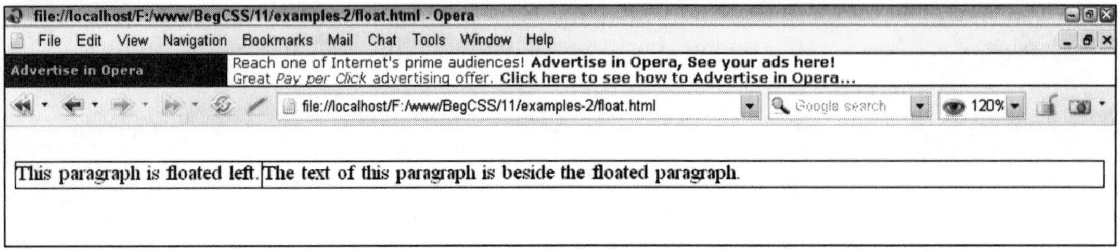

Figure 11-6

Both outputs shown in the preceding figures are correct! In Figure 11-5, the second paragraph appears raised because of margin collapsing — the top margin of the normal paragraph is collapsed with the top margin of the <body> element, and a floated element's margins never collapse. Opera's output (shown in Figure 11-6) is also correct because Opera applies default padding to the <body> element instead of margins — so, no margins, no margin collapsing.

The following code and figure show what happens if the padding and margin of the <body> element are explicitly controlled:

```
body {
    margin: 0;
    padding: 8px;
}
p#floated {
    float: left;
}
p {
    border: thin solid black;
}
```

Figure 11-7 shows that when you control default margins and padding from the style sheet, you can achieve consistent behavior; the output of Mozilla is now identical to the output of Opera.

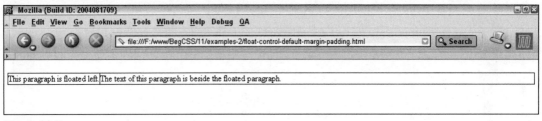

Figure 11-7

The next section examines each of the rules that come together when an element is floated.

Floating Box Model

Because floated elements are repositioned to allow other content to flow around them, they exhibit unique behavior. This behavior is outlined here:

- ❑ The margins of floated elements do not collapse, no matter what they are next to.
- ❑ Only the contents of elements following a floated element are affected by the floated element. That is, the backgrounds, margins, borders, padding, and width (the dimensions) of elements following a floated element are not affected.
- ❑ A floated element is always treated like a block element.

Each of these rules is important in determining how floated elements are positioned and rendered. This section examines each of these rules in depth.

First, the margins of floated elements never collapse. Consider the following diagram in Figure 11-8 showing how the box model is incorporated when an element has been floated.

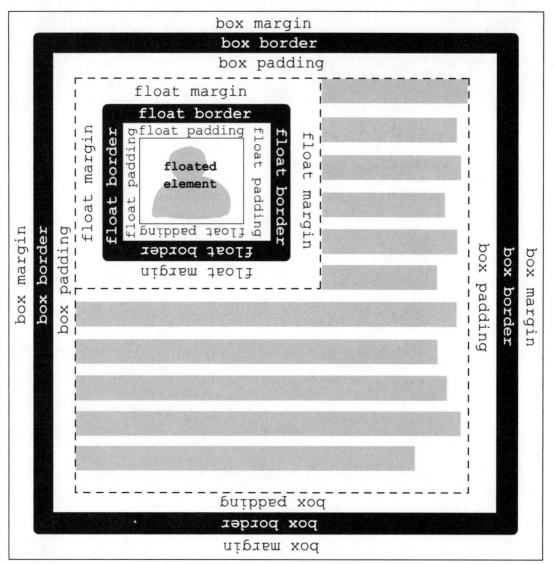

Figure 11-8

The diagram in Figure 11-8 shows the box model of two elements. The *box* is the element that contains the floated element (as shown in Figure 11-5) — that is, the <body> element. The other box is the *float* element (also from Figure 11-5) — that is the floated paragraph. According to the diagram, the margin of the floated element is inside the element that contains it. In Figure 11-5, the <body> element contains the floated <p> element, so its margins do not collapse with the <body> element. To highlight this behavior, consider the following example:

```
div {
    margin: 10px;
    background: rgb(200, 200, 200);
    height: 100px;
}

p#floated {
    background: rgb(220, 220, 220);
    margin: 10px;
    padding: 10px;
    border: 1px solid black;
    float: left;
}
p#normal {
    background: rgb(240, 240, 240);
    border: 1px solid black;
}
```

Combine the preceding code with this markup:

```
<body>
    <div>
        <p id='floated'>
            This paragraph is floated left.
        </p>
        <p id='normal'>
            The text of this paragraph is beside the floated paragraph.
        </p>
    </div>
</body>
```

Figure 11-9 highlights the effects of the diagram presented in Figure 11-8.

Figure 11-9

The normal paragraph appears all the way at the top of the <div> element, meaning that the default top margin of the normal paragraph has collapsed and yielded to the top margin of the <div> element. The default top margin of the <body> element has also collapsed and yielded to the top margin of the <div> element because has the largest margin. The floated paragraph has completely maintained its margins on all four sides, highlighting that the margins of the floated paragraph have not collapsed.

The next thing that is obvious from Figure 11-9 is the behavior outlined in the second bullet point of our rules for floated elements: The dimensions of the normal paragraph have been maintained as though the floated element doesn't even exist. Its dimensions are clearly highlighted as they pass behind the floated element, showing that only the content inside the normal paragraph is affected by the presence of the floated element.

The final rule, which states that all floated elements are treated like block elements, is discussed in the next section.

Floating Inline Elements and the Inline Box Model

The final rule for floated elements is that they're always treated like block elements. Inline elements like <span> or <em> allow some box model properties such as margin, borders, and padding to be applied. Inline elements, however, do not allow dimensional properties such as width and height to be applied. This is understandable because these properties are expected to be contained in the flow of text. The <img/> element is an exception because it allows dimensional properties to be applied. Elements like the <img/> element are known as *replaced* inline elements, and elements like <span> and <em> are known as *non-replaced* inline elements. Replaced inline elements are replaced by something—for example the <img/> element is replaced by the image referenced via the src attribute. After the float property is applied to an element, it doesn't matter if the original element was an inline element or a replaced inline element because a floated element is a block element. This is demonstrated in the following example:

```
div {
    margin: 10px;
    background: rgb(200, 200, 200);
    height: 100px;
}
span#floated {
    background: rgb(220, 220, 220);
    margin: 10px;
    padding: 10px;
    border: 1px solid black;
    float: left;
    width: 100px;
}
span#normal {
    background: rgb(240, 240, 240);
    border: 1px solid black;
    margin: 100px;
    width: 1000px;
}
```

Apply the preceding rule to the following markup:

```
<div>
    <span id='floated'>
        This span is floated left.
    </span>
    <span id='normal'>
        The text of this span is beside the floated span.
    </span>
```

```
          This is extra text. This is extra text. This is extra text.
          This is extra text. This is extra text. This is extra text.
          This is extra text. This is extra text. This is extra text.
          This is extra text. This is extra text. This is extra text.
          This is extra text. This is extra text. This is extra text.
          This is extra text. This is extra text. This is extra text.
   </div>
```

Figure 11-10 shows that when an inline element is floated, it becomes a block element and is fully definable by all box model properties.

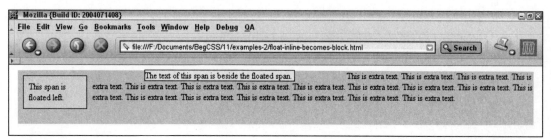

Figure 11-10

The floated `<span>` is given a width of 100 pixels, a top margin, and padding — all of which are present in the rendering in Figure 11-10. The normal `<span>` is given a width of 1000 pixels, and because it is an inline element, the browser ignores the width. A margin of 100 pixels is also specified, but Figure 11-10 shows that only the left and right margin actually affect the surrounding text. In fact, although padding, borders, and margin can be applied to inline elements, these have no effect on the height of the line. They do, however, affect the text to the left and right. If I add a padding of 50 pixels to the normal `<span>`, the top and bottom padding, borders, and margin do not affect the rest of the paragraph, only the area to the left and right of the inline element are affected as is demonstrated by Figure 11-11.

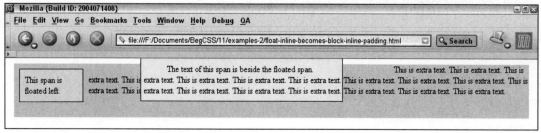

Figure 11-11

Figure 11-11 shows what happens when the padding and margins are increased even more. From this example, you can see that a box appears behind the rest of the paragraph, and the text to the left and right of the normal `<span>` is displaced by the presence of left and right margins, borders, and padding. The dimensions of non-replaced inline elements are defined by the line-height font size, the spacing between letters and words, and the amount of content contained in the inline element. Box model properties can be applied, although the behavior of box model properties for inline elements is somewhat different from that of block elements. Box model properties cannot affect the line-height of inline elements because inline elements may span multiple lines. To demonstrate this concept, study the following styles:

```css
div {
    margin: 10px;
    background: rgb(200, 200, 200);
    height: 100px;
}
span#floated {
    background: rgb(220, 220, 220);
    margin: 10px;
    padding: 10px;
    border: 1px solid black;
    float: left;
    width: 100px;
}
span#normal {
    background: rgb(240, 240, 240);
    border: 1px solid black;
}
```

Apply this to markup that includes more content in the normal `<span>` element:

```html
<body>
    <div>
        <span id='floated'>
            This span is floated left.
        </span>
        <span id='normal'>
            The text of this span is beside the floated span.
            The text of this span is beside the floated span.
            The text of this span is beside the floated span.
            The text of this span is beside the floated span.
            The text of this span is beside the floated span.
            The text of this span is beside the floated span.
            The text of this span is beside the floated span.
        </span>
        This is extra text. This is extra text. This is extra text.
    </div>
</body>
```

Figure 11-12 shows what happens when an inline element that spans multiple lines is given a border and a background color.

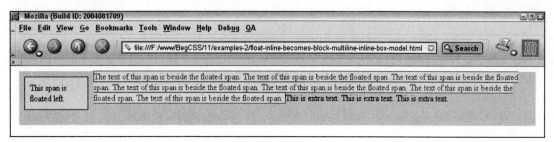

Figure 11-12

Figure 11-12 shows that the box model properties applied to the <span> element are wrapped with each line of content. The box of an inline element is broken at the end of each line and continues on the following line up until the end of the content. The rendering of the normal <span> element in Figure 11-12 is in stark contrast to how the floated <span> element in the figure is rendered. The floated <span> element becomes a block element after the float property is applied to it.

If margin: 20px; and padding: 20px; declarations are applied to the preceding example, the text in the <span> becomes unreadable, which is demonstrated by the following rule.

```
span#normal {
    background: rgb(240, 240, 240);
    border: 1px solid black;
    opacity: 0.7;
    padding: 20px;
    margin: 20px;
}
```

The application of the preceding opacity, padding, and margin declarations are demonstrated in Figure 11-13.

Figure 11-13

The application of margins and padding causes the normal <span> to layer over itself with each new line because line height cannot be affected by the application of box model properties to an inline element. I made the <span> in Figure 11-13 slightly transparent with the opacity: 0.7; declaration, to highlight the unchanging line height. The lighter text of the lines following the first line shows that the text is obstructed by the background of the preceding lines. This, in turn, shows that the background of the preceding line is layered on top of each line that follows.

When any element is given a position with the float property, it takes on the behavior of a block element regardless of what it was previously. The next section continues exploring floats with a look at what happens when several elements are floated in sequence.

Applying Multiple Floats

If several elements are floated in a sequence, each one appears next to the previous one, filling all the space available on the line as the width of each float allows. This is demonstrated by the following rule:

```
p {
    float: left;
    border: 1px solid black;
    padding: 10px;
    background: rgb(218, 218, 218);
    margin: 10px;
}
```

When combined with this markup, you see the results shown in Figure 11-14:

```
<p>
    This is the text of the first paragraph.
</p>
<p>
    This is the text of the second paragraph.
</p>
<p>
    This is the text of the third paragraph.
</p>
```

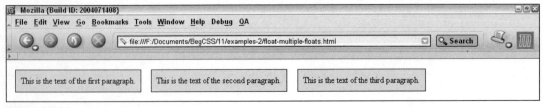

Figure 11-14

The output in Figure 11-14 demonstrates that each paragraph occupies the same line. Figure 11-14 also demonstrates how applying the float property to an element changes how width is applied to block elements. In Chapter 10, you saw how a block element occupies all the space available to it because of the width: auto; declaration. In Figure 11-14, the width of each paragraph is no more than what is contained inside, making the behavior of a floating block similar to what you saw in Chapter 10 for the <table> element. In CSS, this type of width is known as *shrink-to-fit*. Applied here, each <p> only expands horizontally enough to accommodate the content inside when the float property is applied.

The next section looks at an example of what happens when both a left and right float are specified.

Left and Right Floating

If an element floated to the left is followed by an element floated to the right and the width of each element permits, both elements occupy the same line, one on the left side and one on the right side. This is similar to what you saw in Chapter 10 when the margin property was used with an auto keyword to align block elements. The following example demonstrates this:

```
body {
    margin: 0;
    padding: 8px;
}
p {
    border: 1px solid black;
    padding: 10px;
    background: rgb(218, 218, 218);
    margin: 10px;
}
p#left {
    float: left;
}
p#right {
    float: right;
}
```

The preceding rule, applied to this markup, results in the output shown in Figure 11-15:

```
<p id='left'>
    This is the text of the first paragraph.
</p>
<p id='right'>
    This is the text of the second paragraph.
</p>
```

Figure 11-15

Figure 11-15 demonstrates that the left floated element appears on the left side, and it is only as wide as the content inside of it. The right floated element appears on the same line, but on the right side of the browser window. Again, it is only as wide as its content. If the browser window shrinks enough, the left floated element appears above the right floated element. This is demonstrated by the output shown in Figure 11-16.

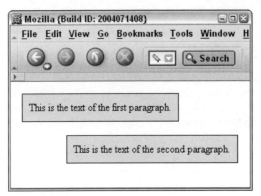

Figure 11-16

If the margins, borders, padding, and width are larger than the free space available on the line, the right floated element gets bumped to the next line down. What happens if a third paragraph is included, but not floated? This is demonstrated by the next example:

```
<p id='left'>
    This is the text of the first paragraph.
</p>
<p id='right'>
    This is the text of the second paragraph.
</p>
<p>
    This is the text of the third paragraph. (repeat this text to observe the
    wrapping effect shown in Figure 11-15)
</p>
```

Using the rules given for Figure 11-15, a third paragraph is applied, resulting in the output shown in Figure 11-17.

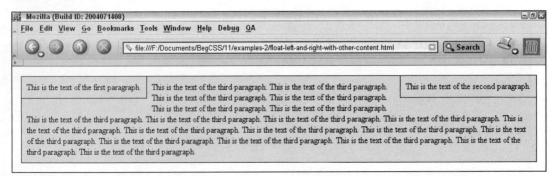

Figure 11-17

Figure 11-17 shows that the third paragraph floats up between the left floated paragraph and the right floated paragraph. The text of the third paragraph fills all the space available between the left floated paragraph and the right floated paragraph. This is the foundation of one technique for achieving a multi-column layout with CSS. This results in a true three-column layout. You apply a left and right margin to the third paragraph and cement the width of the left and right floated paragraphs by supplying an explicit width. The following style sheet demonstrates this concept:

```css
body {
    margin: 0;
    padding: 8px;
}
p {
    border: 1px solid black;
    padding: 10px;
    background: rgb(218, 218, 218);
    margin: 10px;
}
p#left {
    float: left;
    width: 200px;
}
p#right {
    float: right;
    width: 200px;
}
p#center {
    margin: 10px 231px;
}
```

Apply this style sheet to the following markup:

```html
<p id='left'>
    This is the text of the first paragraph.
</p>
<p id='right'>
    This is the text of the second paragraph.
</p>
<p id='center'>
    This is the text of the third paragraph. (repeat this text to observe the
    wrapping effect shown in Figure 11-15)
</p>
```

This results in the output shown in Figure 11-18.

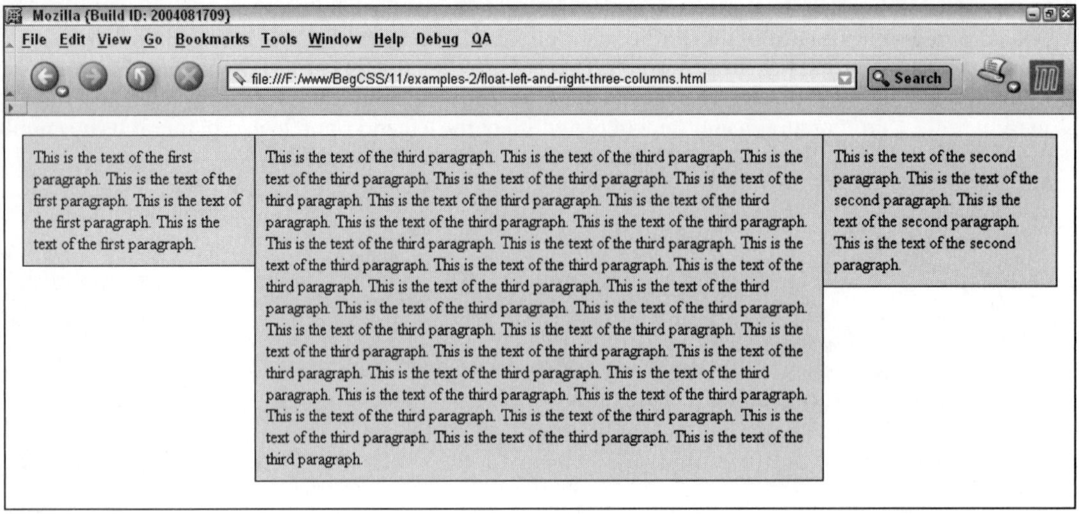

Figure 11-18

Figure 11-18 shows that the design is now a true three-column design. By applying a fixed width to the left and right paragraphs and a left and right margin to the center paragraph, you achieve a three-column layout.

Having seen what the `float` property does, you can work through the following Try It Out, which continues the JT's Island Grill and Gallery website presented in Chapter 10 with the addition of the `float` property.

Try It Out   Applying the float Property

Example 11-1. The following steps show how the `float` property fits into the JT's style sheet.

1. Add the following rules to the menu_system.css style sheet.

```
div#nav > ul > li {
    padding: 0.5em;
    border: 0.05em solid black;
    font-size: 0.9em;
}
ul#gifts > li {
    float: left;
}
ul#food > li {
    float: right;
}
```

2. Save menu_system.css.

3. Add the following declaration to inline style attribute for the dinner_plate.jpg image.

```
<img src='images/photos/dinner_plate.jpg'
     style='width: 9em; height: auto; float: right;'
     alt='dinner plate'/>
```

4. Add the following declaration to the inline style attribute for the meta_playing.jpg image.

```
<img src='images/photos/meta_playing.jpg'
     style='width: 16em; height: auto; float: right;'
     alt='meta playing'/>
```

5. Swap around the following navigation headings so that, in the dinner menu source code, the *Delicious Food* heading comes before the *Employment* heading.

```
<li id='rightedge'>
    Delicious Food
    <ul class='menu'>
        <li><a href=''>Lunch at JT's</a></li>
        <li><a href=''>JT's Lunch Menu</a></li>
        <li><a href=''>Dinner at JT's</a></li>
        <li>
         <a href='dinner_menu.html'>
            JT's Dinner Menu
         </a>
        </li>
    </ul>
</li>
<li>
    Employment
    <ul class='menu'>
        <li><a href=''>Contact JT's</a></li>
        <li><a href=''>Seasonal Employment
                       Opportunities</a></li>
    </ul>
</li>
```

6. Save dinner_menu.html. When you open dinner_menu.html in Mozilla, you see the output in Figure 11-19.

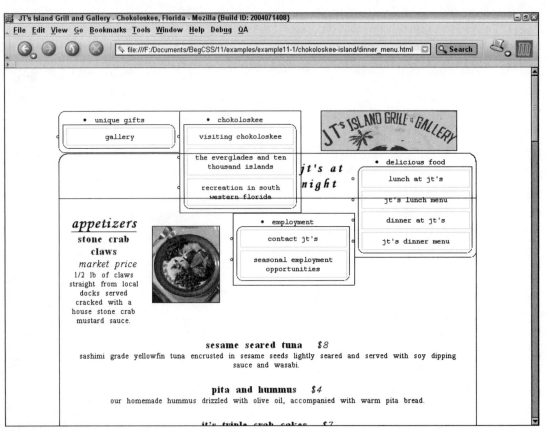

Figure 11-19

How It Works

Figure 11-19 shows what can happen when the float property is applied to the JT's style sheet. Because the objective of the float property is to allow content to flow around the floated element, at this point the JT's dinner menu looks chaotic; but you'll correct the bad side effects of the `float` property in Example 11-2. For the time being, review each modification and explore the theory behind each addition and change. The first change is made so that the *unique gifts* and *chokoloskee* headings appear side by side. This is done by applying the `float: left;` declaration:

```
ul#gifts > li {
    float: left;
}
ul#food > li {
    float: right;
}
```

The second rule does the same thing for the *employment* and *delicious food* headings, but in the opposite way: These are floated to the right instead of to the left. The theory behind these additions is that eventually the unordered list with the *unique gifts* and *chokoloskee* headings will be positioned to the left of the

JT's logo and the *employment* and *delicious food* headings will be positioned to the right of the JT's logo. At this point, I am getting closer to achieving my goal. The application of each float, however, has had unexpected side effects. Floated elements must be placed as high as possible in the document, and the content that follows a float must fill in all the space left over. That puts the top half of the dinner menu right in the middle of the navigation. In the upcoming section on the `clear` property, I discuss how to control the effects of the `float` property. Another unanticipated side effect is that the `float: right;` property causes the *delicious food* heading to appear before the *employment* heading, when I intended it to be the last heading. This is corrected by flip-flopping the list items in the markup itself so that when the *delicious food* list item is right floated, the *employment* heading directly follows to the left of it. The last addition to the JT's markup is floating the images appearing in the menu itself so that the content of the menu wraps around them.

The next section continues `clear` property, which is closely related to the `float` property.

The clear Property

Documented in CSS 2.1 and supported in IE 5.5, IE 6, Mozilla 1.7, Opera 7.5, and Safari 1.2.

In this section, I discuss a property intrinsically related to the `float` property: the `clear` property. The `clear` property is used to control floating content. The following table outlines the `clear` property and its possible values.

Property	Value
clear	none | left | right | both | inherit Initial value: none

The simplest explanation for the `clear` property is that it is used to cancel the effects of one or more floated elements. An example of its use can be observed in the following rules:

```
p {
    border: 1px solid black;
    background: rgb(218, 218, 218);
    line-height: 1em;
    padding: 10px;
}
p#floated {
    float: left;
    margin: 10px;
}
p#cleared {
    clear: left;
}
```

Applying those rules to the following markup renders the image shown in Figure 11-20:

```
<p id='floated'>
    This is the text of the first paragraph.
</p>
<p id='cleared'>
    This is the text of the second paragraph.
</p>
```

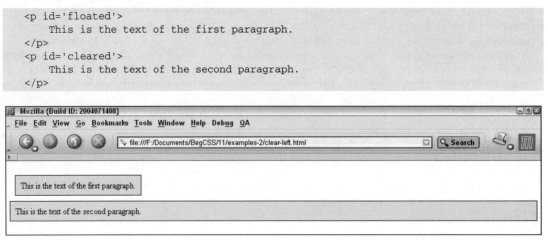

Figure 11-20

Figure 11-20 shows how the `clear: left;` declaration is used to cancel the effects of the left floated paragraph. If the paragraph has been right floated, a `clear: right;` declaration is used to cancel the effects of that float. A declaration of `clear: both;` is used to clear the effects of both left and right floated elements. Based on the example presented in Figure 11-20, the following demonstrates how the `clear: both;` declaration is used to avoid the effects of both left and right floated elements:

```
body {
    margin: 0;
    padding: 8px;
}
p {
    border: 1px solid black;
    background: rgb(218, 218, 218);
    line-height: 1em;
    padding: 10px;
}
p#left {
    width: 200px;
    float: left;
    margin: 10px;
}
p#right {
    width: 200px;
    float: right;
    margin: 10px;
}
p#clear {
    clear: both;
}
```

When the preceding rules are combined with the following markup, you see the results shown in Figure 11-21.

```
<p id='left'>
    This is the text of the first paragraph.
    This is the text of the first paragraph.
    This is the text of the first paragraph.
    This is the text of the first paragraph.
</p>
<p id='right'>
    This is the text of the second paragraph.
    This is the text of the second paragraph.
    This is the text of the second paragraph.
    This is the text of the second paragraph.
    This is the text of the second paragraph.
    This is the text of the second paragraph.
    This is the text of the second paragraph.
    This is the text of the second paragraph.
</p>
<p>
    This is the text of the third paragraph.
</p>
<p id='clear'>
    This is the text of the forth paragraph.
</p>
```

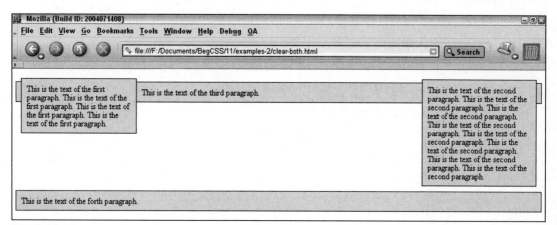

Figure 11-21

Figure 11-21 shows that the *clear* paragraph is below both the left and right floated paragraphs. If I had applied a `clear: left;` declaration instead, the *clear* paragraph would be beside the right floated paragraph and not beside the left floated paragraph. This is demonstrated in the output shown in Figure 11-22.

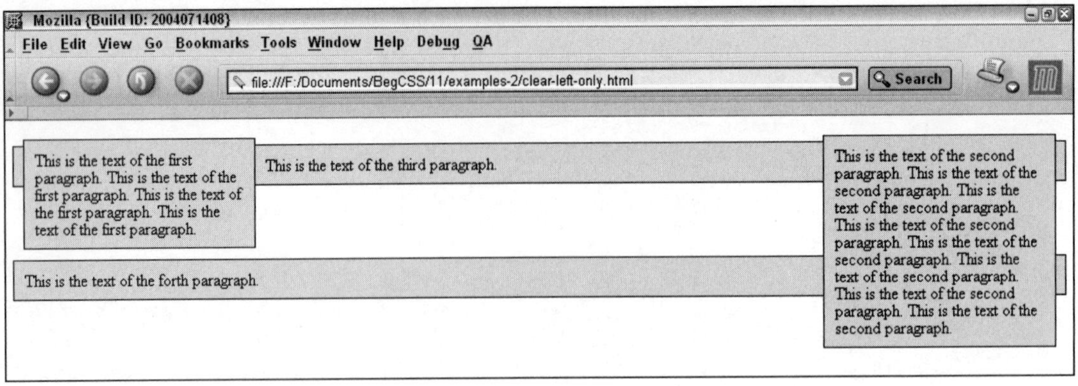

Figure 11-22

Now that you've seen some examples of how the `clear` property is used to control the elements that appear after a floated element, the following Try It Out applies the `clear` property to the JT's Island Grill and Gallery website.

Try It Out · Applying the clear Property

Example 11-2. In the following steps, you can see how the `clear` property controls the effects of the `float` property.

1. Add the following declaration to the base_styles.css style sheet:

```
h1 {
    clear: both;
    padding: 0.5em 1.1em;
    border-top: 0.05em solid black;
    -moz-border-radius-topleft: 0.8em;
    -moz-border-radius-topright: 0.8em;
    font-family: "Monotype Corsiva", cursive;
    letter-spacing: 4px;
    font-size: 1.5em;
}
```

2. Save base_styles.css.

3. Add the following declarations to the menu_system.css style sheet:

```
div#nav > a > img {
    clear: left;
    display: block;
    margin: 0 auto;
    width: 16em;
    height: auto;
}
```

4. Save menu_system.css. When you open dinner_menu.html in Mozilla, you see the output in Figure 11-23.

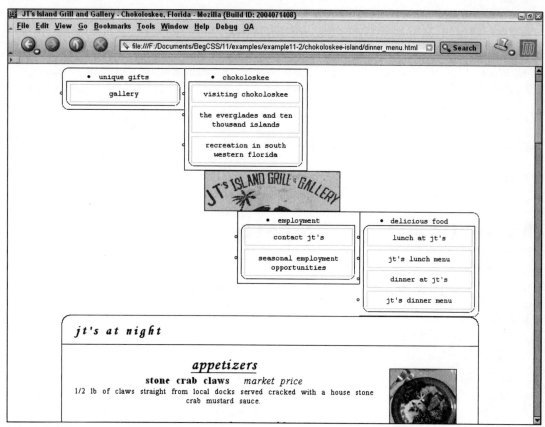

Figure 11-23

How It Works

Figure 11-23 shows that the dinner menu is much more cleanly defined. The left side of the navigation bar appears above the JT's logo. In Chapter 14, I apply CSS positioning properties to place this navigation to the left of the logo, and I apply several declarations to the logo to control both its placement and how it handles the floating elements around it:

```
clear: left;
display: block;
margin: 0 auto;
```

The clear: left; declaration prevents the logo from going to the left of the navigation menu. This is done so that the layout appears clean and organized as additional properties are applied. In Chapter 14 (using other CSS properties), the navigation menu will be positioned explicitly to the left of the logo and the links underneath each heading will become dynamic drop-down menus that appear only when the user's mouse cursor is over a heading. The same will happen to the navigation appearing below the JT's logo, but it will be positioned to the right of the logo. A display: block; declaration was necessary for the image because the clear property can be applied only to block elements. This declaration causes the image to no longer be centered. The `text-align: center;` property applied to the nav `<div>` in Chapter 8 has no effect on block elements. To correct this, the image is centered using the `margin: 0 auto;` declaration, so that no margin is applied to the top or bottom sides of the image, and the `auto` keyword is used to center the image. Next a `clear` property is applied to the `<h1>` element that begins the menu and its content. Here, a `clear: both;` is applied, although simply applying a `clear: right;` declaration would have the same effect.

This example demonstrates how the `clear` property is used to control the flow of content with respect to floated elements. With the `clear` property applied, the floated images in the dinner menu appear in their intended places, with text flowing around them to their left sides.

The next section focuses on the `vertical-align` property.

The vertical-align Property

Documented in CSS 2.1 and supported in IE 5.5, IE 6, Mozilla 1.7, Opera 7.5, and Safari 1.2.

The `vertical-align` property is used primarily in two contexts. In one context, it is used to vertically align text appearing within the lines of a paragraph. One example of this creates subscript or superscript text. The `vertical-align` property may also be used to align the content appearing inside a table cell. The following table outlines the `vertical-align` property and its possible values.

Property	Value
vertical-align	baseline | sub | super | top | text-top | middle | bottom | text-bottom | <percentage> | <length> | inherit Initial value: baseline

The `vertical-align` property applies exclusively to inline elements, such as `<img/>` and `<span>`. It has different meaning when applied to table cells. I discuss its use in cells in an upcoming section. In the next section, however, I look at how to format subscript text with the vertical-align property.

Subscript and Superscript Text

Within a paragraph, you may need several different types of styles that are only applied to snippets of the text, such as bold or italic fonts. Figure 11-12 showed that it is possible to apply a different background color to only one subset of text appearing within a paragraph by using the `<span>` element. Subscript text is an example of styles that often apply only to a selection of text rather than to a whole paragraph. *Subscript* text is text that appears slightly smaller than the text surrounding it and slightly lower than the baseline of the surrounding text. The *baseline* is the invisible line created for each line of text against which the bottom of each letter is aligned. In other words, the baseline is the line that letters "sit" on. *Superscript* text, on the other hand, is text raised above the baseline and that appears slightly smaller than the surrounding text. The following is a demonstration of subscript and superscript text:

```
p {

    font-size: 16px;
}
span {
    font-size: 0.8em;
}
p#sub span {
    vertical-align: sub;
}
p#super span {
    vertical-align: super;
}
```

Apply these rules to the following markup:

```
<p id='sub'>
    This is normal text. <span>This is subscript text.</span> This is normal text.
</p>
<p id='super'>
    This is normal text. <span>This is superscript text.</span> This is normal text.
</p>
```

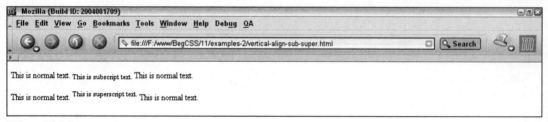

Figure 11-24

Figure 11-24 shows that the content of the <span> element of the first paragraph appears lower than that of the rest of the text and has a smaller font size, which is a result of applying the `vertical-align: sub;` and `font-size: 0.8em;` declarations. The figure also shows that the <span> element of the second paragraph appears slightly higher and with a slightly smaller font size, which is a result of the `vertical-align: super;` and `font-size: 0.8em;` declarations. In the normal text of both paragraphs, you observe the behavior of the `baseline` keyword, which is the default value of the `vertical-align` property.

The next section continues the discussion of the `vertical-align` property with superscript text.

The top, middle, and bottom Keywords

The `top`, `middle`, and `bottom` keywords are used to control vertical alignment of selections of text that are slightly smaller than the surrounding text. This is demonstrated in the following style sheet:

```
p {
    margin: 10px;
    font-size: 40px;
}
span {
    background: lightblue;
}
span.valign {
    font-size: 16px;
    color: white;
    background: steelblue;
    font-weight: bold;
}
span#baseline {
    vertical-align: baseline;
}
span#text-top {
    vertical-align: top;
}
span#middle {
    vertical-align: middle;
}
span#text-bottom {
    vertical-align: bottom;
}
```

Combine the preceding style sheet with the following markup:

```
<p>
    <span>
        Peter Piper picked a peck of
            <span class='valign' id='baseline'>pickled</span>
        peppers.
    </span>
</p>
<p>
    <span>
        Did Peter Piper pick a peck of
            <span class='valign' id='top'>pickled</span>
        peppers?
    </span>
</p>
<p>
    <span>
        If Peter Piper picked a peck of
            <span class='valign' id='middle'>pickled</span>
        peppers,
    </span>
</p>
<p>
    <span>
        where's the peck of
            <span class='valign' id='bottom'>pickled</span>
        peppers Peter Piper picked?
    </span>
</p>
```

This source code results in the rendering depicted in Figure 11-25.

Figure 11-25

The preceding example highlights the differences between the `baseline`, `top`, `middle`, and `bottom` keyword values of the `vertical-align` property. In the output, the text with a light blue (or lighter gray in the black and white screen shot shown in Figure 11-25) background is normal text. The font size of this text is increased to highlight the effects of each `vertical-align` keyword value. The text is given a background to highlight the dimensions of each line box. This is done by wrapping the entire line with `<span>` tags and applying the light blue background to those `<span>` elements to highlight the inline box model. Then, within each line of text, a single word, *pickled,* is wrapped in another set of `<span>` tags and given a different background color, steel blue, and a smaller font size than the text that surrounds it.

The application of these styles highlights the dimensions of the inline box model of the single word, *pickled.* Then a different `vertical-align` keyword is applied to the `<span>` tag wrapping the word *pickled* in each of the four paragraphs. In the first paragraph, you see what happens when *pickled* is given the `baseline` keyword. The letters of *pickled* are aligned with the baseline of the letters of the surrounding text. In the second paragraph, the `top` keyword is applied to the `<span>` tags surrounding *pickled,* which causes the top border of the inline box for *pickled* to be aligned with the top border of the inline box containing it. Then in the third paragraph, the `middle` keyword is applied to the `<span>` tags enclosing *pickled.* This causes the word to be aligned with respect to the middle of the lowercase letters. You may recall from Chapter 4, the x-height or ex unit is a measurement based on the height of the lowercase letter *x.* In this example, the `middle` keyword causes the `<span>` element containing the word *pickled* to be vertically centered based on the height of the lowercase letter *x.* The middle point of the inline box is aligned to the center of the lowercase letter *x.* And finally, in the last paragraph, the `<span>` element containing the word *pickled* is given the `bottom` keyword. This causes the bottom of the inline box containing the word *pickled* to be aligned with the bottom border of the inline box containing it.

The next section discusses the `text-top` and `text-bottom` keywords of the `vertical-align` property.

The text-top and text-bottom Keywords

Like the top, middle, and bottom values, the text-top and text-bottom keywords raise or lower a subset of text. The difference in the text-top keyword as opposed to the top keyword is that the text-top keyword causes alignment to happen with respect to the tallest character of the font of the surrounding text, for instance the lowercase letters *t, l, f,* or the uppercase letters. Likewise the text-bottom keyword aligns with respect to the lowest character, for instance the letters *p, y,* or *g,* which drop below the baseline. The text-top and text-bottom keyword values produce output similar to that produced by the top and bottom keywords. The most important difference between top and text-top is that top causes the border of the inline box to align with the top border of the line containing that inline box, whereas text-top aligns with respect to the tallest character in the font.

The next section discusses percentage and length values as applied to the vertical-align property.

Percentage and Length Value

If the selection of keywords I presented in the previous sections weren't enough for you, the vertical-align property also allows percentage and length values to be applied. The following example demonstrates the vertical-align property with a percentage value:

```
p {
    width: 200px;
    margin: 10px;
    padding: 10px;
    border: 1px solid black;
    font-size: 16px;
}
span {
    background: lightblue;
}
span > span {
    vertical-align: 100%;
    background: lightgray;
}
```

Combine the preceding style sheet with the following markup:

```
<p>
  <span>
    Peter Piper picked a peck of <span>pickled</span> peppers.
    Did Peter Piper pick a peck of <span>pickled</span> peppers?
    If Peter Piper picked a peck of <span>pickled</span> peppers,
    where's the peck of <span>pickled</span> peppers Peter Piper picked?
  </span>
</p>
```

You get the output shown in Figure 11-26.

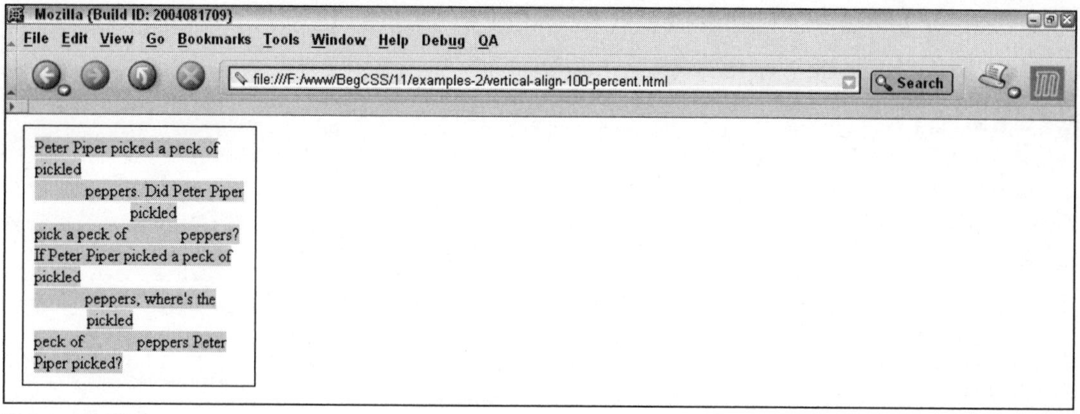

Figure 11-26

Figure 11-26 shows that the `<span>` wrapping all the contents of the paragraph is given a light blue background to highlight the dimensions of each line box. The `<span>` elements containing the word *pickled* are given the `vertical-align: 100%;` declaration. The application of this declaration results in each nested `<span>` element being raised 100% of the line height. Percentage measurements as applied with the `vertical-align` property are based on the height of the line. So if the value of the line-height property is 32 pixels and a `vertical-align: 50%;` declaration is applied, this results in the box being raised 50% of 32 pixels, or 16 pixels. A negative percentage may also be applied. If a negative percentage is applied, the opposite happens. The box is lowered by that percentage amount. A 0% value is the same value as the `baseline` keyword. Likewise, a length measurement may be applied, such as `vertical-align: 1em;`. This declaration causes the box to be raised 1em from the baseline. A negative value may also be applied. A `vertical-align: -1em;` declaration causes the box to be lowered 1em from the baseline.

The next section discusses the `vertical-align` property as applied to table cells.

Vertically Aligning the Contents of Table Cells

The `vertical-align` property has completely different meaning when it is applied to table cells. When applied to table cells only the `baseline`, `top`, `middle`, and `bottom` keywords are applicable, and the `vertical-align` property is used to align the entire contents of the cell. This is demonstrated in the following example:

```
table {
    font: 16px sans-serif;
    border: 1px solid black;
}
td {
    border: 1px solid black;
    width: 125px;
}
td.baseline {
    vertical-align: baseline;
}
```

```
td#largefont {
    font-size: 60px;
    vertical-align: baseline;
}
td#top {
    vertical-align: top;
}
td#middle {
    vertical-align: middle;
}
td#bottom {
    vertical-align: bottom;
}
```

Apply the preceding style sheet to the following markup:

```
<table>
    <tr>
        <td class='baseline'>
            The contents of this cell
            are aligned to the baseline.
        </td>
        <td class='baseline' id='largefont'>
            L
        </td>
        <td id='top'>
            The contents of this cell
            are top aligned.
        </td>
        <td id='middle'>
            The contents of this
            cell are middle aligned.
        </td>
        <td id='bottom'>
            The contents of this
            cell are bottom aligned.
        </td>
    </tr>
</table>
```

Figure 11-27 shows the output from this example.

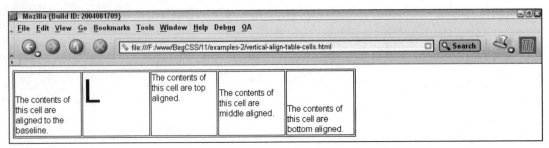

Figure 11-27

The preceding example is a demonstration of the four `vertical-align` properties that are applicable to table cells: `baseline`, `top`, `middle`, and `bottom`. The first two cells are aligned to the baseline. The baseline of a table cell is determined by the baseline of the table row. The baseline of the table row is determined by taking the baseline of the first line of each baseline-aligned table cell in that row. The one with the largest font determines the baseline of the row, which each table cell is aligned against.

In short, this complicated summary of baselining results in the line *The contents of* in the first table cell in Figure 11-27 having the same baseline as the letter *L* that appears in the second cell. In this case, the size of the letter *L* determines where the baseline of the table row is. The third cell is top-aligned, which means the content begins at the top of the cell and flows on downward from there. The fourth cell is middle-aligned, which means that the height of the content is measured to determine the middle point of the content, and then that midpoint is aligned with the midpoint of the cell. Finally, the fifth cell is bottom-aligned, which means that the bottom-most point of the content in the cell is aligned with the bottom of the cell.

Although you might expect the `vertical-align` property to apply to all elements — to block elements, for example, in the same way it is applied to table cells — this isn't the case. The `vertical-align` property is applicable only to inline elements and table cell elements: `<td>` and `<th>`.

Summary

This chapter focused on three key areas of CSS design. In this chapter you learned that

- ❑ Margin collapsing is a phenomenon that occurs when two vertical margins come into contact with one another, regardless of how many margins are present. Margin collapsing can occur between adjacent elements or nested elements; as a rule of thumb, the element with the largest margin wins, and the other margins are collapsed to zero.

- ❑ The `float` property is a seemingly complex property that has a unique place in CSS design. The `float` property is used for layout — for instance, to achieve a multicolumn design and to include content in the flow of paragraph text in such a way that text wraps around the floated element.

- ❑ The `clear` property is used to control the effects of the `float` property in situations where you don't want all the content following a floated element to float beside it.

- ❑ The `vertical-align` property is used to vertically align inline elements such as the `<span>` element or the `<img/>` element relative to the line containing those inline elements; this property can be used, for instance, to create subscript or superscript text.

- ❑ The `vertical-align` property may also be applied to table cells to control vertical alignment of the content within table cells. If the `vertical-align` property is applied to table cells, only a subset of properties are applicable. These include the `baseline`, `top`, `middle`, and `bottom` properties. The behavior of these properties is completely different when applied to table cells as opposed to normal inline content.

Chapter 12 discusses how to control the styling of list elements with CSS.

Exercise

Using the `float` and `clear` properties (and not using tables), design a web page with a four-column layout and a footer that spans all four columns. Apply whatever text or images you like to each column, or create an empty design that simply demonstrates the concept (by adding width, height, borders, background colors, and so on to each column). Give each column a 1-pixel-thick border, 5 pixels of padding, and give three of the four columns a fixed width. Put 5 pixels of space between each column, the footer, and the browser window. You should end up with a design like that shown in Figure 11-28.

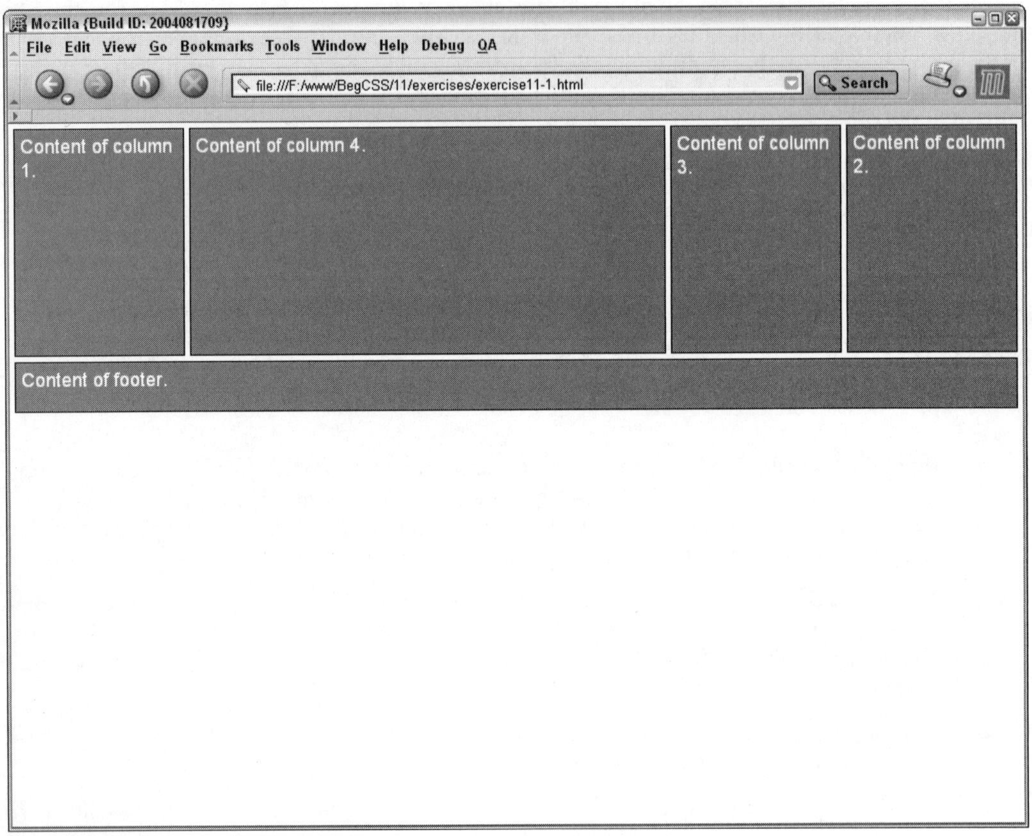

Figure 11-28

Styling Lists and the User Interface

In Chapter 11, you saw how the `float` and `clear` properties are used to control the flow of content in a web document. In this chapter, I look at properties used to control the styling of list elements, as well as special CSS properties used to style certain aspects of the user interface, such as the type of mouse cursor displayed. I cover the following:

❏ The `list-style-type` property and how it's used to present different types of lists through a variety of marker styles for bulleted lists and numbered lists

❏ The `list-style-image` property and how it's used to provide a custom marker for each list item

❏ The `list-style-position` property and how it's used to control the positioning of list item markers

❏ The `cursor` property and how it's used to control mouse cursors

Like the CSS properties I've covered in previous chapters, the CSS list properties give you complete control over the way you present and style list items.

The list-style-type Property

Documented in CSS 2.1 and supported in IE 5.5 (partial)IE 6 (partial), Mozilla 1.7, Opera 7.5, and Safari 1.2.

You use the `list-style-type` property to change the presentation of bulleted and numbered lists. For example, you can change an ordered list to a list using Roman numerals for markers, or you can change a bulleted list to one using squares instead of circles for markers. The following table outlines the `list-style-type` property and its possible values.

Property	Value
list-style-type	disc | circle | square | decimal | decimal-leading-zero | lower-roman | upper-roman | lower-greek | lower-latin | upper-latin | armenian | georgian | none | inherit Initial value: disc

Internet Explorer 6 supports only CSS 1 keyword values: disc | circle | square | decimal | lower-roman | upper-roman | lower-alpha | upper-alpha | none. Netscape 4 supports only CSS 1 values; CSS 2 support began with NS 6.

Naturally, the default list type used also depends on whether <ol> or <ul> list elements are used to structure the list. A variety of keywords allows for a variety of presentational styles. The next series of figures shows what each of these keywords looks like when rendered in a browser. Each of the following renderings is based on a simple test page. For unordered lists, you use a rule like

```
ul {
    font-family: sans-serif;
}
li.square {
    list-style-type: square;
}
li.disc {
    list-style-type: disc;
}
li.circle {
    list-style-type: circle;
}
```

with this markup:

```
<ul>
    <li class='square'>This list item has a square marker.</li>
    <li class='square'>This list item has a square marker.</li>
    <li class='disc'>This list item has a disc marker.</li>
    <li class='disc'>This list item has a disc marker.</li>
    <li class='circle'>This list item has a circle marker.</li>
    <li class='circle'>This list item has a circle marker.</li>
</ul>
```

The list-style-type property is inherited, so it may be applied to either the <li> element or the <ul> element.

For ordered list styles, I've used a test page that includes an <ol> element to keep the structure intuitive. Figure 12-2 shows what the list-style-type: decimal; and list-style-type: decimal-leading-zero; declarations look like.

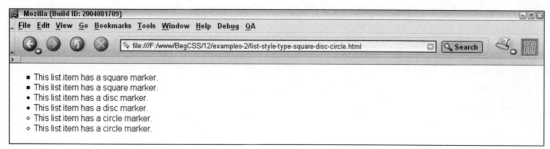

Figure 12-1

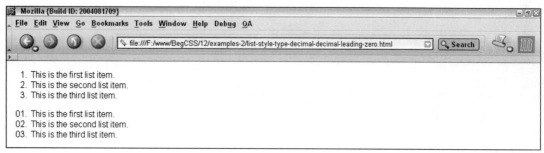

Figure 12-2

As you can see in Figure 12-2, the list markers of the first ordered list include only the number; the second ordered list includes the leading zero in the marker.

Figure 12-3 shows the `list-style-type: lower-roman;` and `list-style-type: upper-roman;` declarations. The top ordered list uses lowercase Roman numerals for the list markers, whereas the bottom list uses uppercase Roman numerals.

Figure 12-3

Figure 12-4 shows the `list-style-type: lower-latin;` and the `list-style-type: upper-latin;` declarations. As you can see, the top ordered list uses lowercase Latin letters for the list markers, and the bottom list uses uppercase Latin letters.

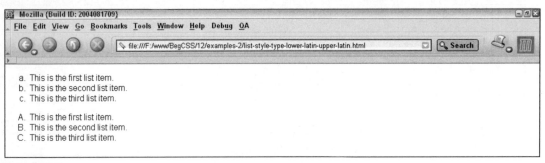

Figure 12-4

The `lower-latin` **and** `upper-latin` **keywords were called** `lower-alpha` **and** `upper-alpha` **in CSS 1.**

Figure 12-5 shows the `list-style-type: lower-greek;` declaration.

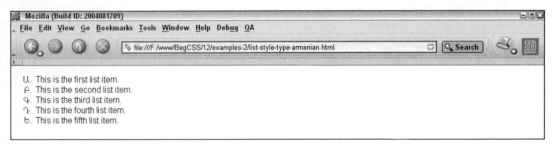

Figure 12-5

Figure 12-6 shows the `list-style-type: armenian;` declaration.

Figure 12-6

Figure 12-7 shows the `list-style-type: georgian;` declaration. The output shown in this figure is from Opera because Mozilla does not support this declaration.

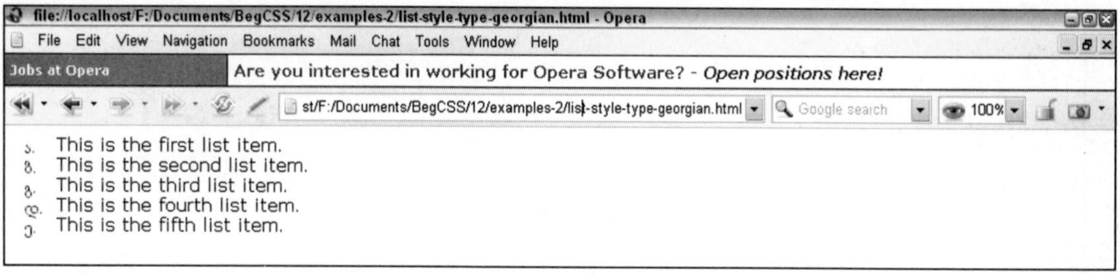

Figure 12-7

In the preceding figures, you saw the various already built-in styling that CSS provides for ordered and unordered list markers. The following Try It Out continues the JT's Island Grill and Gallery website. In this example, the list markers are removed from the navigation lists using the `list-style-none` property.

Try It Out   Removing List Style

Example 12-1. In the following steps, you see how to remove the list item markers from the navigation of the JT's Island Grill and Gallery website.

1.   Add the following declaration to the menu_system.css style sheet:

```
div#nav ul {
    list-style-type: none;
    margin: 0;
    padding: 0;
}
```

2.   Save menu_system.css.

As you can see in Figure 12-8, the list item markers have been removed by the `list-style-type: none;` declaration, which brings the navigation menus one step closer to the desired styles.

How It Works

By removing the list item markers, the navigation of the JT's website resembles menus rather than lists.

The next section continues the discussion of CSS list properties with the introduction of the `list-style-image` property. This property enables you to use a tiny version of an image file as a list marker.

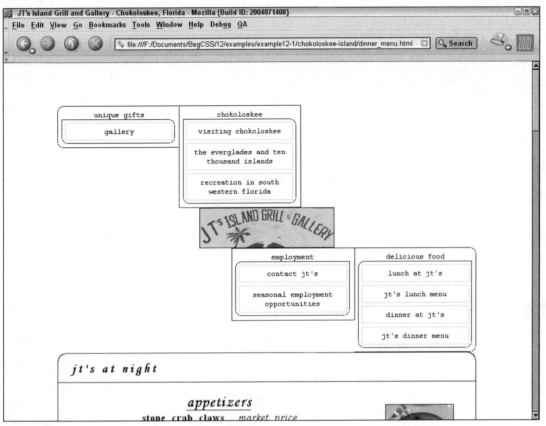

Figure 12-8

The list-style-image Property

Documented in CSS 2.1 and supported in IE 5.5, IE 6, Mozilla 1.7, Opera 7.5, and Safari 1.2.

Like the list-style-type property, you can use the list-style-image property to change the marker used for list items. The list-style-image property is most suited for custom bulleted lists. The following table outlines the list-style-image property and its possible values.

Property	Value
list-style-image	\<uri\> | none | inherit Initial value: none

The `list-style-image` property is quite straightforward; it accepts a file path to the image, which is denoted in the preceding table by the `<uri>` notation. Here is a simple example of the `list-style-image` property in action

```
ul {
    font-family: sans-serif;
    list-style-image: url('download.gif');
}
```

given this markup:

```
<ul>
    <li>Download cat.jpg</li>
    <li>Download myapp.exe</li>
    <li>Download powertools.zip</li>
</ul>
```

This results in the output in Figure 12-9.

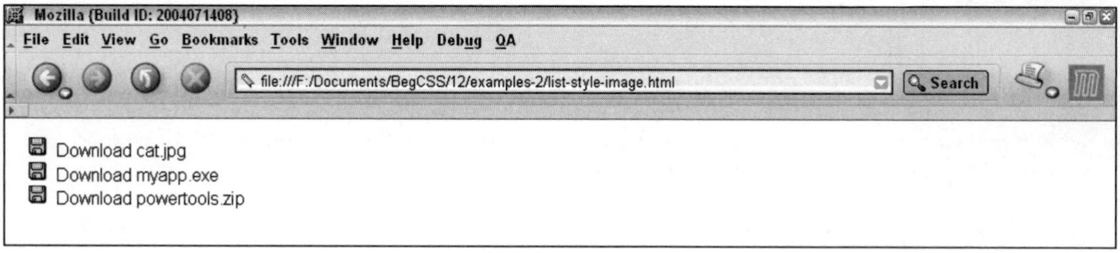

Figure 12-9

As you can see in Figure 12-9, the download.gif icon has replaced the list bullets, making the list marker into a tiny image of a floppy disc.

In the next section, I discuss the `list-style-position` property, which enables you to control the placement of list markers.

The list-style-position Property

Documented in CSS 2.1 and supported in IE 5.5, IE 6, Mozilla 1.7, Opera 7.5, and Safari 1.2.

You can use the `list-style-position` property to control the placement of list item markers and whether the list item marker appears on the inside of the list item element or outside of it. The following table outlines the `list-style-position` property and its possible values.

Property	Value
list-style-position	inside | outside | inherit Initial value: outside

You can highlight the effects of the list-style-position property. Figure 12-10 shows the list item dimensions highlighted using a light gray border.

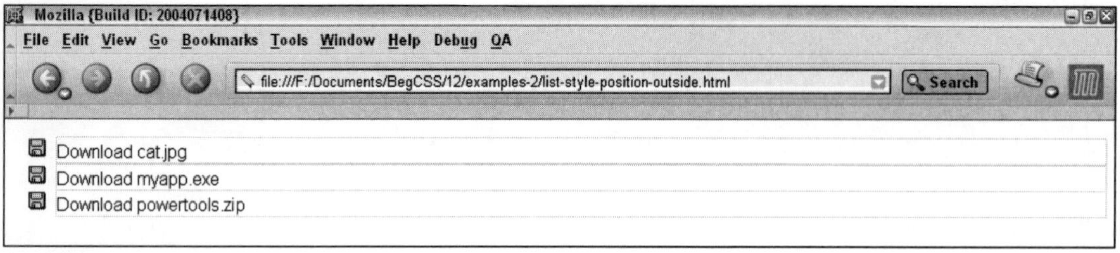

Figure 12-10

Figure 12-10 highlights the dimensions of each list item by applying a border to each <li> element; this demonstrates the behavior of the list-style-position: outside; declaration. Figure 12-11 shows what happens when a list-style-position: inside declaration is applied: The download.gif image now appears inside the list item borders.

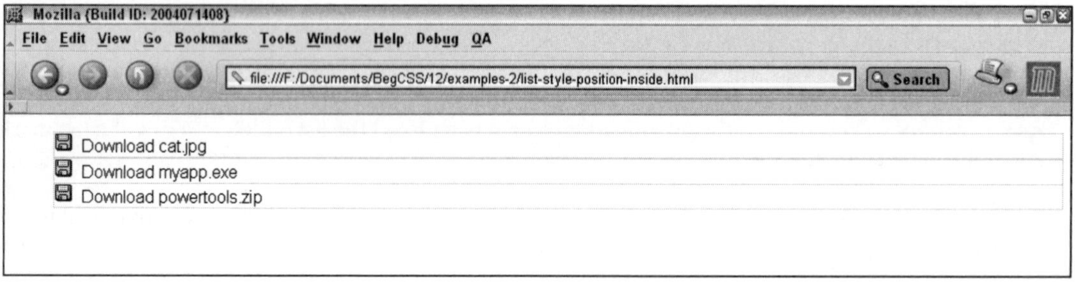

Figure 12-11

The next section wraps up discussion of CSS list properties with the list-style shorthand property. Using this property, you can combine several properties into one.

The list-style shorthand Property

Documented in CSS 2.1 and supported in IE 5.5, IE 6, Mozilla 1.7, Opera 7.5, and Safari 1.2.

Like the shorthand properties I presented in previous chapters, the list-style shorthand property allows multiple properties to be combined into one property. The following table outlines the list-style shorthand property and the possible values it allows.

Property	Value
list-style	[<'list-style-type'> | | <'list-style-position'> | | <'list-style-image'>] | inherit Initial value: n/a

The `list-style` property enables you to specify from one to three values, with each value corresponding to the list style properties I have discussed throughout this chapter: `list-style-type`, `list-style-image`, and `list-style-position`. For example, you could rewrite the example shown in Figure 12-9 like this using the `list-style` property:

```
ul {
    font-family: sans-serif;
    list-style: disc outside url('download.gif');
}
```

This produces the same output as that shown in Figure 12-9. You may be thinking "Why specify both an image and a marker style? Won't the image replace the marker style?" Although that's true, it is also possible that the user has disabled the display of images. Voice synthesizers may also provide a different style of voice for different marker styles to help visually impaired visitors.

You don't have to specify values for all three properties. You can include only two values in the `list-style` property, like this:

```
ul {
    font-family: sans-serif;
    list-style: inside url('download.gif');
}
```

This rule produces output identical to what was shown earlier in Figure 12-11.

Finally, it is also possible to provide only one value for this property, which would be `list-style-type`, `list-style-position`, or `list-style-image`.

```
ul {
    font-family: sans-serif;
    list-style: url('download.gif');
}
```

The preceding rule provides output identical to that shown in Figure 12-9. The final property that I discuss in this chapter is the `cursor` property, which enables you to control the kind of cursor displayed on your page.

The cursor Property

Documented in CSS 2.1 and supported in IE 5.5, IE 6, Mozilla 1.7, Opera 7.5, and Safari 1.2.

CSS provides the `cursor` property to control the type of cursor displayed for a particular element. The following table outlines the `cursor` property and its possible values.

Property	Value
cursor	[[<uri> ,]* [auto | crosshair | default | pointer | move | e-resize | ne-resize | nw-resize | n-resize | se-resize | sw-resize | s-resize | w-resize | text | wait | help | progress]] | inherit Initial value: auto

The notation in the preceding table shows that the cursor property can accept a reference to a custom cursor with the <uri> notation. The table also shows that you can provide more than one URL by giving a comma-separated list of URLs. Alternatively, you can provide a keyword to change the cursor displayed while the user's mouse pointer is hovering over an element. To demonstrate how the cursor can be changed, consider the following rule:

```
div {
    cursor: move;
    border: thin solid black;
    width: 100px;
    height: 100px;
}
```

Figure 12-12 shows that the cursor changes to a crosshair with arrows on all four points when the user's mouse hovers over the <div> element.

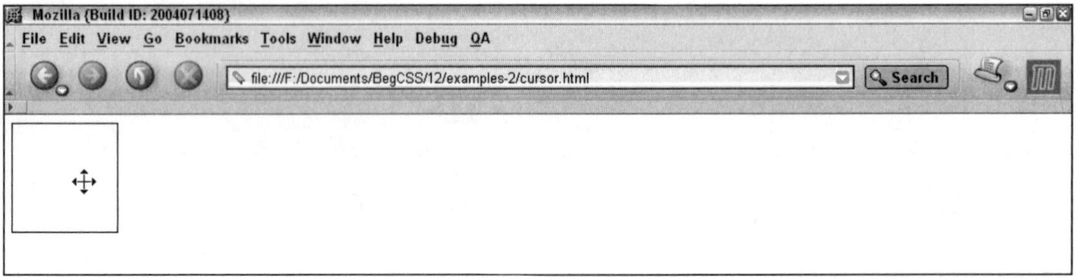

Figure 12-12

The following table shows what type of cursor to expect with each keyword value.

Cursor Keyword	Cursor Image
crosshair	
pointer	
move	

Cursor Keyword	Cursor Image
e-resize / w-resize	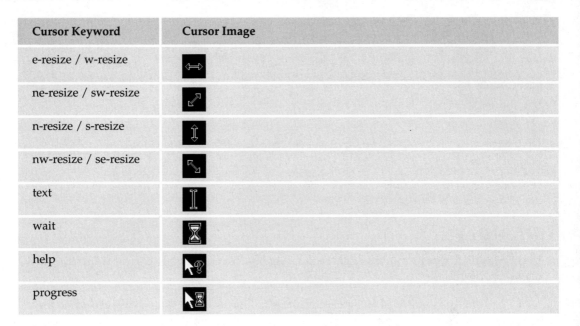
ne-resize / sw-resize	
n-resize / s-resize	
nw-resize / se-resize	
text	
wait	
help	
progress	

The cursors of the preceding table are typical of the Windows OS. If you have a Windows OS, you can find more cursors in the `C:\Windows\Cursors` directory.

Although the table shows cursors specific to the Windows OS, other operating systems provide similar cursors. The type of cursor displayed for each keyword may be different based on the user's cursor preferences. For instance, the user may have installed a theme that includes a different style of cursor. The style of cursor is also different on different operating systems, meaning it would differ from Mac OS X to Windows. Despite the possible differences in the aesthetic appearance of cursors, the cursors provided by the operating system will match the `cursor` keywords provided by CSS.

You can also provide a custom cursor by referencing the file path to the cursor file:

```
div {
    cursor: url('banana.ani');
    border: thin solid black;
    width: 100px;
    height: 100px;
}
```

The rendered output in Figure 12-13 shows an animated banana cursor when viewed in IE 6.

Mozilla, Opera, and Safari do not yet support custom cursors. IE 6 supports only Windows native cursor formats: .cur (a static cursor image) and .ani (an animated cursor image). The W3C specification states that more than one cursor image may be referenced, as in the following, in the event that the browser does not understand the first cursor image provided:

```
cursor: url('cursor.svg'), url('cursor.cur'), pointer;
```

In this example, an .svg file is referenced first. If the browser isn't capable of displaying an .svg file, it attempts to retrieve the cursor.cur image. If it can't display that cursor, it defaults to the `pointer` keyword.

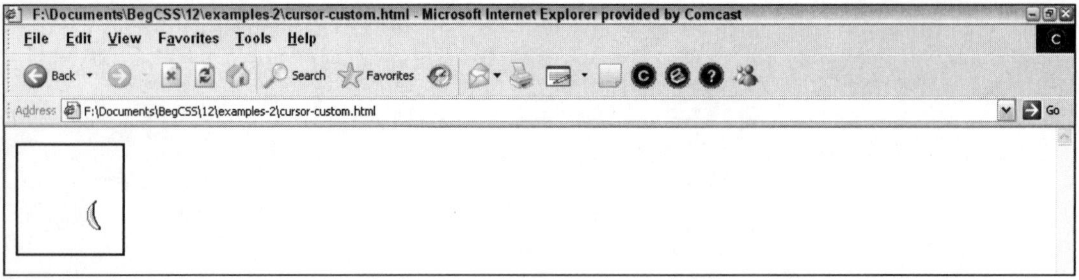

Figure 12-13

Summary

The CSS list properties provide complete control over how list elements are presented. To recap, in this chapter you learned that

❑ A variety of predefined options are available for the display of list item markers using the `list-style-type` property.

❑ The `list-style-image` property may be used to provide a custom image as the list item marker.

❑ The `list-style-position` property dictates whether the markers appear inside the list item element or outside of it.

❑ The `list-style` property provides a shortcut syntax where all three list style properties may be referenced at once.

❑ The `cursor` property may be used to change the cursor displayed to the user, which may be via a predefined list of keywords or by referencing a custom image via a URL, although the latter is only supported (at the time of this writing) by Internet Explorer 6.

In Chapter 13, I explore the properties that CSS provides for control over the presentation of backgrounds.

Exercises

1. Using the `list-style-type` property introduced in this chapter and properties introduced in previous chapters, create a tabbed navigation menu using only lists (`<ul>` and `<li>`) and CSS. Include four links, one in each list-item and lay out the tabs horizontally. Put a thin, solid border below all the tabs and around each individual tab, make each tab 100 pixels wide, center the text of each tab, and space each tab from the other.

> Floated elements are taken out of the normal flow. To place the border on the bottom of the tabs, the `<ul>` element must have an explicit height.

2. Create a list that resembles a folder navigation tree. Use two images: an image representing a closed folder and an image representing an open folder. Place at least five items in your folder tree. Make the last list item positioned on the inside of the list and display an open folder for the list item marker. You may use only one list and only two rules; and you cannot use any class or id names.

> **Use adjacent selectors to select a specific list item.**

Backgrounds: Setting the Scene

In Chapter 12, you learned how CSS lists are styled and how you can control the mouse cursor by using the cursor property. In this chapter, you explore the CSS background properties and see how these provide control over the presentation of the background. In this chapter, I discuss the following:

- ❑ How to use the background-color property to set a background color
- ❑ How to use the background-image property to specify a background image
- ❑ How to use the background-repeat property to control background tiling
- ❑ How to use the background-position property to control how the background is positioned
- ❑ How to use the background-attachment property to control whether the background scrolls with the page or remains fixed in place with respect to the view port
- ❑ How to use the background shorthand property to combine all the separate background properties into a single property

Backgrounds play a large role in CSS design and are often the bread and butter of the overall aesthetic presentation of a web page. This chapter begins the discussion of background properties by exploring the background-color property.

The background-color Property

Documented in CSS 2.1 and supported in IE5.5, IE6, Mozilla 1.7, Opera 7.5, and Safari 1.2.

As I touched on in Chapter 4, you use the background-color property to specify a solid background color. The following table shows the possible values for the background-color property.

Property	Value
background-color	\<color\> | transparent | inherit Initial value: transparent

The `background-color` property allows any of the color values supported by CSS, such as a color keyword, an RGB value, or a hexadecimal, or short hexadecimal value. It may also be given the `transparent` keyword, which indicates that no color should be used.

The following exercise applies the `background-color` property to the JT's Island Grill and Gallery style sheet.

Try It Out   **Applying a Background Color**

Example 13-1. To apply the `background-color` property to the JT's Island Grill website, follow these steps.

1. Add the following declaration to the base_styles.css style sheet to apply background colors for the page heading and footer:

```
h1, h6 {
    background-color: lightsteelblue;
    border-left: 0.05em solid black;
    border-right: 0.05em solid black;
}
```

2. Save base_styles.css.

3. Make the following modifications to the menu_system.css style sheet to apply background colors for each aspect of the site's navigation:

```
div#nav > ul > li {
    background-color: lightblue;
    padding: 0.5em;
    border: 0.05em solid black;
    font-size: 0.9em;
}
div#nav > ul > li:hover {
    background-color: lightsteelblue;
}
```

4. Still modifying the menu_system.css style sheet, make the following changes:

```
ul.menu {
    background-color: lightblue;
    width: 15em;
```

```
    -moz-border-radius-bottomleft: 1em;
    -moz-border-radius-bottomright: 1em;
    border: 0.05em solid black;
}
ul#food ul.menu {
    -moz-border-radius-topleft: 1em;
}
ul#gifts ul.menu {
    -moz-border-radius-topright: 1em;
}
ul.menu li {
    color: black;
}
ul.menu a {
    margin: 0.4em;
    padding: 0.5em;
    color: black;
    display: block;
    border: 0.05em solid lightblue;
}
ul.menu a:hover {
    background-color: lightsteelblue;
    -moz-border-radius: 0.8em;
    border: 0.05em solid black;
    text-decoration: none;
}
div#nav ul a:active {
    background-color: steelblue;
}
```

5. Save menu_system.css.

6. Add the following rule to the dinner_menu.css style sheet to give the dinner menu itself a background color:

```
p.copy {
    padding-top: 0;
}
div#content {
    background-color: lightyellow;
}
```

7. Save dinner_menu.css.

Figure 13-1 shows that a number of background colors have been applied to the JT's dinner menu.

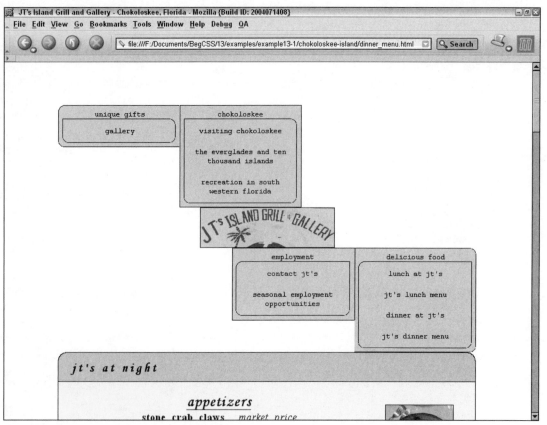

Figure 13-1

How It Works

Different background colors have been applied to each navigational heading and each list of links underneath each heading. A background color has been applied to the <h1> heading containing the page's title, the body of the dinner menu itself, and the <h6> heading containing the page's footer. I've already covered the background-color property fairly extensively in previous chapters, but here's a review of the most important modifications made to the menu_system.css style sheet. The following shows how these modifications impact the presentation of the web page.

The first modification to the menu_system.css style sheet is made to give each heading a light blue background color.

```
div#nav > ul > li {
    background-color: lightblue;
    padding: 0.5em;
```

Okay, straightforward enough. The navigational headings are selected here based on their ancestry with the direct child selector. If the nav <div> element has a <ul> element as a child and that <ul> element has an <li> element as a child, apply a lightblue background color. The next modification changes the color of those <li> item background colors if the user's mouse cursor is over the <li> element.

```
div#nav > ul > li:hover {
    background-color: lightsteelblue;
}
```

This step adds dynamic functionality to each navigational heading. The background color of each list item changes in response to user actions, allowing the JT's menu to feel more like an application and less like a static, unchanging web document. In the old days, such functionality could only be achieved by using complicated client-side scripting languages. Today, simple dynamic functionality, such as a heading that changes color when the user's mouse cursor rolls over it, can be completely created using plain HTML and CSS.

The next modification gives each submenu that contains the links for each heading a light blue background color to complement the background color of each individual heading:

```
ul.menu {
    background-color: lightblue;
    width: 15em;
```

These submenus are provided with their own background colors. When I turn these into drop-down menus in Chapter 14, each menu will have a solid background instead of a transparent background.

Next, as I did for each individual navigation heading, I specified a background color that appears when the user's mouse cursor hovers over the individual links contained in each menu:

```
ul.menu a:hover {
    background-color: lightsteelblue;
    -moz-border-radius: 0.8em;
```

This follows along with the same dynamic principles applied to each heading. The background color of each link changes in response to user action; in this case, the background color of each link changes as the user makes a selection from the menu. Finally, I provide another background color for links that have actually been clicked:

```
div#nav ul a:active {
    background-color: steelblue;
}
```

When clicked, each link briefly changes color (in this case, to steel blue) to indicate that it has been clicked.

In the next section, I discuss the background-image property, which lets you use an image for the background of your page.

The background-image Property

Documented in CSS 2.1 and supported in IE 5.5, IE 6, Mozilla 1.7, Opera 7.5, and Safari 1.2.

As you probably guessed, the `background-image` property enables you to provide an image for the background. The following table outlines the possible values available for the `background-image` property.

Property	Value
background-image	<uri> | none | inherit Initial value: none

Like the `list-style-image` property that I discussed in Chapter 12, the `background-image` property allows you to reference a URL, which is indicated by the `<uri>` notation in the preceding table, a keyword of `none`, or, like all other properties, a keyword of `inherit`. When you specify a background image, by default the image tiles across the entire area available to it. The size of each tile depends on the size of the image itself. Consider the following example:

```
<!DOCTYPE html PUBLIC "-//W3C//DTD XHTML 1.0 Strict//EN"
"http://www.w3.org/TR/xhtml1/DTD/xhtml1-strict.dtd">
<html>
    <head>
        <title></title>
        <style type='text/css'>
            html, body {
                height: 1000px;
            }
            body {
                background-image: url('jts.jpg');
            }
        </style>
    </head>
    <body>
    </body>
</html>
```

Figure 13-2 shows that the image is tiled horizontally and vertically, covering all the available space. To be able to see how the background reacts while scrolling the page I gave the `<html>` and `<body>` elements both an explicit height, overriding their auto height behavior.

The following Try It Out applies two background images to the JT's Island Grill and Gallery style sheet. These images — palms.jpg (1600 pixels in width by 781 pixels in height) and dinner_glass.jpg (1600 pixels in width by 1200 pixels in height) — are available to download from www.wrox.com. If you are unable to download them for any reason, you can substitute your own images.

Figure 13-2

Try It Out   Applying a Background Image

Example 13-2. In the following steps, you apply background images to the JT's Island Grill and Gallery dinner menu.

1. Add the following declaration to the base_styles.css style sheet to apply a background image to the `<body>` of the web page:

```
body {
    background-image: url('../images/backgrounds/palms.jpg');
    padding: 5em 0 1.2em 0;
    margin: 0;
    font-family: "Courier New", Courier, monospace;
    text-transform: lowercase;
}
```

2. Save base_styles.css.

3. Add the following declaration to the dinner_menu.css style sheet to apply a background image to the body of the dinner menu itself:

```
p.copy {
    padding-top: 0;
}
div#content {
    background-color: lightyellow;
    background-image: url('../images/backgrounds/dinner_glass.jpg');
}
```

4. Save dinner_menu.css

In Figure 13-3, you can see that two images have been applied to the JT's dinner menu.

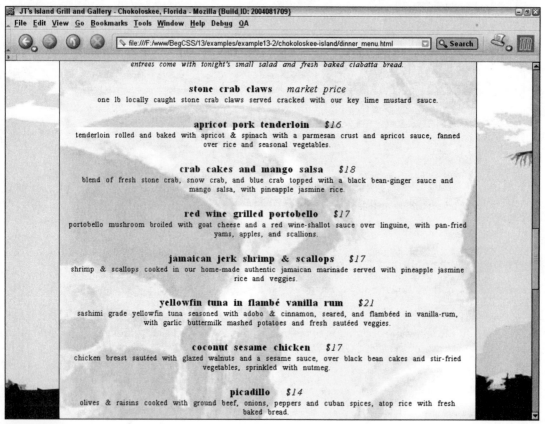

Figure 13-3

How It Works

Figure 13-3 shows that two images have been applied to the JT's dinner menu. One (palms.jpg) to the background of the <body> element, which in essence means the browser view port. This image is a soft-ened representation of a Chokoloskee sunset as viewed from JT's front porch. I created this image with the largest possible screen resolutions in mind, giving it dimensions of 1600 x 781 pixels. This allows the background image to remain stretched across the view port as the screen resolution increases. It isn't the best way to approach the background image, but CSS offers no way to dynamically resize the image with the area available to the image. In other words, you can't dynamically scale the image to 1024 x 768 (if that is the user's screen resolution). In order to size the background image so that it reaches the most screen resolutions, I've made it as wide as the largest screen resolution I'm willing to target: 1600 x 1200.

I also experimented with different JPEG compression rates to get the image as small in file size as possible, selecting the lowest-possible compression resulting in the least artifacts appearing in the image. Compression artifacts are very similar to the effects of pixelization that I discussed in Chapter 4. An image of low-quality compression containing artifacts makes the image ugly, so I settled on a compression rate that produces as few as possible. This technique can be explored with Adobe Photoshop or other graphic editing tools.

I also employed similar techniques for the dinner_glass.jpg image that I used for the background of the dinner menu. Although with this second image, I used Adobe Photoshop with the various filters and the image editing tools it offers to soften the original photo, thereby ensuring that the text of the menu itself would not be difficult to read with the dinner_glass.jpg image behind it. Adobe Photoshop offers a far more powerful range of image-editing capabilities. I also gave this image a size of 1600 x 1200 pixels so that it would respond gracefully to adjustments in the user's screen resolution and the user's default text size. Once more experimenting with different JPEG compression rates, I achieved an image about 60KB in size, which results in acceptable download times for the majority of users.

The final technique employed in this example is the use of a relative file path preceded by two periods and a forward slash:

```
background-image: url('../images/backgrounds/dinner_glass.jpg');
```

The two periods and forward slash before the reference to the images directory tells the browser that the images directory can be found in the parent directory of the style_sheets directory. The parent directory here is the chokoloskee-island directory. This is necessary because, if I specified the file path like this

```
background-image: url('images/backgrounds/dinner_glass.jpg');
```

the browser would expect the images directory to be in the style_sheets directory and would consider `style_sheets/images/backgrounds/dinner_glass.jpg` to be the path to the dinner_glass.jpg. Of course, the browser wouldn't be able to find the image there. So I used the two periods and forward slash to tell it to first go up one directory level before looking for the images directory.

The next section continues the discussion of CSS background properties with the `background-repeat` property. This property enables you to control whether and how an image is tiled.

The background-repeat Property

Documented in CSS 2.1 and supported in IE 5, IE 6, Mozilla 1.7, Opera 7.5, and Safari 1.2.

The `background-repeat` property is used to control how an image is tiled or if it is tiled at all. The following table shows the possible values for the `background-repeat` property.

Property	Value
background-repeat	repeat | repeat-x | repeat-y | no-repeat | inherit Initial value: repeat

As you saw in the last section, by default a background is tiled vertically and horizontally. The back-ground-repeat property offers control over this. For instance, you can limit the tiling of a background image to the x-axis by supplying the repeat-x keyword value to the background-repeat property. Consider this keyword applied to the example shown in Figure 13-2:

```
html, body {
    height: 1000px;
}
body {
    background-image: url('jts.jpg');
    background-repeat: repeat-x;
}
```

Figure 13-4 shows that the jts.jpg image is tiled only along the x-axis.

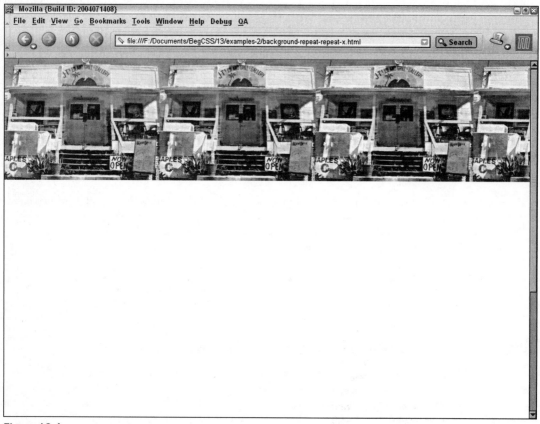

Figure 13-4

Conversely, you can limit the image to tiling along the y-axis by using the `repeat-y` keyword, as is shown in Figure 13-5.

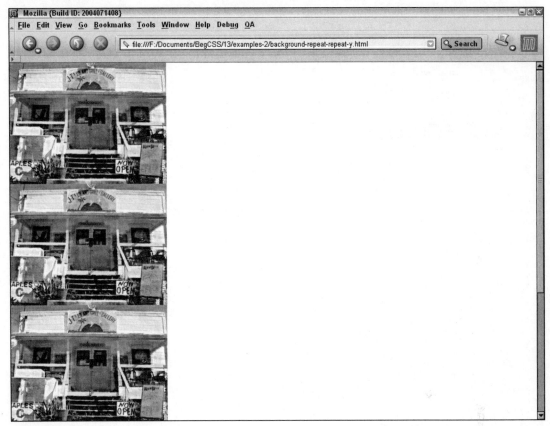

Figure 13-5

Or, you can make the image not repeat (tile) at all by using the `no-repeat` keyword, as depicted in Figure 13-6.

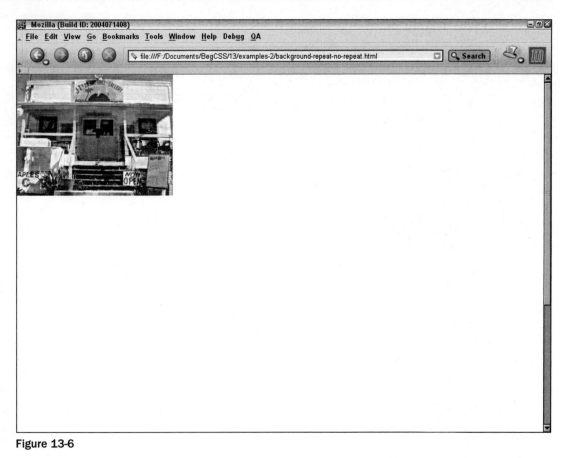

Figure 13-6

The following Try It Out applies the `background-repeat` property to the JT's Island Grill and Gallery style sheet.

Try It Out   Controlling Background Repetition

Example 13-3. In the following steps you can see the effects of the `background-repeat` property.

1. Add the following declaration to the base_styles.css style sheet to turn off tiling of the palms.jpg background image:

```css
body {
    background-image: url('../images/backgrounds/palms.jpg');
    background-repeat: no-repeat;
    padding: 5em 0 1.2em 0;
    margin: 0;
    font-family: "Courier New", Courier, monospace;
    text-transform: lowercase;
}
```

2. Save base_styles.css.

3. Add the following declaration to the dinner_menu.css style sheet to turn off tiling of the dinner_glass.jpg background image:

```
div#content {
    background-color: lightyellow;
    background-image: url('../images/backgrounds/dinner_glass.jpg');
    background-repeat: no-repeat;
}
```

4. Save dinner_menu.css.

How It Works

The effects of this property are not easily captured with a screen shot because the page is simply too long for the space available here. If you're working through these examples with me, however, you can see that when dinner_menu.html is loaded into Mozilla, the palms.jpg and dinner_glass.jpg images appear only once on the page, instead of being tiled as they were when you applied the background-image property.

The next section continues discussion of CSS background properties by introducing the background-position property. The background-position property lets you control the placement of the background.

The background-position Property

Documented in CSS 3 and supported in IE 5.5, IE 6, Mozilla 1.7, Opera 7.5, and Safari 1.2.

The background-position property, as its name implies, allows you to control the placement of the background. The following table shows the possible values for the background-position property.

Property	Value
background-position	[[<percentage> | <length>]{1,2} | [[top | center | bottom] || [left | center | right]]] | inherit Initial value: 0% 0%

At first glance, this property looks a little complicated; in truth, it isn't all that complex. The notation boils down to this: The property allows two values that express the position of the background; one value that gives the position of the background, or a value of inherit. The value must be one of the three possibilities shown in the preceding table, but all three cannot be used at once. Square brackets are used to group the possible values. The following is the first subgrouping of values within the first grouping:

```
[<percentage> | <length> ]{1,2}
```

The first grouping indicates that the value may be a percentage or length value. Either one or two values may be provided; but if two values are provided, both must be percentage values or length values — not a mixture. This is indicated by the presence of a single vertical bar between the `<percentage>` and `<length>` values. The second subgrouping is preceded by a vertical bar, which indicates another possibility for the value:

```
| [ [top | center | bottom] || [left | center | right] ]
```

The second grouping indicates that either one or two keyword values may be provided; if two values are provided, it may be any keyword from the first grouping combined with any of the keywords from the second grouping.

Consider the following example of this in action:

```
<!DOCTYPE html PUBLIC "-//W3C//DTD XHTML 1.0 Strict//EN"
"http://www.w3.org/TR/xhtml1/DTD/xhtml1-strict.dtd">
<html>
    <head>
        <title></title>
        <style type='text/css'>
            html, body {
                height: 1000px;
            }
            body {
                background-image: url('jts.jpg');
                background-repeat: no-repeat;
                background-position: left top;
            }
        </style>
    </head>
    <body>
    </body>
</html>
```

This example results in the same output shown in Figure 13-6; the image is positioned to the left and top of the view port. This use of the `background-position` property is an example of the first grouping of values in which two values are provided to the property. The `background-position: left top;` declaration is the same as saying `background-position: top left;` or what you would get by supplying a percentage measurement of `background-position: 0% 0%;`. Each results in the same output. Here is another example:

```
body {
    background-image: url('jts.jpg');
    background-repeat: no-repeat;
    background-position: top center;
}
```

Figure 13-7 shows the background image centered at the top of the browser window.

You can also express this position with a single keyword: `background-position: top;`. Using this value results in the same output shown in Figure 13-7. In addition, the declaration `background-position: center top;` provides output identical to that shown in Figure 13-7.

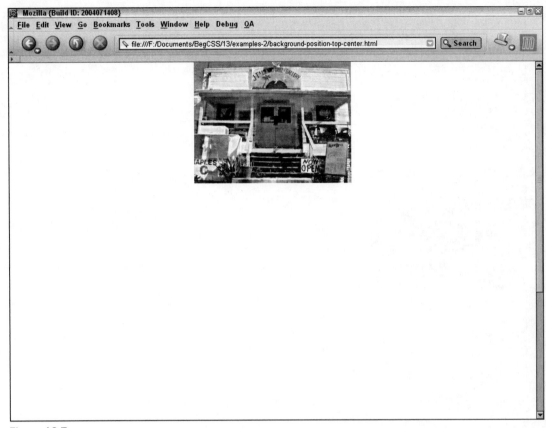

Figure 13-7

If a percentage measurement or a length unit is used, two values must be provided, as is indicated in the first grouping of values in the notation for the background-position property. Consider the following example:

```
body {
    background-image: url('jts.jpg');
    background-repeat: no-repeat;
    background-position: 0% 50%;
}
```

Figure 13-8 shows that the background image is now vertically centered and appears horizontally on the left side of the browser window.

The background-position: 0% 50%; declaration is the same thing as saying background-position: left center; or background-position: center left;.

371

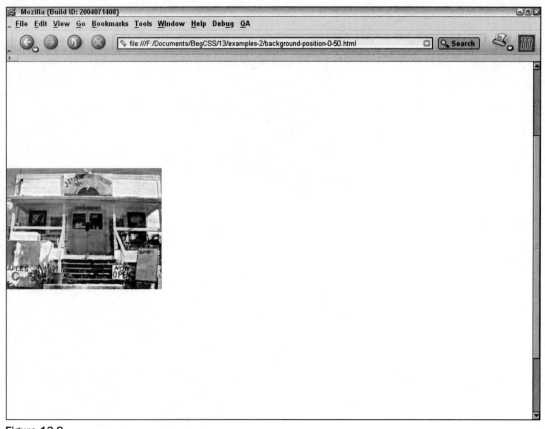

Figure 13-8

The following Try It Out applies the `background-position` property to the JT's Island Grill and Gallery dinner menu.

Try It Out   **Controlling the Background's Position**

Example 13-4. The following steps show how you can use the `background-position` property to position the background on JT's website.

1. Add the following declaration to the base_styles.css style sheet to position the palms.jpg background image:

```
body {
    background-image: url('../images/backgrounds/palms.jpg');
    background-repeat: no-repeat;
    background-position: center bottom;
    padding: 5em 0 1.2em 0;
    margin: 0;
    font-family: "Courier New", Courier, monospace;
    text-transform: lowercase;
}
```

2. Save base_styles.css.

3. Add the following declaration to the dinner_menu.css style sheet to position the dinner_glass.jpg image:

```
div#content {
    background-color: lightyellow;
    background-image: url('../images/backgrounds/dinner_glass.jpg');
    background-repeat: no-repeat;
    background-position: center center;
}
```

4. Save dinner_menu.css

Figure 13-9 shows the dinner_glass.jpg image positioned at the center and bottom of the browser window.

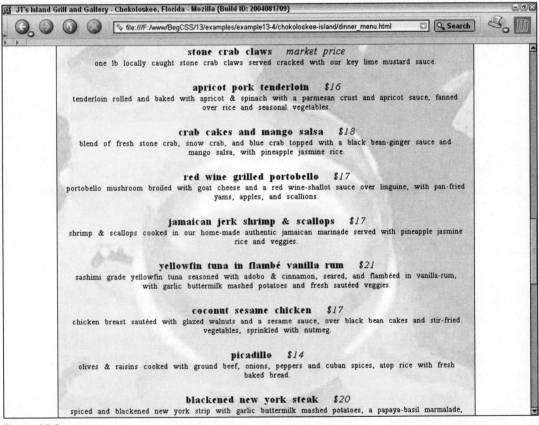

Figure 13-9

Figure 13-10 shows the browser window scrolled down below the dinner menu; you can see that the palms.jpg image is now positioned at the center and bottom of the window.

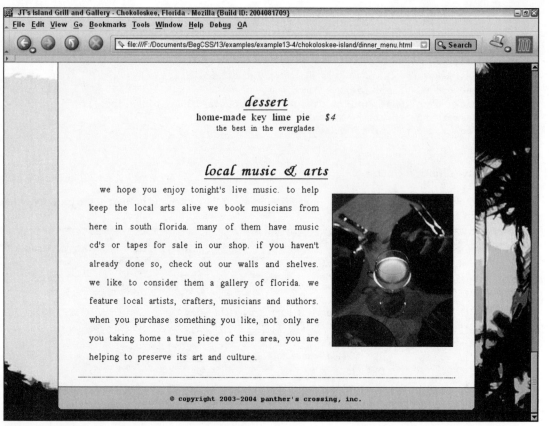

Figure 13-10

How It Works

In Figure 13-9, the dinner_glass.jpg image is centered vertically and horizontally in the output. Positioning it at the center of the content <div> — both horizontally and vertically — allows the wine glass in the picture to take center stage. This image isn't visible in Figure 13-10, however, because the figure shows only the bottom of the dinner menu.

Controlling the positioning of the background image in Figure 13-10 enables the palms.jpg image to be visible in the background. Being centered in the window, it becomes more visible as the screen resolution increases.

The effects of these modifications are brought out even further with the addition of the next property, the background-attachment property. This property lets you control whether an image scrolls with the rest of a page's content.

The background-attachment Property

Documented in CSS 2.1 and supported in IE 5.5, IE 6, Opera 7.5, and Safari 1.2.

You can use the `background-attachment` property to control whether a background image scrolls with the content of a web page (when scroll bars are activated because that content is larger than the browser window). The following table outlines the possible values for the `background-attachment` property.

Property	Value
background-attachment	scroll | fixed | inheri Initial value: scroll

Internet Explorer supports the `fixed` keyword only if applied to the `<body>` element.

The `background-attachment` property provides one very cool effect. By default, the background image scrolls with the content of the web page; this is the behavior of the `background-attachment: scroll;` declaration. If the fixed keyword is provided and the browser in question supports it, the background image remains fixed in place while the page scrolls. Here is an example of this scenario:

```
<!DOCTYPE html PUBLIC "-//W3C//DTD XHTML 1.0 Strict//EN"
"http://www.w3.org/TR/xhtml1/DTD/xhtml1-strict.dtd">
<html>
    <head>
        <title></title>
        <style type='text/css'>
            html, body {
                height: 1000px;
            }
            body {
                background-image: url('jts.jpg');
                background-repeat: no-repeat;
                background-position: 0% 0%;
                background-attachment: fixed;
            }
        </style>
    </head>
    <body>
    </body>
</html>
```

This effect is not easily represented in a screen capture. To view the effect of the preceding code, load up the preceding example into Mozilla and be in awe as the jts.jpg image remains fixed to the left top corner of the browser window while you scroll. You can obtain this image in the book's code download at www.wrox.com and also see the finished .html file (background-attachment-fixed.html). If you don't have Internet access, you may substitute an image of your own.

The following Try It Out implements the `background-attachment` property in JT's dinner menu.

Try It Out   **Fixing the Background in Place**

Example 13-5. To see how the dinner menu background images remain fixed in place while scrolling, follow these steps.

1. Add the following declaration to the base_styles.css style sheet:

```
body {
    background-image: url('../images/backgrounds/palms.jpg');
    background-repeat: no-repeat;
    background-position: center bottom;
    background-attachment: fixed;
    padding: 5em 0 1.2em 0;
    margin: 0;
    font-family: "Courier New", Courier, monospace;
    text-transform: lowercase;
}
```

2. Save base_styles.css.

3. Add the following declaration to the dinner_menu.css style sheet:

```
div#content {
    background-color: lightyellow;
    background-image: url('../images/backgrounds/dinner_glass.jpg');
    background-repeat: no-repeat;
    background-position: center center;
    background-attachment: fixed;
}
```

4. Save dinner_menu.css.

Figure 13-11 shows that both images are fixed in place and remain in place while the menu is scrolled.

How It Works

As you can see, the palms.jpg image is no longer at the very bottom of the page (as it was in Figure 13-10) because the menu has been scrolled down. Being fixed in place, both background images appear as though they are a part of the browser window itself.

The next section wraps up this chapter with a discussion of the background shorthand property. As with the shorthand properties you've been introduced to in other chapters, this property lets you combine several background properties into one.

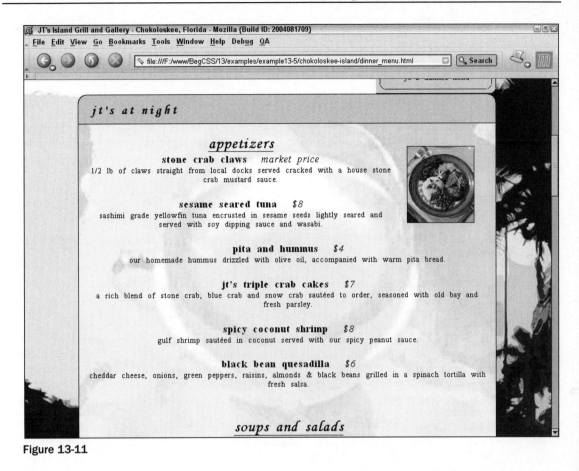

Figure 13-11

The background shorthand Property

Documented in CSS 2.1 and supported in IE 5.5, IE 6, Mozilla 1.7, Opera 7.5, and Safari 1.2.

Like the shorthand properties I introduced in previous chapters, the background property combines each of the individual background properties into a single property. The following table outlines the values allowed by the background property.

Property	Value
background	[<'background-color'> || <'background-image'> || <'background-repeat'> || <'background-attachment'> || <'background-position'>] | inherit Initial value: n/a

With the background property, you can specify anywhere from one to five separate background properties. Consider the following rule:

```
body {
    background: transparent url('jts.jpg') no-repeat scroll top center;
}
```

This rule provides output identical to what you see if you refer back to Figure 13-7. Actually, because `transparent` is the default background color and `scroll` is the default value for `background repeat`, these two values are unnecessary. You could rewrite this rule like this:

```
body {
    background: url('jts.jpg') no-repeat top center;
}
```

And because you can express the `top center` position with only the `top` keyword, you could rewrite this rule as follows:

```
body {
    background: url('jts.jpg') no-repeat top;
}
```

Now even more simplified, the preceding rule still produces the same output as shown in Figure 13-7. As you have seen in examples in previous chapters, the `background` property can be used with only a single value. The `background: red;` declaration is the same as the `background-color: red;` declaration. Likewise, the declaration demonstrated in Figure 13-2, `background-image: url('jts.jpg');`, can also be written as `background: url('jts.jpg');`. The `background` property provides the functionality of all five background properties in one property.

The following Try It Out simplifies the JT's style sheet by rewriting the rules of previous examples into one using the `background` shorthand property.

Try It Out   Applying the Background Shorthand Property

Example 13-6. To see how individual background properties can be rewritten using the `background` property, follow these steps.

1.   Locate the following rule from the base_styles.css style sheet:

```
body {
    background-image: url('../images/backgrounds/palms.jpg');
    background-repeat: no-repeat;
    background-position: center bottom;
    background-attachment: fixed;
    padding: 5em 0 1.2em 0;
    margin: 0;
    font-family: "Courier New", Courier, monospace;
    text-transform: lowercase;
}
```

2. Rewrite the highlighted declarations in Step 1 as the following:

```
body {
    background: url('../images/backgrounds/palms.jpg') no-repeat fixed center
bottom;
    padding: 5em 0 1.2em 0;
    margin: 0;
    font-family: "Courier New", Courier, monospace;
    text-transform: lowercase;
}
```

3. Save base_styles.css.

4. Locate the following rule from the dinner_menu.css style sheet:

```
div#content {
    background-color: lightyellow;
    background-image: url('../images/backgrounds/dinner_glass.jpg');
    background-repeat: no-repeat;
    background-position: center center;
    background-attachment: fixed;
}
```

5. Rewrite the declarations that you located in Step 4 as the following:

```
div#content {
    background: lightyellow url('../images/backgrounds/dinner_glass.jpg') no-repeat
fixed center center;
}
```

6. Save dinner_menu.css.

How It Works

The modifications made to the JT's style sheet in this example provide identical output to that observed in Figure 13-11 using only one declaration where there were previously five. Shorthand properties provide the functionality of many using the syntax of only one.

Summary

The CSS background properties provide a fine-grained control over the presentation of backgrounds in a web document, which allows interesting aesthetic possibilities. To recap in this chapter, you learned that

❑ You can specify a solid background color by using the `background-color` property.

❑ You can use the `background-image` property to provide a background image that tiles all the space available to it by default.

❑ You can use the `background-repeat` property to control the tiling of background images. This can be limited to the x-axis or the y-axis, or you can use the `no-repeat` keyword to prevent the background image from tiling.

❑   You can use the `background-position` property to position the background image.

❑   You can use the `background-attachment` property to control whether a background image scrolls with a page or remains fixed in place. If the image is fixed in place it becomes positioned relative to the browser window itself instead of the element it is applied to.

❑   You can use the `background` shorthand property to put the control of all five properties into one property.

Chapter 14 discusses the properties that CSS provides to position elements.

Exercise

Using the four-column design you created for Chapter 11, Exercise 1, create an image as large as the resolution of your computer screen. For full effect, make two different versions of the same background image using a graphics editing program: a black-and-white version of the original image and the original image itself. The idea is to create two versions of the same image identical in size, with the only difference being that one is black and white and the other is full color. You may obtain an example of this in this book's source code download from www.wrox.com. (See kayaking.jpg, kayaking2.jpg, and exercise13-1.html in the Chapter 13 folder after you download the files.)

Armed with two variations of the same image, add a list of hyperlinks in column #1 enclosing the hyperlinks in unordered lists and removing the default padding, margin, and list styles. Given each list item a height of 50 pixels and a solid black border. Add a bottom margin to each list item so that each list item is separated from the others by a small gap. Set the background image for each list item using the original image. Position the image in the center both vertically and horizontally, but use only one keyword to do so. Fix the background in place as the page scrolls. Turn off tiling of the image. Repeat the same technique for the background of each column 1–4, this time using the black and white version of the original image. Again repeating the same technique set the background of the body of the document with the original image. Finally, give the footer a background using a solid color.

Use only the background shorthand property to set all the backgrounds. You can see a preview of what this should look like in Figure 13-12.

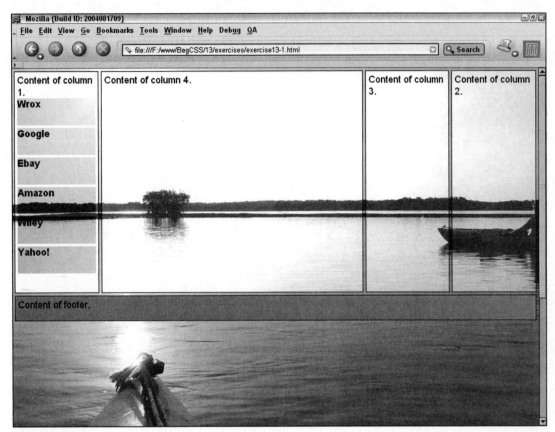

Figure 13-12

Positioning

This chapter examines the various properties that CSS provides to position elements in a document. *Positioning* can be thought of as layering, in that the various elements of a page can be layered on top of others and given specific places to appear in the browser's window. In this chapter I discuss:

❑ The position property and the four types of positioning that CSS has to offer: static, relative, absolute, and fixed

❑ The offset properties top, right, bottom, left and how these are used to deliver an element to a specific position in a web document

❑ The z-index property and how this property is used to layer the elements of a document

Positioning makes CSS a very powerful presentational language, and further enhances its flexibility. Like floating elements, positioning offers some unique characteristics that allow behavior you might not always expect. In Chapter 10, I introduced positioning by demonstrating how combining absolute positioning with the four offset properties can create an element that has margins, borders, and padding with fluid height and width. This chapter begins the discussion of positioning with none other than the position property.

The position Property

Documented in CSS 2 and supported in IE 5.5 (partial), IE 6 (partial), Opera 7.5, Mozilla 1.7, and Safari 1.2.

The position property is used to give an element a certain type of positioning. The following table outlines the position property and its possible values.

Property	Value
position	static | relative | absolute | fixed | inherit Initial value: static

Neither IE 5.5 nor IE 6 supports fixed positioning.

There are four different types of positioning. In the upcoming sections I describe each of the four types of positioning in detail: static, absolute, relative, and fixed. The next section begins this discussion with static positioning.

Static Positioning

By default, all elements are positioned statically, which you do using the position: static; declaration. This is the behavior you've observed in the majority of examples up to this point. Static positioning means that all elements appear in a normal flow; that is, elements appear one after another from the top of the document and flow in sequence to the bottom of the document. A statically positioned element has no special positioning applied and cannot be affected by the use of the four offset properties—top, right, bottom and left—which control the placement of an absolutely, relatively, or fixed positioned element. The four offset properties are discussed in further detail in the upcoming "Offset Properties" section in this chapter.

The next section continues discussion of absolute positioning, which is often used to layer elements in a document.

Absolute Positioning

Absolute positioning is used to deliver an element to a specific place in a web document. The effects of absolute positioning cannot be fully conveyed without also discussing relative positioning, and the four offset properties, top, bottom, left, and right. To those ends, absolute positioning is something I continue to cover throughout this chapter because it can be combined with different types of positioning, the four offset properties, and layering. However, in the meantime, examine what absolute positioning does on its own. Consider the following rules:

```
div {
    position: absolute;
    width: 200px;
    border: 1px solid black;
    opacity: 0.7;
    background: lightyellow;
}
p {
    margin: 0;
}
```

Combine these rules with the following markup:

```
<div>
    <p>
        Paragraph text. Paragraph text. Paragraph text.
        Paragraph text. Paragraph text. Paragraph text.
    </p>
</div>
<div>
    Second div text.
</div>
```

The screen shot in Figure 14-1 shows that something interesting is happening. Both <div> elements are given a position: absolute; declaration, which causes the <div> elements to appear stacked one on top of the other.

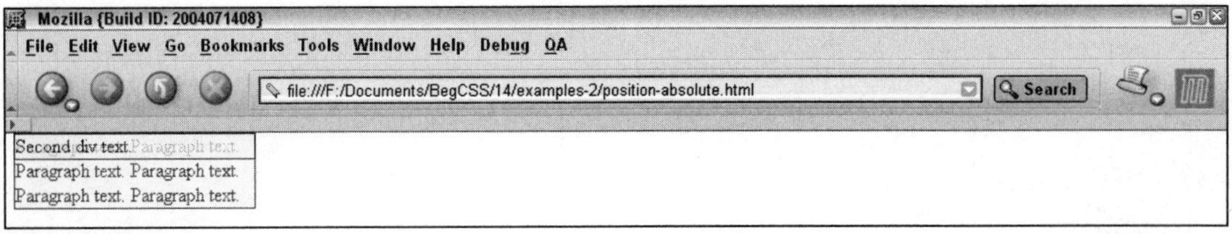

Figure 14-1

Applying a slight opacity to the second `<div>` element further highlights the stacking of the two elements. The `opacity` property is new to CSS 3, and at the time of this writing is only supported by Mozilla 1.7 and Safari 1.2. It accepts a floating-point number between 0 and 1, where 0 is fully transparent and 1 is fully opaque. Applying the opacity property allows you to see that the paragraph text inside of the first `<div>` element is underneath the second `<div>` element. This example demonstrates how absolute positioning is used for layering elements in a document. An element that is absolutely positioned is completely taken out of the normal flow of the document and positioned along an invisible z-axis.

At this point, you know that absolute positioning places elements in a specific place in a document. In the following Try it Out example, you add absolute positioning to the JT's Island Grill and Gallery style sheet to begin the processes of positioning the navigation of the JT's website and making dynamic drop-down menus.

Try It Out   Applying Absolute Positioning

Example 14-1. The following steps show you how to apply absolute positioning.

1. Open menu_system.css and apply the following declarations:

```
div#nav {
    position: absolute;
    margin: auto;
    width: 50em;
    text-align: center;
}
div#nav > a > img {
    clear: left;
    display: block;
    margin: 0 auto;
    width: 16em;
    height: auto;
}
div#nav ul {
    position: absolute;
    list-style-type: none;
    margin: 0;
    padding: 0;
}
```

2. Save menu_system.css.

Figure 14-2 shows that things have turned chaotic in the JT's dinner menu, although it is closer to having dynamic drop-down menus.

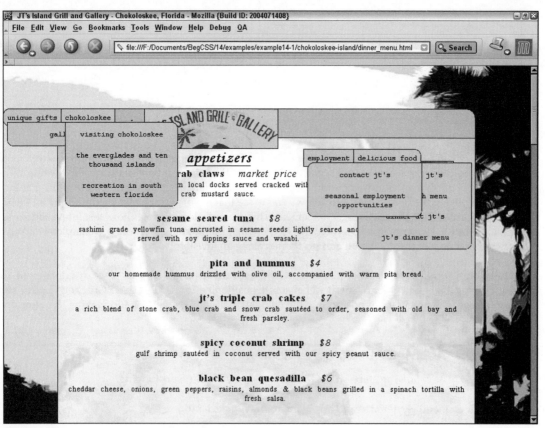

Figure 14-2

How It Works

In this example, you apply absolute positioning to the areas of the dinner menu that you can easily fore-see as positioned. Each of the four navigation headings is split into two pairs. One pair is positioned to the left and one pair is positioned to the right of the logo. This takes you a step closer to the goal of having each of these headings contain a drop-down menu that appears only when the user's mouse hovers over the corresponding heading. The logo and navigation headings are also layered slightly on top of the first heading of the document. According to this plan, absolute positioning is applied to the menu_system.css style sheet for the relevant elements. The nav `<div>` is positioned absolutely so that it can be layered slightly on top of the first heading of the dinner menu. All the `<ul>` elements inside of the nav `<div>` are also positioned absolutely, because both the headings and the menus of links are to be delivered to specific places in the document.

This example highlights how elements that are positioned absolutely are taken out of the normal flow of the document. In Chapter 10 you applied a declaration to base_styles.css that applied 5em of top padding on the `<body>` element:

```
body {
    background: url('../images/backgrounds/palms.jpg') no-repeat fixed center
bottom;
    padding: 5em 0 1.2em 0;
    margin: 0;
    font-family: "Courier New" Courier monospace;
    text-transform: lowercase;
}
```

You applied this padding in Chapter 10, so when the navigation was given positioning here, a small gap appeared between the top heading of the menu and the bottom border of the browser window, reserving a place for that navigation to reside. It should be obvious that the navigation is now layered along an invisible z-axis.

Offset Properties

Documented in CSS 2.1 and supported in IE 5.5, IE 6, Opera 7.5, Mozilla 1.7, and Safari 1.2.

Offset properties are used to precision position elements. In Chapter 10, you saw how specifying all four offset properties stretches content. This chapter demonstrates how offset properties are used in the vast majority of scenarios to control placement of positioned elements. The following table outlines the four offset properties and their possible values.

Property	Value
top	\<length> | \<percentage> | auto | inherit Initial value: auto
right	\<length> | \<percentage> | auto | inherit Initial value: auto
bottom	\<length> | \<percentage> | auto | inherit Initial value: auto
left	\<length> | \<percentage> | auto | inherit Initial value: auto

Offset properties contribute much to understanding exactly what part positioning plays in the design of a web document. Without the four offset properties, positioning isn't very interesting; therefore, these properties have an intrinsic part to play. Consider the following rules:

```
div {
    position: absolute;
    width: 150px;
    height: 150px;
    padding: 10px;
    border: 1px solid black;
```

```
        opacity: 0.7;
        background: lightyellow;
    }
    div#div1 {
        top: 0;
        left: 0;
    }
    div#div2 {
        top: 20px;
        left: 20px;
    }
```

Also consider this markup:

```
<div id='div1'>
    This is the text of the first div.
    This is the text of the first div.
</div>
<div id='div2'>
    This is the text of the second div.
    This is the text of the second div.
</div>
```

Figure 14-3 shows that the position of each <div> element can be controlled precisely with inclusion of the top and left offset properties.

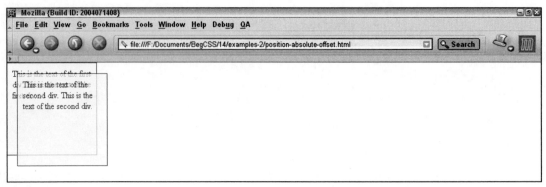

Figure 14-3

The top and left properties in Figure 14-3 show that each <div> element is positioned relative to the browser view port: top refers to the top border of the view port and left to the left side. If you follow along with the markup presented for Figure 14-3, you see what happens when right is specified instead of left:

```
div#div1 {
    top: 0;
    right: 0;
}
div#div2 {
    top: 20px;
    right: 20px;
}
```

Figure 14-4 shows essentially the same concept as Figure 14-3, except this time both are positioned from the right side of the browser's view port.

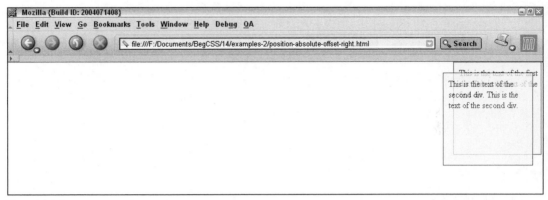

Figure 14-4

Naturally, the next example shows the bottom property instead of the top:

```
div#div1 {
    bottom: 0;
    right: 0;
}
div#div2 {
    bottom: 20px;
    right: 20px;
}
```

Figure 14-5 shows that the element is positioned from the bottom of the browser's view port.

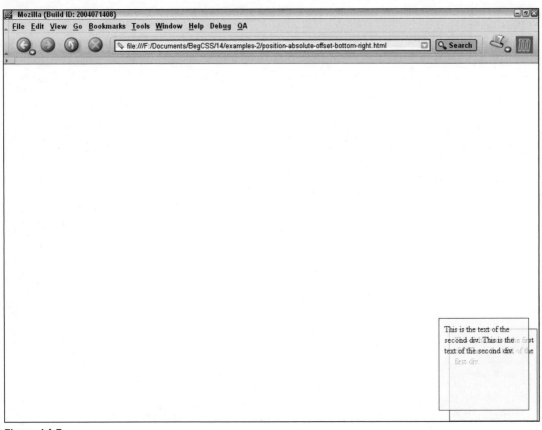

Figure 14-5

I'm sure you can guess what happens when `bottom` and `left` are specified (as shown in Figure 14-6).

From the screen output in Figures 14-3, 14-4, 14-5, and 14-6 you get an idea of what the offset properties do to position an element on the screen. When only two properties are provided, such as `top` and `left` or `top` and `right` or `bottom` and `left` or `bottom` and `right`, this indicates the position of the element on screen. The `top` and `left` properties position the element using the top and left borders of the box and the top and left sides of the browser's view port. So when `top: 0;` and `left: 0;` are provided that tells the browser that the element should appear 0 from the left side and 0 from the topside of the view port. Naturally, the same thing happens with other combinations, such as `bottom` and `right`. If `bottom: 10px;` is provided with `right: 10px;` that tells the browser 10 pixels of space should separate the element's right outside border edge and the right edge of the browser's view port, and 10 pixels of space should separate the element's bottom outside border edge from the bottom of the view port.

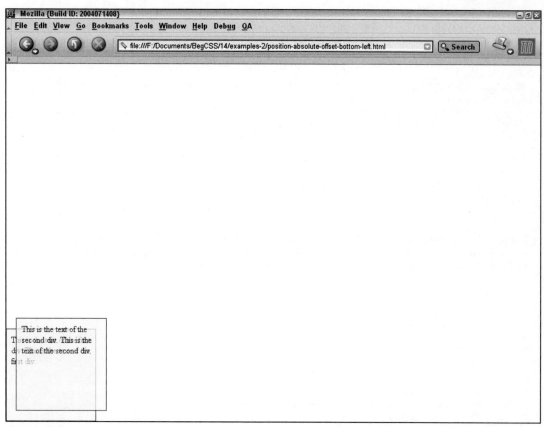

Figure 14-6

Up until now you have observed absolutely positioned <div> elements with a defined width and height. Now, examine what happens when no width or height is defined:

```
div {
    position: absolute;
    padding: 10px;
    border: 1px solid black;
    opacity: 0.7;
    background: lightyellow;
}
div#div1 {
    top: 0;
    left: 0;
}
div#div2 {
    top: 20px;
    left: 20px;
}
```

Figure 14-7 demonstrates something you saw in Chapter 11 with floating elements. When an element is positioned, it takes on the *shrink-to-fit* behavior you saw in Chapter 10 with tables and Chapter 11 with floated elements. The <div> elements only expand enough to accommodate the content contained within.

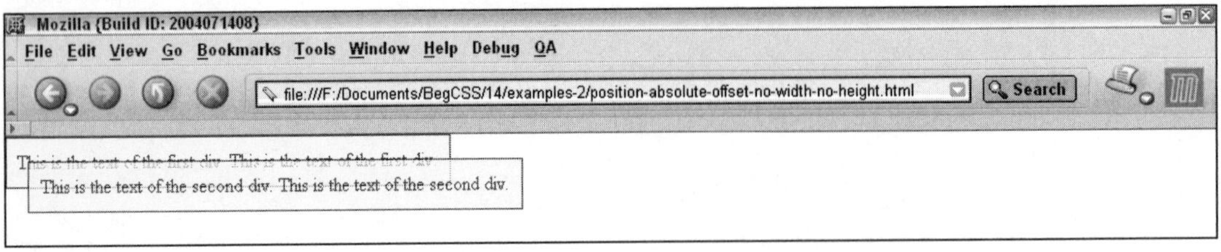

Figure 14-7

Finally, to reiterate what was presented in Chapter 10, if both top and bottom are specified on an absolutely positioned element, height is implied. Likewise, if both left and right are provided, width is implied. Techniques like this can be used to create liquid layout. Consider the following example:

```
div {
    position: absolute;
    padding: 10px;
    border: 1px solid black;
    opacity: 0.7;
    background: lightyellow;
}
div#div1 {
    top: 0;
    right: 0;
    bottom: 0;
    left: 0;
}
div#div2 {
    top: 20px;
    right: 20px;
    bottom: 20px;
    left: 20px;
}
```

Figure 14-8 shows output stretched out vertically and horizontally, demonstrating that if right and left are both provided, the width of the element is implied; if both top and bottom are provided, the height of the element is implied.

The next section continues the discussion of positioning with a discussion of relative positioning.

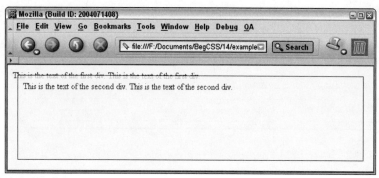

Figure 14-8

Relative Positioning

Unlike in absolute positioning, relatively positioned elements are not removed from the flow of a document. Relatively positioned elements remain in the flow of the document, but can be positioned with offset properties. To demonstrate this, consider the following example:

```
div {
    position: relative;
    padding: 10px;
    border: 1px solid black;
    opacity: 0.7;
    background: lightyellow;
}
div#div1 {
    top: 0;
    left: 0;
}
div#div2 {
    top: 20px;
    left: 20px;
}
```

The preceding is combined with the following markup:

```
<div id='div1'>
    This is the text of the first div.
    This is the text of the first div.
</div>
<div id='div2'>
    This is the text of the second div.
    This is the text of the second div.
</div>
```

Figure 14-9 shows that both <div> elements appear normally because block elements span the window filling the area available to them.

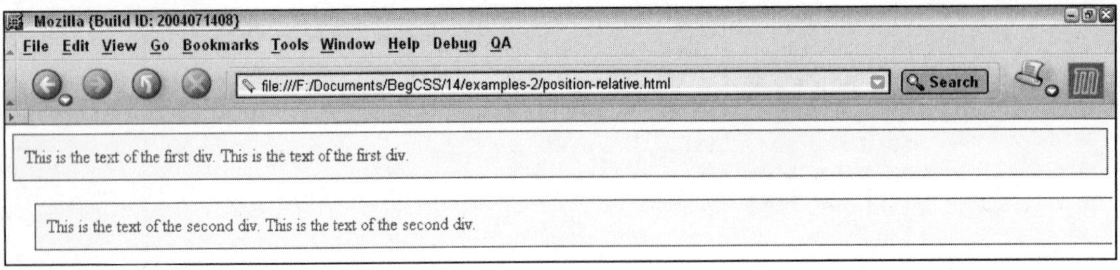

Figure 14-9

Figure 14-9 also shows that the first <div> element is still affected by the default margin of the <body> element. What's interesting in this example is that the second <div> is positioned 20 pixels from the bottom of the first <div> and 20 pixels from the outside margin edge of the <body> element on the left side. At first glance, the position properties when applied to a relatively positioned element appear to have the same effect as margin. However, one very fundamental difference exists: If margin: 20px 0 0 20px; instead of top: 20px; and left: 20px; had been applied to the second <div> element, it would not venture slightly off screen on the right side of the window. The application of the offset properties moves the element, but does not affect its width because, as a block element, it is still as wide as the <body> element allows.

Often times, relative positioning has a single purpose: to cause absolutely positioned elements to position themselves relative to the element with relative positioning. When an element is given a relative position, and an element inside of that element (a descendant element) is given an absolute position, a very cool thing happens. The element with absolute positioning is positioned relative to the element with relative positioning applied, instead of relative to the view port. The case in point is the following:

```
div {
    padding: 10px;
    border: 1px solid black;
    opacity: 0.7;
    background: lightyellow;
}
div#div1 {
    position: relative;
    margin: 30px;
}
div#div2 {
    position: absolute;
    top: 20px;
    left: 20px;
}
```

The preceding is combined with the following markup:

```
<div id='div1'>
    This is the text of the first div.
    This is the text of the first div.
    <div id='div2'>
        This is the text of the second div.
        This is the text of the second div.
    </div>
</div>
```

In Figure 14-10, you see how the absolutely positioned element positions itself relative to the borders of its relatively positioned parent.

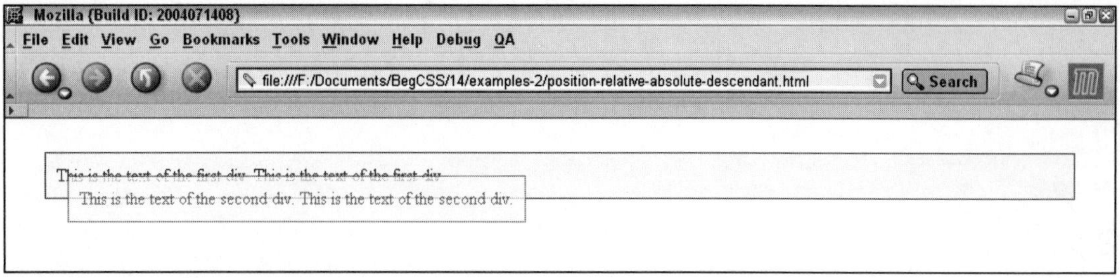

Figure 14-10

The first <div> is supplied a hefty margin of 30 pixels to provide a gap between it and the borders of the view port to highlight the positioning of the second <div>, whereas you can observe that 20 pixels of space separates the second <div> from the top and left borders of the first <div> element.

Having seen a few examples of the uses of relative positioning, you can now use Try It Out to apply relative positioning and the offset properties to the JT's Island Grill and Gallery style sheet.

Try It Out   Applying Relative Positioning and the Four Offset Properties

Example 14-2. You can apply relative positioning with the following steps.

1.   In Example 14-1, you saw how the JT's style sheet turned rather chaotic after you applied absolute positioning. In this step, you add a few declarations to control positioning of those absolutely positioned elements. Open menu_system.css and apply the following modifications:

```
div#nav {
    position: absolute;
    right: 0;
    left: 0;
    top: 0.8em;
}
div#nav > div {
    position: relative;
    margin: auto;
    width: 50em;
    text-align: center;
}
div#nav > div > a > img {
    position: relative;
    clear: left;
    display: block;
    margin: 0 auto;
    width: 17em;
    height: auto;
}
div#nav ul {
    position: absolute;
```

```css
        list-style-type: none;
        margin: 0;
        padding: 0;
}
div#nav > div > ul {
        top: 2.92em;
        width: 50%;
}
ul#gifts {
        left: 0;
}
ul#food {
        right: 0;
}
div#nav span {
        display: block;
        overflow: hidden;
        height: 2.1em;
        line-height: 2.2em;
}
div#nav > div > ul > li {
        position: relative;
        background-color: lightblue;
        padding: 0.5em;
        border: 0.05em solid black;
        font-size: 0.9em;
        padding: 0 0.5em;
        width: 8.35em;
        height: 2.2em;
}
div#nav > div > ul > li:hover {
        background-color: lightsteelblue;
}
ul#gifts > li {
        float: left;
}
ul#food > li {
        float: right;
}
div#nav > div > ul > li#leftedge {
        border-right-width: 0;
        -moz-border-radius-topleft: 1em;
        -moz-border-radius-bottomleft: 1em;
        margin-left: 0.3em;
}
div#nav > div > ul > li#leftedge:hover {
        -moz-border-radius-bottomleft: 0;
}
div#nav > div > ul > li#rightedge {
        border-left-width: 0;
        -moz-border-radius-topright: 1em;
        -moz-border-radius-bottomright: 1em;
        margin-right: 0.3em;
}
```

```
div#nav > div > ul > li#rightedge:hover {
    -moz-border-radius-bottomright: 0;
}
ul.menu {
    top: 2.19em;
    background-color: lightblue;
    width: 15em;
    -moz-border-radius-bottomleft: 1em;
    -moz-border-radius-bottomright: 1em;
    border: 0.05em solid black;
}
ul#food ul.menu {
    -moz-border-radius-topleft: 1em;
    right: -0.07em;
}
ul#gifts ul.menu {
    -moz-border-radius-topright: 1em;
    left: -0.05em;
}
ul.menu li {
    text-align: left;
    color: black;
}
ul.menu a {
    margin: 0.4em;
    padding: 0.5em;
    color: black;
    display: block;
    border: 0.05em solid lightblue;
}
ul.menu a:hover {
    background-color: lightsteelblue;
    -moz-border-radius: 0.8em;
    border: 0.05em solid black;
    text-decoration: none;
}
div#nav ul a:active {
    background-color: steelblue;
}
```

2. Save menu_system.css. The menu_style.css style sheet is presented here in its entirety. Be sure to double-check that your style sheet matches the one presented here.

3. Make the following modifications to dinner_menu.html:

```
<body>
    <div id='nav'>
        <div>
            <ul id='gifts'>
                <li id='leftedge'>
                    <span>Unique Gifts</span>
                    <ul class='menu'>
                        <li><a href=''>Gallery</a></li>
```

```
                    </ul>
                </li>
                <li>
                    <span>Chokoloskee</span>
                    <ul class='menu'>
                        <li><a href=''>Visiting Chokoloskee</a></li>
                        <li>
                            <a href=''>The Everglades and Ten
                                        Thousand Islands</a></li>
                        <li><a href=''>Recreation in South
                                        Western Florida</a></li>
                    </ul>
                </li>
            </ul>
            <a href='index.html'>
                <img src='images/photos/jts_sign.jpg'
                    alt='JTs sign'
                    title='Go home.'/>
            </a>
            <ul id='food'>
                <li id='rightedge'>
                    <span>Delicious Food</span>
                    <ul class='menu'>
                        <li><a href=''>Lunch at JT's</a></li>
                        <li><a href=''>JT's Lunch Menu</a></li>
                        <li><a href=''>Dinner at JT's</a></li>
                        <li>
                          <a href='dinner_menu.html'>
                             JT's Dinner Menu
                          </a>
                          </li>
                    </ul>
                </li>
                <li>
                    <span>Employment</span>
                    <ul class='menu'>
                        <li><a href=''>Contact JT's</a></li>
                        <li><a href=''>Seasonal Employment
                                       Opportunities</a></li>
                    </ul>
                </li>
            </ul>
        </div>
    </div>
    <div id='body'>
        <h1>
            JT's at Night
        </h1>
```

4. Save dinner_menu.html.

Figure 14-11 shows that the navigational headings and submenus are moved into place.

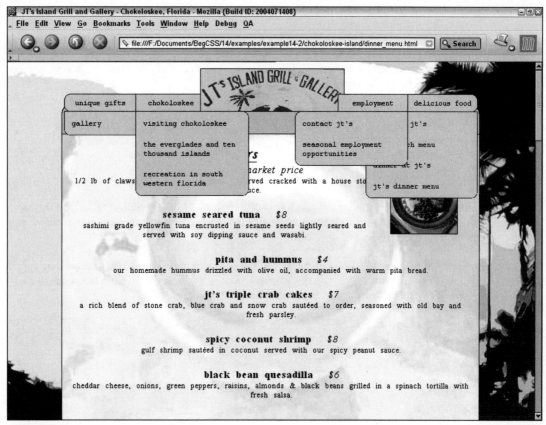

Figure 14-11

How It Works

This example contains lengthy, complicated changes; and each has a very important effect on the final product. Let's review each modification and why it was important. The first involves the addition of a new <div> element in the dinner_menu.html markup. This change was essential because of how positioning works. The <div> with a 'nav' id name was given an absolute position in Example 14-1. Here I've stretched the nav <div> element by specifying both a left and right offset property. This is necessary because the nav <div> is absolutely positioned. The margin: auto; declaration, therefore, no longer centers the element as it did when the nav <div> was positioned statically.

```
div#nav {
    position: absolute;
    right: 0;
    left: 0;
    top: 0.8em;
}
```

Applying both the `right` and `left` offset properties makes the nav `<div>` fluid; it spans the whole window horizontally. Unfortunately, that presents a problem. Because it is fluid, it has a variable width. A variable width that means that elements positioned relative to it won't always appear in the same place. Any elements positioned relative to the nav `<div>` move depending on its width. To remedy this problem, you add another `<div>` element and mov the defined width of 50em, auto margins, and centered text declarations to the selector for that `<div>` element:

```
div#nav > div {
    position: relative;
    margin: auto;
    width: 50em;
    text-align: center;
}
```

The `<ul>` elements that you positioned absolutely in Example 14-1 now reposition relative to this new `<div>`. Because it has a fixed width, those absolutely positioned `<ul>` elements remain in place no matter how wide or narrow the browser window is.

Adding the new `<div>` element means that many of the selectors no longer work because they rely upon a direct child relationship with the nav `<div>` element. So you add the extra `<div>` reference to each selector that requires it. The first is the reference to the JT's logo:

```
div#nav > div > a > img {
    position: relative;
    clear: left;
    display: block;
    margin: 0 auto;
    width: 17em;
    height: auto;
}
```

The JT's logo is given a relative position; this allows the logo to be layered. I cover layering in the upcoming discussion on the `z-index` property. The logo is also increased in width from 16em to 17em; the increase in width corrects an error on my part early in the planning of this example. It also makes the logo consistent with the final product you observed in Chapter 7. The next modification does two things: It positions the two pairs of navigation headings and it fixes positioned floated elements in Opera:

```
div#nav > div > ul {
    top: 2.92em;
    width: 50%;
}
ul#gifts {
    left: 0;
}
ul#food {
    right: 0;
}
```

In the preceding three rules, the addition of the top property places 2.92em of space between the top border of the wrapper `<div>` that you added and the top border of the two `<ul>` elements that contain the main navigational headings, *unique gifts*, *chokoloskee*, *employment*, and *delicious food*. The 2.92 measurement allows the bottom border of the list elements inside those <ul> elements to line up with the bottom of the JT's logo. Because one <ul> is to be positioned to the left and the other <ul> to the right, those properties are added in the separate rules that follow. The <ul> with the 'gifts' id name is positioned to the left of the logo and the <ul> with the 'food' id name is positioned to the right of the logo with the left: 0; and right: 0; declarations, respectively:

```
ul#gifts {
    left: 0;
}
ul#food {
    right: 0;
}
```

A 50% width is given to each <ul> element with the div#nav > div > ul selector to correct Opera's rendering of the navigational toolbar:

```
div#nav > div > ul {
    top: 2.92em;
    width: 50%;
}
```

In Chapter 11, you applied the float property to the list items of both pairs of navigation headings, resulting in one side being floated to the left and the other side being floated to the right. Earlier in this chapter, you learned that positioned elements, by default, apply width using the *shrink-to-fit* algorithm. In Opera, the *shrink-to-fit* algorithm means that because the <ul> doesn't have a defined width, those list elements don't float beside each other. You correct this by giving both <ul> elements a width larger than that of the width for each list item. Mozilla doesn't have this problem; it follows the rule that a floating element must be placed as high as possible and calculates the width of the <ul> element after floating has occurred. So which one is correct? Amazingly enough, according to the W3C specifications both are correct. They simply have different interpretations of the specifications.

The next rule that you apply is a bug fix:

```
div#nav span {
    display: block;
    overflow: hidden;
    height: 2.1em;
    line-height: 2.2em;
}
```

For this rule, you wrap each corresponding navigational heading with <span> elements in the dinner_menu.html markup. The addition of this rule serves two purposes. Its first purpose involves what happens when the user increases the font size. When the font size of the page is increased, sometimes the *delicious food* heading spans two lines instead of only one. This can be observed not only in Mozilla, but in other browsers as well. To keep both design consistency and fluidity with increases or decreases to the font size, the <span> elements are converted to block elements with the display: block; declaration. Then, the overflow: hidden; declaration and an explicit height of 2.1em are used so that if that *delicious food* heading decides to span more than one line, the user will see only *delicious* and the aesthetics of the navigation toolbar are preserved. This behavior is rather obscure and isn't likely to be experienced by the majority of users. But because it is an easy behavior to circumvent, a bug fix is applied.

The second purpose of this rule involves vertically centering the text. Without a line height, the text appears too far toward the top of each list item. Therefore, to center the text vertically, you apply a line-height of 2.2em, which moves the baseline of the text farther down and results in the text of each heading being centered vertically. This is a bug fix that may not apply to every case, but it is acceptable for this scenario. The next rule defines the two pairs of navigational headings to the left and right of the JT's logo:

```
div#nav > div > ul > li {
    position: relative;
    background-color: lightblue;
    padding: 0.5em;
    border: 0.05em solid black;
    font-size: 0.9em;
    padding: 0 0.5em;
    width: 8.35em;
    height: 2.2em;
}
```

The list items on both sides of the JT's logo are given properties that they have in common. First you apply a relative position, so that each submenu containing hyperlinks is positioned relative to its corresponding heading. You also apply a fixed width and height for further consistency. This gives each list item the same dimensions. Left and right padding are also applied to further space each heading apart. The next few modifications involve adding that new <div> element to each selector and applying margins:

```
div#nav > div > ul > li:hover {
    background-color: lightsteelblue;
}
ul#gifts > li {
    float: left;
}
ul#food > li {
    float: right;
}
div#nav > div > ul > li#leftedge {
    border-right-width: 0;
    -moz-border-radius-topleft: 1em;
    -moz-border-radius-bottomleft: 1em;
    margin-left: 0.3em;
}
div#nav > div > ul > li#leftedge:hover {
    -moz-border-radius-bottomleft: 0;
}
div#nav > div > ul > li#rightedge {
    border-left-width: 0;
    -moz-border-radius-topright: 1em;
    -moz-border-radius-bottomright: 1em;
    margin-right: 0.3em;
}
div#nav > div > ul > li#rightedge:hover {
    -moz-border-radius-bottomright: 0;
}
```

Left and right margins are applied to the left pair of navigation headings and the right pair of navigation headings. The application of `margin-left: 0.3em;` causes a small gap to appear between the left side of the menu itself and the beginning of the left pair of navigation headings. The same is done for the right side with the `margin-right: 0.3em;` declaration. The last modifications made to the menu_system.css style sheet position and style each submenu:

```
ul.menu {
    top: 2.19em;
    background-color: lightblue;
    width: 15em;
    -moz-border-radius-bottomleft: 1em;
    -moz-border-radius-bottomright: 1em;
    border: 0.05em solid black;
}
ul#food ul.menu {
    -moz-border-radius-topleft: 1em;
    right: -0.07em;
}
ul#gifts ul.menu {
    -moz-border-radius-topright: 1em;
    left: -0.05em;
}
ul.menu li {
    text-align: left;
    color: black;
}
```

Each menu `<ul>` contains the hyperlinks for each heading. These are now positioned relative to each list-item heading. They are positioned 2.19em from the top border of each list-item heading; then in the two subsequent rules, the menu `<ul>` elements under the left headings are positioned from the left. These are given a position of -0.05em to line up the left borders of the menu `<ul>` elements with the left borders of each heading. Similarly, the right side menu `<ul>` elements are positioned -0.07em to the right, to line up the right borders of these elements with the right borders of their corresponding headings.

Having now covered absolute and relative positioning as well as the four offset properties, I continue in the next section with fixed positioning.

Fixed Positioning

Fixed positioning is very similar to absolute positioning, with two major differences:

❑   Elements that have fixed positioning are always positioned relative to the view port, no matter what type of positioning their parent element may have applied.

❑   Elements that have fixed positioning remain fixed in place as the document is scrolled by the user.

Now that you have an overview of what fixed positioning is, the question becomes what can you use it for? Fixed positioning is useful for creating things like watermarks, a semitransparent logo that remains in place as the page is scrolled. Often times, when this logo is clicked, it takes the user back to the home page of a website. Fixed positioning can be used to create a navigational toolbar that remains fixed in place as the page scrolls, providing the user with easy to access navigational options. To demonstrate fixed positioning, consider the following code:

```
html, body {
    height: 2000px;
}
div {
    position: fixed;
    padding: 10px;
    border: 1px solid black;
    opacity: 0.7;
    background: lightyellow;
}
div#div1 {
    top: 0;
    left: 0;
}
div#div2 {
    top: 20px;
    left: 20px;
}
```

This provides output like that shown in Figure 14-12.

The markup used for the screen shot in Figure 14-12 applies a 2000-pixel height to both the <html> and <body> elements. This forces a scroll bar to appear. You can observe the effects of fixed positioning in that, as the page is scrolled, both <div> elements remain fixed in place.

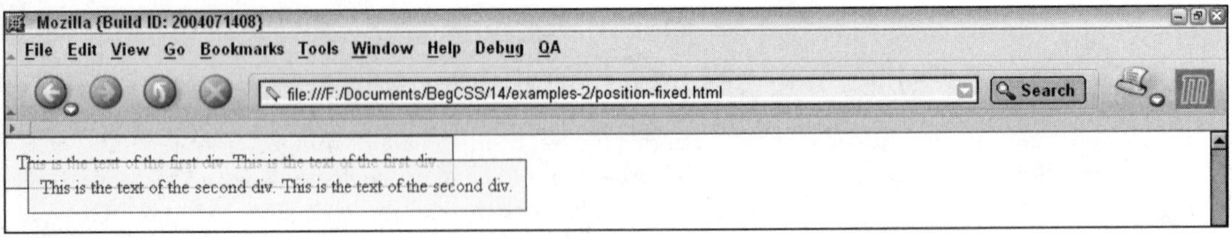

Figure 14-12

In the following Try It Out, you apply fixed positioning to the JT's Island Grill and Gallery style sheet.

Try It Out   Applying Fixed Positioning

Example 14-3. Follow these steps to apply fixed positioning.

1.   Open menu_system.css and replace the `position: absolute;` declaration in the selector for the nav <div> with a `position: fixed;` declaration to observe the effects of a fixed position navigation on the JT's Island Grill and Gallery website:

```
div#nav {
    position: fixed;
    right: 0;
    left: 0;
    top: 0.8em;
}
```

2. Save menu_system.css. When this is opened in Mozilla, you see output like that shown in Figure 14-13.

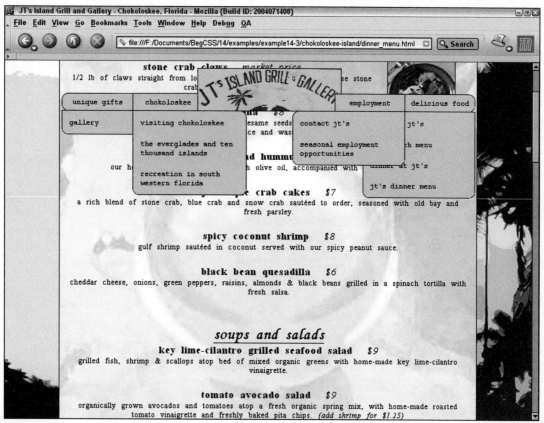

Figure 14-13

How It Works

Figure 14-13 shows that now when the page is scrolled, the JT's logo and navigation remains fixed in place. This gives the user convenient access to the navigation from any place on the dinner menu page.

The next section finishes the discussion of positioning with the z-index property.

Controlling Layering with the z-index Property

Documented in CSS 2.1 and supported in IE 5.5, IE 6, Opera 7.5, Mozilla 1.7, and Safari 1.2.

As I mentioned earlier in this chapter, the z-index property is used to control the layering of elements in a web document. The following table outlines the z-index property and the values that it allows.

Property	Value
z-index	auto | <integer> | inherit Initial value: auto

The z-index property is fairly straightforward; it can accept a positive or negative integer value. By default the value of z-index is the auto keyword. With the auto keyword, each new positioned element receives a higher z-index value than the one before it. Using an integer value, you can control an element's placement along an invisible z-axis. This is demonstrated by the following rules:

```
div {
    position: absolute;
    padding: 10px;
    border: 1px solid black;
    opacity: 0.9;
    background: lightyellow;
    width: 100px;
    height: 100px;
    top: 20px;
    left: 20px;
    z-index: 4;
}
div + div {
    background: lightblue;
    top: 40px;
    left: 40px;
    z-index: 3;
}
div + div + div {
    background: lightgreen;
    top: 60px;
    left: 60px;
    z-index: 2;
}
div + div + div + div {
    background: pink;
    top: 80px;
    left: 80px;
    z-index: 1;
}
```

The preceding code is combined with the following markup:

```
<div></div>
<div></div>
<div></div>
<div></div>
```

Figure 14-14 shows that because the z-index value of each <div> element is specified explicitly, layering of each element is controlled.

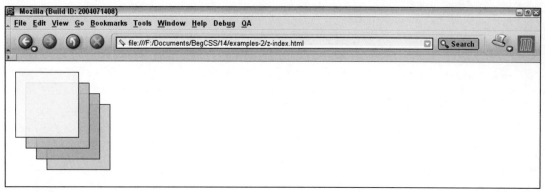

Figure 14-14

The first <div> in the sequence of four is given a light yellow background and some basic dimensions and properties that also apply to the other <div> elements. Then, by using the adjacent sibling selector, I select the subsequent <div> elements and provide those with different backgrounds and a decrementing z-index value. This results in the <div> with a light yellow background being displayed on top, followed by the <div> with the light blue background, followed by the <div> with the light green background, and finally the <div> with a pink background is shown at the back of the stack. This example demonstrates that the highest z-index value appears highest on the z-axis, or if you envision an invisible line perpendicular to the computer screen, the highest z-index appears furthest toward the user on that invisible line. If I omit the z-index property from the example shown in Figure 14-14, the value of the z-index property becomes auto, and the stack along the z-axis is determined by the document flow. For instance, the first element with positioning applied appears on the bottom of the stack, and each subsequent element appears one higher. The last element in the document with positioning receives the highest z-index value. Omitting the z-index value is demonstrated in Figure 14-15.

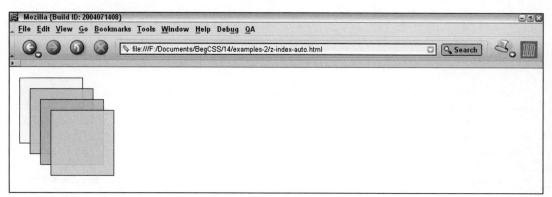

Figure 14-15

In Figure 14-15, you see that with the `z-index` property omitted, the auto keyword is assumed for the value of the `z-index`, which causes the `<div>` element with the pink background to appear on top of the stack, and the `<div>` element with a light yellow background to appear on the bottom. The `z-index` also works differently based on an element's ancestry. Consider the following example:

```css
div {
    position: absolute;
    padding: 10px;
    border: 1px solid black;
    opacity: 0.9;
    background: lightyellow;
    width: 100px;
    height: 100px;
    top: 20px;
    left: 20px;
    z-index: 4;
}
div > div {
    background: lightblue;
    z-index: 3;
}
div > div > div {
    background: lightgreen;
    z-index: 2;
}
div > div > div > div {
    background: pink;
    z-index: 1;
}
```

The preceding is combined with this markup:

```html
<div>
    <div>
        <div>
            <div>
            </div>
        </div>
    </div>
</div>
```

This time, each `<div>` element is placed inside the last. The result is very similar to that shown in Figure 14-15 with the auto `z-index`, but I set up the test case with the same `z-index` values used for Figure 14-14. The result shown in Figure 14-16 demonstrates that child elements are forbidden to have a lower `z-index` value than their parent element.

You have been introduced to the concept of layering. The following Try It Out lets you control layering by applying the z-index property. You also convert each list of navigation into dynamic drop-down menus.

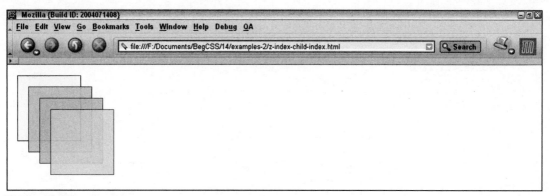

Figure 14-16

Try It Out   **Applying Layering and Creating Drop-Down Menus**

Example 14-4. The following steps show you how to apply layering and create drop-down navigational menus.

1. Modify the following rule in menu_system.css, applying the highlighted declaration to control layering of JT's logo:

```
div#nav > div > a > img {
    position: relative;
    clear: left;
    display: block;
    margin: 0 auto;
    width: 17em;
    height: auto;
    z-index: 1;
}
```

2. Still modifying menu_system.css, make the following highlighted modifications to convert each list of hyperlinks into dynamic drop-down menus:

```
ul.menu {
    top: 2.19em;
    background-color: lightblue;
    width: 15em;
    -moz-border-radius-bottomleft: 1em;
    -moz-border-radius-bottomright: 1em;
    border: 0.05em solid black;
    display: none;
}
div#nav > div > ul > li:hover > ul.menu,
ul.menu:hover {
    display: block;
}
```

```
ul#food ul.menu {
    -moz-border-radius-topleft: 1em;
     right: -0.07em;
}
ul#gifts ul.menu {
    -moz-border-radius-topright: 1em;
    left: -0.05em;
}
```

3. Save menu_system.css. The result is shown in Figure 14-17.

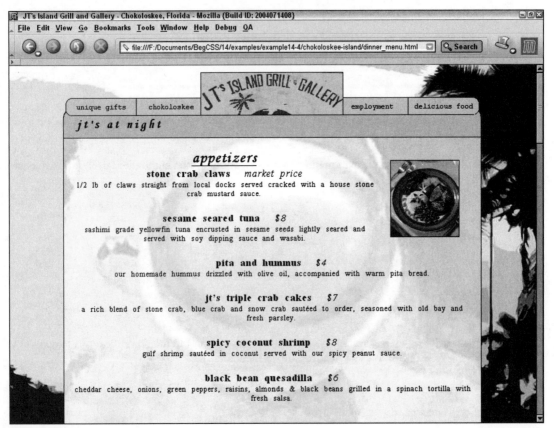

Figure 14-17

How It Works

You modify the menu_system.css style sheet in two key areas. The first modification involved controlling the layering of the JT's logo, so that the JT's logo is always on top. To do this, you apply a z-index: 1; declaration to the rule for the JT's logo. This demonstrates that an integer provided to the z-index property, which specifies layering by providing a number, takes precedence over the auto z-index. This means that the auto z-index is determined first, and then elements with a numbered z-index appear above those with an auto z-index. In this scenario, this eliminates the need to explicitly specify a z-index for any of the other elements.

The second round of modifications to the menu_style.css style sheet in this example involves making each list of navigation links into drop-down menus. First a display: none; declaration is supplied to the ul.menu selector to hide all the menus. The display: none; declaration prevents the browser from rendering the menu <ul> elements. Then, the :hover pseudo-class is applied to make those menus reappear if the user's mouse cursor hovers over a navigational heading:

```
div#nav > div > ul > li:hover > ul.menu,
ul.menu:hover {
    display: block;
}
```

The first selector in this example works using the same direct child relationship that you've observed before. Essentially what you are stating here is the following: If the nav <div> element has a child <div> element, and that child <div> element has a <ul> child element, and that child <ul> element has a <li> element that the user's mouse is hovering over, and that <li> element has a <ul> element with a menu class name, display it as a block element. This creates the effect of dynamic drop-down menus using CSS. The second selector is applied merely as a logical precaution. If the user's mouse is hovering over a <ul> element with a menu class name, for example any submenu, you continue to display that element as a block element.

Summary

This chapter presented some important CSS properties used to control positioning. Positioning, like the box model presented in Chapter 10, is a cornerstone of CSS development. In this chapter you learned the following:

❑ The position property is used to specify different types of positioning for an element.

❑ By default, elements are positioned statically.

❑ Absolutely positioned elements can be positioned in a specific place in a document, or positioned relative to the borders of the browser window or relative to the borders of a specific element.

❑ The four offset properties, top, right, bottom, and left are used to precision position any positioned element, with the exception of statically positioned elements.

❑ Relative positioned elements do not leave the flow of text. The position of a relatively positioned element can be fine-tuned by providing offset properties. Relative positioning can be used to cause a descendant absolutely-positioned element to position relative to its relatively positioned parent.

❑ Fixed positioning is similar to absolute positioning, except that elements with fixed positioning are always positioned relative to the view port and remain fixed in that position when the user scrolls the page.

❑   The z-index property is used to control the layering of positioned elements. When a z-index property is not supplied, the auto keyword is assumed, which causes the z-index to increase with each positioned element in a document. The z-index property works differently when it is applied to descendant elements that are positioned than when it is applied to adjacent elements. Positioning applied to descendant elements causes the z-index to increase with each descendant, and this cannot be overridden.

In Chapter 15, I show you how to create style sheets for print and handheld devices.

Exercises

1.   Using the Widgets and What's-its FAQ page that you completed in Chapter 10, Exercise 1, add dynamic text to each of the five links for the Widget's and What's-its navigation that describes what it located at each link. Position the text so that it appears in the upper-right–hand corner of the page, layered above the "Widgets and What's-its" heading. Use the combination of the :hover psuedo-class and display property technique that you observed for the JT's dynamic drop-down menus to accomplish this.

2.   Add a semi-transparent watermark logo to the Widgets and What's-its FAQ page, positioning the watermark in the lower-right–hand corner of the page. Determine that it stays in place as the page is scrolled, and add any decorative styles that you like.

Styling for Handheld Devices and Print

In this chapter, I present some of the techniques you can use to style a web document for devices other than traditional personal computers. As I mentioned in Chapters 8 and 10, part of the target audience for the JT's Island Grill and Gallery website are those people accessing the site via a cellular phone or PDA device. Additionally, it's important that each page be given specific styling for presentation as a printed document. In this chapter, I discuss

❑ How to present web documents for handheld devices

❑ How to present web documents for print

The portion of the JT's website that I focus on here is a dinner menu, so it naturally makes sense that you might want to print or access the menu using a mobile device. These options provide convenience to JT's customers, who are primarily tourists and are likely to have done some Internet research before visiting the Chokoloskee area. The first types of devices I tackle in this chapter are handheld devices such as PDAs and cell phones.

Styling Web Documents for Handheld Devices

In recent years, the technology used to view web content using a cellular phone or PDA device has improved by leaps and bounds. Improved technology, combined with the falling cost of the cellular phones that use it, should tell you that styling web documents for presentation on a handheld device makes a great deal of sense. Doing so increases the potential audience of a website, as well as provides end users with the additional convenience these devices offer.

Like personal computers, different mobile devices use different browsers to present content. Mobile device vendors often provide emulators for previewing web content styled for their devices. I chose three emulators to preview content styled for handheld devices instead of going through the expense and trouble of physically obtaining each handheld device. An *emulator* is software designed to replicate the functionality of something else — in this case, the functionality of a handheld device. To facilitate developing content for handheld devices, most mobile phone manufactures provide free software capable of replicating what a user would see using an actual phone. I chose the following emulators:

❑   **Motorola emulator:** Software capable of previewing content as it would appear on a Motorola phone; available from www.motocoder.com

❑   **Openwave emulator:** Software capable of previewing content as it would appear on an Openwave phone; available from http://developer.openwave.com

❑   The **Opera 7.5 browser:** Contains a built-in, handheld emulator called Small Screen capable of previewing content styled for a variety of handheld devices made by manufactures such as Nokia and Sony Ericsson; certain models use a special mobile device version of the Opera browser.

In Chapter 10, you learned that a style sheet could be designated for a specific device using the media attribute with either the <link/> or <style> elements, an @media rule within the style sheet itself, or by specifying the media when importing a style sheet using the @import rule. For instance, you can target a handheld device by applying the media='handheld' attribute to a style sheet via the <link/> or <style> element. The rules inside that style sheet are then limited only to handheld devices, whereas the media='screen' attribute applies rules for normal personal computers.

For the purposes of this book, the emulator built into Opera 7.5 works perfectly for previewing content designated for the 'handheld' media type. In Opera 7.5, the mobile browser emulator is activated by selecting Small Screen from the View menu. Figure 15-1 shows the JT's website on the Opera 7.5 emulator.

Some mobile device browsers — such as the NetFront browser developed by Access, which happens to be in my Sanyo Sprint PCS phone — try to render content intended for full-sized computer screens by using the 'screen' media type with absolutely no support for the 'handheld' media type intended for mobile devices. Although the NetFront browser has impressive CSS support, mobile devices with this browser have serious limitations. This is because this particular browser attempts to render a web document the same way that a personal computer would. That makes the content difficult to read and access because the screen is simply too small. In fact, when I loaded up JT's dinner menu into my Sprint PCS phone, I was surprised to find the browser even supported fixed positioning. Unfortunately, this also made all the navigation completely inaccessible because the navigation remained fixed in place while I was scrolling horizontally.

In the real world, I would turn to a server-side technology, such as PHP or ASP, to sniff out the type of browser attempting to access data and then dynamically change the content so that everyone can access the website using a mobile device. Unfortunately, server-side technologies are beyond the scope of this book. With that in mind, the solutions I present here can be expected to work with any mobile device browser that supports the 'handheld' media type. You can find out if the browser in your mobile device supports the 'handheld' media type by using your mobile device's browser to visit www.htmldog.com/test/handheld.html.

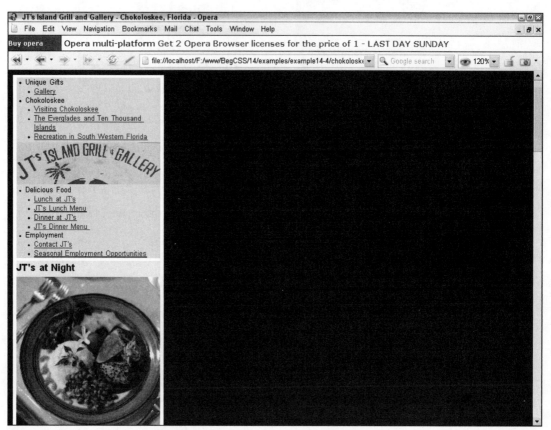

Figure 15-1

In Figure 15-2, the JT's web site is displayed on the Motorola emulator. You can see that it produces similar results to that of Opera's built-in Small Screen feature, in that it applies the handheld style sheet, if one is present.

Figure 15-2

The Openwave emulator is also capable of reading handheld style sheets. Figure 15-3 shows JT's website displayed in the Openwave emulator.

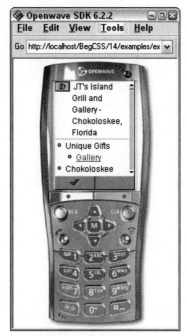

Figure 15-3

If a handheld style sheet is not present, the Opera browser uses a special proprietary formatting to control presentation for handheld devices. The best way to observe how Opera changes formatting using the Small Screen feature is to visit a website that does not have a handheld style sheet defined. Whereas Opera reformats the page to completely remove any horizontal scrolling, this built-in rendering for handheld devices is overridden by the presence of a handheld style sheet. Opera also limits the CSS properties available in handheld mode. A complete table of the CSS features supported in the handheld version of Opera is available at www.opera.com/docs/specs/css/.

In the following Try It Out, you can see some of the techniques used to control presentation of a web document for a handheld device by applying a handheld style sheet to the JT's Island Grill and Gallery website.

Try It Out   Applying a Style Sheet for Handheld Devices

Example 15-1. The following steps show you how to apply a handheld style sheet.

1.   Enter the following rules into a new style sheet:

```
body {
    font: 0.6em sans-serif;
    max-width: 20em;
}
```

```
h1, h2, h3, h4, h5, h6 {
    margin: 0;
    padding: 0;
    background: #ccc;
}
h1 {
    font-size: 1.3em;
    margin-top: 2em;
}
p {
    margin-top: 0;
}
img {
    width: 100%;
    height: auto;
    border: none;
}
ul {
    margin: 0.5em 0;
    padding-left: 1em;
    background: #ccc;
}
ul ul {
    margin: 0;
}
h5 {
    font-weight: normal;
}
h3, h4 {
    margin-top: 1em;
}
h5 {
    font-size: 1em;
    background: transparent none;
}
a:focus {
    color: white;
    background: black;
}
```

2. Save the new style sheet in the style_sheets directory as handheld.css.

3. Make the following modifications to the dinner_menu.html file:

```
<html>
    <head>
        <title>
            JT's Island Grill and Gallery - Chokoloskee, Florida
        </title>
        <link rel='stylesheet'
            type='text/css'
            href='style_sheets/base_styles.css' media='screen'/>
```

```
<link rel='stylesheet'
      type='text/css'
      href='style_sheets/menu_system.css' media='screen'/>
<link rel='stylesheet'
      type='text/css'
      href='style_sheets/dinner_menu.css' media='screen'/>
<link rel='stylesheet'
      type='text/css'
      href='style_sheets/handheld.css' media='handheld'/>
</head>
```

4. The styles included in dinner_menu.html for elements using the `style` attribute conflict with the new handheld style sheet, so you need to relocate these styles. Remove the `style` attribute from this element and add an `id` attribute:

```
<img src='images/photos/dinner_plate.jpg'
     id='dinnerplate'
     alt='dinner plate'/>
```

5. As you did in Step 4, remove the `style` attribute and add an `id` attribute:

```
<img src='images/photos/dinner.jpg'
     id='dinner'
     alt='Dinner Table'/>
```

6. Save dinner_menu.html.

7. Add the following rules to the dinner_menu.css style sheet:

```
div#content {
    background: lightyellow url('../images/backgrounds/dinner_glass.jpg') no-repeat
fixed center center;
}
div#body img {
    float: right;
    height: auto;
}
img#dinnerplate {
    width: 9em;
}
img#dinner {
    width: 16em;
}
```

8. Save dinner_menu.css

Figure 15-4 shows output from the Opera Small Screen mobile device emulator.

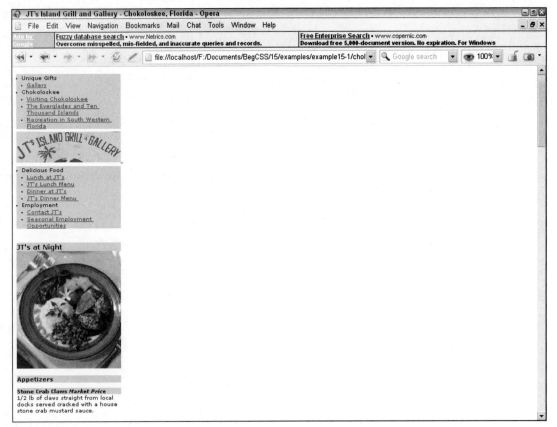

Figure 15-4

How It Works

As you can see from the output in Figure 15-4, the handheld style sheet that you wrote for this example does much to emulate the look and feel you observed in Figure 15-1, where the Opera small screen technology adjusted the styles of the page automatically. In this example, a handheld style sheet, which overrides automatic formatting, is explicitly provided. Handheld devices have tiny screens, so formatting features such as fixed-width, positioning, and the various textual effects aren't as effective when viewed on a small screen. These types of effects more often than not cause the user to have to scroll horizontally to view the content. Additionally, the number of colors available on a handheld device is limited, which makes a barebones design that presents only the necessary information the most effective. If you recall from Chapter 4, a web-safe color pallet exists for devices with limited color display capabilities (think *shorthand hexadecimal colors = web-safe pallet*), but for some devices, even the web-safe pallet may be too much. Keep in mind that most handheld devices are capable of displaying around 256 colors, some even less than that. This is one area where the device emulator is very useful. Be sure to check colors using the emulator for your target device to ensure that the colors you have chosen will display properly.

The style sheet provided for handheld devices in this example does little more than control the spacing of elements in the JT's dinner menu and control the sizes of fonts. Each image in the document is also limited to a 15em width or less to accommodate tiny screen sizes. By using a 100% width on the image and an auto height, the image scales to the available screen size. This type of formatting allows the user to access the information in the document in an organized fashion. Figure 15-4 shows output similar to that shown in Figure 8-2, before any CSS is applied. Because the handheld medium is limited in what it can display, the design is adjusted to accommodate those limitations. Horizontal scrolling makes the information more difficult to access, so it is completely avoided to provide the user with the easiest experience.

In this example, you also modified the dinner_menu.html file itself: First you changed it to link to the handheld style sheet and then to remove all style attributes from the body of the document. Even though handheld devices are limited in size and color, most still interpret properties like float. Naturally, in some cases, this adversely affected the design. So the styles for each image are relocated to the dinner_menu.css file, where they cannot affect presentation on handheld devices.

In the next sections, I discuss some of the techniques involved in styling content for print.

Styling Web Documents for Print

Like handheld devices, a specific style sheet can be used to style content for print. In Chapter 4, you saw the differences between length units used for a computer screen and length units used for print. This is one of the key reasons that separate style sheets for print exist. Specifying measurements designated for computer screens, such as pixel units, can potentially be inconsistent in printed documents, whereas real-world, absolute length units such as inches, centimeters, points, and so on are ideally suited for print.

A style sheet written explicitly for print enables developers to exclude irrelevant portions of a web document from the printed version. For example, no document navigation is required in a printed version. Additionally, because color documents have some expense associated with them, depending on the type of printer and what type of ink or toner the printer users, it is also often better to exclude background images or other aspects of the design that result in greater consumption of expensive ink or toner. For these reasons, print versions of web documents are often simplified to simple black and white productions of the original document. Only foreground images relevant to the document are retained.

CSS 2 provides several properties for controlling the presentation of paged media, although at the time of this writing a sparse selection of those features is actually implemented in current browsers. CSS 2 properties control such things as where page breaks occur, the size of the page margins, and the size of the page itself. In this area, Opera 7.5 boasts the best support for the CSS 2 paged media properties.

Controlling page breaks

`page-break-before` *and* `page-break-after`: *Documented in CSS 2 and supported in IE 6 (Partial), Mozilla 1.7 (Partial), Opera 7.5, and Safari 1.2 (Partial).*

Two properties that most browsers (Internet Explorer, Mozilla, Opera, and Safari) have in common are `page-break-before` and `page-break-after`. These properties are outlined in the following table.

Property	Value
page-break-before	auto | always | avoid | left | right | inherit
	Initial value: auto
page-break-after	auto | always | avoid | left | right | inherit
	Initial value: auto

The page-break-before and page-break-after properties control where page breaks are made. Unfortunately, even though different browsers offer support for these two properties, they do not support all the values that CSS 2 allows. Mozilla, Safari, and Internet Explorer support only the keywords always and auto.

The page-break-before and page-break-after properties dictate where a page break should be made depending on where an element appears in a document. For example, the following rule causes a page break to happen before the start of any <p> elements in a document:

```
p {
    page-break-before: always;
}
```

Apply this rule to the following markup:

```
<body>
    This text appears on the first printed page.
    <p>
        This text appears at the start of the second printed page.
    </p>
    <p>
        This text appears at the start of the third printed page.
    </p>
</body>
```

Figure 15-5 shows the print preview screen of Mozilla. Here the text before the first <p> element appears on the first page.

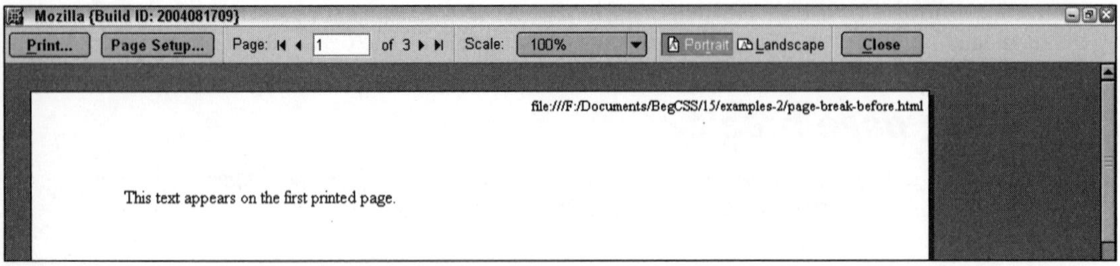

Figure 15-5

Figure 15-6 shows Mozilla's print preview screen advanced to the second page, which shows the text inside the first <p> element.

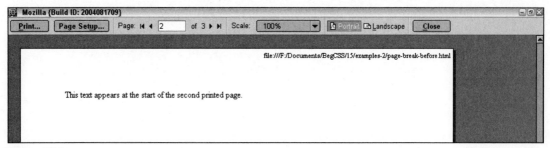

Figure 15-6

Figure 15-7 shows Mozilla's print preview screen advanced to the third page, which shows the text inside the second <p> element.

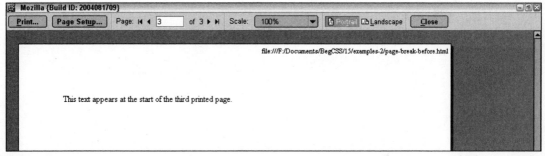

Figure 15-7

Figures 15-5, 15-6, and 15-7 show that the page-break-before: always; declaration forces a page break before the start of the <p> element. The page-break-after: always; declaration performs the same function, with the exception that page breaks come after the element.

> **The print properties that CSS provides should be used in situations where you have control over the actual printing of a document (size of the paper and the printer settings), such as in a corporate intranet application. For a public website, you should provide a print version of the document that exhibits as much flexibility as possible.**

In the following Try It Out, you apply a print style sheet to the JT's Island Grill and Gallery website.

Applying a Style Sheet for Print

Example 15-2. The following steps show you how to apply a print style sheet.

1. Open your text editor and enter the following styles:

```
body {
    letter-spacing: 1pt;
}
div#nav ul {
    display: none;
}
div#nav img {
    width: 3in;
    display: block;
    margin: auto;
}
img {
    border: thin solid black;
}
h1 {
    font-size: 14pt;
    border-bottom: thin dotted black;
}
img#dinnerplate, img#dinner {
    float: right;
    width: 2in;
    height: auto;
    margin: 0.25in;
}
div#content {
    text-align: center;
}
p {
    margin-top: 0;
}
h2, h3, h4, h5, h6 {
    margin: 0;
}
h3 {
    text-decoration: underline;
}
h1, h3 {
    font: 16pt "Monotype Corsiva" cursive;
}
h5 + h3 {
    margin-top: 0.25in;
}
h4 > em, h5 > em {
    font-weight: normal;
    margin-left: 0.20in;
}
```

```
h5 {
    font-weight: normal;
    font-size: 12pt;
}
h6 {
    border-top: thin dotted black;
    text-align: center;
}
p.copy {
    text-align: justify;
    text-indent: 0.25in;
    margin-top: 0;
    line-height: 24pt;
}
```

2.   Save this style sheet in the style_sheets directory as print.css.

3.   To link to the new print style sheet, open dinner_menu.html and apply the following markup:

```
<html>
    <head>
        <title>
            JT's Island Grill and Gallery - Chokoloskee, Florida
        </title>
        <link rel='stylesheet'
              type='text/css'
              href='style_sheets/base_styles.css' media='screen'/>
        <link rel='stylesheet'
              type='text/css'
              href='style_sheets/menu_system.css' media='screen'/>
        <link rel='stylesheet'
              type='text/css'
              href='style_sheets/dinner_menu.css' media='screen'/>
        <link rel='stylesheet'
              type='text/css'
              href='style_sheets/handheld.css' media='handheld'/>
        <link rel='stylesheet'
              type='text/css'
              href='style_sheets/print.css' media='print'/>
    </head>
```

4.   Save dinner_menu.html.

Open the file dinner_menu.html in Mozilla and choose File ⇨ Print Preview to see the screen shown in Figure 15-8.

Figure 15-8

How It Works

Like the handheld style sheet that you created for Example 15-1, the print style sheet is a stripped-down representation of the dinner menu. Background images and background colors are avoided, as the user is unlikely to want these in the printed document.

Some of the styles presented in this style sheet are redundant because some of the same techniques are used in the style sheets for screen. In a real-world project, it would make sense to combine styles that apply to all types of media devices in a style sheet with media='all' specified. However, the styles presented in the handheld style sheet are vastly different from those in the screen and media style sheets, and the print style sheet uses real-world measurement units instead of those intended for screen. A little redundancy, therefore, isn't too bad in this case.

Another technique likely to be deployed in a real-world project is separating the print style sheet into different style sheets, as you did with the screen style sheets. By creating a base_styles.css, menu_system.css, and dinner_menu.css style sheet, you have one for the entire website, one specifically for navigation, and one for styles specific to the dinner menu. I lumped these together for print to keep the example simple.

Other techniques deployed in the print style sheet include avoiding fixed widths and using real-world measurements to design a print dinner menu that looks similar to the one presented on-screen. Fixed widths especially should be avoided because you, as the designer, have no way of knowing what size paper the user intends to print on.

Print style sheets provide a version of a web page optimized for print. Print style sheets are best approached by avoiding background colors and images and keeping to a simple black and white design. Real-world length units should also be utilized to avoid possible inconsistencies with length units designed for the computer screen, such as the px unit.

Summary

Media-specific style sheets open up doors to a much larger potential audience for a website. In this chapter, you leaned the following:

❑ With handheld technology progressing in the way it is, more and more people have the capability to access the web using a handheld device.

❑ When you plan to present content for specific mediums, you should take into account the limitations and possible expense of using each medium.

❑ The limitations of handheld devices include a tiny screen, potentially longer loading times, and a limited selection of color.

❑ For print, you should consider the cost of ink. Because ink and toner are expensive, avoiding high color designs is considered best practice in the formulation of print style sheets.

❑ Navigation is useless for a printed document. For a print style sheet, the parts of the document most useful to the user should be included and the rest should be hidden using the display: none; declaration.

❑ The print properties that CSS provides should not be used unless you have control over the actual printing of the document.

In Chapter 16, I take a look at the properties that CSS provides for styling tabular data.

Exercises

1. Write a handheld style sheet for the Widgets and What's-it's FAQ page. Use the markup that you completed for Chapter 14, Exercise 2. Things like floating and positioning should be avoided. Use the Small Screen feature offered in the Opera 7 browser as a guide for how the handheld style sheet should be styled. Convert the embedded style sheet to an external style sheet and limit it to screen media.

2. Write a print style sheet for the Widgets and What's-it's FAQ page. Use all real-world measurements and remove the navigation, colored backgrounds, and watermark from the printed version. Create the print style sheet so that it is a simple black and white representation of the same page, with a similar look and feel to its screen counterpart.

16

Styling Tables

In Chapter 15, I showed some examples of how to create style sheets for specific mediums like print and handheld devices. In this chapter, I discuss some odds and ends related to styling HTML/XHTML table elements and the controls that CSS provides for flexibility.

In Chapter 10, I told you how using tables to lay out a web page can be inefficient and, perhaps, make your website inaccessible for visually impaired users. However, tables are not all bad and not completely taboo. Tables are primarily a method to show the relationship between data, much as a spreadsheet application does. As I explore some acceptable uses of tables in this chapter, I discuss

❑   The optional table elements that can make it easier to style a table and that make the structure more intuitive

❑   Controlling placement of the table caption

❑   Controlling the layout of the table

❑   Controlling the spacing between table cells

❑   Controlling whether empty cells are displayed

Tables can be complex creatures in HTML/XHTML. If used properly, they allow information to be presented in a neat, organized, and consistent manner. Put simply, data that needs to show relation and logic should be placed into tables because that is what tables are for. The discussion presented in this chapter also plays heavily into the discussion about styling XML in Chapter 17. The examples presented in Chapter 17 are identical to those presented in this chapter with one very important difference: They're written in XML.

Tables have several optional tags that may be used to further enhance the structure and presentation of a table. This is where I start the discussion.

Optional Table Elements

The `<table>` element has a number of optional tags that can be utilized to enhance the presentation of a table, including captions, columns, headings, and footers. Take a look at a `<table>` element that makes use of all these optional tags. When I get into the discussion of styling tables, beginning with the section "Table Captions," you must understand what is possible in a table. I also present CSS 2 properties that are table-specific, allowing more control over table presentation. The following markup is a `<table>` element complete with all the optional bells and whistles:

```
<table>
    <caption>
        Table: My favorite records.
    </caption>
    <colgroup>
        <col id='album' />
        <col id='artist' />
        <col id='released' />
    </colgroup>
    <thead>
        <tr>
            <th> album          </th>
            <th> artist         </th>
            <th> released       </th>
        </tr>
    </thead>
    <tbody>
        <tr>
            <td> Rubber Soul      </td>
            <td> The Beatles      </td>
            <td> 1965             </td>
        </tr>
        <tr>
            <td> Brown Eyed Girl  </td>
            <td> Van Morrison     </td>
            <td> 1967             </td>
        </tr>
        <tr>
            <td> Queen II         </td>
            <td> Queen            </td>
            <td> 1974             </td>
        </tr>
        <tr>
            <td> Mellon Collie and the Infinite Sadness </td>
            <td> The Smashing Pumpkins                   </td>
            <td> 1995                                    </td>
        </tr>
        <tr>
            <td></td>
            <td></td>
            <td></td>
        </tr>
    </tbody>
    <tfoot>
        <tr>
```

```
                    <td> album        </td>
                    <td> artist       </td>
                    <td> released     </td>
              </tr>
          </tfoot>
      </table>
```

Next, I have some CSS to apply to this markup. After the CSS is applied, I show you what it looks like in a browser. In the next few sections, I refer back to this example, which is also available if you download this book's files from www.wrox.com. (The file is named html-table.html, and if you download the entire directory structure, you can find this file under Chapter 16\Examples.) Using this example, I present different properties that allow manipulation of how a table is presented and explain the different elements that structure the various parts of a table. If you don't have access to the Wrox website, you can type the preceding markup in an XHTML document and save the file as html-table.html so that you can follow along with the examples.

In the next few sections I discuss

- ❑ Table captions — the caption-side property
- ❑ Table columns — what they are and how to style them
- ❑ Grouping table data with the <thead>, <tbody>, and <tfoot> elements
- ❑ Other table styles for controlling table layout, borders, and cell spacing using CSS

To complement the preceding example, I've prepared a style sheet that allows some basic presentation to be applied. In the next few sections, I add to this style sheet to demonstrate the different properties that allow control over table presentation.

```
* {
    font-family: monospace;
}
body {
    margin: 0;
}
table {
    width: 100%;
    border: thin solid black;
}
th, tfoot td {
    border: thin solid black;
    text-align: center;
    font-weight: bold;
}
tbody td {
    font-size: 120%;
}
caption {
    font-size: 90%;
    text-align: right;
}
td, th, caption {
    padding: 5px;
}
```

This style sheet can be embedded in the XHTML document or saved to be referenced externally as html-table.css. Before you apply any additional styles to the table, the document appears as it does in Figure 16-1.

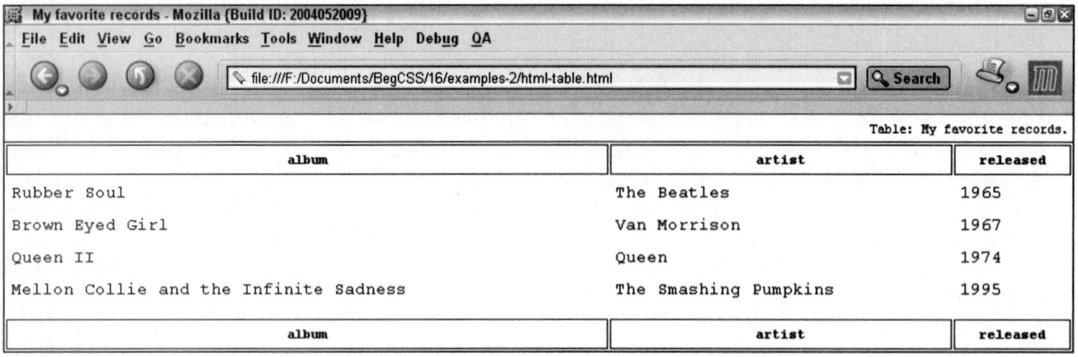

Figure 16-1

Each section starts with the example file presented here. Therefore, at the beginning of each section, start with the original html-table.html and html-table.css example files shown here and modify the original files to see the examples presented in that section in action. Each variation of the html-table.html and html-table.css file is also available in the code download at the Wrox website.

Table Captions

Captions are presented in the `<caption>` element. By default, these are rendered above the table in the document. You use the `caption-side` property to control the placement of the table caption.

caption-side

Documented in CSS 2.1 and supported in Mozilla 1.7, Opera 7.5, and Safari 1.2.

The following table shows the `caption-side` property and its possible values.

Property	Value
caption-side	top | bottom | inherit

Using the `caption-side` property, you can control whether the caption appears above or below the table. If you use the html-table.css file, here's what the inclusion of the `caption-side` property looks like.

```
* {
    font-family: monospace;
}
body {
```

```
    margin: 0;
}
table {
    width: 100%;
    border: thin solid black;
    caption-side: bottom;
}
```

I have saved the variation of the html-table.css and html-table.html file as html-table-1.html, and html-table-1.css respectively. With the inclusion of the caption-side property in the html-table.css file, the caption is moved to the bottom of the table, as depicted in Figure 16-2.

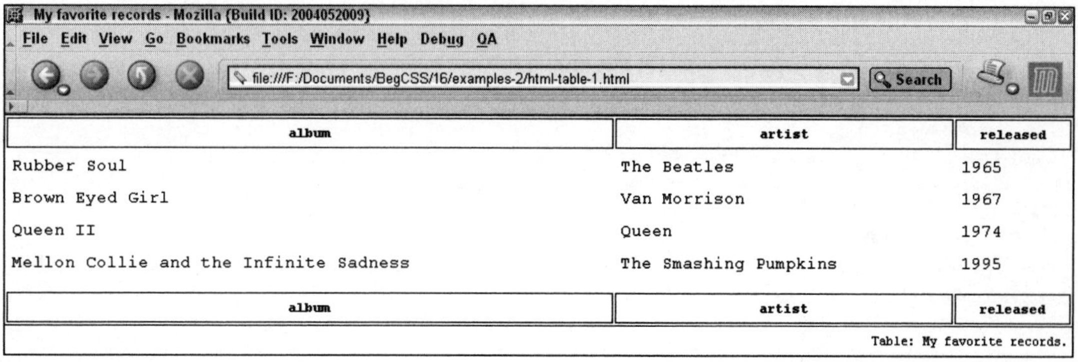

Figure 16-2

Table Columns

In HTML/XHTML, the <colgroup> and <col> elements allow the vertical columns of a table to be controlled. This is useful for controlling the width of a column of data or other aspects of presentation, such as background color or text color.

By using these elements, you can span more than one column or have one column defined for each actual column, as in the following example:

```
<table>
    <colgroup>
        <col span='2' />
        <col />
    </colgroup>
    <tbody>
        <tr>
            <td> column 1 </td>
            <td> column 2 </td>
            <td> column 3 </td>
        </tr>
    </tbody>
</table>
```

`<col span='2' />` controls the presentation of the `<td>` elements containing the text of column 1 and column 2, the first two columns of the table. The last `<col />` element (without the span attribute) controls the presentation of column 3, contained in the last `<td>` element.

Using CSS, I can continue the example containing my favorite records (using the html-table.html markup and style sheet). This example shows a column defined for each actual column of data, or in other words, each `<td>` element appearing in a row. In this html-table.html example, a column is defined for each cell, and each row has three cells; consequently, there are three columns. Adding the following CSS to the style sheet enables me to control the styles of each column in the html-table.html markup using CSS:

```
col#album {
    background: lightgrey;
}
col#artist {
    width: 250px;
}
col#released {
    width: 100px;
    background: lightgrey;
}
```

I've saved this variation as html-table-2.html and html-table-2.css. After I apply these rules, the table now looks like Figure 16-3.

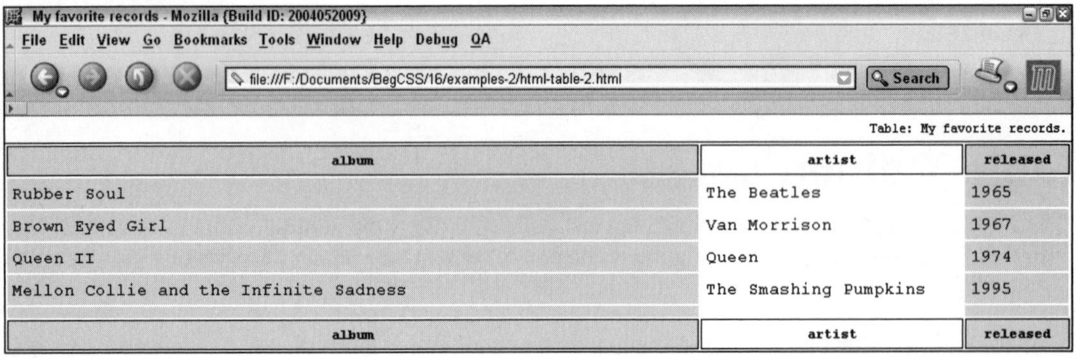

Figure 16-3

Each column is given a different background color. The first column is `lightgrey`, spelled according to the British spelling to accommodate Internet Explorer, which does not allow *lightgray*, the U.S. spelling. The next column is given no background and a fixed width of 250 pixels. The last column is also given a `lightgrey` background and a fixed width of 100 pixels.

> Internet Explorer allows more flexibility with the `<col>` element and allows the text color to be changed. Mozilla is slightly more restrictive, allowing the width and a background color to be specified, but not much else. The W3C specs don't elaborate specifically on what is allowed, leaving this to the individual browsers to decide for themselves.

Grouping Table Data

Table data is grouped using four elements, including <colgroup>, which you saw in the table columns section earlier in this chapter. Here are the four elements for grouping table data:

❑   <colgroup>: Used to control aspects of the vertical columns of a table, such as column width, background color, and text color

❑   <thead>: Used to designate the table headings; using this element generally results in a bold-faced font and the text being centered in the rows and cells contained inside it

❑   <tbody>: Designates the portion of the table that is the body where all the tabular data is contained

❑   <tfoot>: Used on the footer cells of the table; provides no special styles on the cells it encapsulates

Grouping table data is useful from both a structural and a presentational perspective. Because the table data is grouped, you don't add class or id attributes to the table to differentiate between cells contained in the heading, in the body, or in the footer; additionally, the structure of the document is more intuitive. Grouping table data also provides special functionality for printed documents. When a table with heading, body, and footers designated with <thead>, <tbody> and <tfoot> is printed, the table headers and footers are repeated for each page of the table.

From a CSS standpoint, this structure enables you to use descendant selectors and a named table instead of creating individual class and id names for each cell of the table. For instance, if I have this markup

```
<table id='beatles'>
    <tbody>
        <td> John   </td>
        <td> Paul   </td>
        <td> George </td>
        <td> Ringo  </td>
    </tbody>
</table>
```

and this CSS,

```
table#beatles tbody td {
    font: 12pt sans-serif;
}
```

I can use descendant selectors to select cells in the body of the table. Using this selector, the <td> element must be nested inside a <tbody> element, and the <tbody> element must be nested inside a <table> element that has an id of 'beatles'. With this approach, I can limit the selector to the cells contained in the <tbody> element of a table with the id of 'beatles'. I can also invent similar rules for the <thead> and <tfoot> elements and give them different styles from those cells contained inside the <tbody> element.

In the following Try It Out, I show how all the extra bells and whistles available for <table> elements work in a real-world project and how these elements help you take advantage of CSS. This Try It Out continues the example, which I used in Chapter 2, which demonstrates placing a recipe in a table. I'm also adding a little eye candy here with CSS background images to enhance the look and feel of the document. This example is also important in Chapter 17, where I show you how it can be ported to XML and styled with CSS as an XML document.

Try It Out **Applying Tables to a Real Project**

Example 16-1. In the following steps, you apply tables to a real-world project.

1. Type the following XHTML markup into your text editor:

```
<!DOCTYPE html PUBLIC "-//W3C//DTD XHTML 1.0 Strict//EN"
"http://www.w3.org/TR/xhtml1/DTD/xhtml1-strict.dtd">
<html>
    <head>
        <title> Spicy Thai Peanut Sauce </title>
        <link rel='stylesheet' type='text/css' href='example16.css'/>
    </head>
    <body>
        <table class='recipe'>
            <caption>
                Spicy Thai Peanut Sauce
            </caption>
            <colgroup>
                <col/>
                <col/>
                <col/>
                <col/>
            </colgroup>
            <thead>
                <tr>
                    <th> quantity     </th>
                    <th> measurement  </th>
                    <th> product      </th>
                    <th> instructions </th>
                </tr>
            </thead>
            <tbody>
                <tr>
                    <td> .5            </td>
                    <td> CUPS          </td>
                    <td> Peanut Oil    </td>
                    <td></td>
                </tr>
                <tr>
                    <td> 12            </td>
                    <td> Each          </td>
                    <td> Serrano Peppers </td>
                    <td> Sliced        </td>
                </tr>
                <tr>
```

```
            <td> 16          </td>
            <td> Each         </td>
            <td> Garlic Cloves </td>
            <td> Minced       </td>
        </tr>
        <tr>
            <td> 2            </td>
            <td> CUPS         </td>
            <td> Peanut Butter </td>
            <td></td>
        </tr>
        <tr>
            <td> 1            </td>
            <td> CUPS         </td>
            <td> Soy Sauce    </td>
            <td></td>
        </tr>
        <tr>
            <td> .5           </td>
            <td> CUPS         </td>
            <td> Lime Juice   </td>
            <td></td>
        </tr>
        <tr>
            <td> 4            </td>
            <td> TABLESPOONS  </td>
            <td> Sesame Oil   </td>
            <td></td>
        </tr>
        <tr>
            <td> 4            </td>
            <td> CUPS         </td>
            <td> Coconut Milk </td>
            <td></td>
        </tr>
        <tr>
            <td> .5           </td>
            <td> CUPS         </td>
            <td> Honey        </td>
            <td></td>
        </tr>
        <tr>
            <td>  .5          </td>
            <td>  CUPS        </td>
            <td> Brown Sugar  </td>
            <td></td>
        </tr>
    </tbody>
    <tfoot>
        <tr>
            <td colspan='4'>
```

```
                    <ul>
                        <li>
                            Sautee sliced serranos and garlic in peanut oil
                            till lightly browned.
                        </li>
                        <li>
                            Add all other ingredients and stir till dissolved.
                        </li>
                        <li>
                            Simmer for 5 minutes.
                        </li>
                        <li>
                            Puree all in blender.
                        </li>
                    </ul>
                    <p>
                        Sautee your favorite vegetables; onions, mushrooms,
                        green peppers and squash work best, sprinkle with
                        allspice, salt and pepper. Optionally add walnuts
                        or pine nuts. Add browned chicken or tofu and glaze
                        with sauce. Serve with jasmine rice.
                    </p>
                </td>
            </tr>
        </tfoot>
    </table>
    </body>
</html>
```

2.   Save the file as example16-1.html.

3.   Write the following CSS into your text editor in a separate document:

```
* {
    font-family: monospace;
}
html {
    background: #fff url('fruit_veg_web.jpg') no-repeat fixed center center;
}
body {
    padding: 10px;
    margin: 10px auto;
    min-width: 500px;
    max-width: 900px;
    /* Moz proprietary opacity property */
    -moz-opacity: 0.7;
    /* Safari / KHTML proprietary opacity property */
    -khtml-opacity: 0.7;
    /* Microsoft proprietary filter property */
    filter:progid:DXImageTransform.Microsoft.Alpha(opacity=70);
    /* CSS 3 opacity property */
```

```
        opacity: 0.7;
        background: url('cross_hatch.jpg') repeat;
    }
    table.recipe {
        width: 100%;
        margin-bottom: 5px;
    }
    caption {
        text-align: left;
        margin-bottom: 5px;
        text-transform: lowercase;
        font-size: 160%;
        padding: 5px;
        letter-spacing: 10px;
        font-weight: bold;
    }
    table.recipe thead th {
        font-weight: bold;
        font-size: 150%;
        color: black;
    }
    table.recipe thead th, table.recipe tbody td {
        padding: 5px;
        text-transform: lowercase;
    }
    table.recipe tbody td, table.recipe tfoot td {
        font-size: 130%;
    }
    table.recipe tfoot td {
        padding: 5px;
    }
    table.recipe tbody td:hover,
    table.recipe thead th:hover,
    table.recipe tfoot td ul:hover,
    table.recipe caption:hover,
    table.recipe tfoot td p:hover {
        background: black;
        color: white;
        font-weight: bold;
    }
    table.recipe tfoot td p {
        padding: 5px;
    }
    li {
        margin-left: 30px;
        padding-left: 30px;
    }
```

4. Save the file as example16-1.css.

This results in the output shown in Figure 16-4.

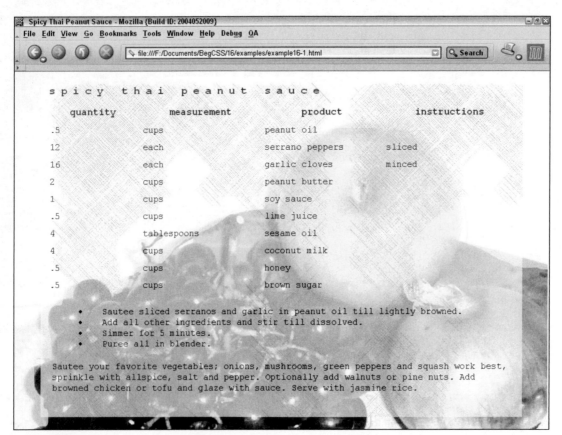

Figure 16-4

How It Works

This example is a lot to digest. Take a look at each part of it in detail to see how it comes together. First, explore the markup of the document. I have included a `<caption>` element inside the table to house the name of the recipe:

```
<table class='recipe'>
    <caption>
        Spicy Thai Peanut Sauce
    </caption>
    <colgroup>
        <col/>
        <col/>
```

I could just as easily have put the name of the recipe in a heading tag like `<h1>` and placed it outside the table. I chose the caption so the name of the recipe is bound to the table of ingredients. Later, if I choose to, I can include the name of the website or a logo above the table of ingredients. Next, I've added `<colgroup>` and `<col/>` tags. These can be used to control the layout of each column, although I haven't chosen to take advantage of this capability yet. Although you can use these tags, they are not absolutely necessary. I can leave them out, causing no impact on the table's final rendered layout. Next, I added the table headings, placed inside <thead> tags, and I used <th> instead of <td> to house the contents of each cell:

```
      <col/>
      <col/>
   </colgroup>
   <thead>
      <tr>
         <th> quantity    </th>
         <th> measurement </th>
         <th> product     </th>
         <th> instructions </th>
      </tr>
   </thead>
   <tbody>
```

I added the <tbody> element to house the contents of the recipe itself, and near the bottom of the recipe I listed the instructions in an unordered list (<ul>) element. I placed final suggestions in a paragraph at the bottom of the document.

Look more closely at how the CSS comes together with the markup to produce the final rendered output in Figure 16-4. The first rule styles the <body> element, and there's quite a bit going on here:

```
body {
     padding: 10px;
     margin: 10px auto;
     min-width: 500px;
     max-width: 900px;
     /* Moz proprietary opacity property */
     -moz-opacity: 0.7;
     /* Safari / KHTML proprietary opacity property */
     -khtml-opacity: 0.7;
     /* Microsoft proprietary filter property */
     filter:progid:DXImageTransform.Microsoft.Alpha(opacity=70);
     /* CSS 3 opacity property */
     opacity: 0.7;
     background: url('cross_hatch.jpg') repeat;
}
```

First things, first. The <body> element is a block-level element, and it behaves identically to the <div> element. Its width expands to fill the entire available area by default, and its height expands only enough to accommodate the content inside. I take advantage of that behavior here, using the margin: 10px auto; declaration, which adds 10 pixels of margin to the top and bottom of the element. It is centered horizontally with the auto value. Because the <body> element expands to fill the entire available area by default, I decided that I want it to stop expanding at a certain point for those visitors viewing the page using a high-resolution monitor. I use the max-width: 900px; declaration to stop the element from expanding when it reaches 900 pixels. Conversely, I don't want the element to shrink past a certain point if the document is being viewed on a low-resolution monitor. This causes nasty things to happen. I stop the element from shrinking by using the min-width: 500px; declaration.

The next four declarations all deal with opacity. At the time of this writing, the opacity property is an official part of CSS 3. Before the CSS 3 implementation, each browser had its own way of handling opacity, with the exception of Opera, which does not support opacity in any form. The Mozilla proprietary CSS opacity property is -moz-opacity;; -khtml-opacity is the Safari proprietary opacity property. Microsoft has a completely different method for specifying opacity: it's handled through a proprietary filter property. The use of these opacity properties produces an aesthetically pleasing transparency effect that allows the background specified for the <html> element in this rule to bleed through:

```
html {
    background: #fff url('fruit_veg_web.jpg') no-repeat fixed center center;
}
```

I discuss special effects like this in great detail in Chapter 18.

Lastly, for the <body> element, I've applied a background that uses a cross-hatching effect. The backgrounds I've chosen for this document are purely aesthetical. The image 'fruit_veg_web.jpg' is quite large in size, over 100KB. On first download, this image takes a while to load on a low-bandwidth connection. However, with browser caching, the technique that saves a local copy of all the documents and components of the web page, the bite caused by this large file is limited to the first visit. As visitors view subsequent pages with the same background, the browser remembers that this file is the same one requested from the page before and simply displays that local copy instead of requesting it again from the server.

The next rule on the style sheet is the <table> containing the Spicy Thai Peanut Sauce recipe:

```
table.recipe {
    width: 100%;
    margin-bottom: 5px;
}
```

Here the table is told to take up 100% of the available space horizontally. Because it resides inside of the <body> element, the amount of free space is what's available inside of that element. A margin is applied to the bottom of the table to provide more spacing from the end of the <table> and the start of the <ul>. The caption, containing the name of the recipe, renders above the table by default. Therefore, the table appears in Figure 16-4 just as if you had written the following:

```
table.recipe {
    caption-side: top;
    width: 100%;
    margin-bottom: 5px;
}
```

If I wanted the caption to appear below the table, after the data contained in the <table> element and before the <ul> element, I would have included caption-side: bottom; instead. For this example, it made more sense for the caption to appear above the table because it contains the name of the recipe.

The next group of style sheet rules style the cells of the table:

```
table.recipe thead th {
    font-weight: bold;
    font-size: 150%;
```

```
        color: black;
    }
table.recipe thead th, table.recipe tbody td {
    padding: 5px;
    text-transform: lowercase;
}
table.recipe tbody td, table.recipe tfoot td {
    font-size: 130%;
}
table.recipe tfoot td {
    padding: 5px;
}
```

For the cells of the table, I have chosen to take advantage of grouping elements to differentiate the styles for table headings (<thead> element), the body of the table (<tbody> element), and the footer of the table (<tfoot> element). This approach allows me to apply style to the table without adding additional id or class attributes. I use the descendant selector here to ensure that styles are applied only to tables containing the recipe class name. This allows me to include more than one recipe per page or possibly introduce other tables of data without affecting the styles for those tables. Again, the descendant selector works by looking at the element's ancestry. For instance, table.recipe thead th says to look first for a <table> that contains a recipe class name; then look for a <thead> element inside that table; look for a <th> element inside the <thead> element; and finally, apply the declarations contained inside the rule.

Next, I add some effects to the page using the :hover pseudo-class:

```
table.recipe tbody td:hover,
table.recipe thead th:hover,
table.recipe tfoot td ul:hover,
table.recipe caption:hover,
table.recipe tfoot td p:hover {
    background: black;
    color: white;
    font-weight: bold;
}
```

If you recall from Chapter 6, the :hover pseudo-class is a selector that applies style when the user's mouse is hovering over an element. For example, the table.recipe tbody td:hover selector uses the descendant selector that I just discussed. It says that if a <table> element has a class name of "recipe" and if inside that <table> element is a <tbody> element, and if inside that <tbody> element is a <td> element, when the user's mouse hovers over that <td> element these declarations should be applied. I have grouped several selectors here using commas, and this allows me to select the <td> elements contained in the <tbody>, the <th> elements contained in the <thead> element, the <ul> element containing preparation instructions in the table footer, and the paragraph containing the suggestions for use. I included this effect so that when the user's mouse is over an element, the cell gets a semi-transparent black background, white text, and bold font — for both clarity and aesthetic effect. The semitransparent effect is achieved because the opacity properties that I included in the selector for the <body> element are inherited, meaning that all elements inside the <body> element are made semi-transparent, including the text, borders, and backgrounds.

Now, that you have seen the various elements available for use in a <table> element, the following section explores what else is possible with CSS and tables.

Other Table Styles

Besides the table styles I've discussed so far, you can also use the properties shown in the following table. With these properties, you can control table layout with the `table-layout` property, control how table cells are spaced using the `border-collapse` and `border-spacing` properties, and choose whether the browser should render empty cells with the `empty-cells` property.

Property	Value
table-layout	auto | fixed | inherit Initial value: auto
border-collapse	collapse | separate | inherit Initial value: separate
border-spacing	<length> <length>? | inherit Initial value: 0
empty-cells	show | hide | inherit Initial value: show

These properties control the more trivial aspects of presenting HTML/XHTML tables. The following sections look at each property in detail.

table-layout

Documented in CSS 2.1 and supported in IE 5.5, IE 6, Opera 7.5, Mozilla 1.7 (partial), and Safari 1.2.

By default, a table expands and contracts to accommodate the data contained inside. As data fills the table, it continues to expand as long as there is space. When you look at them this way, tables are inherently fluid. Here's what happens if I remove the `width: 100%;` declaration from the `<table>` element in the html-table.html example (remember to use the original example file to create the variation).

```
table {
    border: thin solid black;
}
```

This rule is the same as saying:

```
table {
    border: thin solid black;
    table-layout: auto;
}
```

The `table-layout: auto;` declaration is the default behavior of a table. Save this variation as html-table-3.html and html-table-3.css; this code results in the output depicted in Figure 16-5.

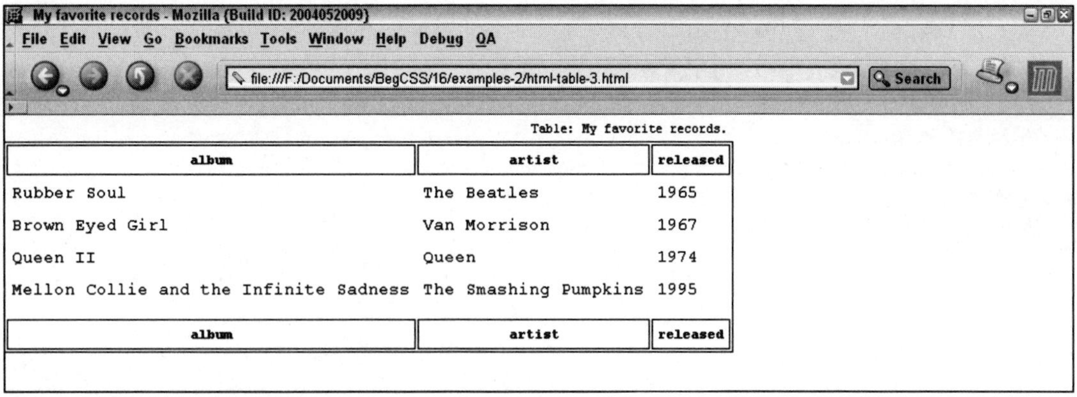

Figure 16-5

By default, the table expands only enough for the content that it contains, and this is the same as `table-layout: auto;`. Sometimes, however, it is necessary to force a table into a fixed width for both the table and the cells. Here's what happens when I specify a fixed width for the table:

```
table {
    width: 200px;
    border: thin solid black;
}
```

To see what a 200-pixel width looks like, add this snippet of markup to the body of the html-table.html document:

```
<body>
    <div style='width: 200px;
                height: 30px;
                background: gray;
                color: white;
                text-align: center;'>
        &lt; -- 200 pixels -- &gt;
    </div>
    <table>
        <caption>
            Table: My favorite records.
        </caption>
```

Save this variation as html-table-4.html and html-table-4.css. This code results in the output depicted in Figure 16-6.

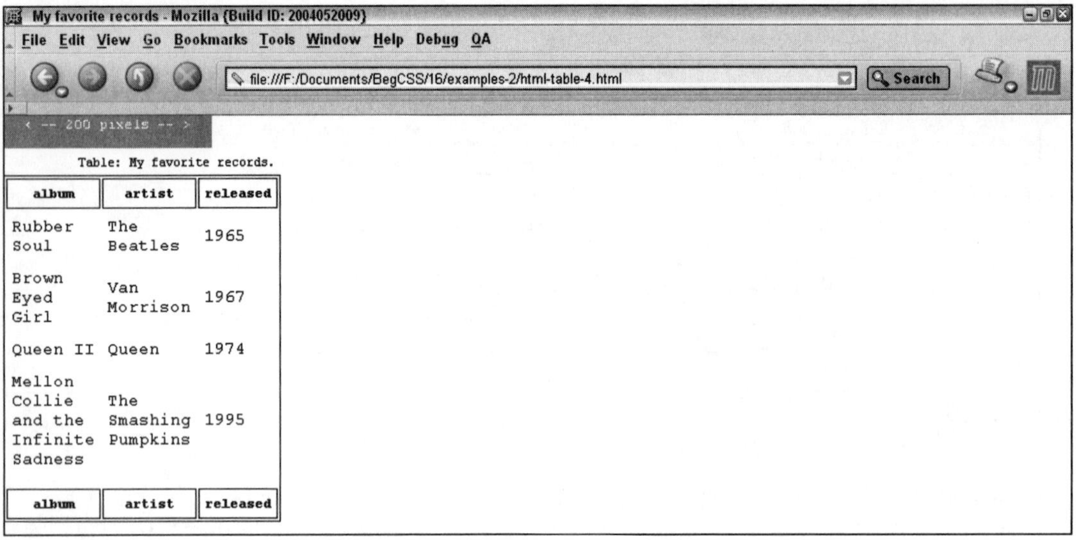

Figure 16-6

The table is larger than 200 pixels because the text contained in the cells results in a width larger than 200 pixels. You can use the `table-layout: fixed;` declaration to force the table into a 200-pixel width. Incorporate the following change into the html-table example:

```
table {
    width: 200px;
    border: thin solid black;
    table-layout: fixed;
}
```

Save this variation as html-table-5.html and html-table-5.css. Figure 16-7 shows the result when rendered in a browser.

The table is forced to maintain its width of 200 pixels, regardless of how much data is contained in its table cells. If the content inside the cells results in a width larger than 200 pixels, the content gets clipped. The clipped content is not visible when the document is viewed using Internet Explorer or Opera 7, which is what is supposed to happen. As you see in Figure 16-7, however, the clipped content is visible. You can correct this with the following:

```
th, td {
    overflow: hidden;
}
```

Save this as html-table-6.html and html-table-6.css. The result is shown in Figure 16-8.

This is what the output is supposed to look like. In contrast, as you saw in Chapter 10, the `overflow` property may also be used to add scroll bars so that the clipped content can be viewed.

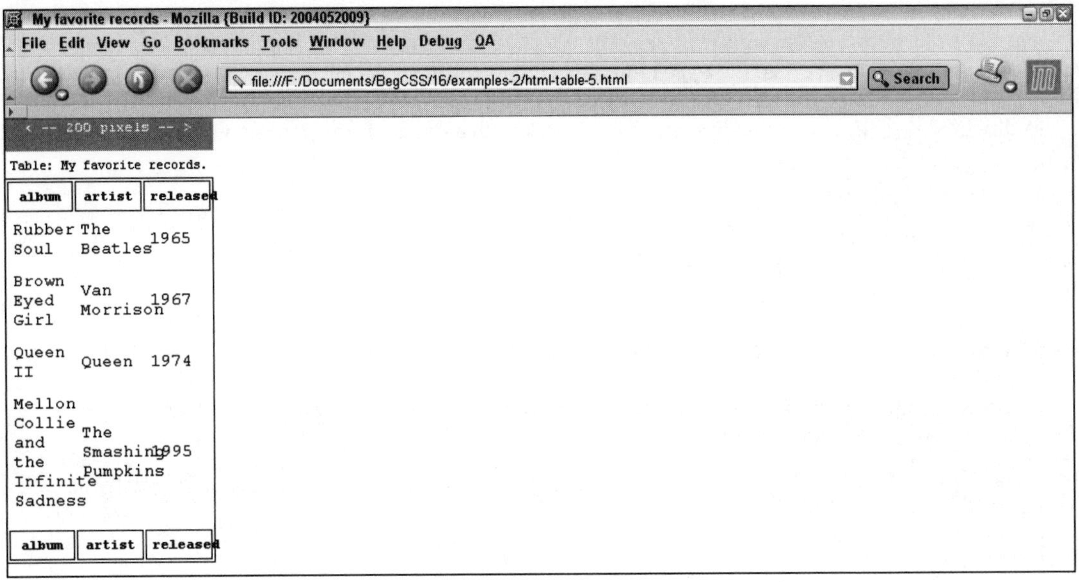

Figure 16-7

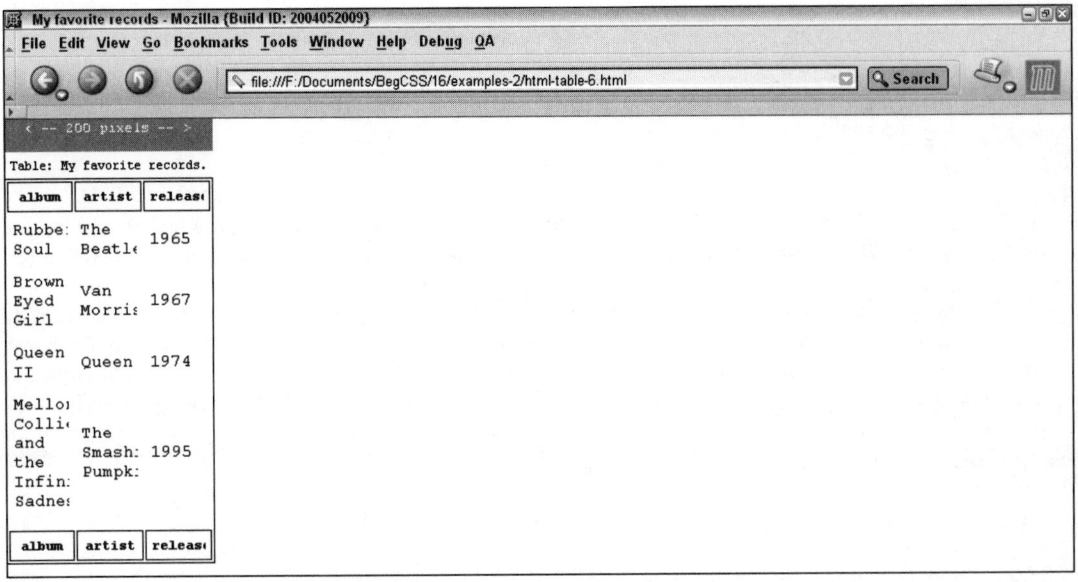

Figure 16-8

The `table-layout: fixed;` declaration goes by the width defined for the `<table>` element. In this example, the width is 200 pixels, so the table is forced into having a 200 pixel width. If a width isn't defined for the `<table>` element, it goes by the width for each `<col>` element. If no width is defined there, it goes by the width for the `<td>` elements in the first row of the table.

By default, tables are rendered with `table-layout: auto;`, which in essence means that the table can expand and contract to accommodate the data contained in its cells. What happens if a percentage width is specified for the table? When the table has a percentage width, each cell is given an equal width that expands and contracts, depending on the space available to it. If the content of the cell is larger than the width, however, the content is clipped, just as it was with a fixed width. Here's an example of this in action:

```
table {
    width: 100%;
    border: thin solid black;
    table-layout: fixed;
}
```

Save this variation as html-table-7.html and html-table-7.css. The result is shown in Figure 16-9.

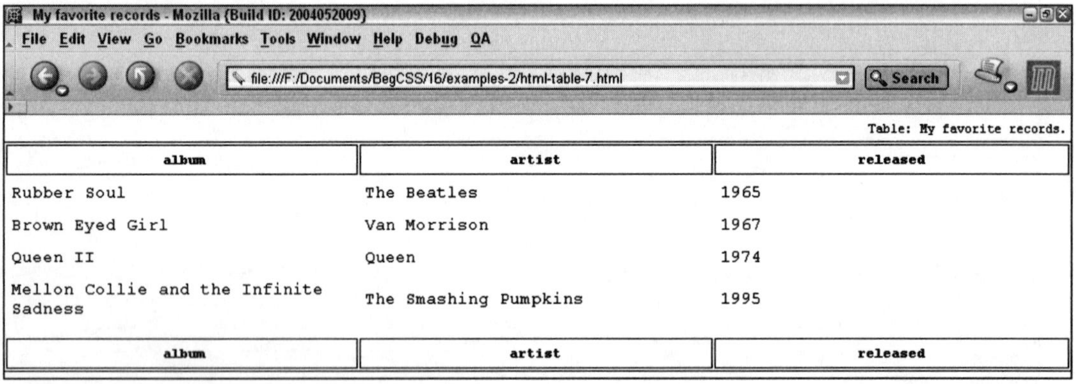

Figure 16-9

Each cell is spaced evenly. When the browser window is resized, the table gets smaller. As it gets smaller and the content of the cells become larger than the cell, the content gets clipped as it did in Figure 16-8.

Now that I've presented what the `table-layout` property does, I want to demonstrate the results of this property when it's applied to the Spicy Thai Peanut Sauce recipe table. Before I apply the `table-layout` property, however, I first need to apply a temporary rule that adds a border to each cell so that you can see the effect of the `table-layout` property. In the following Try It Out, you add this rule to the style sheet.

Try It Out   Highlighting Cell Widths

Example 16-2. The following steps show you how to add a rule that applies a border to each cell.

1. Open example16-1.css and add the following rule to the style sheet:

```
th, td {
    border: thin solid lightgrey;
}
```

2. Save the file as example16-2.css.

3. Make the following changes to example16-1.html to reference the new style sheet:

```
<!DOCTYPE html PUBLIC "-//W3C//DTD XHTML 1.0 Strict//EN"
"http://www.w3.org/TR/xhtml1/DTD/xhtml1-strict.dtd">
<html>
    <head>
        <title> Spicy Thai Peanut Sauce </title>
        <link rel='stylesheet' type='text/css' href='example16-2.css'/>
    </head>
```

4. Save the file as example16-2.html. The result is depicted in Figure 16-10.

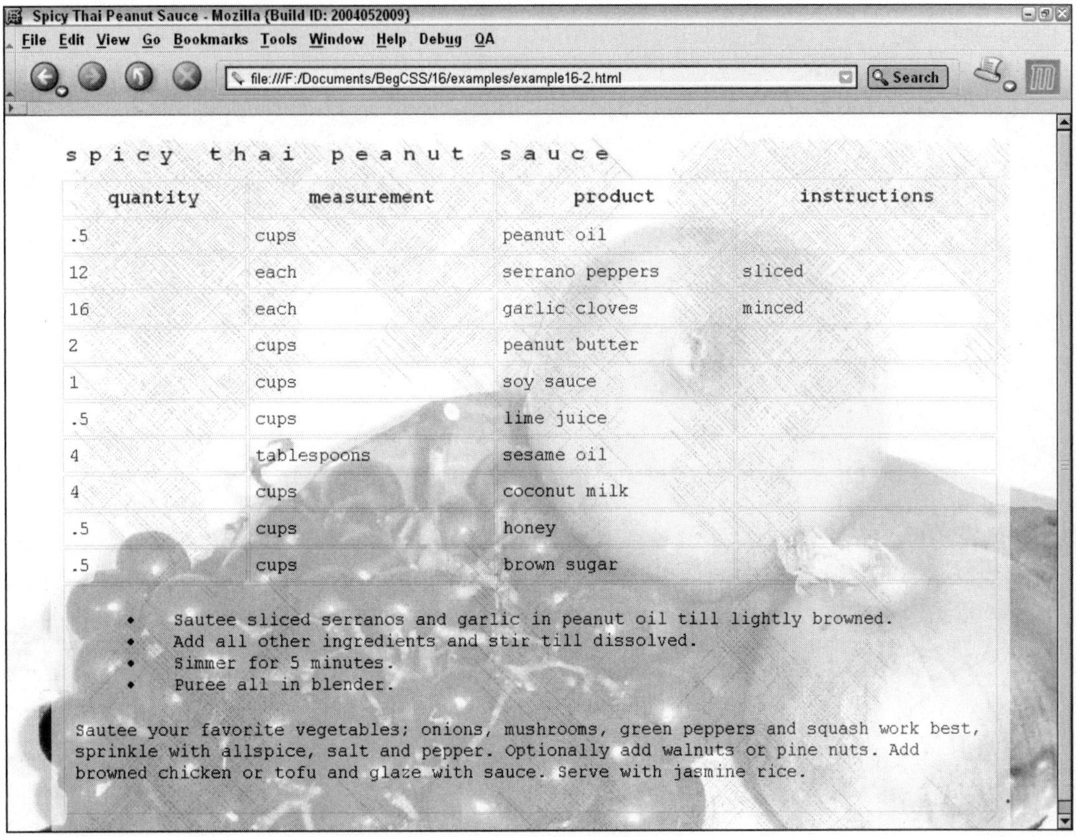

Figure 16-10

How It Works

The borders highlight the fact that the cells of the table are uneven. Each cell has a different width depending on the contents of the cell; by default, a table expands just enough to accommodate its content. This table has a 100% width, which only alters that behavior slightly. The cells themselves still expand and contract depending only on how much content is in each cell. The more content a cell is given, the more its column width expands.

Temporary style rules like this are often helpful in highlighting the effects of rendering that are difficult to see. Keeping the highlighted borders, examine the following Try It Out to see what this example looks like when the `table-layout: fixed` declaration is applied.

Try It Out   Applying the table-layout Property

Example 16-3. In the following steps, you apply the `table-layout: fixed;` property.

1. Open example16-2.css and add the highlighted declaration to the style sheet:

```
table.recipe {
    width: 100%;
    margin-bottom: 5px;
    table-layout: fixed;
}
```

2. Save the file as example16-3.css.

3. Make the following changes to modify example16-2.html so that it references the new style sheet:

```
<!DOCTYPE html PUBLIC "-//W3C//DTD XHTML 1.0 Strict//EN"
"http://www.w3.org/TR/xhtml1/DTD/xhtml1-strict.dtd">
<html>
    <head>
        <title> Spicy Thai Peanut Sauce </title>
        <link rel='stylesheet' type='text/css' href='example16-3.css'/>
    </head>
```

4. Save the file as example16-3.html. The result is shown in Figure 16-11.

How It Works

The addition of the `table-layout: fixed;` declaration gives the table a very clean, organized look. All the columns have equal, consistent widths. With this particular design, the table fills the area available inside the <body> element because it has a width of 100%. With the minimum and maximum widths I applied to the <body> element, no possibility exists that the cell data will be clipped if the viewing area becomes too small.

The `table-layout: fixed;` declaration allows a table's layout to be more consistent by forcing a table to honor the value contained in the `width` property. The `width` property may be applied to the <table> element itself, to the <col/> elements inside the table, or to the cells themselves.

Now that I've thoroughly explored the `table-layout` property, in the following sections I examine the other CSS properties that exist for controlling table layout.

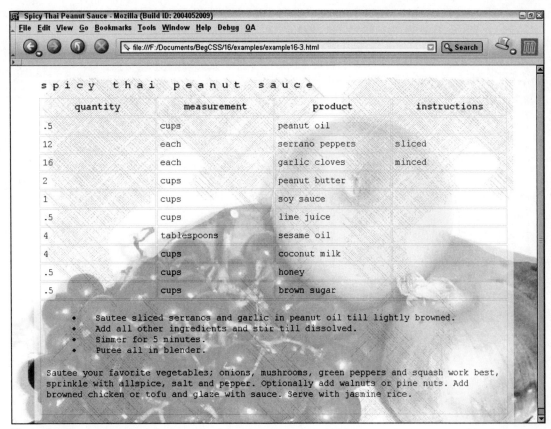

Figure 16-11

border-collapse

Documented in CSS 2.1 and supported in IE 5.5, IE 6, Mozilla 1.7, Opera 7.5, and Safari 1.2

Just as you did with the file you created earlier in Example 16-2, you need to add extra borders here for clarification so that you can truly see the effect of the border-collapse property when it's added to the html-table example.

```
td {
    border: thin solid black;
}
```

Save this variation as html-table-8.html and html-table-8.css. Figure 16-12 shows the result.

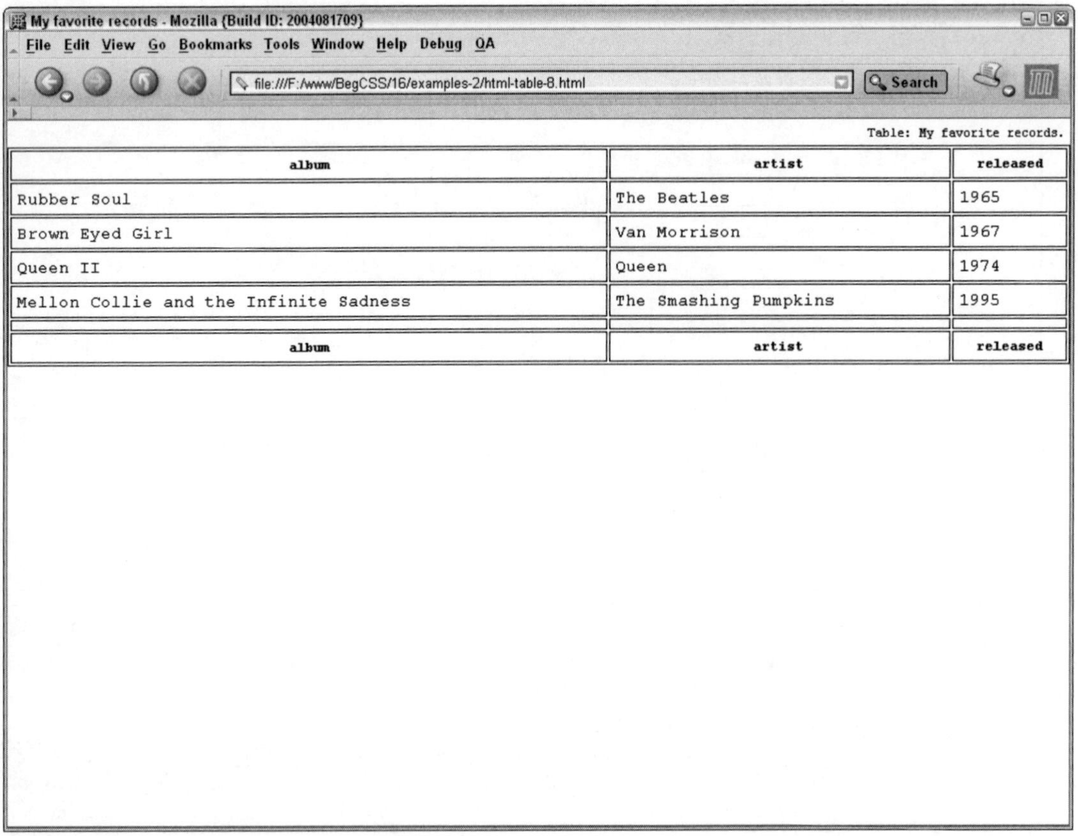

Figure 16-12

The edges of each cell are now clearly visible. Tables, by default, include some spacing between each of the cells appearing in the table. In HTML this was controlled with the `cellspacing` attribute. CSS 2 replaces this attribute with the `border-collapse` property and the `border-spacing` property. By default, the `border-collapse` property has a value of `separate`. If you set the value to `collapse`, you remove the spacing between each cell. Using the My Favorite Records table example (again, start with the original html-table.html file and style sheet), add the following style declaration:

```
table {
    width: 100%;
    border: thin solid black;
    border-collapse: collapse;
}
td {
    border: thin solid black;
}
```

The border around each cell adds clarity to the table. If you apply the `collapse` value, all the cells are squeezed tightly together. Save this variation as html-table-9.html and html-table-9.css. Figure 16-13 shows the result.

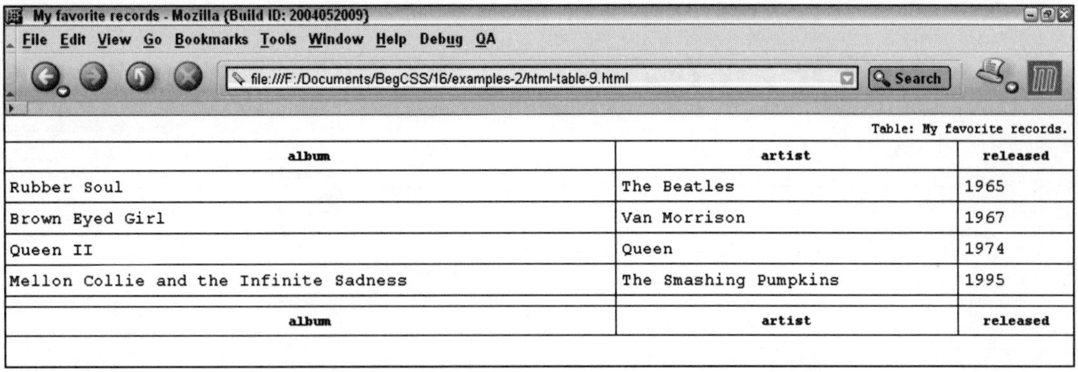

Figure 16-13

border-spacing

Documented in CSS 2.1 and supported in Mozilla 1. 7, Opera 7.5, and Safari 1.2.

To control the spacing between cells, the `border-spacing` property was added in CSS 2. A `border-spacing: 0;` declaration is identical to the behavior of the `border-collapse: collapse;` declaration in the last example. The `border-spacing` property, however, allows more control over cell spacing than `border-collapse` because it allows the length to be specified.

If, as in the following example, you provide a single length value of 15px, 15 pixels of space are added between each cell, both vertically and horizontally:

```
table {
    width: 100%;
    border: thin solid black;
    border-spacing: 15px;
}
```

Save this variation as html-table-10.html and html-table-10.css. The result is shown in Figure 16-14.

The `border-spacing` property has the following syntax:

```
border-spacing: <vertical spacing length> <horizontal spacing length>;
```

If the optional second value is present, this property allows the vertical and horizontal spacing to be specified. The following snippet results in 15 pixels of space between the top and bottom of each cell:

```
table {
    width: 100%;
    border: thin solid black;
    border-spacing: 0 15px;
}
```

Save the variation as html-table-11.html and html-table-11.css. The result is shown in Figure 16-15.

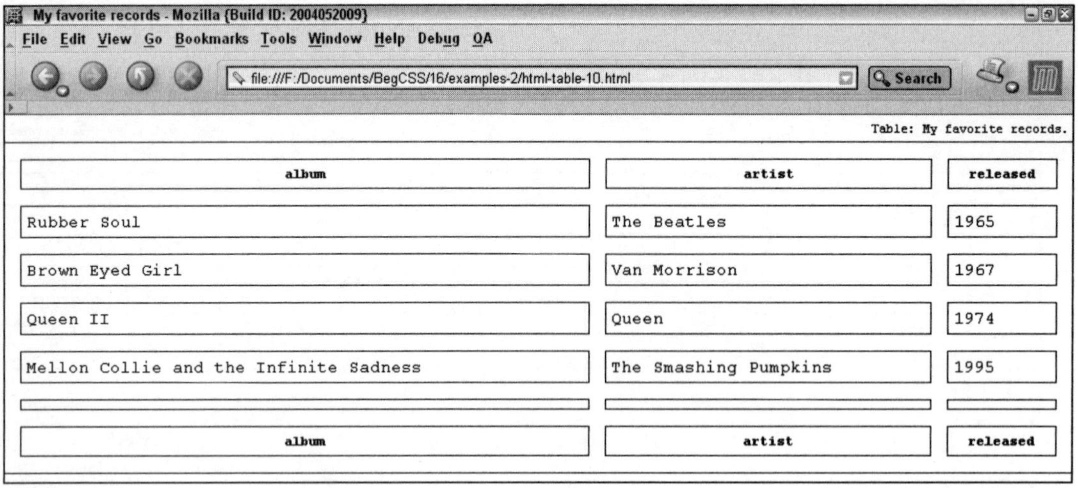

Figure 16-14

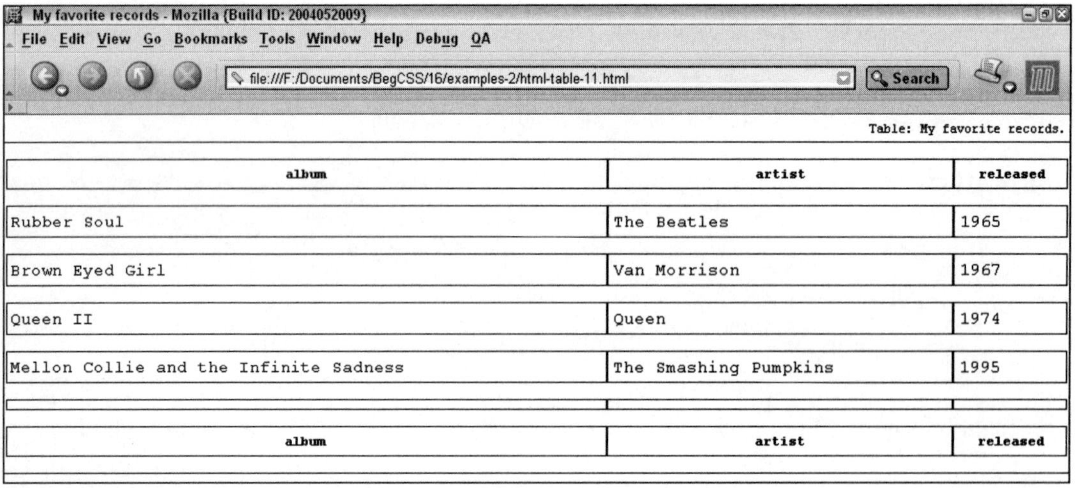

Figure 16-15

Whereas, if I flip the values around, as in the following

```
table {
    width: 100%;
    border: thin solid black;
    border-spacing: 15px 0;
}
```

I get 15 pixels of space between the left and right edges of each cell. Save this variation as html-table-12.html and html-table-12.css. The result is shown in Figure 16-16.

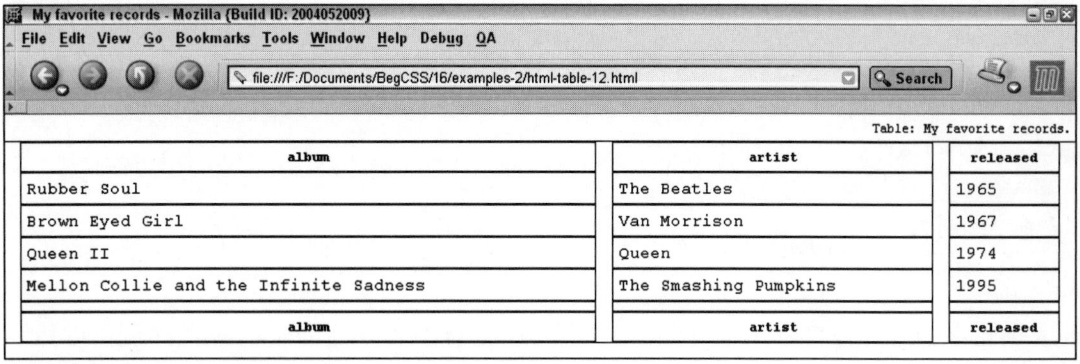

Figure 16-16

empty-cells

Documented in CSS 2.1 and supported in Mozilla 1.7, Opera 7.5, and Safari 1.2.

By default, browsers render empty table cells. Using the `empty-cells` property, however, you can override this default:

```
table {
    width: 100%;
    border: thin solid black;
}
td:empty {
    background: gray;
}
```

Save the variation as html-table-13.html and html-table-13.css. The result is shown in Figure 16-17.

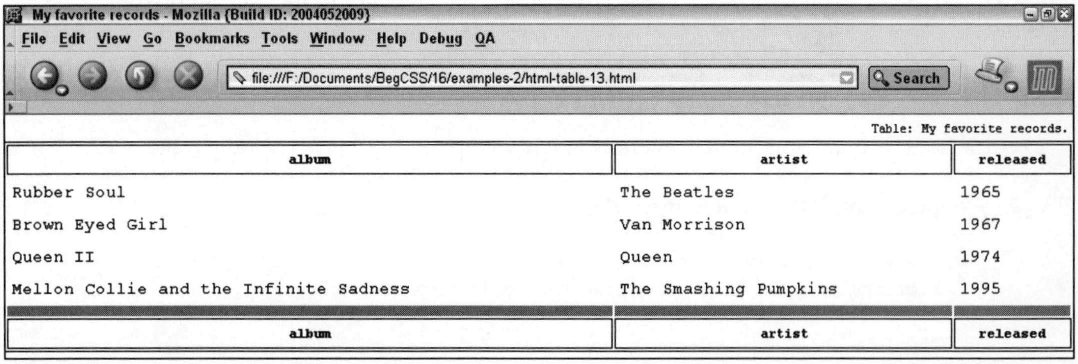

Figure 16-17

In the preceding example I added the `td:empty` selector, which (if you recall from Chapter 6) selects only empty table cells. I did this to highlight the effects of the `show` keyword, which is the default value of the `empty-cells` property. The `td:empty` selector applies a gray background so that it is obvious where the empty cells appear in the table.

When I apply `empty-cells: hide;` the cells are not rendered, but the space where they should appear remains open:

```
table {
    width: 100%;
    border: thin solid black;
    empty-cells: hide;
}
td:empty {
    background: gray;
}
```

Save this variation as html-table-14.html and html-table-14.css. The result is shown in Figure 16-18.

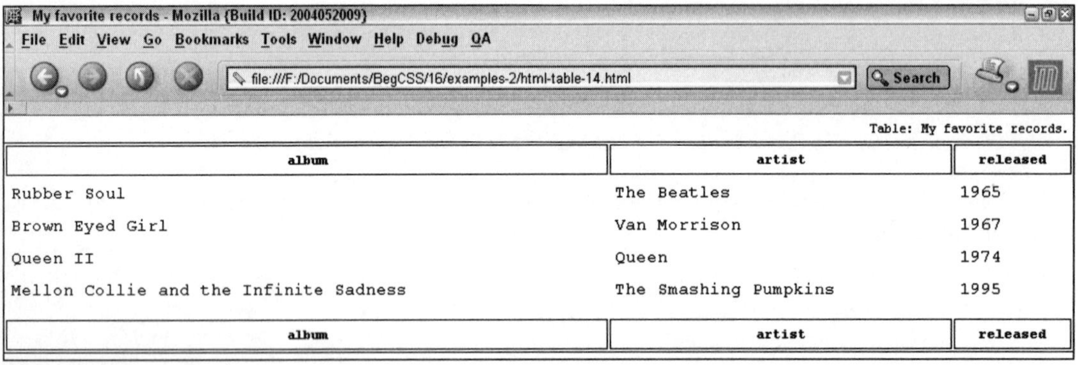
My favorite records - Mozilla (Build ID: 2004052009)
File Edit View Go Bookmarks Tools Window Help Debug QA
file:///F:/Documents/BegCSS/16/examples-2/html-table-14.html
Search
Table: My favorite records.
album
artist
released
Rubber Soul
The Beatles
1965
Brown Eyed Girl
Van Morrison
1967
Queen II
Queen
1974
Mellon Collie and the Infinite Sadness
The Smashing Pumpkins
1995
album
artist
released

Figure 16-18

The gray background added by the `td:empty` selector has been hidden.

Now that I've shown you how to control the spacing between cells and whether empty cells are rendered, you can apply this knowledge to the Spicy Thai Peanut Sauce recipe. The following Try It Out demonstrates a practical use of these properties in action.

Try It Out — Cell Spacing and Empty Cells

Example 16-4. The following steps show how to work with cell spacing and empty cells.

1. Open example16-3.css and make the following modifications to the file:

```
    /* Microsoft proprietary filter property */
    filter:progid:DXImageTransform.Microsoft.Alpha(opacity=70);
    /* CSS 3 opacity property */
    opacity: 0.7;
    background: url('cross_hatch.jpg') repeat;
}
table.recipe {
    width: 100%;
    margin-bottom: 5px;
    table-layout: fixed;
```

```
        border-collapse: collapse;
        empty-cells: hide;
    }
    th, td {
        border: thin solid lightgrey;
    }
    caption {
        text-align: left;
        margin-bottom: 5px;
```

2. Save the file as example16-4.css.

3. Update the markup in example16-3.html to reflect the new style sheet:

```
<!DOCTYPE html PUBLIC "-//W3C//DTD XHTML 1.0 Strict//EN"
"http://www.w3.org/TR/xhtml1/DTD/xhtml1-strict.dtd">
<html>
    <head>
        <title> Spicy Thai Peanut Sauce  </title>
        <link rel='stylesheet' type='text/css' href='example16-4.css'/>
    </head>
```

4. Save the file as example16-4.html. The result of these changes is shown in Figure 16-19.

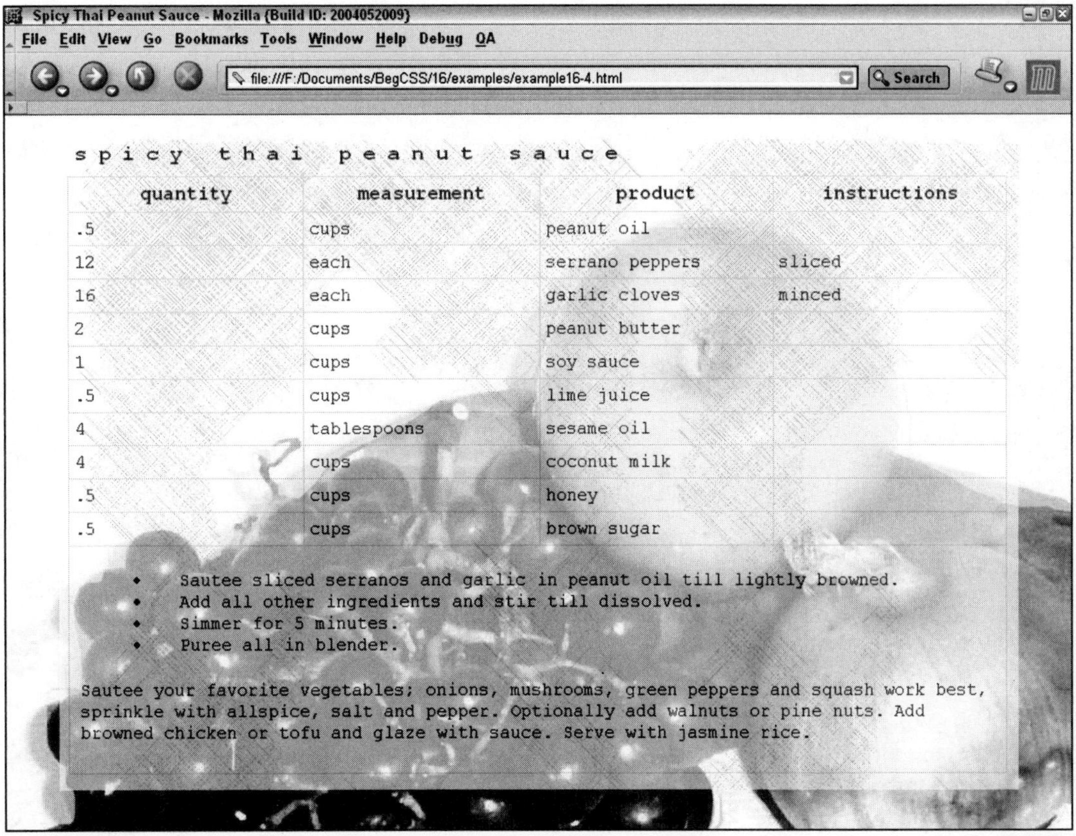

Figure 16-19

How It Works

As you can see in the output, the addition of `border-collapse: collapse;` and `empty-cells:`
`hide;` fine-tunes the design for the Spicy Thai Peanut Sauce recipe. Removing the extra space between
the cells tightens up the design. With the inclusion of the `empty-cells: hide;` declaration, the background no longer turns semitransparent black when the user's mouse rolls over cells that don't contain
any data. This enhances the purpose of the roll-overs, which exist both for clarification (the data is easier
to see against the high-contrast background) and for aesthetic design. At this point, I can remove the
temporary borders that I included to make the cell edges obvious:

```
th, td {
    border: thin solid lightgrey;
}
```

With this rule removed, the page looks like what's shown in Figure 16-20.

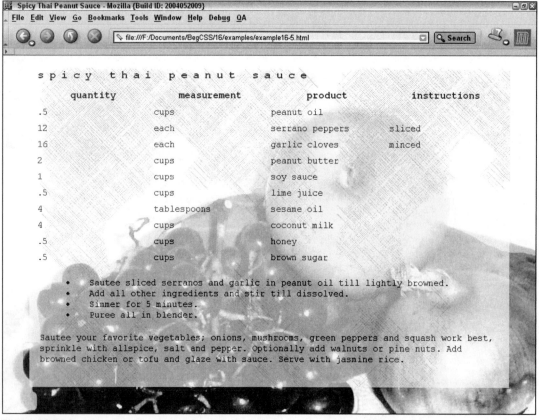

Figure 16-20

The final product shown in Figure 16-20, with the temporary border removed, is saved in the source
code files for download at www.wrox.com. After downloading the entire folder structure, you can find
the files, example16-5.html and example16-5.css, under Chapter 16\Try It Out.

Summary

In this chapter, I showed you what is possible with HTML/XHTML tables. Here is what I covered:

❑ Tables have lots of optional elements that make the structure easier to style. These include columns, heading groupings, body groupings, and footer groupings.

❑ You control the placement of a table's caption by using the `caption-side` property.

❑ You control a table's layout by using the `table-layout` property. With this property, it is possible to force a table into a certain width.

❑ You can remove the spacing between table cells by using the `border-collapse` property.

❑ You can adjust the spacing between table cells by using the `border-spacing` property.

❑ You can hide or show empty cells contained in a table by using the `empty-cells` property.

In the next chapter, I begin discussing how to style an XML document. As I mentioned earlier in this chapter, Chapter 17 relies heavily on the content presented in this chapter because it focuses on how to create tables using CSS and XML

Exercise

Write an HTML table containing your favorite movies. Include the name of the movie, its genre, a few of the stars of each movie, along with the year it was released. Define a width of 300 pixels for the table and force the table to maintain that width. Also place a caption on the table, position the caption to render below the table, and remove all spacing between table cells. Include headings for each column describing the data contained in each column. Use groupings and columns. Use borders, padding, background colors, and other CSS presentational controls to enhance visual clarity.

17

Styling XML

In Chapter 16, I demonstrated the various options available to structure and style tables. In this chapter, I discuss how CSS can be combined with XML to style XML documents. This chapter covers the following:

- ❏ What XML is
- ❏ How to create an XML document structure suitable for presentation
- ❏ The XML declaration
- ❏ The CSS display property
- ❏ Displaying block-level boxes with XML and CSS
- ❏ Displaying inline-level boxes with XML and CSS
- ❏ Recreating the structure, layout, and behavior of HTML tables using XML and CSS

XML is a robust and flexible markup language. Its uses extend to desktop applications such as spreadsheets and music jukebox software. It is also used heavily on the Internet for a plethora of applications. Many people see XML as the web language of tomorrow, one that will eventually replace HTML as the mainstream markup language of choice for building websites. In the following sections you look further into XML.

XML Documents

As you learned in Chapter 2, XML documents have a number of uses. For example, an XML document can be used to store data (like a database) because in an XML document you invent the tags and attributes. You have the advantage of creating tags in an XML document that describe the data they contain. Because you have the freedom to create tags and attributes as you wish, the data contained in the document can be organized much more efficiently than by using HTML alone. Your ability to invent tags and attributes makes using XML advantageous in another way as well. It creates a document structure that makes sense to both humans and computers. Placing a recipe between `<recipe>` tags makes much more sense than using the various tags of HTML and

XHTML. Placing a recipe between `<recipe>` tags makes it easier for a webmaster to design a search that looks for pages that contain only recipes. He can also share or transport those recipes to a variety of applications, such as spreadsheet programs and word processors, or by syndication to thousands or even millions of websites worldwide. XML's most impressive benefit is that it can be used for a variety of applications, not just for display on a web page.

This use of XML to syndicate data is typically called Really Simple Syndication (RSS), a specification that uses the XML language to describe syndicated data. RSS is in use today by thousands (perhaps even millions) of websites, and this is just one of the many uses of XML.

XML can also be used to present data on the web like an HTML or XHTML document does. This isn't, however, the most common use of XML; in fact, the world's most popular browser, Internet Explorer 6, offers only mediocre support for XML display using CSS. Mozilla, Opera, and Safari, in contrast, have excellent support for the CSS required to display an XML document, and the examples in this chapter display very well if viewed in one of these browsers. Note that CSS is not the only solution in the works for displaying XML in a browser. Another solution is the Extensible Stylesheet Language (XSL), a style-sheet language designed specifically for XML.

XSL isn't a replacement for CSS in XML documents; XSL is a more complicated style-sheet language that uses XML syntax. XSL is capable of much more than CSS. For instance, XSL is capable of completely transforming documents. Both languages have advantages for particular tasks and may both be utilized to present XML documents.

For the sake of staying on topic and simplicity, I cover styling XML using only CSS with what's available in today's browsers.

XML most closely resembles HTML; however, the angle bracket is about the only thing the two languages have in common. Let's review XML document structure.

❑ XML must be well-formed. *Well-formed* means that the document contains an XML declaration and all tags have both an opening and closing tag. Each of the rules for XHTML document structure covered in Chapter 2 also applies to XML and defines much of what it means for an XML document to be well-formed. The only exception is that XML tags don't have to be in all lowercase letters.

❑ XML documents can contain only one root element.

❑ XML is case-sensitive.

Here's a brief example of an XML document.

```
<?xml version="1.0"?>
<page>
    <books>
        <book favorite="true">
            The Alchemist <cover art="alchemist.jpg"/>
        </book>
        <book>Dante's Inferno</book>
    </books>
</page>
```

When you view this in a browser, the browser displays a tree of the XML source code as shown in Figure 17-1.

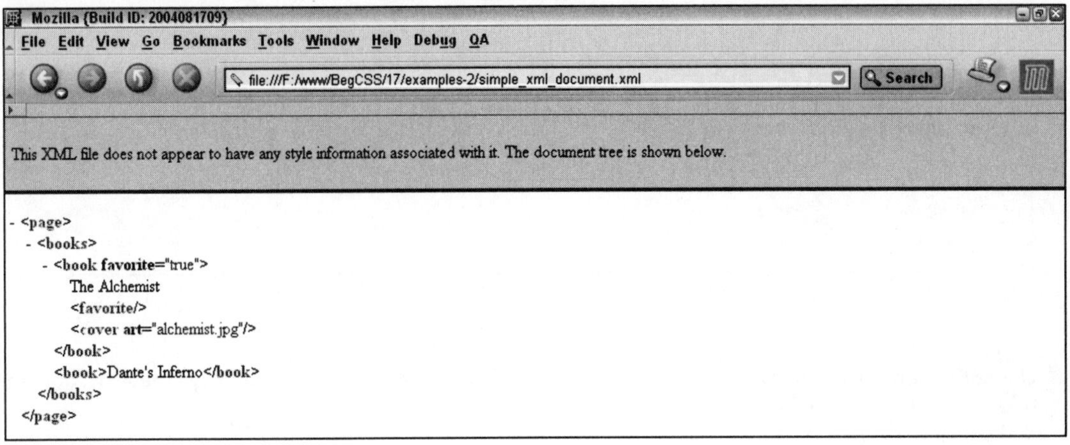

Figure 17-1

XML is said to be well-formed when the document contains an XML declaration — the `<?xml version="1.0"?>` in this example — all tags have both an opening and closing tag, any attributes in the document are quoted, and only one root element exists. I cover the XML declaration in more detail later in this chapter. As with XHTML, you can use the shortcut syntax to close a tag, as shown in the `<cover/>` element in this example.

Next, an XML document can only contain one root element. The root element in this example is the `<page>` element; in HTML and XHTML the root element is the `<html>` element. Therefore, the following is not valid a XML document because it contains two root elements.

```
<?xml version="1.0"?>
<library>
    <books>
        <book>The Alchemist <favorite/></book>
        <book>Dante's Inferno</book>
    </books>
</library>
<library>
    <books>
        <book>The Stand <favorite/></book>
        <book>The Poet</book>
    </books>
</library>
```

If an XML document is not well-formed, the browser refuses to display it and instead displays some error text indicating what went awry. This error text is depicted in Figure 17-2.

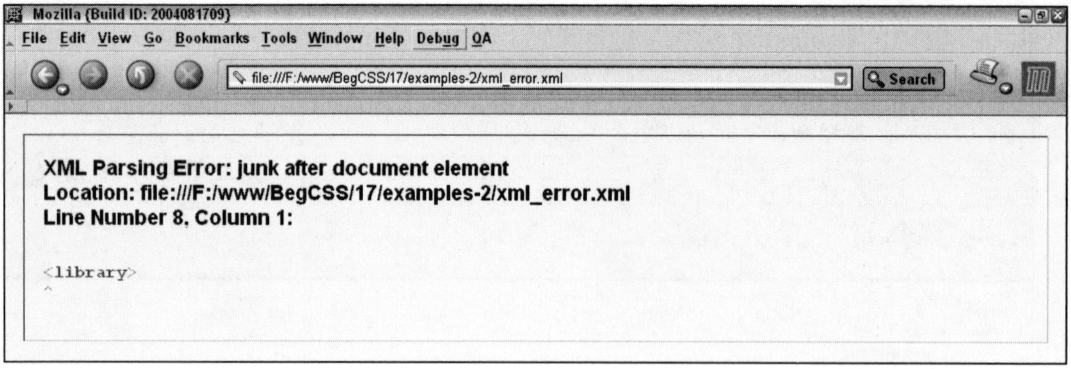

Figure 17-2

Using this error text you can correct the document, after which the browser displays the XML document tree like that shown in Figure 17-1.

Finally, XML is case-sensitive. So `<PAGE>` and `<page>` are two different tags in XML.

As you've just seen here and in Chapter 2, XML's markup structure can describe the data it contains. This is a benefit of XML but not a requirement. In the following section, I discuss creating an XML schema that you can use to structure the data contained in an XML document.

Creating an XML Schema

The term *schema* refers to the structure and naming of XML elements that work together to produce a well-formed XML document. In this section, you require a schema that is optimized for display on the web.

Some requirements that I have to consider are the following:

❑ Defining a page structure that resembles tabular data or list data, such as HTML/XHTML `<table>`, `<tr>`, and `<td>` elements and list elements like `<ul>` and `<li>`.

❑ Determining which elements are block-level elements (like the `<div>` element in HTML/XHTML) and which are inline-level elements (like `<span>`).

This schema business really isn't difficult. Let's look at how the "My Favorite Records" example from Chapter 16 is written as an XML document.

```
<favorites>
    <title>
        Table: My favorite records.
    </title>
    <cols>
        <album/>
        <artist/>
        <released/>
    </cols>
```

```
    <headings>
        <record>
            <album>    album        </album>
            <artist>   artist       </artist>
            <released> released     </released>
        </record>
    </headings>
    <records>
        <record>
            <album>    Rubber Soul    </album>
            <artist>   The Beatles    </artist>
            <released> 1965           </released>
        </record>
        <record>
            <album>    Brown Eyed Girl </album>
            <artist>   Van Morrison    </artist>
            <released> 1967            </released>
        </record>
        <record>
            <album>    Queen II        </album>
            <artist>   Queen           </artist>
            <released> 1974            </released>
        </record>
        <record>
            <album>    Mellon Collie and the Infinite Sadness    </album>
            <artist>   The Smashing Pumpkins                     </artist>
            <released> 1995                                      </released>
        </record>
    </records>
    <footers>
        <record>
            <album>    album        </album>
            <artist>   artist       </artist>
            <released> released     </released>
        </record>
    </footers>
</favorites>
```

This example is used again later in the chapter and is referred to as xml-table.xml.

Like the example presented in Chapter 16, this markup is available for downloading at the book's source code site at www.wrox.com.

This is the entire XML document. In this version of the document, the XML tags that structure the data also describe the data contained in the document. Instead of the `<table>` element, there is the `<favorites>` element; instead of the `<caption>` element, the `<title>` element is used. Instead of the `<colgroup>` element, the `<cols>` element is used to group the columns; and the columns themselves are named for what type of columns they are: `<album/>`, `<artist/>`, and `<released/>` instead of `<col>`. `<headings>` replaces the `<thead>` element, and `<record>` replaces the `<tr>` element. `<album>`, `<artist>`, and `<released>` are used here as cells, replacing the `<th>` elements. You can use the same names for the cells as for columns here because CSS offers options to distinguish between the two. Likewise, the rest of the table elements in Chapter 16's *My Favorite Records* example are also represented here with an XML counterpart. Finally, unlike the example in Chapter 16, the XML document here is complete — you don't add

`<html>` or `<body>` elements. This is the complete document. However, before the XML version of the *My Favorite Records* example is complete it needs two more things: an XML declaration and an XML `stylesheet` declaration, both of which I add later in this chapter.

Now that you've seen an example of converting an HTML document to an XML document, the following Try It Out presents the Spicy Thai Peanut Sauce recipe that you saw in Chapter 16. Here the recipe is reformatted as an XML document.

Try It Out   Creating an XML Schema

Example 17-1. In the following steps, you create an XML version of Chapter 16's Spicy Thai Peanut Sauce recipe.

1.   Enter the following XML into your text editor:

```
<page>
    <recipe>
        <ingredients>
            <title>
                Spicy Thai Peanut Sauce
            </title>
            <columns>
                <quantity/>
                <measurement/>
                <product/>
                <instructions/>
            </columns>
            <headings>
                <heading>
                    <quantity>        quantity        </quantity>
                    <measurement>     measurement     </measurement>
                    <product>         product         </product>
                    <instructions>    instructions    </instructions>
                </heading>
            </headings>
            <ingredientsbody>
                <ingredient>
                    <quantity>        .5              </quantity>
                    <measurement>     CUPS            </measurement>
                    <product>         Peanut Oil      </product>
                    <instructions></instructions>
                </ingredient>
                <ingredient>
                    <quantity>        12              </quantity>
                    <measurement>     Each            </measurement>
                    <product>         Serrano Peppers </product>
                    <instructions>    Sliced          </instructions>
                </ingredient>
                <ingredient>
                    <quantity>        16              </quantity>
                    <measurement>     Each            </measurement>
                    <product>         Garlic Cloves   </product>
                    <instructions>    Minced          </instructions>
```

```
            </ingredient>
            <ingredient>
                <quantity>        2            </quantity>
                <measurement>     CUPS         </measurement>
                <product>         Peanut Butter </product>
                <instructions></instructions>
            </ingredient>
            <ingredient>
                <quantity>        1            </quantity>
                <measurement>     CUPS         </measurement>
                <product>         Soy Sauce    </product>
                <instructions></instructions>
            </ingredient>
            <ingredient>
                <quantity>        .5           </quantity>
                <measurement>     CUPS         </measurement>
                <product>         Lime Juice   </product>
                <instructions></instructions>
            </ingredient>
            <ingredient>
                <quantity>        4            </quantity>
                <measurement>     TABLESPOONS  </measurement>
                <product>         Sesame Oil   </product>
                <instructions></instructions>
            </ingredient>
            <ingredient>
                <quantity>        4            </quantity>
                <measurement>     CUPS         </measurement>
                <product>         Coconut Milk </product>
                <instructions></instructions>
            </ingredient>
            <ingredient>
                <quantity>        .5           </quantity>
                <measurement>     CUPS         </measurement>
                <product>         Honey        </product>
                <instructions></instructions>
            </ingredient>
            <ingredient>
                <quantity>        .5           </quantity>
                <measurement>     CUPS         </measurement>
                <product>         Brown Sugar  </product>
                <instructions></instructions>
            </ingredient>
        </ingredientsbody>
    </ingredients>
    <directions>
        <direction>
            Sautee sliced serranos and garlic in peanut oil
            till lightly browned.
        </direction>
        <direction>
            Add <really>all</really> other ingredients and stir till
            dissolved.
        </direction>
```

```
            <direction>
                Simmer for 5 minutes.
            </direction>
            <direction>
                Puree all in blender.
            </direction>
        </directions>
        <suggestions>
            Sautee your favorite vegetables; onions, mushrooms,
            green peppers and squash work best, sprinkle with allspice,
            salt and pepper. Optionally add walnuts or pine nuts. Add
            browned chicken or tofu and glaze with sauce. Serve with
            jasmine rice.
        </suggestions>
    </recipe>
</page>
```

2. Save the file as example17-1.xml.

3. Open it in the browser and see what you've created.

How It Works

Nothing fancy here just yet. When viewed in a browser, the Try It Out code example simply shows a tree of the XML source file similar to that depicted in Figure 17-1. The differences here are important because each has an effect on how the document is presented with CSS, and each offers further flexibility in the presentation of the document.

First, the `<page>` tag is added so that the `<recipe>` element can be styled independently. The `<page>` element is to this XML document as the `<html>` element is to an HTML/XHTML document, with one major difference: The `<page>` tag can be given any name you like. If you recall from Chapter 16, I applied a background to the `<html>` element using CSS, which is why I have created a `<page>` element for this example. The `<recipe>` element emulates the behavior of the `<body>` element presented in Chapter 16, and it has the semitransparent crosshatch background that was used there.

Next is the `<ingredients>` element, a table that contains the recipe's ingredients. All the table elements presented in Chapter 16 are represented here using an XML counterpart with one minor difference: In Chapter 16, I included the directions and suggestions as part of the table footers. When you are using only XML and CSS, this presents a problem. At the time of this writing, you have no way to span multiple columns with the CSS implemented in today's browsers. However, here I can simply move portions of the recipe that span multiple columns outside of the table.

Now that the Spicy Thai Peanut Sauce recipe has a viable XML document structure, let's continue the discussion. In the next section I discuss the XML declaration.

The XML Declaration

Most XML documents contain an XML declaration. If one is included, it's the very first tag in the document, and it looks like this:

```
<?xml version="1.0"?>
```

This declaration announces which version of XML is contained in the document. This is not very complicated, and it isn't required. In an XML document it simply says, "Hey, I'm an XML document!" When an XML document encounters a browser or any other type of application that is able to read XML documents, the browser or application doesn't have to guess what kind of document is being presented. I say *encounter* in this context because, as I discussed earlier, an XML document is not restricted to web browsers.

XML Declaration Attributes

An XML declaration can contain three attributes, two of which are optional. These are called *pseudo-attributes* because they resemble markup attributes. The first attribute is the version attribute (see the previous example). This denotes which version of the XML specification is being referenced. Currently, two versions, 1.0 and 1.1 exist. Version 1.1 was only recently made a candidate recommendation by the W3C. As a candidate recommendation (and not a standard), Version 1.1 is still shiny and new, meaning it isn't yet widely available. For the purpose of this discussion I'll stick with 1.0. Which version I use is moot because the differences between the two versions do not affect the basic syntactical presentation of XML documents in the examples of this chapter. The features in the XML 1.1 specification affect more complicated uses of XML that are beyond this immediate discussion.

The next attribute is an optional *encoding* attribute:

```
<?xml version="1.0" encoding="ISO-8859-1"?>
```

The encoding attribute tells the parser (the program interpreting the XML) about the characters contained in the document. The value `"ISO-8859-1"` is computer gibberish for characters common to the Americas and Western Europe. This can also go by the much simpler name of `"LATIN-1"`, as in the following:

```
<?xml version="1.0" encoding="LATIN-1"?>
```

> **The inclusion of the encoding attribute is very important because the default encoding value is not `"LATIN-1"` but an even smaller set of characters. You must include the proper encoding type in order to have all characters correctly translated to their proper display equivalents.**

The third attribute is the *standalone* attribute, which looks like this:

```
<?xml version="1.0" encoding="LATIN-1" standalone="yes"?>
```

The standalone attribute has to do with the inclusion of a Document Type Declaration, which you saw in Chapter 2. Document Type Declarations may also be included in XML documents, but they require the DTD to be custom written because the tags of an XML document can be invented. Creating a Document Type Declaration is beyond the scope of this book, so for the purpose of this discussion the standalone attribute with a value of `"yes"` tells the browser that no Document Type Declaration is accompanying the XML document.

> An XML declaration should always be included in XML documents because it helps both humans and the computer program that is interpreting the XML to determine what kind of XML appears in the document.

The pseudo-attributes of an XML declaration must also appear in a particular order: The first attribute must always be the version attribute, followed by the optional encoding attribute, followed by the optional standalone attribute.

The XML stylesheet Declaration

The syntax for including a style sheet in an XML document closely resembles a cross between the XML declaration itself and the `<link>` tag in HTML/XHTML:

```
<?xml-stylesheet type="text/css" href="test.css"?>
```

Like the `<link>` element in an HTML or XHTML document, this references the external style sheet which styles the XML document. The XML `stylesheet` declaration must appear after the XML declaration. The declaration must appear first in the document and before the document markup itself. By including a style sheet, you gain access to the full range of CSS properties and values in an XML document, just as you gain access in an HTML or XHTML document.

Now that you are familiar with the XML declaration and the `stylesheet` declaration, append the syntax to the My Favorite Records example:

```
<?xml version="1.0" encoding="ISO-8859-1" standalone="yes"?>
<?xml-stylesheet type="text/css" href="xml-table-1.css"?>
<favorites>
    <title>
        Table: My favorite records.
    </title>
```

Save the file as xml-table-1.xml. This results in the output depicted in Figure 17-3.

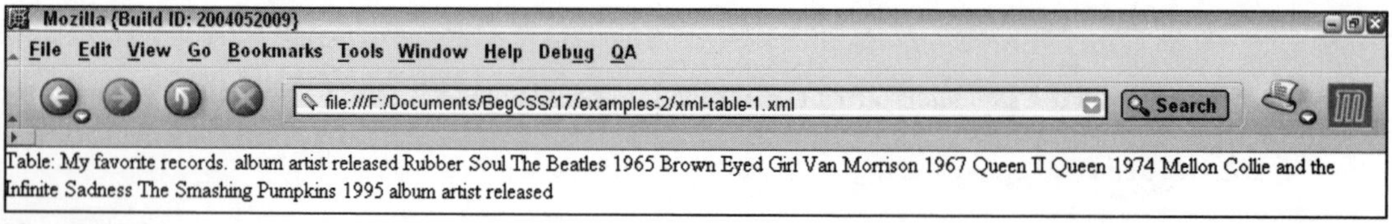

Figure 17-3

I'll be using the My Favorite Records example again later in the chapter, but for now just put it aside.

Because the `stylesheet` declaration has been added even though no actual style sheet is created, the text is run together. You can now include style-sheet rules in the external CSS file to format the text of the XML document.

You've just seen what including both the XML declaration and the XML `stylesheet` declaration does to an XML document. In the following Try It Out you'll update the Spicy Thai Peanut Sauce recipe presented in your example17-1.xml file so that it has an XML declaration and a reference to an XML style sheet.

Try It Out — Adding an XML Declaration and Style Declaration

Example 17-2. The steps below add an XML declaration and style-sheet reference to the Spicy Thai Peanut Sauce recipe document.

1. Open example17-1.xml and add the following modifications:

```
<?xml version="1.0" encoding="ISO-8859-1" standalone="yes"?>
<?xml-stylesheet type="text/css" href="example17-2.css"?>
<page>
    <recipe>
```

2. Save this file as example17-2.xml
3. Create a blank style sheet and save it as example17-2.css

This results in the output depicted in Figure 17-4.

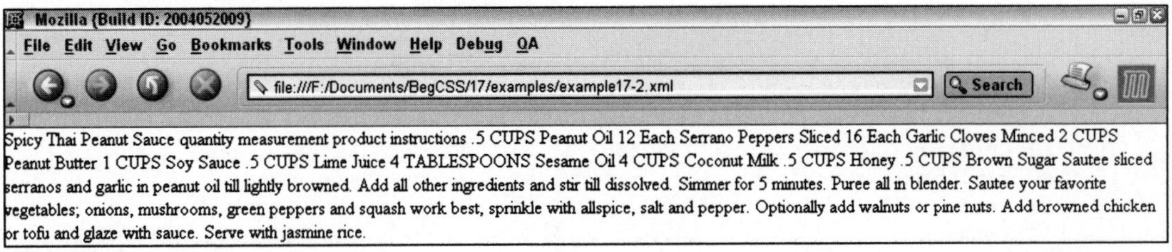

Mozilla {Build ID: 2004052009}
File Edit View Go Bookmarks Tools Window Help Debug QA
file:///F:/Documents/BegCSS/17/examples/example17-2.xml
Search
Spicy Thai Peanut Sauce quantity measurement product instructions .5 CUPS Peanut Oil 12 Each Serrano Peppers Sliced 16 Each Garlic Cloves Minced 2 CUPS Peanut Butter 1 CUPS Soy Sauce .5 CUPS Lime Juice 4 TABLESPOONS Sesame Oil 4 CUPS Coconut Milk .5 CUPS Honey .5 CUPS Brown Sugar Sautee sliced serranos and garlic in peanut oil till lightly browned. Add all other ingredients and stir till dissolved. Simmer for 5 minutes. Puree all in blender. Sautee your favorite vegetables; onions, mushrooms, green peppers and squash work best, sprinkle with allspice, salt and pepper. Optionally add walnuts or pine nuts. Add browned chicken or tofu and glaze with sauce. Serve with jasmine rice.

Figure 17-4

How It Works

By referencing a style sheet, you have taken the first step for applying style to an XML document. Now when you view the XML document in a browser, it no longer appears with the tree structure of the XML source code, as it would if you had not specified a style sheet. At this point the document isn't very pretty — it is displayed as one long string of text. This is why the CSS `display` property is essential. It explains to the browser how to display each tag contained in the XML document.

The display Property

Documented in CSS 2.1 and supported in: IE 5.5 (partial), IE 6 (partial), Mozilla 1.7 (partial), Opera 7.5, Safari 1.2.

Displaying XML documents with CSS requires heavy use of the CSS `display` property, a property that has the capability to define an element's behavior when it is rendered in a browser. The following table shows the `display` property and its possible values.

Property	Value
display	inline | block | list-item | run-in | inline-block | table | inline-table | table-row-group | table-header-group | table-footer-group | table-row | table-column-group | table-column | table-cell | table-caption | none | inherit

The display property can have one of 17 different values (as of CSS 2.1). Internet Explorer 6 is behind the times in terms of supporting the full list of display value possibilities. Mozilla, Netscape 7, Opera, and Safari 1.2 have fantastic support of the CSS 2 display values. Opera, in this case, supports the full set of possible display property values, and Mozilla supports most of the possible values, but not all. Look at each possible value individually, what display mode each triggers when applied to an XML element, and what elements with the same rendering behavior are found in HTML and XHTML.

Styling Inline Elements with display: inline

Documented in CSS 2.1 and supported in IE 5.5, IE 6, Mozilla 1.7, Opera 7.5, and Safari 1.2.

The display: inline value emulates elements like <span>; that means it causes the target element to behave like an inline level element, enabling it to appear in the flow of text. In an XML document it might be necessary to emphasize a word or phrase in the context of the text. This is done by assigning the element a display: inline; declaration in the CSS style sheet. The following XML document and style sheet demonstrate how inline elements are displayed in XML.

```
<?xml version="1.0" encoding="ISO-8859-1" standalone="yes"?>
<?xml-stylesheet type="text/css" href="xml-inline.css"?>
<observation>
    The quick brown fox <wow>devoured</wow> a cat's carcass whole.
</observation>
```

In the CSS style sheet the <wow> element can be defined to have whatever emphasis you deem appropriate.

```
wow {
    display: inline;
    font-weight: bold;
    font-style: italic;
    color: red;
}
```

Now the browser has explicit instructions for displaying any <wow> elements appearing in XML documents. The effects of this are depicted in Figure 17-5.

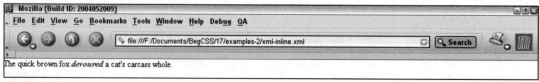

Figure 17-5

Styling Block Elements with display: block

Documented in CSS 2.1 and supported in IE 5.5, IE 6, Opera 7.5, and Safari 1.2.

After looking over the first bit of code in the previous section, naturally I'll bet your next question is, "What about the <observation> element?" The answer is that you can give the browser a variety of explicit instructions for how to display this element. For this example, you can make the <observation> element a block-level element with the display: block; declaration:

```
observation {
    display: block;
    background: lightgrey;
}
```

This results in the output depicted in Figure 17-6. (Note, it will look slightly different in Internet Explorer.)

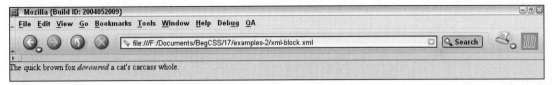

Figure 17-6

Just as in HTML/XHTML, block-level element default behaviors still apply: The output will automatically span the entire window unless told to do differently, because its default width value is auto. With this declaration, the <observation> element emulates the behavior of the <html> element found in HTML and XHTML because it is the root element of the document. This is why you see the light gray background taking up the whole screen. In fact it's the same thing as writing:

```
<html>
    The quick brown fox <span>devoured</span> a cat's carcass whole.
</html>
```

Styling List Items with display: list-item

Documented in CSS 2.1 and supported in IE 6, Mozilla 1.7, Opera 7.5, and Safari 1.2.

The display: list-item; declaration causes an element to appear with a default bullet character next to it, as is the case with the <li> element in HTML and XHTML. When combined with the list-style-type property or list-style-image properties, the list can be numbered, bulleted, or have a custom image applied. Consider the following snip of XML:

```
<list>
    <item>Rubber Soul</item>
    <item>Sgt. Pepper's Lonely Hearts Club Band</item>
    <item>Revolver</item>
</list>
```

When combined with the right CSS, this is transformed into a list:

```
list {
    display: block;
    margin-left: 20px;
    list-style-type: disc;
}
item {
    display: list-item;
}
```

This results in the output shown in Figure 17-7.

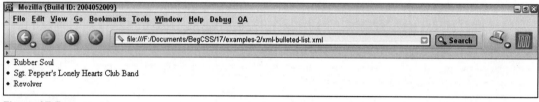

Figure 17-7

This is the same thing as writing in HTML/XHTML:

```
<ul>
    <li>Rubber Soul</li>
    <li>Sgt. Pepper's Lonely Heart's Club Band</li>
    <li>Revolver</li>
</ul>
```

The `<list>` element is made into a block-level element to emulate the behavior of a `<ul>` HTML element. It's also given some margin on the left side to indent the list. Next, the `list-style-type: disc;` declaration makes the list into a bulleted list. The `<item>` element is told to be a list-item with the `display: list-item;` declaration. Without the `list-style-type: disc;` declaration, the list still appears with bullets because a bulleted list is the default behavior of the `display: list-item;` declaration.

Generating Numbered Lists

Creating numbered lists is a more difficult undertaking in XML documents than it is in HTML given current browser limitations. Applying a simple `list-style-type: decimal;` declaration should produce a numbered list, and it does so if you're viewing the output in Opera 7 or even in Internet Explorer 6. However, a bug in Mozilla 1.7 prevents it from producing a numbered list. When viewed in Mozilla 1.7 the list appears with all zeros.

This is the required CSS to generate numbered lists:

```
list {
    display: block;
    margin-left: 20px;
    list-style-type: decimal;
}
```

```
item {
    display: list-item;
}
```

Using Opera 7, you get the results depicted in Figure 17-8.

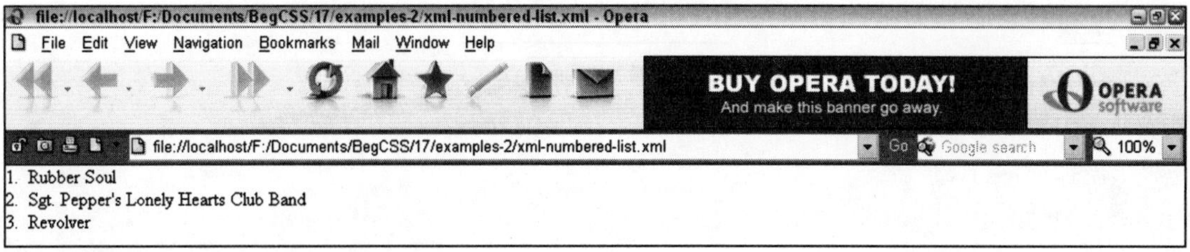

Figure 17-8

This is the same as if you wrote the following in HTML/XHTML:

```
<ol>
    <li>Rubber Soul</li>
    <li>Sgt. Pepper's Lonely Heart's Club Band</li>
    <li>Revolver</li>
</ol>
```

Using the `display` and `list-style-type` allows for emulation of the HTML `<ol>` element.

Now that you have some idea of what is involved with using the `display` property to dictate the behavior of XML elements, the following Try It Out example continues the Spicy Thai Peanut Sauce recipe with the addition of some style sheet rules.

Try It Out   Applying inline, block, and list Styles

Example 17-3. Follow these steps to apply `display` property values to the Spicy Thai Peanut Sauce recipe.

1.   Enter the following CSS into your text editor:

```
* {
    font-family: monospace;
}
page {
    display: block;
    background: #fff url('fruit_veg_web.jpg') no-repeat fixed center center;
}
recipe {
    display: block;
    padding: 10px;
    margin: 10px auto;
    min-width: 500px;
    max-width: 900px;
    /* Moz proprietary opacity property */
    -moz-opacity: 0.7;
```

```
        /* Safari / KHTML proprietary opacity property */
        -khtml-opacity: 0.7;
        /* Microsoft proprietary filter property */
        filter:progid:DXImageTransform.Microsoft.Alpha(opacity=70);
        /* CSS 3 opacity property */
        opacity: 0.7;
        background: url('cross_hatch.jpg') repeat;
}
directions, suggestions {
        display: block;
        font-size: 130%;
}
directions {
        list-style-type: disc;
}
direction {
        display: list-item;
}
really {
        display: inline;
        font-weight: bold;
}
```

2.   Save the file as example17-3.css.

3.   Modify example17-2.xml to reference the new CSS file:

```
<?xml-stylesheet type="text/css" href="example17-3.css"?>
<page>
    <recipe>
```

4.   Save the result as example17-3.xml.

This results in the output depicted in Figure 17-9.

How It Works

As you can see after viewing the output in a browser, after you add just a few XML declarations to the XML document, the recipe is beginning to take shape. At this point, the example looks similar when viewed in IE, Opera, or Mozilla. IE 6 has a bug that prevents the display of the background image, and as I've pointed out in previous chapters, it does not support the min/max width properties. Opera 7 only displays a portion of the background image, but it corrects this if the browser window is resized. The recipe renders best in Mozilla, which displays the document as intended.

Let's go through the example line by line:

```
page {
    display: block;
    background: #fff url('fruit_veg_web.jpg') no-repeat fixed center center;
}
```

The <page> element is intended to emulate the <html> element in HTML/XHTML. This is defined as a block-level element, and it is given a background image, as it was Example 16-1 from Chapter 16.

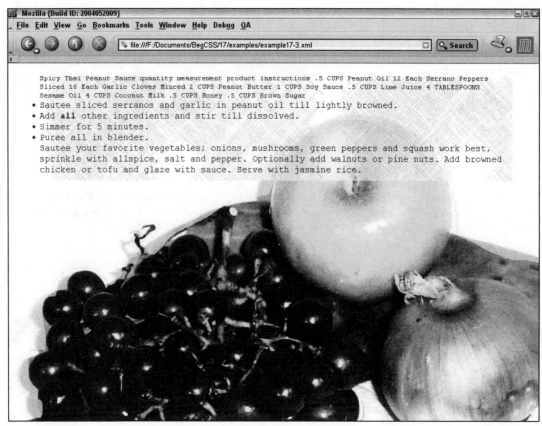

Figure 17-9

Next is the <recipe> element, which contains all the ingredients and other information for the Spicy Thai Peanut Sauce recipe:

```
recipe {
    display: block;
    padding: 10px;
    margin: 10px auto;
    min-width: 500px;
    max-width: 900px;
    /* Moz proprietary opacity property */
    -moz-opacity: 0.7;
    /* Safari / KHTML proprietary opacity property */
    -khtml-opacity: 0.7;
    /* Microsoft proprietary filter property */
    filter:progid:DXImageTransform.Microsoft.Alpha(opacity=70);
    /* CSS 3 opacity property */
    opacity: 0.7;
    background: url('cross_hatch.jpg') repeat;
}
```

Once more, the element is made into a block-level element with the `display: block;` declaration. Here, the same properties are applied to the `<recipe>` element as were applied to the `<body>` element in Chapter 16 in Example 16-1. They include the semitransparent effect, and they specify a minimum and maximum width to accommodate users with high-resolution displays as well as those with low-resolution displays.

Next are the `<directions>` and `<suggestions>` elements:

```
directions, suggestions {
    display: block;
    font-size: 130%;
}
```

Each of these is made into a block-level element. The `<directions>` element emulates the HTML/XHTML `<ul>` element, and the `<suggestions>` element emulates a plain `<div>` or `<p>` element. Because the `<directions>` element emulates a `<ul>` element, it is given a list-style–type declaration:

```
directions {
    list-style-type: disc;
}
```

Next, the list items themselves are styled:

```
direction {
    display: list-item;
}
```

The `display: list-item;` declaration lets the `<direction>` element emulate a `<li>` element. Finally, each `<really>` element is told to be an inline-level element with the `display: inline;` declaration:

```
really {
    display: inline;
    font-weight: bold;
}
```

Here the `<really>` element is bold for emphasis.

The `display` property gives an element its behavior, and block-level elements like `<html>`, `<body>`, `<div>`, and `<ul>` can be emulated using the `display: block;` declaration. Inline-level elements like `<a>`, `<span>`, `<em>`, `<strong>` can be emulated using the `display: inline;` declaration. List elements (`<li>`) can be emulated using the `display: list-item;` declaration. You now need to style only the table containing the recipe's ingredients. This part of the styling is also taken care of using the `display` property and the table display values.

Table Display Values

Documented in CSS 2.1 and supported in Mozilla 1. 7, Opera 7.5, and Safari 1.2.

The table set of display values enables you to emulate HTML tables. With these tools, it's possible to fully recreate the behavior of an HTML table using XML elements. The following table shows the display value and the table element that it emulates.

Display Value	Emulated Element
`display: table;`	`<table>`
`display: table-caption;`	`<caption>`
`display: table-column-group;`	`<colgroup>`
`display: table-column;`	`<col/>`
`display: table-header-group;`	`<thead>`
`display: table-row-group;`	`<tbody>`
`display: table-row;`	`<tr>`
`display: table-cell;`	`<td>`, `<th>`
`display: table-footer-group;`	`<tfoot>`

Each table keyword for the display property has an XHTML/HTML element counterpart. Look at each value individually and how each is applied to an XML document.

The next sections each rely on the xml-table-1.xml file created earlier in this chapter. You use this XML file and add to the style sheet as each new rule is presented. These files are also available in the book's source code download at www.wrox.com and are named xml-table-2.xml and xml-table-2.css.

Applying display: table

If you add the following rules to the xml-table-2.css file, the `<favorites>` element emulates an HTML/XHTML `<table>` element:

```
* {
    font-family: monospace;
}
favorites {
    display: table;
    width: 100%;
    border: thin solid black;
    border-spacing: 2px;
}
```

This is done with the `display: table;` declaration. The `<favorites>` element now behaves just like the `<table>` element found in HTML/XHTML. As I did in Chapter 16, I've also added some other declarations so that xml-table-2.xml renders identically to html-table.html from Chapter 16. Additionally, as in HTML/XHTML, other display properties can be applied, such as the `border: thin solid black;` declaration and `width: 100%;` that I've added to the rule.

Adding a Caption with display: table-caption

Just as was the case with `display: table;`, the caption can be displayed with the `display: table-caption;` declaration. In the XML source for xml-table.xml, the caption is the `<title>` element. I could have just as easily called it `<caption>`, as it is in XHTML/HTML. However I have chosen to take advantage of XML's capability that allows me to invent any tag name I like.

Append the following rule to the xml-table-2.css file:

```
title {
    display: table-caption;
    font-size: 90%;
    text-align: right;
    padding: 5px;
}
```

The `<title>` element is made to behave like a table caption and now has behavior that is identical to the `<caption>` element found in HTML/XHTML.

Applying display: table-column-group and display: table-column

Table columns are styled next. In XML, styling is accomplished in the same way as with the table columns example presented earlier in this chapter, except that the elements have to be told they are columns. I append these two rules to the xml-table-2.css file as shown here:

```
cols {
    display: table-column-group;
}
cols album, cols artist, cols released {
    display: table-column;
}
```

The `display: table-column-group;` declaration causes the `<cols>` element to emulate the `<colgroup>` element found in XHTML/HTML; it is used to group the columns. Secondly, the individual columns are displayed in the same way as the `<col />` element in XHTML/HTML with the `display: column;` declaration.

Styling Groupings, Table Rows, and Table Cells

The styles required to create groupings, table rows, and table cells are just as intuitive as the other table display values. The declaration `display: table-header-group;` causes the target element to take on the behavior of the `<thead>` element found in HTML and XHTML, as demonstrated by the following style rule. Append this rule to the xml-table-2.css file:

```
headings {
    display: table-header-group;
}
```

The `<thead>` element does little more than center the table headers and make them boldfaced. Next, the `<tbody>` element found in HTML and XHTML is emulated with the CSS declaration `display: table-row-group;`, and again this element doesn't offer any changes in presentation other than further distinction in the structure of the document. This rule makes the `<records>` element emulate the `<tbody>` element:

```
records {
    display: table-row-group;
}
```

Now that you've distinguished the different groupings of table data, the next step is to make table rows. This is done with the `display: table-row;` declaration. Here, the purpose is mimicking the behavior of the `<tr>` element:

```
record {
    display: table-row;
}
```

Table cells are styled with the `display: table-cell;` declaration to obtain the behavior of the `<td>` element:

```
record > * {
    display: table-cell;
    padding: 5px;
}
```

I have chosen the universal and the direct child combination of selectors here so that if, in the future, I decide to add additional cells I will not be required to modify the style sheet. The `record > *` selector chooses all the child elements of the `<record>` elements. I could have just as easily written the rule this way:

```
album, artist, released {
    display: table-cell;
    padding: 5px;
}
```

I would have achieved an identical result. The next element in the "My Favorite Records" example is the `<footers>` element. Here, my intention is to emulate the `<tfoot>` element. As was the case with the `<tbody>` element, this offers no change in presentation, but places further distinctions in the structure of the document:

```
footers {
    display: table-footer-group;
}
footers > record > *, headings > record > * {
    border: thin solid black;
    text-align: center;
    font-weight: bold;
}
records > record > * {
    font-size: 120%;
}
```

The remaining styles contribute further to giving the XML version of "My Favorite Records" the same look and feel as the XHTML version. With the addition of table styles, the document renders as it is depicted in Figure 17-10 (xml-table-2.xml and xml-table-2.css).

Now that you have some idea of how tables are styled in XML, you can apply the information to an example with more real-world merit and pizzazz. The following Try It Out continues building on the Spicy Thai Peanut Sauce recipe presented in earlier examples and applies the table set of display values.

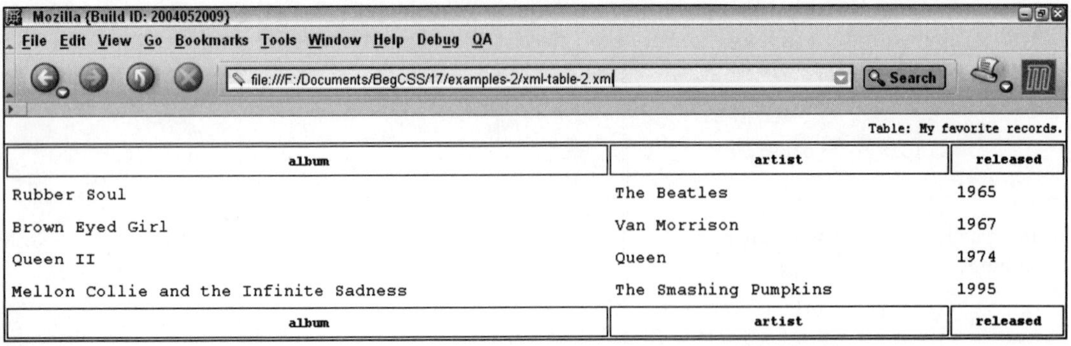

Figure 17-10

| Try It Out | Styling XML Tables |

Example 17-4. With these steps, you apply table style formatting to the spicy Thai Peanut Sauce recipe.

1. Open example17-3.css and modify the CSS document to reflect the following highlighted changes:

```
* {
    font-family: monospace;
}
page {
    display: block;
    background: #fff url('fruit_veg_web.jpg') no-repeat fixed center center;
}
recipe {
    display: block;
    padding: 10px;
    margin: 10px auto;
    min-width: 500px;
    max-width: 900px;
    /* Moz proprietary opacity property */
    -moz-opacity: 0.7;
    /* Safari / KHTML proprietary opacity property */
    -khtml-opacity: 0.7;
    /* Microsoft proprietary filter property */
    filter:progid:DXImageTransform.Microsoft.Alpha(opacity=70);
    /* CSS 3 opacity property */
    opacity: 0.7;
    background: url('cross_hatch.jpg') repeat;
}
ingredients {
    display: table;
    width: 100%;
    margin-bottom: 5px;
    table-layout: fixed;
    border-collapse: collapse;
    empty-cells: hide;
}
```

```css
title {
    display: table-caption;
    text-align: left;
    margin-bottom: 5px;
    text-transform: lowercase;
    font-size: 160%;
    padding: 5px;
    letter-spacing: 10px;
    font-weight: bold;
}
columns {
    display: table-column-group;
}
columns > * {
    display: table-column;
}
headings {
    display: table-header-group;
}
ingredientsbody {
    display: table-row-group;
}
heading, ingredient {
    display: table-row;
}
heading > * {
    font-weight: bold;
    font-size: 150%;
    color: black;
    text-align: center;
}
heading > *, ingredient > * {
    display: table-cell;
    padding: 5px;
    text-transform: lowercase;
}
ingredient > * {
    font-size: 130%;
}
ingredient > *:hover,
heading > *:hover,
directions:hover,
suggestions:hover,
title:hover {
    background: black;
    color: white;
    font-weight: bold;
}
directions, suggestions {
    display: block;
    font-size: 130%;
}
directions {
    margin: 17px 0 15px 0;
    padding: 0 0 0 45px;
```

```
        list-style-type: disc;
}
suggestions {
        margin: 22px 0 32px 0;
        padding: 0 5px 0 10px;
}
direction {
        display: list-item;
        margin-left: 30px;
        padding-left: 30px;
}
really {
        display: inline;
        font-weight: bold;
}
```

2. Save the file as example17-4.css.

3. Modify example17-3.xml to point to the new CSS document and save as example17-4.xml.

This results in the output depicted in Figure 17-11.

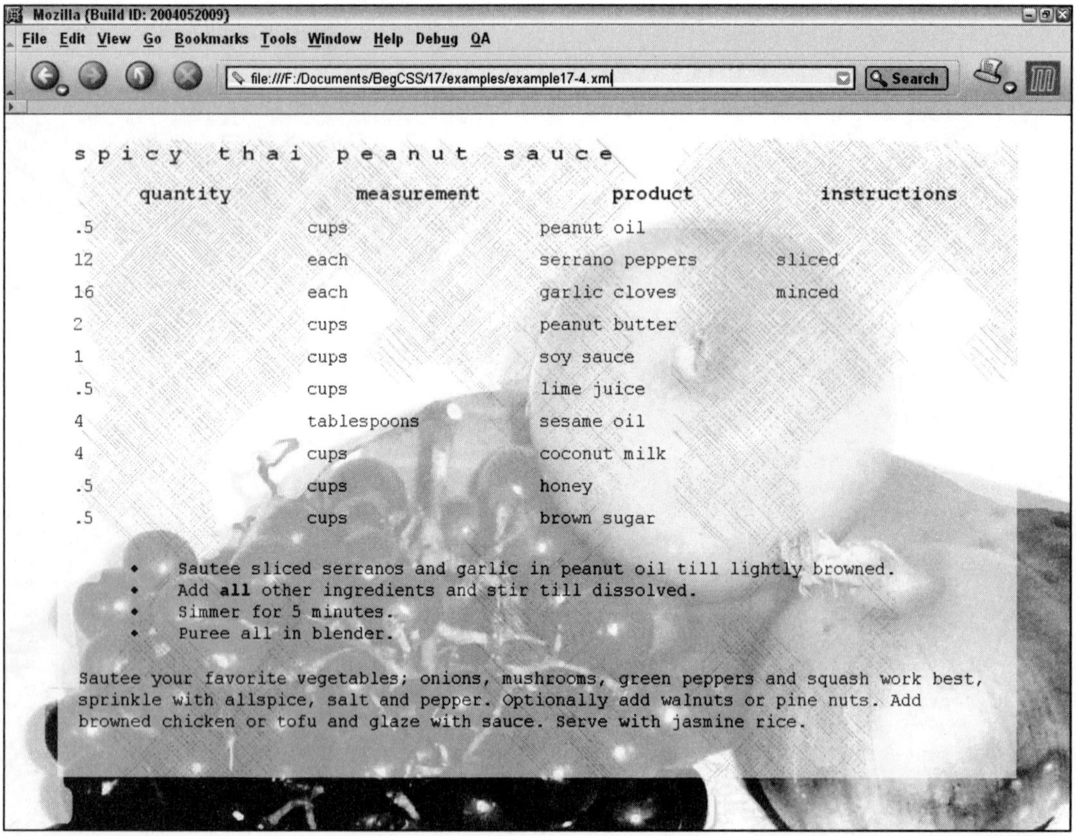

Figure 17-11

How It Works

Here, you applied a number of rules to style the table portion of the Spicy Thai Peanut Sauce recipe:

```
ingredients {
    display: table;
    width: 100%;
    margin-bottom: 5px;
    table-layout: fixed;
    border-collapse: collapse;
    empty-cells: hide;
}
```

The `<ingredients>` element is made into a table here with the `display: table;` declaration. This essentially makes the `<ingredients>` element the same as the `<table>` element found in HTML/XHTML. The table display properties that I discussed in Chapter 16 are now available to apply additional formatting. I've chosen to hide empty cells with the `empty-cells: hide;` declaration, and I removed spacing between the cells contained in the table with the `border-collapse: collapse;` declaration. Next the `<title>` element is made into the table caption with the `display: table-caption;` declaration. This makes the `<title>` element in this document the same as the `<caption>` element I discussed in Chapter 16:

```
title {
    display: table-caption;
    text-align: left;
    margin-bottom: 5px;
    text-transform: lowercase;
    font-size: 160%;
    padding: 5px;
    letter-spacing: 10px;
    font-weight: bold;
}
```

The `<title>` element contains the recipe's title and several styles that are applied to format the text. Next, the column-grouping element `<columns>` is given its behavior via the `display: table-column-group;` declaration. The columns themselves are given their behavior via the `display: table-column;` declaration:

```
columns {
    display: table-column-group;
}
columns > * {
    display: table-column;
}
```

At this point in the design, I have chosen to not take advantage of column styling, but I hold these elements in reserve for possible future enhancements to the document. In a real-world application it's perfectly fine to omit elements that have no effect on the document's final presentation; I have included this here simply to demonstrate its possibility.

As for the table headings, the `<thead>` element is emulated in this document with the `<headings>` element, and this element is given its style via the `display: table-header-group;` declaration:

```
headings {
    display: table-header-group;
}
```

The <tbody> element is also represented with the <instructionsbody> element, and this is given its style using the display: table-row-group; declaration:

```
ingredientsbody {
    display: table-row-group;
}
```

So far, nothing other than the <ingredients> and <title> elements contribute to the actual presentation of the document.

Next, table rows are given their behavior:

```
heading, ingredient {
    display: table-row;
}
```

Unlike the columns, heading groupings, and row groupings, table rows are very important for the structure of the document. These keep the cells in their places.

Next the cells in the heading are styled with a bold font, centering, black text, and 150% font size, which, in this case, is 50% larger than the browser's default font size:

```
heading > * {
    font-weight: bold;
    font-size: 150%;
    color: black;
    text-align: center;
}
```

The cells inside the <heading> element are selected using two selectors, the direct child selector and the universal selector. The direct child selector is the > character, which selects only elements that are children of the <heading> element. In this example, that could be the <quantity> element, the <measurement> element, the <product> element, or the <instructions> element: All these are direct children of the <heading> element. The universal selector is the asterisk. As you learned in Chapter 5, using the universal selector by itself selects all elements. Here the principal is the same. I want to select all children of the <heading> element without calling them by name, so I use heading > * as the selector. This selects all the children without having to type each element's name. The cells contained in the <heading> element haven't been made into cells yet. That is handled by the next rule:

```
heading > *, ingredient > * {
    display: table-cell;
    padding: 5px;
    text-transform: lowercase;
}
```

Here again I've chosen the universal and direct child combination of selectors, which provides me with flexibility should I chose to add additional elements to the recipe in the future. Here I am selecting the children of the `<heading>` element, as I did for the last rule, and the children of the `<ingredient>` element, which selects all remaining cells in the table. The cells of the table's body that actually contain the ingredients are styled with the next rule:

```
ingredient > * {
    font-size: 130%;
}
```

This next rule should look familiar. It creates the same hover effect that I presented in Chapter 16, although I am using different syntax for the selectors:

```
ingredient > *:hover,
heading > *:hover,
directions:hover,
suggestions:hover,
title:hover {
    background: black;
    color: white;
    font-weight: bold;
}
```

The direct child and universal selectors can be used with pseudo-classes like `:hover`, too. This rule has a grouping of five different selectors all separated using commas. The first selector is `ingredient > *:hover`. This selector chooses all cells in the table body, just like the `ingredient > *` selector did in the previous rule. This rule says that if a mouse cursor hovers over a child element of the `<ingredient>` element, apply these styles to the cell with the cursor hovering over it. Likewise, the same is done for the cells inside of the `<heading>` element, the `<directions>` and `<suggestions>` elements, and the `<title>` element. The last additions to the style sheet are put in place so that the XML version of The Spicy Thai Peanut Sauce recipe is a pixel-for-pixel perfect emulation of its HTML cousin:

```
directions {
    margin: 17px 0 15px 0;
    padding: 0 0 0 45px;
    list-style-type: disc;
}
suggestions {
    margin: 22px 0 32px 0;
    padding: 0 5px 0 10px;
}
direction {
    display: list-item;
    margin-left: 30px;
    padding-left: 30px;
}
```

The padding and margin values here were determined using trial and error, switching back and forth between the document presented in example16-5.html and this example, example17-4.xml.

Other Display Values

I have chosen not to cover other display values at this time because browser support for these is incredibly marginal. Opera 7 and Safari 1.2 do support the remaining display values: run-in, inline-block, and inline-table.

I also want to mention that, although I chose to use XML as the vehicle for demonstrating the various display values covered in this chapter, their use is not limited to XML. For clarity in presenting the material, I felt XML was the cleanest and most intuitive approach. It is perfectly acceptable to use the display property and its various values in HTML or XHTML documents. These values can be applied, conceivably, to any element. For instance:

```
<!DOCTYPE html PUBLIC "-//W3C//DTD XHTML 1.0 Strict//EN"
"http://www.w3.org/TR/xhtml1/DTD/xhtml1-strict.dtd">
<html>
    <head>
        <style type="text/css">
            html {
                display: table;
                border-spacing: 5px;
            }
            body {
                display: table-row;
            }
            div {
                display: table-cell;
                padding: 5px;
                border: thin solid black;
            }
        </style>
        <title> HTML display property  </title>
        <link rel='stylesheet' type='text/css' href='example16-5.css'/>
    </head>
    <body>
        <div> table cell </div>
        <div> table cell </div>
    </body>
</html>
```

This results in the output shown in Figure 17-12.

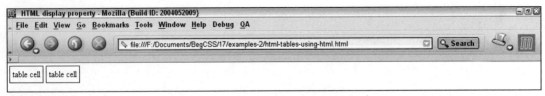

Figure 17-12

Using an HTML document, I have essentially recreated the behavior of tables using as little extra HTML code as is possible. This is a perfectly acceptable use of the `display` property. And I might also add an acceptable use of table-based layouts.

Summary

XML is a flexible, robust markup language with multiple applications. CSS provides powerful control over how an XML document is presented. CSS can emulate any type of HTML/XHTML element. XML declarations provide the browser with important information about the XML document, including the XML version and the encoding. This, in turn, provides information about the characters contained in the document. The display property can be used to create block-level and inline-level boxes as well as the various elements used in tables.

In this chapter you learned

❑ What XML is and some of its uses.

❑ How to create an XML schema, and the document structure necessary to emulate HTML tables, block-level, inline-level, and list elements.

❑ What the XML declaration and the pseudo-attributes inside of it mean.

❑ How to style an XML document.

❑ How to create block-level boxes like the `<div>` element in HTML/ XHTML.

❑ How to create inline-level boxes like the `<span>` element in HTML/XHTML.

❑ How to style lists in XML.

❑ How to style tables in XML.

In Chapter 18, I wrap up my discussion of CSS with a look at how to address specific bugs and lack of CSS support in Microsoft Internet Explorer.

Exercise

Write an XML document containing your favorite movies and style it identically to the scenario presented in Chapter 16, Exercise 1.

Using XML and CSS, write a table containing your favorite movies. Include the name of the movie, its genre, a few of the stars of each movie, and the year it was released. Define a width of 300 pixels for the table and force the table to maintain that width, place a caption on the table, position the caption to render below the table, and remove all spacing between table cells. Include headings for each column that describe the data contained in each column. Use groupings and columns. Use borders, padding, background colors, and other CSS presentational controls to enhance visual clarity.

18

Cross-Browser Compatibility

Chapter 17 focused on how to style XML documents with CSS and how to emulate HTML using the Display property. In this chapter I explore some very useful solutions for getting CSS to work in most browsers in use today. In this chapter I discuss the following:

❑ IE7 (not the next major browser from Microsoft), an open source package used to implement CSS standards in Internet Explorer browsers without upgrading the browser itself

❑ Installation of an HTTP server, the software used to transmit web pages from server to browser, which is required to use the IE7 package

❑ Internet Explorer rendering bugs

❑ Additional places on the web to go to for help

At the time of this writing, Microsoft Internet Explorer exhibits more problems than any other browser in terms of support for CSS standards. This chapter focuses on techniques that web designers use to bring Internet Explorer up to speed with its competitors. This discussion is necessary because the majority of Internet users are using Internet Explorer for Windows in one form or another.

Bugs in Microsoft Internet Explorer

Bugs are an unfortunate fact of designing web pages. In a perfect world, no hacks or work-arounds would be necessary. Unfortunately, this isn't a perfect world. A couple of years ago, designers were grumbling about having to support Netscape Navigator 4. Today, use of Netscape Navigator 4 is virtually non-existent, and the browser designers are complaining about Microsoft Internet Explorer 6. IE 5.5 still has a marginal number of users, however (and of course, even more bugs than IE 6).

In the upcoming sections, you learn about a few of the most important bugs you may encounter when rendering a web page for Microsoft Internet Explorer, and I show you how to smash them. Although other browsers, such as Mozilla, Opera, and Safari, have their share of bugs, the biggest problem today is Microsoft Internet Explorer for Windows. The majority of the bug fixes presented in this chapter involve floating elements in Internet Explorer. I also present a unique package that corrects some of Internet Explorer's rendering bugs and implements CSS functionality in Internet Explorer 5, 5.5, and 6. This solution is called IE7, and it is the focus of the next section.

IE7

No, IE7 in this context isn't the next major version of the Microsoft Internet Explorer browser. To review from Chapter 2, Microsoft discontinued the standalone IE browser and announced it would be completely integrating the IE browser with its next operating system, code named Longhorn. Where does that leave web designers who would like to see the IE browser continue to implement CSS and other web standards now? The answer is IE7, an open source project focused on repairing Microsoft's faulty and non-existent CSS support features in IE 5, 5.5 and 6. The IE7 package was developed by London, UK native Dean Edwards. Commenting on the lack of CSS 2 support in the current IE browser (see his website at http://dean.edwards.name/ie7) Dean contends, "We need a level playing field." The coming sections explain what IE7 is and how to deploy this solution in a website.

What IE7 Is

IE7 is a client-side solution written completely in JavaScript, a programming language that can be included directly in a web document. Because IE7 is developed using JavaScript, the end-user accessing a website need not download, update, or install anything. This makes IE7 an attractive solution. Consequently, because of its ambitious goals and impressive functionality, many have hailed IE7 as the Holy Grail of website design.

Getting the IE7 Source Code

You can find the IE7 home page at http://dean.edwards.name/ie7, and you can download IE7 from Source Forge at https://sourceforge.net/projects/ie7/. IE7 is available under a Creative Commons license, meaning that the source may be modified or redistributed, provided that the original author is always credited. For more information on the Creative Commons License, visit http://creativecommons.org/licenses/by/2.0/.

CSS Features Provided by IE7

The goal of IE7 is to provide working CSS 2 and some CSS 3 selector syntax, as well as support for a small subset of properties. It focuses on providing the same features offered by Gecko, Opera, and Safari, all of which have far more advanced CSS support than the current Internet Explorer. At the time of this writing, the majority of web surfers use Internet Explorer, but it has slowly become a thorn in the sides of developers who want to take advantage of the features offered in CSS 2 and the emerging CSS 3 standards.

Here is a brief summary of some of the features provided by IE7:

❑   Attribute, direct child, and adjacent sibling selectors

❑   Support for pseudo-classes: `:active`, `:hover`, `:focus`, `:first-child`, `:last-child`, `:root` and `:empty`

❑   Support for pseudo-elements: `::before` and `::after` as well as the `content` property

❑   Consistent box model rendering between IE 5, 5.5 and 6, per the W3C specifications

❑   Support for `min-width`, `max-width` and `min-height` properties

❑   Support for the `background-attachment: fixed;` declaration

❑   Support for the `position: fixed;` declaration

❑   PNG transparency

IE7's developer Dean Edwards doesn't have immediate plans to integrate additional functionality, having stated that "It's important that IE7 not be better than standard browsers." However, he has expressed a willingness to accept bribes for the implementation of additional features and a willingness to accept assistance to develop this solution. Because IE7 is a continuously evolving solution, it will probably support many more features by the time you read this. In an upcoming Try It Out I explain how to find out exactly what functionality is provided by IE7.

At the time of this writing, IE7 is considered alpha software. *Alpha* software is software in an early stage of development. Generally, software deemed in an alpha state has been tested only by its developer and may be subject to bugs and changes in its design. *Beta* software is a step above alpha; beta software has been tested by a larger group, but it may still contain bugs in its functionality. Its design, however, is typically rooted and stable. *Stable* software is what you find most in use. It has been tested extensively; it may have a few bugs, but it does what is expected by its developer in the majority of scenarios. The beauty of IE7 is that no special software is required for the user to take advantage of its features. All the necessary code is included directly in the web page. The end user needs no plug-ins or complicated downloads. Furthermore, after it is downloaded, the IE7 files reside in the browser's cache, so other than the initial download of the required files, IE7 does not affect download times.

How IE7 Works

IE7 is written in JavaScript, a special programming language that executes in the browser itself. JavaScript files can be embedded directly into a web document or referenced externally using a URL, just like external style sheets. The IE7 package arrives in .zip format; .zip is a file format used to compress files for download or archival storage. The files inside of the IE7 zip archive must be saved to the root directory of your website. For instance, if you have the domain `http://www.example.com`, the IE7 files must appear at `http://www.example.com/ie7`. Therefore, before I can demonstrate the functionality of IE7, you must install or have access to an HTTP server.

Installing an HTTP Server

In Chapter 1, you saw an overview of how web pages are accessed and stored. This is accomplished using something called an HTTP server. An HTTP server is software used to deliver a web page from the server computer, for example, `http://www.example.com`, to the browser of the client computer. In order to use IE7, you must have a web server installed on your computer to serve the files. This has to do with how the files of the IE7 package are structured and makes implementation of this solution much more painless. A myriad of different HTTP servers are available; in this example, I walk you through the process of installing the Apache HTTP server step by step. Apache is a popular, open source HTTP server used to serve up millions of websites for both individuals and businesses large and small. This example provides instructions for how to download and install the Apache HTTP server for a Windows operating system. If you're using Mac OS X or Linux, chances are Apache is already installed on your system.

Try It Out   **Installing the Apache HTTP Server**

Example 18-1. To install the Apache web server, follow these steps:

1.   Download Apache 2 from `http://httpd.apache.org`. More than one download package is available; select the Win32 MSI Installer for Apache 2.

2.   After the package is downloaded, double-click the downloaded file to initiate the installation wizard.

3. Read and accept the terms of the Apache license agreement; then, click Next.

4. If you desire, read the next pane on installing Apache for Windows; then, click Next.

5. The next screen (see Figure 18-1) is very important because it determines what you will type to access your web pages through a browser. Under Network Domain, type localhost, and under Server Name, type localhost again. Under Administrator's Email Address, you may include either your real e-mail address or simply type admin@localhost. After you have typed this information, click Next.

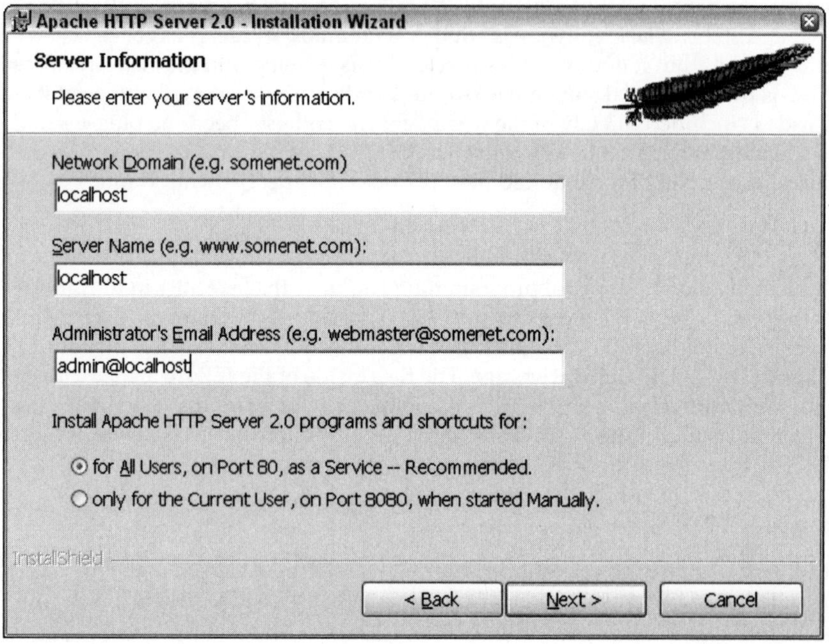

Figure 18-1

6. In the next screen, select the Typical installation option (see Figure 18-2); then, click Next.

7. On the next screen, select the directory where Apache should be installed, or use the default path of C:\Program Files\Apache Group\ (see Figure 18-3). After selecting the directory, click Next.

8. Finally, click the Install button to begin installing the Apache server.

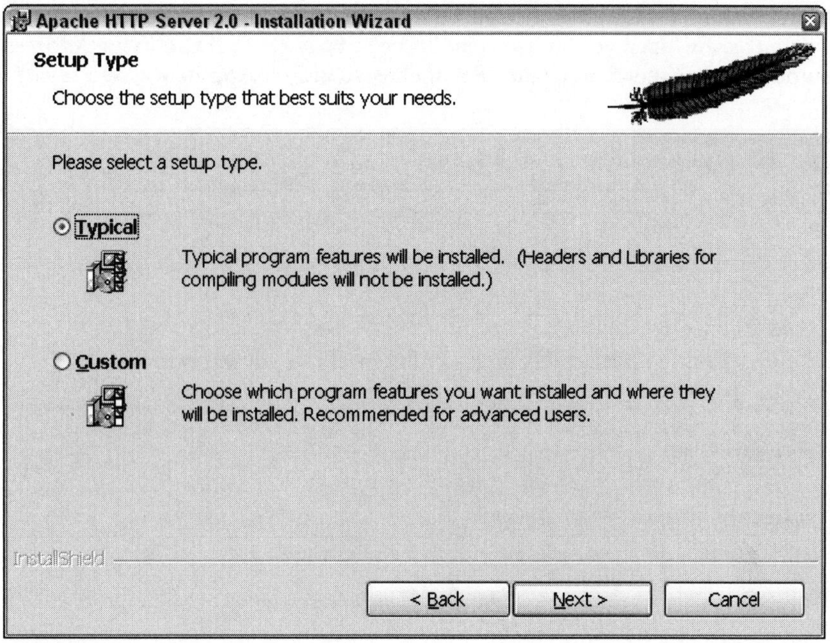

Figure 18-2

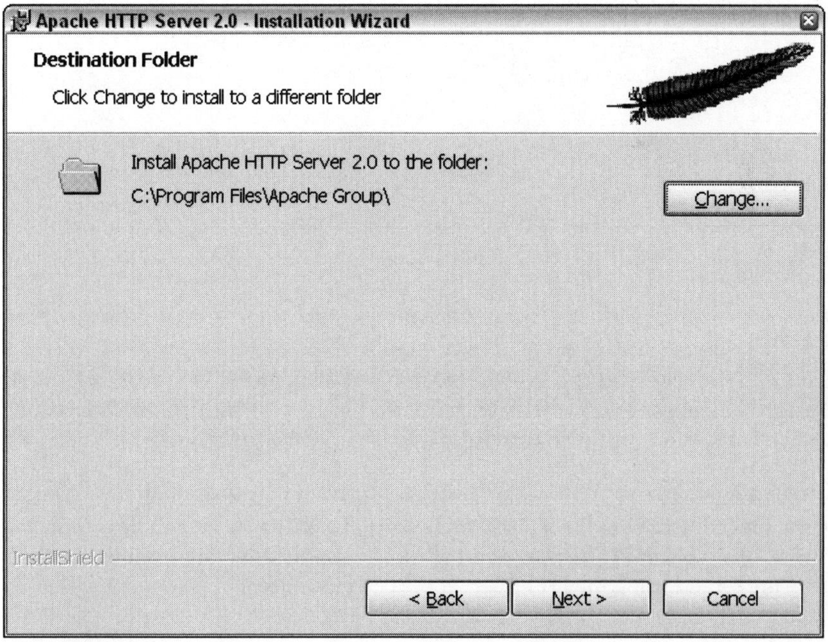

Figure 18-3

9. After finishing the installation, Apache should be good to go. To see if the installation of Apache was successful, open your browser and type `http://localhost` in the Address bar. If you see output like that shown in Figure 18-4, the installation of Apache was successful!

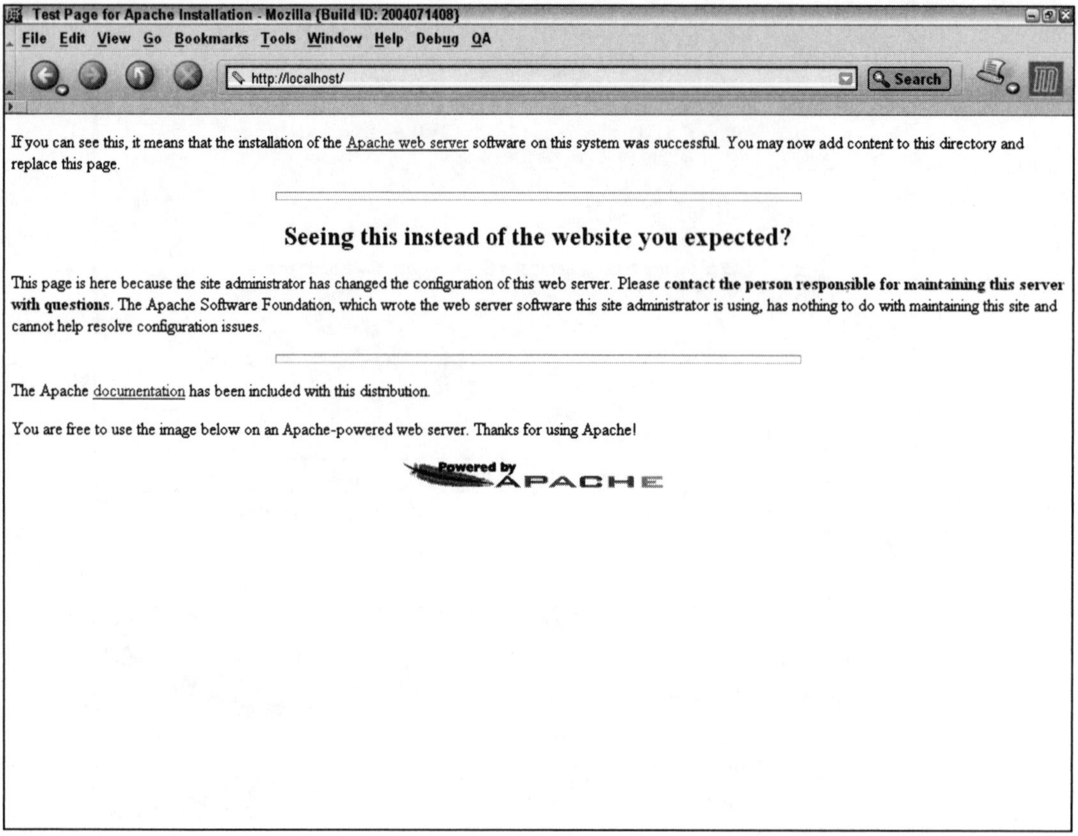

Figure 18-4

How It Works

Apache is an HTTP server used to serve web pages. Installing an HTTP server, such as Apache, is the first step toward hosting your own website, although for the purposes of this discussion you're going to use it to test web pages on your own computer and observe the functionality offered by the IE7 package.

After you have installed an HTTP server, the following Try It Out walks you through the process of extracting the files contained in the IE7 .zip archive. It also instructs you on how to install those files to the root directory of your HTTP server (or, in other words, the directory from which the documents of your website are served using the HTTP server you just installed).

Try It Out   Installing IE7

Example 18-2. To extract the files of IE7, follow these steps:

1. Download IE7 from
   https://sourceforge.net/project/showfiles.php?group_id=109983.

2. Open the zip archive using Windows Explorer. If you're using Windows XP, do this by double-clicking the archive file. If your operating system does not natively support zip archive extraction, you may obtain third-party software from www.download.com by supplying the search term *zip* to the download.com search box in conjunction with your operating system (use the advanced search option to select a specific operating system). Several third-party software solutions are available free of charge.

3. In Windows XP, click the Extract All Files link in the left pane of the window under Folder Tasks, as shown in Figure 18-5.

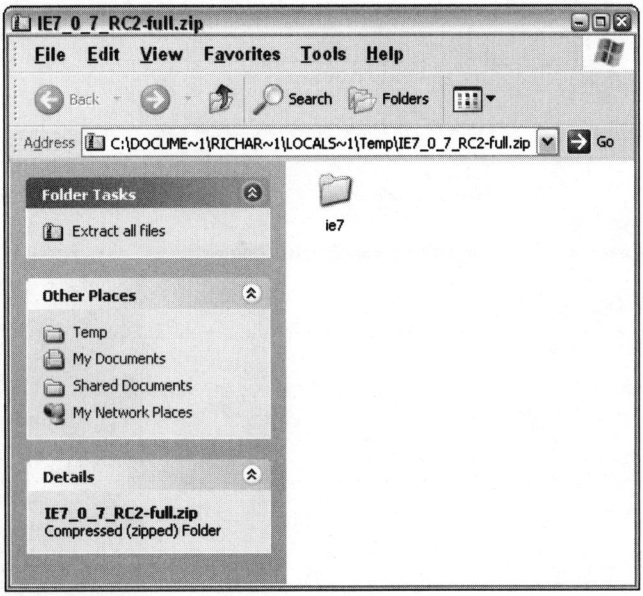

Figure 18-5

4. This opens the native Windows XP zip archive extraction wizard.

5. Select the directory to which you wish to save the extracted files. For these files to be served by Apache through the http://localhost URL, they must be stored in a special directory known as the root www directory. By default, Apache creates an htdocs directory for this purpose. Therefore, the files must be extracted to C:\Program Files\Apache Group\Apache2\htdocs. Update the file path accordingly if you chose to install Apache to a different location. This window is shown in Figure 18-6.

6. Type http://localhost/ie7. If you see a page like that in Figure 18-7, you are successful.

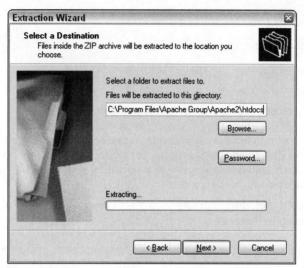

Figure 18-6

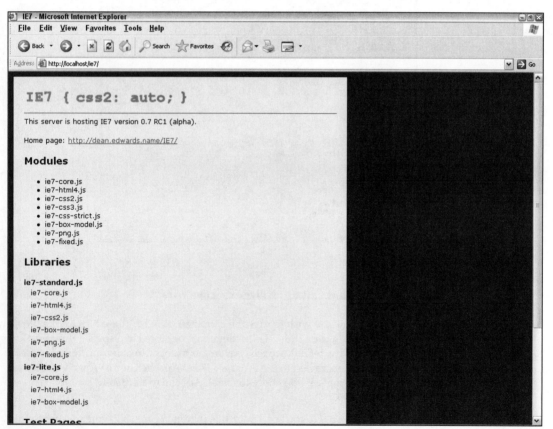

Figure 18-7

How It Works

The IE7 solution works most painlessly if the files are installed to the root directory of your HTTP server. The files arrive in a special compressed zip format. This reduces the size of the files so they can be downloaded in less time or stored on a hard drive using less space. Windows XP has a built-in zip archive extraction utility capable of reading this special format. Additionally, several software solutions are available at `http://www.download.com` if your operating system does not support zip archive extraction.

To see the features currently offered by IE7, click the Compatibility Suite link at the bottom of the page at `http://localhost/ie7`. This page shows a table of the features currently offered by IE7.

Now that you've installed IE7, as well as an HTTP server, this example demonstrates how to apply the IE7 solution to the JT's Island Grill and Gallery website. However, before you apply this solution, open up the JT's Island Grill and Gallery website in Internet Explorer 6. You should see output like that in Figure 18-8.

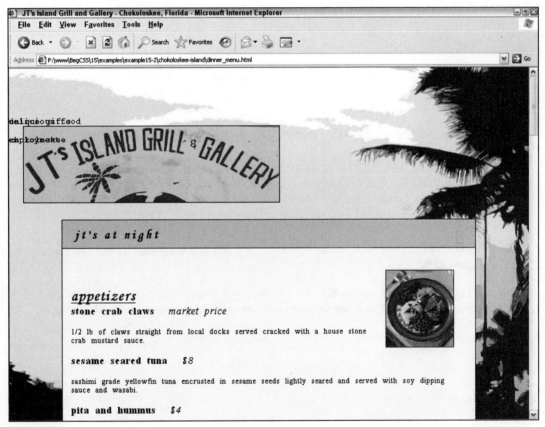

Figure 18-8

At this point, the dinner menu doesn't appear to have been designed by a professional developer, and it certainly won't fly with the clients if your website doesn't work in the majority of browsers, such as Internet Explorer. The IE7 solution — which you work with in the following Try It Out — is an ideal starting point to correct the bugs present in the design. This is especially true because so many of the features provided by IE7 are exactly the features this project requires.

Try It Out   Applying the IE7 solution

Example 18-3. In the following steps, you apply the IE7 package to the JT's dinner menu:

1.   Open up the dinner_menu.html file and add the following markup:

```
<!DOCTYPE html PUBLIC "-/pp/W3C//DTD XHTML 1.0 Strict//EN"
"http://www.w3.org/TR/xhtml1/DTD/xhtml1-strict.dtd">
<html>
    <head>
        <title>
            JT's Island Grill and Gallery - Chokoloskee, Florida
        </title>
        <!-- compliance patch for microsoft browsers -->
        <!--[if lt IE 7]>
        <script src="/ie7/ie7-standard-p.js" type="text/javascript">
        </script>
        <![endif]-->
```

2.   Save dinner_menu.html to C:\Program Files\Apache Group\Apache2\htdocs\ dinner_menu.html.

3.   Move each file and directory of the JT's website to the htdocs directory, keeping intact the directory structure that you've used throughout the book. Relocate each style sheet to C:\Program Files\Apache Group\Apache2\htdocs\style_sheets and the images to C:\Program Files\ Apache Group\Apache2\htdocs\images. This makes the JT's website available at `http://localhost` url.

4.   Type `http://localhost/dinner_menu.html`, and you should see output like that shown in Figure 18-9.

At the time of this writing, the handheld and print style sheets that you applied in Chapter 15 interfere with the application of IE7, so it may be necessary to remove these style sheets to properly observe the effects of IE7.

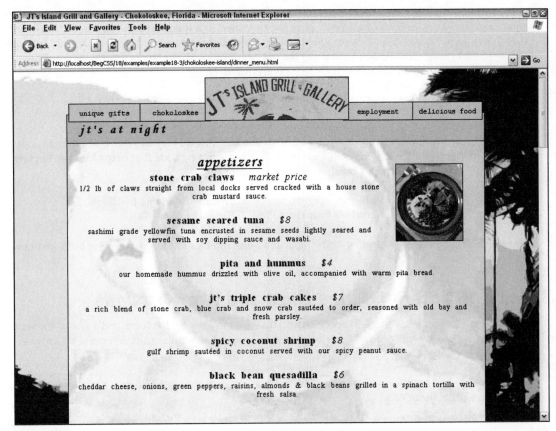

Figure 18-9

How It Works

Figure 18-14 shows the results of applying the IE7 style sheet. The design is still not quite perfect, but it now much more closely resembles how Mozilla and Opera render the page. A myriad of bugs still remain in IE 5 and 5.5 and just a few more subtle bugs in IE 6.

The IE7 files are included using a proprietary Microsoft feature called conditional comments. Conditional comments are used to hide content from other browsers. In this example, the conditional comments say if the version number of Internet Explorer is less than 7, include this markup in the document. This involves a special syntax.

```
<!--[if lt IE 7]>
```

As you've seen in earlier chapters, the `<!--` and `-->` tags are usually used to include comments in the source of an HTML or XHTML document. Here they are used in a special context to prevent browsers other than Internet Explorer from seeing the markup inside the comment tags. Currently, only Internet Explorer 5 and greater for Windows supports the use of conditional comments. Inside the conditional comments a `<script>` tag is used to include a JavaScript file.

```
<script src="/ie7/ie7-standard-p.js" type="text/javascript">
</script>
```

This preceding code references an external JavaScript file in the same way as you've seen external style sheets referenced. The external JavaScript file includes programming code that helps Internet Explorer interpret CSS syntax that it wasn't capable of understanding before.

> If you'd like to learn more about JavaScript, you may be interested in Beginning JavaScript, 2nd Edition, by Paul Wilton, also available from Wrox Press (ISBN: 0-7645-5587-1).

The next section takes a look at some of the most annoying Internet Explorer rendering bugs and how to work around them.

Specific IE CSS Rendering Bugs and Work-Arounds

The following section takes a look at specific bugs that arise in Internet Explorer and a few of the techniques you can use to work around these bugs. The following list, with snappy titles and all, covers which bugs I will discuss.

- ❑ **Peek-a-boo bug:** As the name implies, this bug involves the use of floats where certain content on a page disappears and occasionally reappears.
- ❑ **Guillotine bug:** Another bug that comes up in IE when using floats, where content is cut in half.
- ❑ **Three-pixel jog:** This bug causes 3 pixels of space to mysteriously appear when using floats in IE.
- ❑ **Double-margin bug:** Causes the left or right margins of a floated box to double when using floats in IE.

The Peek-A-Boo Bug

The peek-a-boo bug can come up in several different contexts, in fact, in far too many to list here. It involves content that disappears and reappears seemingly at random (hence its aptly applied name). The following example demonstrates the peek-a-boo bug:

```
<!DOCTYPE html PUBLIC "-//W3C//DTD XHTML 1.0 Strict//EN"
"http://www.w3.org/TR/xhtml1/DTD/xhtml1-strict.dtd">
<html>
    <head>
        <title></title>
        <style type='text/css'>
            div#container {
                border: thick dotted black;
                margin: 0 20px;
                background: ghostwhite;
            }
```

```
            a:hover {
                background: orange;
            }
            div#float {
                text-align: center;
                float: left;
                border: 1px solid black;
                width: 150px;
                height: 150px;
            }
            div.content {
                background: lightyellow;
                border: 1px solid black;
            }
            div#clear {
                border: 1px solid black;
                background: lightgreen;
                clear: both;
            }
        </style>
    </head>
    <body>
        <div id='container'>
            <div id='float'>
                Float text. <a href='#'>Link text</a>.
            </div>
                Content text. <a href='#'>Link text</a>.
            <div class='content'>
                Content text. <a href='#'>Link text</a>.
            </div>
                Content text. <a href='#'>Link text</a>.
            <div class='content'>
                Content text. <a href='#'>Link text</a>.
            </div>
                Content text. <a href='#'>Link text</a>.
            <div class='content'>
                Content text. <a href='#'>Link text</a>.
            </div>
                Content text. <a href='#'>Link text</a>.
            <div id='clear'>
                Clear text. <a href='#'>Link text</a>.
            </div>
            <div>
                Another div.
            </div>
        </div>
    </body>
</html>
```

Figure 18-10 shows that when this document is loaded into Internet Explorer 6, none of the content beside the floated element is visible until you hover your mouse over a link. Hovering causes the lost content to reappear. If you hover your mouse cursor over the links that have reappeared, you find some of the content disappears again.

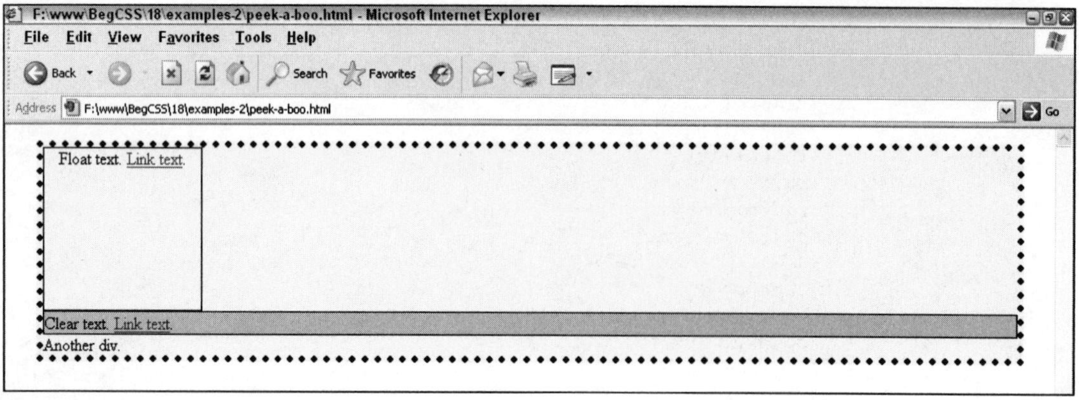

Figure 18-10

Three properties present in the style sheet trigger this bug:

❑ Floating an element by applying a `float: left;` declaration (`float: right;` also triggers the bug).

❑ Including a background on the containing element. In this example, this is the `background: ghostwhite;` declaration.

❑ Including a Clear on an element following the float, where the margins of the clearing element come into contact with the floating element.

So, with an overview of what causes the peek-a-boo bug and what it is, what do you do to work around the bug? You have more than one option:

❑ Apply a `position: relative;` declaration to the containing element and floating element.

❑ Prevent the margins of the clearing element from coming into contact with the floating element.

❑ Avoid applying a background to the containing element.

❑ Apply a fixed width to the containing element.

The next section continues discussion of Internet Explorer bugs with the guillotine bug.

The Guillotine Bug

The guillotine bug is another aptly named bug where only part of the content disappears. The guillotine bug is demonstrated in the following document:

```
<!DOCTYPE html PUBLIC "-//W3C//DTD XHTML 1.0 Strict//EN"
"http://www.w3.org/TR/xhtml1/DTD/xhtml1-strict.dtd">
<html>
    <head>
        <title></title>
```

```
        <style type='text/css'>
            div#container {
                border: thick dotted black;
                margin: 0 20px;
                background: lightyellow;
            }
            a:hover {
                background: orange;
            }
            div#float {
                background: lightgrey;
                float: left;
                border: 1px solid black;
                width: 150px;
                height: 150px;
            }
            ul {
                margin: 0;
                list-style: none;
            }
        </style>
    </head>
    <body>
        <div id='container'>
            <div id='float'>
                <p>
                    Float text. <a href='#'>Content on</a>.
                    Float text. Float text. Float text. Float text.
                    Float text. Float text. Float text. Float text.
                </p>
                <p>
                    This text is chopped off!  This text is chopped off!
                    This text is chopped off!  This text is chopped off!
                </p>
            </div>
            <ul>
                <li><a href='#'>Content on.</a></li>
                <li><a href='#'>Content on.</a></li>
                <li><a href='#'>Content off.</a></li>
                <li><a href='#'>Content off.</a></li>
                <li><a href='#'>Content off.</a></li>
            </ul>
        </div>
    </body>
</html>
```

After you load the preceding in Internet Explorer, when you hover your mouse cursor over the Content Off links, part of the content inside the floating element is chopped off! You can see this in the output in Figure 18-11.

505

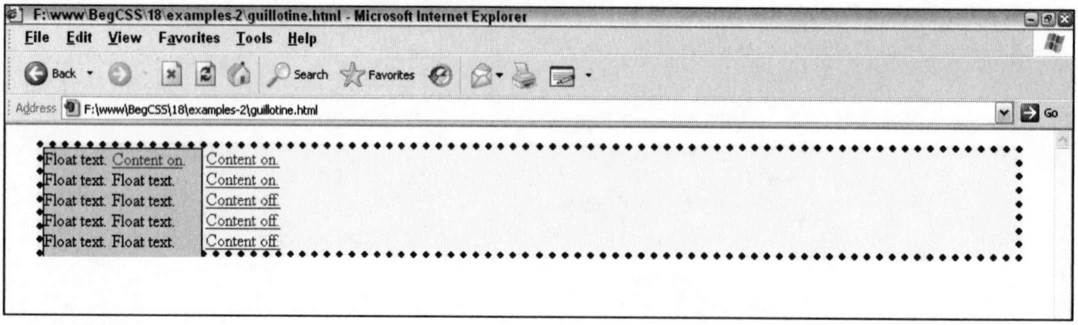

Figure 18-11

The guillotine bug occurs when the following conditions are present:

❑   An element is floated inside of a container element.

❑   Links exist inside the container element in non-floated content that appears after the float.

❑   A `:hover` pseudo-class is applied to `<a>` elements that change certain properties.

The guillotine bug is yet another bizarre IE rendering bug. The fix is not nearly as elegant as that for the peek-a-boo bug. To fix the guillotine bug, a clearing element must appear after the containing element. The best method to apply this clearing element without affecting the original design is to apply the following rule to the clearing element:

```
div#clearing {
    clear: both;
    visibility: hidden;
}
```

Then in the markup, add the clearing element:

```
                <li><a href='#'>Content off.</a></li>
            </ul>
        </div>
        <div id='clearing'></div>
    </body>
</html>
```

After you apply this rule and markup, the guillotine bug is corrected without any effects on the intended design. The `visibility: hidden;` declaration is similar to the `display: none;` declaration. The key difference is that an element with `display: none;` is not rendered and does not appear in a document, whereas an element with `visibility: hidden;` is rendered, does appear in the document, but is invisible. The easiest way to distinguish between the two is that the `display` property with a `none` keyword makes it seem an element doesn't exist at all. If you use the `display: none;`, declaration properties are not applied and the element takes up no space. If you use `visibility: hidden;` instead with this declaration, the element still exists; properties are applied and the dimensions of the element are still honored, even though the element is invisible.

The nest section continues the discussion of Internet Explorer bugs with the three-pixel jog.

The Three-Pixel Jog

The next Internet Explorer rendering bug, which also involves floated elements, is called the three-pixel jog. As the name implies, this bug causes 3 pixels of space to appear between text inside an element that follows a floated element and the inner border of that element. This bug is demonstrated by the following markup:

```
<!DOCTYPE html PUBLIC "-//W3C//DTD XHTML 1.0 Strict//EN"
"http://www.w3.org/TR/xhtml1/DTD/xhtml1-strict.dtd">
<html>
    <head>
        <title></title>
        <style type='text/css'>
            div#container {
                margin: 0 20px;
                background: lightyellow;
                width: 300px;
            }
            div#float {
                background: lightgrey;
                float: left;
                border: 1px solid black;
                width: 75px;
                height: 50px;
            }
            p {
                margin-left: 76px;
                border: 1px solid black;
            }
        </style>
    </head>
    <body>
        <div id='container'>
            <div id='float'>
                Float text.
            </div>
            <p>
                Paragraph text. Paragraph text. Paragraph text.
                Paragraph text. Paragraph text. Paragraph text.
                Paragraph text. Paragraph text. Paragraph text.
            </p>
        </div>
    </body>
</html>
```

Figure 18-12 shows the subtle effects of the three-pixel jog. If you look closely in the screen shot, you can see that the first three lines of the paragraph are 3 pixels farther to the right than the two lines that follow, which corresponds directly to the height of the floated element.

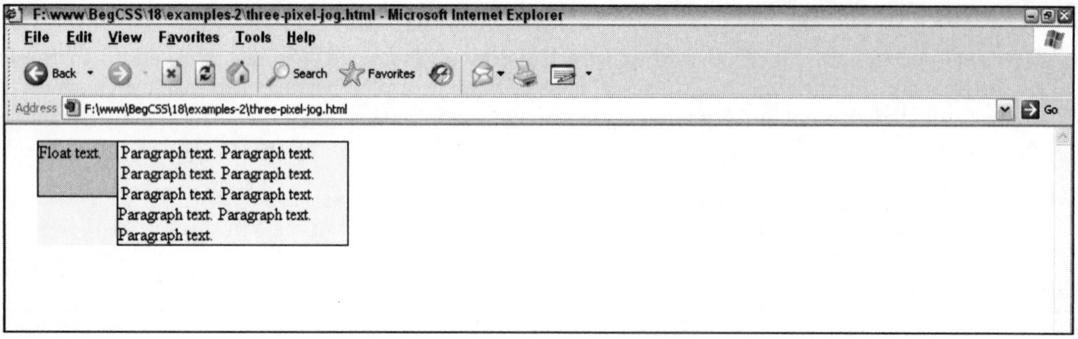

Figure 18-12

The three-pixel jog doesn't look like much of a big deal, but it can be — especially if a design must be the same, pixel for pixel, in all browsers. The three-pixel jog can be corrected by applying either a width or height (other than auto) to the element that follows the float. Because an explicit width or height is not always desirable, a few methods target IE browsers specifically. The first method uses conditional comments like those you saw in use for the IE7 package.

```
<!--[if lt IE 7]>
<style type='text/css'>
    p {
        height: 1%;
    }
</style>
<![endif]-->
```

This is a very clean, acceptable method to target IE for Windows explicitly, and because IE 6 and earlier versions have incorrect support for the height property, the content isn't adversely affected by including this declaration. Other browsers won't be so forgiving, however, so this solution must only be applied to Internet Explorer to avoid complications. The next section continues discussion of Internet Explorer rendering bugs with the double-margin bug.

The Double-Margin Bug

Here's yet another Internet Explorer rendering bug involving floated elements. This bug is currently addressed by the IE7 package, so including the IE7 package fixes this bug without need of additional CSS or markup. The double-margin bug is demonstrated in the following document:

```
<!DOCTYPE html PUBLIC "-//W3C//DTD XHTML 1.0 Strict//EN"
"http://www.w3.org/TR/xhtml1/DTD/xhtml1-strict.dtd">
<html>
    <head>
        <title></title>
        <style type='text/css'>
            div#container {
                margin: 0 20px;
                background: lightyellow;
                width: 300px;
            }
```

```
        div#float {
            margin-left: 50px;
            background: lightgrey;
            float: left;
            border: 1px solid black;
            width: 75px;
            height: 50px;
        }
    </style>
</head>
<body>
    <div id='container'>
        <div id='float'>
            Float text.
        </div>
    </div>
</body>
</html>
```

Figure 18-13 shows the double-margin bug in action.

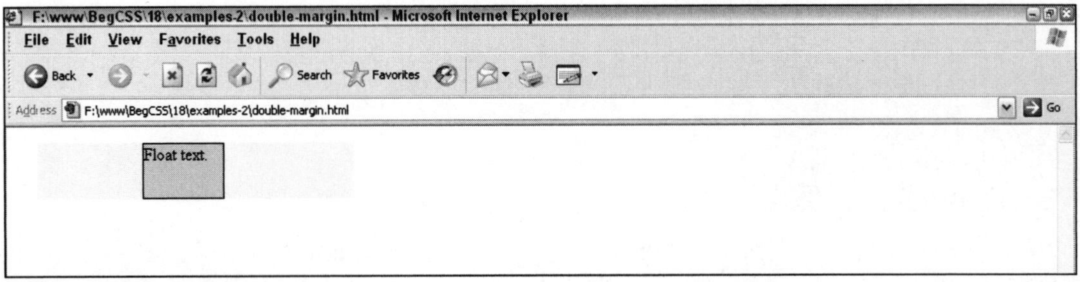

Figure 18-13

Three ingredients are required to reproduce this bug:

❑   A containing element

❑   A floated element inside the containing element

❑   A left margin specified on the floated element

When these ingredients are present, the left margin of the floated element doubles, so Figure 18-13 shows the floated element with 100 pixels of left margin instead of only 50, as is specified in the style sheet. The fix for this bug is very simple. All you need to do is apply a display: inline; declaration to the floated element. If you recall from Chapter 11, all floated elements are always block elements. Using the display: inline; declaration somehow tricks Internet Explorer into correct behavior. Be sure to test this fix with different browsers to ensure that unexpected side effects are not encountered. As is the case with the three-pixel jog, you can target Internet Explorer specifically by including this declaration within a rule inside of a style sheet that resides in conditional comments. Figure 18-14 shows the results of applying display: inline; to the floated element.

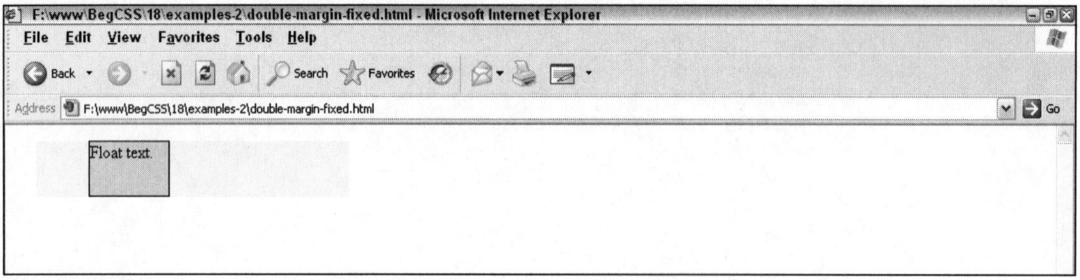

Figure 18-14

Figure 18-14 shows that when display: inline; is applied to the floated element, the left margin of the floated element is 50 pixels, as you expected it to be.

Floating Elements and Percentage Widths

The last bug that I have chosen to profile is also a bug that arises with the use of floating elements. This bug, as far as I am aware, has no official name, but it exists nonetheless. This bug occurs when a 100% width is used on an element that follows a floated element:

```
<!DOCTYPE html PUBLIC "-//W3C//DTD XHTML 1.0 Strict//EN"
"http://www.w3.org/TR/xhtml1/DTD/xhtml1-strict.dtd">
<html>
    <head>
        <title></title>
        <style type='text/css'>
            div#container {
                margin: 0 20px;
                background: lightyellow;
            }
            div#float {
                background: lightgrey;
                float: left;
                border: 1px solid black;
                width: 75px;
                height: 50px;
            }
            div#follow {
                margin-left: 77px;
            }
            table {
                border: 1px solid black;
                width: 100%;
            }
            td {
                border: 1px solid black;
            }
        </style>
    </head>
    <body>
        <div id='container'>
```

```
                    <div id='float'>
                        Float text.
                    </div>
                    <div id='follow'>
                        <table>
                            <tr>
                                <td>
                                    Table text.
                                </td>
                            </tr>
                        </table>
                    </div>
                </div>
            </body>
        </html>
```

Figure 18-15 shows that the `<table>` element does not appear beside the floated element.

Figure 18-15

This is a bug that can arise in a number of different contexts. If you apply a 100% width to an element that follows a floating element, it causes a top margin to appear above the element following the floated element. The solutions for this bug are as follows:

❑ If the element is a table (as it is in the preceeding example), a `table-layout: fixed;` declaration often provides the desired result. Remember from Chapter 16, however, that this declaration affects the column size and can lead to content being clipped. Using `table-layout: fixed;` with Internet Explorer causes the table to behave as though it has a 100% width. This isn't the same case for Mozilla, which still treats the table as shrink-to-fit, so Internet Explorer should be targeted explicitly, or all browsers except Internet Explorer should be given the `width: 100%;` declaration in addition to the `table-layout: fixed;` declaration. If `table-layout: fixed;` and `width: 100%;` are applied in the style sheet that all browsers see, you can apply a `width: auto;` declaration in a style sheet that appears in Internet Explorer only. You can use conditional comments to prevent Internet Explorer from seeing the `width: 100%;` declaration because the cascade overrides the original `width: 100%;` declaration.

❑ If the element is a block element, like a `<div>` or `<p>` element, avoid applying the 100% width at all because a block-level element expands to fill all available space.

❑ Specify a smaller percentage to correct the bug.

Any of the preceding solutions prevent the top margin from appearing above elements that follow a floating element with 100% width. In fact, all these solutions involve completely avoiding applying a 100% width. The next section discusses how to install multiple versions of Internet Explorer using only one installation of Windows.

Installing Multiple Versions of Internet Explorer

When designing content for the web, it is helpful if you install multiple versions of browsers so that a design can be tested as extensively as possible against as many environments as possible. The problem is Internet Explorer. The most popular browser at the time of this writing, by design, cannot be installed more than once; although browsers like Mozilla and Netscape can be. For Mozilla, Firefox, and Netscape, all that you have to do is simply change the name of the destination directory while installing the browser. Multiple versions of Netscape and Mozilla can even be run at the same time, provided that a different user profile is given for each browser running. With Internet Explorer, the process isn't quite so obvious and involves downloading a hacked version of older Internet Explorer browsers.

To test your design on multiple versions of Internet Explorer using the same Windows computer, visit one of the following URLs and follow the instructions provided. I have included more than one URL. In the event that one website is no longer available, an alternative will likely still be available. The multiple IE solution presented on both websites is identical.

- ❑ Quirks Mode - `http://www.quirksmode.org/index.html?/browsers/multipleie.html`
- ❑ Chicago Web design - `http://www.insert-title.com/web_design/?page=articles/dev/multi_IE`

All you have to do to install the older versions of Internet Explorer is download the required zip archive, unzip the archive to the directory of your choice, and then open the IEXPLORE.EXE file. Presto, you have a functioning multiple IE set-up. To make things easier, you can create shortcuts to the IEXPLORE.EXE file, giving each shortcut its appropriate version number.

Installing multiple versions of Internet Explorer is necessary if you want to perform the next Try It Out exercise; however, if you don't have access to the Internet or are not using a Windows computer, you can follow along with the exercise in principle.

The Caveats

There are but a few caveats if you use this method of installing older versions of Internet Explorer on the same installation of Windows. The first is that, no matter which Internet Explorer you are using, Internet Explorer says that it is IE 6. This affects the use of conditional comments; conditional comments also say that the version of IE is version 6. This makes it impossible to test conditional comments using this solution. Other browser features, like Favorites, Print Preview, and so on, may cause IE to crash.

Now that you've seen how a website can be tested on the same computer using multiple versions of Internet Explorer, the following Try It Out finishes up the JT's Island Grill and Gallery website by addressing a few anomalies between IE 5, 5.5, and 6 for Windows.

Try It Out   **Finalizing the JT's Island Grill and Gallery Website**

Example 18-4. With these steps, you can complete the JT's dinner menu.

1.   Start a new document in your text editor and enter the following CSS:

```
ul.menu a {
    width: 100%;
}
div#nav > div > ul {
    top: 2.89em;
}
```

2.   Create a new directory in the `style_sheets` directory and call this directory `ie`.

3.   Save the preceding CSS as `ie6.css` in the `ie` directory that you just created.

4.   Start a new document, and enter the following CSS:

```
* {
    text-align: left;
}
body {
    text-align: center;
}
ul#gifts, ul#food {
    top: 60px;
}
div#nav {
    width: 100%;
    text-align: center;
}
div#nav > div > a > img {
    text-align: center;
}
div#nav > div > ul {
    top: 48px;
}
div#nav > div > ul > li {
    width: 117px;
}
div#nav span {
    text-align: center;
}
ul.menu {
    top: 30px;
    width: 225px;
}
ul.menu a {
    margin-left: -10px;
}
ul#food ul.menu {
    right: -2px;
}
```

5. Save this document in the `ie` directory as `ie5-5.css`.

6. Make the following modifications to dinner_menu.html to link up to the style sheets that you just created:

```
<!DOCTYPE html PUBLIC "-/pp/W3C//DTD XHTML 1.0 Strict//EN"
"http://www.w3.org/TR/xhtml1/DTD/xhtml1-strict.dtd">
<html>
    <head>
        <title>
            JT's Island Grill and Gallery - Chokoloskee, Florida
        </title>
        <!-- compliance patch for microsoft browsers -->
        <!--[if lt IE 7]>
        <script src="/ie7/ie7-standard-p.js" type="text/javascript">
        </script>
        <![endif]-->
        <link rel='stylesheet' type='text/css'
            href='style_sheets/base_styles.css' media='screen'/>
        <link rel='stylesheet' type='text/css'
            href='style_sheets/menu_system.css' media='screen'/>
        <link rel='stylesheet' type='text/css'
            href='style_sheets/dinner_menu.css' media='screen'/>
        <link rel='stylesheet' type='text/css'
            href='style_sheets/handheld.css' media='handheld'/>
        <link rel='stylesheet' type='text/css'
            href='style_sheets/print.css' media='print'/>
        <!--[if lt IE 7]>
        <link rel='stylesheet' type='text/css'
            href='style_sheets/ie/ie6.css' media='screen'/>
        <![endif]-->
        <!--[if lt IE 6]>
        <link rel='stylesheet' type='text/css'
            href='style_sheets/ie/ie5-5.css' media='screen'/>
        <![endif]-->
    </head>
```

7. Save dinner_menu.html. See the end result in Figure 18-16.

How It Works

This example addresses a number of inconsistencies with the presentation of the JT's Island Grill and Gallery dinner menu in Internet Explorer for Windows. Each modification has made the design more consistent with how Mozilla 1.7 and Opera 7.5 render the page. The first modifications were targeted at Internet Explorer 6 specifically:

```
ul.menu a {
    width: 100%;
}
div#nav > div > ul {
    top: 2.89em;
}
```

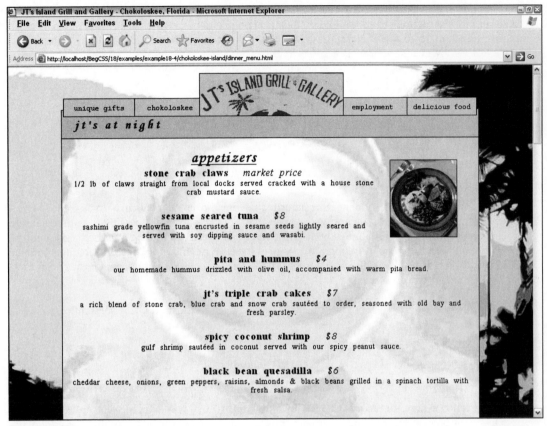

Figure 18-16

The first rule fixes a bug with the links in each drop-down menu. By adding the `width: 100%;` declaration, you make the links are clickable from anywhere in the highlighted box, instead of only when the mouse cursor is hovering over text. You may have noticed in Example 18-3 that when the IE7 solution was applied, a slight inconsistency existed in the positioning of the JT's logo in Internet Explorer versus Mozilla's positioning of the logo. This inconsistency is corrected with a tweak of the top offset property for IE 6, which is shown in the second rule of the preceding code.

Like the IE7, conditional comments are used to target Internet Explorer 6 and earlier versions specifically.

```
<!--[if lt IE 7]>
<link rel='stylesheet' type='text/css'
    href='style_sheets/ie/ie6.css' media='screen'/>
<![endif]-->
```

The fixes applied in the IE 6 style sheet are likely to apply to IE 5.5 and 5 as well, so the conditional comments allow IE 5.5 and 5 to see the style sheet, as well, by specifying all Internet Explorers less than version 7. Conditional comments were introduced in Internet Explorer 5, so IE 4 won't see anything at all.

The next modifications address IE 5.5. IE 5.5 has trouble with a few areas of the JT's dinner menu. First, it has trouble interpreting the em unit when it is used on positioned elements. Secondly, IE 5.5 does not support the margin: auto; declaration, which if you recall from Chapter 10 is used to center block elements. It does however support use of text-align: center; to accomplish the same thing, even though this is incorrect per the W3C CSS specifications. To center the dinner menu, a text-align: center; declaration is applied to the <body> element:

```
*  {
    text-align: left;
}
body {
    text-align: center;
}
```

Remember that text-align: center; is inherited by all children elements in a document. To circumvent the effects of inheritance, you apply a text-align: left; declaration using the universal selector. This gives *all* elements left-aligned text. Then, you must specify explicitly anywhere text must be center aligned, which is done by taking advantage of the cascade. If you recall from Chapter 7, the universal selector has a specificity of zero, so rules with a greater specificity can override the declarations specified using the universal selector.

The next rule specifies the position of the gifts <ul> element and the food <ul> element in pixels instead of em:

```
ul#gifts, ul#food {
    top: 60px;
}
```

This modification is necessary to make the design appear consistent with IE 6, Mozilla, and Opera, because IE 5.5 has some bugs when applying em units to positioned elements. The next modification adds 100% width to the nav <div> element, which corrects IE 5 and 5.5's positioning of the navigation bar.

```
div#nav {
    width: 100%;
    text-align: center;
}
```

Before you add the 100% width and text-align: center; declaration, the navigation is on the left side of the screen. With these modifications applied, it is centered. The next modification centers the JT's logo.

```
div#nav > div > a > img {
    text-align: center;
}
```

Although it seems strange to apply text-align: center; on an image to make it centered, it works here because the logo image was converted to a block-level element in the menu_system.css style sheet. Because margin: auto; doesn't work in IE 5 and 5.5, the image is centered with a text-align: center; declaration.

The next modifications do two things. First, they reimplement center-aligned text in the headings of the navigation because inheritance was overridden via the universal selector. Next, em measurements are converted into pixel measurements.

```
div#nav > div > ul {
    top: 48px;
}
div#nav > div > ul > li {
    width: 117px;
}
div#nav span {
    text-align: center;
}
ul.menu {
    top: 30px;
    width: 225px;
}
```

Without pixel measurements, IE 5.5 renders a very unprofessional-appearing navigation; with these in place, everything goes where it is supposed to go. The final two modifications tweak positioning of elements.

```
ul.menu a {
    margin-left: -10px;
}
ul#food ul.menu {
    right: -2px;
}
```

The first modification prevents a gap from appearing on the left of each link in each drop-down menu. The second tweaks the positioning of the drop downs to the right of the logo, so the right border of drop downs on the right side of the logo line up with the right border of each heading on the right side of the logo.

> It's important to note that some of the design inconsistencies between IE 5.5 and IE 6 also resulted from application of the IE7 package. Remember this solution is an alpha software package at the time of writing. Even in this early state of development, it provides impressive and immediate help with IE CSS support quandaries. That being said, because IE7 is an evolving solution, some of the modifications applied in this style sheet may become unnecessary using a newer version of the IE7 package. The examples in this chapter use version 0.7.2 alpha.

Additional CSS Resources

A multitude of websites exists for CSS how-to, articles, experiments, and other general discussion. A few of the websites that I frequent most and personally recommend are:

❏ A List Apart - http://www.alistapart.com

❏ Position is Everything - http://www.positioniseverything.net

❏ Quirks Mode - http://www.quirksmode.org

❑ CSS Zen Garden - `http://www.csszengarden.com`

❑ Eric Meyer's website - `http://www.meyerweb.com`

There are also a few venues that exist to help newcomers and veterans alike through forums and mailing lists. The two that I use most frequently are:

❑ Wrox Programmer to Programmer (P2P) - `http://p2p.wrox.com`

❑ CSS Discussion (mailing list): `http://css-discss.incutio.com`

Summary

CSS designs go far beyond what HTML alone is capable of. In this chapter, you've seen that CSS can often be used to overcome differences in how browsers render web pages. In this chapter, you've learned the following:

❑ How to install an HTTP server to server and test web pages on your own computer.

❑ What the IE7 package is and how to deploy this solution in a web page.

❑ How to recognize and fix a few of the most common CSS bugs in Internet Explorer.

❑ How to use conditional comments to target specific versions of Internet Explorer for Windows.

Exercises

1. Apply the IE7 package to the Widgets and What's-its FAQ page that you completed for Chapter 15, Exercise 2.

2. Identify and fix the Internet Explorer 6 rendering bugs in the following document:

```
<!DOCTYPE html PUBLIC "-/pp/W3C//DTD XHTML 1.0 Strict//EN"
"http://www.w3.org/TR/xhtml1/DTD/xhtml1-strict.dtd">
<html>
    <head>
        <title>Oops</title>
        <style type='text/css'>
            body {
                font: 1em sans-serif;
            }
            div#content {
                background: lightblue;
                padding: 10px;
                border: 1px solid black;
            }
            div#nav {
                float: left;
                margin-left: 10px;
```

```
                    background: lightsteelblue;
                    width: 150px;
                    border: 1px solid black;
                }
            div#nav ul {
                    list-style: none;
                    padding: 0;
                    margin: 0;
                }
            div#nav a {
                    color: black;
                    display: block;
                    width: 100%;
                    margin: 4px;
                    padding: 4px;
                    text-decoration: none;
                    border: 1px solid lightsteelblue;
                }
            div#nav a:hover {
                    border: 1px solid black;
                    background: steelblue;
                    color: white;
                }
            div#gallery {
                    margin-left: 200px;
                    padding: 10px;
                    border: 1px solid black;
                    text-align: center;
                }
            div#gallery a:hover {
                    background: seagreen;
                    color: white;
                }
            div#gallery img {
                    border: 1px solid black;
                    width: 10em;
                    height: auto;
                }
        </style>
    </head>
    <body>
        <div id='content'>
            <div id='nav'>
                <ul>
                    <li><a href='#'>Home</a></li>
                    <li><a href='#'>About us</a></li>
                    <li><a href='#'>Products</a></li>
                    <li><a href='#'>Services</a></li>
                    <li><a href='#'>FAQ</a></li>
                    <li><a href='#'>Privacy Statement</a></li>
                    <li><a href='#'>Site Usage Agreement</a></li>
                </ul>
```

```
            </div>
            <div id='body'>
                <div id='gallery'>
                        <a href='oops.jpg'><img src='oops.jpg'/></a><br/>
                        <a href='oops.jpg'>Larger image</a>
                    </div>
                </div>
            </div>
        </body>
    </html>
```

A

Exercise Answers

Chapter 2

Exercise 1 solution

An HTML page:

```
<!DOCTYPE HTML PUBLIC "-//W3C//DTD HTML 4.01 Transitional//EN">
    <HTML>
        <HEAD>
            <TITLE>My favorite Movies</TITLE>
        </HEAD>
        <BODY>
            <TABLE BORDER=0 WIDTH=500>
                <TR>
                    <TH COLSPAN=3 BGCOLOR=#000000>
                        <FONT COLOR=#FFFFFF>
                            My Favorite Movies
                        </FONT>
                    </TH>
                </TR>
                <TR>
                    <TH BGCOLOR=#000000>
                        <FONT COLOR=#FFFFFF>
                            Title
                        </FONT>
                    </TH>
                    <TH BGCOLOR=#000000>
                        <FONT COLOR=#FFFFFF>
                            Actor/Actress
                        </FONT>
                    </TH>
                    <TH BGCOLOR=#000000>
                        <FONT COLOR=#FFFFFF>
                            Genre
                        </FONT>
```

```
                    </TH>
                </tr>
                <TR>
                    <TD>What Dreams May Come</TD>
                    <TD>Robin Williams, Annabella Sciorra</TD>
                    <TD>Drama</TD>
                </TR>
                <TR>
                    <TD>Stir of Echoes</TD>
                    <TD>Kevin Bacon, Kathryn Erbe</TD>
                    <TD>Horror</TD>
                </TR>
                <TR>
                    <TD>Groundhog Day</TD>
                    <TD>Bill Murray, Andie MacDowell</TD>
                    <TD>Comedy</TD>
                </TR>
            </TABLE>
        </BODY>
    </HTML>
```

An XML page:

```
<?xml version="1.0" encoding="ISO-8859-1" ?>
<movies>
    <title>My favorite Movies</title>
    <movie>
        <picture>What Dreams May Come</picture>
        <talent>Robin Williams, Annabella Sciorra</talent>
        <genre>Drama</genre>
    </movie>
    <movie>
        <picture>Stir of Echoes</picture>
        <talent>Kevin Bacon, Kathryn Erbe</talent>
        <genre>Horror</genre>
    </movie>
    <movie>
        <picture>Groundhog Day</picture>
        <talent>Bill Murray, Andie MacDowell</talent>
        <genre>Comedy</genre>
    </movie>
</movies>
```

An XHTML page:

```
<!DOCTYPE html PUBLIC "-//W3C//DTD XHTML 1.0 Strict//EN"
"http://www.w3.org/TR/xhtml1/DTD/xhtml1-strict.dtd">
    <html>
        <head>
            <title>My favorite Movies</title>
            <style type='text/css' media='all'>
             table {
                 border-width: 0px;
                 width: 500px;
```

```
            }
            th {
                background: black;
                color: white;
            }
            #footer {
                background: darkgray;
                color: white;
            }
            </style>
    </head>
    <body>
        <table>
            <tr>
                <th colspan='3'>
                    My Favorite Movies
                </th>
            </tr>
            <tr>
                <th>
                    Title
                </th>
                <th>
                    Actor/Actress
                </th>
                <th>
                    Genre
                </th>
            </tr>
            <tr>
                <td>What Dreams May Come</td>
                <td>Robin Williams, Annabella Sciorra</td>
                <td>Drama</td>
            </tr>
            <tr>
                <td>Stir of Echoes</td>
                <td>Kevin Bacon, Kathryn Erbe</td>
                <td>Horror</td>
            </tr>
            <tr>
                <td>Groundhog Day</td>
                <td>Bill Murray, Andie MacDowell</td>
                <td>Comedy</td>
            </tr>
        </table>
    </body>
</html>
```

Exercise 2 solution

Quirks mode relies on nonstandard methods of delivering presentational content. For instance, in Internet Explorer, quirks mode initiates an incorrect interpretation of the CSS box model, whereas standards mode interprets the box model correctly. Standards mode is intended to follow the W3C recommendations to the letter.

Chapter 3

Exercise 1 solution

```
<!DOCTYPE html PUBLIC "-//W3C//DTD XHTML 1.0 Strict//EN"
"http://www.w3.org/TR/xhtml1/DTD/xhtml1-strict.dtd">
<html>
    <head>
        <meta http-equiv="content-type" content="text/xhtml; charset=windows-1252" />
        <meta http-equiv="content-language" content="en-us" />
        <title>Exercise 1</title>
        <style type="text/css" media="all">

            /* Paragraph text is black and in 12pt font */
            p {
                font-size: 12pt;
                color: black;
            }

            /* h1, h2 and p are in Times New Roman font */
            h1, h2, p {
                font-family: Times New Roman;
            }

            /* h1 and h2 have green text and 22pt font */
            h1, h2 {
                color: green;
                font-size: 22pt;
            }

        </style>
    </head>
    <body>
        <h1>
            Heading 1
        </h1>
        <h2>
            Heading 2
        </h2>
        <p>
            Some paragraph text.
        </p>
    </body>
</html>
```

Exercise 2 solution

Create an external CSS file; save it as exercise3-2.css:

```
/* Paragraph text is black and in 12pt font */
p {
    font-size: 12pt;
    color: black;
}
```

```
    /* h1, h2 and p are in Times New Roman font */
    h1, h2, p {
        font-family: Times New Roman;
    }

    /* h1 and h2 have green text */
    h1, h2 {
        color: green;
        font-size: 22pt;
    }
```

Next, link to the file using the `<link>` tag or `@import` notation; either is acceptable.

Using the `<link>` tag:

```
<!DOCTYPE html PUBLIC "-//W3C//DTD XHTML 1.0 Strict//EN"
"http://www.w3.org/TR/xhtml1/DTD/xhtml1-strict.dtd">
<html>
    <head>
     <meta http-equiv="content-type" content="text/xhtml; charset=windows-1252" />
     <meta http-equiv="content-language" content="en-us" />
        <title>Exercise 1</title>
        <link rel="stylesheet" href="exercise3-2.css" type="text/css" />
    </head>
    <body>
        <h1>
            Heading 1
        </h1>
        <h2>
            Heading 2
        </h2>
        <p>
            Some paragraph text.
        </p>
    </body>
</html>
```

Using the `@import` notation:

```
<!DOCTYPE html PUBLIC "-//W3C//DTD XHTML 1.0 Strict//EN"
"http://www.w3.org/TR/xhtml1/DTD/xhtml1-strict.dtd">
<html>
    <head>
     <meta http-equiv="content-type" content="text/xhtml; charset=windows-1252" />
     <meta http-equiv="content-language" content="en-us" />
        <title>Exercise 1</title>
        <style type="text/css">
            @import url(exercise3-2.css);
        </style>
    </head>
    <body>
        <h1>
            Heading 1
```

```
        </h1>
        <h2>
            Heading 2
        </h2>
        <p>
            Some paragraph text.
        </p>
    </body>
</html>
```

Exercise 3 solution

```
<!DOCTYPE html PUBLIC "-//W3C//DTD XHTML 1.0 Strict//EN"
"http://www.w3.org/TR/xhtml1/DTD/xhtml1-strict.dtd">
<html>
    <head>
     <meta http-equiv="content-type" content="text/xhtml; charset=windows-1252" />
     <meta http-equiv="content-language" content="en-us" />
        <title>Exercise 1</title>
    </head>
    <body>
        <h1 style='font-family: Times New Roman; color: green; font-size: 22pt;'>
            Heading 1
        </h1>
        <h2 style='font-family: Times New Roman; color: green; font-size: 22pt;'>
            Heading 2
        </h2>
        <p style='font-family: Times New Roman; color: black; font-size: 12pt;'>
            Some paragraph text.
        </p>
    </body>
</html>
```

Chapter 4

Exercise 1 solution

Your text and the value of the em units might be different, but your document should be similar in appearance to that generated by the following code:

```
<!DOCTYPE html PUBLIC "-//W3C//DTD XHTML 1.0 Strict//EN"
"http://www.w3.org/TR/xhtml1/DTD/xhtml1-strict.dtd">
<html>
    <head>
        <title> exercise 4-1 </title>
        <style type='text/css' media='all'>
            body {
                font-size: 12px;
            }
            h1 {
                font-size: 2.1em;
                background: pink;
                padding: 1em;
```

```
                    border: thin solid black;
            }
            p {
                font-size: 0.9em;
                padding: 1em;
                border: thin solid black;
                background: gray;
                color: white;
            }
        </style>
    </head>
    <body>
        <h1>
            This is a heading
        </h1>
        <p>
            This is a paragraph of text.
        </p>
    </body>
</html>
```

Exercise 2 solution

Again, as in Exercise 1, the value you use for the em units might be different than the one I use, so their conversion to pixel units might be different as well.

```
<!DOCTYPE html PUBLIC "-//W3C//DTD XHTML 1.0 Strict//EN"
"http://www.w3.org/TR/xhtml1/DTD/xhtml1-strict.dtd">
<html>
    <head>
        <title> exercise 4-2 </title>
        <style type='text/css' media='all'>
            body {
                font-size: 12px;
            }
            h1 {
                font-size: 25px;
                background: rgb(255, 192, 203);
                padding: 25px;
                border: thin solid rgb(0, 0, 0);
            }
            p {
                font-size: 11px;
                padding: 11px;
                border: thin solid rgb(0, 0, 0);
                background: rgb(128, 128, 128);
                color: rgb(255, 255, 255);
            }
        </style>
    </head>
    <body>
        <h1>
            This is a heading
        </h1>
```

```
        <p>
            This is a paragraph of text.
        </p>
    </body>
</html>
```

Chapter 5

Exercise 1 solution

```
<!DOCTYPE html PUBLIC "-//W3C//DTD XHTML 1.0 Strict//EN"
"http://www.w3.org/TR/xhtml1/DTD/xhtml1-strict.dtd">
<html>
    <head>
        <style type="text/css">
            * {
                font-family: sans-serif;
                color: white;
            }
            h1, form h2 {
                background: gray;
            }
            h1, h2, form {
                margin: 0;
            }
            h1 {
                font-size: 24px;
                padding: 5px;
                border-bottom: 5px solid black;
                letter-spacing: -2px;
                width: 510px;
                -moz-border-radius-topleft: 10px;
                -moz-border-radius-topright: 10px;
            }
            form {
                background: lightgrey;
                padding: 10px;
                width: 500px;
                -moz-border-radius-bottomleft: 10px;
                -moz-border-radius-bottomright: 10px;
            }
            form label {
                display: block;
                font-weight: bold;
                margin: 5px;
                width: 225px;
                text-align: right;
                background: black;
                float: left;
            }
            form h2, form label {
                font-size: 15px;
                -moz-border-radius: 10px;
```

```
        padding: 3px;
}
form div {
    clear: left;
}
div input, div select, div textarea {
    margin: 3px;
    padding: 4px;
    background: darkgray;
    font-weight: bold;
}
select {
    color: darkgreen;
}
option {
    padding: 4px;
    letter-spacing: 2px;
}
#newspaper {
    background: orange;
}
#magazine {
    background: red;
}
#radio {
    background: green;
}
#other {
    background: blue;
}
#name {
    color: darkred;
}
#email {
    color: darkblue;
}
#address {
    color: purple;
}
#television, #message {
    color: black;
}
label.spanform {
    float: none;
    width: auto;
    text-align: left;
}
div.spanform {
    text-align: center;
}
div#buttons {
    text-align: right;
}
input#button {
```

```
                    background: black;
                    font-weight: bold;
                    border: 1px solid white;
                }
            div#copyright {
                    margin-top: 10px;
                    border-top: 1px dashed black;
                    padding-top: 10px;
                    font-size: 10px;
                    text-align: center;
                    color: black;
                }
        </style>
        <title>Feedback Form - Widgets and What's-its</title>
    </head>
    <body>
        <h1>Widgets and What's-its</h1>
        <form>
            <h2>Tell us what's on your mind..</h2>
            <div>
                <label for='feedback[name]'>Name:</label>
                <input type='text' size='25' id='name' name='feedback[name]' />
            </div>
            <div>
                <label for='feedback[email]'>Email:</label>
                <input type='text' size='25' id='email' name='feedback[email]' />
            </div>
            <div class='spanform'>
                <label for='feedback[address]' class='spanform'>Address:</label>
                <textarea name='feedback[address]'
                        id='address' cols='40' rows='3' wrap='virtual'>
                </textarea>
            </div>
            <div class='spanform'>
                <label for='feedback[message]' class='spanform'>Comments:</label>
                <textarea name='feedback[message]'
                        id='message' cols='40' rows='6' wrap='virtual'>
                </textarea>
            </div>
            <div>
                <label for='feedback[heard]'>How'd you hear about us?</label>
                <select name='feedback[heard]'>
                    <option value=''>Choose...</option>
                    <option id='newspaper' value='newspaper'>Newspaper</option>
                    <option id='magazine' value='magazine'>Magazine</option>
                    <option id='television' value='television'>Television</option>
                    <option id='radio' value='radio'>Radio</option>
                    <option id='other' value='other'>Other</option>
                </select>
            </div>
            <div id='buttons'>
                <input type='submit'
                        name='feedback[action]' value='Submit' id='button' />
            </div>
```

```
            <div id='copyright'>
                &copy; Copyright 2004 What's-its and Widgets, All Rights Reserved.
            </div>
        </form>
    </body>
</html>
```

Exercise 2 solution

```
<!DOCTYPE html PUBLIC "-//W3C//DTD XHTML 1.0 Strict//EN"
"http://www.w3.org/TR/xhtml1/DTD/xhtml1-strict.dtd">
<html>
    <head>
        <style type="text/css">
            * {
                font-family: sans-serif;
                color: honeydew;
            }
            form h2 {
                background: seagreen;
            }
            h1, h2, form {
                margin: 0;
            }
            h1 {
                background: black;
                font-size: 18pt;
                padding: 5px;
                border-bottom: 5px dashed seagreen;
                letter-spacing: -2px;
                -moz-border-radius-topleft: 10px;
                -moz-border-radius-topright: 10px;
            }
            form {
                background: teal;
                padding: 10px;
                -moz-border-radius-bottomleft: 10px;
                -moz-border-radius-bottomright: 10px;
            }
            form label {
                display: block;
                margin: 5px;
                width: 50%;
                text-align: right;
                background: black;
                float: left;
            }
            form h2, form label {
                font-size: 11pt;
                -moz-border-radius: 10px;
                padding: 3px;
            }
            form div {
                clear: left;
```

```
            }
        div input, div textarea {
            margin: 3px;
            padding: 4px;
            background: yellowgreen;
            font-weight: bold;
            -moz-border-radius: 10px;
            color: black;
        }
        label.spanform {
            float: none;
            width: auto;
            text-align: left;
        }
        div.spanform {
            text-align: center;
        }
        div#buttons {
            text-align: right;
        }
        input#button {
            background: black;
            font-weight: bold;
            -moz-border-radius: 10px;
            color: white;
        }
        div#copyright {
            margin-top: 10px;
            border-top: 2px dashed black;
            padding-top: 10px;
            font-size: 8pt;
            text-align: center;
        }
    </style>
    <title>Feedback Form - Tuff Stuff</title>
</head>
<body>
    <h1>Tuff Stuff</h1>
    <form>
        <h2>What up? You have something to say?</h2>
        <div>
            <label for='feedback[name]'>Name:</label>
            <input type='text' size='25' name='feedback[name]' />
        </div>
        <div>
            <label for='feedback[email]'>Email:</label>
            <input type='text' size='25' name='feedback[email]' />
        </div>
        <div class='spanform'>
            <label for='feedback[message]' class='spanform'>
                Comments:
            </label>
            <textarea name='feedback[message]'
                    cols='40' rows='6' wrap='virtual'>
```

```
                </textarea>
            </div>
            <div id='buttons'>
                <input type='submit' name='feedback[action]'
                        value='Submit' id='button' />
            </div>
            <div id='copyright'>
                &copy; Copyright 2004 Tuff Stuff, All Rights Reserved.
            </div>
        </form>
    </body>
</html>
```

Chapter 6

Exercise 1 solution

Using the exercise file you made for Chapter 5, Exercise 1, make the following changes to the document.

1.   Add the following CSS to the embedded style sheet:

```
div#copyright {
    margin-top: 10px;
    border-top: 1px dashed black;
    padding-top: 10px;
    font-size: 8pt;
    text-align: center;
    color: black;
}
ul#navigation {
    list-style: none;
    background: gray;
    margin: 2px;
    padding: 0;
}
ul#navigation li {
    float: left;
    margin: 5px;
}
form {
    clear: left;
}

ul#navigation li a {
    padding: 5px;
}
ul#navigation li a:link {
    background: gray;
}
ul#navigation li a:active {
    background: orange;
}
ul#navigation li a:visited {
```

```
            background: black;
        }
        ul#navigation li a:hover, li a:focus {
            background: white;
            color: black;
        }
        input:focus, textarea:focus, select:focus {
            background: white;
        }

    </style>
    <title>Feedback Form - Widgets and What's-its</title>
</head>
```

2. Add the following markup to the body of the document:

```
<body>
    <h1>Widgets and What's-its</h1>

    <ul>
        <li><a href=''>home</a></li>
        <li><a href=''>contact us</a></li>
        <li><a href=''>products</a></li>
        <li><a href=''>services</a></li>
        <li><a href=''>faq</a></li>
    </ul>

    <form>
        <h2>Tell us what's on your mind..</h2>
        <div>
            <h3>Name:</h3>
            <input type='text' size='25' id='name' name='feedback[name]' />
        </div>
```

Exercise 2 solution

```
<!DOCTYPE html PUBLIC "-//W3C//DTD XHTML 1.0 Strict//EN"
"http://www.w3.org/TR/xhtml1/DTD/xhtml1-strict.dtd">
<html>
    <head>
      <meta http-equiv="content-type" content="text/xhtml; charset=windows-1252" />
      <meta http-equiv="content-language" content="en-us" />
        <style type="text/css">
            * {
                font-family: sans-serif;
                color: white;
            }
            h1, h2 {
                margin: 0;
                background: gray;
            }
            h1 {
                font-size: 18pt;
                padding: 5px;
```

```
        border-bottom: 5px solid black;
        letter-spacing: -2px;
        width: 510px;
        -moz-border-radius-topleft: 10px;
        -moz-border-radius-topright: 10px;
}
div {
        background: lightgrey;
        padding: 10px;
        width: 500px;
        -moz-border-radius-bottomleft: 10px;
        -moz-border-radius-bottomright: 10px;
        clear: left;
}
h2 {
        font-size: 11pt;
        -moz-border-radius: 10px;
        padding: 3px;
}
ul#navigation {
        list-style: none;
        background: gray;
        margin: 2px;
        padding: 0;
}
ul#navigation li {
        float: left;
        margin: 5px;
}
ul#navigation li a {
        padding: 5px;
}
ul#navigation li a:link {
        background: gray;
}
ul#navigation li a:active {
        background: orange;
}
ul#navigation li a:visited {
        background: black;
}
ul#navigation li a:hover, li a:focus {
        background: white;
        color: black;
}

ul#top {
        color: black;
}

h3, p {
        color: black;
}

p {
```

```
                border: 1px solid black;
                padding: 10px;
            }
            h3:target {
                color: yellow;
                background: red;
            }

            ul#top li a {
                color: black;
            }

    </style>
    <title>FAQ - Widgets and What's-its</title>
</head>
<body>
    <h1>Widgets and What's-its</h1>
    <ul id='navigation'>
        <li><a href=''>home</a></li>
        <li><a href=''>contact us</a></li>
        <li><a href=''>products</a></li>
        <li><a href=''>services</a></li>
        <li><a href=''>faq</a></li>
    </ul>
    <div>
        <h2>faq</h2>
        <ul id='top'>
            <li><a href='#widgets'>Q. What are widgets?</a></li>
            <li><a href='#why'>Q. Why should I buy a widget?</a></li>
            <li><a href='#where'>Q. Where do widgets come from?</a></li>
            <li><a href='#what'>Q. What are widgets made of?</a></li>
            <li><a href='#how'>Q. How do I use my widget?</a></li>
            <li><a href='#who'>Q. Who uses widgets?</a></li>
        </ul>
        <h3 id='widgets'>Q. What are widgets? <a href='#top'>top</a></h3>
        <p>
            A. Widgets are a smaller, more compact version of what's its.
        </p>
        <h3 id='why'>Q. Why should I buy a widget? <a href='#top'>top</a></h3>
        <p>
            A. Because widgets will solve all of you problems.
        </p>
        <h3 id='where'>
            Q. Where do widgets come from? <a href='#top'>top</a>
        </h3>
        <p>
            A. Widgets are harvested from the Amazon rain forest by
            little green gnomes.
        </p>
        <h3 id='what'>Q. What are widgets made of? <a href='#top'>top</a></h3>
        <p>
            A. Widgets are made of primordial, esoteric matter, and as
            such could cause your head to explode into one of seven
            fun-filled colors.
```

```
            </p>
            <h3 id='how'>Q. How do I use my widget? <a href='#top'>top</a></h3>
            <p>
                A. You must summon a troll using our proprietary magic wand and
                book of spells who will teach you everything you need to know
                about your widget.
            </p>
            <h3 id='who'>Q. Who uses widgets? <a href='#top'>top</a></h3>
            <p>
                A. Day traders and postal workers, primarily.
            </p>
        </div>
    </body>
</html>
```

Chapter 7

Exercise 1 solution

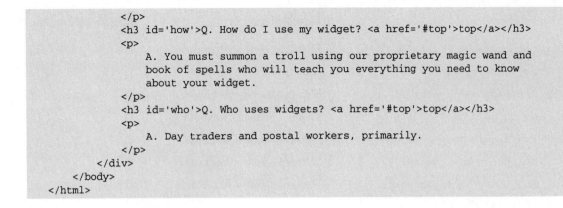

Selector	Selector type	Specificity
*	Universal	0
h1, form h2	Element name, Descendant	1 (for the first selector) 2 (for the second selector)
h1, h2, form	Element name	1 (for each selector)
h1	Element name	1
form	Element name	1
form h3	Descendant	2
form h2, form h3	Descendant, Descendant	2 (for each selector)
form > div > h3	Direct Child	3
form > div	Direct Child	2
div > input, div > select	Direct Child	2 (for each selector)
select > option	Direct Child	2
h3 + input, h3 + select, h3 + textarea	Adjacent Sibling	2 (each selector)
option[value]	Element Name + Attribute	11
option[value='newspaper']	Element Name + Attribute	11
option[value='television']	Element Name + Attribute	11
option[value='radio']	Element Name + Attribute	11

Table continued on following page

Selector	Selector type	Specificity
`option[value='other']`	Element Name + Attribute	11
`input[name$='[name]']`	Element Name + Attribute	11
`input[name$='[email]']`	Element Name + Attribute	11
`textarea[name$='[address]']`	Element Name + Attribute	11
`textarea[name$='[message]']`	Element Name + Attribute	11
`select[name$='[heard]']`	Element Name + Attribute	11

`input[name^='feedback'],`
`select[name^='feedback'],`
`textarea[name^='feedback']`
	Element Name + Attribute	11 (each selector)

`h3.spanform`	Element Name + Class Name	11
`div.spanform`	Element Name + Class Name	11
`div#buttons`	Element Name + ID Name	101
`input#button`	Element Name + ID Name	101
`div#copyright`	Element Name + ID Name	101

Exercise 2 solution

```
* {
    color: black !important;
    -moz-border-radius: 0 !important;
}
a:link, a {
    color: royalblue !important;
}
a:active {
    color: red !important;
}
a:visited {
    color: purple !important;
}
body {
    background: white !important;
}
div, table, td, h1, h2, h3, h4, h5, h6 {
    background: inherit !important;
}
input, select, textarea {
    padding: 5px !important;
    border: thin solid black !important;
    background-color: white !important;
    margin: 5px !important;
}
input:focus {
```

```
    background-color: red !important;
}
input[type='image'] {
    display: none !important;
}
img {
    display: none !important;
}
```

Chapter 8

Exercise 1 solution

The logical approach is to organize the website's files based on their usage in the website. Create a directory for the website's images. Within that directory, create one subdirectory dedicated to photos and another dedicated to paintings or artwork in general. Next, create a directory for style sheets, and within that directory create a subdirectory for each skin.

Exercise 2 solution

The solution is to use the white-space property.

```
<!DOCTYPE html PUBLIC "-/pp/W3C//DTD XHTML 1.0 Strict//EN"
"http://www.w3.org/TR/xhtml1/DTD/xhtml1-strict.dtd">
<html>
    <head>
        <title></title>
        <style type='text/css'>
            body {
                white-space: pre;
            }
        </style>
    </head>
    <body>
ode

we are the music-makers,
and we are the dreamers of dreams,
wandering by lone sea-breakers,
and sitting by desolate streams.
world-losers and world-forsakers,
upon whom the pale moon gleams;
yet we are the movers and shakers,
of the world forever, it seems.

with wonderful deathless ditties
we build up the world's great cities,
and out of a fabulous story
we fashion an empire's glory:
one man with a dream, at pleasure,
shall go forth and conquer a crown;
and three with a new song's measure
can trample an empire down.
```

```
we, in the ages lying
in the buried past of the earth,
built Nineveh with our sighing,
and Babel itself with our mirth;
and o'erthrew them with prophesying
to the old of the new world's worth;
for each age is a dream that is dying,
or one that is coming to birth.

Arthur O'Shaughnessy
    </body>
</html>
```

Exercise 3 solution

```
<!DOCTYPE html PUBLIC "-/pp/W3C//DTD XHTML 1.0 Strict//EN"
"http://www.w3.org/TR/xhtml1/DTD/xhtml1-strict.dtd">
<html>
    <head>
        <title></title>
        <style type='text/css'>
            body {
                width: 200px;
            }
            h1::first-letter, p::first-letter {
                text-transform: capitalize;
            }
            h1 {
                text-align: center;
                text-decoration: underline;
            }
            p {
                text-indent: 25px;
                text-align: justify;
                letter-spacing: 1px;
                word-spacing: 5px;
            }

        </style>
    </head>
    <body>
        <h1>ode</h1>
        <p>we are the music-makers,</p>
        <p>And we are the dreamers of dreams,</p>
        <p>wandering by lone sea-breakers,</p>
        <p>and sitting by desolate streams.</p>
        <p>world-losers and world-forsakers,</p>
        <p>upon whom the pale moon gleams;</p>
        <p>yet we are the movers and shakers,</p>
        <p>of the world forever, it seems.</p>

        <p>with wonderful deathless ditties</p>
        <p>We build up the world's great cities,</p>
        <p>And out of a fabulous story</p>
```

```
        <p>We fashion an empire's glory:</p>
        <p>One man with a dream, at pleasure,</p>
        <p>Shall go forth and conquer a crown;</p>
        <p>And three with a new song's measure</p>
        <p>Can trample an empire down.</p>

        <p>We, in the ages lying</p>
        <p>In the buried past of the earth,</p>
        <p>Built Nineveh with our sighing,</p>
        <p>And Babel itself with our mirth;</p>
        <p>And o'erthrew them with prophesying</p>
        <p>To the old of the new world's worth;</p>
        <p>For each age is a dream that is dying,</p>
        <p>Or one that is coming to birth.</p>
        Arthur O'Shaughnessy
    </body>
</html>
```

Chapter 9

Exercise 1 solution

```
<!DOCTYPE html PUBLIC "-/pp/W3C//DTD XHTML 1.0 Strict//EN"
"http://www.w3.org/TR/xhtml1/DTD/xhtml1-strict.dtd">
<html>
    <head>
        <title></title>
        <style type='text/css'>
            h1::first-letter, p::first-letter {
                text-transform: capitalize;
            }
            h1 {
                font-weight: normal;
                text-align: center;
                text-decoration: underline;
                font-family: "Monotype Corsiva";
            }
            p {
                text-indent: 25px;
                text-align: justify;
                letter-spacing: 1px;
                word-spacing: 5px;
            }
            p::first-letter {
                font-style: italic;
                font-size: 120%;
            }
        </style>
    </head>
    <body>
        <h1>ode</h1>
        <p>we are the music-makers,</p>
        <p>And we are the dreamers of dreams,</p>
```

```
<p>wandering by lone sea-breakers,</p>
<p>and sitting by desolate streams.</p>
<p>world-losers and world-forsakers,</p>
<p>upon whom the pale moon gleams;</p>
<p>yet we are the movers and shakers,</p>
<p>of the world forever, it seems.</p>

<p>with wonderful deathless ditties</p>
<p>We build up the world's great cities,</p>
<p>And out of a fabulous story</p>
<p>We fashion an empire's glory:</p>
<p>One man with a dream, at pleasure,</p>
<p>Shall go forth and conquer a crown;</p>
<p>And three with a new song's measure</p>
<p>Can trample an empire down.</p>

<p>We, in the ages lying</p>
<p>In the buried past of the earth,</p>
<p>Built Nineveh with our sighing,</p>
<p>And Babel itself with our mirth;</p>
<p>And o'erthrew them with prophesying</p>
<p>To the old of the new world's worth;</p>
<p>For each age is a dream that is dying,</p>
<p>Or one that is coming to birth.</p>
Arthur O'Shaughnessy
    </body>
</html>
```

Exercise 2 solution

The second question includes some trickery if you used the Monotype Corsiva font: It doesn't have an italic style!

```
<!DOCTYPE html PUBLIC "-/pp/W3C//DTD XHTML 1.0 Strict//EN"
"http://www.w3.org/TR/xhtml1/DTD/xhtml1-strict.dtd">
<html>
    <head>
        <title></title>
        <style type='text/css'>
            h1::first-letter, p::first-letter {
                text-transform: capitalize;
            }
            h1 {
                font-weight: normal;
                text-align: center;
                text-decoration: underline;
            }
            p {
                text-indent: 25px;
                text-align: justify;
                letter-spacing: 1px;
                word-spacing: 5px;
            }
            p::first-letter {
```

```
                        font: 120% "Monotype Corsiva";
                }
        </style>
    </head>
    <body>
        <h1>ode</h1>
        <p>we are the music-makers,</p>
        <p>And we are the dreamers of dreams,</p>
        <p>wandering by lone sea-breakers,</p>
        <p>and sitting by desolate streams.</p>
        <p>world-losers and world-forsakers,</p>
        <p>upon whom the pale moon gleams;</p>
        <p>yet we are the movers and shakers,</p>
        <p>of the world forever, it seems.</p>

        <p>with wonderful deathless ditties</p>
        <p>We build up the world's great cities,</p>
        <p>And out of a fabulous story</p>
        <p>We fashion an empire's glory:</p>
        <p>One man with a dream, at pleasure,</p>
        <p>Shall go forth and conquer a crown;</p>
        <p>And three with a new song's measure</p>
        <p>Can trample an empire down.</p>

        <p>We, in the ages lying</p>
        <p>In the buried past of the earth,</p>
        <p>Built Nineveh with our sighing,</p>
        <p>And Babel itself with our mirth;</p>
        <p>And o'erthrew them with prophesying</p>
        <p>To the old of the new world's worth;</p>
        <p>For each age is a dream that is dying,</p>
        <p>Or one that is coming to birth.</p>
        Arthur O'Shaughnessy
    </body>
</html>
```

Chapter 10

Exercise 1 solution

```
<!DOCTYPE html PUBLIC "-//W3C//DTD XHTML 1.0 Strict//EN"
"http://www.w3.org/TR/xhtml1/DTD/xhtml1-strict.dtd">
<html>
    <head>
        <meta http-equiv="content-type" content="text/xhtml; charset=windows-1252" />
        <meta http-equiv="content-language" content="en-us" />
        <style type="text/css">
            * {
                font-family: sans-serif;
                color: white;
            }
            body {
                margin: 0;
            }
```

```
h1, h2 {
    margin: 0;
    background: gray;
}
h1 {
    font-size: 1.6em;
    padding: 0.3em;
    border-bottom: 5px solid black;
    letter-spacing: -0.08em;
}
div {
    background: lightgrey;
    padding: 0.7em;
    clear: left;
}
h2 {
    font-size: 1em;
    padding: 0.2em;
}
ul#navigation {
    list-style: none;
    background: gray;
    margin: 0.1em;
    padding: 0;
}
ul#navigation li {
    float: left;
    margin: 0.4em;
}
ul#navigation li a {
    padding: 0.3em;
}
ul#navigation li a:link {
    background: gray;
}
ul#navigation li a:active {
    background: orange;
}
ul#navigation li a:visited {
    background: black;
}
ul#navigation li a:hover, li a:focus {
    background: white;
    color: black;
}

ul#top {
    color: black;
}

h3, p {
    color: black;
}
```

```
        p {
            border: 0.05em solid black;
            padding: 0.8em;
        }
        h3:target {
            color: yellow;
            background: red;
        }

        ul#top li a {
            color: black;
        }

    </style>
    <title>FAQ - Widgets and What's-its</title>
</head>
<body>
    <h1>Widgets and What's-its</h1>
    <ul id='navigation'>
        <li><a href=''>home</a></li>
        <li><a href=''>contact us</a></li>
        <li><a href=''>products</a></li>
        <li><a href=''>services</a></li>
        <li><a href=''>faq</a></li>
    </ul>
    <div>
        <h2>faq</h2>
        <ul id='top'>
            <li><a href='#widgets'>Q. What are widgets?</a></li>
            <li><a href='#why'>Q. Why should I buy a widget?</a></li>
            <li><a href='#where'>Q. Where do widgets come from?</a></li>
            <li><a href='#what'>Q. What are widgets made of?</a></li>
            <li><a href='#how'>Q. How do I use my widget?</a></li>
            <li><a href='#who'>Q. Who uses widgets?</a></li>
        </ul>
        <h3 id='widgets'>Q. What are widgets? <a href='#top'>top</a></h3>
        <p>
            A. Widgets are a smaller, more compact version of what's its.
        </p>
        <h3 id='why'>Q. Why should I buy a widget? <a href='#top'>top</a></h3>
        <p>
            A. Because widgets will solve all of you problems.
        </p>
        <h3 id='where'>Q. Where do widgets come from?
            <a href='#top'>top</a></h3>
        <p>
            A. Widgets are harvested from the Amazon rain forest by
            little green gnomes.
        </p>
        <h3 id='what'>Q. What are widgets made of? <a href='#top'>top</a></h3>
        <p>
            A. Widgets are made of primordial, esoteric matter, and as
            such could cause your head to explode into one of seven
            fun-filled colors.
```

```
        </p>
        <h3 id='how'>Q. How do I use my widget? <a href='#top'>top</a></h3>
        <p>
            A. You must summon a troll using our proprietary magic wand and
            book of spells who will teach you everything you need to know
            about your widget.
        </p>
        <h3 id='who'>Q. Who uses widgets? <a href='#top'>top</a></h3>
        <p>
            A. Day traders and postal workers, primarily.
        </p>
    </div>
  </body>
</html>
```

Exercise 2 solution

This rule is applied to the solution for Exercise 1.

```
body {
    margin: 0 auto;
    max-width: 50em;
    min-width: 30em;
}
```

Exercise 3 solution

```
<!DOCTYPE html PUBLIC "-//W3C//DTD XHTML 1.0 Strict//EN"
"http://www.w3.org/TR/xhtml1/DTD/xhtml1-strict.dtd">
<html>
    <head>
      <meta http-equiv="content-type" content="text/xhtml; charset=windows-1252" />
      <meta http-equiv="content-language" content="en-us" />
        <style type="text/css">
            * {
                font-family: sans-serif;
                color: white;
            }
            body {
                margin: 0;
            }
            div#body {
                margin: auto;
                max-width: 50em;
                min-width: 30em;
                max-height: 30em;
                overflow: auto;
            }
            h1, h2 {
                margin: 0;
                background: gray;
            }
            h1 {
```

```
        font-size: 1.6em;
        padding: 0.3em;
        border-bottom: 5px solid black;
        letter-spacing: -0.08em;
    }
    div#content {
        background: lightgrey;
        padding: 0.7em;
        clear: left;
    }
    h2 {
        font-size: 1em;
        padding: 0.2em;
    }
    ul#navigation {
        list-style: none;
        background: gray;
        margin: 0.1em;
        padding: 0;
    }
    ul#navigation li {
        float: left;
        margin: 0.4em;
    }
    ul#navigation li a {
        padding: 0.3em;
    }
    ul#navigation li a:link {
        background: gray;
    }
    ul#navigation li a:active {
        background: orange;
    }
    ul#navigation li a:visited {
        background: black;
    }
    ul#navigation li a:hover, li a:focus {
        background: white;
        color: black;
    }

    ul#top {
        color: black;
    }

    h3, p {
        color: black;
    }

    p {
        border: 0.05em solid black;
        padding: 0.8em;
    }
```

```
        h3:target {
            color: yellow;
            background: red;
        }

        ul#top li a {
            color: black;
        }

    </style>
    <title>FAQ - Widgets and What's-its</title>
</head>
<body>
    <div id='body'>
        <h1>Widgets and What's-its</h1>
        <ul id='navigation'>
            <li><a href=''>home</a></li>
            <li><a href=''>contact us</a></li>
            <li><a href=''>products</a></li>
            <li><a href=''>services</a></li>
            <li><a href=''>faq</a></li>
        </ul>
        <div id='content'>
            <h2>faq</h2>
            <ul id='top'>
                <li><a href='#widgets'>Q. What are widgets?</a></li>
                <li><a href='#why'>Q. Why should I buy a widget?</a></li>
                <li><a href='#where'>Q. Where do widgets come from?</a></li>
                <li><a href='#what'>Q. What are widgets made of?</a></li>
                <li><a href='#how'>Q. How do I use my widget?</a></li>
                <li><a href='#who'>Q. Who uses widgets?</a></li>
            </ul>
            <h3 id='widgets'>Q. What are widgets? <a href='#top'>top</a></h3>
            <p>
                A. Widgets are a smaller, more compact version of what's its.
            </p>
            <h3 id='why'>Q. Why should I buy a widget?
                <a href='#top'>top</a></h3>
            <p>
                A. Because widgets will solve all of you problems.
            </p>
            <h3 id='where'>Q. Where do widgets come from?
                <a href='#top'>top</a></h3>
            <p>
                A. Widgets are harvested from the Amazon rain forest by
                little green gnomes.
            </p>
            <h3 id='what'>Q. What are widgets made of?
                <a href='#top'>top</a></h3>
            <p>
                A. Widgets are made of primordial, esoteric matter, and as
                such could cause your head to explode into one of seven
                fun-filled colors.
            </p>
```

```
                        <h3 id='how'>Q. How do I use my widget? <a href='#top'>top</a></h3>
                        <p>
                            A. You must summon a troll using our proprietary magic wand and
                            book of spells who will teach you everything you need to know
                            about your widget.
                        </p>
                        <h3 id='who'>Q. Who uses widgets? <a href='#top'>top</a></h3>
                        <p>
                            A. Day traders and postal workers, primarily.
                        </p>
                    </div>
                </div>
            </body>
        </html>
```

Chapter 11

Exercise solution

```
<!DOCTYPE html PUBLIC "-//W3C//DTD XHTML 1.0 Strict//EN"
"http://www.w3.org/TR/xhtml1/DTD/xhtml1-strict.dtd">
    <html>
        <head>
            <title></title>
            <style type='text/css'>
                body {
                    margin: 0;
                    padding: 5px;
                }
                div {
                    font: 18px sans-serif;
                    color: white;
                    border: 1px solid black;
                    background: gray;
                    height: 200px;
                    padding: 5px;
                }
                div#column1 {
                    float: left;
                    width: 150px;
                    margin: 0 5px 0 0;
                }
                div#column2, div#column3 {
                    float: right;
                    width: 150px;
                    margin: 0 0 0 5px;
                }
                div#column4 {
                    margin: 0 334px 0 167px;
                }
                div#footer {
                    height: 35px;
                    margin: 5px 0 0 0;
```

```
                                clear: both;
                        }
                </style>
        </head>
        <body>
                <div id='column1'>
                        Content of column 1.
                </div>
                <div id='column2'>
                        Content of column 2.
                </div>
                <div id='column3'>
                        Content of column 3.
                </div>
                <div id='column4'>
                        Content of column 4.
                </div>
                <div id='footer'>
                        Content of footer.
                </div>
        </body>
</html>
```

Chapter 12

Exercise 1 solution

```
<!DOCTYPE html PUBLIC "-//W3C//DTD XHTML 1.0 Strict//EN"
"http://www.w3.org/TR/xhtml1/DTD/xhtml1-strict.dtd">
<html>
    <head>
        <title></title>
        <style type='text/css'>
            ul {

                list-style: none;
                border-bottom: thin solid black;
                height: 21px;
            }
            li {
                text-align: center;
                float: left;
                margin: 0 10px;
                border: thin solid black;
                width: 100px;
            }
        </style>
    </head>
    <body>
        <ul>
            <li><a href='http://www.google.com'>Google</a></li>
            <li><a href='http://www.yahoo.com'>Yahoo</a></li>
            <li><a href='http://www.ebay.com'>Ebay</a></li>
```

```
                <li><a href='http://www.wrox.com'>Wrox</a></li>
            </ul>
        </body>
</html>
```

Exercise 2 solution

```
<!DOCTYPE html PUBLIC "-//W3C//DTD XHTML 1.0 Strict//EN"
"http://www.w3.org/TR/xhtml1/DTD/xhtml1-strict.dtd">
<html>
    <head>
        <title></title>
        <style type='text/css'>
            li {
                list-style-image: url('collapsed_folder.gif');
            }
            li + li + li + li + li {
                list-style: inside url('exploded_folder.gif');
            }
        </style>
    </head>
    <body>
        <ul>
            <li> My Pictures</li>
            <li> My Music</li>
            <li> My Documents</li>
            <li> My Computer</li>
            <li> Control Panel</li>
        </ul>
    </body>
</html>
```

Chapter 13

Exercise solution

```
<!DOCTYPE html PUBLIC "-//W3C//DTD XHTML 1.0 Strict//EN"
"http://www.w3.org/TR/xhtml1/DTD/xhtml1-strict.dtd">
    <html>
        <head>
            <title></title>
            <style type='text/css'>
                body {
                    height: 1000px;
                    margin: 0;
                    padding: 5px;
                    background: url('kayaking.jpg') no-repeat center fixed;
                }
                div {
                    font: 18px sans-serif;
                    border: 1px solid black;
                    background: gray;
                    height: 400px;
```

```
                            padding: 5px;
                        }
                        div#column1 {
                            float: left;
                            width: 150px;
                            margin: 0 5px 0 0;
                            background: url('kayaking2.jpg') no-repeat center fixed;
                        }
                        div#column2, div#column3 {
                            float: right;
                            width: 150px;
                            margin: 0 0 0 5px;
                            background: url('kayaking2.jpg') no-repeat center fixed;
                        }
                        div#column4 {
                            margin: 0 334px 0 167px;
                            background: url('kayaking2.jpg') no-repeat center fixed;
                        }
                        div#footer {
                            height: 35px;
                            margin: 5px 0 0 0;
                            clear: both;
                        }
                        ul {
                            list-style: none;
                            margin: 0;
                            padding: 0;
                        }
                        li {
                            margin-bottom: 5px;
                            height: 50px;
                            background: url('kayaking.jpg') no-repeat center fixed;
                            border: 1px solid black;
                        }
                        a {
                            text-decoration: none;
                            color: black;
                            font-weight: bold;
                        }
                    </style>
                </head>
                <body>
                    <div id='column1'>
                        Content of column 1.
                        <ul>
                            <li><a href='http://www.wrox.com'>Wrox</a></li>
                            <li><a href='http://www.google.com'>Google</a></li>
                            <li><a href='http://www.ebay.com'>Ebay</a></li>
                            <li><a href='http://www.amazon.com'>Amazon</a></li>
                            <li><a href='http://www.wiley.com'>Wiley</a></li>
                            <li><a href='http://www.yahoo.com'>Yahoo!</a></li>
                        </ul>
                    </div>
                    <div id='column2'>
```

```
              Content of column 2.
          </div>
          <div id='column3'>
              Content of column 3.
          </div>
          <div id='column4'>
              Content of column 4.
          </div>
          <div id='footer'>
              Content of footer.
          </div>
      </body>
  </html>
```

Chapter 14

Exercise 1 solution

```
<!DOCTYPE html PUBLIC "-//W3C//DTD XHTML 1.0 Strict//EN"
"http://www.w3.org/TR/xhtml1/DTD/xhtml1-strict.dtd">
<html>
    <head>
      <meta http-equiv="content-type" content="text/xhtml; charset=windows-1252" />
      <meta http-equiv="content-language" content="en-us" />
        <style type="text/css">
            * {
                font-family: sans-serif;
                color: white;
            }
            body {
                margin: 0;
            }
            h1, h2 {
                margin: 0;
                background: gray;
            }
            h1 {
                font-size: 1.6em;
                padding: 0.3em;
                border-bottom: 5px solid black;
                letter-spacing: -0.08em;
            }
            div {
                background: lightgrey;
                padding: 0.7em;
                clear: left;
            }
            h2 {
                font-size: 1em;
                padding: 0.2em;
            }
            ul#navigation {
                list-style: none;
```

```
            background: gray;
            margin: 0.1em;
            padding: 0;
        }
        ul#navigation li {
            float: left;
            margin: 0.4em;
        }
        ul#navigation li a {
            padding: 0.3em;
        }
        ul#navigation li a:link {
            background: gray;
        }
        ul#navigation li a:active {
            background: orange;
        }
        ul#navigation li a:visited {
            background: black;
        }
        ul#navigation li a:hover, li a:focus {
            background: white;
            color: black;
        }
        /* Dynamic link descriptions */
        ul#navigation div {
            position: absolute;
            right: 0;
            top: 0;
            background: gray;
            display: none;
        }
        ul#navigation li:hover > div {
            display: block;
        }
        ul#top {
            color: black;
        }
        h3, p {
            color: black;
        }
        p {
            border: 0.05em solid black;
            padding: 0.8em;
        }
        h3:target {
            color: yellow;
            background: red;
        }
        ul#top li a {
            color: black;
        }
    </style>
    <title>FAQ - Widgets and What's-its</title>
</head>
```

```
<body>
    <h1>Widgets and What's-its</h1>
    <ul id='navigation'>
        <li>
            <a href=''>home</a>
            <div>Go to the Widgets and What's-its home page.</div>
        </li>
        <li>
            <a href=''>contact us</a>
            <div>Widgets and What's-its contact information.</div>
        </li>
        <li>
            <a href=''>products</a>
            <div>Browse our complete line of Widgets and What's-its.</div>
        </li>
        <li>
            <a href=''>services</a>
            <div>Quality Widgets and What's-its service and support.</div>
        </li>
        <li>
            <a href=''>faq</a>
            <div>Frequently asked questions about our Widgets and
            What's-its.</div>
        </li>
    </ul>
    <div>
        <h2>faq</h2>
        <ul id='top'>
            <li><a href='#widgets'>Q. What are widgets?</a></li>
            <li><a href='#why'>Q. Why should I buy a widget?</a></li>
            <li><a href='#where'>Q. Where do widgets come from?</a></li>
            <li><a href='#what'>Q. What are widgets made of?</a></li>
            <li><a href='#how'>Q. How do I use my widget?</a></li>
            <li><a href='#who'>Q. Who uses widgets?</a></li>
        </ul>
        <h3 id='widgets'>Q. What are widgets? <a href='#top'>top</a></h3>
        <p>
            A. Widgets are a smaller, more compact version of what's its.
        </p>
        <h3 id='why'>Q. Why should I buy a widget? <a href='#top'>top</a></h3>
        <p>
            A. Because widgets will solve all of you problems.
        </p>
        <h3 id='where'>Q. Where do widgets come from?
            <a href='#top'>top</a></h3>
        <p>
            A. Widgets are harvested from the Amazon rain forest by
            little green gnomes.
        </p>
        <h3 id='what'>Q. What are widgets made of? <a href='#top'>top</a></h3>
        <p>
            A. Widgets are made of primordial, esoteric matter, and as
            such could cause your head to explode into one of seven
            fun-filled colors.
        </p>
```

```
         <h3 id='how'>Q. How do I use my widget? <a href='#top'>top</a></h3>
         <p>
             A. You must summon a troll using our proprietary magic wand and
             book of spells who will teach you everything you need to know
             about your widget.
         </p>
         <h3 id='who'>Q. Who uses widgets? <a href='#top'>top</a></h3>
         <p>
             A. Day traders and postal workers, primarily.
         </p>
     </div>
  </body>
</html>
```

Exercise 2 solution

Add the following rules to the CSS for Exercise 1:

```css
/* Watermark */

div#watermark {
    position: fixed;
    bottom: 10px;
    right: 10px;
    font-size: 4em;
    padding: 0.1em;
    background: white;
    color: gray;
    opacity: 0.5;
}
div#watermark a {
    color: black;
    text-decoration: none;
}
```

Add the following markup to the XHTML for Exercise 1.

```html
     </div>
     <div id='watermark'>
         <a href=''>W</a>
     </div>
  </body>
</html>
```

Chapter 15

Exercise 1 solution

If you use the markup that you completed for Chapter 14, Exercise 2, the style sheets should be linked in the markup like this:

```
<!DOCTYPE html PUBLIC "-//W3C//DTD XHTML 1.0 Strict//EN"
"http://www.w3.org/TR/xhtml1/DTD/xhtml1-strict.dtd">
```

```
<html>
    <head>
        <meta http-equiv="content-type" content="text/xhtml; charset=windows-1252" />
        <meta http-equiv="content-language" content="en-us" />
        <link rel='stylesheet' type='text/css'
            href='exercise15-1-screen.css' media='screen'/>
        <link rel='stylesheet' type='text/css'
            href='exercise15-1-handheld.css' media='handheld'/>
        <title>FAQ - Widgets and What's-its</title>
    </head>
    <body>
```

The embedded style sheet shown in Chapter 14, Exercise 2 should be saved as an external style sheet, shown in this example as exercise15-1-screen.css. A handheld style sheet resembling Opera's Small Screen rendering of the Widgets and What's-its FAQ should also be provided. The styles for that style sheet should look something like the following.

```
body {
    font: 0.8em sans-serif;
    max-width: 17em;
}
h1, h2 {
    padding: 0.2em 0;
    font-size: 0.9em;
    margin: 0;
}
h1, div {
    background: #eee;
}
ul {
    font-size: 0.8em;
    padding: 0;
    margin: 0.5em 0 0.5em 1.2em;
}
ul#top {
    margin-left: 1.6em;
}
h3 {
    font-size: 0.8em;
    margin: 0;
}
p {
    font-size: 0.8em;
    margin: 0 0 1em 0;
}
```

Exercise 2 solution

If you use the updated markup that you completed for Exercise 1, the print style sheet should be linked in the markup like so:

```
<!DOCTYPE html PUBLIC "-//W3C//DTD XHTML 1.0 Strict//EN"
"http://www.w3.org/TR/xhtml1/DTD/xhtml1-strict.dtd">
```

```
<html>
    <head>
     <meta http-equiv="content-type" content="text/xhtml; charset=windows-1252" />
     <meta http-equiv="content-language" content="en-us" />
     <link rel='stylesheet' type='text/css'
           href='exercise15-2-screen.css' media='screen'/>
     <link rel='stylesheet' type='text/css'
           href='exercise15-2-handheld.css' media='handheld'/>
     <link rel='stylesheet' type='text/css'
           href='exercise15-2-print.css' media='print'/>
     <title>FAQ - Widgets and What's-its</title>
    </head>
```

The following is the print style sheet:

```
* {
    font-family: sans-serif;
    color: black;
}
body {
    margin: 0;
}
h1, h2 {
    margin: 0;
    background: gray;
}
h1 {
    font-size: 16pt;
    padding: 1pt;
    border-bottom: 3pt solid black;
    letter-spacing: -1pt;
}
div {
    background: lightgrey;
    padding: 0.7em;
    clear: left;
}
h2 {
    font-size: 14pt;
    padding: 2pt;
}
ul#navigation {
    display: none;
}
div#watermark {
    display: none;
}
p {
```

```
        border: thin solid black;
        padding: 3pt;
    }

    ul#top li a {
        color: black;
    }
```

Chapter 16

Exercise solution

```
<!DOCTYPE html PUBLIC "-//W3C//DTD XHTML 1.0 Strict//EN"
"http://www.w3.org/TR/xhtml1/DTD/xhtml1-strict.dtd">
<html>
    <head>
        <title> HTML tables </title>
        <style type='text/css'>
            * {
                font-family: monospace;
                font-size: 100%;
            }
            table {
                width: 300px;
                caption-side: bottom;
                border: thin solid black;
                table-layout: fixed;
                /* border-collapse: collapse; is also acceptable */
                border-spacing: 0;
            }
            th, td {
                border: thin solid black;
                text-align: center;
                font-weight: bold;
                /* Kudos if you thought of fixing
                   table-layout: fixed; in Mozilla
                   with the overflow: hidden;
                   declararion. */
                overflow: hidden;
            }
            th {
                background: lightgrey;
            }
            td {
                vertical-align: top;
            }
            caption {
                font-size: 90%;
                text-align: right;
            }
```

```
                    td, th, caption {
                        padding: 5px;
                    }
                </style>
            </head>
            <body>
                <table>
                    <caption>
                        Table: My favorite movies.
                    </caption>
                    <colgroup>
                        <col id='movie' />
                        <col id='cast' />
                        <col id='genre' />
                        <col id='year' />
                    </colgroup>
                    <thead>
                        <tr>
                            <th> movie          </th>
                            <th> stars          </th>
                            <th> genre          </th>
                            <th> year           </th>
                        </tr>
                    </thead>
                    <tbody>
                        <tr>
                            <td> Bruce Almighty              </td>
                            <td> Jim Carrey, Jennifer Aniston.. </td>
                            <td> Comedy                      </td>
                            <td> 2003                        </td>
                        </tr>
                        <tr>
                            <td> The Lord of the Rings, the
                                 Fellowship of the Ring
                                 (Extended Edition)          </td>
                            <td> Elijah Wood,  Viggo Mortensen..</td>
                            <td> Action / Adventure          </td>
                            <td> 2002                        </td>
                        </tr>
                        <tr>
                            <td> The Last Samurai            </td>
                            <td> Ken Watanabe, Tom Cruise..  </td>
                            <td> Action / Drama              </td>
                            <td> 2004                        </td>
                        </tr>
                    </tbody>
                </table>
            </body>
        </html>
```

The result should look like Figure A-1.

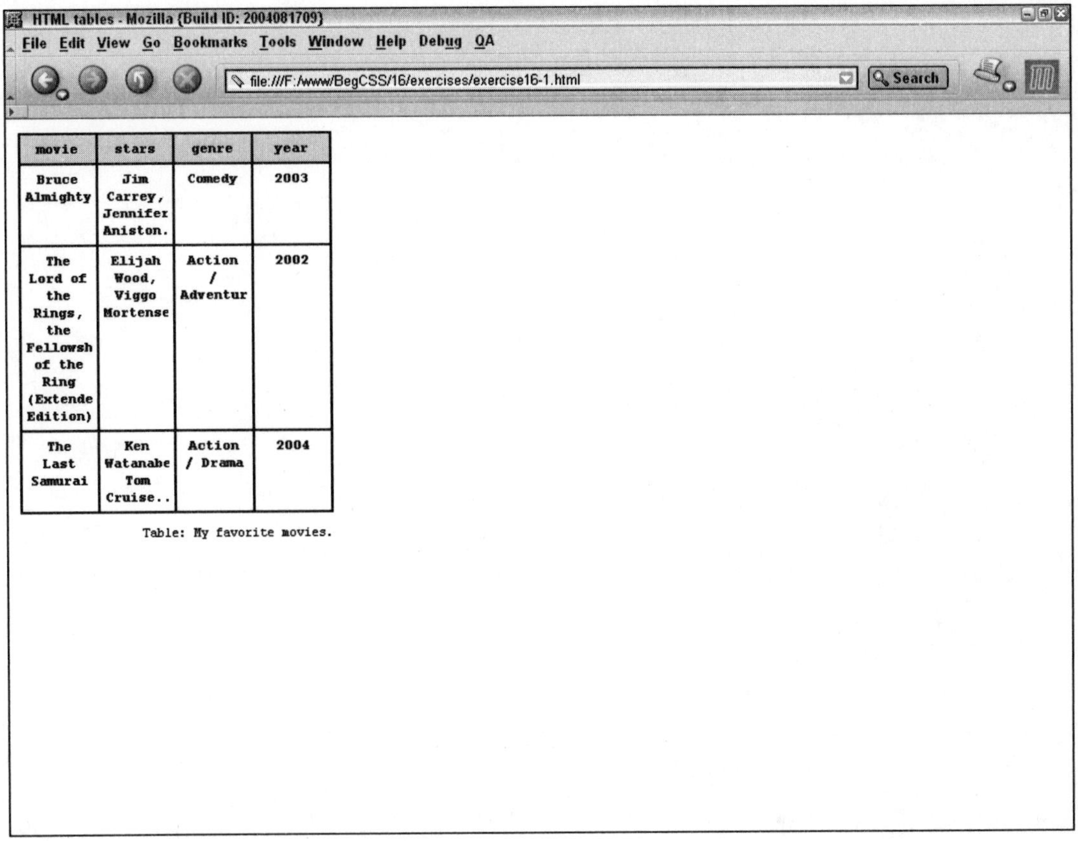

Figure A-1

Chapter 17

Exercise solution

Although you can use any XML schema, it should resemble what I show you here. I've used markup with HTML names here to demonstrate what the document structure should look like, but this is also valid XML. Remember, this is an XML file, not an HTML file. This file appears in the book's code download as exercise17-1.xml and exercise17-1.css, respectively.

Note that Internet Explorer becomes very confused by the use of HTML syntax in an XML document. IE attempts to render the table as though it were HTML, but does so incorrectly.

```
<?xml version="1.0" encoding="ISO-8859-1"?>
<?xml-stylesheet type="text/css" href="exercise16-2.css"?>
<body>
    <table>
        <caption>
```

```
            Table: My favorite movies.
        </caption>
        <colgroup>
            <col id='movie' />
            <col id='cast' />
            <col id='genre' />
            <col id='year' />
        </colgroup>
        <thead>
            <tr>
                <th> movie          </th>
                <th> stars          </th>
                <th> genre          </th>
                <th> year           </th>
            </tr>
        </thead>
        <tbody>
            <tr>
                <td> Bruce Almighty              </td>
                <td> Jim Carrey, Jennifer Aniston.. </td>
                <td> Comedy                      </td>
                <td> 2003                        </td>
            </tr>
            <tr>
                <td> The Lord of the Rings, the
                     Fellowship of the Ring
                     (Extended Edition)          </td>
                <td> Elijah Wood,  Viggo Mortensen..</td>
                <td> Action / Adventure          </td>
                <td> 2002                        </td>
            </tr>
            <tr>
                <td> The Last Samurai            </td>
                <td> Ken Watanabe, Tom Cruise..  </td>
                <td> Action / Drama              </td>
                <td> 2004                        </td>
            </tr>
        </tbody>
    </table>
</body>
```

And the accompanying style sheet:

```
* {
    font-size: 100%;
    font-family: monospace;
}
body {
    display: block;
    margin: 13px;
}
table {
    display: table;
    width: 300px;
```

```
        caption-side: bottom;
        border: thin solid black;
        table-layout: fixed;
        /* border-collapse: collapse; is also acceptable */
        border-spacing: 0;
    }
    colgroup {
        display: table-column-group;
    }
    col {
        display: table-column;
    }
    thead {
        display: table-header-group;
    }
    tbody {
        display: table-row-group;
    }
    tr {
        display: table-row;
    }
    th, td {
        display: table-cell;
        border: thin solid black;
        text-align: center;
        font-weight: bold;
        overflow: hidden;
    }
    th {
        background: lightgrey;
    }
    td {
        vertical-align: top;
    }
    caption {
        display: table-caption;
        font-size: 90%;
        text-align: right;
    }
    td, th, caption {
        padding: 5px;
    }
```

Chapter 18

Exercise 1 solution

```
<!DOCTYPE html PUBLIC "-//W3C//DTD XHTML 1.0 Strict//EN"
"http://www.w3.org/TR/xhtml1/DTD/xhtml1-strict.dtd">
<html>
    <head>
     <meta http-equiv="content-type" content="text/xhtml; charset=windows-1252" />
     <meta http-equiv="content-language" content="en-us" />
```

```
    <!-- compliance patch for microsoft browsers -->
    <!--[if lt IE 7]>
    <script src="/ie7/ie7-standard-p.js" type="text/javascript">
    </script>
    <![endif]-->
    <link rel='stylesheet' type='text/css'
          href='exercise18-1-screen.css' media='screen'/>
    <link rel='stylesheet' type='text/css'
          href='exercise18-1-handheld.css' media='handheld'/>
    <link rel='stylesheet' type='text/css'
          href='exercise18-1-print.css' media='print'/>
    <title>FAQ - Widgets and What's-its</title>
</head>
```

Exercise 2 solution

The document presented suffers from two Internet Explorer rendering bugs. The first bug is the double-margin bug, caused by the left margin applied to the floated nav <div> element. The second bug is the guillotine bug, which is caused by using background effects on links and floated content that stretches larger than its containing element.

Two fixes are required; the first is for the double-margin bug.

```
div#nav {
    float: left;
    display: inline;
    margin-left: 10px;
    background: lightsteelblue;
    width: 150px;
    border: 1px solid black;
}
```

The second fix is for the guillotine bug. The first step to fix the guillotine bug is to apply an empty element after the content:

```
        </div>
    </div>
    <div id='guillotine'>
    </div>
</body>
</html>
```

The second step is to apply the following rule in the style sheet.

```
div#guillotine {
    visibility: hidden;
    clear: both;
}
```

B

CSS Reference

Reference Conventions

The following conventions are used to outline browser compatibility for each CSS feature:

- ❑ **Y = Yes.** The feature is implemented completely per the W3C specification of what that feature is.
- ❑ **N = No.** The feature is not implemented.
- ❑ **B = Buggy.** The feature is implemented but has unexpected side effects.
- ❑ **P = Partial.** The feature is partially implemented.
- ❑ **A = Alternative.** The feature is not implemented but an alternative proprietary feature is available that provides the same functionality.
- ❑ **I = Incorrect.** The feature is implemented but does not conform to the W3C definition of what that feature provides.

The CSS level that reference material refers to is provided in the CSS column. At the time of this writing, there are four CSS specifications:

- ❑ **CSS Level 1:** The reference material provided is outlined in the CSS Level 1 Recommendation made 17 December 1996.
- ❑ **CSS Level 2:** The reference material provided is outlined in the W3C CSS Level 2 Recommendation made 12 May 1998.
- ❑ **CSS Level 2.1:** The reference material provided is outlined in the W3C CSS Level 2.1 Candidate Recommendation made 25 February 2004.
- ❑ **CSS Level 3:** The reference material provided refers to a W3C CSS Level 3 Candidate Recommendation (at the time of this writing portions of CSS 3 are still in development; references refer to those parts of CSS 3 in Candidate Recommendation status).

Selectors

Selector	CSS	IE 5.5	IE 6.0	Mozilla 1.7	Opera 7.5	Safari 1.2
Universal `* {color: blue;}`	3	Y	Y	Y	Y	Y
Type `div {color: blue;}`	3	Y	Y	Y	Y	Y
Descendant `div p {color: blue;}`	3	Y	Y	Y	Y	Y
Direct Child `div > p {color: blue;}`	3	N	N	Y	Y	Y
Direct Adjacent Sibling `p + p {color: blue}`	3	N	N	Y	Y	Y
Indirect Adjacent Sibling `p ~ p {color: blue;}`	3	N	N	Y	Y	Y
Attribute Existence `input[type] {color: blue;}`	3	N	N	Y	Y	Y
Attribute's value matches value exactly. `input[type=text] {color: blue;}`	3	N	N	Y	Y	Y

Attribute's value is a space-separated list of words.
`input[type~=text file password] {`
`    color: blue;`
`}`
	3	N	N	Y	Y	Y

Attribute's value begins with a value or is the value exactly; value provided may be a hyphen-separated list of words.
`input[name|=value1-value2] {`
`    color: blue;`
`}`
	3	N	N	Y	Y	Y

Attribute's value begins with...
`a[href^=http://www.somesite.com] {`
`    color: blue;`
`}`
	3	N	N	Y	N	Y

Attribute's value contains...
`a[href*=somesite] {`
`    color: blue;`
`}`
	3	N	N	Y	N	Y

Selector	CSS	IE 5.5	IE 6.0	Mozilla 1.7	Opera 7.5	Safari 1.2

Attribute's value ends with...
`a[href$=html] {`
`    color: blue;`
`}`
	3	N	N	Y	N	Y

Class `div.class {color: blue;}`	3	Y	Y	Y	Y	Y
Multiple Classes `div.class1.class2 {color: blue;}`	3	B	B	Y	Y	Y
IE 5.5 and 6 support multiple class syntax on the element, but not chaining class selectors in the style sheet.						
ID `div#id {color: blue;}`	3	Y	Y	Y	Y	Y

Pseudo-Classes

Pseudo-Class	CSS	IE 5.5	IE 6.0	Mozilla 1.7	Opera 7.5	Safari 1.2
:link	3	Y	Y	Y	Y	Y
:visited	3	Y	Y	Y	Y	Y
:hover	3	P	P	Y	Y	Y
:active	3	P	P	Y	Y	Y
:focus	3	N	N	Y	Y	Y
:target	3	N	N	Y	N	Y
:lang	3	N	N	Y	N	N
:root	3	N	N	Y	N	Y
:first-child	3	N	N	Y	Y	Y
:last-child	3	N	N	Y	N	Y
:empty	3	N	N	I	N	Y
Mozilla incorrectly applies :empty to elements that contain white space.						
:not	3	N	N	Y	N	Y

Pseudo-Elements

Pseudo-Element	CSS	IE 5.5	IE 6.0	Mozilla 1.7	Opera 7.5	Safari 1.2
CSS 3 :: (double-colon) syntax.	3	Y	Y	Y	Y	Y
::first-line	3	Y	Y	Y	Y	Y
::first-letter	3	Y	Y	Y	Y	Y
::before	3	N	N	Y	Y	Y
::after	3	N	N	Y	Y	Y
::selection	3	N	N	A	N	Y

Mozilla provides a proprietary `::-moz-selection` pseudo-element.

Color Properties

Property	CSS	IE 5.5	IE 6.0	Mozilla 1.7	Opera 7.5	Safari 1.2
color	2.1	Y	Y	Y	Y	Y
Value:	<color> | inherit					
Initial value:	Depends on browser					
Applies to:	All elements					
Inherited:	Yes					

<color> refers to one of the following:

A color keyword:	`body {color: black;}`
A hexadecimal value:	`body {color: #000000;}`
Short hexadecimal value:	`body {color: #000;}`
RGB value:	`body {color: rgb(0, 0, 0);}`
RGB percentage:	`body {color: rgb(0% ,0%, 0%);}`

Property	CSS	IE 5.5	IE 6.0	Mozilla 1.7	Opera 7.5	Safari 1.2
opacity	3	A	A	I	N	Y
Value:	<alphavalue> | inherit					
Initial value:	1					

Property	CSS	IE 5.5	IE 6.0	Mozilla 1.7	Opera 7.5	Safari 1.2
Applies to:	All elements					
Inherited:	No					

Introduced in CSS 3, the `opacity` property accepts a floating integer between 0.0 (fully transparent) and 1.0 (fully opaque)

Mozilla 1.7 incorrectly allows this property to inherit to children elements.

IE 5.5 and 6 provide an alternative, proprietary `filter` property to achieve a similar effect (see entry for the Microsoft `filter` property). Mozilla prior to 1.7 provides an alternative proprietary `-moz-opacity` property (see entry for Mozilla `-moz-opacity` property).

Font Properties

Property	CSS	IE 5.5	IE 6.0	Mozilla 1.7	Opera 7.5	Safari 1.2
font-family	2.1	Y	Y	Y	Y	Y
Value:	[[<family-name> | <generic-family>] [, <family-name> | <generic-family>]*] | inherit					
Initial value:	Varies from browser to browser					
Applies to:	All elements					
Inherited:	Yes					

`<family-name>` Refers to the name of a font installed on the user's operating system and supported by the browser, for instance: Arial and Times New Roman. A comma-separated list of fonts may be provided, font names containing spaces must be enclosed with quotations.

`<generic-family>` Refers to fonts not native to a particular operating system and provided by the browser. The following are all of the generic font families:

* serif (Times New Roman, or Times)

* sans-serif (Arial or Helvetica)

* cursive (Zapf-Chancery)

* fantasy (Western)

* monospace (Courier)

font-style	2.1	Y	Y	Y	Y	Y
Value:	normal | italic | oblique | inherit					
Initial value:	normal					

Table continued on following page

Property	CSS	IE 5.5	IE 6.0	Mozilla 1.7	Opera 7.5	Safari 1.2
Applies to:	All elements					
Inherited:	Yes					
font-variant	2.1	Y	Y	Y	Y	P
Value:	normal | small-caps | inherit					
Initial value:	normal					
Applies to:	All elements					
Inherited:	Yes					
Safari 1.2 does not support the small-caps keyword.						
font-weight	2.1	Y	Y	Y	Y	Y
Value:	normal | bold | bolder | lighter | 100 | 200 | 300 | 400 | 500 | 600 | 700 | 800 | 900 | inherit					
Initial value:	normal					
Applies to:	All elements					
Inherited:	Yes					
font-size	2.1	Y	Y	Y	Y	Y
Value:	<absolute-size> | <relative-size> | <length> | <percentage> | inherit					
Initial value:	medium					
Applies to:	All elements					
Inherited:	Yes					
Percentage value:	Refers to parent element's font size					
<absolute-size> refers to one of the keywords:						
	xx-small | x-small | small | medium | large | xx-large					
<relative-size> refers to one of the keywords:						
	larger | smaller					
font	2.1	Y	Y	Y	Y	Y
Value:	[[<font-style> || <font-variant> || <font-weight>]? <font-size> [/ <line-height>]? <font-family>] | caption | icon | menu | message-box | small-caption | status-bar | inherit					
Initial value:	Not defined for shorthand properties					
Applies to:	All elements					
Inherited:	Yes					

Background Properties

Property	CSS	IE 5.5	IE 6.0	Mozilla 1.7	Opera 7.5	Safari 1.2
background-color	2.1	Y	Y	Y	Y	Y
Value:	<color> | transparent | inherit					
Initial value:	transparent					
Applies to:	All elements					
Inherited:	No					
background-image	2.1	Y	Y	Y	Y	Y
Value:	<uri> | none | inherit					
Initial value:	none					
Applies to:	All elements					
Inherited:	No					
background-repeat	2.1	Y	Y	Y	Y	Y
Value:	repeat | repeat-x | repeat-y | no-repeat | inherit					
Initial value:	repeat					
Applies to:	All elements					
Inherited:	No					
background-attachment	2.1	Y	P	Y	Y	Y
Value:	scroll | fixed | inherit					
Initial value:	repeat					
Applies to:	All elements					
Inherited:	No					
IE 5.5 and 6 only support the `fixed` keyword when applied to the <body> element.						
background-position	3	Y	Y	Y	Y	Y
Value:	[[<percentage> | <length>]{1,2} | [[top | center | bottom] | | [left | center | right]]] | inherit					
Initial value:	0% 0%					
Applies to:	All elements					
Inherited:	No					
Percentage values:	Are determined based on the size of the element itself.					

Table continued on following page

Property	CSS	IE 5.5	IE 6.0	Mozilla 1.7	Opera 7.5	Safari 1.2
background	2.1	Y	Y	Y	Y	Y
Value:	[<background-color> || <background-image> || <background-repeat> || <background-attachment> || <background-position>] | inherit					
Initial value:	Not defined for shorthand properties					
Applies to:	All elements					
Inherited:	No					
Percentage values:	Are determined based on the size of the element itself					

Text Properties

Property	CSS	IE 5.5	IE 6.0	Mozilla 1.7	Opera 7.5	Safari 1.2
word-spacing	2.1	Y	Y	Y	Y	Y
Value:	normal | <length>					
Initial value:	normal					
Applies to:	All elements					
Inherited:	Yes					
letter-spacing	2.1	Y	Y	Y	Y	Y
Value:	normal | <length>					
Initial value:	normal					
Applies to:	All elements					
Inherited:	Yes					
text-decoration	2.1	Y	Y	Y	Y	Y
Value:	none | [underline || overline || line-through || blink]					
Initial value:	none					
Applies to:	All elements					
Inherited:	No					
text-transform	2.1	Y	Y	Y	Y	Y
Value:	capitalize | uppercase | lowercase | none					
Initial value:	none					
Applies to:	All elements					

Property	CSS	IE 5.5	IE 6.0	Mozilla 1.7	Opera 7.5	Safari 1.2
Inherited:	Yes					
text-align	2.1	Y	Y	Y	Y	Y
Value:	left | right | center | justify					
Initial value:	left					
Applies to:	Block-level elements, table cells and inline blocks					
Inherited:	Yes					
text-indent	2.1	Y	Y	Y	Y	Y
Value:	<length> | <percentage>					
Initial value:	0					
Applies to:	Block-level elements, table cells and inline blocks					
Inherited:	Yes					
Percentage value:	Refers to the width of the containing block					
line-height	2.1	Y	Y	Y	Y	Y
Value:	normal | <number> | <length> | <percentage>					
Initial value:	normal					
Applies to:	All elements					
Inherited:	Yes					
Percentage value:	Refers to the font size of the element the line-height is applied to					
vertical-align	2.1	Y	Y	Y	Y	Y
Value:	baseline | sub | super | top | text-top | middle | bottom | text-bottom | <percentage>					
Initial value:	baseline					
Applies to:	Inline-level and 'table-cell' elements					
Inherited:	No					
Percentage value:	Is determined by the line-height of the element					
white-space	2	P	Y	Y	Y	Y
Value:	normal | pre | nowrap | inherit					
Initial value:	normal					
Applies to:	All elements					
Inherited:	Yes.					
Internet Explorer 5.5 does not support the pre keyword.						

Box Model Properties

Property	CSS	IE 5.5	IE 6.0	Mozilla 1.7	Opera 7.5	Safari 1.2
margin-top **margin-right** **margin-bottom** **margin-left**	2.1	Y	Y	Y	Y	Y
Value:	<length> | <percentage> | auto					
Initial value:	0					
Applies to:	All elements					
Inherited:	No					
Percentage value:	Refers to the width of the containing block					
margin	2.1	Y	Y	Y	Y	Y
Value:	[<length> | <percentage> | auto] {1, 4}					
Initial value:	Not defined for shorthand properties					
Applies to:	All elements					
Inherited:	No					
Percentage value:	Refers to the width of the containing block					
padding-top **padding-right** **padding-bottom** **padding-left**	2.1	Y	Y	Y	Y	Y
Value:	<length> | <percentage>					
Initial value:	0					
Applies to:	All elements					
Inherited:	No					
Percentage value:	Refers to the width of the containing block					
padding	2.1	Y	Y	Y	Y	Y
Value:	[<length> | <percentage>] {1,4}					
Initial value:	Not defined for shorthand properties					
Applies to:	All elements					
Inherited:	No					
Percentage value:	Refers to the width of the containing block					

Property	CSS	IE 5.5	IE 6.0	Mozilla 1.7	Opera 7.5	Safari 1.2
border-top-width **border-right-width** **border-bottom-width** **border-left-width**	2.1	Y	Y	Y	Y	Y
Value:	thin | medium | thick | <length>					
Initial value:	medium					
Applies to:	All elements					
Inherited:	No					
border-width	2.1	Y	Y	Y	Y	Y
Value:	[thin | medium | thick | <length>] {!,4}					
Initial value:	Not defined for short-hand properties					
Applies to:	All elements					
Inherited:	No					
border-top-color **border-right-color** **border-bottom-color** **border-left-color**	2.1	P	P	Y	Y	Y
Value:	<color> | transparent | inherit					
Initial value:	The value of the color property					
Applies to:	All elements					
Inherited:	No					
IE 5.5 and 6 do not support the transparent keyword.						
border-color	2.1	P	P	Y	Y	Y
Value:	[<color> | transparent] {1,4} inherit					
Initial value:	See individual properties					
Applies to:	All elements					
Inherited:	No					
IE 5.5 and 6 do not support the transparent keyword.						
border-top-style **border-right-style** **border-bottom-style** **border-left-style**	2.1	P	P	Y	Y	Y
Value:	none | dotted | dashed | solid | double | groove | ridge | inset | outset					

Table continued on following page

Property	CSS	IE 5.5	IE 6.0	Mozilla 1.7	Opera 7.5	Safari 1.2
Initial value:	none					
Applies to:	All elements					
Inherited:	No					
IE 5.5 and 6 render the dotted keyword as dashed.						
border-style	2.1	P	P	Y	Y	Y
Value:	[none | dotted | dashed | solid | double | groove | ridge | inset | outset] {!,4}					
Initial value:	Not defined for short-hand properties					
Applies to:	All elements					
Inherited:	No					
IE 5.5 and 6 render the dotted keyword as dashed.						
border-top **border-right** **border-bottom** **border-left**	2.1	Y	Y	Y	Y	Y
Value:	[<border-width> || <border-style> || <border-color>] | inherit					
Initial value:	Not defined for short-hand properties					
Applies to:	All elements					
Inherited:	No					
border	2.1	Y	Y	Y	Y	Y
Value:	[<border-width> || <border-style> || <border-color>] | inherit					
Initial value:	Not defined for short-hand properties					
Applies to:	All elements					
Inherited:	No					
Width	2.1	Y	Y	Y	Y	Y
Value:	<length> | <percentage> | auto | inherit					
Initial value:	auto					
Applies to:	All elements, but non-replaced inline elements, table rows, and row groups					
Inherited:	No					
IE incorrectly resizes elements if the content inside of the element is larger than its width.						

Property	CSS	IE 5.5	IE 6.0	Mozilla 1.7	Opera 7.5	Safari 1.2
min-width	2.1	N	N	Y	Y	P
Value:	<length> | <percentage> | inherit					
Initial value:	0					
Applies to:	All elements, but non-replaced inline elements and table elements					
Inherited:	No					
Safari does not support min-width when applied to positioned elements.						
max-width	2.1	N	N	Y	Y	P
Value:	<length> | <percentage> | none | inherit					
Initial value:	none					
Applies to:	All elements, but non-replaced inline elements and table elements					
Inherited:	No					
Safari does not support max-width when applied to positioned elements.						
height	2.1	P	P	Y	Y	Y
Value:	<length> | <percentage> | auto | inherit					
Initial value:	auto					
Applies to:	All elements, but non-replaced inline elements, table rows, and row groups					
Inherited:	No					
IE incorrectly resizes elements if the content inside of the element is larger than its height.						
min-height	2.1	N	P	Y	Y	N
Value:	<length> | <percentage> | inherit					
Initial value:	0					
Applies to:	All elements, but non-replaced inline elements, table rows, and row groups					
Inherited:	No					
IE 6 only supports the min-height property when applied to <td>, <th> or <tr> elements.						
max-height	2.1	N	N	Y	Y	N
Value:	<length> | <percentage> | none | inherit					
Initial value:	none					

Table continued on following page

Property	CSS	IE 5.5	IE 6.0	Mozilla 1.7	Opera 7.5	Safari 1.2
Applies to: and row groups	All elements, but non-replaced inline elements, table rows,					
Inherited:	No					

Visual Effects

CSS Property	CSS	IE 5.5	IE 6.0	Mozilla 1.7	Opera 7.5	Safari 1.2
overflow	2.1	Y	Y	Y	Y	Y
Value:	visible | hidden | scroll | auto | inherit					
Initial value:	visible					
Applies to:	Block-level and replaced elements					
Inherited:	No					
Clip	2.1	Y	Y	Y	Y	Y
Value:	<shape> | auto | inherit					
Initial value:	auto					
Applies to:	Absolutely positioned elements					
Inherited:	No					

Under CSS 2 the only valid <shape> value is rect(<top>, <right>, <bottom>, <left>), where rect() provides the dimensions of a rectangle and <top>, <right>, <bottom>, <left> are <length> values.

visibility	2.1	P	P	P	P	P
Value:	visible | hidden | collapse | inherit					
Initial value:	visible					
Applies to:	All elements					
Inherited:	Yes					

No browser supports the collapse keyword, since it essentially provides the same effect as display: none;

Positioning

Property	CSS	IE 5.5	IE 6.0	Mozilla 1.7	Opera 7.5	Safari 1.2
display	2.1	P	P	P	Y	Y
Values:	inline | block | list-item | run-in | inline-block | table | inline-table | table-row-group | table-header-group | table-footer-group | table-row | table-column-group | table-column | table-cell | table-caption | none | inherit					
Initial value:	inline					
Applies to:	All elements					
Inherited:	No					

IE 5.5 and 6 only support the keywords `block`, `none`, `inline`, `inline-block`, `table-header-group` and `table-footer-group`. IE 6 additionally supports the `list-item` keyword. Mozilla does not support the keywords `inline-block`, `run-in` or `compact`.

Property	CSS	IE 5.5	IE 6.0	Mozilla 1.7	Opera 7.5	Safari 1.2
position	2.1	P	P	Y	Y	Y
Value:	static | relative | absolute | fixed | inherit					
Initial value:	static					
Applies to:	All elements					
Inherited:	No					

IE 5.5 and 6 do not support the `fixed` keyword.

Property	CSS	IE 5.5	IE 6.0	Mozilla 1.7	Opera 7.5	Safari 1.2
Top	2.1	Y	Y	Y	Y	Y
Value:	<length> | <percentage> | auto | inherit					
Initial value:	auto					
Applies to:	Positioned elements					
Inherited:	No					
Percentage value:	Refers to height of containing block					
Right	2.1	Y	Y	Y	Y	Y
Value:	<length> | <percentage> | auto | inherit					
Initial value:	auto					
Applies to:	Positioned elements					
Inherited:	No					
Percentage value:	Refers to width of containing block					
Bottom	2.1	Y	Y	Y	Y	Y

Table continued on following page

Property	CSS	IE 5.5	IE 6.0	Mozilla 1.7	Opera 7.5	Safari 1.2
Value:	<length> | <percentage> | auto | inherit					
Initial value:	auto					
Applies to:	Positioned elements					
Inherited:	No					
Percentage value:	Refers to height of containing block					
Left	2.1	Y	Y	Y	Y	Y
Value:	<length> | <percentage> | auto | inherit					
Initial value:	auto					
Applies to:	Positioned elements					
Inherited:	No					
Percentage value:	Refers to width of containing block					
Float	2.1	Y	Y	Y	Y	Y
Value:	left | right | none | inherit					
Initial value:	none					
Applies to:	All elements					
Inherited:	No					
Clear	2.1	Y	Y	Y	Y	Y
Value:	none | left | right | both | inherit					
Initial value:	none					
Applies to:	Block-level elements					
Inherited:	No					
z-index	2.1	Y	Y	Y	Y	Y
Value:	auto | <integer> | inherit					
Initial value:	auto					
Applies to:	Positioned elements					
Inherited:	No					

Table Properties

Property	CSS	IE 5.5	IE 6.0	Mozilla 1.7	Opera 7.5	Safari 1.2
caption-side	2.1	N	N	Y	N	Y
Value:	top | bottom | inherit					
Initial value:	top					
Applies to:	'table-caption' elements					
Inherited:	Yes					
table-layout	2.1	Y	Y	Y	Y	Y
Value:	auto | fixed | inherit					
Initial value:	auto					
Applies to:	'table' and 'inline-table' elements					
Inherited:	No					
border-collapse	2.1	Y	Y	Y	Y	Y
Value:	collapse | separate | inherit					
Initial value:	separate					
Applies to:	'table' and 'inline-table' elements					
Inherited:	Yes					
border-spacing	2.1	N	N	Y	Y	Y
Value:	<length> <length> ? | inherit					
Initial value:	0					
Applies to:	'table' and 'inline-table' elements					
Inherited:	Yes					
empty-cells	2.1	N	N	Y	Y	Y
Value:	show | hide | inherit					
Initial value:	show					
Applies to:	'table-cell' elements					
Inherited:	Yes					

User Interface

Property	CSS	IE 5.5	IE 6.0	Mozilla 1.7	Opera 7.5	Safari 1.2
cursor	2.1	Y	Y	P	P	P
Value:	[[<uri> ,]* [auto | crosshair | default | pointer | move | e-resize | ne-resize | nw-resize | n-resize | se-resize | sw-resize | s-resize | w-resize | text | wait | help | progress]] | inherit					
Initial value:	auto					
Applies to:	All elements					
Inherited:	Yes					
Mozilla, Opera and Safari do not support custom cursors supplied via a <uri>.						
outline-width	2.1	N	N	A	Y	Y
Value:	<border-width> | inherit					
Initial value:	medium					
Applies to:	All elements					
Inherited:	No					
See the proprietary -moz-outline-width property.						
outline-style	2.1	N	N	A	Y	Y
Value:	<border-style> | inherit					
Initial value:	none					
Applies to:	All elements					
Inherited:	No					
See the proprietary -moz-outline-style property.						
outline-color	2.1	N	N	A	Y	Y
Value:	<color> | invert | inherit					
Initial value:	invert					
Applies to:	All elements					
Inherited:	No					
See the proprietary -moz-outline-color property.						
outline	2.1	N	N	A	Y	Y
Value:	[<'outline-color'> | | <'outline-style'> | | <'outline-width'>] | inherit					

Property	CSS	IE 5.5	IE 6.0	Mozilla 1.7	Opera 7.5	Safari 1.2
Initial value:	Not defined for shorthand properties					
Applies to:	All elements					
Inherited:	No					
See the proprietary -moz-outline property.						

Generated Content, Automatic Numbering, and Lists

Property	CSS	IE 5.5	IE 6.0	Mozilla 1.7	Opera 7.5	Safari 1.2
content	2.1	N	N	Y	Y	Y
Value:	normal | [<string> | <uri> | <counter> | attr(<identifier>) | open-quote | close-quote | no-open-quote | no-close-quote]+ | inherit					
Initial value:	normal					
Applies to:	::before and ::after pseudo-elements					
Inherited:	No					
quotes	2.1	N	N	Y	Y	N
Value:	[<string> <string>]+ | none | inherit					
Initial value:	Varies from browser to browser					
Applies to:	All elements					
Inherited:	Yes					
counter-reset	2.1	N	N	N	Y	N
Value:	[<identifier> <integer>?]+ | none | inherit					
Initial value:	none					
Applies to:	All elements					
Inherited:	No					
counter-increment	2.1	N	N	N	Y	N
Value:	[<identifier> <integer>?]+ | none | inherit					
Initial value:	none					

Table continued on following page

Property	CSS	IE 5.5	IE 6.0	Mozilla 1.7	Opera 7.5	Safari 1.2
Applies to:	All elements					
Inherited:	No					
list-style-type	2.1	P	P	P	P	Y
Value:	disc | circle | square | decimal | decimal-leading-zero | lower-roman | upper-roman | lower-greek | lower-latin | upper-latin | armenian | georgian | none | inherit					
Initial value:	disc					
Applies to:	Elements with 'display: list-item'					
Inherited:	Yes					

Mozilla 1.7 does not support the georgian keyword. IE 5.5 and 6 only support CSS 1 keyword values: disc \| circle \| square \| decimal \| lower-roman \| upper-roman \| lower-alpha \| upper-alpha \| none

Property	CSS	IE 5.5	IE 6.0	Mozilla 1.7	Opera 7.5	Safari 1.2
list-style-image	2.1	Y	Y	Y	Y	Y
Value:	<uri> | none | inherit					
Initial value:	none					
Applies to:	Elements with 'display: list-item'					
Inherited:	Yes					
list-style-position	2.1	Y	Y	Y	Y	Y
Value:	inside | outside | inherit					
Initial value:	outside					
Applies to:	Elements with 'display: list-item'					
Inherited:	Yes					
list-style	2.1	P	P	P	P	Y
Value:	[<'list-style-type'> || <'list-style-position'> || <'list-style-image'>] | inherit					
Initial value:	Not defined for shorthand properties.					
Applies to:	Elements with 'display: list-item'					
Inherited:	Yes					

Paged Media

Property	CSS	IE 5.5	IE 6.0	Mozilla 1.7	Opera 7.5	Safari 1.2
Size	2.1	N	N	N	Y	N
Value:	<length>{1,2} | auto | portrait | landscape | inherit					
Initial value:	auto					
Applies to:	Page (via @page rule)					
Marks	2.1	N	N	N	N	N
Value:	[crop | | cross] | none | inherit					
Initial value:	none					
Applies to:	Page (via @page rule)					
page-break-before	2.1	P	P	P	Y	P
Value:	auto | always | avoid | left | right | inherit					
Initial value:	auto					
Applies to:	Block-level elements					
IE, Mozilla, and Safari only support the auto and always keywords.						
page-break-after	2.1	P	P	P	Y	P
Value:	auto | always | avoid | left | right | inherit					
Initial value:	auto					
Applies to:	Block-level elements					
IE, Mozilla. and Safari only support the auto and always keywords.						
page-break-inside	2.1	N	N	N	Y	N
Value:	avoid | auto | inherit					
Initial value:	auto					
Applies to:	Block-level elements					
Page	2.1	N	N	N	N	N
Value:	<identifier> | auto					
Initial value:	auto					
Applies to:	Block-level elements.					
orphans	2.1	N	N	N	Y	N
Value:	<integer> | inherit					
Initial value:	2					

Table continued on following page

Property	CSS	IE 5.5	IE 6.0	Mozilla 1.7	Opera 7.5	Safari 1.2
Applies to:	Block-level elements					
widows	2.1	N	N	N	Y	N
Value:	<integer> | inherit					
Initial value:	2					
Applies to:	Block-level elements					

Microsoft Proprietary Extensions to CSS

The following selections of properties are Microsoft proprietary extensions to CSS and are not part of any W3C standard.

Visual Effects

Property	Supported Since
Filter	IE 5.5
Value:	See below
Applies to:	All elements
Inherited:	No
The filter property is a complicated property that provides effects like transparency, gradients, or an array of other effects that are only available for Windows versions of Internet Explorer. For a complete reference, visit the following URLs.	
Introduction to filters: http://msdn.microsoft.com/workshop/author/filter/filters.asp	
Filter reference: http://msdn.microsoft.com/workshop/author/filter/reference/reference.asp	
overflow-x	IE 4
Value:	visible | hidden | scroll | auto
Initial value:	visible
Applies to:	Block-level and replaced elements
Inherited:	No
This property is proposed for inclusion in CSS 3.	
overflow-y	IE 4

Property	Supported Since
Value:	visible | hidden | scroll | auto
Initial value:	visible
Applies to:	Block-level and replaced elements
Inherited:	No
This property is proposed for inclusion in CSS 3.	

User-Interface

Property	Supported Since
scrollbar-3dlight-color **scrollbar-arrow-color** **scrollbar-base-color** **scrollbar-darkshadow-color** **scrollbar-face-color** **scrollbar-highlight-color** **scrollbar-shadow-color**	IE 5.5, Opera 7
Value:	<color>
Applies to:	Any object where a scroll bar is applied
Inherited:	Yes
In Opera, custom scroll bar colors are turned off by default. Custom scroll bar colors are only applied if the user has them turned on in the Opera preferences panel.	
Zoom	IE 5.5
Value:	normal | <number> | <percentage>
Applies to:	Any object where a scroll bar is applied
Inherited:	Yes

Backgrounds

Property	Supported Since
background-position-x	IE 4
Value:	<length> | <percentage> | left | center | right
Applies to:	All elements
Inherited:	Yes

Table continued on following page

Property	Supported Since
background-position-y	IE 4
Value:	<length> | <percentage> | top | center | bottom
Applies to:	All elements
Inherited:	Yes

Gecko Proprietary Extensions to CSS

The following selections of CSS features are Gecko proprietary extensions to CSS, which apply to the Mozilla, Netscape, and Firefox family of browsers and are not part of any W3C standard.

When new CSS features are added in Gecko, they usually undergo a testing period where they are prefixed with the Mozilla vendor specific prefix "-moz-", which is the W3C recommended method of deploying proprietary extensions to CSS, or CSS features not yet finalized in an official W3C CSS recommendation. This prefix remains in place until the functionality is finalized in a W3C CSS recommendation, or until bugs can be worked out with the implementation in such a way that Gecko's (or any other browser's) implementation can be expected to follow the W3C definition of what that feature provides.

Features such as these should be used with the understanding that they can be completely changed or removed without notice in future Gecko releases.

The following tables show the version of Gecko in which a particular feature was added. If previous to Mozilla 1.0, Netscape 6 is provided as the version; if the feature was added in Mozilla 1.0 or later, the version of Mozilla is indicated. Be sure to keep in mind the relationships between the Netscape, Mozilla, and Firefox browsers as shown in the tables in Chapter 2.

Pseudo-Elements

Pseudo-Element	Supported Since
::-moz-selection	Mozilla 1.5
Identical to the CSS 3 ::selection pseudo-element.	

Visual Effects

Property	Supported Since
-moz-opacity	NS 6
Value	<alphavalue> | <percentage> | inherit
Initial value:	visible

Property	Supported Since
Applies to:	Block-level and replaced elements
Inherited:	Yes

Similar to the CSS 3 opacity property, except the CSS 3 opacity property is not inherited. <alphavalue> refers to a floating integer between 0.0 (fully transparent) and 1.0 (fully opaque).

```
table {opacity: 0.9;}
```

Box Model

Property	Supported Since
-moz-border-radius-topleft -moz-border-radius-topright -moz-border-radius-bottom-left -moz-border-radius-bottom-right	NS 6
Value	<length> | <percentage> | inherit
Initial value:	0
Applies to:	All elements
Inherited:	No

Applies rounded corners to box borders. Similar to the border-top-left-radius, border-top-right-radius, border-bottom-left-radius and border-bottom-right-radius properties proposed for inclusion in CSS 3.

-moz-border-radius	NS6
Value	[<length> | <percentage>] {!,4} | inherit
Initial value:	0
Applies to:	All elements
Inherited:	No

Applies rounded corners to box borders. A similar border-radius property is proposed for inclusion in CSS 3.

-moz-border-top-colors -moz-border-right-colors -moz-border-bottom-colors -moz-border-left-colors	NS6
Value	<color>+ | none | inherit
Initial value:	none
Applies to:	All elements
Inherited:	No

Property	Supported Since
Provides a color striping effect for borders, where one or more <color> values are provided. Each color is applied in 1 pixel-width increments from the outside border to the inside border. If there are not enough colors specified for each pixel width, the value of the border-color property colors the remaining border.	

User-Interface

Property	Supported Since
-moz-outline-color	NS 6
Value:	<color> | invert | inherit
Applies to:	All elements
Inherited:	No
-moz-outline-style	NS 6
Value:	<border-style> | inherit
Applies to:	All elements
Inherited:	No
-moz-outline-width	NS 6
Value:	<border-width> | inherit
Applies to:	All elements
Inherited:	No
-moz-outline	NS 6
Value:	[<-moz-outline-color> | | <-moz-outline-style> | | <-moz-outline-width>] | inherit
Applies to:	All elements
Inherited:	No

-moz-outline, -moz-outline-color, -moz-outline-style and -moz-outline-width are intended to mirror the CSS outline properties, Mozilla has implemented these properties as such until their implementation of the outline property can be said to conform to the W3C definition of what the outline property provides.

C

CSS Colors

This appendix references the available CSS color keywords as documented in the W3C CSS 3 candidate recommendation. With the exception of Internet Explorer not supporting spelling of *gray* with an *a*, as in its American spelling, all the following keywords are supported by Internet Explorer 5.5 and 6, Mozilla 1.7, Opera 7.5, and Safari 1.2.

Colors Sorted Alphabetically

Color Keyword	Hexadecimal Value	RGB
aliceblue	#F0F8FF	240, 248, 255
antiquewhite	#FAEBD7	250, 235, 215
aqua	#00FFFF	0, 255, 255
aquamarine	#7FFFD4	127, 255, 212
azure	#F0FFFF	240, 255, 255
beige	#F5F5DC	245, 245, 220
bisque	#FFE4C4	255, 228, 196
black	#000000	0, 0, 0
blanchedalmond	#FFEBCD	255, 235, 205
blue	#0000FF	0, 0, 255
blueviolet	#8A2BE2	138, 43, 226
brown	#A52A2A	165, 42, 42
burlywood	#DEB887	222, 184, 135
cadetblue	#5F9EA0	95, 158, 160

Table continued on following page

Color Keyword	Hexadecimal Value	RGB
chartreuse	#7FFF00	127, 255, 0
chocolate	#D2691E	210, 105, 30
coral	#FF7F50	255, 127, 80
cornflowerblue	#6495ED	100, 149, 237
cornsilk	#FFF8DC	255, 248, 220
crimson	#DC143C	220, 20, 60
cyan	#00FFFF	0, 255, 255
darkblue	#00008B	0, 0, 139
darkcyan	#008B8B	0, 139, 139
darkgoldenrod	#B8860B	184, 134, 11
darkgray	#A9A9A9	169, 169, 169
darkgreen	#006400	0, 100, 0
darkgrey	#A9A9A9	169, 169, 169
darkkhaki	#BDB76B	189, 183, 107
darkmagenta	#8B008B	139, 0, 139
darkolivegreen	#556B2F	85, 107, 47
darkorange	#FF8C00	255, 140, 0
darkorchid	#9932CC	153, 50, 204
darkred	#8B0000	139, 0, 0
darksalmon	#E9967A	233, 150, 122
darkseagreen	#8FBC8F	143, 188, 143
darkslateblue	#483D8B	72, 61, 139
darkslategray	#2F4F4F	47, 79, 79
darkslategrey	#2F4F4F	47, 79, 79
darkturquoise	#00CED1	0, 206, 209
darkviolet	#9400D3	148, 0, 211
deeppink	#FF1493	255, 20, 147
deepskyblue	#00BFFF	0, 191, 255
dimgray	#696969	105, 105, 105
dimgrey	#696969	105, 105, 105
dodgerblue	#1E90FF	30, 144, 255

Color Keyword	Hexadecimal Value	RGB
firebrick	#B22222	178, 34, 34
floralwhite	#FFFAF0	255, 250, 240
forestgreen	#228B22	34, 139, 34
fuchsia	#FF00FF	255, 0, 255
gainsboro	#DCDCDC	220, 220, 220
ghostwhite	#F8F8FF	248, 248, 255
gold	#FFD700	255, 215, 0
goldenrod	#DAA520	218, 165, 32
gray	#808080	128, 128, 128
green	#008000	0, 128, 0
greenyellow	#ADFF2F	173, 255, 47
grey	#808080	128, 128, 128
honeydew	#F0FFF0	240, 255, 240
hotpink	#FF69B4	255, 105, 180
indianred	#CD5C5C	205, 92, 92
indigo	#4B0082	75, 0, 130
ivory	#FFFFF0	255, 255, 240
khaki	#F0E68C	240, 230, 140
lavender	#E6E6FA	230, 230, 250
lavenderblush	#FFF0F5	255, 240, 245
lawngreen	#7CFC00	124, 252, 0
lemonchiffon	#FFFACD	255, 250, 205
lightblue	#ADD8E6	173, 216, 230
lightcoral	#F08080	240, 128, 128
lightcyan	#E0FFFF	224, 255, 255
lightgoldenrodyellow	#FAFAD2	250, 250, 210
lightgray	#D3D3D3	211, 211, 211
lightgreen	#90EE90	144, 238, 144
lightgrey	#D3D3D3	211, 211, 211
lightpink	#FFB6C1	255, 182, 193
lightsalmon	#FFA07A	255, 160, 122

Table continued on following page

Color Keyword	Hexadecimal Value	RGB
lightseagreen	#20B2AA	32, 178, 170
lightskyblue	#87CEFA	135, 206, 250
lightslategray	#778899	119, 136, 153
lightslategrey	#778899	119, 136, 153
lightsteelblue	#B0C4DE	176, 196, 222
lightyellow	#FFFFE0	255, 255, 224
lime	#00FF00	0, 255, 0
limegreen	#32CD32	50, 205, 50
linen	#FAF0E6	250, 240, 230
magenta	#FF00FF	255, 0, 255
maroon	#800000	128, 0, 0
mediumaquamarine	#66CDAA	102, 205, 170
mediumblue	#0000CD	0, 0, 205
mediumorchid	#BA55D3	186, 85, 211
mediumpurple	#9370DB	147, 112, 219
mediumseagreen	#3CB371	60, 179, 113
mediumslateblue	#7B68EE	123, 104, 238
mediumspringgreen	#00FA9A	0, 250, 154
mediumturquoise	#48D1CC	72, 209, 204
mediumvioletred	#C71585	199, 21, 133
midnightblue	#191970	25, 25, 112
mintcream	#F5FFFA	245, 255, 250
mistyrose	#FFE4E1	255, 228, 225
moccasin	#FFE4B5	255, 228, 181
navajowhite	#FFDEAD	255, 222, 173
navy	#000080	0, 0, 128
oldlace	#FDF5E6	253, 245, 230
olive	#808000	128, 128, 0
olivedrab	#6B8E23	107, 142, 35
orange	#FFA500	255, 165, 0
orangered	#FF4500	255, 69, 0

Color Keyword	Hexadecimal Value	RGB
orchid	#DA70D6	218, 112, 214
palegoldenrod	#EEE8AA	238, 232, 170
palegreen	#98FB98	152, 251, 152
paleturquoise	#AFEEEE	175, 238, 238
palevioletred	#DB7093	219, 112, 147
papayawhip	#FFEFD5	255, 239, 213
peachpuff	#FFDAB9	255, 218, 185
peru	#CD853F	205, 133, 63
pink	#FFC0CB	255, 192, 203
plum	#DDA0DD	221, 160, 221
powderblue	#B0E0E6	176, 224, 230
purple	#800080	128, 0, 128
red	#FF0000	255, 0, 0
rosybrown	#BC8F8F	188, 143, 143
royalblue	#4169E1	65, 105, 225
saddlebrown	#8B4513	139, 69, 19
salmon	#FA8072	250, 128, 114
sandybrown	#F4A460	244, 164, 96
seagreen	#2E8B57	46, 139, 87
seashell	#FFF5EE	255, 245, 238
sienna	#A0522D	160, 82, 45
silver	#C0C0C0	192, 192, 192
skyblue	#87CEEB	135, 206, 235
slateblue	#6A5ACD	106, 90, 205
slategray	#708090	112, 128, 144
slategrey	#708090	112, 128, 144
snow	#FFFAFA	255, 250, 250
springgreen	#00FF7F	0, 255, 127
steelblue	#4682B4	70, 130, 180
tan	#D2B48C	210, 180, 140
teal	#008080	0, 128, 128

Table continued on following page

Color Keyword	Hexadecimal Value	RGB
thistle	#D8BFD8	216, 191, 216
tomato	#FF6347	255, 99, 71
turquoise	#40E0D0	64, 224, 208
violet	#EE82EE	238, 130, 238
wheat	#F5DEB3	245, 222, 179
white	#FFFFFF	255, 255, 255
whitesmoke	#F5F5F5	245, 245, 245
yellow	#FFFF00	255, 255, 0
yellowgreen	#9ACD32	154, 205, 50

Colors Sorted by Color

The following sections show colors as sorted from light hue to dark hue.

Reds

Color Keyword	Hexadecimal	RGB
lavenderblush	#FFF0F5	255, 240, 245
mistyrose	#FFE4E1	255, 228, 225
pink	#FFC0CB	255, 192, 203
lightpink	#FFB6C1	255, 182, 193
orange	#FFA500	255, 165, 0
lightsalmon	#FFA07A	255, 160, 122
darkorange	#FF8C00	255, 140, 0
coral	#FF7F50	255, 127, 80
hotpink	#FF69B4	255, 105, 180
tomato	#FF6347	255, 99, 71
orangered	#FF4500	255, 69, 0
deeppink	#FF1493	255, 20, 147
fuchsia	#FF00FF	255, 0, 255
magenta	#FF00FF	255, 0, 255
red	#FF0000	255, 0, 0

Color Keyword	Hexadecimal	RGB
salmon	#FA8072	250, 128, 114
lightcoral	#F08080	240, 128, 128
violet	#EE82EE	238, 130, 238
darksalmon	#E9967A	233, 150, 122
plum	#DDA0DD	221, 160, 221
crimson	#DC143C	220, 20, 60
palevioletred	#DB7093	219, 112, 147
orchid	#DA70D6	218, 112, 214
thistle	#D8BFD8	216, 191, 216
indianred	#CD5C5C	205, 92, 92
mediumvioletred	#C71585	199, 21, 133
mediumorchid	#BA55D3	186, 85, 211
firebrick	#B22222	178, 34, 34
darkorchid	#9932CC	153, 50, 204
darkviolet	#9400D3	148, 0, 211
mediumpurple	#9370DB	147, 112, 219
darkmagenta	#8B008B	139, 0, 139
darkred	#8B0000	139, 0, 0
purple	#800080	128, 0, 128
maroon	#800000	128, 0, 0

Blues

Color Keyword	Hexadecimal	RGB
azure	#F0FFFF	240, 255, 255
aliceblue	#F0F8FF	240, 248, 255
lavender	#E6E6FA	230, 230, 250
lightcyan	#E0FFFF	224, 255, 255
powderblue	#B0E0E6	176, 224, 230
lightsteelblue	#B0C4DE	176, 196, 222
paleturquoise	#AFEEEE	175, 238, 238

Table continued on following page

Color Keyword	Hexadecimal	RGB
lightblue	#ADD8E6	173, 216, 230
blueviolet	#8A2BE2	138, 43, 226
lightskyblue	#87CEFA	135, 206, 250
skyblue	#87CEEB	135, 206, 235
mediumslateblue	#7B68EE	123, 104, 238
slateblue	#6A5ACD	106, 90, 205
cornflowerblue	#6495ED	100, 149, 237
cadetblue	#5F9EA0	95, 158, 160
indigo	#4B0082	75, 0, 130
mediumturquoise	#48D1CC	72, 209, 204
darkslateblue	#483D8B	72, 61, 139
steelblue	#4682B4	70, 130, 180
royalblue	#4169E1	65, 105, 225
turquoise	#40E0D0	64, 224, 208
dodgerblue	#1E90FF	30, 144, 255
midnightblue	#191970	25, 25, 112
aqua	#00FFFF	0, 255, 255
cyan	#00FFFF	0, 255, 255
darkturquoise	#00CED1	0, 206, 209
deepskyblue	#00BFFF	0, 191, 255
darkcyan	#008B8B	0, 139, 139
blue	#0000FF	0, 0, 255
mediumblue	#0000CD	0, 0, 205
darkblue	#00008B	0, 0, 139
navy	#000080	0, 0, 128

Greens

Color Keyword	Hexadecimal	RGB
mintcream	#F5FFFA	245, 255, 250
honeydew	#F0FFF0	240, 255, 240

Color Keyword	Hexadecimal	RGB
greenyellow	#ADFF2F	173, 255, 47
yellowgreen	#9ACD32	154, 205, 50
palegreen	#98FB98	152, 251, 152
lightgreen	#90EE90	144, 238, 144
darkseagreen	#8FBC8F	143, 188, 143
olive	#808000	128, 128, 0
aquamarine	#7FFFD4	127, 255, 212
chartreuse	#7FFF00	127, 255, 0
lawngreen	#7CFC00	124, 252, 0
olivedrab	#6B8E23	107, 142, 35
mediumaquamarine	#66CDAA	102, 205, 170
darkolivegreen	#556B2F	85, 107, 47
mediumseagreen	#3CB371	60, 179, 113
limegreen	#32CD32	50, 205, 50
seagreen	#2E8B57	46, 139, 87
forestgreen	#228B22	34, 139, 34
lightseagreen	#20B2AA	32, 178, 170
springgreen	#00FF7F	0, 255, 127
lime	#00FF00	0, 255, 0
mediumspringgreen	#00FA9A	0, 250, 154
teal	#008080	0, 128, 128
green	#008000	0, 128, 0
darkgreen	#006400	0, 100, 0

Yellows

Color Keyword	Hexadecimal	RGB
lightgoldenrodyellow	#FAFAD2	250, 250, 210
ivory	#FFFFF0	255, 255, 240
lightyellow	#FFFFE0	255, 255, 224
floralwhite	#FFFAF0	255, 250, 240

Table continued on following page

Color Keyword	Hexadecimal	RGB
lemonchiffon	#FFFACD	255, 250, 205
cornsilk	#FFF8DC	255, 248, 220
khaki	#F0E68C	240, 230, 140
yellow	#FFFF00	255, 255, 0
gold	#FFD700	255, 215, 0
darkkhaki	#BDB76B	189, 183, 107

Browns

Color Keyword	Hexadecimal	RGB
snow	#FFFAFA	255, 250, 250
seashell	#FFF5EE	255, 245, 238
oldlace	#FDF5E6	253, 245, 230
linen	#FAF0E6	250, 240, 230
antiquewhite	#FAEBD7	250, 235, 215
beige	#F5F5DC	245, 245, 220
papayawhip	#FFEFD5	255, 239, 213
blanchedalmond	#FFEBCD	255, 235, 205
bisque	#FFE4C4	255, 228, 196
moccasin	#FFE4B5	255, 228, 181
navajowhite	#FFDEAD	255, 222, 173
peachpuff	#FFDAB9	255, 218, 185
wheat	#F5DEB3	245, 222, 179
sandybrown	#F4A460	244, 164, 96
palegoldenrod	#EEE8AA	238, 232, 170
burlywood	#DEB887	222, 184, 135
goldenrod	#DAA520	218, 165, 32
tan	#D2B48C	210, 180, 140
chocolate	#D2691E	210, 105, 30
peru	#CD853F	205, 133, 63
rosybrown	#BC8F8F	188, 143, 143
darkgoldenrod	#B8860B	184, 134, 11

Color Keyword	Hexadecimal	RGB
brown	#A52A2A	165, 42, 42
sienna	#A0522D	160, 82, 45
saddlebrown	#8B4513	139, 69, 19

Grays

Color Keyword	Hexadecimal	RGB
white	#FFFFFF	255, 255, 255
ghostwhite	#F8F8FF	248, 248, 255
whitesmoke	#F5F5F5	245, 245, 245
gainsboro	#DCDCDC	220, 220, 220
lightgray	#D3D3D3	211, 211, 211
lightgrey	#D3D3D3	211, 211, 211
silver	#C0C0C0	192, 192, 192
darkgray	#A9A9A9	169, 169, 169
darkgrey	#A9A9A9	169, 169, 169
gray	#808080	128, 128, 128
grey	#808080	128, 128, 128
lightslategray	#778899	119, 136, 153
lightslategrey	#778899	119, 136, 153
slategray	#708090	112, 128, 144
slategrey	#708090	112, 128, 144
dimgray	#696969	105, 105, 105
dimgrey	#696969	105, 105, 105
darkslategray	#2F4F4F	47, 79, 79
darkslategrey	#2F4F4F	47, 79, 79
black	#000000	0, 0, 0

User-Interface Color Keywords

User-interface color keywords (CSS 2 & 3) enable an author to reference colors present in the user-interface. They are referenced like any other color keyword. These color keywords allow an author to design a website with the same look and feel as the operating system.

Color Keyword	Description
ActiveBorder	Border of the active window.
ActiveCaption	Caption of the active window.
AppWorkspace	Background color of multiple document interface.
Background	Desktop background.
ButtonFace	Face color of three-dimensional display elements.
ButtonHighlight	Dark shadow for three-dimensional display elements (for edges facing away from the light source).
ButtonShadow	Shadow color for three-dimensional display elements.
ButtonText	Text on push buttons.
CaptionText	Text in caption, size box, and scrollbar arrow box.
GrayText	Grayed (disabled) text. This color is set to #000 if the current display driver does not support a solid gray color.
Highlight	Item(s) selected in a control.
HighlightText	Text of item(s) selected in a control.
InactiveBorder	Inactive window border.
InactiveCaption	Inactive window caption.
InactiveCaptionText	Color of text in an inactive caption.
InfoBackground	Background color for tooltip controls.
InfoText	Text color for tooltip controls.
Menu	Menu background.
MenuText	Text in menus.
Scrollbar	Scrollbar gray area.
ThreeDDarkShadow	Dark shadow for three-dimensional display elements.
ThreeDFace	Face color for three-dimensional display elements.
ThreeDHighlight	Highlight color for three-dimensional display elements.
ThreeDLightShadow	Light color for three-dimensional display elements (for edges facing the light source).
ThreeDShadow	Dark shadow for three-dimensional display elements.
Window	Window background.
WindowFrame	Window frame.
WindowText	Text in windows.

D

Browser Rendering Modes

S = Standards mode

A = Almost standards mode

Q = Quirks mode

Doctype / Document	IE6 (Win)	IE5 (Mac)	Moz NS7	O	S
Pre HTML 4.0 DTD `<!DOCTYPE HTML PUBLIC "-//W3C//DTD HTML 3.2 Final//EN">`	Q	Q	Q	Q	Q
HTML 4.0					
HTML 4.0 Transitional DTD without DTD URL `<!DOCTYPE HTML PUBLIC "-//W3C//DTD HTML 4.0 Transitional//EN">`	Q	Q	Q	Q	Q
HTML 4.0 Transitional DTD with DTD URL `<!DOCTYPE HTML PUBLIC "-//W3C//DTD HTML 4.01 Transitional//EN" "http://www.w3.org/TR/html4/loose.dtd">`	S	S	Q	S	S
HTML 4.0 Frameset DTD without DTD URL `<!DOCTYPE HTML PUBLIC "-//W3C//DTD HTML 4.0 Frameset//EN">`	Q	Q	Q	Q	Q
HTML 4.0 Frameset DTD with DTD URL `<!DOCTYPE HTML PUBLIC "-//W3C//DTD HTML 4.0 Frameset//EN" "http://www.w3.org/TR/REC-html40/frameset.dtd">`	S	S	Q	S	Q

Table continued on following page

Doctype / Document	IE6 (Win)	IE5 (Mac)	Moz NS7	O	S

HTML 4.0 Strict DTD without DTD URL
 	
`<!DOCTYPE HTML PUBLIC "-//W3C//`
`DTD HTML 4.0//EN">`
	S	S	S	S	S

HTML 4.0 Strict DTD with DTD URL
 	
`<!DOCTYPE HTML PUBLIC "-//W3C//DTD HTML 4.0//`
`EN" "http://www.w3.org/TR/html4/strict.dtd">`
	S	S	S	S	S

HTML 4.01					

HTML 4.01 Transitional DTD without DTD URL
 	
`<!DOCTYPE HTML PUBLIC "-//W3C//DTD HTML 4.01`
`Transitional//EN">`
	Q	Q	Q	Q	Q

HTML 4.01 Transitional DTD with DTD URL
 	
`<!DOCTYPE HTML PUBLIC "-//W3C//DTD HTML 4.01`
`Transitional//EN" "http://www.w3.org/TR/`
`html4/loose.dtd">`
	S	S	A	S	S

HTML 4.01 Frameset DTD without DTD URL
 	
`<!DOCTYPE HTML PUBLIC "-//W3C//DTD HTML 4.01`
`Frameset//EN">`
	Q	Q	Q	Q	Q

HTML 4.01 Frameset DTD with DTD URL
 	
`<!DOCTYPE HTML PUBLIC "-//W3C//DTD HTML 4.01`
`Frameset//EN" "http://www.w3.org/TR/html4/`
`frameset.dtd">`
	S	S	A	S	A

HTML 4.01 Strict DTD without DTD URL
 	
`<!DOCTYPE HTML PUBLIC "-//W3C//`
`DTD HTML 4.01//EN">`
	S	Q	S	S	S

HTML 4.01 Strict DTD with DTD URL
 	
`<!DOCTYPE HTML PUBLIC "-//W3C//`
`DTD HTML 4.01//EN" "http://www.w3.org/TR/`
`html4/strict.dtd">`
	S	S	S	S	S

XHTML 1.0					

XHTML 1.0 Transitional DTD without an XML Declaration
 	
`<!DOCTYPE html PUBLIC "-//W3C//DTD XHTML 1.0`
`Transitional//EN" "http://www.w3.org/TR/`
`xhtml1/DTD/xhtml1-transitional.dtd">`
	S	S	A	S	S

Doctype / Document	IE6 (Win)	IE5 (Mac)	Moz NS7	O	S

XHTML 1.0 Transitional DTD with an XML Declaration
 	
`<?xml version="1.0" encoding="LATIN-1"?>`
`<!DOCTYPE html PUBLIC "-//W3C//DTD XHTML 1.0`
`Transitional//EN" "http://www.w3.org/TR/`
`xhtml1/DTD/xhtml1-transitional.dtd">`
	Q	S	A	S	S

XHTML 1.0 Frameset DTD with a DTD URL
 	
`<!DOCTYPE html PUBLIC "-//W3C//DTD XHTML 1.0`
`Frameset//EN" "http://www.w3.org/TR/xhtml1/`
`DTD/xhtml1-frameset.dtd">`
	S	S	A	S	A

XHTML 1.0 Strict DTD without an XML Declaration
 	
`<!DOCTYPE html PUBLIC "-//W3C//DTD XHTML 1.0`
`Strict//EN" "http://www.w3.org/TR/xhtml1/DTD/`
`xhtml1-strict.dtd">`
	S	S	S	S	S

XHTML 1.0 Strict DTD with an XML Declaration
 	
`<?xml version="1.0" encoding="LATIN-1"?>`
`<!DOCTYPE html PUBLIC "-//W3C//DTD XHTML 1.0`
`Strict//EN" "http://www.w3.org/TR/xhtml1/DTD/`
`xhtml1-strict.dtd">`
	Q	S	S	S	S

Other					
XML Documents	S	S	S	S	S
No DOCTYPE	Q	Q	Q	Q	Q
Unrecognized DOCTYPE	S	S	S	S	S

Index

SYMBOLS AND NUMERICS

* (asterisk), 77–78, 204
*/ (asterisk, forward slash), 54
\ (backslash), 61
^ (caret), 95
: (colon), 108
$ (dollar sign), 96
:: (double colon), 108
" (double quotes)
  in strings, 60–61
  XHTML, enclosing attribute values in, 31–32
/* (forward slash, asterisk), 54
> (greater-than symbol)
  HTML tags, 23
  relationship between elements, showing, 86
< (left angle bracket), 23
< (less-than symbol), 23
- (minus sign), 68–69
+ (plus sign), 68–69
? (question mark), 230
> (right angle bracket), 23
' (single quote), 61
~ (tilde), 92
100 percent width, 510–512

A

absolute font values
  size, 222–223
  weight, 218
absolute path, external style sheet, 50
absolute positioning, 384–387

accessibility
  custom style sheet, specifying, 156
  HTML tables versus CSS, 240
  liquid design and, 238–239
  list marker styles, 351
:active pseudo-class, 115–116
Administrator's Email address, 494
::after content, inserting, 111–113
Agaramond font, 218
aligning text
  blocks of slightly smaller text (top, middle and
    bottom keywords), 335–337
  described, 185–190, 334
  floating block elements, 323–328
  by percentage and length values, 338–339
  subscript and superscript text, 334–335
  table cells, 339–341
  on tallest character (text-top and text-bottom
    keywords), 338
alpha software, 493
America Online (AOL), 21
anatomy, CSS
  comments, 54
  declaration, grouping with selectors, 44–48
  embedded style sheet, 49–50
  external style sheet, linking to, 50
  importing style sheets, 50–52
  inline styles, 52–54
  rules described, 43–44
  selectors, 44
ancestral relationship
  custom style sheets, 156–161
  descendent elements, 153–154
  described, 85–89, 135–137

ancestral relationship (continued)

direct adjacent sibling combinator, 89–92

examples, 152, 154

float property, 313

inherit keyword, 137

navigational headings, colors for, 361

overriding (!important syntax), 155

selectors, precedence of, 139–151

style sheet, origination of, 137–139

anchor, pseudo-class based on (::target), 128–132

AOL (America Online), 21

Apache HTTP server, installing, 493–496

Apple Mac OS

Apache HTTP server, 493

Internet Explorer, future of, 20, 21

Safari browser, 23

text editors, 19

archive file, opening, 497, 499

Arial font, 206

Armenian letters, 346

arrow cursor images, 353

asterisk (*), 77–78, 204

asterisk, forward slash (*/), 54

attribute selectors

described, 93

mechanics, 98–99

presence of, 93–94

substring, 95–98

value of, 94–95

attributes

declaration, XML, 469–470

HTML, 25–28

minimization preventing with XHTML, 32

aural synthesizer, 243

author discussion, 7

auto handling, overflowing content, 302–304

auto **keyword, 58**

automatic numbering, 583–584

B

backgrounds

browser-compatible properties, 571–572

color

inline elements, 320–321

property, 357–361

table columns, 433–434

combining properties, 377–379

images

background-image property, 362–365

including with URI, 74

scrolling (background-attachment property), 375–377

tiling (background-repeat property), 365–369

inline elements, 320–321

Microsoft proprietary extensions, 587–588

navigational headings, 361

placing (background-position property), 369–374

table cells, 442

z-index positioning, 407–408

backslash (\), 61

banana cursor, 353, 354

baseline, table cell, 341

::before **content, inserting, 111–113**

Berners-Lee, Tim (Web inventor), 12

beta software, 493

blocks, text

centering, 291–293

characters, aligning on tallest (text-top and text-bottom keywords), 338

floating, 323–328

slightly smaller, aligning (top, middle and bottom keywords), 335–337

XML elements, displaying, 473

blue colors, 597–598

bold font (font-weight property), 216–221

borders

color, 255–256

content, space padding

applying, 275–276, 297–302

CSS box model, 84, 247–248

elements, grouping, 48–49

inline elements, 319

margin collapse, preventing, 311–312

right floated elements, 324

inline elements, 319

list elements, 350

margin collapse, preventing, 311

style, 250–255

tables, adding extra (border-collapse), 451–453

width, CSS box model, 248–250

Bos, Bert (CSS creator), 13

bottom alignment, 335–337

bottom margin

collapsing, 310–313

setting, 290–291

box model

borders

color, 255–256

combined properties, 259–260

future CSS 3 properties, 260–264

sides, shorthand for, 256–259
style, 250–255
width, 248–250
browser-compatible properties, 574–578
described, 84
dimensions described, 268
example, 264–268
Gecko proprietary extensions, 589–590
height, 270–274
illustrated, 246–248
inheritance versus, 136
line-height property, 282–288
margins
applying, 297–302
described, 290–297
minimum and maximum dimensions, 277–282
overflowing content, handling, 302–305
padding
applying, 297–302
described, 288–290
percentage width and height measurements, 274–276
width, 269–270
Braille devices, 243
break, line
HTML, 23–24
tag, avoiding, 241
white space, ignoring, 200
XHTML, 32–33
brown colors, 600–601
browsers
compatibility
background properties, 571–572
backward, XHTML and, 33
box model properties, 574–578
color properties, 568–569
conventions, 565
font properties, 569–570
generated content, automatic numbering, and lists, 583–584
indirect adjacent sibling selector, 93
paged media, 585–586
positioning, 579–580
pseudo-classes, 567
pseudo-elements, 568
selectors, 77, 100, 566–567
structural pseudo-classes, 120
table properties, 581
text properties, 572–573
user interface, 582–583
visual effects, 578
W3C role, 10

Gecko-based, 21–22
IE7 open source project
CSS features, 492–493
HTTP server, installing, 493–496
installing, 497–498
sample, 499–501
source code, obtaining, 492
style sheet, sample applying, 501–502
Internet Explorer
bugs, fixing, 502–510
content property and, 62
CSS box model quirk mode, 246
CSS, early support for, 13
custom style sheets, specifying, 156
described, 20–21
DTD, invoking rendering mode with, 37–39
multiple versions, installing, 512–517
Netscape Navigator versus, 491
overflow models limited to, 305
percentage widths and floating elements, 510–512
XML support, 462
KHTML, 22–23
Netscape Communicator, 239
Netscape Navigator
described, 21–22
multiple versions, running, 512
skepticism about CSS, 13
use of, 21, 491
Opera
content property and, 59, 62
described, 22
handheld emulator, 414, 417, 420–421
quirks mode and standards mode, 37
XML display values, nonsupported, 488
rendering modes, 603–605
Safari
described, 22–23
quirks mode and standards mode, 37
XML display values, nonsupported, 488
W3C specifications, 10–11
bugs
double-margin, 508–510
guillotine, 504–506
peek-a-boo, 502–504
software, stages of, 493
three-pixel jog, 507–508
bulleted and numbered (list-style-type **property)**
lists, 343–348

C

caching external style sheets, 242

candidate recommendation, W3C, 10

capitalization (`text-transform` **property**), 196–198

caption font, 232

captions

HTML tables, emulating, 479–480

tables, placing (`caption-side` property), 432–433

caret (^), 95

Cascading HTML Style Sheets, 13

Cascading Style Sheets. *See* CSS; CSS anatomy and syntax; CSS box model

Cascading Style Sheets (CSS 3)

border properties, 260–264

text changes in, 200–201

case-sensitivity

HTML 4.01 transitional, 40

XHTML, 31

XML, 28, 462

cell phone browser emulators, 414

cells

aligning text, 339–341

background, 442

coloring empty (`empty-cells`), 455–458

HTML data, 24

opacity, 442

spacing between (`border-spacing`), 453–455

XML emulating, 480–484

centering

background images, 370–373

block-level elements, 291–293

text, vertical, 402–403

centimeters, 63

Cerf, Vinton (IP creator), 12

character spacing

form input, 98

sample website, 175–178

characters

coding for Americas and Western Europe, 469

sequence of, 59–63

tallest, aligning text blocks on (`text-top` and `text-bottom` keywords), 338

child selectors

described, 85–89

navigational headings, colors for, 361

class and ID selectors, 100–105

class names, chained, 101

`clear` **property, 329–334**

clicked element (`:active` **pseudo-class), 115–116**

client-side computer, 12

clipping overflow content, 305

closing tags, 32–33

colon (:), 108

color

background

inline elements, 320–321

property, 357–361

table columns, 433–434

browser compatibility properties, 568–569

computer screen presentation, 243

hexadecimal, 71–72

keywords, 57–58, 70

listings

alphabetical, 591–596

blues, 597–598

browns, 600–601

grays, 601

greens, 598–599

reds, 596–597

user-interface keywords, 601–602

yellows, 599–600

RGB, 70–71

short hexadecimal and web-safe, 72–73

specifying, 69–70

text, grouping formatting, 48

updating, 165

columns

grouping data, 435

HTML tables, emulating, 480

multiple, 325–326

text color, 433–434

width and colors (`colgroup` and `col` elements), 433–434

combined `border` **properties, 259–260**

comments

adding, 49

conditional, IE7, 501–502, 515–516

in embedded style sheets, 49–50

multiline CSS, 54

Communicator (Netscape), 239

compatibility, browser

background properties, 571–572

backward, XHTML and, 33

box model properties, 574–578

color properties, 568–569

conventions, 565

font properties, 569–570

generated content, automatic numbering, and lists, 583–584

indirect adjacent sibling selector, 93

paged media, 585–586

positioning, 579–580
pseudo-classes, 567
pseudo-elements, 568
selectors, 77, 100, 566–567
structural pseudo-classes, 120
table properties, 581
text properties, 572–573
user interface, 582–583
visual effects, 578
W3C role, 10
computer monitor
element stretching larger than, 276
fonts, rendering in absolute measurement, 64
pixel measurements, 67
scaling to fit, 277–282
conditional comments, 501–502, 515–516
conditions, special, 107
content
adding
inside elements (`::before` and `::after` pseudo-elements), 111–113
strings, 59–63
border, space padding
applying, 275–276, 297–302
CSS box model, 84, 247–248
elements, grouping, 48–49
inline elements, 319
margin collapse, preventing, 311–312
right floated elements, 324
problems
partial disappearance, 504–506
random disappearance and reappearance, 502–504
side by side (`float` property)
canceling (`clear` property), 89, 329–334
content, randomly disappearing and reappearing, 502–504
described, 313–315
double margin, 508–510
example, 328–329
floating box model, 315–318
inline box model, 318–322
input form, 88–89, 104–105
left and right, 323–328
multiple, applying, 322–323
100 percent width and, 510–512
partial content disappearance, 504–506
percentage widths, 510–512
three pixels of space, 323–328
contextual/descendent selectors, 78–85
Courier/Courier New font, 206

Creative Commons License, 492
cross-browser compatibility
automatic numbering, 583–584
background properties, 571–572
backward, XHTML and, 33
box model properties, 574–578
color properties, 568–569
conventions, 565
font properties, 569–570
generated content, 583–584
indirect adjacent sibling selector, 93
lists, 583–584
paged media, 585–586
positioning, 579–580
pseudo-classes, 567
pseudo-elements, 568
selectors, 77, 100, 566–567
structural pseudo-classes, 120
table properties, 581
text properties, 572–573
user interface, 582–583
visual effects, 578
W3C role, 10
crosshair cursor, 352
CSS (Cascading Style Sheets)
advantages of, 14
creation and maintenance, 10–11
described, 9
hiding from older browsers, 49–50
history of, 13–14
IE7 open source features, 492–493
levels, 565
websites, 517–518
CSS (Cascading Style Sheets) anatomy and syntax
comments, 54
declaration, grouping with selectors, 44–48
embedded style sheet, 49–50
external style sheet, linking to, 50
importing style sheets, 50–52
inline styles, 52–54
rules described, 43–44
selectors, 44
CSS (Cascading Style Sheets) box model
borders
color, 255–256
combined properties, 259–260
future CSS 3 properties, 260–264
sides, shorthand for, 256–259
style, 250–255
width, 248–250

CSS (Cascading Style Sheets) box model (continued)
browser-compatible properties, 574–578
described, 84
dimensions described, 268
example, 264–268
Gecko proprietary extensions, 589–590
height, 270–274
illustrated, 246–248
inheritance versus, 136
line-height property, 282–288
margins
applying, 297–302
described, 290–297
minimum and maximum dimensions, 277–282
overflowing content, handling, 302–305
padding
applying, 297–302
described, 288–290
percentage width and height measurements, 274–276
width, 269–270
CSS (Cascading Style Sheets) Working Group, 10
CSS 3 (Cascading Style Sheets)
border properties, 260–264
text changes in, 200–201
cursive font, 206–207
cursor type, lists (cursor property), 351–354
custom style sheets
Mozilla, specifying with, 156–161
MSIE, specifying with, 156

D

data
accommodating (table-layout), 444–451
grouping, 435–443
width, accommodating, 58
data type, 59
data-entry form
basic look and feel, 80–84
boldface text, 99
colored labels, 90–92
field, focus on, 116–118
input fields, adding, 86–88
letter spacing, 98–99
questions, 85
Submit button, adding, 105
declaration, XML
attributes, 469–470
described, 468–469
grouping with selectors, 44–48
style sheet, including, 470–471

default style, applying (auto keyword), 58
descendent elements, 153–154
design, liquid
borders
color, 255–256
combined properties, 259–260
future CSS 3 properties, 260–264
sides, shorthand for, 256–259
style, 250–255
width, 248–250
browser-compatible properties, 574–578
described, 84, 237–238
dimensions described, 268
example, 264–268
external style sheets, advantages of, 242–245
Gecko proprietary extensions, 589–590
ground rules, 238–239
height, 270–274
HTML tables, limitations of, 239–241
illustrated, 246–248
inheritance versus, 136
line-height property, 282–288
margins
applying, 297–302
described, 290–297
minimum and maximum dimensions, 277–282
overflowing content, handling, 302–305
padding
applying, 297–302
described, 288–290
percentage width and height measurements, 274–276
unnecessary or useless markup, 241–242
width, 269–270
design strategy
described, 237–238
external style sheets, advantages of, 242–245
ground rules, 238–239
HTML tables, limitations of, 239–241
navigational menu, 174–175
sample website, 164–165
unnecessary or useless markup, 241–242
desktop icon font, 232
devices, designing for multiple
borders
color, 255–256
combined properties, 259–260
future CSS 3 properties, 260–264
sides, shorthand for, 256–259
style, 250–255
width, 248–250
browser-compatible properties, 574–578

described, 84, 237–238
dimensions described, 268
example, 264–268
external style sheets, advantages of, 242–245
Gecko proprietary extensions, 589–590
ground rules, 238–239
height, 270–274
HTML tables, limitations of, 239–241
illustrated, 246–248
inheritance versus, 136
line-height property, 282–288
margins
    applying, 297–302
    described, 290–297
minimum and maximum dimensions, 277–282
overflowing content, handling, 302–305
padding
    applying, 297–302
    described, 288–290
percentage width and height measurements, 274–276
unnecessary or useless markup, 241–242
width, 269–270
dimensions, CSS box
described, 268
height, 270–274
width, 269–270
direct adjacent sibling combinator, 89–92
direct child selectors
described, 85–89
navigational headings, colors for, 361
directory structure, 165–167
disabled, designing for
custom style sheet, specifying, 156
HTML tables versus CSS, 240
liquid design and, 238–239
list marker styles, 351
display values, 488–489
displaying XML documents
block elements, 473
described, 471–472
inline level elements, 472
list items, 473–478
dithering, 72–73
DOCTYPE sniffing, 37–38
document
pseudo-element formatting, 107–113
rule, applying to entire, 77–78
document standards
browser, choosing, 19–23
DTD
    DOCTYPE sniffing, 37–38
    HTML 4.01 frameset, 40–41

HTML 4.01 strict, 41
HTML 4.01 transitional, 40
mechanics of, 39–40
sample, 36–37
XHTML 1.0 frameset, 41
XHTML 1.0 strict, 41
XHTML 1.0 transitional, 41
HTML
    attributes, 25–28
    single tags and line breaks, 23–24
markup language, 17–19
XHTML
    attribute minimization, preventing, 32
    benefits of using, 18, 33–36
    case-sensitivity, 31
    mechanics, 36
    opening and closing tags, 32–33
    quotes, enclosing attribute values in, 31–32
XML, 28–30
Document Type Declaration. See DTD
dollar sign ($), 96
double colon (::), 108
double quotes (")
in strings, 60–61
XHTML, enclosing attribute values in, 31–32
double-margin bug, 508–510
download time, 33
drop-down menus
bug, correcting, 515
navigational, layers creating, 409–411
styling, 89
DTD (Document Type Declaration)
DOCTYPE sniffing, 37–38
HTML 4.01 frameset, 40–41
HTML 4.01 strict, 41
HTML 4.01 transitional, 40
mechanics of, 39–40
sample, 36–37
XHTML 1.0 frameset, 41
XHTML 1.0 strict, 41
XHTML 1.0 transitional, 41
XML standalone attribute, 469
dynamic pseudo-classes, 113–120

E

Edwards, Dean (IE7 creator), 492, 493
Einstein, Albert, quotation web page
clicking on heading, 131–132
dynamic pseudo-classes, 117–118
formatting, 109–110
inserting content, 112–113

Einstein, Albert, quotation web page (continued)

negation pseudo-class, 126–127

picture and `:target` effects, 129–131

root pseudo-classes, 124–126

structural pseudo-classes, 122–124

element

content and border, space between, CSS box model, 288–290

HTML, 24

without child elements, text, or content (`:empty`), 122–124

em unit

described, 65

measuring, 65–66

scaling and use of, 286–288

e-mail address, 494

embedded style sheet, 49–50

embossed Braille devices, 243

emphasis tag (`em`), 242

emulator, mobile phone browser, 414

encoding attribute, 469

e-resize / w-resize cursor image, 353

errata, book, 6

errors

double-margin, 508–510

guillotine, 504–506

peek-a-boo, 502–504

software, stages of, 493

three-pixel jog, 507–508

expand-to-fit elements, 58

eXtensible HyperText Markup Language. *See* XHTML

eXtensible Markup Language. *See* XML

eXtensible Stylesheet Language (XSL), 462

extensions, Microsoft proprietary

backgrounds, 587–588

conditional comments, 501–502

user interface, 587

visual effects, 586–587

external style sheet

linking to, 50

presentation method (`media` attribute and `@media` rule), 242–245

F

fantasy font, 206–207

Firefox browser, 22

first letter and first line of element containing text (`::first-letter` and `::first_line`), 108–110

first-child of element (`:first-child`), 121

fixed positioning, 403–405

fixing bugs

double-margin, 508–510

guillotine, 504–506

peek-a-boo, 502–504

software, stages of, 493

three-pixel jog, 507–508

`float` **property**

canceling (`clear` property), 89, 329–334

content, randomly disappearing and reappearing, 502–504

described, 313–315

double margin, 508–510

example, 328–329

floating box model, 315–318

inline box model, 318–322

input form, 88–89, 104–105

left and right, 323–328

multiple, applying, 322–323

100 percent width and, 510–512

partial content disappearance, 504–506

percentage widths, 510–512

three pixels of space, 323–328

floating box model, 315–318

floppy disc list marker, 349

focus element (input field or form button), 116–120

font

absolute lengths, 63–64

bold (`font-weight` property), 216–221

browser compatibility, 569–570

ex measurement, 67

first line or first element, formatting, 108–110

generic, 83, 206–208

properties, grouping, 46–48

shorthand property, 230–232

size

absolute values, 222–223

percentage values, 225–230

property overview, 221–222

relative values, 223–225

small caps (`font-variant` property), 215–216

specifying (`font-family` property), 203–205, 209–211

styles, switching (`font-style` property), 211–214

system, operating system keywords, 232–234

footer cells, table, 435

form button, 116–118

form, input

basic look and feel, 80–84

boldface text, 99

colored labels, 90–92

input fields, adding, 86–88
letter spacing, 98–99
questions, 85
Submit button, adding, 105
formatting
blocks
centering, 291–293
characters, aligning on tallest (`text-top` and
`text-bottom` keywords), 338
floating, 323–328
slightly smaller, aligning (`top`, `middle` and `bottom`
keywords), 335–337
XML elements, displaying, 473
lowercase letters as small caps, 216
multiple, enabling, 46–48
text
aligning, 185–190, 334–341
capitalizing (`text-transform` property), 196–198
changes ahead in CSS 3 Text module, 200–201
described, 163–164
design strategy, 164–165
directory structure, creating, 165–167
extra spaces, collapsing, 200
first line or first element as different size, 108–110
form questions, 85
indenting paragraphs, 181–185
`letter-spacing` property, 175–178
lowercase letters as small caps, 216
mouse-highlighted, 110–111
properties, grouping, 46–48
subset, raising and lowering (`text-top` and
`text-bottom`), 338
table of contents, 167–175
underlining, overlining, and strikethrough
(`text-decoration` property), 191–196
`white-space` property, 199–200
`word-spacing` property, 179–181
forward slash, asterisk (/*), 54
framesets, 40–41
FrontPage (Microsoft), 18
functions, negation pseudo-class, 126–128

G

Gecko-based browsers
box model, 589–590
described, 21–22
pseudo-elements, 588
user interface, 590
visual effects, 588–589

generated content
browser compatibility, 583–584
strings, 583–584
generic font families, 206–208
Georgian letters, 347
glitches
double-margin, 508–510
guillotine, 504–506
peek-a-boo, 502–504
software, stages of, 493
three-pixel jog, 507–508
graphics
backgrounds
`background-image` property, 362–365
including with URI, 74
scrolling (`background-attachment` property),
375–377
tiling (`background-repeat` property), 365–369
border side and corner, setting, 261
cursors, 352–353
as list markers, 349
text, alternate, 240
gray/grey colors
Internet Explorer spelling, 84, 434
listed, 601
tables, coloring empty cells (`empty-cells`), 455–458
greater-than symbol (>)
HTML tags, 23
relationship between elements, showing, 86
Greek letters, 346
green colors, 598–599
grouping
emulating HTML tables, 480–484
HTML table data, 435–443
XML declaration with selectors, 44–48
guillotine bug, 504–506

H

handheld devices
style, 243
styling web documents for, 413–421
headings
backgrounds, 361
clicking on, 131–132
colored, 360–361
navigational hyperlinks, 403
table, grouping, 435
hearing impaired
liquid design and, 238
list marker styles, 351

help cursor image, 353
Helvetica font, 206
hexadecimal colors, 71–72
highlighting
  cell widths, 448–450
  list markers, 350
home page, return element, 403
horizontal rows
  HTML data, 24
  table cell, aligning, 341
  XML emulating, 480–484
horizontal scroll bar, 304–305, 305
horizontal tiling, background images, 366
hourglass cursor images, 353
hovering mouse pointer (`:hover` pseudo-class),
  114–115
HTML 4.0 (HyperText Markup Language) rendering
  modes, 603–604
HTML 4.01 (HyperText Markup Language)
  DTD, 40–41
  rendering modes, 604
  strict, 41
  transitional, 40
HTML (HyperText Markup Language)
  anchors, pseudo-class based on (`::target`),
    128–132
  attribute selectors, 93
  attributes, 25–28
  benefits of using, 18
  conditional comment tags, 502
  creation of, 12
  display values, 488–489
  document display values, 488–489
  DTD, 36–37
  files, creating, 19
  limitations, 13
  one-word attributes, 32
  root element, pseudo-class referring to, 120, 124–125
  sample page, 521–522
  single tags and line breaks, 23–24
  XHTML versus, 9, 31, 33
  XML versus, 28
HTML (HyperText Markup Language) tables
  benefits of, 429
  borders, adding extra (`border-collapse`), 451–453
  captions, 432–433
  cells
    content, `vertical-align` property, 339–341
    empty, coloring grey (`empty-cells`), 455–458
    spacing between (`border-spacing`), 453–455

  columns
    vertical (`colgroup` and `col` elements), 433–434
    width and colors, 433–434
  data
    accommodating (`table-layout`), 444–451
    grouping, 435–443
  HTML sample, 23–24
  limitations of, 239–241
  liquid design, barring, 238
  optional elements, 430–432
  placing captions (`caption-side` property), 432–433
  styling overview, 429
  XML emulating
    applying, 479
    captioning, 479–480
    columns, 480
    described, 478–479
    example, 485–487
    groupings, table rows, and table cells, 480–484
HTTP (HyperText Transfer Protocol), 12
HTTP (HyperText Transfer Protocol) server
  installing for IE7, 493–496
  Internet mechanics, 11–12
hummus recipe
  HTML table, creating, 25–28
  XHTML, rewriting in, 34–36
  XML document, creating, 29–30
hyperlinks
  focus, shifting, 116
  navigational headings, 403
  pseudo-classes for visited and unvisited (`:link` and
    `:visited`), 113–114
HyperText Markup Language. See HTML
HyperText Markup Language tables. See HTML tables
HyperText Transfer Protocol (HTTP), 12
HyperText Transfer Protocol (HTTP) server
  installing for IE7, 493–496
  Internet mechanics, 11–12

I

icon font, 232
IE7 open source project
  CSS features, 492–493
  HTTP server, installing, 493–496
  installing, 497–498
  sample, 499–501
  source code, obtaining, 492
  style sheet, sample applying, 501–502
image-editing software, 167–172

images
backgrounds
`background-image` property, 362–365
including with URI, 74
scrolling (`background-attachment` property), 375–377
tiling (`background-repeat` property), 365–369
border side and corner, setting, 261
cursors, 352–353
as list markers, 349
text, alternate, 240
`!important` **syntax, 155**
importing style sheets, 50–52
inches, absolute length in, 63
indenting
incorrect three-pixel jog, 507–508
markup, 175
paragraphs, 181–185
indirect adjacent sibling combinators, 92–93
inheritance
custom style sheets
Internet Explorer, 156
Mozilla, 156–161
descendent elements, 153–154
described, 135–137
examples, 152, 154
`float` property, 313
`inherit` keyword, 137
overriding (`!important` syntax), 155
selectors, precedence of, 139–151
style sheet, origination of, 137–139
inline box model, 318–322
inline level elements, 472
inline styles, 52–54
input form
basic look and feel, 80–84
boldface text, 99
colored labels, 90–92
field, focus on, 116–118
input fields, adding, 86–88
letter spacing, 98–99
questions, 85
Submit button, adding, 105
inserting content (`::before` and `::after`), 111–113
installing
HTTP server, 493–496
IE7 open source project, 497–498
Internet Explorer, multiple versions, 512–517
integers and real numbers, 68–69

interface, user
browser compatibility, 582–583
color keywords, 601–602
defined, 238
Gecko proprietary extensions, 590
Microsoft proprietary extensions, 587
Internet
mechanics of, 11–12
W3C role, 10
Internet Explorer (Microsoft)
bugs, fixing
double-margin, 508–510
guillotine, 504–506
peek-a-boo bug, 502–504
three-pixel jog, 507–508
`content` property and, 62
CSS box model quirk mode, 246
CSS, early support for, 13
custom style sheets, specifying, 156
described, 20–21
DTD, invoking rendering mode with, 37–39
IE7 open source project
CSS features, 492–493
HTTP server, installing, 493–496
installing, 497–498
sample, 499–501
source code, obtaining, 492
style sheet, sample applying, 501–502
multiple versions, installing, 512–517
Netscape Navigator versus, 491
overflow models limited to, 305
percentage widths and floating elements, 510–512
XML support, 462
IP (Internet Protocol), 12
italic font
oblique, switching, 211–214
tag, avoiding, 241

J
JavaScript file, referencing, 502
JPEG (Joint Photographic Experts Group) background images, 365
JT's Island Grill and Gallery website
background
color property, 358–361
fixing, 376–377
images, adding, 363–365
positioning, 372–374

JT's Island Grill and Gallery website (continued)

borders, 261–268

cascade and inheritance, effects of, 141–151

design strategy, 164–165

dimensions, adding to style sheet, 283–288

directory structure, 165–167

drop-down navigational menus, 409–411

fixed positioning, 404–405

`float` property, 326–329, 332–334

font formatting

  applying throughout, 208–211

  boldface letters, 220–221

  capital and lowercase letters (`text-transform` property), 197–198

  italic and oblique, switching (`font-style` property), 211–214

  `letter-spacing` property, 177–178

  sizes, 227–230

layering, 409–411

list item markers, removing, 347–348

markup, 168–173

Motorola emulator displaying, 415

navigational menu, 174–175, 189

Openwave emulator displaying, 416

padding and margins, 293–302

positioning

  absolute, 385–387

  relative, 395–403

style sheets

  handheld device, applying, 417–421

  print, 424–427

  separating by media, 244–245

table of contents, 167–168

text formatting

  alignment, 187–189

  indenting, 184–185

  `text-decoration` property, 193–195

  `word-spacing` property, 180–181

justifying text, 186–189, 190

K

Kahn, Robert (IP creator), 12

keywords

colors, 70

described, 57–59

strings versus, 60

KHTML browsers

Konqueror , 22–23

Safari

  described, 22–23

  quirks mode and standards mode, 37

  XML display values, nonsupported, 488

L

last-child of element (`:last-child`), 121–122

Latin letters

encoding, 469

as list markers, 346

layering

absolute, 276, 384–387

backgrounds, 369–374

browser compatibility, 579–580

defined, 383–384

example, 399–403

fixed, 403–405

layering (z-index property), 405–411

offset, 387–393

relative, 393–399

static, 384

left angle bracket (<), 23

left `float` property

canceling, 330–332

described, 323–328

left margin, 290–291

lengths

absolute measurements, inconsistencies with, 64

`background-position` property, 369–374

box borders, 248

listed, 63

measurements based on height of lowercase letter *x*, 67

metric measurements, 64

percentage measurements, 68

pixel measurements, 67

relative length measurements, 65–67

typographical measurements, 65

`vertical-align` property, 338–339

less-than symbol (<), 23

letter spacing

form input, 98

sample website, 175–178

letters

coding for Americas and Western Europe, 469

sequence of, 59–63

tallest, aligning text blocks on (`text-top` and `text-bottom` keywords), 338

Lie, Håkon Wium (CSS creator), 13

line around window
color, 255–256
content, space padding
applying, 275–276, 297–302
CSS box model, 84, 247–248
elements, grouping, 48–49
inline elements, 319
margin collapse, preventing, 311–312
right floated elements, 324
inline elements, 319
list elements, 350
margin collapse, preventing, 311
style, 250–255
tables, adding extra (`border-collapse`), 451–453
width, CSS box model, 248–250
line break
HTML, 23–24
tag, avoiding, 241
white space, ignoring, 200
XHTML, 32–33
`line-height` **property**
CSS box model, 282–288
inline elements, 320
lines, paragraph spacing, 180
lining up text
blocks of slightly smaller text (`top`, `middle` and bottom `keywords`), 335–337
described, 185–190, 334
floating block elements, 323–328
by percentage and length values, 338–339
subscript and superscript text, 334–335
table cells, 339–341
on tallest character (`text-top` and `text-bottom` keywords), 338
links
focus, shifting, 116
navigational headings, 403
pseudo-classes for visited and unvisited (`:link` and `:visited`), 113–114
Linux operating system
Apache HTTP server, 493
browser, 22–23
liquid design
borders
color, 255–256
combined properties, 259–260
future CSS 3 properties, 260–264
sides, shorthand for, 256–259
style, 250–255
width, 248–250

browser-compatible properties, 574–578
described, 84, 237–238
dimensions described, 268
example, 264–268
external style sheets, advantages of, 242–245
Gecko proprietary extensions, 589–590
ground rules, 238–239
`height`, 270–274
HTML tables, limitations of, 239–241
illustrated, 246–248
inheritance versus, 136
`line-height` property, 282–288
margins
applying, 297–302
described, 290–297
minimum and maximum dimensions, 277–282
overflowing content, handling, 302–305
padding
applying, 297–302
described, 288–290
percentage width and height measurements, 274–276
unnecessary or useless markup, 241–242
`width`, 269–270
lists
browser compatibility, 583–584
bulleted (`list-style-type` property), 343–348
cursor type (`cursor` property), 351–354
drop-down
bug, correcting, 515
navigational, layers creating, 409–411
styling, 89
items, displaying in XML documents, 473–478
marker
changing (`list-style-type` property), 348–349
placing (`list-style-position` property), 349–350
multiple properties, shorthand controlling (`list-style` property), 350–351
numbered (`list-style-type` property), 343–348, 474–476
XML schema, 464
logo
`float` property, 328–329, 332–334
positioning problem, 515
watermarks, 403–405
Longhorn operating system, 492
lowercase letters
capitalizing (`text-transform` property), 196–198
case-sensitivity, 28, 31, 40, 462
small caps, formatting as, 216

M

Mac OS
Apache HTTP server, 493
Internet Explorer, future of, 20, 21
Safari browser, 23
text editors, 19
margins
canceling (clear property), 334
collapsing, 309–313, 314, 317
CSS box model, 275–276, 290–302
inline elements, 319
navigation headings, 403
right floated elements, 324
marker, list
item, placing (list-style-position property), 349–350
styling (list-style-type property), 345–346, 348–349
markup
language
described, 17–19
writing, 18–19
unnecessary or useless, 241–242
max-height **property, 280–282**
maximum dimensions, CSS box model, 277–282
max-width **property, 278–279**
measurements based on height of lowercase letter x, 67
media **attribute and** @media **rule, 242–245**
media, designing for multiple
described, 237–238
external style sheets, advantages of, 242–245
ground rules, 238–239
HTML tables, limitations of, 239–241
unnecessary or useless markup, 241–242
menu
drop-down
bug, correcting, 515
navigational, layers creating, 409–411
styling, 89
navigational
aligning, 189
building with pseudo-classes, 118–120
colored headings, 360–361
designing, 174–175
drop-down menus, 409–411
hyperlinks, 403
mobile phone browser, 414
underlining, removing from, 196
menu font, 232

message-box font, 232
methods, negation pseudo-class, 126–128
metric lengths, 64
Microsoft FrontPage, 18
Microsoft Internet Explorer
bugs, correcting
double-margin, 508–510
guillotine, 504–506
peek-a-boo, 502–504
three-pixel jog, 507–508
content property and, 62
CSS box model quirk mode, 246
CSS, early support for, 13
custom style sheets, specifying, 156
described, 20–21
DTD, invoking rendering mode with, 37–39
IE7 open source project
CSS features, 492–493
HTTP server, installing, 493–496
installing, 497–498
sample, 499–501
source code, obtaining, 492
style sheet, sample applying, 501–502
multiple versions, installing, 512–517
Netscape Navigator versus, 491
overflow models limited to, 305
percentage widths and floating elements, 510–512
XML support, 462
Microsoft proprietary extensions
backgrounds, 587–588
conditional comments, 501–502
user interface, 587
visual effects, 586–587
Microsoft Windows
cursor images, 353
text editors, 18
middle alignment, 335–337
millimeter lengths, 63
min-height **property, 279–280**
minimization attributes, preventing with XHTML, 32
minimum and maximum dimensions, CSS box model, 277–282
minus sign (-), 68–69
min-width **property, 277–278**
mobile phone browser emulators, 414
mockup, 167–172
monitor
element stretching larger than, 276
fonts, rendering in absolute measurement, 64
pixel measurements, 67
scaling to fit, 277–282

monospace font, 206–207
Monotype Corsiva font, 213
Motorola phone emulator, 414, 415
mouse
    hovering pointer (:hover pseudo-class), 114–115
    text, highlighted
        coloring, 361
        formatting (::selection), 110–111
    visited/unvisited hyperlinks, 113–114
move cursor, 352
Mozilla browser
    content property and, 59, 62
    custom style sheets, specifying with, 156–161
    described, 21–22
    form input letter spacing, 98
    multiple versions, running, 512
    quirks mode and standards mode, 37
    unsupported list marker, 347
Mozilla Firefox browser, 21–22
multiline comments, 54
multi-platform design
    borders
        color, 255–256
        combined properties, 259–260
        future CSS 3 properties, 260–264
        sides, shorthand for, 256–259
        style, 250–255
        width, 248–250
    browser-compatible properties, 574–578
    described, 84, 237–238
    dimensions described, 268
    example, 264–268
    external style sheets, advantages of, 242–245
    Gecko proprietary extensions, 589–590
    ground rules, 238–239
    height, 270–274
    HTML tables, limitations of, 239–241
    illustrated, 246–248
    inheritance versus, 136
    line-height property, 282–288
    margins
        applying, 297–302
        described, 290–297
    minimum and maximum dimensions, 277–282
    overflowing content, handling, 302–305
    padding
        applying, 297–302
        described, 288–290
    percentage width and height measurements, 274–276
    unnecessary or useless markup, 241–242
    width, 269–270

multiple browsers, preparing for
    automatic numbering, 583–584
    background properties, 571–572
    backward, XHTML and, 33
    box model properties, 574–578
    color properties, 568–569
    conventions, 565
    font properties, 569–570
    generated content, 583–584
    indirect adjacent sibling selector, 93
    lists, 583–584
    paged media, 585–586
    positioning, 579–580
    pseudo-classes, 567
    pseudo-elements, 568
    selectors, 77, 100, 566–567
    structural pseudo-classes, 120
    table properties, 581
    text properties, 572–573
    user interface, 582–583
    visual effects, 578
    W3C role, 10
multiple lines, 320
multiple versions, Internet Explorer (Microsoft), 512–517
multiple-column layout, 325–326

N
name, Apache HTTP server, 494
navigational menu
    aligning, 189
    building with pseudo-classes, 118–120
    colored headings, 360–361
    designing, 174–175
    drop-down menus, 409–411
    hyperlinks, 403
    mobile phone browser, 414
    underlining, removing from, 196
negation, pseudo-class, 126–128
NetFront phone browser, 414
Netscape Communicator, 239
Netscape Navigator
    described, 21–22
    multiple versions, running, 512
    skepticism about CSS, 13
    use of, 21, 491
Network Domain, 494
non-replaced inline elements, 318–319
Notepad, 18
numbered lists, 343–348, 474–476
numbering, automatic, 583–584

O

oblique type style, 211–214

offset positioning, 276, 387–393

older browsers, hiding CSS from, 49–50

one-word HTML attributes, 32

opacity, table cell, 442

open source project, IE7

  CSS features, 492–493

  HTTP server, installing, 493–496

  installing, 497–498

  sample, 499–501

  source code, obtaining, 492

  style sheet, sample applying, 501–502

opening tags, XHTML, 32–33

Openwave phone emulator, 414, 416

Opera browser

  content property and, 59, 62

  described, 22

  handheld emulator, 414, 417, 420–421

  quirks mode and standards mode, 37

  XML display values, nonsupported, 488

operating system

  fonts

    available families, 205

    keywords, 232–234

    predetermined by, 232–234

  Internet Explorer, integrating, 20

  Linux

    Apache HTTP server, 493

    browser, 22–23

  Mac OS

    Apache HTTP server, 493

    Internet Explorer, future of, 20, 21

    Safari browser, 23

    text editors, 19

  Windows

    cursor images, 353

    text editors, 18

overflowing content

  auto handling, 302–304

  background, attaching, 375–377

  clipping content, 305

  horizontal and vertical scrolling, 305

  scrolling, 304–305

overlining text, 191–196

overrides

  inheritance (!important syntax), 155

  system font, aspects of, 234

P

padding

  applying, 275–276, 297–302

  CSS box model, 84, 247–248

  elements, grouping, 48–49

  inline elements, 319

  margin collapse, preventing, 311–312

  right floated elements, 324

page breaks, print, 421–423

page layout rules

  borders

    color, 255–256

    combined properties, 259–260

    future CSS 3 properties, 260–264

    sides, shorthand for, 256–259

    style, 250–255

    width, 248–250

  browser-compatible properties, 574–578

  described, 84

  dimensions described, 268

  example, 264–268

  Gecko proprietary extensions, 589–590

  height, 270–274

  illustrated, 246–248

  inheritance versus, 136

  line-height property, 282–288

  margins

    applying, 297–302

    described, 290–297

  minimum and maximum dimensions, 277–282

  overflowing content, handling, 302–305

  padding

    applying, 297–302

    described, 288–290

  percentage width and height measurements, 274–276

  width, 269–270

paged media, 585–586

paragraphs

  indenting, 181–185

  margin collapsing, 311

parent-child relationship

  described, 85–89

  navigational headings, colors for, 361

peek-a-boo bug, 502–504

peer discussion, 7

percentage font size values, 225–230

percentage measurements

  background-position property, 369–374

  CSS box model, 274–276

  floating elements, 510–512

lengths, 68

`vertical-align` property, 338–339

Phoenix browser, 21–22

picas length measurement, 63

pictures

as alternative to text, 240

background

`background-image` property, 362–365

including with URI, 74

scrolling (`background-attachment` property), 375–377

tiling (`background-repeat` property), 365–369

border side and corner, setting, 261

cursors, 352–353

as list markers, 349

pixels

described, 65

length measurement, 67

plus sign (+), 68–69

pointer cursor, 352

points length measurement, 63

portable devices

style, 243

styling web documents for, 413–421

positioning

absolute, 276, 384–387

backgrounds, 369–374

browser compatibility, 579–580

defined, 383–384

example, 399–403

fixed, 403–405

layering (z-index property), 405–411

offset, 387–393

relative, 393–399

static, 384

P2P forums, 7

presentation method (media **attribute and** @media **rule), 242–245**

print

example, 426–427

page breaks, controlling, 421–423

printer output, 243

style overview, 421

style sheet, applying, 424–426

progress cursor image, 353

projection presentation, 243

pseudo-attributes, 469

pseudo-classes

browser compatibility, 567

clicked element (`:active` pseudo-class), 115–116

dynamic, 113–120

focus element, 116–120

hovering mouse pointer (`:hover` pseudo-class), 114–115

negation, 126–128

structural

elements without child elements, text, or content (`:empty`), 122–124

first-child of element (`:first-child`), 121

last-child of element (`:last-child`), 121–122

root element, document (`:root`), 120

style, applying based on HTML anchors (`:target`), 128–132

visited and unvisited hyperlinks (`:link` and `:visited`), 113–114

pseudo-elements

browser compatibility, 568

described, 107–108

first letter and first line of element containing text (`::first-letter` and `::first_line`), 108–110

Gecko proprietary extensions, 588

inserting content (`::before` and `::after`), 111–113

mouse highlighted text, user-selected (`::selection`), 110–111

publishing-industry fonts, cost of, 221

Q

query string, 96

question mark (?), 230

questions, form, 85

quotation marks (")

in strings, 60–61

XHTML, enclosing attribute values in, 31–32

quotation web page

clicking on heading, 131–132

dynamic pseudo-classes, 117–118

formatting, 109–110

inserting content, 112–113

negation pseudo-class, 126–127

picture and `:target` effects, 129–131

root pseudo-classes, 124–126

structural pseudo-classes, 122–124

R

Really Simple Syndication (RSS), 462

recommendations, W3C, 10

red colors, 596–597

relative font size values, 223–225

relative length measurements, 65–67

relative path, external style sheet, 50

relative positioning, 393–399

rendering modes
> browser, 603–605
> choice, importance of, 37

repeating background images, 365–369

replaced inline elements, 318–319

resolution
> fonts, rendering in absolute measurement, 64
> pixel measurements, 67

RGB colors, 70–71

right angle bracket (>), 23

right `float` **property**
> canceling, 329–332
> described, 323–328

right margin, 290–291

Roman numeral list markers, 345

root directory, 166

root element, document (`:root`**)**
> pseudo-class referring to, 120, 124–125
> XML document, 463

rounding box edges (`border-radius` **properties), 260**

rows
> HTML data, 24
> table cell, aligning, 341
> XML emulating, 480–484

RSS (Really Simple Syndication), 462

rule, applying to entire document, 77–78

S

Safari browser
> described, 22–23
> quirks mode and standards mode, 37
> XML display values, nonsupported, 488

sans-serif font, 206–207, 210

schema, 464–468

screen size
> element stretching larger than, 276
> fonts, rendering in absolute measurement, 64
> pixel measurements, 67
> scaling to fit, 277–282

scrolling
> background images (`background-attachment` property), 375–377
> fixed positioning, 404–405
> horizontal and vertical, 305
> overflowing content, 303–305

`::selection` **text, highlighting, 110–111**

selectors
> attribute
>> described, 93
>> mechanics, 98–99

> presence of, 93–94
> substring, 95–98
> value of, 94–95
> browser compatibility, 566–567
> class and ID, 100–105
> contextual/descendent
>> described, 78–80
>> input form, 80–84
> CSS anatomy and syntax, 44
> declaration, grouping with, 44–48
> direct adjacent sibling combinator, 89–92
> direct child, 85–89
> indirect adjacent sibling combinators, 92–93
> precedence of
>> described, 139–141
>> website illustrating, 141–151
> universal (*), 77–78

serif font, 206–207

server-side computer
> described, 12
> sniffing browsers, 415

SGML (Standard Generalized Markup Language), 17

shorthand properties
> backgrounds, 377–379
> box sides, 256–259
> font, 230–232, 233
> list (`list-style` property), 350–351

short hexadecimal colors, 72–73

shrink-to-fit elements, 58, 323, 392, 401

side-by-side content (`float` **property)**
> canceling (`clear` property), 89, 329–334
> described, 313–315
> double margin, 508–510
> example, 328–329
> floating box model, 315–318
> inline box model, 318–322
> input form, 88–89, 104–105
> left and right, 323–328
> multiple, applying, 322–323
> 100 percent width and, 510–512
> partial content disappearance, 504–506
> percentage widths, 510–512
> randomly disappearing and reappearing, 502–504
> three pixels of space, 323–328

sides, border shorthand for, 256–259

single colon (:), 108

single quotes ('), 61

single tags and line breaks, 23–24

size, font
> absolute values, 222–223
> first line or first element, 108–110

percentage values, 225–230

property overview, 221–222

relative values, 223–225

small caps (`font-variant` property), 215–216

small-caption font, 232

sniffing browsers, 415

software

HTTP server, described, 493

stages of, 493

source code

IE7 open source project, obtaining, 492

Internet mechanics, 11

spacing

between cells (`border-spacing`), 453–455

input form, adjusting, 89

margins

canceling (`clear` property), 334

collapsing, 309–313, 314, 317

CSS box model, 275–276, 290–302

inline elements, 319

navigation headings, 403

right floated elements, 324

padding

applying, 275–276, 297–302

CSS box model, 84, 247–248

elements, grouping, 48–49

inline elements, 319

margin collapse, preventing, 311–312

right floated elements, 324

text (`white-space` property), 199–200

specifications, W3C, 10

specifying font (`font-family` property), 209–211

speech synthesizer, 243

Spicy Thai Peanut Sauce recipe

XHTML table, creating, 436–443

XML version, 466–468, 471, 476–478, 482–487

stable software, 493

standalone attribute, 469

Standard Generalized Markup Language (SGML), 17

standards, document

browser, choosing, 19–23

DTD

DOCTYPE sniffing, 37–38

HTML 4.01 frameset, 40–41

HTML 4.01 strict, 41

HTML 4.01 transitional, 40

mechanics of, 39–40

sample, 36–37

XHTML 1.0 frameset, 41

XHTML 1.0 strict, 41

XHTML 1.0 transitional, 41

HTML

attributes, 25–28

single tags and line breaks, 23–24

markup language, 17–19

XHTML

attribute minimization, preventing, 32

benefits of using, 18, 33–36

case-sensitivity, 31

mechanics, 36

opening and closing tags, 32–33

quotes, enclosing attribute values in, 31–32

XML, 28–30

static positioning, 384

status-bar font, 232

strikethrough text, 191–196

strings, 59–63

structural pseudo-classes

elements without child elements, text, or content (`:empty`), 122–124

first-child of element (`:first-child`), 121

last-child of element (`:last-child`), 121–122

root element, document (`:root`), 120

style

applying

attribute, 93–99

based on HTML anchors (`:target`), 128–132

browser compatibility, 566–567

class and ID, 100–105

contextual/descendent, 78–85

CSS anatomy and syntax, 44

declaration, grouping with, 44–48

default (`auto` keyword), 58

direct adjacent sibling combinator, 89–92

direct child, 85–89

to entire document, 77–78

indirect adjacent sibling combinators, 92–93

precedence of, 139–151

style, applying (continued)

relationships, dependent, 78–85

universal selector (*), 77–78

font, switching (`font-style` property), 211–214

print overview, 421

table overview, 429

style sheet

IE7 open source project, sample applying, 501–502

inheritance, 137–139

print, applying, 424–426

standardization, need for, 13

URI, including with, 74

XML declaration, including, 470–471

Submit button, 105

subscript text, aligning, 334–335
substring attribute selectors, 95–98
superscript text, aligning, 334–335
syntax, CSS
  comments, 54
  declaration, grouping with selectors, 44–48
  embedded style sheet, 49–50
  external style sheet, linking to, 50
  importing style sheets, 50–52
  inline styles, 52–54
  rules described, 43–44
  selectors, 44
synthesizer, voice
  liquid design and, 238
  list marker styles, 351
system
  fonts
    available families, 205
    keywords, 232–234
    predetermined by, 232–234
  Internet Explorer, integrating, 20
  Linux
    Apache HTTP server, 493
    browser, 22–23
  Mac OS
    Apache HTTP server, 493
    Internet Explorer, future of, 20, 21
    Safari browser, 23
    text editors, 19
  Windows
    cursor images, 353
    text editors, 18

T

Tab key focus, 116
table of contents, 167–175
tables
  borders, adding extra (border-collapse), 451–453
  browser compatibility, 581
  captions, placing (caption-side property), 432–433
  cells
    content, vertical-align property, 339–341
    empty, coloring grey (empty-cells), 455–458
    spacing between (border-spacing), 453–455
  columns, vertical (colgroup and col elements), 433–434
  data
    accommodating (table-layout), 444–451, 464
    grouping, 435–443
  HTML sample, 23–24

  liquid design, barring, 238
  optional elements, 430–432
  styling overview, 429
tag soup, 241–242
tags
  attribute selectors, 93
  HTML, 23
  liquid design, avoiding, 238
  XHTML, restricted from, 32–33
  XML, well-formed, 28, 462–464
::target pseudo-class, 128–132
television, display on, 243
text
  alternate for images, 240
  browser compatibility, 572–573
  color, 99, 433–434
  cursor image, 353
text blocks
  centering, 291–293
  characters, aligning on tallest (text-top and text-bottom keywords), 338
  floating, 323–328
  slightly smaller, aligning (top, middle and bottom keywords), 335–337
  XML elements, displaying, 473
text editors, 18–19
text headings
  backgrounds, 361
  clicking on, 131–132
  colored, 360–361
  navigational hyperlinks, 403
  table, grouping, 435
three-column layout, 325–326
three-pixel jog bug, 507–508
tilde (~), 92
Times/Times New Roman font, 206
top alignment, 335–337
top margin
  collapsing, 310–313
  described, 290–291
transferable design
  borders
    color, 255–256
    combined properties, 259–260
    future CSS 3 properties, 260–264
    sides, shorthand for, 256–259
    style, 250–255
    width, 248–250
  browser-compatible properties, 574–578
  described, 84, 237–238
  dimensions described, 268

example, 264–268
external style sheets, advantages of, 242–245
Gecko proprietary extensions, 589–590
ground rules, 238–239
height, 270–274
HTML tables, limitations of, 239–241
illustrated, 246–248
inheritance versus, 136
line-height property, 282–288
margins
    applying, 297–302
    described, 290–297
minimum and maximum dimensions, 277–282
overflowing content, handling, 302–305
padding
    applying, 297–302
    described, 288–290
percentage width and height measurements, 274–276
unnecessary or useless markup, 241–242
width, 269–270
tty devices, 243
typeface
    absolute lengths, 63–64
    bold (font-weight property), 216–221
    browser compatibility, 569–570
    ex measurement, 67
    first line or first element, formatting, 108–110
    generic, 83, 206–208
    properties, grouping, 46–48
    shorthand property, 230–232
    size (font-size property), 221–230
    small caps (font-variant property), 215–216
    specifying (font-family property), 203–205,
        209–211
    styles, switching (font-style property), 211–214
    system, operating system keywords, 232–234
typographical length measurements, 65

U
underlining text, 191–196
universal selector (*), 77–78
unnecessary or useless markup, 241–242
unvisited hyperlinks, 113–114
URI (Universal Resource Indicator), 73–74
URL (Uniform Resource Locator)
    custom cursors, 352
    matching, 96
    navigational headings, 403
URN (Universal Resource Name), 73

user input form
    basic look and feel, 80–84
    boldface text, 99
    colored labels, 90–92
    input fields, adding, 86–88
    letter spacing, 98–99
    questions, 85
    Submit button, adding, 105
user interface
    browser compatibility, 582–583
    color keywords, 601–602
    defined, 238
    Gecko proprietary extensions, 590
    Microsoft proprietary extensions, 587
users, style dictated by
    active document element, 116–118
    current click, 115–116
    events, 107
    font size, 228
    hovering mouse pointer, 114–115
    hyperlinks, visited and unvisited, 113–114
    Internet Explorer, 156
    mouse-highlighted text, formatting, 110–111
    Mozilla, 156–161
    navigational heading colors, 361
    need for, 138
    selectors defined by, 102–104

V
vertical columns
    grouping data, 435
    HTML tables, emulating, 480
    multiple, 325–326
    width and colors (colgroup and col elements),
        433–434
vertical scroll bar
    fixed positioning, 404–405
    overflowing content, 303, 304–305
vertical tiling, background images, 366, 367
vertical-align **property**
    described, 334
    percentage and length values, 338–339
    subscript and superscript text, 334–335
    table cell content, 339–341
    text subset, raising and lowering (text-top and
        text-bottom), 338
    top, middle and bottom keywords, 335–337
visited hyperlinks, 113–114

visitors

input form

basic look and feel, 80–84

boldface text, 99

colored labels, 90–92

field, focus on, 116–118

input fields, adding, 86–88

letter spacing, 98–99

questions, 85

Submit button, adding, 105

style dictated by

active document element, 116–118

current click, 115–116

events, 107

font size, 228

hovering mouse pointer, 114–115

hyperlinks, visited and unvisited, 113–114

Internet Explorer, 156

mouse-highlighted text, formatting, 110–111

Mozilla, 156–161

navigational heading colors, 361

need for, 138

selectors defined by, 102–104

visual effects

browser compatibility, 578

Gecko proprietary extensions, 588–589

Microsoft proprietary extensions, 586–587

voice synthesizer

liquid design and, 238

list marker styles, 351

W

wait cursor image, 353

watermarks, 403–405

W3C (World Wide Web Consortium), 10

web

colors safe for use on, 72–73

history of, 12

W3C, 10–11

web browsers

compatibility

background properties, 571–572

backward, XHTML and, 33

box model properties, 574–578

color properties, 568–569

conventions, 565

font properties, 569–570

generated content, automatic numbering, and lists, 583–584

indirect adjacent sibling selector, 93

paged media, 585–586

positioning, 579–580

pseudo-classes, 567

pseudo-elements, 568

selectors, 77, 100, 566–567

structural pseudo-classes, 120

table properties, 581

text properties, 572–573

user interface, 582–583

visual effects, 578

W3C role, 10

Gecko-based, 21–22

IE7 open source project

CSS features, 492–493

HTTP server, installing, 493–496

installing, 497–498

sample, 499–501

source code, obtaining, 492

style sheet, sample applying, 501–502

Internet Explorer

bugs, fixing, 502–510

content property and, 62

CSS box model quirk mode, 246

CSS, early support for, 13

custom style sheets, specifying, 156

described, 20–21

DTD, invoking rendering mode with, 37–39

multiple versions, installing, 512–517

Netscape Navigator versus, 491

overflow models limited to, 305

percentage widths and floating elements, 510–512

XML support, 462

KHTML, 22–23

Netscape Communicator, 239

Netscape Navigator

described, 21–22

multiple versions, running, 512

skepticism about CSS, 13

use of, 21, 491

Opera

content property and, 59, 62

described, 22

handheld emulator, 414, 417, 420–421

quirks mode and standards mode, 37

XML display values, nonsupported, 488

rendering modes, 603–605

Safari

described, 22–23

quirks mode and standards mode, 37

XML display values, nonsupported, 488

W3C specifications, 10–11

web page layout rules

borders

color, 255–256

combined properties, 259–260

future CSS 3 properties, 260–264

sides, shorthand for, 256–259

style, 250–255

width, 248–250

browser-compatible properties, 574–578

described, 84

dimensions described, 268

example, 264–268

Gecko proprietary extensions, 589–590

`height`, 270–274

illustrated, 246–248

inheritance versus, 136

`line-height` property, 282–288

margins

applying, 297–302

described, 290–297

minimum and maximum dimensions, 277–282

overflowing content, handling, 302–305

padding

applying, 297–302

described, 288–290

percentage width and height measurements, 274–276

`width`, 269–270

web page, sample quotation

clicking on heading, 131–132

dynamic pseudo-classes, 117–118

formatting, 109–110

inserting content, 112–113

negation pseudo-class, 126–127

picture and `:target` effects, 129–131

root pseudo-classes, 124–126

structural pseudo-classes, 122–124

website, JT's Island Grill and Gallery

background

color property, 358–361

fixing, 376–377

images, adding, 363–365

positioning, 372–374

borders, 261–268

cascade and inheritance, effects of, 141–151

design strategy, 164–165

dimensions, adding to style sheet, 283–288

directory structure, 165–167

drop-down navigational menus, 409–411

fixed positioning, 404–405

`float` property, 326–329, 332–334

font formatting

applying throughout, 208–211

boldface letters, 220–221

capital and lowercase letters (`text-transform` property), 197–198

italic and oblique, switching (`font-style` property), 211–214

`letter-spacing` property, 177–178

sizes, 227–230

layering, 409–411

list item markers, removing, 347–348

markup, 168–173

Motorola emulator displaying, 415

navigational menu, 174–175, 189

Openwave emulator displaying, 416

padding and margins, 293–302

positioning

absolute, 385–387

relative, 395–403

style sheets

handheld device, applying, 417–421

print, 424–427

separating by media, 244–245

table of contents, 167–168

text formatting

alignment, 187–189

indenting, 184–185

`text-decoration` property, 193–195

`word-spacing` property, 180–181

Weinman, Lynda (Web-safe color identifier), 72

Western font, 206

width

columns, 433–434

enlarging tables to fit window, 444–448

fitting data, 58

fixed tables, 450–451

highlighting cells, 448–450

paragraph indent, 183

shrink-to-fit floating block, 323

wild card attribute string value, 96

window, elements larger than

auto handling, 302–304

background, attaching, 375–377

clipping content, 305

horizontal and vertical scrolling, 305

scrolling, 304–305

window, enlarging tables to fit, 444–448

Windows (Microsoft)

cursor images, 353

text editors, 18

wireless browser emulators, 414

word blocks
centering, 291–293
characters, aligning on tallest (`text-top` and `text-bottom` keywords), 338
floating, 323–328
slightly smaller, aligning (`top`, `middle` and `bottom` keywords), 335–337
XML elements, displaying, 473
words
alternate for images, 240
browser compatibility, 572–573
color, 99, 433–434
cursor image, 353
formatting
aligning, 185–190, 334–341
capitalizing (`text-transform` property), 196–198
changes ahead in CSS 3 Text module, 200–201
described, 163–164
design strategy, 164–165
directory structure, creating, 165–167
extra spaces, collapsing, 200
first line or first element as different size, 108–110
form questions, 85
indenting paragraphs, 181–185
justifying, 186–189, 190
`letter-spacing` property, 175–178
lowercase letters as small caps, 216
mouse-highlighted, 110–111
properties, grouping, 46–48
subset, raising and lowering (`text-top` and `text-bottom`), 338
table of contents, 167–175
underlining, overlining, and strikethrough (`text-decoration` property), 191–196
`white-space` property, 199–200
`word-spacing` property, 179–181
word-spacing **property, 179–181**
World Wide Web Consortium (W3C), 10

X

x-axis, tiling background images, 366
x-height relative units, 65
XHTML 1.0 (eXtensible HyperText Markup Language)
frameset, DTD, 41
rendering modes, 604–605
strict DTD, 41
transitional DTD, 41
XHTML (eXtensible HyperText Markup Language)
attribute minimization, preventing, 32
attribute selectors, 93

benefits of using, 18, 33–36
case-sensitivity, 31
conditional comment tags, 502
CSS, including in document, 52–54
document display values, 488–489
document standards, 31–36
DTD, 36–37
HTML and, 9
integers, rendering, 68–69
mechanics, 36
opening and closing tags, 32–33
quotes, enclosing attribute values in, 31–32
root element, pseudo-class referring to, 120
sample exercise solution, 522–523
table style sheet, embedding, 432
XHTML (eXtensible HyperText Markup Language) tables. *See* HTML tables
XML (eXtensible Markup Language)
attribute selector, 93
declaration
attributes, 469–470
described, 468–469
style sheet, including, 470–471
described, 461–464
displaying
block elements, 473
described, 471–472
inline level elements, 472
list items, 473–478
HTML tables, emulating
applying, 479
captioning, 479–480
columns, 480
described, 478–479
example, 485–487
groupings, table rows, and table cells, 480–484
rendering modes, 605
root element, pseudo-class referring to, 124–125
sample page, 522
schema, creating, 464–468
standards, 28–30
XSL (Extensible Stylesheet Language), 462

Y

y-axis, tiling background images, 366, 367
yellow colors, 599–600

Z

Zapf-Chancery font, 206
zip archive file, opening, 497, 499